gmax® Bible

Kelly Murdock

WILEY

Wiley Publishing, Inc.

gmax® Bible

Published by
Wiley Publishing, Inc.
909 Third Avenue
New York, NY 10022
www.wiley.com

Copyright © 2003 by Wiley Publishing, Inc., Indianapolis, Indiana

Library of Congress Control Number: 2003101836

ISBN: 0-7645-3757-1

Manufactured in the United States of America

10 9 8 7 6 5 4 3 2 1

1B/SR/QT/QT/IN

Published by Wiley Publishing, Inc., Indianapolis, Indiana
Published simultaneously in Canada

About the Author

Kelly Murdock has been involved with more computer books than he cares to count — so many that he gets very nostalgic when visiting the computer book section of the bookstore. His book credits include a host of Web, graphics, and multimedia titles, including three editions of *3ds max Bible, Adobe Atmosphere Bible, Master HTML and XHTML Visually, JavaScript Blueprints,* and co-authoring two editions of *Illustrator Bible.* Kelly also co-authored *Laura Lemay's Web Workshop: 3D Graphics and VRML 2* at a time when we all thought VRML was going somewhere.

With a background in engineering and computer graphics, Kelly has been all over the 3D industry from high-level CAD workstations and large-scale visualization projects to creating 3D models for feature films, working as a freelance 3D artist, and even some 3D programming.

Kelly's been using 3D Studio since version 3 for DOS and has been a serious gamer even longer. His favorite games are first person shooters, and he can stand his own in most deathmatches.

Credits

Acquisitions Editor
Tom Heine

Project Editor
Martin V. Minner

Technical Editor
Chris Murdock

Copy Editor
Gwenette Gaddis Goshert

Editorial Manager
Rev Mengle

Vice President and Executive Group Publisher
Richard Swadley

Vice President and Executive Publisher
Bob Ipsen

Vice President and Publisher
Barry Pruett

Project Coordinator
Regina Snyder

Graphics and Production Specialists
Amanda Carter
Jennifer Click
Kristin McMullan
Heather Pope
Janet Seib
Mary Virgin

Quality Control Technicians
John Tyler Connoley
John Greenough
Andy Hollandbeck
Angel Perez

Senior Permissions Editor
Carmen Krikorian

Media Development Specialist
Travis Silvers

Proofreading and Indexing
TECHBOOKS Production Services

Cover Image
Anthony Bunyan
3D rendering by Kelly Murdock
Model from Curious Labs' Poser

Playing games is the process of practicing for reality.

The more someone plays, the better suited to face real life.

To Eric and Thomas, 2003

Foreword

Let's face it — most people who have played any kind of PC game have wondered how they could get a job working with games all day. Like becoming a movie director or globe-trotting photographer, achieving the position of game designer, game creator, level designer, or 3D modeler seems too good to be true. But bright minds in the games industry recognized the opportunity to tap the creative potential of game fans. In a spirit of openness unknown in all other software forms outside of the Linux open-source message, game developers have made tools available to their fans and encouraged contributions and extensions to some huge game franchises.

This community spirit has encouraged thousands of fans to get involved. A vast number have scored jobs at major game development studios as a result of the work they did in bedrooms, in spare time, with faceless friends on the Internet, and for the fun of being involved in the game community's creative environment.

Becoming a world-class photographer or movie director may seem out of reach, but a tangible and even professional involvement in game development is much closer than you might think. That's thanks, in part, to products like gmax.

Discreet Software's 3ds max graphics modeling package is a cornerstone of hundreds of game development studios. The gmax initiative took that high-end program and crafted a program sufficiently accessible and powerful that any game enthusiast could start creating new character models, levels, and functions for some of the biggest games on the market.

gmax Bible provides an incredibly comprehensive guide to getting started, becoming proficient, and ultimately achieving expertise with gmax. With practical applications for some current chart-topping games including Quake III Arena, Flight Simulator 2002, Dungeon Siege, C&C: Renegade, and Trainz, any gamer can start to understand the processes involved in game creation and acquire the skills that development studios look for daily.

Offering a clear understanding of this software package's application to gaming, *gmax Bible* covers every detail that a wannabe game designer could need. Gamers are constantly astonished by the stories of fellow fans manipulating current games, having their talents spotted by studios, and then, individually or with their online team friends, being offered professional contracts to create game mods or even full projects.

All you need are the dedication to learn the mechanics of the game world; the freely available, powerful, and comprehensive gmax software; and this friendly, approachable reference work to answer any questions that appear on your way to game mod greatness.

If you've ever played a game and thought you could do better, here is your chance. Take it.

Rob Smith
Editor-in-Chief, *PC Gamer*

Preface

I'm getting much smarter when it comes to writing these computer books. For this project, I actually had to play games to prepare. "It's research," I'd claim to my family, and they would buy it. It wasn't hard for my kids to accept. They were very interested in the progress I made at Dungeon Siege, but my major failure was that I wasn't successful in getting my wife hooked on Flight Simulator (even though she loves planes and is working on her private pilot's license).

Although I enjoy playing games, I'm not near the hard-core gamer that many of you are, so why am I writing this book? The answer lies in my experience with another piece of software that isn't even a game, a little program called 3ds max. 3ds max (or Max for short) is the big brother of gmax, and I have had the good fortune of writing a well-received book on it titled *3ds max Bible*. This book is based roughly on that book.

I guess I could have slapped a sticker on the front of *3ds max Bible* that said, "Covers gmax. Gamers welcome," but that wouldn't have been enough. Deep down, I would be haunted by dissatisfied gamers, and I'd be the target in every online deathmatch I entered. So, I decided that *gmax Bible* would need more.

The more that is needed comes in many different forms. First, I revisited every section of *3ds max Bible* that I'd previously written to sync it up with gmax. When Discreet made gmax, they made lots of little tweak changes that combine elements of all the various versions of Max. Finding these changes has been quite a task, but the end result is a complete book that is technically accurate for gmax.

Secondly, I've revisited many of the tutorials found throughout the Max book and made them unique to gmax. The third and most noticeable change was the addition of Part V where the individual game packs are covered. All the chapters in this part cover the game specific features and tools added to the various gmax game packs. So if you're a hard-core Dungeon Siege player, you'll find a hefty chapter just for you covering the specific aspects of creating scenery, characters, and objects to use in your own Siegelet.

The final new addition to this book is Caryn Law. As I sat down to write this book, I quickly realized that I needed to become an expert in five different games — an enjoyable but daunting task. So I enlisted the help of someone who really knows her way around the gaming industry. Caryn works for Activision and is tied in tightly to the Quake community where she is known as the formidable Hellchick. Caryn is responsible for writing the game pack chapters on Quake III Arena and Command & Conquer: Renegade (not that I really wanted to give up the first-person shooter games, but she kicked my tail in a deathmatch).

About This Book

Games are lots of fun, and being part of the gaming community is great, but this book isn't for the general gamer — it is for an important part of the gaming community, the game content creator. If this book were for gamers, it would be a thin, 100-page, large format book in full color and full of cheat codes and strategies. But this book is quite different; it is thick and heavy and void of any color except for the cover and the impressive color insert pages.

This book is thick on purpose. gmax is an advanced piece of software with more capability than you can learn in a week or even a month. I had lots to cover, and I made sure that I turned over every rock and pebble as I covered it. The result is a book that is a complete reference to every feature and command in gmax.

If you're so excited to be working with gmax that you can't decide where to start, head straight for Part V and read the game pack chapter for your game of choice. This will get you started with creating content; from there, you can branch into the various aspects of gmax. On the other hand, if you want to learn gmax and gain some 3D skills that will potentially land you in the gaming industry, I suggest starting at the front of the book and methodically moving through it, covering and learning from each tutorial. Then, when you hit the game pack chapters, you can decide which game to attack and you'll already have the skills to accomplish whatever you want.

As this book has come together, I've tried to write the type of book that I'd like to read. I've tried to include a variety of examples that are infused with creativity. It is my hope that these examples will not only teach you how to use the software, but provide a creative springboard for you in the creation of your own worlds.

Be warned as you begin to read that this book suffers from multiple personalities. Of the games that have available game packs, I've decided to focus on five unique games — Quake III Arena, Dungeon Siege, Command & Conquer: Renegade, Flight Simulator, and Trainz. References to all these games are scattered throughout the book. If you feel slighted because Trainz is your game and I seem to be referencing Flight Simulator in all my jokes, then be sure to visit the Trainz chapter in Part V. It is just for you.

Tutorials aplenty

I've always been a very visual learner — the easiest way for me to gain knowledge is by doing things for myself while exploring at the same time. Other people learn by reading and comprehending ideas. In this book, I've tried to present information in a number of ways to make the information usable for all types of learners. That is why you'll see detailed discussions of the various features along with tutorials that show these concepts in action.

The tutorials appear throughout the book and are clearly marked with the "Tutorial" label in front of the section title. They always include a series of logical steps, typically ending with a figure for you to study and compare to your creation. These tutorial examples are provided on the book's CD-ROM to give you a firsthand look and a chance to get some hands-on experience.

I've attempted to "laser focus" all the tutorials down to one or two key concepts. This means that you probably won't want to load the results into your games. For example, many of the early tutorials don't have any materials applied because I felt that using materials before they've been explained would only confuse you.

I've attempted to think of and use examples that are diverse, unique, and interesting, while striving to make them simple, light, and easy to follow. Many of them would fit nicely in a game, but then just about any item can be used in a game depending on how it is designed. For most of the tutorials, the CD-ROM includes a starting point. This approach lets me focus the tutorials even more and with fewer, more relevant steps, you can learn and experience the concepts without the complexity. On the book's CD-ROM, you'll find the gmax files that are referenced in Step 1 of most tutorials. The completed tutorial's gmax file is saved with the word *final* tacked on the end. If you get lost midway through the tutorial, you can open the final resulting file and see for yourself how it is supposed to work. I'm happy to report that every example in the book is included on the CD-ROM, along with the models and textures required to complete the tutorial.

I've put lots of effort into this book, and I hope it helps you in your efforts. I present this book as a starting point. In each tutorial, I've purposely left all the creative spice out, leaving room for you to put it in—you're the one with the vision.

How this book is organized

The book is organized to flow logically through the various aspects of gmax, moving from simple, highly used features to the more complex, obscure ones. Each part and chapter covers a logical grouping of features, but some features require much more discussion than others, so the chapter sizes aren't really uniform. You may get the most benefit by jumping around to different sections as needed, but if you're new to gmax, you may want to check out Part I because it familiarizes you with the interface and basic features. The book is divided into the following parts:

+ **Part I: Attacking gmax Hard and Fast**—Whether it's understanding and configuring the interface, dealing with files, or learning the basics of positioning objects, the chapters in this part get you comfortable with the interface so you won't get lost moving about this mammoth package.

+ **Part II: Building an Empire of Objects**—gmax includes several different ways to model objects. This part includes chapters on working with primitives, splines, shapes, meshes, patches, and a variety of specialized compound objects like lofts and morphs.

✦ **Part III: Changing Object Appearance Inside and Out** — After you create an object, you want to modify and dress it up. This part deals with modifiers, bones, and IK systems, and the gmax Material Editor for applying materials to objects.

✦ **Part IV: Lights, Camera, Action** — This part describes how to control lights and cameras, and then its on to animation. Getting objects to move just right using keyframing, the Track View, constraints, and controllers is one of the most creative parts of the process.

✦ **Part V: Creating mods with the gmax Game Packs** — The game-specific details are covered in this part. For loading new characters into Dungeon Siege, creating a new level with traps for Quake, or putting a custom paint job on your favorite Flight Sim airplane, these are the chapters to visit.

At the very end of this book, you'll find three appendixes that cover system installation and configuration, gmax keyboard shortcuts, and the contents of the book's CD-ROM.

Using the book's icons

The following margin icons are used to help you get the most out of this book:

Note icons highlight useful information that you should take into consideration.

Tips provide an additional bit of advice that make a particular feature quicker or easier to use.

Cautions warn you of a potential problem before you make a mistake.

Watch for this icon to learn where in another chapter you can go to find more information on a particular feature.

This icon points you toward related materials that are included on the book's CD-ROM.

The book's CD-ROM

Computer book CD-ROMs are sometimes just an afterthought that includes a handful of examples and product demos. This book's CD-ROM, however, is much more than that. Its content was carefully selected to provide you with an additional resource that can supplement the book. Appendix C, "What's on the CD-ROM," supplies the details of the content on the CD-ROM.

Perhaps the main benefit of the CD-ROM is that it includes gmax and several of the game packs. With these items, you will be able to complete almost all the tutorials in the book. gmax and most of the game packs are also available on the Web, so check the Web site for the latest version of these items.

The CD-ROM also includes all the tutorial files that are shown in the figures throughout the book, including all the models. If you see a model in the book that you want to use, you should be able to find it on the CD-ROM. If you haven't noticed yet, most of this book is printed in black and white. This can make seeing the details and colors of the figures difficult. The CD-ROM includes a complete searchable version of the book along with all the figures in color.

Acknowledgments

I have a host of people to thank for their involvement in this work. The order in which they are mentioned doesn't necessarily represent the amount of work they did.

First of all, thanks to my family — Angie, Eric, and Thomas. They were frightfully supportive of the times when I needed to write, especially Eric, who at age 9 is so ready to play Teen-rated games that he can't stand it. It was especially hard when Dad loaded a new game that he couldn't play. He even tried to convince me that E-rated games were for Eric and that T-rated games were for Thomas (I guess Mom would get the M-rated games). Thank heavens that Flight Simulator and Trainz weren't Teen-rated, but Eric and Thomas took turns to see who could produce the most disastrous crash. (I'm going to have to think twice about ever letting them get a driver's license.) When I asked Eric about this book, he thought it was pretty cool, unlike the other "boring" books that I write. With this type of approval, how could I fail?

My second big thanks goes out to Caryn Law, who did an excellent job writing the game pack chapters that were assigned to her. She brought a true gamer's perspective to the writing and a voice of authority that was much needed.

I'd also like to thank Dave Brueck, who wrote some of the earlier chapters in *3ds max Bible* for me including the coverage of MAXScript found in Chapter 8. Some of his excellent work remains and carries his spirit with it.

My thanks also go to all the editors at Wiley. Tom Heine was instrumental and encouraging in seeing this proposal through to approval. At times when I felt like dropping the whole project, he provided the power that kept the plane from stalling and crashing.

Another of my long-time cohorts is Marty Minner, who served as project editor. He deserves oodles of thanks. He was, as always, meticulous in his editing work and helpful in keeping all the pieces in line. I must also thank him for his patience because as I got behind on my submissions, he would feel the pain. Thanks also to the triple G, also known as Gwenette Gaddis Goshert, the copy editor.

I'd also like to thank Carmen Krikorian for managing to pull together an incredible CD-ROM of content while wrestling with the egos of several major game companies. Yes, Carmen, there really is a company named Id Software. Thanks to Anthony Bunyan for producing a great cover. I'd also like to thank all the publishing experts that had a hand in this book including the production staff, marketing, and the project coordinator.

Kudos to Chris Murdock (my out-of-control brother who actually got me hooked on rock climbing this last summer) for taking over the technical editing for this monster. Chris is great to work with because I could call up (or down) to him from some precarious perch on the side of rock wall and tell him that I think I missed something in the latest chapter and that he should watch for it. To which he'd always respond, "No worries." But I never could figure out if he was talking about rock climbing or the book project, both of which I worried over immensely.

On the corporate side, thanks to Discreet for building gmax and for thinking of all of us gamers. And thanks to the game companies, especially Steve Yates, Tony Hilliam, and Vaughan Kidd at Auran; Mike Biddlecombe at Gas Powered Games; Amy Farris at Westwood Studios; and Eric Kwan for Microsoft Games and Id Software. I'd also like to thank the wonderful modelers at Viewpoint Datalabs, Zygote Media, and Hou Soon Ming at the 3D Toon Shop for their excellent models that are featured in the book's examples. Also, thanks to Tori Porter and Marc Keohane at Curious Labs.

For the excellent color insert pages that inspire readers everywhere, I'd like to thank the following for supplying images:

♦ Jan Visser and his cohorts of dedicated FS2002 modelers

♦ The various characters at Team Evolve including g1zm0, sock, Inflict, Sgt. Hulka Minty Fresh, and ThinG (I mean, Mike Burbidge, Simon O'Callaghan, Dan Haigh, Robert Waring, Mike Reed, and Time Smith) for images of their amazing custom Quake levels

♦ Marco "Rox" Pantozzi, Matthew Williams, Andy Quaas, Mark Hoffman, Chris Caswell and Peter Pardoe-Matthews for their excellent Trainz images (and apologies to all the Trainz users who submitted images that I didn't have room for—maybe next time)

♦ David Goldfarb and Team Elemental (www.the-elemental.net) for their Dungeon Siege images

Contents

● ●

Foreword vii

Preface. ix

About This Book x
Tutorials aplenty. x
How this book is organized xi
Using the book's icons. xii
The book's CD-ROM xiii
Acknowledgments xv

Part I: Attacking gmax Hard and Fast   1

Chapter 1: gmax — The Possibilities 3

Learning the History of gmax. 4
Understanding the Relationship Between gmax and 3ds max 4
gmax and the Gaming Industry. 5
Pursuing a Career in the Gaming Industry 5
gmax Enabled Games 6
Quake III Arena. 6
Flight Simulator 2002 Professional Edition 7
Trainz 8
Dungeon Siege 9
Command & Conquer: Renegade. 10
Combat Flight Simulator 3. 10
Train Simulator 11
And more to come 11
Understanding the Limitations of gmax 12
Modeling limitations — the stuff you don't need 13
Animation limitations 13
Material Editor limitations 13
Effects limitations 14
No rendering or compositing. 14
Other limitations 14
Summary. 15

Chapter 2: Using the In-Your-Face Interface 17

The Interface Elements. 18
    Visible interface elements. 18
    Non-visible interface elements 20
Using the Menus 20
    The File menu. 21
    The Edit menu 21
    The Tools menu 23
    The Group menu 25
    The Views menu 25
    The Create menu 28
    The Modifiers menu 28
    The Animation menu. 28
    The Graph Editors menu 29
    The Track View menu 29
    The Customize menu 29
    The MAXScript menu 30
    The Help menu 30
Using the Main Toolbar 32
Using the Tab Panel. 35
Using the Command Panel. 36
    Create panel. 38
    Modify panel 39
    Hierarchy panel. 39
    Motion panel 40
    Display panel 41
    Utilities panel 41
Using the Additional Interface Controls 42
    Using the Time Controls. 43
    Time Slider 44
    Track Bar 44
    Learning from the Status Bar and the Prompt Line 44
    MAXScript Listener 45
Interacting with the Interface 46
    Right-click quadmenus 46
    Floating and docking panels 47
    Understanding the color cues 48
    Drag-and-drop features 48
    Controlling spinners 48
    Keyboard shortcuts 49
    Modeless and persistent dialog boxes. 49
Working with the Viewports. 49
    Understanding 3D space. 49
    Using the viewport navigation controls 51
    Tutorial: Navigating the active viewport 53
    Working with viewport backgrounds 55
Summary. 58

Chapter 3: Making a Custom Face, er, Interface 59

Using the Customize User Interface Window 59
    Customizing keyboard shortcuts. 60
    Tutorial: Assigning keyboard shortcuts 61
    Customizing toolbars 62
    Tutorial: Creating a custom toolbar 63
    Customizing quadmenus 66
    Customizing menus 68
    Tutorial: Adding a new menu 69
    Customizing colors. 71
Customizing the Tab Panel. 72
Customizing Command Panel Buttons 73
Working with Custom Interfaces 74
    Saving and loading a custom interface 74
    Tutorial: Saving a custom interface 75
    Locking the interface 75
    Reverting to the startup interface 75
Configuring Paths 75
Selecting System Units 77
Configuring the Viewports 78
    Setting the viewport rendering method 79
    Altering the Viewport layout 86
Setting Preferences 86
    Inverse Kinematics preferences 89
    Animation preferences. 90
    Files panel preferences 92
    Gamma preferences 94
    Viewport preferences 95
    MAXScript preferences. 101
Summary 102

Chapter 4: Getting Files In and Out of gmax 103

Working with gmax Scene Files 103
    Saving files 104
    Opening files 105
    Merging and replacing objects 106
    Archiving files 107
    Getting out 107
Importing and Exporting 107
    Importing geometric objects 108
    Importing from external applications 110
    Exporting geometric objects 114
Referencing External Objects 115
    Using XRef Scenes 116
    Using XRef Objects 120
    Tutorial: Using an XRef proxy 122

XRef Objects in the Modifier Stack 124
Configuring XRef paths. 124
Using the File Utilities. 125
Using the Asset Browser utility 125
Finding files with the gmax File Finder utility 127
Collecting files with the Resource Collector utility. 128
Using the Map Path Utility. 129
Accessing File Information 130
Displaying scene information 130
Viewing file properties 131
Viewing files 132
Using the Virtual Frame Buffer 133
Summary 134

Chapter 5: Choosing Your Poison — Selecting Objects 135

Selecting Objects 136
Working with selection filters 137
Using the select buttons 138
Selecting with the Edit menu 138
Selecting multiple objects 141
Tutorial: Selecting objects 142
Locking selection sets 143
Using named selection sets 143
Isolating the current selection 144
Selecting objects in other interfaces 145
Setting Object Properties. 146
Viewing object information 146
Setting Display properties 147
Using the User-Defined panel 149
Hiding and freezing objects 149
Using the Display Floater dialog box 149
Using the Display panel 150
Tutorial: Playing hide and seek 152
Summary 153

**Chapter 6: Cloning, Grouping, and Linking Objects,
and Other –ings 155**

Cloning Objects 156
Using the Clone command. 156
Using the Shift-clone method 157
Tutorial: Cloning cows 157
Understanding Cloning Options 158
Working with copies, instances, and references 158
Tutorial: Copied, instanced, and referenced Genie's lamps 159
Mirroring Objects 161
Using the Mirror command 161
Tutorial: Mirroring a broadsword. 162

Cloning Over Time. 163
    Using the Snapshot command. 163
    Tutorial: Following a mouse through a maze 164
Spacing Cloned Objects. 165
    Using the Spacing tool 165
    Tutorial: Building a roller coaster. 166
Creating Arrays of Objects 168
    Linear arrays 168
    Tutorial: Building a white picket fence. 169
    Circular arrays 170
    Tutorial: Building a Ferris wheel 171
    Spiral arrays 172
    Tutorial: Building a spiral staircase. 172
    Working with a ring array 174
    Tutorial: Using a ring array to create a carousel 175
Working with Groups 177
    Creating groups 177
    Ungrouping objects. 178
    Opening and closing groups. 178
    Attaching and detaching objects 178
    Tutorial: Grouping the deer parts together 178
Understanding Parent, Child, and Root Relationships 180
Building Links between Objects 180
    Linking objects 180
    Unlinking objects 181
    Tutorial: Creating a solar system 181
Displaying Links and Hierarchies 182
    Displaying links in the viewport. 182
    Viewing hierarchies. 183
Working with Linked Objects. 184
    Selecting hierarchies 185
    Linking to dummies. 185
    Tutorial: Creating the two-cars-in-a-sphere stunt 185
Summary 187

**Chapter 7: Moving, Rotating, and Scaling Objects –
Return of the –ings** **189**

Moving, Rotating, and Scaling Objects 190
    Moving objects 190
    Rotating objects. 190
    Scaling objects 190
    Using the transform buttons 192
Transformation Tools. 192
    Working with the Transform Gizmos 192
    Using the Transform Type-In dialog box 194
    Using the status bar Type-In fields 195
    Understanding the Transform Managers 196

Tutorial: Re-creating a chess game 200
Tutorial: Setting the dining room table. 202
Tutorial: Building a snowman 204
Using Pivot Points 205
Positioning pivot points 205
Aligning pivot points 206
Transform adjustments 207
Using the Reset XForm utility 207
Using the Align Commands. 207
Aligning objects 208
Aligning normals 208
Tutorial: Aligning a kissing couple 209
Aligning to a view 210
Using Grids 211
The Home Grid 211
Creating and activating new grids 212
Using AutoGrid 212
Using Snap Options 213
Setting snap points 214
Setting snap options 214
Tutorial: Creating a lattice for a methane molecule 215
Summary 216

Chapter 8: Placing gmax on Autopilot with MAXScript 219
What Is MAXScript? 219
Using MAXScript Tools 220
The MAXScript menu. 220
The MAXScript Utility rollout 221
Tutorial: Using the SphereArray script. 222
The MAXScript Listener window 223
Tutorial: Talking to the MAXScript interpreter 225
MAXScript editor windows 228
The Macro Recorder 228
Tutorial: Recording a simple script. 230
Understanding the Different Types of Scripts 232
Macro scripts 232
Scripted utilities. 233
Scripted right-click menus 233
Scripted mouse tools 233
Writing Your Own MAXScripts 233
Variables and data types 233
Tutorial: Using variables 235
Expressions 237
Conditions 240
Collections and arrays 240
Loops. 242
Functions. 243
Tutorial: Creating a school of fish. 245

Using the Visual MAXScript Editor 250
The editor interface 251
The menus and the main toolbar 252
Toolbar elements 252
Laying out a rollout 254
Aligning and spacing elements 254
Tutorial: Building a custom rollout with the
Visual MAXScript editor 254
Summary 258

Part II: Building an Empire of Objects   259

Chatper 9: Beginning with the Basic Building Blocks 261

Exploring the Modeling Types 262
Converting objects 262
Parametric vs. non-parametric 263
Working with Subobjects 263
Using Soft Selection. 264
Tutorial: Soft selecting a heart from a plane. 266
Creating Primitive Objects 267
Using the Create panel 267
Using the Create menu 269
Naming objects, renaming objects, and assigning colors 269
Using different creation methods 271
Using the Keyboard Entry rollout for precise dimensions. 273
Altering object parameters 273
Recovering from mistakes and deleting objects 273
Primitive Object Types 274
Standard Primitives. 274
Modifying object parameters 279
Tutorial: Filling a treasure chest with gems 279
Modeling Helpers 281
Using Dummy and Point objects 281
Measuring coordinate distances 281
Tutorial: Testing the Pythagorean Theorem. 282
Summary 283

Chapter 10: Starting with Simple Splines and Shapes. 285

Drawing in 2D 285
Working with shape primitives 286
Tutorial: Drawing a company logo 295
Editing Splines 296
Editable Splines versus the Edit Spline modifier 297
Selecting spline subobjects 297
Controlling spline geometry 299
Editing vertices 302

Editing segments 307
Editing spline subobjects 308
Using Spline Modifiers 313
Spline-specific modifiers 313
Moving Splines to 3D 314
Summary 318

Chapter 11: Moving On with Marvelous Meshes **319**

Creating Editable Mesh and Poly Objects 319
Converting objects 320
Collapsing to a mesh object 320
Applying the Edit Mesh modifier 320
Editable Mesh versus Editable Poly objects 320
Editing Mesh and Poly Objects 321
Editable Mesh subobjects modes 321
Editable Poly subobject modes 322
Selection rollout 322
Edit Geometry rollout 324
Editing vertices 325
Tutorial: Modeling a clown head 330
Editing edges 331
Editing Face, Border, Polygon, and Element subobjects 333
Tutorial: Building a beveled pyramid 336
Tutorial: Cleaning up imported meshes 340
Creating Low-Res Models 342
The Polygon Counter utility 342
Using the Optimize modifier 342
Summary 343

Chapter 12: Performing with Perfect Patches **345**

Introducing Patch Grids 345
Creating a patch grid 345
Tutorial: Creating a checkerboard 346
Editing Patches 348
Editable patches versus the Edit Patch modifier 348
Selecting patch subobjects 348
Working with Patch Geometry 350
Relaxing a patch 359
Tutorial: Modeling a shell 360
Tutorial: Creating a maple leaf from patches 361
Summary 363

Chapter 13: Continuing with Crazy Compound Objects **365**

Understanding Compound Object Types 365
Morphing Objects 366
Creating Morph keys 367
Morph objects versus the Morpher modifier 367
Tutorial: Morphing an alien head 367

Creating Connect Objects 368
    Filling object holes 368
    Tutorial: Creating a park bench 370
Creating a ShapeMerge Object. 371
    Cookie Cutter and Merge options. 372
    Tutorial: Using the ShapeMerge compound object 373
Modeling with Boolean Objects 375
    Union 376
    Intersection 376
    Subtraction 376
    Cut 376
    Tips for working with Booleans 377
    Tutorial: Creating a Lincoln Log set 377
Creating a Loft Object. 379
    Using the Get Shape and Get Path buttons 379
    Controlling surface parameters. 380
    Changing path parameters. 381
    Setting skin parameters 381
    Tutorial: Designing a slip-proof hanger 382
    Deforming Loft objects. 383
    The Deformation window interface. 384
    Scale Deformation 387
    Twist Deformation 387
    Teeter Deformation 387
    Bevel Deformation 388
    Fit Deformation 388
    Modifying Loft subobjects 390
    Comparing shapes 390
    Editing Loft paths 391
    Tutorial: Creating drapes 391
    Loft objects versus surface tools 392
Summary 393

Part III: Changing Object Appearance Inside and Out   395

Chapter 14: Controlled Destruction with Modifiers 397

Exploring the Modifier Stack. 397
    Applying modifiers 397
    Using the Modifier Stack 398
    Reordering the Stack 400
    Tutorial: Learning the effect of Stack order 401
    Collapsing the Stack 402
    Using gizmo subobjects 402
    Modifying subobjects. 402
    Topology dependency warning 403
    Holding and fetching a scene 403

Exploring Modifier Types. 403
    Selection modifiers 404
    Using Modifiers on Patch and Spline Objects 408
    Using Mesh Editing Modifiers 413
    Animation modifiers 417
    Subdivision Surface modifiers. 421
    Free Form Deformer modifiers 423
    Parametric Deformer modifiers 426
Summary 438

Chapter 15: Skeletons Rule: Building with Bones and IK 439

Building a Bones System 440
    Assigning an IK Solver 440
    Setting bone parameters. 441
    Refining bones. 442
    Tutorial: Making a simple puppet using bones 442
    Making objects into bones. 444
    Tutorial: Making a linked teddy bear into a bones system 444
Using the Skin Modifier 446
    Skin subobjects 446
    Editing envelopes 446
    Working with weights. 448
    Display and Advanced settings 449
    Tutorial: Applying the Skin modifier to a flamingo 449
    Using deformers. 450
Forward versus Inverse Kinematics. 451
Creating an Inverse Kinematics System. 452
    Building and linking a system 452
    Selecting a terminator 452
    Defining joint constraints 453
    Copying, pasting, and mirroring joints. 454
    Binding objects 454
    Understanding precedence 455
    Tutorial: Building an extensible arm linkage 455
Using the Inverse Kinematics Methods. 457
    Interactive IK 457
    Applied IK 459
    IK Limb Solver. 460
Summary 464

Chapter 16: Putting on the Ritz with the gmax Material Editor . . . 467

Understanding Material Properties 467
    Colors 468
    Opacity and transparency. 468
    Reflection and refraction. 469
    Shininess and specular highlights 469

Working with the gmax Material Editor 469
   Creating a new material 471
   Using the sample slot. 471
   Naming materials 473
   Assigning materials to objects 473
   Picking materials from a scene 474
   Resetting a material 474
   Removing materials and maps 475
   Tutorial: Coloring Easter eggs 475
Using the gmax Material Navigator 476
   Getting new materials 478
   Working with libraries 479
   Tutorial: Loading a custom material library 479
   Understanding Material/Map Hierarchies 480
Using the Standard Material 482
   Using shading types 482
   Maps rollout 486
   Tutorial: Coloring a dolphin 486
Using Multi-Materials 487
   Multi-Material rollouts 487
   Tutorial: Creating a patchwork quilt 489
Applying Multiple Materials 490
   Using material IDs. 490
   Tutorial: Mapping die faces 491
Understanding Maps 492
Using the Bitmap Map. 494
   The Coordinates rollout 494
   The Noise rollout 496
   Bitmap map 497
   The Time rollout 500
   The Output rollout 500
   Checker map. 501
Using the Maps Rollout 502
   Ambient mapping. 503
   Diffuse mapping. 503
   Specular mapping. 503
   Specular Level mapping 504
   Glossiness mapping 504
   Self-Illumination mapping 504
   Opacity mapping 504
   Filter color mapping 504
   Bump mapping 504
   Reflection mapping. 505
   Refraction mapping. 505
   Displacement mapping 505

Mapping Modifiers 505
    UVW Map modifier 505
    Tutorial: Using the UVW Map modifier to apply decals 507
    UVW XForm modifier. 508
    Unwrap UVW modifier 509
    Creating Planar Maps. 511
    Tutorial: Mapping a house. 512
    Material modifier 515
    Vertex Paint modifier. 515
    Tutorial: Marking heart tension. 516
Removing Materials and Maps 517
Summary 518

Part IV: Lights, Camera, Action   519

Chapter 17: Creating Ambiance and Mood with Lights 521

Understanding the Basics of Lighting. 521
    Natural and artificial light 522
    Shadows 522
Getting to Know the Light Types 523
    Default lighting 524
    Ambient light 524
    Omni light 525
    Spot light. 525
    Direct light 525
Creating and Positioning Light Objects 525
    Transforming lights. 526
    Listing lights. 526
    Placing highlights 527
    Tutorial: Lighting the snowman's face 527
Viewing a Scene from a Light. 528
    Light viewport controls 528
    Tutorial: Lighting a lamp. 530
Altering Light Parameters 531
    General parameters. 531
    Attenuation parameters 532
    Spot and directional light parameters 533
    Projection maps. 533
    Shadow parameters 534
    Manipulating Hotspot and Falloff cones 535
    Tutorial: Creating twinkling stars 535
    Tutorial: Showing car headlights 536
    Using projector maps and raytraced shadows 538
    Tutorial: Projecting a trumpet image onto a scene 538
    Tutorial: Creating a stained-glass window 538
Summary 540

Chapter 18: If You Could See What I See —
Controlling Cameras **541**

Working with Cameras 541
Creating a camera object 542
Creating a camera view 543
Tutorial: Setting up an opponent's view 544
Controlling a camera 545
Aiming a camera 547
Tutorial: Watching a rocket 547
Aligning cameras 549
Tutorial: Seeing the snowman's good side. 549
Setting Camera Parameters 550
Lens settings and field of view 550
Camera type and display options. 551
Environment ranges and clipping planes 552
Summary 553

Chapter 19: Getting the Prop to Spin — Animation Basics. **555**

Using the Time Controls 555
Setting frame rate. 557
Setting speed and direction 557
Using Time Tags. 558
Working with Keys. 558
Using the Animate button 559
Tutorial: Rotating an airplane propeller 559
Creating keys with the Time Slider 560
Copying parameter animation keys. 561
Using the TrackBar 561
Viewing and Editing Key Values 562
Using the Motion Panel 564
Setting parameters 564
Using trajectories 565
Tutorial: Making an airplane follow a looping path. 566
Using Ghosting. 567
Animating Objects. 569
Animating cameras 569
Animating lights. 569
Animating materials 569
Tutorial: Animating darts hitting a dartboard. 570
Merging Animations 571
Wiring Parameters. 572
Adding custom parameters 572
Using the Parameter Wiring dialog box 574
Manipulator helpers 575
Tutorial: Controlling a crocodile's bite. 576
Summary 577

Chapter 20: Graphing Animations with the Track View **579**

Learning the Track View Interface. 579
   The Track View toolbar 580
   Tracks 581
   Status bar 583
Track View Modes. 584
   Edit keys mode 584
   Edit time mode 586
   Edit ranges mode 587
   Position ranges mode 587
   Function curves mode 588
Working with Keys. 590
   Adding and deleting keys 590
   Moving, sliding, and scaling keys 590
   Aligning keys 590
   Editing keys 590
   Using visibility tracks. 591
Editing Time 591
   Selecting time 591
   Deleting, cutting, copying, and pasting time 591
   Reversing, inserting, and scaling time 592
   Reducing keys. 592
   Setting ranges 592
Adjusting Function Curves 592
   Inserting new keys 593
   Moving keys 593
   Scaling keys and values 593
   Working with tangents 593
   Applying ease and multiplier curves 594
   Tutorial: Animating a hyper pogo stick 595
Filtering Tracks 597
Working with Controllers. 598
Using Out-of-Range Types 599
Adding Note Tracks 599
Synchronizing to a Sound Track. 600
   Using the Sound Options dialog box 601
   Tutorial: Adding sound to an animation 601
Summary 603

Chapter 21: Whoa, Betty! Constraining Motion **605**

Using Constraints 605
Working with the Constraints 606
   Attachment constraint. 606
   Tutorial: Attaching a boat to the sea 607
   Surface constraint 608

Tutorial: Rolling a tire down a hill with the Surface constraint 608
Path constraint 609
Tutorial: Creating a dragonfly flight path 610
Position constraint 611
Link constraint 612
Tutorial: Skating a figure eight 613
LookAt constraint. 614
Tutorial: Watching a dragonfly fly 615
Orientation constraint 617
Summary 617

Chapter 22: Creating Automatic Actions with Controllers. 619
Understanding Controller Types 619
Assigning Controllers 620
Automatically assigned controllers. 620
Assigning controllers in the Motion panel. 621
Assigning controllers in Track View 623
Setting Default Controllers 623
Examining the Various Controllers 625
Transform controllers 625
Position track controllers 627
Rotation and Scale track controllers 633
Parameter controllers 634
Working with Expressions in Spinners 641
Understanding the Expression Controller Interface. 641
Defining variables. 642
Building expressions 643
Debugging and evaluating expressions 644
Managing expressions 645
Tutorial: Creating following eyes 645
Expression Elements 647
Predefined variables 647
Operators 648
Functions. 650
Return types. 652
Sample expressions. 653
Using Expression Controllers 654
Animating transforms with the Expression controller 654
Animating parameters with the Float Expression controller 655
Tutorial: Inflating a balloon 655
Animating materials with the Expression controller 656
Tutorial: Controlling a stoplight. 656
Summary 658

Part V: Creating Mods with the gmax Game Packs   661

Chapter 23: Making Worlds with Tempest for Quake III Arena . . . 663

Installing and Configuring Tempest for gmax 664
  Setting up paths. 665
  Testing it all out 666
  Load it up! 666
Brushes, Textures, and Entities: Learning Level-Speak 667
  Brushes 667
  Textures 667
  Shaders. 667
  Entities 668
  Triggers and functions 668
Getting a Handle on the Tempest Interface. 668
Setting It Up: Getting Ready to Work 672
  Tutorial: Creating the building blocks 673
  Tutorial: Applying textures 674
  Tutorial: Adding the player start 678
  Tutorial: Compiling and loading a level 679
Adding the Good Stuff. 680
  Tutorial: Adding lights 681
  Tutorial: Adding a weapon. 683
  Tutorial: Bringing on the pain
    (Or adding lava and other triggers) 685
Advanced Editing: Slicing, Dicing, and the Fine Art of Texturing 688
  Tutorial: A gothic skylight 688
  Tutorial: Getting into gear 691
  Tutorial: Multi-textured brushes 694
More on Functions. 695
  Tutorial: Adding a door 695
  Working with angles 697
Importing Models 698
  Tutorial: Adding torches 698
  Tutorial: Advanced texture manipulation 700
Enter the Arena: Finding Help in the Map Community 702
  Tempest discussion at gmax support forums 703
  Quake3World forums 703
  ..::LvL 703
  QMap 703
  Claudec's Tutorial Index 703
Summary 704

Chapter 24: Creating Custom Content for Flight Simulator 2002. . . 705

Using the Flight Simulator Editing Tools 705
  Using the MakeMDL Tool 706
  MakeMDL Recognized Names 710
  Working with Textures 711

Creating Scenery Objects 712
Working with Aircraft. 715
Tutorial: Exporting an MDL Aircraft 715
Finding Online Resources for Flight Simulator 2002. 716
Developer's Desk at Flight Simulator Insider 717
Combat Flight Simulator Insider 717
FSPlanet 717
FlightSim.com 717
AVSim. 717
Train Simulator Insider. 717
Summary 718

Chapter 25: Creating Adventures with Dungeon Siege®. 719

Using the Dungeon Siege Tool Kit™ 720
Siege Editor™ 720
Siege Max™ 721
DS Anim Viewer™ and DS Mod™ 721
Working with the Siege Editor™ 722
Learning the Siege Editor™ interface. 723
Navigating the view window. 723
Working with maps, regions, and nodes 724
Placing and positioning objects. 730
Working with monsters and triggers 734
Setting lighting and mood 736
Exporting maps to Dungeon Siege® 737
Working with Siege Max™. 738
Setting units and snap settings 738
Creating custom terrain nodes 739
Creating custom objects 742
Defining object characteristics through Template files 748
Working with characters. 750
Finding Dungeon Siege® Online Resources 755
Dungeon Siege® 755
Planet Dungeon Siege. 755
SiegeNetwork 756
The Dungeon Siege 'Net Guide 756
Dungeon Siege Realms 756
Summary 756

Chapter 26: Creating New Scenery for Trainz 757

Content Creation Tools 758
Editing Trainz 759
Working with the Surveyor 760
Adding graphics to the Surveyor 762
Creating config files. 762
Creating image reference files 766
Using the Content Foundry 766
Tutorial: Creating a green water texture 768

Installing the Trainz Asset Creation Studio. 770
Working with Trainz Objects. 772
    Setting and measuring units 772
    Editing existing source files 772
    Tutorial: Adding a windmill object 772
    Creating Trainz objects 775
    Mapping Trainz objects 775
    Positioning Trainz objects. 776
    Exporting Trainz objects. 776
    Loading Trainz objects. 777
    Tutorial: Adding a cow scenery object. 778
Creating Trains. 781
Adding Sound and Smoke Effects 782
Sharing Content 783
    Working with the Content Dispatcher 783
    Debugging with the Content Dispatcher 783
Locating Online Trainz Resources. 784
    Auran's Trainz Web site 784
    Trainz Luvr 784
    Train Simulator Insider. 785
Summary 785

Part VI: Appendixes   787

Appendix A: Installing and Configuring gmax. 789

Appendix B: gmax Keyboard Shortcuts 795

Appendix C: What's on the CD-ROM 805

Glossary 809

Index 821

Attacking gmax Hard and Fast

In This Part

Chapter 1
gmax — The
Possibilities

Chapter 2
Using the In-Your-Face
Interface

Chapter 3
Making a Custom
Face, er, Interface

Chapter 4
Getting Files In and
Out of gmax

Chapter 5
Choosing Your
Poison — Selecting
Objects

Chapter 6
Cloning, Grouping,
and Linking Objects,
and Other –ings

Chapter 7
Moving, Rotating, and
Scaling Objects —
The Return of the –ings

Chapter 8
Placing gmax on
Autopilot with
MAXScript

gmax –
The Possibilities

Do you remember the first time you played an arcade game? How about the first time you played a computer game at home? Do you remember the first adventure or scenario-based game that you finished? How about the first one you finished without cheating? Do you remember the first game that you completed with all settings on the most difficult level? Do you remember the first time that you stopped playing a game because no more levels were available? Do you remember your joy of finding some additional levels online? Have you ever thought of creating your own mod or levels?

If you've answered yes to most of these questions, then you truly are a gamer at heart. If you've answered yes to the last question, then you're about to embark on an interesting journey.

gmax is a complex piece of software that makes creating custom game content and levels possible. Throughout the chapters that follow, you'll learn to use the exact tool that the game developers use to create their games. Building game mods isn't for the faint at heart (as the thickness of this book would indicate). It takes patience and skill, a little bit of study, and a lot of practice, but the end result can be very rewarding. There is nothing like challenging other players to a death-match on a level you designed and built yourself. Talk about home field advantage.

Before we dive into the details on gmax, this chapter gives you a high-altitude view of gmax and its games. From this viewpoint, you'll be able to see how gmax fits into the gaming industry and what options lie ahead of you as a gamer and a game developer.

✦　✦　✦　✦

In This Chapter

Learning the history of gmax

Understanding gmax's relationship to 3ds max

gmax and the gaming community

Pursuing a career in the gaming industry

Introducing the gmax game packs

Understanding the limitations of gmax

✦　✦　✦　✦

Learning the History of gmax

At the Game Developer's Conference (GDC) in 2001, Discreet dropped an announcement on the gaming community that had generally had one of two different effects on the listeners. Attendees were either rendered immobile from shock or set into a frenzy of giddy excitement. Essentially, the announcement was that Discreet was going to make an optimized version of 3ds max for gamers, and they were going to give it away for free. At the time, this was an amazing bit of news, because 3ds max sold for around $2,500 to $3,000.

The excitement for gamers was significant because 3ds max is the software package that most game companies use to create their games, and now game content creators can use the same tool that the game companies use.

Once gmax appeared as a free download on the Discreet site, the number of downloads began to take off and entire Web sites sprang up overnight devoted to gmax and custom game content. Today the total number of downloads of gmax is over a half million. That's a lot of game content creators.

Understanding the Relationship Between gmax and 3ds max

To understand gmax, you first need to understand where it came from. gmax is based on 3ds max, version 4, which just happens to be the best selling 3d modeling, animation, and rendering package available. Combined with Character Studio, it's the product of choice for most gaming companies.

Note   Even though 3ds max 5 is currently available, most of the functions found in gmax are the same as those found in 3ds max 4. Version 5 includes many high-end enhancements that wouldn't be included in gmax anyway. Over time, some of these improvements will find their way to gmax.

gmax actually comes in two flavors — regular and extra crunchy. The normal gmax version is available for free from Discreet (or you can get it off the CD-ROM that came with this book). Discreet also has a development version of gmax available, affectionately called gmax dev. This later version enables game companies to create game packs that ship with their games. If you're looking to get your hands on gmax dev, then be warned that it is very expensive (unless you own a game company), but for most users, gmax is more than enough.

On the CD-ROM   The latest version of gmax at the time of publishing, version 1.2, is included on the book's CD-ROM.

gmax and the Gaming Industry

With gmax, the gaming companies have a way to give their game legs. The term "legs" is used to define the length of time that the game remains on the shelves. For these companies, the longer the game stays on the shelf, the more money it makes. (Come to think of it, book publishing works the same way.)

Have you ever played a game and ripped through all the levels in a matter a days and then felt jipped because it held your interest for only two weekends? Thank heavens for mod builders who enabled gamers to create new and devious levels, many of which were much better than the levels shipped with the game.

gmax lets mod creators use the same tool that was used to create the game in the first place, along with all the customization needed to output the content to the format that the game uses.

So the game companies get a game that stays around longer, the game hobbyists get an advanced mod builder, and the normal gamer gets more levels than he or she can shake a joystick at. It's a win-win-win situation.

Pursuing a Career in the Gaming Industry

If you speak of the gaming industry in Las Vegas, they will immediately think of gambling games, but because you're reading this book (even if you live in Las Vegas), I assume that you aren't interested in the odds of winning for a royal flush. I frequently tempt my young son with a career in the gaming industry. I ask him, "How would it be to play games for a living or even better, to make games for a living?" His answer is always the same: "Ooh, yeah!"

If you're anything like my son, then you were probably one of the first to download gmax and probably know more tricks than anyone on your block for beating games. If you're considering getting a job in the gaming industry, then learning gmax (and 3ds max) is a good start.

 Note Another good feather to have in your 3d cap is getting experience with the 3d program called Maya. Alias/Wavefront has recently made a learning edition of Maya available for free. You may want to check this tool out also. You can find details on the Maya Personal Learning Edition at www.aliaswavefront.com.

Many positions are open to game developers. You can become a modeler, an animator, or an effects specialist. One of the nice things about using gmax is that you get experience in all these areas. As you work with gmax to create a custom gaming level, pay attention to which area of development you most look forward to.

When you begin interviewing with game companies, you're going to need a portfolio of your work, so as you build levels, be sure to save images of your best work to show off later. Chances are the interviewer will not fire up Quake to see your custom level, but they will take time to look at your images. You can always take screenshots of your game in progress using the Print Screen key on your keyboard.

Another avenue that leads to the game industry is to choose one of the many schools that offer degrees in game development. You can find a good list of schools that will prepare you for the gaming industry at www.gamedev.net.

Every year there are several conferences and events that bring the gaming industry together. Attending these conferences gives you some valuable exposure to the industry. For games, the big one to attend is the E3 Expo. This conference takes place in the spring and is the place where all the new games are announced. Another good conference that is more technical is the Game Developer's Conference (GDC). For computer graphics as a whole, the place to be is Siggraph. You can usually volunteer as a student to get into conferences free of charge.

You can find out about these conferences online. E3 Expo is at www.e3expo.com, GDC info can be found at www.gdconf.com, and Siggraph info is at www.siggraph.org.

gmax Enabled Games

Just because gmax is out there and available doesn't mean you'll be able to use it with all the games that you want. Discreet is making money on gmax by licensing its use to the game companies. These game companies need to pay Discreet for the right to tie their game into gmax, so the list of games that you can use gmax on is short, but growing.

As part of licensing the right to use gmax, the game companies can develop their own interface pieces that work within gmax; these pieces are called game packs. These game packs enable the stuff you create in gmax to be loaded and used within the game.

Quake III Arena

When Quake was initially released by Id Software, it shook up the gaming market and single-handedly defined the first-person shooter genre. As Discreet was looking for a game to use to prototype gmax, Quake, which was up to version III by then, was a natural fit.

The Discreet engineers created a Quake game pack for gmax by pushing and poking all the functionality of gmax. The result was called Tempest, shown in Figure 1-1, and it was released alongside gmax as a proof-of-concept.

Cross-
Reference   You can find all the excruciating details on the Tempest game pack in Chapter 23, "Making Worlds with Tempest for Quake III Arena."

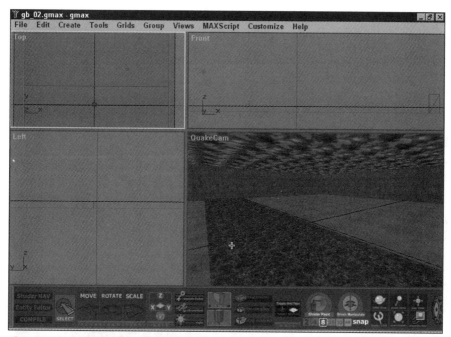

Figure 1-1: Tempest has its own toolbar full of commands that are unique to building Quake levels.

The Tempest game pack is still available for download at the Discreet site, www.discreet.com/products/gmax.

If you look closely at Tempest, you'll see the rough edges. Many Quake content creators use other tools to create their nightmares, but Tempest is still extremely useful as a first look at gmax and provides a quick and easy way to get your feet wet.

Flight Simulator 2002 Professional Edition

When Microsoft released Flight Simulator 2002 Professional, it was heralded in the burgeoning gmax community as the first gmax-compatible game. Flight Simulator users were excited about the possibilities that gmax offered, but many of them ran into a steep learning curve that sent them running back to their standby content creation tools.

In the Flight Simulator arsenal of tools, gmax is just one of many unique SDKs that enable customization. The integration with gmax consisted simply of an export feature that converted the gmax file into a format that Flight Simulator could use.

The Flight Simulator game pack didn't push gmax as far as Tempest did, but it was a good, important first step. Over time, Flight Simulator content creators have accepted and used gmax happily.

Figure 1-2 shows an aircraft being updated in gmax for Flight Simulator.

Cross-Reference   Details on using the Flight Simulator game pack can be found in Chapter 24, "Creating Custom Content for Flight Simulator 2002."

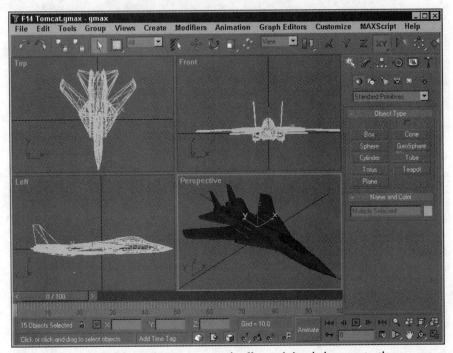

Figure 1-2: The Flight Simulator game pack offers minimal changes to the gmax interface.

Trainz

As Flight Simulator was making its big splash in the gmax market, another simulation game with a dedicated group of users appeared with a fairly robust implementation that relied on gmax. Trainz, created by Auran, is a simulator for trains.

With all the appropriate tools in place, the learning curve was manageable. Trainz users now boast one of the largest online repositories of gmax custom content available.

Figure 1-3 shows a sample engine created in gmax by Jean-Luc Benard.

Cross-Reference   For details on using the Flight Simulator game pack, turn to Chapter 26, "Creating New Scenery for Trainz."

Figure 1-3: The Trainz game pack changes the gmax interface slightly and adds some exporting features.

Dungeon Siege

After Flight Simulator, Microsoft released a game created by Gas Powered Games that relied heavily on gmax and allowed users to customize every aspect of the game to create their own adventures. The game was Dungeon Siege and gmax has made possible the creation of Siegelets that number in the hundreds.

The Dungeon Siege game pack is called Siege Max. Alongside a separate Siege Editor, it forms part of the Dungeon Siege Tool Kit. With these tools, you can create all the objects needed to populate the world of your adventure.

Figure 1-4 shows an image of a Sand Golem character created by Team Elemental, a group assembled to create a unique Dungeon Siege adventure.

 Cross-Reference   The various tools included in the Dungeon Siege Tool Kit are discussed in Chapter 25, "Creating Adventures with Dungeon Siege."

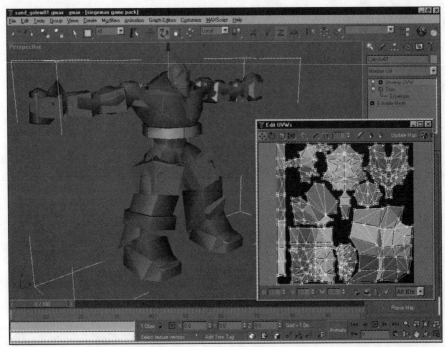

Figure 1-4: The Dungeon Siege game pack includes many interface enhancements that prepare objects and characters to interact with other characters within the game.

Command & Conquer: Renegade

Westwood Studios decided to create a gmax game pack for their Command & Conquer: Renegade release. This game takes the hugely popular Command & Conquer game concept and adds a first-person shooter element.

The resulting game pack, named RenX, overhauled many aspects of gmax and added lots of new functionality that made it easy to produce objects, weapons, vehicles, and characters for the Renegade game.

Combat Flight Simulator 3

Following on the success of Flight Simulator, Microsoft developed a gmax game pack for Combat Flight Simulator. This game's integration takes a step beyond its predecessor. The Combat Flight Simulator 3 game pack can export to the CFS .M3D file format. Figure 1-5 shows a sample plane in the Combat Flight Simulator game pack.

Cross-Reference   Combat Flight Simulator is similar to Flight Simulator, which is covered in Chapter 24, "Creating Custom Content for Flight Simulator 2002."

Figure 1-5: The Combat Flight Simulator game pack is similar in most respects to the Flight Simulator game pack.

Train Simulator

Answering the call of Trainz, Microsoft released its Train Simulator game. Train Simulator, like Flight Simulator, enables you to export gmax models into a format the game engine can use, as shown in Figure 1-6.

Note   Because of the extensive coverage of Trainz, this book does not cover Train Simulator, but the Train Simulator game pack is different from Trainz and is fairly similar to Flight Simulator.

And more to come

In addition to these games, several more games have been announced to appear during 2003 with gmax support, including the following:

✦ Microsoft's Impossible Creatures

✦ Microid's Tennis Master Series

✦ Unreal Tournament 2003

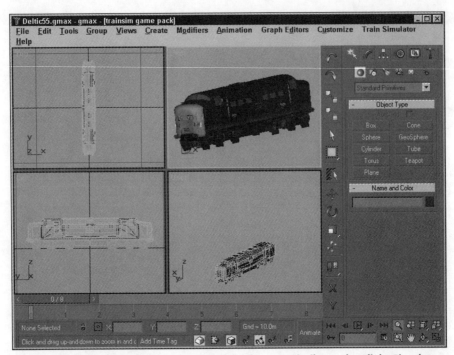

Figure 1-6: The Train Simulator game pack is also very similar to the Flight Simulator game pack.

Tip

Discreet keeps a list on its Web site of games that users have voted to provide with gmax support. If your favorite games aren't on the list, you can make your voice heard at the Discreet site.

Understanding the Limitations of gmax

Nobody likes to hear that software has limitations, and you may be screaming, "Hey, don't tell me what I don't have." But gmax may be just the starting point to a lifetime of work with 3ds max, and knowing where one ends and the other begins can help you in the long run. Also, by knowing the limits of gmax, you won't be spinning your wheels looking for a feature that isn't there.

Now that you're armed with a lame excuse, I'll give you the real excuse. Much of the features left out of gmax were excluded on purpose because games don't need them. For example, gmax doesn't include a way to render your scenes because the game engine has an optimized renderer built into it. The main purpose of gmax is to build and animate additional content for games, and almost all the modeling and animation features remain. See, someone is watching out for you.

Modeling limitations—the stuff you don't need

With all the various modeling features, you probably won't even miss these few limitations. These few limitations can be addressed easily using the available modeling types.

gmax has no Pyramid primitive object. Why is the pyramid missing? It probably has something to do with the power of pyramids, and such an object is just too dangerous in the hands of gamers. All the Extended primitives are also missing including equally dangerous objects such as the Hedras and the Torus Knots. (But they left the teapot for you, so what else do you need?)

For 2D drawing tools, the Section spline tool is missing.

NURBS modeling is also removed. NURBS is an acronym that stands for Non-Uniform Rational B-Splines. You can think of a NURBS object as a model that is made from a net and at each intersecting point is a handle that you can grab onto to push or pull the net. Using these control points, you can change the surface of the model. In some ways, working with NURBS is like modeling with clay.

NURBS are very useful for modeling organic objects like flowers and cloth. I guess Discreet assumes that we don't need any of these objects in our games. NURBS objects usually don't work in real-time games because they take longer to render.

3ds gmax has many other objects that it groups together as compound objects. These include Loft, Boolean, ShapeMerge, Morph, Connect, Conform, Scatter, Terrain, and Mesher objects. gmax includes only the first five of these. The latter four (Conform, Scatter, Terrain, and Mesher) can yield very large objects that wouldn't work well in games.

Animation limitations

Although 3ds gmax includes several different Inverse Kinematics solvers, only the Interactive and Applied IK methods and the IK Limb Solver is included in gmax. The HI IK Solver and the HD IK Solvers are missing. These solvers enable Hierarchy Independent and Hierarchy Dependent IK solutions.

Also missing in gmax is the Dynamics module that enables users to animate using defined physical properties like gravity, friction, etc.

Material Editor limitations

The Material Editor has been redesigned for gmax and it looks quite a bit different than the Material Editor found in 3ds max. Of all the various material and map types, only Standard and Multi-Material materials are available in gmax. For maps, you'll have to make do with the Bitmap and Checker map types. All other procedural materials and maps are gone, but you can simulate any of these other types using a Bitmap map, so Discreet left the one that counts.

Several complex materials have also been removed, including most of the Shaders, Reflection Mapping, Raytrace Materials, and Displacement Mapping. These materials are used to produce detailed looks that take a long time to render and would slow down your game. (You wouldn't want that, would you?)

Most of the material modifiers are absent, but the mapping modifiers of UVW Map, UVW Xform, and UVW Unwrap are still available. So gmax includes all that you need to work with and manipulate maps.

Effects limitations

gmax can't do Atmospheric effects like fog or Environment Mapping. Again, the reason is probably because these effects would take too long to render effectively. gmax allows backgrounds, but you can't animate them.

3ds max also includes Particle Systems and Space Warps, which sound like B-grade science fiction movies, but they let you create special effects by controlling the movement of thousands of tiny particles. A Space Warp is a tool used to create forces within a scene such as wind, torque, gravity, etc.

No rendering or compositing

There are no rendering limitations in gmax because there are no rendering features at all. Because the game engine is used to render the objects, rendering objects in gmax isn't necessary. gmax does include a flat shade renderer that is used within the viewport. This renderer can render objects as wireframes, smooth, or smooth with highlights. For the work you'll be doing, this is sufficient.

The Video Post interface is also missing. In 3ds max, this interface lets you combine different animation sequences and edit them in different ways.

Other limitations

3ds gmax includes a Sunlight system, which can simulate the effect of sunlight at any time during the year in any part of the world. This is missing in gmax.

The Camera Tracker and Camera Match utilities are missing in gmax. These utilities let you match a camera to a section of video or to an image. The Motion Capture controllers are also missing.

The Schematic View is also missing in gmax. This view displays all objects as nodes (small boxes) and includes all the links, groups, and instances of an object in a single view. It's good for getting a macro look at your scene and can even be used to move and define relationships between objects.

Summary

Understanding what gmax is and what it can and can't do is crucial as you begin to build game levels. With this understanding, you are ready to move to the next level.

This chapter covered the following topics:

✦ The history of gmax

✦ gmax-enabled games

✦ gmax limitations

Hey, this gmax thing sounds pretty cool, so let's look at it. The next chapter presents and (more importantly) explains the gmax user interface.

✦   ✦   ✦

Using the In-Your-Face Interface

◆　◆　◆　◆

In This Chapter

Learning the interface
elements

Becoming familiar
with the menus and
the main toolbar
buttons

Using the Command
Panels

Discovering
additional interface
controls

Understanding 3D
space

Using the Viewport
Navigation buttons

Loading a viewport
background image

◆　◆　◆　◆

Your first question may be "Why do you call it an In-Your-Face interface?" The answer is that the chapter title sounds cool, and because gamers like cool things, I figured it would help convince you to buy this book. Apparently, it worked. But seriously, the interface has been designed to make immediately accessible the commands that you use the most. This is no easy task because gmax has a ton (let me emphasize, a whole lot) of commands.

All of these tasks can be accessed in a number of ways. You can use a menu, a button in a dialog box, a keyboard shortcut, or a right-click pop-up menu. The commands are everywhere and are never more than a few short clicks away. And if you don't like the interface, you can customize it to be exactly what you want.

How important is a software interface? Well, consider this. The interface is the set of controls that enable you to access the program's features. Without a good interface, you may never use many of the best features of the software. A piece of software can have all the greatest features, but if the user can't find or access them, then the software won't be used to its full potential. gmax includes some amazing features, and luckily, the interface makes them easy to find and use.

The interface is all about making the features accessible, and gmax gives you many different ways to access the same command. Some of these access methods are faster than others. This is intended to give beginning users an intuitive command and advanced users direct access. For example, to undo a command, you can select Edit ⇨ Undo, which requires two mouse clicks, but as you gain more experience, you can simply click on the Undo icon on the toolbar (only one click. And an expert with his hands on the keyboard will press Ctrl+Z without even reaching for the mouse. These methods all have the same result, but you can use the one that is easiest for you.

This chapter explains all of the various elements of the gmax interface, but I'll warn you that this chapter has lots going on and you'll often find several paths leading to the goal. My advice is to find the path that works for you and stick with it.

The Interface Elements

If you're new to the gmax interface, the first order of business is to take a stroll around the block and meet your new neighbors. The gmax interface has a number of interface elements that neatly group all the similar commands together. For example, all the commands for controlling the viewports are grouped together in the Viewport Navigation Controls found in the lower-right corner of the interface.

Caution   If you are using gmax as part of a game pack, all interface bets are off. The various game packs can change the interface in a number of ways. The Tempest game pack for Quake, for example, has a new toolbar at the bottom of the interface that includes the main functions used by Tempest. To learn about Tempest and its interface changes, see Chapter 23, "Making Worlds with Tempest for Quake III Arena."

The interface is made up of the standard elements that you can see and elements that magically appear when you need them. First, we'll look at the visible controls and then talk about the magical ones that come when you call them.

The interface is all about making the features accessible, and gmax provides many different ways to access the various commands. The commands are roughly grouped into several different areas. For example, creating objects is done in the Create panel, and the Animation controls are grouped in the Time Controls.

For a quick overview of the various interface elements, see Figure 2-1.

Visible interface elements

The visible interface elements are the ones that you can point to with your finger while you ask, "What happens if I click here?" I cover each of these interface elements in the sections that follow. The visible interface elements include the following:

✦ **Menus:** Default menus at the top of the window offer a host of features. The application wouldn't look right without them.

✦ **Main Toolbar:** A toolbar of icons at the top of the window contains the commonly used features, and yes, you can swap these buttons with other ones. You can hide the entire main toolbar by pressing Alt+6.

✦ **Viewports:** Four separate windows show the Top, Front, Left, and Perspective views. This is your view into the scene.

✦ **Command Panel:** The major panel is located to the right. This panel is like a dialog box that never goes away, but you can hide it with the 3 keyboard shortcut. All the parameters for the selection or mode are displayed here, and you'll spend lots of time rifling through this panel.

✦ **Track Bar:** This long horizontal slider and time line at the bottom of the viewports lets you move between the animation frames.

✦ **Status Bar:** The bottom of the window offers information and settings for the scene. It can help you to know what gmax is expecting next.

✦ **Time Controls:** This set of VCR-like controls is used for playing, rewinding, and fast-forwarding through an animation sequence.

✦ **Viewport Navigation Controls:** These controls are for manipulating the view seen in the viewports.

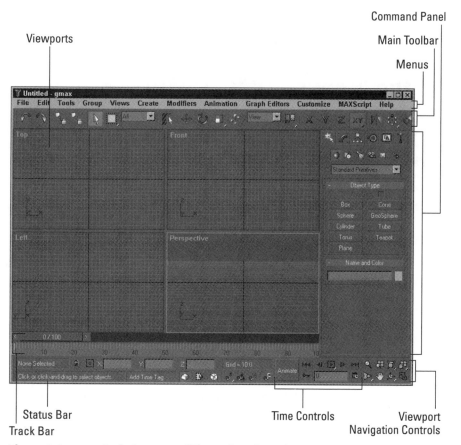

Figure 2-1: gmax includes many different interface elements.

Non-visible interface elements

Just because something is not visible doesn't mean it isn't valuable. You'll quickly find that these interface elements are very useful. These non-visible elements are initially not visible, but appear in response to a command. They include the following:

✦ **Tab Panel:** This is an expanded toolbar divided into many tabs containing icons for every major feature. You can open the Tab Panel by choosing Customize ➪ Show UI ➪ Show Tab Panel or by pressing the Y (or 2) keyboard shortcut.

✦ **Floating Toolbars:** These are custom toolbars that float above the interface or that can be docked to an edge. You access them by choosing Customize ➪ Show UI ➪ Show Floating Toolbars or by pressing 4.

✦ **Quadmenus:** Right-clicking on the active viewport makes these pop-up menus appear. They offer context-sensitive commands based on the object or location being clicked.

✦ **Dialog Boxes and Editors:** Some commands open a separate window of controls. These dialog boxes may contain their own menus, toolbars, and interface elements.

Using the Menus

The pull-down menus at the top of the gmax interface include most of the features available in gmax and are a great place for beginners to start. Several of the menu commands have corresponding toolbar buttons and keyboard shortcuts. To execute a menu command, you can choose it from the menu where it resides, click its corresponding toolbar button if it has one, or press its keyboard shortcut.

The main menu includes the following options: File, Edit, Tools, Group, Views, Create, Modifiers, Animation, Graph Editors, Customize, MAXScript, and Help.

If a keyboard command is available for a menu command, it will be shown to the right of the menu item. If an ellipsis (three dots) appears after a menu item, that menu command will cause a dialog box to be opened. A small black arrow to the right of a menu item indicates that a submenu for this item exists. Clicking the menu item or holding the mouse over the top of a menu item makes the submenu appear. Toggle menu options (such as Views ➪ Show Ghosting) change state every time they are executed. If a toggle menu option is enabled, a small check mark appears to its left; if disabled, no check mark appears.

You can also navigate the menus using the keyboard by pressing the Alt key by itself. Doing so selects the File menu, and then you can use the arrow keys to move up and down and among menus. With a menu selected, you can press the keyboard letter that is underlined to select and execute a menu command, or you can navigate to a menu command and press Enter to execute that command. For example, pressing Alt, then F (for File) and N (for New) executes the File ⇨ New command; or you may press Alt and then use the down arrow to select the New command and press the Enter key.

Not all menu commands are available at all times. If a menu command is unavailable, it is grayed out and cannot be selected. For example, the Clone command is available only when an object is selected, so if no objects are selected, the Clone command will be grayed out and unavailable. After you select an object, this command becomes available.

The File menu

The File menu includes commands for working with gmax files. These commands enable you to create a new scene, open and save scene files, and work with external referenced (XRefs) objects and scenes. You can also merge scenes, merge animation sequences, and replace objects in the current scene. The File menu also includes commands to import and export objects.

Because most of the commands found in the File menu affect files, these commands are covered mostly in Chapter 4, "Getting Files In and Out of gmax."

The Archive command copies all files used in the scene to an easily portable archive file format. The Summary Info and File Properties commands open dialog boxes where you can get information about the current scene file. The View Image File command opens a dialog box where you can view an image before loading it, and the Exit command exits the application.

The Edit menu

The Edit menu wins an award for having the most listed keyboard shortcuts per menu item than any other menu. It includes commands for recovering from mistakes (Undo and Redo), preparing for catastrophe (Hold and Fetch), and the ubiquitous Delete. It also includes a Clone command for making copies of an object.

The Edit menu also includes several commands for selecting objects — Select All, Select None, Select Invert, and Select By Color and/or Name. You can also specify the type of selection region and whether the region simply needs to cross the object or needs to window the object to select it. The Edit Named Selection command opens a dialog box where you can name a selected set of objects for easy recall. Finally, the Object Properties command opens a dialog box where all the properties for the selected object can be found.

The Clone command is covered in (no surprise) Chapter 6, "Cloning, Grouping, and Linking Objects, and Other –ings," and the selecting features are covered in Chapter 5, "Choosing Your Poison — Selecting Objects."

Recovering from mistakes

The first commands on the Edit menu are Undo (Ctrl+Z) and Redo (Ctrl+A). You can set the levels of undo in the Preference Settings dialog box. The Undo command lets you reverse an operation. By right-clicking the Undo and Redo buttons, you can see a list of recent operations and undo (or redo) several operations at once.

Caution

Many operations, such as applying or deleting modifiers and changing parameters, cannot be undone.

The Hold command saves the scene into a temporary buffer for easy recovery. After a scene is set with the Hold command (Alt+Ctrl+H), you can bring it back instantly with the Fetch command (Alt+Ctrl+F). These commands provide a quick way to backtrack on modifications to a scene or project without having to save and reload the project.

Tip

Along with saving your file often, you should get in the habit of using the Hold command before applying any complex modifier to an object.

Viewing object properties

Object Properties, the final command in the Edit menu, opens the Object Properties dialog box, shown in Figure 2-2, for the current selection. This dialog box includes information about the object and settings for Rendering Control, Display Properties, and Motion Blur. You can also use the Object Properties dialog box with multiple objects selected, but only the common properties are displayed. Right-clicking an object and selecting Properties from the pop-up menu can also open the Object Properties dialog box.

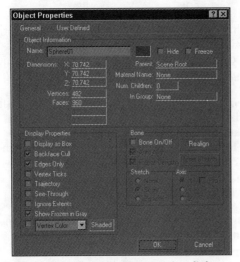

Figure 2-2: The Object Properties dialog box displays information about the object.

Cross-Reference

Chapter 5, "Choosing Your Poison — Selecting Objects," covers the various settings found in the Object Properties dialog box.

The Tools menu

The Tools menu provides access to most of the main dialog boxes in gmax. These dialog boxes, along with the Command Panel, hold many of the main functions of gmax. I briefly describe them here and cover them throughout the remaining chapters in more detail.

Object dialog boxes

The Tools menu includes several commands for controlling individual objects. Transform Type-In (F12) lets you input precise values for moving, rotating, and scaling objects. This command provides more exact control over the placement of objects than dragging with the mouse.

Cross-Reference

I cover Transform Type-In in more detail in Chapter 7, "Moving, Rotating, and Scaling Objects — The Return of the –ings."

The Display Floater command opens a dialog box with the same name that lets you hide, freeze, and control display properties. The Selection Floater command also opens a dialog box with the same name that lists all the objects in a scene sorted alphabetically, or by type, color, or size. From the list, you can select several objects, groups, or sets.

Cross-Reference

I talk about the floater dialog boxes in Chapter 5, "Choosing Your Poison — Selecting Objects."

The Isolate command hides all objects except for the selected object. It also opens a simple dialog box with an Exit Isolation button in it. Clicking this button or selecting the Isolate command again exits isolation mode and displays all the objects again.

Additional cloning commands

The Tools menu has several additional methods for cloning objects — in addition to the Clone command. The Mirror command uses the Mirror dialog box to create a symmetrical copy of an object across a designated axis. The Array command opens an Array dialog box in which you can create multiple instances of an object with each instance offset from the others. The Snapshot command clones objects over time using the Snapshot dialog box.

Cross-Reference

I cover the Mirror, Array, and Snapshot commands in Chapter 6, "Cloning, Grouping, and Linking Objects, and Other –ings."

Aligning objects

The Tools menu includes several ways to align objects. The Align command (Alt+A) opens an Align dialog box in which you can line up objects by axis, edges, or centers. The Align Normals command (Alt+N) enables you to align the face normals of two objects. A *normal* is a vector that extends perpendicular from an object face.

Place Highlight (Ctrl+H) moves the selected light in order to reproduce a highlight in the location you specify. Align Camera moves the selected camera in order to be directly in front of the point you select. The Align to View command aligns the object to one of the axes.

Cross-Reference
I explain most of the alignment commands in Chapter 7, "Moving, Rotating, and Scaling Objects — The Return of the –ings." I talk about the Place Highlight command in Chapter 17, "Creating Ambiance and Mood with Lights," and the Align Camera command in Chapter 18, "If You Could See What I See — Controlling Cameras."

Other dialog boxes

The Light Lister command opens the Light Lister dialog box, shown in Figure 2-3, where you can see at a quick glance all the details for all the lights in the scene. This dialog box also lets you change the light settings. It includes rollouts for Global Settings, which are the settings that affect all lights, and for Lights, which holds details on each individual light.

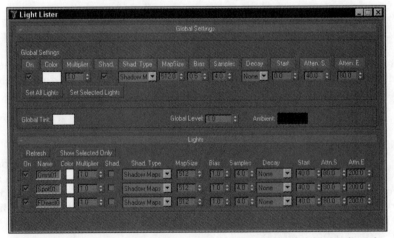

Figure 2-3: The Light Lister dialog box includes a comprehensive list of light settings in one place.

The Spacing Tool command (Shift+I) opens the Spacing Tool dialog box, which creates and spaces objects along a path. This is perhaps the easiest way to hang laundry out to dry.

I talk about the Light Lister in Chapter 17, "Creating Ambiance and Mood with Lights," and the Spacing Tool in Chapter 6, "Cloning, Grouping, and Linking Objects, and Other –ings."

The Group menu

The Group menu commands let you control how objects are grouped together. Selecting several objects and using the Group command opens a simple dialog box where you can type a name for the group. The Ungroup command disassembles the group and is active only if a group is selected. You can nest groups one inside another. You can also open groups, which enables individual group objects to be transformed or deleted. You can attach or detach objects from a group; the Explode command ungroups all nested group objects.

 For a more complete examination of groups and grouping, check out Chapter 6, "Cloning, Grouping, and Linking Objects, and Other –ings."

The Views menu

The Views menu controls all aspects of the viewports. Separately from manipulating an object, you can manipulate a view with the Viewport Navigation Controls in the lower-right corner of the interface. I cover these controls in a later section ("Using the Additional Interface Controls").

Undo View Change (Shift+Z) and Redo View Change (Shift+A) give you control over viewport changes, enabling you to undo and redo any changes made with the Viewport Navigation Controls.

You can also save and restore each viewport's active view with the Save Active View and Restore Active View commands.

 Saving an active view uses a buffer, so it remembers only one view for each viewport.

Controlling the viewport display

Grids are helpful in establishing your bearings in 3D space. The Grids command opens a submenu with the following options: Show Home Grid, Activate Home Grid, Activate Grid Object, and Align to View.

 Chapter 7, "Moving, Rotating, and Scaling Objects — The Return of the –ings," covers grids in more detail.

The Viewport Background command (Alt+B) opens a dialog box in which you can select an image or animation to appear behind a viewport. The displayed background image is helpful for aligning objects in a scene, but it is for display purposes only and will not be rendered. To create a background image to be rendered, use the Environment command in the Rendering menu.

Tip   Viewport Background can come in handy when you want to load as a reference an image or sketch of an object you're modeling.

If the background image changes, you can update the viewport using the Update Background Image command (Alt+Shift+Ctrl+B). The Reset Background Transform command automatically rescales and recenters the background image to fit the viewport.

Next on the Views menu are several commands that control what is displayed in the viewport. If these commands are enabled, a check mark will appear to the left of the command. The Show Transform Gizmo command displays axes and special handles to move, rotate, and scale the object in different directions.

The Show Ghosting command displays the position of the selected object in the previous several frames, the next several frames, or both. This feature lets you see the path and motion of objects as they are animated. Set the Ghosting settings in the Viewport panel of the Preference Settings dialog box. The Show Key Times command displays frame numbers along the trajectory where every animation key is located.

Cross-Reference   I cover ghosting and animation techniques in general in Chapter 19, "Getting the Prop to Spin — Animation Basics."

The Shade Selected command turns on shading for the selected object in all viewports. The Show Dependencies command shows any objects that are linked or instanced from a parent object.

Miscellaneous viewport settings

Several miscellaneous commands in the Views menu control the viewport. The Match Camera to View command (Ctrl+C) repositions a selected camera to match the current scene (you first need to have a camera in the scene and selected). Using the Viewport Navigation Controls to interactively line up a perspective view is often easier. After the view is correct, the Match Camera to View command can position and point a camera at exactly what you want to see.

The Add Default Lights to Scene command converts the default lights to actual light objects in the scene. This feature lets you start with the default lights and modify them as needed.

Cross-Reference   You can find more details on the Match Camera to View command in Chapter 18, "If You Could See What I See — Controlling Cameras," and more details on controlling lights in Chapter 17, "Creating Ambiance and Mood with Lights."

The Redraw All Views command (keyboard shortcut 1) refreshes each viewport and makes everything visible again (as objects get moved around, they will often mask one another and lines will disappear).

Deactivate All Maps turns off all maps. Material maps can take up lots of memory and can slow down a machine. If you're positioning or animating items, then turning off all maps makes sense.

Update During Spinner Drag causes a viewport to interactively show the results of a parameter value change set with spinner controls. Spinners are fields with up and down arrows to their right.

Running in Expert Mode

The Expert Mode command (Ctrl+X) maximizes viewport space by removing the menus, main toolbar, Command Panel, Viewport Navigation buttons, Status Bar, and Prompt Line from the interface.

You use features in Expert Mode by accessing the keyboard shortcuts. To re-enable the default interface, click the Cancel Expert Mode button in the lower right of the gmax window or press Ctrl+X again. Figure 2-4 shows the interface in Expert Mode.

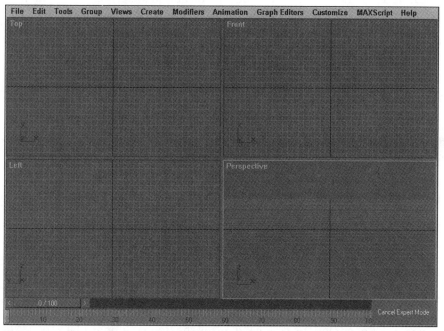

Figure 2-4: Expert Mode maximizes the viewports and shows only the Time Slider control and Cancel Expert Mode button.

The Create menu

The Create menu includes an easy way to create objects without your having to open the Create panel. Selecting an object from the Create menu automatically opens the Create panel and selects the correct category, subcategory, and button needed to create the object. After selecting the menu option, you simply need to click in one of the viewports to create the object.

The Create menu includes the following categories: Standard Primitives, Shapes, and Lights. You can find more details on each of these object types in later chapters.

The Modifiers menu

The Modifiers menu offers a way to apply modifiers without your having to go to the Modify panel. Before you can apply a modifier, you must select an object. Only the modifiers that you can apply to the selected object will be enabled.

Selecting a modifier from the Modifiers menu automatically opens the Modify panel, in which you can adjust the Parameters for the applied modifier. The modifiers in the Modifiers menu are grouped into several categories, including Selection Modifiers, Patch/Spline Editing, Mesh Editing, Animation Modifiers, UV Coordinates, Subdivision Surfaces, Free Form Deformers, Parametric Deformers, and Surface.

 You can find details on most of these modifiers in Chapter 14, "Controlled Destruction with Modifiers."

The Animation menu

The Animation menu contains many commands that help in producing animation sequences such as IK Solvers and Constraints. The IK Solvers menu lets you select the IK Limb Solver.

The Constraints submenu includes options that limit the motion of an object during an animation sequence. This feature is helpful for keeping the movement of objects within certain boundaries. The available constraints include Attachment, Surface, Path, Position, Link, Look-At, and Orientation.

The Create Bones menu command opens the Systems category in the Create panel and selects the Bones button. This command lets you quickly and easily make bones. The Bones Options command opens the Bones Options dialog box, where you can set the bone properties.

 I cover constraints in Chapter 21, "Whoa, Betty! Constraining Motion," and I cover bones and IK Solvers in Chapter 15, "Skeletons Rule: Building with Bones and IK."

The Dummy and Point commands, like the Create menu options, allow you to quickly create dummy or point objects. Dummy objects are useful if you need a non-renderable object to which you can link other objects. Point objects are useful if you want to mark a specific point in space.

The Add Custom Attribute command opens the Add Parameter dialog box. Using this dialog box, you can add new parameters to an object. These new parameters, once defined, show up in the Custom Attributes rollout of the Command Panel.

You can use the Wire Parameters and Parameter Wire dialog box commands to make objects respond to the changes of another object. For example, you can specify that the radius of one sphere increase as another sphere is moved.

 I cover adding custom attributes and wiring parameters in Chapter 19, "Getting the Prop to Spin — Animation Basics."

The Graph Editors menu

The Graph Editors menu includes the Track View menu. This menu lets you open the current Track View, create a new Track View, or delete an existing Track View.

The Track View menu

The Track View presents all the aspects of a project in a hierarchical form, letting you control the objects, transformations, and materials.

 I discuss the Track View dialog box in Chapter 20, "Graphing Animations with the Track View."

The Customize menu

The Customize menu provides commands for controlling and customizing the gmax interface. It opens the new Customize User Interface dialog box. This dialog box includes panels for Keyboard, Toolbars, Quads, Menus, and Colors, enabling you to customize almost every aspect of the gmax interface.

The Load Custom UI and Save Custom UI As commands let you load and save different custom interfaces. The Lock UI Layout prevents an interface from being changed. This feature is helpful if you accidentally keep dragging toolbars out of place. If your customization gets confusing, you can reset the layout with the Revert to Startup UI Layout command.

The Show UI menu contains a submenu of interface elements that you can toggle on or off. Elements that you can toggle include the Command Panel (3), Floating Toolbars (4), the main toolbar (Alt+6), the Tab Panel (Y or 2), and the Track Bar.

The Configure Paths command opens the Configure Paths dialog box where you can define all the default paths. The Preferences command opens the Preference Settings dialog box for controlling many aspects of gmax.

Chapter 3, "Making a Custom Face, er, Interface," explains how to customize many aspects of the interface and how to use the Preference Settings dialog box.

The Viewport Configuration command lets you configure the viewport using the Viewport Configuration dialog box. The Units Setup command opens the Units Setup dialog box for establishing system units. The Grid and Snap Settings command opens the Grid and Snap Settings dialog box for controlling grid objects and determining which points to snap to.

The MAXScript menu

From the MAXScript menu, you can create, open, and run scripts. You can also open the MAXScript Listener (F11) and enable the Macro Recorder.

Chapter 8, "Placing gmax on Auto Pilot with MAXScript," covers the basics of MAXScript.

The Help menu

The Help menu is a valuable resource that provides access to reference materials and tutorials. The User Reference, shown in Figure 2-5, and the MAXScript Reference are comprehensive help systems based on Microsoft's Internet Explorer.

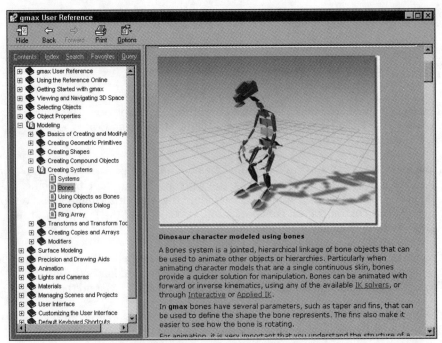

Figure 2-5: The User Reference includes hyperlinked words that link to other topics.

The References are split into two panels — the left panel includes a hierarchical list of topics and the right panel includes the details for the selected topic. The tabs at the top of the left panel can switch among Contents, Index, Search, Favorites and Query. Using these different tabbed panels, you can see an indexed list of topics, search for keywords, save and recall favorite topics, and query the pages for specific information.

The Help ⇨ Tutorial menu command loads the tutorial pages into the same browser-based help system.

Note   The References and Tutorials are not installed along with the default gmax installation, but can be downloaded as separate files and extracted into the \help and \tutorials directories where gmax is installed.

The Asset Browser command opens the Asset Browser, which is an Explorer-like look at the file directories where you can see thumbnails of images and gmax files. The gmax Community and gmax Support menu options open to their respective Web pages in the default browser.

Additional Help presents help systems for any external plug-ins that are loaded. The About gmax command opens the About dialog box shown in Figure 2-6. This dialog box displays the current version and display driver.

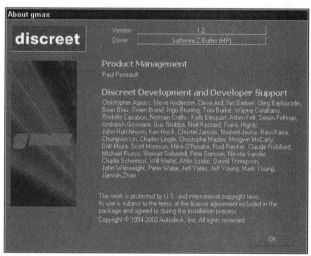

Figure 2-6: The About gmax dialog box shows the current driver.

Using the Main Toolbar

The main toolbar appears at the top of the gmax window by default. gmax includes many toolbars, but the main toolbar is perhaps most useful for managing the major functions of gmax. Figure 2-7 shows the main toolbar as a floating panel.

Tip   You can make the main toolbar disappear with Customize ➪ Show UI ➪ Show Main Toolbar or by pressing the Alt+6 keyboard shortcut.

You can make the main toolbar a floating panel by clicking and dragging the two vertical lines on the left end of the toolbar. After you separate it from the window, you can resize the floating toolbar by dragging on its edges or corners. You can then drag the toolbar and dock it to any of the window edges or double-click the toolbar title to automatically dock the toolbar to the closest edge.

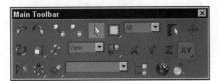

Figure 2-7: The main toolbar includes buttons for controlling many of the most popular gmax functions.

On smaller resolution screens, the entire toolbar will not be visible. To view the entire toolbar, position the cursor on the toolbar away from the buttons (the cursor will change to a hand). Then click and drag the toolbar in either direction. Using the hand cursor to scroll also works in the Command Panel, Material Editor, and any other place where the panel exceeds the given space.

Note   The General panel in the Preference Settings dialog box includes an option for using Large Toolbar Buttons or the small buttons from the previous versions. If you select a different button size, you will need to restart gmax in order to see the new button size.

All toolbar buttons include tooltips, which are identifying text labels. Hold the cursor over the icon to display the tooltip label. This feature is useful for identifying buttons.

The toolbar buttons with a small triangle in the lower-right corner are flyouts. A flyout is a button that holds additional buttons. Click and hold on the flyout to reveal the additional icons and drag to select one.

The icons on the main toolbar are described in Table 2-1. Buttons with flyouts are separated with commas.

Table 2-1
Main Toolbar Buttons

Toolbar Button	Name	Description
	Undo	Removes the last performed command. You can set the levels of Undo in the Preferences dialog box.
	Redo	Brings back the last command that was undone.
	Select and Link	Establishes links between objects.
	Unlink Selection	Breaks links between objects.
	Select Object	Chooses an object.
	Rectangular Selection Region, Circular Selection Region, Fence Selection Region	Determines the method for selecting objects.
	Selection Filter drop-down list	Limits the type of objects that can be selected.
	Select by Name	Opens a dialog box for selecting objects by name.
	Select and Move	Selects an object and allows positional transforms.
	Select and Rotate	Selects an object and allows rotational transforms.
	Select and Uniform Scale, Select and Non-Uniform Scale, Select and Squash	Selects an object and allows scaling transforms.
	Select and Manipulate	Selects an object and allows parameter manipulation.
	Reference Coordinate System drop-down list	Specifies the coordinate system used for transforms.
	Use Pivot Point Center, Use Selection Center, Use Transform Coordinate Center	Specifies the center about which rotations are completed.

Continued

Toolbar Button	Name	Description
X	Restrict to X	Allows objects to move only along the X axis.
Y	Restrict to Y	Allows objects to move only along the Y axis.
Z	Restrict to Z	Allows objects to move only along the Z axis.
XY YZ ZX	Restrict to XY Plane, Restrict to YZ Plane, Restrict to XZ Plane	Allows objects to move only along a specified plane.
	Mirror Selected Objects	Creates a mirrored copy of the selected object.
	Array, Snapshot, Spacing Tool	Creates an array of the selected objects, or copies over time.
	Align, Normal Align, Place Highlight, Align to Camera, Align to View	Opens the alignment dialog box for positioning objects, allows objects to be aligned by their normals (which is a vector that extends perpendicular from an object face), determines the location of highlights, or aligns an object to a camera or view.
	Named Selection Set drop-down list	Selects a set of named objects.
	Open Track View	Opens the Track View.
	gmax Material Editor	Opens the Material Editor window for editing and applying materials.
	gmax Material Navigator	Opens the Material Navigator window for selecting materials.

Cross-Reference Chapter 3, "Making a Custom Face, er, Interface," explains how to create custom toolbars.

Using the Tab Panel

The Tab Panel is like a super toolbar with tabs across the top that let you switch between many different toolbars, as shown in Figure 2-8. This toolbar is an efficient use of space if you want toolbar access to all commands. You can make the Tab Panel appear by choosing Customize ➪ Show UI ➪ Show Tab Panel, by right-clicking any toolbar (away from the buttons) and choosing Tab Panel from the pop-up menu, or by pressing the Y or 2 keyboard shortcuts.

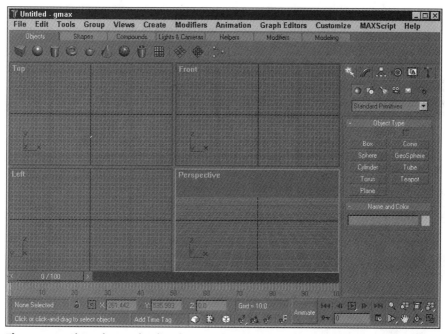

Figure 2-8: The Tab Panel splits the icon buttons into several tabbed toolbars.

The toolbars included in the default Tab Panel include the following: Objects, Shapes, Compounds, Lights & Cameras, Helpers, Modifiers, and Modeling. You can remove any of these individual toolbars from the Tab Panel or reposition it by dragging its tab away from the Tab Panel; however, you cannot remove the Tab Panel itself from the top of the window (but you can hide it).

Cross-Reference

Chapter 3, "Making a Custom Face, er Interface," provides more information on customizing the Tab Panel.

Using the Command Panel

If the gmax interface had a heart, it would be the Command Panel. This is where most of the functions and parameters are located. The features are split into six panels, each accessed via a tab icon located at the top of the Command Panel. These six tabs used to open the various panels are Create, Modify, Hierarchy, Motion, Display, and Utilities. Figure 2-9 shows the Command Panel.

Figure 2-9: The Command Panel includes six separate panels accessed via tab icons.

Tip   You can make the Command Panel hide and reappear with the 3 key.

The empty space at the bottom of the Command Panel dynamically fills with rollouts that include settings and parameters associated with each function. Each rollout includes a title bar with a plus or minus sign. Clicking the rollout title displays or retracts the rollout. You can also reposition the order of the rollouts by dragging the rollout name and dropping it above or below the other rollouts.

Note   You cannot reposition the Object Type or the Name and Color rollouts.

Displaying all the rollouts for a given function will often exceed the screen space allotted to the Command Panel. If the rollouts exceed the given space, then a small vertical scroll bar appears at the right edge of the Command Panel. You can drag this scroll bar to access the rollouts at the bottom of the Command Panel, or you can move the cursor around the Command Panel until a hand cursor appears. With the hand cursor, left-click and drag in either direction to scroll the Command Panel. Right-clicking within the rollouts section displays a pop-up menu that enables you to open or close any or all rollouts or reset the rollup order. Dragging the left edge of the Command Panel increases the column space that is used to display the Command Panel, as shown in Figure 2-10.

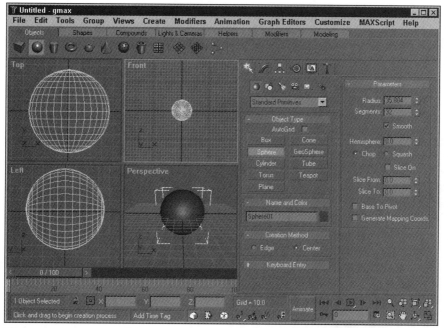

Figure 2-10: Increase the size of the Command Panel by dragging its left edge.

Cross-Reference   You can pull away the Command Panel from the right window edge as a floating dialog box. You can also dock it to the other window edges. You can customize the Command Panel like the other toolbars. I cover customizing the Command Panel in Chapter 3, "Making a Custom Face, er, Interface."

Create panel

You use the Create panel to create a variety of scene objects. The panel includes several categories and subcategories of objects. The categories, shown in Figure 2-11, are displayed as icons directly under the Command Panel tabs and include Geometry, Shapes, Lights, Cameras, Helpers, and Systems. Subcategories are displayed in the drop-down list under the category icons. I present these subcategories in their respective chapters.

Note   The Create menu options will open the Create panel and automatically select the requested object type.

Geometry

Shapes Cameras

Lights   Systems

Helpers

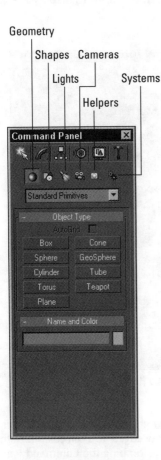

Figure 2-11: The Create panel includes six different categories of objects.

The parameters for newly created objects are displayed in the Create panel below the Name and Color rollout. The buttons in the Object Type rollout change depending on which category and subcategory are selected. Every object created with the Create panel is given a default name and color. The default color specifies the color used to display the object in the viewports if no material is applied. You can alter both of these parameters using the Name and Color rollout.

Modify panel

You can use the Modify panel, shown in Figure 2-12, to apply modifiers to the selected object. Modifiers are functions that modify objects in predefined ways. These modifiers can be controlled via parameters displayed in the Command Panel. All modifiers that are applied to an object are displayed in the Modifier Stack, which appears at the top of the Modify panel. You apply modifiers using the Modifier menu or by selecting the modifier from the Modifier List.

Look for more information on the Modify panel in Chapter 14, "Controlled Destruction with Modifiers."

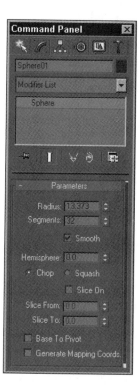

Figure 2-12: Use the Modify panel to apply modifiers and to modify object parameters.

The Modifier Stack displays all modifiers that have been applied to the current selected object. This stack lets you revisit any modifier and change its parameters, reorder it in the stack, or delete it.

Hierarchy panel

The Hierarchy panel, shown in Figure 2-13, includes three buttons for accessing settings for Pivots, Inverse Kinematics, and Link Information. The Pivots button lets you move and reorient an object's pivot point. A pivot point is the point about which transformations are applied. Inverse Kinematics is a method of defining the connections between parts for easier animation.

Check out the details on links in Chapter 6, "Cloning, Grouping, and Linking Objects, and Other –ings." I talk about pivots in Chapter 7, "Moving, Rotating, and Scaling Objects—The Return of the –ings," and Inverse Kinematics in Chapter 15, "Skeletons Rule: Building with Bones and IK."

Figure 2-13: The Hierarchy panel offers controls for adjusting pivot points.

Motion panel

The Motion panel, shown in Figure 2-14, includes two buttons: Parameters and Trajectories. One common way of modifying object motion is to apply Controllers and Constraints. The Parameters button opens an interface that enables you to access animation Controllers and Constraints. Controllers affect the position, rotation, and scaling of objects in preset ways, and Constraints limit the motion of an object. You can access a list of Controllers by clicking the Assign Controller button positioned at the top of the Assign Controller rollout or by choosing Animation ➪ Constraints.

The Trajectories button displays the motion path of an object as a spline and opens a rollout for controlling its parameters.

Cross-Reference Trajectories and Controllers are the subject of Chapter 22, "Creating Automatic Actions with Controllers," and I cover Constraints in Chapter 21, "Whoa, Betty! Constraining Motion."

Figure 2-14: The Motion panel offers an interface for assigning animation Controllers to an object.

Display panel

The Display panel, shown in Figure 2-15, controls how objects are seen within the viewports. You can set display parameters for individual objects. Using this panel, you can hide or freeze objects and modify all display parameters.

 Cross-Reference I cover many aspects of the Display panel in Chapter 5, "Choosing Your Poison — Selecting Objects."

Utilities panel

The Utilities panel, shown in Figure 2-16, includes an assortment of miscellaneous tools such as Asset Browser, gmax File Finder, Resource Collector, Assign Vertex Color, and MAXScript. To execute a utility, simply click its button or select it from the list. The functions of these utilities are diverse and are covered in various chapters throughout the book.

 Cross-Reference This panel also includes the Configure Button Sets button for customizing which buttons appear in the default Utilities rollout. See Chapter 3, "Making a Custom Face, er, Interface" for more information.

Figure 2-15: The Display panel includes Display Properties options for the viewport.

Figure 2-16: Click a utility button to access the various utilities.

Using the Additional Interface Controls

At the bottom of the gmax window are several elements that help you control what's displayed while you're working with the program. These elements are the Viewport Navigation Controls, the Time Controls, the Track Bar, the Status Bar, the

Prompt Line, and the MAXScript Listener. This section describes how to use each of these control elements.

Using the Time Controls

Although the Time Controls sound like an interface to a time machine, you use them in gmax to control animation sequences, as explained in Table 2-2.

	Table 2-2	
	Time Controls	
Toolbar Button	*Name*	*Description*
Animate	Toggle Animation Mode (N)	Turns animation mode on and off. This button is the largest in the whole interface and changes to red when active.
	Go to Start (Home)	Sets the time to frame 1.
	Previous Frame	Decreases the time by one frame.
	Play/Pause Animation, Play/Pause Selected (/)	Cycles through the frames. This button becomes a Stop button when an animation is playing.
	Next Frame	Advances the time by one frame.
	Go to End (End)	Sets the time to the final frame.
	Key Mode Toggle	Alters the controls to move between keys. With Key Mode on, the icon turns light blue and the Previous Frame and Next Frame buttons change to Previous Key and Next Key.
	Current Frame field	Indicates the current frame. A frame number can be typed in this field for more exact control than the Time Slider.
	Time Configuration	Opens the Time Configuration dialog box where settings like frame rate, time display, and animation length can be set.

Time Slider

The Time Slider is actually part of the Time Controls. It is the scrollable bar along the bottom of the window that identifies the current frame. The arrows surrounding the slider function the same as the Previous Frame and Next Frame buttons. You can drag the slider to quickly locate a frame.

Track Bar

Directly below the Time Slider is the Track Bar. This bar displays the animation keys. You can select, move, and delete these keys using the Track Bar. You can hide the Track Bar with the Customize ➪ Show UI ➪ Show Track Bar menu command.

Cross-Reference   See Chapter 19, "Getting the Prop to Spin—Animation Basics," for more on the Time Controls, Time Slider, and Track Bar.

Learning from the Status Bar and the Prompt Line

As you work, the Status Bar provides valuable information, such as the number and type of objects selected, coordinates, and grid size. There is also a Lock Selection Set button. Clicking this button will prevent the selection of any additional objects. The button is yellow when selected.

Tip   The Spacebar is a keyboard shortcut for toggling the Lock Selection Set button.

The Coordinate fields display the world coordinates or the cursor, unless an object is being transformed. For transformation, these fields show the offset dimensions of the transformation (units for moves, degrees for rotation, percentages for scaling).

Tip   When gmax first appears, the MAXScript Mini Listener (the pink and white bar to the lower left of the interface) conceals half of the Status Bar and Prompt Line. You can resize this interface element by dragging on the edge between the Mini Listener and the Status Bar.

The Prompt Line is directly below the Status Bar. If you're stuck as to what to do next, look at the Prompt Line for information on what gmax is expecting. To the right of the Prompt Line are seven buttons, as shown in Table 2-3.

Tip   Right-clicking the Degradation Override button opens the Viewpoint Configuration dialog box and displays the Adaptive Degradation settings. Right-clicking the snap toggles opens the Grid and Snap Settings dialog box, except for the Spinner Snap Toggle, which opens the Preference Settings dialog box.

Table 2-3
Prompt Line Buttons

Toolbar Button	Name	Description
	Plug-In Keyboard Shortcut Toggle	Enables keyboard shortcuts specified by plug-ins instead of gmax's defaults.
	Crossing/Window Selection	Determines how multiple objects are selected. For an object to be selected using Crossing Selection, it must intersect the dragged window. Window Selection requires that the entire object be included. The button default setting is Crossing Selection; depressing the button enables Window Selection.
	Degradation Override	Tells gmax to ignore the degradation settings when rendering an animation in a viewport.
	3D Snap Toggle, 2.5D Snap Toggle, 2D Snap Toggle	Specifies the snap mode. 2D snaps only to the active construction grid, 2.5 snaps to the construction grid or to geometry projected from the grid, and 3D snaps to anywhere in 3D space.
	Angle Snap Toggle	Causes rotations to snap to specified angles.
	Percent Snap	Causes scaling to snap to specified percentages.
	Spinner Snap Toggle	Determines the amount a spinner value changes with each click.

MAXScript Listener

At the left end of the Status Bar is the MAXScript Mini Listener control, as shown in Figure 2-17. This can be opened by dragging the Status Bar to the right. By right-clicking in this control, you can open a Listener Window and view all the current commands recorded by the Listener.

Cross-
Reference

See Chapter 8, "Placing gmax on Auto Pilot with MAXScript," for information on how to use this valuable tool.

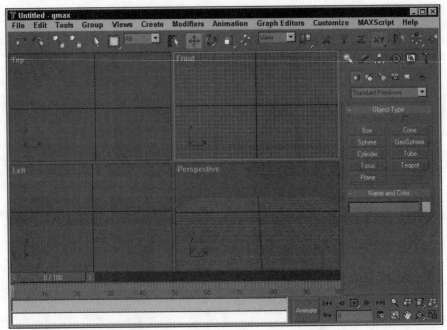

Figure 2-17: The MAXScript Mini Listener can be opened in the Status Bar.

Interacting with the Interface

Knowing where all the interface elements are located is only the start. gmax includes several interactive features that make the interface work. Learning these features will make a difference between an interface that works for you and one that doesn't.

Right-click quadmenus

Right-click menus have always been a part of the gmax interface, but in release 4, their function has been greatly expanded with the new quadmenus. Right-clicking in the active viewport displays up to four pop-up menus positioned around the cursor. The contents of the menus depend on the object selected. The four default quad-menus are Display, Transform, Tools1, and Tools2, as shown in Figure 2-18.

Clicking with the left mouse button away from the quadmenu closes the quadmenu. For each menu, the last menu item selected will be displayed in blue. To quickly access the blue menu item again, simply click the quadmenu title. Using Customize ⇨ Customize User Interface, you can specify which commands appear on the quad-menus.

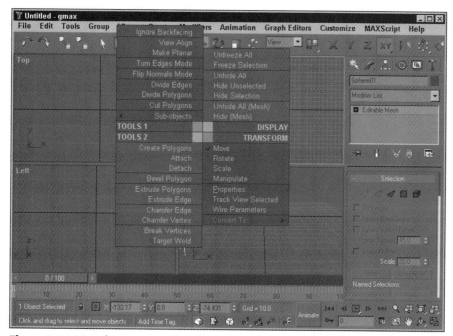

Figure 2-18: Quadmenus contain a host of commands in an easily accessible location.

Floating and docking panels

You can float and dock all toolbars and the Command Panel along the edges of the window. To float a toolbar, drag its title bar into the center of the window. You can resize floating toolbars and position them anywhere on the screen. They will always appear above the default gmax window. You can toggle floating toolbars on and off with the 4 key.

Note   gmax doesn't include any floating toolbars by default.

Figure 2-19 shows an interface where the Command Panel has been moved to the left and the main toolbar has been positioned at the right.

To dock a floating toolbar, move it close to the edge of gmax's window and release the mouse. Or right-click the title and select Dock and the location where it should be located. After a toolbar has been docked and then floated again, double-clicking the title bar will return it to its former docked location.

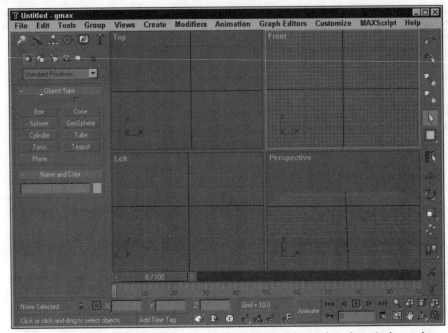

Figure 2-19: You can dock toolbars and the Command Panel to the window edges.

Understanding the color cues

gmax's interface uses color cues to help remind you of the current mode. For example, when the Animate button is depressed, it turns red. The edge of the current viewport being animated also turns red. This reminds you that any modifications will be saved as a key.

Working in Inverse Kinematics mode is denoted by the color blue. Yellow and orange warns of non-default settings, such as working with a subobject. Knowing what the current mode is at all times can keep you out of trouble.

Drag-and-drop features

Dialog boxes that work with files benefit greatly from gmax's drag-and-drop features. The Material Editor, Background Image, and View File dialog boxes all use drag and drop. One of the best places to use drag and drop is with the Asset Manager utility, which I describe later in this section.

Controlling spinners

Spinners are those little controls throughout the Command Panel with a value field and two arrows to its right. As you would expect, clicking the up arrow increases the value and the down arrow decreases the value. The amount of the increase or decrease depends on the setting in the General tab of the Preference Settings dialog box. Another way to control the spinner value is to click the arrows and drag with the mouse. Dragging up increases the value and down decreases it.

Keyboard shortcuts

Many features include keyboard shortcuts. These shortcuts can give you direct access to a command without moving the mouse. The default shortcuts for the menu commands are listed to the right of the command. You can use the Keyboard panel of the Customize User Interface dialog box to view and change the keyboard shortcuts for any feature.

Cross-Reference

Appendix B lists all the default keyboard shortcuts.

Modeless and persistent dialog boxes

Many dialog boxes in gmax are *modeless,* which means that the dialog box doesn't need to be closed before you can work with objects in the background viewports. The Material Editor is an example of a modeless dialog box. With the Material Editor open, you can create, select, and transform objects in the background. Other modeless dialog boxes include the Material/Map Browser, the Transform Type-In dialog box, the Display and Selection Floaters, and the Track View.

Another feature of many, but not all, dialog boxes is *persistence,* which means that values added to a dialog box remain set when the dialog box is reopened. This feature only applies within a given gmax session. Choosing the File ⇨ Reset command button or exiting and restarting gmax will reset all the dialog boxes.

Working with the Viewports

Before we leave this interesting chapter on the gmax interface, we need to spend some time with the interface element that consumes the most space and which you'll probably be looking at most of the time — the viewports.

Understanding 3D space

It seems silly to be talking about 3D space because we live and move in 3D space. If we stop and think about it, 3D space is natural to us. For example, consider a filing cabinet with four drawers. Within each drawer, you can stuff papers in the front, back, or sides, as well as in the drawers above or below. These positions represent three unique directions.

When I ask my wife where our passports are and she says, "They're in the top drawer toward the back on the left side," I know exactly where they are and can find them immediately (unless, of course, my kids have been in the cabinet). The concept of three dimensions is comfortable and familiar.

Now consider the computer screen, which is inherently 2D. If I have many windows open, including a scanned image of my passport, and I ask my wife where the scanned image is, she would reply, "It's somewhere behind the large window where you're writing that book." And I would look and search before locating it. In 2D space, I understand top and bottom and left and right and a little notion of above and below.

This conundrum is what 3D computer artists face — how do you represent 3D objects on a 2D device? The answer that 3ds gmax provides is to present several views, called *viewports*, of the scene. A viewport is a small window that displays the scene from one perspective. These viewports are the windows into gmax's 3D world. Each viewport has numerous settings and viewing options.

Orthographic views

Orthographic views are displayed from the perspective of looking straight down an axis at an object. This reveals a view in only one plane. Because orthographic viewports are constrained to one plane, they show the actual height and width of the object. Available orthographic viewports in gmax include Front, Back, Top, Bottom, Left, and Right. gmax starts up with the Top, Front, and Left orthographic viewports visible, as shown in Figure 2-20. The top-left corner of the viewport displays the viewport name.

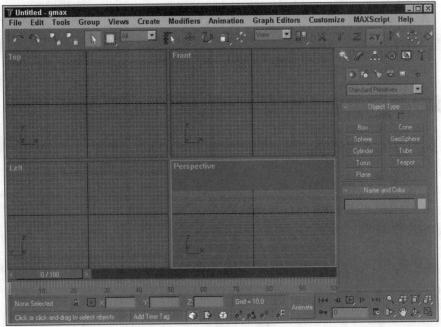

Figure 2-20: The gmax interface includes four viewports, each with a different view.

gmax includes several keyboard shortcuts for quickly changing the view in the active viewport. Use the W key to expand the active viewport to fill the screen (the same as the Min/Max toggle in the Viewport Navigation controls). Pressing W a second time returns the viewport to its normal size. Other keyboard shortcuts include T (Top View), B (Bottom View), F (Front View), K (Back View), L (Left View), R (Right View), C (Camera View), $ (Spotlight View), P (Perspective View), U (User View), G (Grid View), and E (Track View).

Perspective view

The fourth viewport is a Perspective view. Although not as precise when manipulating objects, this view is the closest to what we see in reality and gives a more intuitive definition of the relationship between objects.

Using the viewport navigation controls

The standard viewports will show you several different views of your current project; to alter these basic views, you'll need to use the Viewport Navigation buttons. These eight buttons are located at the bottom-right corner of the window. With these buttons, you can Zoom, Pan, and Rotate views. In Table 2-4, the keyboard shortcut for each button is listed in parentheses next to its name.

Table 2-4 Viewport Navigation Controls		
Toolbar Button	**Name**	**Description**
	Zoom (Z or [or])	Simulates moving closer to or farther from the objects in the active viewport.
	Zoom All	Zooms in or out of all the viewports simultaneously.
	Zoom Extents (Ctrl+Alt+Z), Zoom Extents Selected	Zooms in on the objects or the selected object until it fills the current viewport.
	Zoom Extents All (Ctrl+Shift+Z), Zoom Extents All Selected	Zooms in on the objects or the selected object until it fills all the viewports.
	Region Zoom (Ctrl+W)	Zooms into the region selected by dragging the mouse.
	Pan (Ctrl+P), Interactive Pan (I, held down)	Moves the view to the left, right, up, or down.

Continued

Table 2-4 *(continued)*

Toolbar Button	Name	Description
	Arc Rotate (Ctrl+R or V), Arc Rotate Selected, Arc Rotate SubObject	Rotates the view around the global axis or selected object. You can spin the base plane by dragging on the viewport or rotate along the perpendicular planes by dragging the green handles shown in the viewport.
	Min/Max Toggle (W)	Makes the current viewport fill the screen. Clicking this button a second time shows all four viewports again.

Most Viewport Navigation controls affect only the active viewport, but the controls that refer to all, such as Zoom All, will affect all the viewports. If you right-click on any of the viewports that aren't currently active, then the clicked viewport becomes the active viewport.

Note   If you select a non-orthogonal view, such as the Perspective viewport, the Region Zoom button has a flyout called the Field of View. Using this button, you can control how wide or narrow the view is. This is like using a wide angle or telephoto lens on your camera. This feature is different from zoom in that the perspective is distorted as the Field of View is increased.

When a Viewport Navigation button is selected, its outline turns dark yellow. You cannot select, create, or transform objects while one of these buttons is active.

After you've moved, rotated, and zoomed in a viewport until you have a view that you're happy with, you can save the view using Views ➪ Save Active Viewport. This command saves the Viewport Navigation settings for recall. To restore these settings, use Views ➪ Restore Active Viewport.

Note   The Save and Restore Active Viewport commands do not save any viewport configuration settings, just the navigated view.

You can undo and redo viewport changes with Views ➪ Undo View Change (Shift+Z) and Views ➪ Redo View Change (Shift+A). These commands are different from the Edit ➪ Undo and Edit ➪ Redo commands, which can undo or redo geometry changes.

The Viewport Navigation flyout buttons are color-coded. These colors tell you which object level you are working on. All buttons that include solid white apply only to the selected objects. Icons without any white apply to all objects. Yellow applies to subobject selections.

You can set any viewport to be a camera view or a light view. When either of these views is active, the Viewport Navigation buttons change. In camera view, controls for dolly, roll, truck, pan, orbit, and field of view become active. The light view includes controls for falloff and hotspots.

Chapter 18, "If You Could See What I See — Controlling Cameras," and Chapter 17, "Setting Ambiance and Mood with Lights," cover these changes in more detail.

Tutorial: Navigating the active viewport

Over time, working with the Viewport Navigation controls will become second nature to you, but you'll need to practice to get to that point. In this tutorial, you'll get a chance to take the viewports for a spin — literally.

To practice navigating a viewport, follow these steps:

1. Open dog.gmax from the Chap 02 directory on the CD-ROM.

   This file includes a model of a dog imported from Poser. It will provide a reference as we navigate the viewport. The active viewport is the Perspective viewport. You can tell this by looking for the light gray border that surrounds the viewport.

2. Click the Min/Max Toggle (or press the W key) to make the Perspective viewport fill the space of all four viewports.

3. Click the Zoom button and drag in the Perspective viewport to zoom in on the dog; then click the Pan button and drag the window until the dog's head fills the viewport, as shown in Figure 2-21.

4. Choose Views ⇨ Save Active Perspective View to save the current view of the dog's head.

5. Click the Zoom Extents button to size the entire dog body in the current viewport.

6. Click the Rotate button.

   A circle with small rotating markers at the top, bottom, left, and right appears.

7. Rotate the view by clicking one of these markers and dragging.

   The left and right markers rotate the view side to side, and the top and bottom markers rotate the view up and down. Clicking and dragging outside of the circle spins the view about its center point. Figure 2-22 shows the dog view after rotating it.

8. Click the Region Zoom button, and drag an outline over the dog's head and nose.

   Figure 2-23 shows the result of this zoom.

Figure 2-21: The Perspective viewport zoomed in on the dog's head using the Zoom and Pan controls

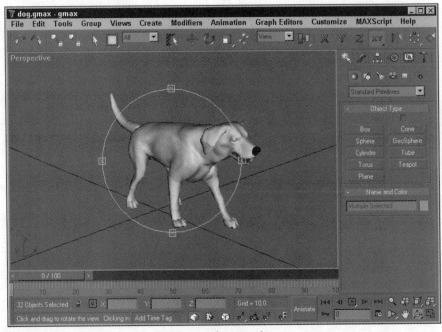

Figure 2-22: The Perspective viewport after rotation

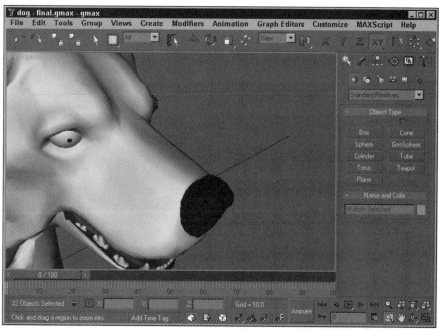

Figure 2-23: The Perspective viewport after zooming in on a region

Working with viewport backgrounds

Remember in grade school when you realized that you could immediately draw really well using tracing paper (where all you needed to do was follow the lines)? Well, it's not quite tracing paper, but you can load background images into a viewport that can help as you create and position your objects.

Loading viewport background images

The Views ➪ Viewport Background menu command (Alt+B) opens a dialog box, shown in Figure 2-24, in which you can select an image or animation to appear behind a viewport. The displayed background image is helpful for aligning objects in a scene.

If the background image changes, you can update the viewport using the Views ➪ Update Background Image menu command (Alt+Shift+Ctrl+B). The Views ➪ Reset Background Transform menu command automatically rescales and recenters the background image to fit the viewport.

Each viewport can have a different background image. To load and configure a viewport background image, choose Views ➪ Viewport Background (or press the Alt+B keyboard shortcut). This opens the Viewport Background dialog box, shown previously.

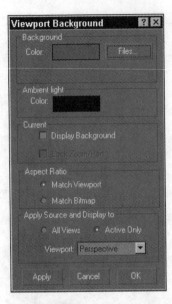

Figure 2-24: The Viewport Background dialog box lets you select a background source image or animation.

The Files button opens the Select Background Image dialog box, where you can select the image to load.

The Aspect Ratio section offers options for setting the size of the background image. You can select to Match Viewport or Match Bitmap.

The Lock Zoom/Pan option is available if the Match Bitmap option is selected. This option will lock the background image to the geometry so that when the objects in the scene are zoomed or panned, the background image follows. If the background gets out of line, you can reset its position with the Views ➪ Reset Background Transform command.

Caution   When the Lock Zoom/Pan option is selected, the background image is resized when you zoom in on an object. Resizing the background image fills the virtual memory, and if you zoom in too far, the background image could exceed your virtual memory. If this happens, a dialog box appears that informs you of the problem and gives you the option of not displaying the background image.

You can set the Apply Source and Display to option to display the background in All Views or in the Active Only.

Tutorial: Loading reference images for modeling

When modeling a physical object, you can get a jump on the project by taking pictures with a digital camera of the front, top, and left views of the object, and then load them as background images in the respective viewports. The background images can then be a reference for your work. This is especially helpful with models that need to be precise. You can even work from CAD drawings.

To load the background images of a brass swan sculpture, follow these steps:

1. Choose File ➪ New (or press Ctrl+N) to open a blank scene file.

2. Right-click the Front viewport to make it the active viewport, and choose Views ➪ Viewport Background (or press Alt+B).

   The Viewport Background dialog box opens.

3. Click the Files button, and in the file dialog box that opens, select the Brass swan-front view.jpg image from the Chap 02 directory on the CD-ROM.

4. Select the Match Viewport, Display Background, and Active Only options, and click OK to close the dialog box.

   The image now appears in the background of the Front viewport.

5. Repeat Steps 2 through 4 for the Top and Left viewports.

Figure 2-25 shows the gmax interface with background images loaded in the Front, Top, and Left viewports.

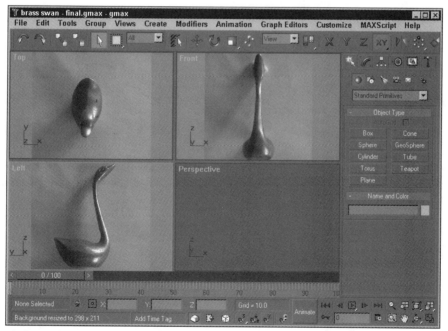

Figure 2-25: Adding a background image to a viewport can help as you begin to model objects.

Summary

You should now be familiar with the major elements that make up the interface for gmax. Understanding the interface is one of the keys to success in using gmax. gmax includes a variety of different interface elements. Among the menus, toolbars, and keyboard shortcuts, several ways to perform the same command exist. Discover the method that works best for you.

Viewports are the window into the gmax world. Learning to navigate the viewports allows you to work effectively with objects. You can configure viewports to display just the way you desire.

This chapter covered the following topics:

✦ The interface elements

✦ Working with menus and the main toolbar

✦ Using the Command Panel

✦ Learning the other interface controls

✦ Controlling animation sequences with Time Controls

✦ Getting information from the Status Bar and the Prompt Line

✦ Interfacing with the gmax interface

✦ Using and navigating the various viewports

✦ Loading a viewport background image

In the next chapter, you'll find out all the details about working with files, including loading, saving, and merging scene files. You'll also learn about External References (XRefs) and how to use them to manage scene creation in a workgroup. The next chapter also covers import and export options for interfacing with other software packages.

✦   ✦   ✦

Making a Custom Face, er, Interface

◆ ◆ ◆ ◆

In This Chapter

Using the Customize
User Interface
dialog box

Creating custom
keyboard shortcuts,
toolbars, quadmenus,
menus, and colors

Customizing the Tab
Panel and the
Command Panel
buttons

Loading and saving
custom interfaces

Configuring paths

Setting up units

Controlling the
viewport settings
with the Viewport
Configuration
dialog box

Setting preferences

◆ ◆ ◆ ◆

When you get into a new car, one of the first things you do is rearrange the seat and mirrors. You do this to make yourself comfortable. The same principle can apply to software packages — arranging or customizing an interface makes it more comfortable to work with.

The gmax interface can be customized to show only the icons and tools that you want to see. You can also play with a rather bulky set of preferences and set almost every aspect of gmax. This chapter covers various ways to make the gmax interface more comfortable for you. Now, if we could only get cars that save a custom setup.

Using the Customize User Interface Window

The key to customizing the interface is the Customize ⇨ Customize User Interface menu command. This command opens the Customize User Interface dialog box. This dialog box includes five panels including Keyboard, Toolbars, Quads, Menus, and Colors. You can also access this dialog box by right-clicking any toolbar away from the buttons and selecting Customize from the pop-up menu.

Note

The game packs will do their share of customizing too, so you may want to familiarize yourself with the default gmax setup before you customize it.

Customizing keyboard shortcuts

If used properly, keyboard shortcuts can increase your efficiency dramatically. Figure 3-1 shows the Keyboard panel of the Customize User Interface dialog box. In this panel, you can assign shortcuts to any command and define sets of shortcuts. You can assign keyboard shortcuts for any of the interfaces listed in the Group drop-down list. When an interface is selected from the Group drop-down list, all of its commands are listed below along with their current keyboard shortcut. You can disable the keyboard shortcuts for any of these interfaces using the Active option located next to the drop-down list.

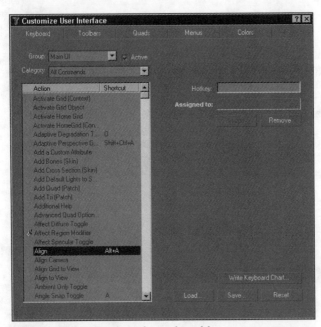

Figure 3-1: The Keyboard panel enables you to create keyboard shortcuts for any command.

Groups that have a large number of commands will be split into categories. You can use the Category drop-down list to filter only select types of commands. This helps you to quickly locate a specific type of commands such as controllers or modifiers. Entering a keyboard shortcut into the Hotkey field will show in the Assigned To field if that key is currently assigned to a command. You can Assign the hotkey to the selected command or Remove the hotkey from its current assignment.

Note   Assigned hotkeys for menu commands will be displayed to the right of the menu.

You can use the Write Keyboard Chart button to output all the keyboard commands to a text file. Using this feature, you can print and post a chart of keyboard shortcuts next to your computer monitor. You can also Load, Save, and Reset selected keyboard shortcut sets. The default installation includes DefaultUI, MaxKeys, and MaxKeysClassic sets that can be loaded. Keyboard shortcut sets are saved as .kbd files in the UI directory where gmax is installed.

 Cross-Reference   You can find a reference of the available default keyboard shortcuts in Appendix B.

Tutorial: Assigning keyboard shortcuts

Do you use both hands to control the mouse? If not, then you have one hand that is idle most of the time. If you can train this hand to control features using the keyboard, then you will be much more efficient.

To assign a new keyboard shortcut to create a Sphere object, follow these steps:

1. Open the Customize User Interface dialog box by choosing Customize ➪ Customize User Interface.

2. Open the Keyboard panel, select Main UI in the Group drop-down list, scroll through the list, and select the Sphere Object command.

Tip   With a list of objects available, you can quickly jump close to a desired item by typing the first letter of the item. For example, pressing the S key will jump to the first item that begins with an *S*.

3. Place the cursor in the Hotkey field, and press Alt+Shift+Ctrl+S keys together.

   This will enter the hotkey into the field. In the default interface, this key isn't assigned to any command.

4. Click the Assign button to assign the hotkey to the command.

5. Click the Save button to save the keyboard shortcut set as myShortcuts.kbd.

   You can load the resulting set from the Chap 03 directory on the CD-ROM.

Figure 3-2 shows the Keyboard panel of the Customize User Interface dialog box before you've assigned the hotkey.

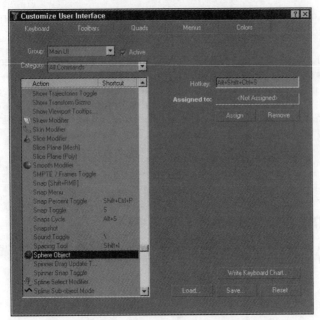

Figure 3-2: You can assign the Sphere object to the Alt+Ctrl+S keyboard shortcut.

Customizing toolbars

You can use the Customize User Interface dialog box's Toolbar panel to create custom toolbars. Figure 3-3 shows this panel.

The Toolbars panel of the Customize User Interface dialog box includes the same Group and Category drop-down lists and command list as the Keyboard panel. Clicking the New button opens a simple dialog box where you can name the new toolbar. The Delete button lets you delete toolbars. You can delete only toolbars that you've created. The Rename button lets you rename the current toolbar.

Use the Load and Save buttons to load and save your newly created interface, including the new toolbar, to a custom interface file. Saved toolbars have the .cui extension; the default installation includes toolbars named DefaultUI and MaxStart.

After you create a new toolbar, you can drag the commands in the Action list to either a new blank toolbar created with the New button or to an existing toolbar. While holding down the Alt key, you can drag a button from another toolbar and move it to your new toolbar. Holding down the Ctrl key and dragging a button retains a copy of the button on the first toolbar.

If you drag a command that has an icon associated with it, the icon will appear on the new toolbar. If the command doesn't have an icon, then the text for the command will appear on the new toolbar.

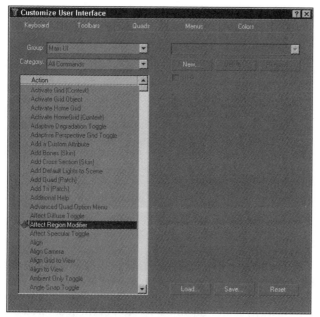

Figure 3-3: The Customize User Interface dialog box enables you to create new toolbars.

Tutorial: Creating a custom toolbar

If you've been using gmax for a while, you probably have several favorite commands that you use extensively.

To create a custom toolbar with your favorite commands, follow these steps:

1. Open the Customize User Interface dialog box by choosing Customize ➪ Custom User Interface.

2. Open the Toolbars panel, and click the New button.

   The New Toolbar dialog box appears where you can name the new toolbar.

3. Type a name and click OK, and a new blank toolbar appears.

4. From the Action list on the left, select and drag the commands to place on your toolbar to the new blank toolbar.

5. Continue to drag commands to the toolbar until you have all the commands you need.

6. Click the Save button to save the changes to the customized interface file.

Figure 3-4 shows the new toolbar. With the new toolbar created, you can float, dock, or add this toolbar to the Tab panel just like the other toolbars.

Figure 3-4: This is the new toolbar I created using the Customize User Interface dialog box.

You can right-click on any of the buttons on the new custom toolbar (when not inside the Customize User Interface dialog box) to access a pop-up menu. This menu enables you to change the button's appearance, delete the button, edit the button's macro script, or open the Customize User Interface dialog box.

Cross-Reference   To learn more about editing macro scripts, see Chapter 8, "Placing gmax on Autopilot with MAXScript."

Changing a button's appearance

Selecting the Edit Button Appearance command from the pop-up menu opens the Edit Macro Button dialog box, shown in Figure 3-5. This dialog box enables you to quickly change the button's icon, tooltip, or text label. Each icon group will show both the standard icon and the grayed-out disabled version of the icon. Default buttons can also be changed. The Odd Only check box shows only the standard icons.

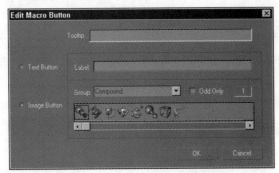

Figure 3-5: The Edit Macro Button dialog box provides a quick way to change an icon, tooltip, or text label.

Note   If a text label doesn't fit within the toolbar button, you can increase the button width using the Fixed Width Text Buttons spinner in the General tab of the Preference Settings dialog box.

Tutorial: Adding custom icons

The gmax interface uses two different sizes of icons. Large icons are 24×24 pixels, and small icons are 16×15 pixels. Large icons can be 24-bit color, and small ones must be only 16-bit. The easiest way to create some custom toolbars is to copy an existing set of icons into an image-editing program, make the modifications, and save them under a different name. You can find all the icons saved as .BMP and used by gmax in the UI/Icons directory where gmax is installed.

To create a new group of icons, follow these steps:

1. Select a group of current icons to edit from the UI directory and open them in Photoshop.

   I've selected the Cameras group, which includes all the files that start with the word *Cameras*. This group includes only two icons.

2. To edit icons used for both large and small icon settings and both active and inactive states, open the following four files: Cameras_16a.bmp, Cameras_16i.bmp, Cameras_24a.bmp, and Cameras_24i.bmp.

   In each file, the icons are all included side by side in the same file, so the first two files are 32×15, and the second two are 48×24.

3. Edit the files, being sure to keep each icon within its required dimensions.

4. When you've finished editing or creating the icons, save each file with the name of the icon group in front of the underscore character.

   My files were saved as Kels_16a.bmp, Kels_16i.bmp, Kels_24a.bmp, and Kels_24i.bmp, so they will show up in Kels group in the Edit Macro Button dialog box. Make sure the files are placed in the UI\Icons directory. You can find the icons I created in the Chap 03 directory on the CD-ROM.

5. After the files are saved to the correct directory, you'll need to restart gmax.

   The icon group will then be available within the Customize User Interface dialog box when assigned to a command.

Figure 3-6 shows the Edit Macro Button dialog box with my custom icon group named "Kels" open.

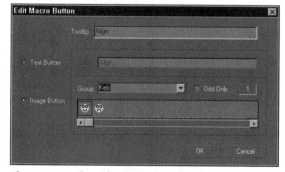

Figure 3-6: The Edit Macro Button dialog box with a custom icon group selected

Customizing quadmenus

The third panel in the Customize User Interface dialog box allows you to customize the quadmenus. You can open quadmenus by right-clicking one of the viewports or in certain interfaces. Figure 3-7 shows this panel.

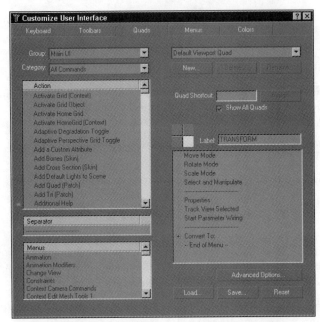

Figure 3-7: The Quads panel of the Customize User Interface dialog box lets you modify pop-up quadmenus.

To the left of the panel are the Group and Category drop-down lists and a list of actions that are the same as the Keyboard and Toolbars panels, but the Quads panel also includes a Separator and a list of Menu commands. Quadmenus can include separators to divide the commands into different sections and menus that appear at the top of the standard interface.

The drop-down list at the top right of the Quads panel includes many different Quadmenu sets. These different quadmenus appear in different locations, such as with the ActiveShade window. Not only can you customize the default viewport quadmenus, but you can also create your own named custom quadmenus with the

New button or Rename an existing quadmenu. The Quad Shortcut field lets you assign a keyboard shortcut to a custom quadmenu.

Tip   Several quadmenus have keyboard shortcuts applied to them. Right-clicking with the Shift key held down opens the Snap quadmenu. Other shortcuts include Alt+right-click for the Animation quadmenu and Ctrl+right-click for the Modeling quadmenu.

If the Show All Quads option is disabled, it causes only a single quadmenu to be shown at a time when unchecked. Although only one quadmenu is shown at a time, the corner of each menu is shown and you can switch between the different menus by moving the mouse over the corner of the menu.

The four quadrants of the current quadmenu are shown as four boxes. The currently selected quadmenu is highlighted yellow, and its label and commands are shown in the adjacent fields. Click the gray boxes to select one of the different quadmenus.

To add a command to the selected quadmenu, drag an action, separator, or menu from the panes on the left to the quadmenu commands pane on the right. You can reorder the commands in the quadmenu commands pane by dragging the commands and dropping them in their new location. To delete a command, just select it and press the Delete key or select Delete Menu Item from the right-click pop-up menu.

The right-click pop-up menu also lets you edit the command name or flatten a submenu, which will display all submenu commands on the top level with the other commands.

Custom quadmenus can be loaded and saved as menu files (with the .mnu extension).

The Quads panel also includes an Advanced Options button. Clicking this button opens the Advanced Quad Menu Options dialog box, shown in Figure 3-8. Using this dialog box, you can set options such as the colors used in the quadmenus.

Changes to the Advanced Quad Menu Options dialog box affect all quadmenus. You can load and save these settings to files (with the .qmo extension). The Starting Quadrant determines which quadrant is first to appear when the quadmenu is accessed. You can select to change the colors for each quadmenu independent of the others. The column with the L locks the colors so they are consistent for all quadmenus if enabled.

The remainder of the Advanced Quad Menu Options dialog box includes settings for controlling how the quadmenus are displayed and positioned, as well as the fonts that are used.

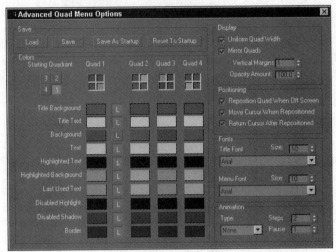

Figure 3-8: The Advanced Quad Menu Options dialog box lets you change quadmenu fonts and colors.

The Animation section lets you define the animation style that is used when the quadmenus appear. The animation types include None, Stretch, and Fade. The Stretch style slowly stretches out the quadmenus until they are full size over the designated number of steps, and the Fade style slowly makes the quadmenus appear.

Tip   I personally don't like to wait for the quadmenus to appear and like to keep the Animation setting set to None.

Customizing menus

The Menus panel of the Customize User Interface dialog box allows you to customize the menus used at the top of the gmax window. Figure 3-9 shows this panel.

This panel includes the same Group and Category drop-down lists and the Action, Separator, and Menus panes found in the Quads panel. You can drag and drop these commands on the menu pane to the right. Menus can be saved as files (with the .mnu extension). In the menu pane on the right, you can delete menu items with the Delete key or by right-clicking and selecting Delete Item from the pop-up menu.

Figure 3-9: You can use the Menus panel of the Customize User Interface dialog box to modify menus.

Tutorial: Adding a new menu

Adding a new menu is easy to do with the Customize User Interface dialog box. For this example, you'll tack another menu on the end of the current default menu.

To add another menu item, follow these steps:

1. Choose Customize ⇨ Customize User Interface to open the Customize User Interface dialog box.

2. Click the Menus tab to open the Menus panel.

3. In the top-right drop-down list, select Main Menu Bar.

   The current main menu bar opens in the right pane.

4. Click the New button.

   A New Menu dialog box opens.

5. Type the name of the new menu, "myMenu."

   This name will be added to the Menus pane on the left.

6. Drag the myMenu menu item from the Menus pane on the left to the command pane on the right, and drop it right after the Help menu item.

7. Click the plus sign to the left of the new menu item to expand it.

   As you drag, a blue line will indicate where the menu will be located.

8. Select several commands from the Action pane on the left, and drag and drop them under the myMenu item in the right pane.

9. Click the Save button to save the menu as a file.

Figure 3-10 shows the menu before it is saved. You can reset the default UI by choosing Customize ➪ Revert to Startup Layout.

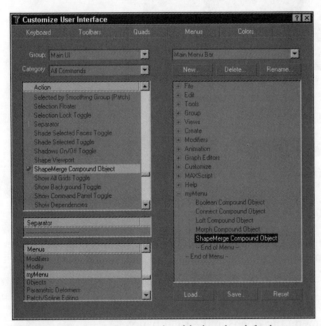

Figure 3-10: A custom menu is added to the default menu, compliments of the Customize User Interface dialog box.

Customizing colors

Within gmax, the colors often indicate the mode that you're working in. For example, red marks animation mode. Using the Colors panel of the Customize User Interface dialog box, you can set custom colors for all gmax interface elements. This panel, shown in Figure 3-11, includes two panes. The upper pane displays the available items for the interface selected in the Elements drop-down list. Selecting an item in the list displays its color in the color swatch to the right.

The lower pane displays a list of the custom colors that can be changed that will affect the appearance of the interface. For example, Highlight Text isn't an element; it's an interface appearance. The Scheme drop-down list can alter the color scheme between custom colors and the Windows Default Colors.

You can save custom color settings as files with the .clr extension. You can use the Apply Colors Now button to immediately update the interface colors. In the \ui directory where gmax is installed, you will find three color interface schemes — defaultUI, MaxColors, and MaxColorsGrey. Figure 3-12 shows the MaxColorsGrey color interface scheme.

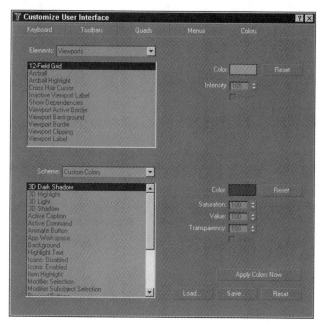

Figure 3-11: You can use the Colors panel of the Customize User Interface dialog box to set the colors used in the interface.

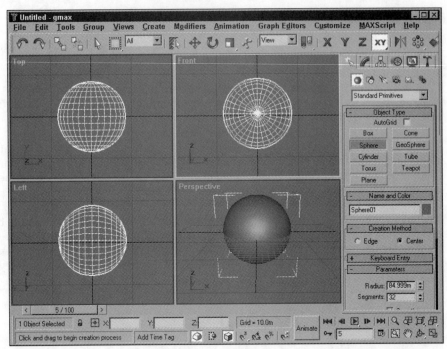

Figure 3-12: The MaxColorsGrey color scheme is considerably lighter than the default colors.

Customizing the Tab Panel

The Tab Panel (keyboard shortcut Y or 2) makes all possible toolbars available. When you click a tab, its toolbar appears. The default toolbars include the following: Objects, Shapes, Compounds, Lights & Cameras, Particles, Helpers, Space Warps, Modifiers, Modeling, and Rendering.

By right-clicking any tab, you can modify the Tab Panel. From the pop-up menu, you can choose to add a tab, delete a tab, or rename a tab. You also have options to move tabs to the left or the right.

You can convert tabs on the Tab Panel to floating toolbars by selecting Copy to Toolbar from the tab's right-click menu, or simply by dragging the tab away from the Tab Panel.

Customizing Command Panel Buttons

The Modify and the Utilities panels in the Command Panel both include a button called Configure Button Sets that allows you to configure how the modifiers are grouped and which utility buttons appear in the Utilities panel.

In the Modify panel, the Configure Modifier Sets button is the right-most button directly under the Modifier Stack. This button opens the Configure Modifier Sets dialog box, shown in Figure 3-13, where you can control which modifiers are grouped with which sets.

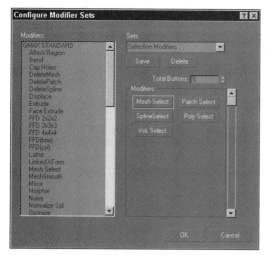

Figure 3-13: The Configure Modifier Sets dialog box lets you group the modifiers as you want.

To add a modifier to a set, select the set from the Sets drop-down list and drag the modifier from the list of Modifiers on the left to the button set on the right. To create a new set, simply type a new name into the Sets field. After a set has changed, you need to save it with the Save button.

You can find the same Configure Button Sets button on the Utilities panel. Clicking this button opens a similar dialog box where you can drag from a list of Utilities on the left to a list of buttons on the right. These buttons will then be displayed in the Utilities panel.

Working with Custom Interfaces

If you've changed your interface, you'll be happy to know that the Customize menu includes a way for you to save and then reload your custom setup.

Saving and loading a custom interface

Custom interface schemes are saved with the .ui extension using the Customize ⇨ Save Custom UI Scheme menu command. When you save a custom scheme, gmax asks which icon set to use. The options are Flash, Icons, and 2d Icons, as shown in Figure 3-14.

Figure 3-14: The Icon Directory dialog box appears when you're saving a custom interface and lets you select which icon set to use.

You can load saved user interface schemes with Customize ⇨ Load Custom UI. The default gmax install includes several predefined interface setups that are located in the UI directory. The standard available interfaces include the following:

✦ **DefaultUI:** Default interface that opens when gmax is first installed

✦ **MaxStart:** The interface that gmax loads when it starts, which includes any changes you've made to the interface

You can use both the load and save menu commands to save and load any of the custom user interface files types, including these:

✦ UI files (.cui)

✦ Menu files (.mnu)

✦ Color files (.clr)

✦ Keyboard Shortcut files (.kbd)

✦ Quadmenu Options files (.qmo)

Tutorial: Saving a custom interface

You can save personalized interfaces for later recall in the UI directory where gmax is installed. To do so, choose Customize ⇨ Save Custom UI. If you save your custom settings to the MaxStart.ui file, then your custom file will be loaded when gmax starts.

To have gmax start with your custom interface, follow these steps:

1. Customize your interface by making any desired changes.

2. Choose Customize ⇨ Save Custom UI Scheme.

   The Save Custom UI Scheme dialog box opens.

3. Open the UI subdirectory (if you are not already there), select the MaxStart.ui file, and click OK.

4. Click OK to replace the existing file.

You can set gmax to automatically save your interface changes when exiting. Select the Save UI Configuration on Exit option in the General tab of the Preference Settings dialog box.

Locking the interface

After you're comfortable with your interface changes, locking the interface to prevent accidental changes is a good idea. To lock the current interface, choose Customize ⇨ Lock UI Layout (or press the Alt+0 keyboard shortcut).

Reverting to the startup interface

When you're first playing around with gmax's customization features, really messing things up can be easy. If you get in a bind, you can reload the default startup interface (MaxStart.ui) with the Customize ⇨ Revert to Startup UI Layout command. Using the File ⇨ Reset menu command will not reset changes to the layout.

If your MaxStart.ui file gets messed up, you can reinstate the original default interface setup by deleting the MaxStart.ui file before starting gmax.

Configuring Paths

When strolling through a park, you can be assured that any paths you encounter lead somewhere. One might take you to the lake and another to the playground. Knowing where the various paths lead can help you as you navigate around the park. Paths in gmax lead, or point to, various resources, either locally or across the network.

All paths can be configured using the Configure Paths dialog box, shown in Figure 3-15. Choose Customize ➪ Configure Paths to open this dialog box. The dialog box includes four panels: General, Plug-Ins, Bitmaps, and XRefs.

When you install gmax, all the paths are set to point to the default subdirectories where gmax is installed. To modify a path, select the path and click the Modify button. A file dialog box will let you locate the new directory.

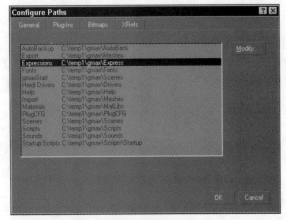

Figure 3-15: The Configure Paths dialog box specifies where to look for various resources.

The General tab includes paths for the following:

✦ **AutoBackup:** Directory where backups are saved

✦ **Export:** Directory where exported files are saved

✦ **Expressions:** Directory containing expression files

✦ **Fonts:** Directory containing fonts

✦ **gmaxStart:** Directory containing programs to execute when gmax is started

✦ **Heidi Drivers:** Directory containing the Heidi Drivers

✦ **Help:** Directory containing help files

✦ **Import:** Directory to open when importing geometry

✦ **Materials:** Directory containing material files

✦ **PlugCFG:** Directory containing plug-in configuration files

✦ **Scenes:** Directory where saved scene files are stored

✦ **Scripts:** Directory where scripts are stored

✦ **Sounds:** Directory to open when sound files are loaded

✦ **Startup Scripts:** Directory containing scripts that load when gmax is started

Tip Personally, I like to keep all my content in a separate directory from where the application is installed. That way, new installs or upgrades won't risk overwriting my files. To do this, I typically change the paths to AutoBackup, Export, Import, Materials, Scenes, and Scripts.

Under the Plug-Ins, Bitmaps, and XRefs tabs, you can add and delete paths. The XRefs panel specifies where to look for external resources and can include several paths. All paths will be searched when you're looking for resources such as plug-ins, but file dialog boxes will open only to the first path. Use the Move Up and Move Down buttons to realign path entries.

Caution Using the Customize ➪ Revert to Startup UI Layout command will not reset path configuration changes.

Selecting System Units

Max supports several different measurement systems, including Metric and U.S. Standard units. You can also define a Custom units system. Working with a units system enables you to work with precision and accuracy using realistic values.

Note Most game packs require a specific set of units to be set up. If you forget to set up the units correctly, the content that you create for your game will be mis-scaled (and nobody wants to drive a tank that is the size of a doghouse, no matter how cool it is).

To specify a units system, choose Customize ➪ Units Setup to display the Units Setup dialog box, shown in Figure 3-16. For the Metric system, options include Millimeters, Centimeters, Meters, and Kilometers. The U.S. standard units system can be set to the default units of Feet or Inches. You can also select to work with fractional inches or decimal inches from the drop-down list. Fractional inches can be set to be $\frac{1}{1}$, $\frac{1}{2}$, $\frac{1}{4}$, $\frac{1}{8}$, $\frac{1}{10}$, $\frac{1}{16}$, $\frac{1}{32}$, $\frac{1}{64}$, or $\frac{1}{100}$.

To define a Custom units system, modify the fields under the Custom option, including a units label and its equivalence to known units. The final option is to use the default Generic units. Generic units relate distances to each other, but the numbers themselves are irrelevant.

Regardless of the units that you specify, you can use other units in parameter fields as long as you designate the units type. gmax automatically converts the units to the units that are set up. For example, if you set the units to meters and then create a sphere with a radius of 3', the value of 0.914m appears in the parameter field.

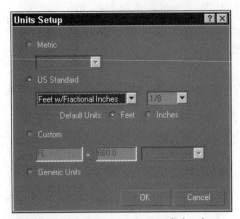

Figure 3-16: The Units Setup dialog box lets you set the units that are used for the scene.

For units, you can use the following designations to represent the various unit types:

✦ double quotes (") for U.S. inches

✦ single quote (') for U.S. feet

✦ mm for millimeters

✦ cm for centimeters

✦ m for meters

✦ km for kilometers

You also can enter fractional units. For example, ½m would convert to 1 foot, 7.685 inches, and ⁷⁄₁₆" would compute to 0.011m. Finally, if you include a space in between several different unit values, the values will be summed together. For example, entering 2 4 5 converts to 11 in the set up units.

By default, all units in gmax equate to one unit measured in the selected units, but you can change this scaling in the General panel of the Preference Settings dialog box covered later in this chapter. You also can enable the Automatic Unit Conversion option, which converts all imported and merged files to the current units.

Configuring the Viewports

If the Viewport Navigation Controls help define what you see, then the Viewport Configuration dialog box helps define how you see objects in the viewports. You can configure each viewport using this dialog box. To open this dialog box, choose the Customize ⇨ Viewport Configuration menu command. You can also open this dialog box by right-clicking the viewport's name located in the upper-left corner of each viewport and choosing Configure from the pop-up menu. The pop-up menu itself includes many of the settings found in the Viewport Configuration dialog box, but the dialog box lets you alter several settings at once. You can also make this dialog box appear for the active viewport by right-clicking any of the Viewport Navigation buttons in the lower-right corner.

The Viewport Configuration dialog box includes two panels — Rendering Method and Layout. I cover each of these panels in the sections that follow. The Preference Settings dialog box (covered later in this chapter) also includes many settings for controlling the behavior and look of the viewports.

Setting the viewport rendering method

Since gmax doesn't include a rendering option (it relies on the game engine to do that), the viewports are the only place to see your content before it appears in your game, so these rendering levels are the key to seeing your content.

If every viewport is set to display the highest-quality view, then updating each viewport can slow the program to a crawl even on a fast machine. The Viewport Configuration dialog box's Rendering Method panel, shown in Figure 3-17, lets you set the rendering settings for the Active Viewport, All Viewports, or All but Active viewport.

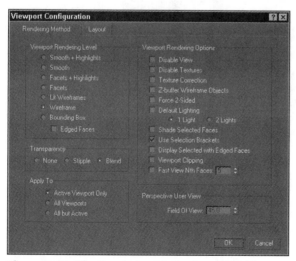

Figure 3-17: The Rendering Method panel holds controls for specifying the Rendering Level and several other rendering options.

Viewport Rendering Levels

The Viewport Rendering Level options, from slowest to fastest include the following:

✦ **Smooth+Highlights:** Shows smooth surfaces with lighting highlights. This rendering type is the slowest.

✦ **Smooth:** Shows smooth surfaces without any lighting effects.

✦ **Facets+Highlights:** Shows individual polygon faces and lighting highlights.

✦ **Facets:** Shows individual polygon faces without any lighting effects.

✦ **Lit Wireframes:** Shows polygon edges with lighting effects.

✦ **Wireframe:** Shows polygon edges.

✦ **Bounding Box:** Shows a box that encloses the object. This rendering type is the quickest.

 Note   Although it really isn't a rendering method, the Edged Faces option shows the edges for each face when a shaded rendering method is selected. You can enable and disable this option with the F4 keyboard shortcut.

Figure 3-18 shows all the various viewport rendering methods applied to a simple sphere side by side.

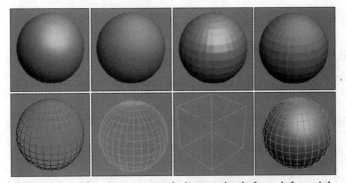

Figure 3-18: The viewport rendering methods from left to right are: Top Row: Smooth+Highlights, Smooth, Facets+Highlights, Facets. Bottom Row: Lit Wireframes, Wireframe, Bounding Box, and Edged Faces applied to Smooth+Highlights.

The most common rendering setting is Wireframe. Faceted rendering displays every face as a flat plane, but it shows the object as a solid model and is good for checking whether objects overlap. The Smooth rendering level shows a rough approximation of the final rendering. Setting the rendering level to include highlights shows the effect of the lights in the scene.

Viewing transparency

In addition to these shading types, you can set the viewport to display objects that contain transparency (which is set in the Object Properties dialog box). The three Transparency options are None, which doesn't display any transparency; Stipple, which cross-hatches the transparent object; and Blend, which includes a transparency effect for a smooth look. Figure 3-19 shows these three transparency options with the help of a Pacman-like creature and his ghostly rival (we need to pay tribute to the older games from time to time).

Tip   Some video cards have trouble with the Blend transparency options. If transparency doesn't appear in the viewport, change the transparency option to Stipple.

Figure 3-19: The viewport transparency options include None, Stipple, and Blend.

Viewport Rendering Options

The Viewport Rendering Options section within the Rendering Method panel includes several other options, such as Disable View (D) and Disable Textures. These options can help speed up viewport updates or increase the visual detail of the objects in the viewport. At any time, you can also choose Views ➪ Redraw All Views (or press the 1 key) to force all viewports to be immediately redrawn. (As objects are moved around, they often mask one another and lines disappear.)

Tip   At any time during a viewport update, you can click the mouse or press a key to cancel the redraw. gmax doesn't make you wait for a screen redraw to be able to execute commands with the mouse or keyboard shortcuts.

The Disable View (D) option causes a viewport not to be updated when changes are made, unless the viewport is active. Setting this option increases the speed with which the other viewports update. To reactivate the viewport, simply select Disable View again (or press the D key). When a viewport is disabled, the word *Disabled* is placed next to the viewport name.

Disable Textures turns off texture rendering for quick viewport updates. Texture Correction speeds rendering updates by interpolating the current texture rather than re-rendering. Texture Correction (along with Disable View) is an option available in the pop-up menu accessed by right-clicking the viewport name.

A Z-Buffer is used to keep track of each object's distance from the camera. Enabling Z-Buffer Wireframe Objects takes advantage of this buffer for quicker updates.

Force 2-Sided makes both sides of all faces visible. For example, suppose you have a sphere with a hole in it. This setting would enable you to see the interior surface of the sphere through the hole.

The Default Lighting toggle deactivates your current lights and uses the default lights. This option can be helpful when you're trying to view objects in a dark setting. You can also specify whether default lighting uses one light or two. Scenes with one light update more quickly than scenes with two.

You use Shade Selected Faces (F2) to shade chosen faces in a red, semitransparent look, which enables you to see what's behind the shaded faces.

Note   The Shade Selected Faces (F2) option, which shades selected subobject faces is different from the Views ⇨ Shade Selected menu command, which turns on shading for the selected object in all viewports.

The Use Selection Brackets (J) option displays white corners around the current selection. Selection brackets are useful for helping you see the entire size of a grouped object, but they can be annoying if left on with many objects selected. Uncheck this option to make these brackets disappear.

The option to Display Selected with Edged Faces helps to highlight the selected object. If this option is enabled, the edges of the current selection are displayed regardless of whether the Edged Faces check box is enabled. Figure 3-20 shows a dog model with his upper torso selected with the Display Selected with Edged Faces option and Use Selection Brackets enabled. These options make the current selection easy to see.

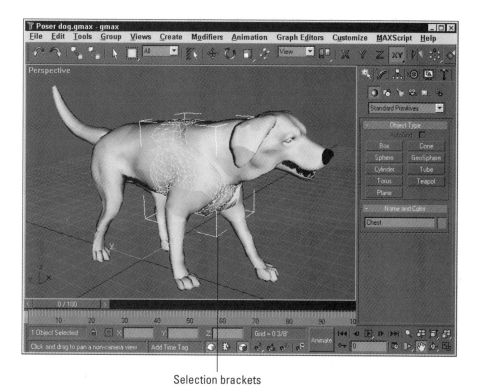

Selection brackets

Figure 3-20: The Display Selected with Edged Faces and Use Selection Brackets options makes identifying the current selection easy.

A clipping plane defines an invisible barrier beyond which all objects are invisible. For example, if you have a scene with many detailed mountain objects in the background, working with an object in the front of the scene can be difficult. By setting the clipping plane between the two, you can work on the front objects without having to update the mountain objects every time you update the scene.

Viewport Clipping places a yellow line with two arrows on the right side of the viewport, as shown in Figure 3-21. The top arrow represents the back clipping plane, and the bottom arrow is the front clipping plane. Drag the arrows to set the clipping planes. You can quickly turn viewport clipping on or off by right-clicking the viewport name and choosing Viewport Clipping from the pop-up menu.

Clipping Plane markers

Figure 3-21: The clipping plane is hiding the grid plane directly behind the dog.
Run, boy, run!

Fast View speeds viewport updates by drawing only a limited number of faces. The
spinner value determines how often faces are drawn. For example, a setting of 5
draws only every fifth face. Fast View renders viewport updates much more quickly
and gives you an idea of the objects without displaying the entire object.

Tutorial: Creating interesting patterns with the Fast View setting

You can use the Fast View setting in the Viewport Configuration dialog box to create
some interesting patterns.

To create patterned spheres, follow these steps:

1. Open the Patterned sphere.max file from the Chap 03 directory on the
   CD-ROM.

   This file has a simple smooth sphere.

2. Click in the Top view, and choose Customize ⇨ Viewport Configuration to
   open the Viewport Configuration dialog box.

3. Select the Smooth Rendering Level and the Fast View Nth Faces options; set the Fast View Nth Faces value to 2.

4. Repeat Step 2 for the Front, Left, and Perspective viewports, setting the Fast View Nth Faces values to 3, 4, and 5, respectively.

Figure 3-22 shows a sphere rendered using the Fast View option. Notice how the settings for each viewport can be different.

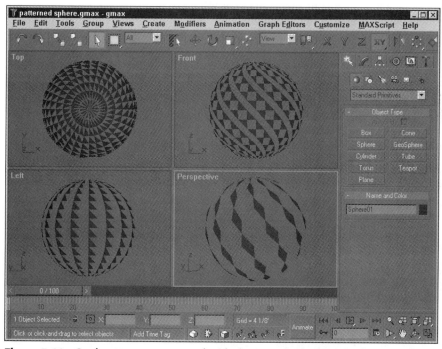

Figure 3-22: Cool patterns are created with the Fast View setting in the Viewport Configuration dialog box.

Note

If any of these spheres were rendered in a game engine, the entire sphere would be visible. The Fast View option affects only the viewport display.

Setting the Field of View

You can also alter the Field of View for the Perspective view in the Viewport Configuration dialog box. To create a fish-eye view, set the FOV value to 10 or less. The maximum FOV value is 180 and the default value is 45. You can also change the Field of View using the button in the Viewport Navigation Controls. The Viewport Configuration dialog box, however, lets you enter precise values.

Cross-Reference See Chapter 18, "If You Could See What I See — Controlling Cameras" for more coverage on Field of View.

Altering the Viewport layout

Now that you've started to figure out the viewports, you might want to change the number and size of viewports that are displayed. The Layout panel, shown in Figure 3-23, in the Viewpoint Configuration dialog box offers several layouts as alternatives to the default layout (not that there is anything wrong with the default and its four equally sized viewports).

Figure 3-23: The Layout panel offers many layout options.

After selecting a layout from the options at the top of the panel, you can assign each individual viewport a different view by clicking the viewport and choosing a view from the pop-up menu. The view options include Perspective, User, Front, Back, Top, Bottom, Left, Right, ActiveShade, Track, Schematic, Grid, Extended, and Shape.

Views can also be set to Camera and Spotlight if they exist in the scene. Each camera and light that exists is listed by name at the top of the pop-up menu.

Setting Preferences

The Preference Settings dialog box lets you configure gmax so it works in a way that is most comfortable for you. You open it by choosing Customize ➪ Preferences. The dialog box includes seven panels: General, Files, Viewports, Gamma, Animation, Inverse

Kinematics, and MAXScript. The first panel in the Preference Settings dialog box is for General settings. Figure 3-24 shows the dialog box with the General panel selected.

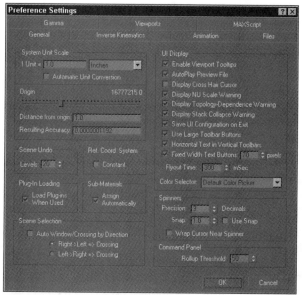

Figure 3-24: The General panel enables you to change the unit scale, among other options.

The General panel includes many global settings that affect the entire interface.

Tip   The quickest way I've found to open the Preference Settings dialog box is to right-click on the Spinner Snap Toggle located at the bottom of the screen.

Setting the System Unit Scale

The System Unit Scale option enables you to define the measurement system used by gmax. Options include Inches, Feet, Miles, Millimeters, Centimeters, Meters, and Kilometers. Units directly relate to parameters entered with the keyboard. For example, with the units set to meters, a sphere created with the radius parameter of 2 would be 4 meters across.

You may also use the multiplier field to alter the value of each unit. The Automatic Unit Conversion toggle converts all existing objects to a new unit system, so you can change all objects in a scene from feet to meters.

The Origin control helps you determine the accuracy of an object as it is moved away from the scene origin. If you know how far objects will be located from the origin, then entering that value will tell you the Resulting Accuracy. You can use this feature to determine the accuracy of your parameters. Objects farther from the origin will have a lower accuracy.

Undo Levels and Loading Plug-Ins

The Scene Undo spinner sets the number of commands that can be kept in a buffer for undoing. A smaller number will free up memory, but will not let you backtrack through your work. The default Undo Levels is 20.

The Load Plug-Ins When Used option keeps plug-ins out of memory until they are accessed. This saves valuable memory and still makes the plug-ins accessible.

Reference Coordinate System and Sub-Material settings

The Reference Coordinate System setting makes all transform tools use the same coordinate system when the Constant option is enabled. If disabled, each transform uses the coordinate system last selected.

The Automatic Sub-Material Assignment option, when enabled, enables materials to be dragged and dropped directly onto a subobject selection.

Scene Selection settings

The Auto Window/Crossing by Direction option lets you select scene objects using the windowing method (the entire object must be within the selected windowed area to be selected) and the crossing method (which selects objects if their borders are crossed with the mouse) at the same time, depending on the direction in which the mouse is dragged. If you select the first option, then the Crossing method will be used when the mouse is dragged from right to left and the Window method will be used when the mouse is dragged from left to right.

Interface Display settings

Finally, toggle switches in the UI Display section control additional aspects of the interface. Enable Viewport Tooltips toggles tooltips on and off. Tooltips are helpful when you're first learning the gmax interface, but they quickly become annoying and you'll want to turn them off.

The AutoPlay Preview File setting automatically plays Preview Files in the default media player when they are finished. The Display Cross Hair Cursor option changes the cursor from the Windows default arrow to a crosshair cursor similar to the one used in AutoCAD.

For some actions, such as nonuniform scaling, gmax displays a warning dialog box asking whether you are sure of the action. To disable these warnings, uncheck this option (or you could check the Disable this Warning box in the dialog box). Actions with warnings include nonuniform scaling, topology-dependence, and collapsing the Modifier Stack.

The Save UI Configuration on Exit switch automatically saves any interface configuration changes. You can deselect Use Large Toolbar Buttons option, enabling the use of smaller toolbar buttons and icons that will reclaim valuable screen real estate.

The Horizontal Text in Vertical Toolbars options fixes the problem of text buttons that take up too much space, especially when printed horizontally on a vertical toolbar. You can also specify a width for text buttons. Any text larger than this value will be clipped off at the edges of the button.

The Flyout Time spinner adjusts the time the system waits before displaying flyout buttons. The Color Selection drop-down list lets you choose which color selector interface gmax uses.

The Rollup Threshold value sets how many pixels can be scrolled before the rollup is shifted to another column. This is used only if you've made the Command Panel wider.

Spinner settings

Spinners are interface controls that enable you to enter values or interactively increase or decrease the value by clicking arrows to the right of the spinner box. The Preferences Settings dialog box includes settings for changing the number of decimals displayed in spinners and for changing the increment or decrement value when clicking an arrow. The Use Spinner Snap option enables the snap mode. You can also enable the snap mode using the Spinner Snap button on the main toolbar.

You can change the values in the spinner by clicking on the spinner and dragging up to increase the value or down to decrease it. The Wrap Cursor Near Spinner option keeps the cursor close to the spinner when you change values by dragging with the mouse, so you can drag the mouse continuously without worrying about hitting the top or bottom of the screen.

Note   You can quickly access these spinner settings by right-clicking the Spinner Snap Toggle button on the main toolbar.

Inverse Kinematics preferences

The Inverse Kinematics panel, shown in Figure 3-25, includes Positional, Rotational, and Iteration Thresholds for both Applied IK and Interactive IK.

Cross-Reference   I cover Applied IK and Interactive IK in greater detail in Chapter 15, "Skeletons Rule: Building with Bones and IK."

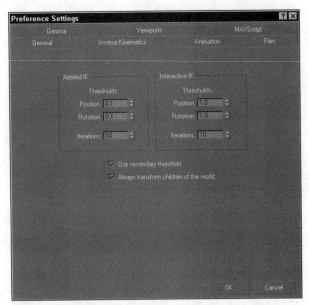

Figure 3-25: The Inverse Kinematics panel of the Preference Settings dialog box includes threshold values for Inverse Kinematics systems.

Animation preferences

The Animation panel, shown in Figure 3-26, contains options dealing with animations. When a specific frame is selected, all objects with keys for that frame are surrounded with white brackets. The Animation panel offers options that specify which objects get these brackets. Options include All Objects, Selected Objects, and None. You can also limit the brackets to only those objects with certain transform keys.

The Local Center During Animate option causes all objects to be animated around their local centers. Turning this option off enables animations around other centers (such as screen and world).

The MIDI Time Slider Controls include an On option and a Setup button. The Setup button opens the MIDI Time Slider Control Setup dialog box shown in Figure 3-27. After this control is set up, you can control an animation using a MIDI device.

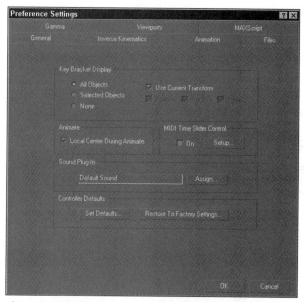

Figure 3-26: The Animation panel includes settings for displaying Key Brackets.

Figure 3-27: The MIDI Time Slider Control Setup dialog box lets you set up specific notes to start, stop, and step through an animation.

You can use the Animation panel to assign a new Sound Plug-In, as well as to set the default values for all animation controllers. Clicking the Set Defaults button opens the Set Controller Defaults dialog box. This dialog box includes a list of all the controllers and a Set button. When you select a controller and click the Set button, another dialog box appears with all the values for that controller.

Cross-Reference You can learn more about specific controllers in Chapter 22, "Creating Automatic Actions with Controllers."

Files panel preferences

The Files panel holds the controls for backing up, archiving, and logging gmax files. You can set files to be backed up, saved incrementally, or compressed when saved. Figure 3-28 shows this panel.

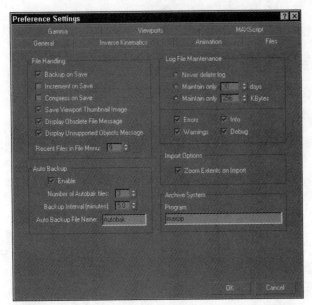

Figure 3-28: The Files panel includes an Auto Backup feature.

Handling files and archives

The Files panel includes several options that define how to handle files. You can enable an option to Backup on Save. This causes the existing copy of a file to be saved as a backup (with the .bak extension) before saving the new file. This option always retains two copies of the file.

The Increment on Save option adds an incremented number to the end of the existing file every time it is saved. This retains multiple copies of the file and is an easy way to version-control your scene files. This way, you can always go back to an earlier file when the client changes his or her mind.

The Compress on Save option compresses the file automatically when it is saved. Compressed files require less file space but take longer to load. If you're running low on hard drive space, then you'll want to enable this option.

The Save Viewport Thumbnail Image option saves a 64×64 pixel thumbnail of the active viewport along with the file. This thumbnail is displayed in the Open dialog box.

Tip The Save Viewport Thumbnail Image option is another good option to keep enabled. Thumbnails make it easier to find scene files later, and nothing is more frustrating than seeing a scene without a thumbnail.

When a gmax file created in a previous version of gmax is opened, a warning dialog box appears that says, "Obsolete data format found — Please resave file." To eliminate this warning, disable the Display Obsolete File Message option.

The Recent Files in File Menu option determines the number of recently opened files that appear at the bottom of the File menu.

Tip I like to set the Recent Files in File Menu option at its highest value because I find that this is the easiest way to open the latest scenes.

Backing up files

The Auto Backup feature in Max can save you from the nightmare of losing all your work due to a system crash. With Auto Backup enabled, you can select the number of Autobak Files and how often the files are backed up. The backup files are saved to the directory specified by the Configure Paths dialog box. The default is to save these backups to the AutoBack directory.

Tip I highly recommend that you keep the Auto Backup option enabled. This feature has saved my bacon more than once.

Tutorial: Setting Auto Backup

Now that it has been stressed that setting up Auto Backup is an important step to do, let's run through exactly how to set it up.

To set up this feature, follow these steps:

1. Open the Preferences Settings dialog box by choosing Customize ⇨ Preferences, and click the Files panel.

2. Turn on Auto Backup by selecting the Enable option in the Auto Backup section.

3. Set the number of Autobak files to 3.

Note To maintain version control of your gmax scenes, use the Increment on Save feature instead of increasing the Number of Autobak Files.

4. Set the Backup Interval to the amount of time to wait between backups.

   The Backup Interval should be set to the maximum amount of work that you are willing to redo. (I keep my settings at 15 minutes.) You can also give the Auto Backup file a name.

5. Auto Backup will save the files in the directory specified by the Auto Backup path. To view where this path is located, choose Customize ⇨ Configure Paths.

Maintaining log files

You can also use the Files panel to control log files. Log files keep track of any errors, general command info, and any debugging information. You can set log files to never be deleted, expire after so many days, or keep a specified file size with the latest information. If your system is having trouble, checking the error log will give you some idea as to what the problem is. Logs are essential if you plan on developing any custom scripts or plug-ins. You can select that the log contain all Errors, Warnings, Info, and Debug statements.

The name of the log file is gmax.log. It is saved in the "network" subdirectory.

Import options

The Import Options group has only a single option: Zoom Extents on Import. When this option is enabled, it automatically zooms all viewports to their extents. Imported objects often can be scaled so small that they aren't even visible. This option helps you to locate an object when imported.

Note   If you are importing an object into a scene with several objects, then this option will not necessarily make the imported object visible.

The Archive System lets you specify which archive program gmax will use to archive your files. Maxzip is the default, but you can change it to whichever program you want to use.

Gamma preferences

The Gamma panel, shown in Figure 3-29, controls the gamma correction for the display and for bitmap files.

Setting screen gamma

Have you ever noticed in an electronics store that television screen displays vary in color? Colors on monitor screens may be fairly consistent for related models, but may vary across brands. Gamma settings are a means by which colors can be consistently represented regardless of the monitor that is being used.

Gamma value is a numerical offset required by an individual monitor in order to be consistent with a standard. To enable gamma correction for gmax, open the Gamma panel in the Preference Settings dialog box, and click the Enable Gamma Correction option. To determine the gamma value, use the spinner or adjust the Gamma value until the gray square blends in with the background.

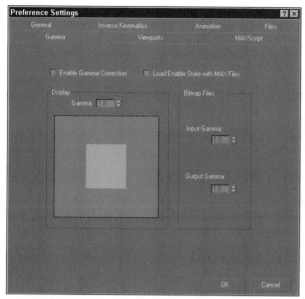

Figure 3-29: Enabling gamma correction makes colors consistent regardless of the monitor.

Setting bitmap gamma

Many bitmap formats, such as TGA, contain their own gamma settings. The Input Gamma setting for Bitmap files sets the gamma for bitmaps that don't have a gamma setting. The Output Gamma setting is the value set for bitmaps being output from gmax.

Note   Match the Input Gamma value to the Display Gamma value so that bitmaps loaded for textures will be displayed correctly.

Viewport preferences

The viewports are your window into the scene. The Viewports panel, shown in Figure 3-30, contains many options for controlling these viewports.

Viewport Parameters options

In the Viewport Parameters group are several options specific to viewports. The Use Dual Planes option enables a method designed to speed up viewport redraws. Objects close to the scene are included in a front plane and objects farther back are included in a back plane. When this option is enabled, only the objects on the front plane are redrawn.

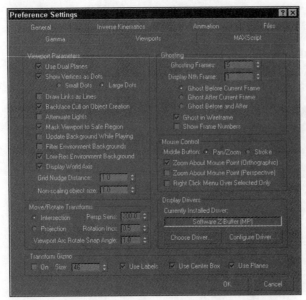

Figure 3-30: The Viewports panel contains several viewport parameter settings.

In subobject mode, the default is to display vertices as small plus signs. The Show Vertices as Dots option displays vertices as either Small or Large dots. The Draw Links as Lines option shows all displayed links as lines that connect the two linked objects.

Caution   I've found that keeping the Draw Links as Lines option can make it confusing to clearly see objects, so I tend to keep it turned off.

The Backface Cull on Object Creation option shows the backfaces of objects when viewed in wireframe mode. The Attenuate Lights option causes objects farther back in a viewport to appear darker. Attenuation is the property that causes lights to diminish over distance.

Note   There is also a Backface Cull display option in the Object Properties dialog box.

In the Viewport Configuration dialog box, you can set Safe Regions, which are borders that the renderer will include. The Mask Viewport to Safe Region option causes the objects beyond the Safe Region border to be invisible.

The Update Background While Playing option causes viewport background bitmaps to be updated while an animation sequence plays. Viewport backgrounds can be filtered if the Filter Environment Backgrounds option is enabled, but this slows the update time. If this option is disabled, the background image appears aliased and pixelated. For quicker refresh times, enable the Low-Res Environment Background option. This reduces the resolution of the background image by half and resizes it to fill the viewport. Enabling this option results in a blocky appearance, but the viewport updates much more quickly.

The Display World Axis option displays the axes in the lower-left corner of each viewport. You can use the arrow keys to nudge objects into position. The Grid Nudge Distance is the distance that an object moves when an arrow key is pressed. Objects without scale, such as lights and cameras, appear in the scene according to the Non-Scaling Object Size value.

Transforms and Gizmo options

The Viewports panel includes several options for controlling viewport transforms. There are two options for moving objects in a Perspective view: Intersection and Projection. Intersection moves the object a greater distance into the scene as the cursor approaches the horizon. It can move the object a great distance quickly. The Projection option moves the object slowly and consistently, but it requires mouse movement. The sensitivity of the movements in Projection mode is controlled by the Perspective Sensitivity value. The Rotation Increment value controls the sensitivity of the mouse for rotations. The Viewport Arc Rotate Snap Angle is the angle that is used by the Angle Snap button in the Status Bar.

Transform Gizmo is an apparatus that enables you to visually constrain the transform motion of an object. The On option enables the gizmo in all viewports, and the Size value determines how big it appears. The Use Labels option labels each axis with a letter. The Use Center Box displays a box in the center of the gizmo. Dragging the box moves the object along the axis that is active in the main toolbar. The Use Planes option displays corner markers for transforming an object in a plane.

Enabling ghosting

Ghosting is similar to the use of "onion-skins" in traditional animation, making an object's prior position and next position to be displayed. When producing animation, knowing where you're going and where you've come from is helpful. Enabling ghosting enables you to produce better animations.

gmax offers several ghosting options. You can set whether a ghost appears before the current frame, after the current frame, or both before and after the current frame. You can set the total number of ghosting frames and how often they should appear. You can also set an option to show the frame numbers.

Cross-Reference

I discuss ghosting in more detail in Chapter 19, "Getting the Prop to Spin — Animation Basics."

Using the middle mouse button

If you're using a mouse that includes a middle button (this includes a mouse with a scrolling wheel), then you can define how the middle button is used. The two options are Pan/Zoom and Stroke. The Pan/Zoom option will pan the active viewport if the middle button is held down, will zoom in and out if you move the scrolling wheel, and will rotate the view if you hold down the Alt key while dragging. You can select options to zoom about the mouse point in the orthographic and perspective viewports.

The Stroke option enables another interface that lets you execute commands by dragging a predefined stroke in a viewport. With the Stroke option selected, close the Preference Settings dialog box and drag with the middle mouse button held down in one of the viewports. A simple dialog box will identify the stroke and execute the command associated with it. If no command is associated, then a simple dialog box appears that lets you Continue (do nothing) or Define the stroke.

Another way to work with strokes is to enable the Strokes Utility. This is done by selecting the Utility panel, clicking the More button, and selecting Strokes from the pop-up list of utilities. This utility will make a Draw Strokes button active. When the button is enabled, it turns yellow and allows you to draw strokes with the left or middle mouse buttons.

If you select to define the stroke, the Define Stroke dialog box, shown in Figure 3-31, is opened. You can also open this dialog box directly by holding down the Ctrl key while dragging a stroke with the middle mouse button. In the upper-left corner of this dialog box is a grid. Strokes are identified by the lines they cross on this grid as they are drawn. For example, an "HK" stroke would be a horizontal line that is dragged from the top of the viewport straight down to the bottom.

With a stroke identified, you can select a command in the upper-right pane. This is the command that executes when you drag the stroke with the middle mouse button in the viewport. For each command, you can set the options found below the stroke grid. These options define what the command is executed on.

All defined strokes are saved in a set, and you can review the current set of defined strokes with the Review button. Clicking this button opens the Review Strokes dialog box where all defined strokes and their commands are displayed. The only default defined stroke is one that opens this dialog box, as shown in Figure 3-32.

One of the commands available in the list of commands is Stroke Preferences. Using this command opens the Stroke Preferences dialog box, where you can save and delete different stroke sets, specify to list commands or strokes in the Review Strokes dialog, set the time that the stroke grid and extents appear, and set the Stroke Point Size.

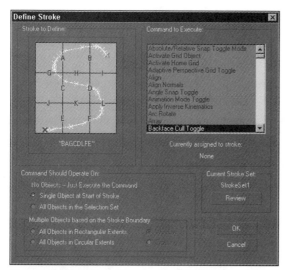

Figure 3-31: The Define Stroke dialog box can associate strokes dragged with the middle mouse button with a command.

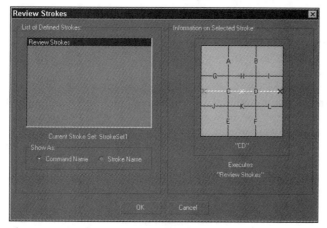

Figure 3-32: The Review Strokes dialog box lists all defined strokes and their respective commands.

Tutorial: Defining a stroke

As you get some experience with the gmax interface, you'll find that for some commands you'll always use keyboard shortcuts, for others you'll use the main toolbar, and for others the menus. Strokes offer another way to quickly execute commands without the pain of searching the menus for a given command.

To assign a stroke to a command, follow these steps:

1. Open the Preference Settings dialog box with the Customize ⇨ Preferences menu command.

2. Select the Viewports panel, and in the Mouse Control section, select the Stroke option; then close the Preference Settings dialog box.

3. With the middle mouse button, drag a U-shaped stroke in the active viewport.

   A dialog box will identify the stroke as not found.

4. Click the Define button to open the Define Stroke dialog box.

   The stroke (as you drew it) will be displayed in the upper-left grid, and if you drew it correctly, it should be identified as 'GJEFLI.'

5. In the Command list, select the Unhide All command and click the OK button to close the dialog box.

6. Use the Tools ⇨ Display Floater to hide some objects in the current scene, and then drag a U-shaped stroke with the middle mouse button.

   All the hidden objects will become visible.

Choosing and configuring display drivers

When gmax was first launched, a simple dialog box, like the one shown in Figure 3-33, asked you which display driver to use. If you were anxious to get a look at gmax, you probably didn't pay much attention to this dialog box. However, weeks later when you happen to be looking through your video card information, you realize that your card supports other drivers like OpenGL and Direct 3D.

Caution   The gmax Driver Setup dialog box displays only the options for the drivers that it finds on your system, but just because an option exists doesn't mean it will work correctly. If a driver hangs your system, you can restart it from a command line with the –h flag after 3dsmax.exe to force gmax to present the gmax Driver Setup dialog box again.

If you want to try out or configure the different display drivers, you can use the Viewports panel of the Preference Settings dialog box. The Viewports panel includes a field that displays the currently installed driver along with two buttons to Choose Driver and Configure Driver. The Choose Driver button opens the gmax Driver Setup dialog box again. If you change the display driver, you will need to restart gmax.

Note   The driver you use really depends on the video card that you have in your system. Check the documentation that came with your video card to see what drivers it supports. If you're unsure, use the default Heidi drivers.

The Configure Driver button opens a dialog box of configurations for the driver that is currently installed. The various configuration dialog boxes include options such as specifying the Texture Size, which is the size of the bitmap used to texture map objects. Larger maps have better image quality but can slow down your display.

Figure 3-33: You use the gmax Driver Setup dialog box to select the display drivers.

All the display driver configuration settings present trade-offs between image quality and speed of display. By tweaking the configuration settings, you can optimize these settings to suite your needs. In general, the more memory available on your video card, the better the results.

Cross-Reference

You can find more details on the various display drivers in Appendix A, "Installing and Configuring gmax."

MAXScript preferences

Settings for working with MAXScript are included in the MAXScript panel, shown in Figure 3-34. These commands include options for loading Startup scripts, controlling the Macro Recorder, the font used in the MAXScript window, and the amount of Memory to use.

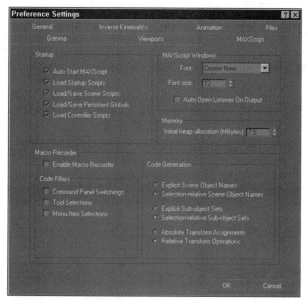

Figure 3-34: The MAXScript panel includes options for controlling MAXScript.

Cross-Reference Check out Chapter 8, "Placing gmax on Autopilot with MAXScript" for more information on MAXScript commands and preferences.

Summary

You can customize the gmax interface in many ways. Most of these customization options are included under the Customize menu. In this chapter, you learned how to use this menu and its commands to customize many aspects of the gmax interface. Customizing the gmax interface makes the interface more efficient and comfortable for you.

Specifically, this chapter covered the following topics:

✦ Using the Customize User Interface dialog box to customize keyboard shortcuts, toolbars, quadmenus, menus, and colors

✦ Customizing the Tab panel and the Command Panel buttons

✦ Saving and loading custom interfaces

✦ Configuring paths and setting up units

✦ Setting the Rendering Level and Display options in the Viewport Configuration dialog box

✦ Using the other panels of the Viewport Configuration dialog box to change the layout, safe frames, and regions

✦ Setting preferences

The next chapter will enable you to make your gmax work portable. Moving files in and out of gmax will enable you to save your work and load it into the game engine. This is a necessary step for seeing your finished work in the gaming world.

✦　　✦　　✦

Getting Files In and Out of gmax

✦   ✦   ✦   ✦

In This Chapter

Saving, opening, merging, and archiving files

Importing and exporting objects

Importing objects from external packages like Poser

Externally referencing objects and scenes

Working with file utilities such as the Asset Browser

Accessing scene files information

✦   ✦   ✦   ✦

Complex game scenes can end up being a collection of hundreds of files, and misplacing any of them will affect the final look of the game objects, so learning to work with files is critical. This chapter focuses on working with files whether they be object files, texture images, or backgrounds. Files enable you to move scene pieces into and out of gmax. You can also export and import files to and from different formats for loading in the various games.

gmax scenes can also be created using several different objects that have been created by a team. Using external references (XRefs), you can pull all the different pieces together into a single scene.

Working with gmax Scene Files

Of all the different file types and formats, there is one file type that you will probably work with more than any other — the gmax format. gmax has its own proprietary format for its scene files. These files have the .gmax extension and allow you to save your work as a file and return to it at a later time.

Tip   Even if you export the object to a unique format that a specific game engine recognizes, you should still save the gmax file in case you want to return to the original object to make some changes.

When gmax starts, a new scene opens. You can start a new scene at any time with the File ➪ New (Ctrl+N) command, but gmax can have only one scene open at a time. Starting a new scene deletes the current scene, but gmax asks you whether you want to keep the objects and hierarchy, keep the objects, or make everything new, as shown in Figure 4-1. Starting a new scene with the File ➪ New command maintains all the current interface settings, including the viewports and Command Panel. To reset the interface, choose File ➪ Reset. When reset, all interface settings return to their default states, but interface changes aren't affected.

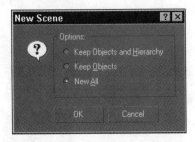

Figure 4-1: When creating a new scene, you can keep the current objects.

Saving files

After you start up gmax, the first thing you should learn is how to save your work. After a scene has changed, you can save it as a file. Choose File ➪ Save (Ctrl+S) to save the scene to the current name. If the scene hasn't been saved yet, then a Save File As dialog box appears, as shown in Figure 4-2. You can also make this dialog box appear using the File ➪ Save As command. Pretty simple — just don't forget to do it often.

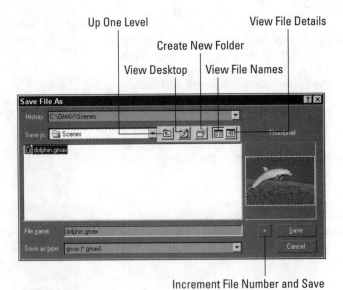

Figure 4-2: Use the Save File As dialog box to save a scene as a file.

The Save File As dialog box keeps a history list of the last five directories that you've opened. You can select these directories from the History drop-down list at the top of the dialog box. The buttons in this dialog box are the standard Windows File dialog box buttons used to go up one directory, view the desktop, or create a new folder, and toggle buttons to view the directory as a list of file names or with all the file details.

Note   If you try to save a scene over the top of an existing scene, then gmax presents a dialog box confirming this action.

Clicking the button with a plus (+) sign to the left of the Save button automatically appends a number to the end of the current filename and saves the file. For example, if you select the myScene.gmax file and click the plus button, then a file named myScene01.gmax is saved.

Tip   Use the auto increment file number and Save button to save progressive versions of a scene. This is an easy version control system. If you ever need to backtrack to an earlier version, you can.

The File menu also includes an option to Save Selected. This option saves the current selected objects to a separate scene file.

Another useful feature for saving files is to enable the Auto Backup feature in the File panel of the Preference Settings dialog box. This dialog box can be accessed with the Customize ➪ Preferences menu command.

Cross-Reference   I talk about the Auto Backup feature in Chapter 3, "Making a Custom Face, er, Interface."

Opening files

After you've saved a file, it might be important to know how to open it again. Choosing File ➪ Open (Ctrl+O) opens a dialog box that is the same as the one used to save files, shown in Figure 4-2. Selecting a file and clicking on the plus (+) button opens a copy of the selected file with a new version number appended to its name.

Note   If gmax cannot locate resources used within a scene (such as maps) when you open a gmax file, then a dialog box appears enabling you to locate or skip the missing files.

The most recently opened scenes are listed at the bottom of the File menu. Selecting these scenes from the list opens the scene file.

Tip   In the Files panel of the Preference Settings dialog box, you can set the number of recent files (up to a maximum of nine) to display at the bottom of the File menu.

Merging and replacing objects

If you happen to create the perfect prop in one scene that you want to integrate with another scene, you can save the prop and then load it into another scene, or you can use the Merge menu command. Choose File ➪ Merge to load objects from another scene into the current scene. Using this command opens a dialog box that is exactly like the Save File As dialog box, but after you select a scene and click the Open button, the Merge dialog box, shown in Figure 4-3, appears. This dialog box displays all the objects found in the selected scene file. It also has options for sorting the objects and filtering certain types of objects. Selecting an object and clicking the OK button loads the object into the current scene.

Tip   If you drag a gmax file from Windows Explorer and drop in on a viewport, then a small menu appears with options to Open File, Merge File, XRef File, or Cancel.

Figure 4-3: The Merge dialog box lists all the objects from a merging scene.

If any of the objects that you are trying to merge with the existing scene have the same names as objects already in the scene, the Duplicate Name dialog box, shown in Figure 4-4, appears. Using this dialog box, you can give the object a new name and merge it, skip the object, or delete the old object in place of the new merging object. The Apply to All Duplicates option applies the specified action to all duplicates found in the scene.

If you ever get involved in a modeling duel, then you'll probably be using the replace command at some time. A modeling duel is when two modelers work on the same rough model of named objects and the animator (or boss) gets to choose which object parts to use. With the File ➪ Replace command, you can replace a named object with an object of the same name in a different scene. The objects are selected using the same dialog box shown in Figure 4-3, but only the objects with identical names in both scene files are displayed. If no objects with the same name appear in both scene files, a warning box is displayed.

Figure 4-4: The Duplicate Name dialog box lets you deal with merging objects that have the same name as an object in the current scene.

The File menu also includes a Merge Animation menu command. I cover this command in Chapter 19, "Getting the Prop to Spin – Animation Basics."

Archiving files

By archiving a gmax scene along with its reference bitmaps, you can ensure that it includes all the necessary files. This is especially useful if you need to send the project to your cousin to show off or to your boss and you don't want to miss any ancillary files. Choose File ➪ Archive to save scene files as a compressed archive. The default archive format is .zip, but you can change it in the Preference Settings dialog box to use whatever archive format you want. Saving an archive as a .zip file compiles all external files, such as bitmaps, into a single compressed file. The File Type drop-down list of the File Archive dialog box also includes an option to create a List of Files. When you select this file type, a text file is created that lists all relevant files and their paths.

Getting out

As you can probably guess, you use the File ➪ Exit command to exit the program, but only after it gives you a chance to save your work. Clicking on the window icon with an X on it in the upper right has the same affect (but I'm sure you knew that).

Importing and Exporting

The number of import options in gmax is frightfully limited, but they are enough. Using the limited number of import formats, you can move almost any 3d object into gmax.

None of the game engines use the gmax file format, so to get your cool new monster in front of the guns in your game, you'll need to use the exporting features enabled by the game pack. You can find both import and export commands in the File menu.

Most game packs use an exclusive export option to convert the gmax content into a format that the game engine understands. The various game pack formats aren't covered here, but you can learn about them in the game pack chapters found in Part V.

Importing geometric objects

Choose File ➪ Import to open the Import dialog box. This dialog box looks like a typical Windows file dialog box. The real power comes with the various Import Settings dialog boxes that are available for each format. The settings in the Import Settings dialog box are different for the various format types.

gmax can import several formats, including these:

✦ 3D Studio Mesh and Projects (3DS, PRJ)

✦ 3D Studio Shape (SHP)

✦ AutoCAD (DXF)

In addition to importing, you may want to export gmax objects for use in other programs. You access the Export command by choosing File ➪ Export. You also have the option to Export Selected (available only if an object is selected). The only export file supported by the default installation of gmax is Plasma (P3D).

Although Plasma is the only export format supported in the default installation of gmax, other formats will become available for certain game packs. For details on the various game packs, check out Part V.

Importing 3D Studio files (3DS, PRJ, SHP)

It shouldn't be a surprise that gmax can import 3D Studio (3DS) files without much headache—after all, 3D Studio was the predecessor to 3ds max and gmax.

3D Studio mesh files are saved using the 3DS format, 3D Studio project files are saved as PRJ files, and 3D Studio shape files are saved as SHP files. Mesh and project files can import 3d data, but they can't hold 2D shapes or splines. Imported SHP files convert 2D polygons created with 3D Studio's Shaper tool into Bézier splines. The shapes can be imported as a single object or as multiple objects. PRJ files are simply 3DS files that include shapes. Or you can select to not import shapes.

Importing a 3D Studio file opens a simple dialog box, shown in Figure 4-5. The dialog box offers options to merge or replace the current scene. It also includes an option to Convert Units. With the Convert Units option selected, gmax assumes that the 3DS file is based in inches and converts it to the currently defined units.

Before loading the file, gmax asks whether you want to set the animation length of the current scene to match the animation length in the 3DS file.

Tip   You can set gmax to reorient all the viewports by automatically zooming to the extents of the imported object. You do this by setting the Zoom Extents on Import option in the Files panel of the Preference Settings dialog box.

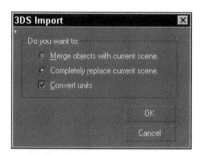

Figure 4-5: The 3DS Import dialog box enables you to merge objects into or completely replace the current scene.

Importing AutoCAD files (DXF)

AutoCAD is a sister product to gmax, aimed at the Computer-Aided Design market. It was produced by the same parent company and, for that reason, interacts very well with 3ds max and gmax. Of the various formats that AutoCAD uses, only the older DXF (which stands for Drawing Exchange Format) can be imported into gmax.

After importing a DXF file, the initial merge/replace dialog box appears. This dialog box is followed by the Import DXF File dialog box, shown in Figure 4-6. This dialog box also includes settings for extracting different objects within the DXF file. You can also separate DXF models into different parts with the Layer, Color, and Entity options. The most common way of separating various parts is by Layer. If your object appears as one solid mass, try importing again and changing this setting to Color or Entity.

The Weld Vertices section welds all vertices that are within the specified threshold together. This can typically cause problems if the units for the file being imported are different than the scene units. It is best to leave the Weld option disabled and to perform any welding operations in gmax.

The Auto Smooth option smoothes all adjacent faces whose normals make an angle that is less than the Smooth Angle value. For example, a Smooth Angle value of 90 smoothes the corners of a cube, but a Smooth Angle value of 0.1 makes almost every face and edge visible.

The Arc Subdivision section specifies degree values between successive vertices required to begin a new mesh or spline on imported polygon meshes and splines. A setting of 90 for splines means that if the difference between this node and the next node is less than 90 degrees, then the node will be part of the existing spline.

Figure 4-6: The Import DXF File dialog box offers settings for making the file import correctly.

The Miscellaneous options can fix common problems with DXF files such as duplicate faces, noncapped meshes being mistaken for splines, and normals that point toward the center of the object, producing a hole when rendered.

Importing from external applications

Although the number of import formats that gmax supports is limited, it still can be used to import 3d objects from external packages. Even if gmax could import several times the current number of import formats, new formats are being created for new products all the time, many of which gmax wouldn't support. This situation does not mean that gmax cannot use objects created in these new products. The trick is to find a common format that both products support.

Importing human figures from Poser

Many animation projects require human figures. Modeling a human figure from scratch can require the same patience and artistic skill that Michelangelo exercised when painting the ceiling of the Sistine Chapel. Luckily (for those of us facing deadlines), this level of commitment isn't necessary. Curious Labs offers a tool devoted to modeling the human body. It is named Poser, and its features include posing and animating lifelike characters. Importing Poser models into gmax can save you from some major modeling headaches.

With Poser, you can choose from a variety of male and female human figures, both unclothed and clothed in all sorts of attire. Even animal models are available. You can easily position these figures to any pose. Figure 4-7 shows the Business Man model posed as if hailing a taxi. This pose was created by simply dragging the man's hand upward into the air.

Poser can also be used to animate characters by setting beginning and ending poses. To change the pose, simply click and drag a body part to its desired location. Poser also includes modules for controlling basic facial expressions and hand gestures.

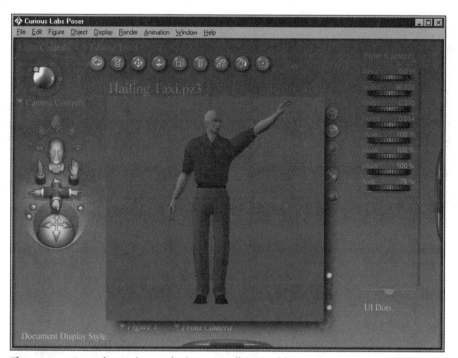

Figure 4-7: Poser by Curious Labs is an excellent tool for working with human figures.

Tutorial: Using Poser models in gmax

Poser makes modeling and positioning human figures easy, but to get the figures into gmax, you need to export them from Poser and import them into gmax. Poser can export several formats, but only two coincide with gmax—3DS and DXF.

To use Poser models in gmax, follow these steps:

1. Position your figure in Poser, and export it by choosing Poser's File ⇨ Export command.

2. In the Export dialog box, select the 3DS file type and save the file.

3. In gmax, import the file by choosing File ⇨ Import.

4. Select the Completely Replace Current Scene and Convert Units options, and click OK.

   The figure appears in the viewports.

5. Save the scene as a gmax file by choosing File ⇨ Save.

Figure 4-8 shows the imported figure.

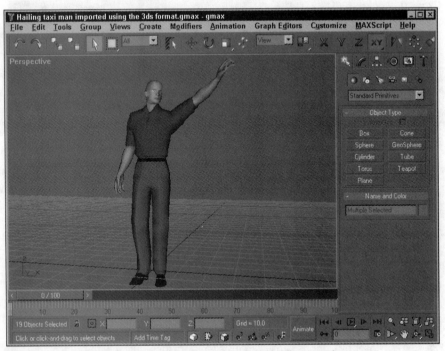

Figure 4-8: A Poser model imported into gmax using the 3DS format

If you repeat the preceding steps using the DXF format, you can see the results in Figure 4-9. Notice how the details of the face have disappeared.

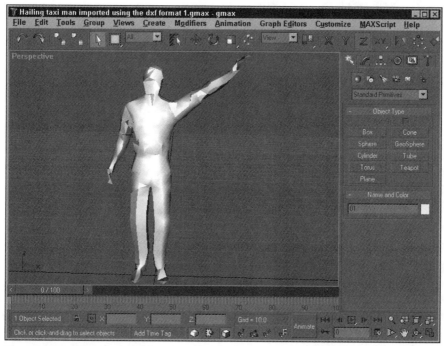

Figure 4-9: A Poser model imported into gmax using the DXF format with Weld Vertices set to 0.01

You can fix the face problems by turning off the Weld Vertices option in the Import DXF File dialog box. Turning off this option results in the model in Figure 4-10.

Although disabling the Weld Vertices option fixed the face detail, you can still see some problems on the man's raised arm and his feet. The black areas are caused by some misaligned normal vectors. The importer couldn't figure out which way was up for these faces. Try importing the man one more time, but this time, disable the Unify Normals option. The result is displayed in Figure 4-11.

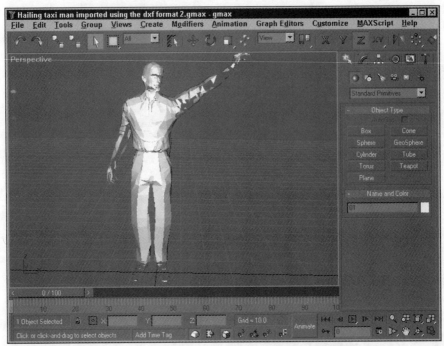

Figure 4-10: A Poser model imported into gmax using the DXF format with Weld Vertices turned off

The lesson to learn from this simple exercise is that the import options can be tricky. It is best to import the models using the minimum number of options as possible. You can then clean up the mesh using the gmax editing features rather than relying on the importer's functionality.

The 3DS format is clearly a better choice for importing models from Poser, but for some software products, the DXF format may be the only choice.

Exporting geometric objects

Choose File ➪ Export to open the Export dialog box. The only file type available is Plasma (P3D). Plasma is another derivative of 3ds max that is geared to the web graphics market. Exporting to Plasma offers no settings, which isn't surprising because it is created by the same basic engine.

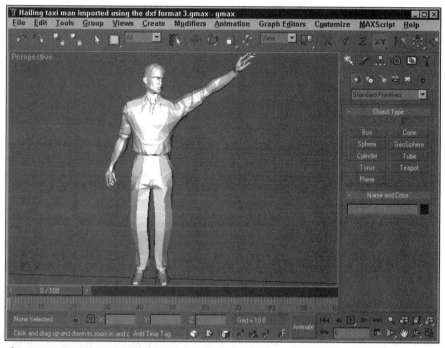

Figure 4-11: A Poser model imported into gmax using the DXF format with the Weld Vertices and Unify Normals options turned off

Other export options will become available depending on the game pack that you use. For example, the Trainz game pack enables you to export gmax files to the .IM, KIN, and PM file formats. Using these formats, you can load gmax objects into Trainz.

Referencing External Objects

No man is an island, and if Discreet has its way, no gmax user will be an island either. XRefs (which stands for eXternal Reference) make it easy for creative teams to collaborate on a project without having to wait for any group member to finish his or her respective production tasks. External references are objects and scenes contained in separate gmax files and made available for reference during a gmax session. This arrangement enables several artists on a team to work on separate sections of a project without interfering with one another or altering each other's work.

gmax includes two different types of XRefs — XRef Scenes and XRef Objects.

Using XRef Scenes

An externally referenced scene is one that appears in the current gmax session, but that is not accessible for editing or changing. The scene can be positioned and transformed when linked to a parent object and can be set to update automatically as changes are made to the source file.

As an example of how XRef Scenes facilitate a project, let's say a design team is in the midst of creating an environment for a project while the animator is animating a character model. The animator can access the in-production environment as an XRef Scene in order to help him move the character correctly about the environment. The design team will be happy because the animator didn't modify any of their lights, terrain models, maps, and props. The animator will be happy because he won't have to wait for the design team to finish all their tweaking before he can get started. The end result is one large, happy production team (if they can meet their deadlines).

Choose File ➪ XRef Scenes to open the XRef Scenes dialog box (shown in Figure 4-12), which you use to load XRef Scenes into a file.

XRef Scene options

In the XRef Scenes dialog box are several options for controlling the appearance of the scene objects, how often the scene is updated, and to which object the scene is bound. This dialog box is modeless, and you can open and change the options in this dialog box at any time.

The pane on the left lists all XRef Scenes in the current scene. To the right are the settings, which can be different for each XRef Scene in the list. To view or apply a setting, you first must select the scene from the list. You can remove any scene by selecting it from the list and clicking the Remove button.

Caution   If an XRef Scene in the list is displayed in red, then the scene could not be loaded. If the path or name is incorrect, you can change it in the Path field at the bottom of the list.

The Convert Selected button converts any selected objects in the current scene to XRef objects by saving them as a separate file. This button opens a dialog box to let you name and save the new file. If no objects are selected in the current scene, then this option is disabled.

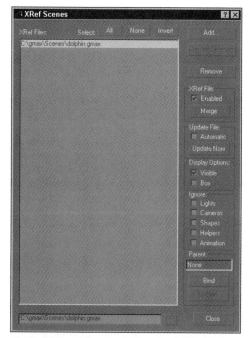

Figure 4-12: The XRef Scenes dialog box lets you specify which scenes to load as external references.

Use the Enabled option to enable or disable all XRef Scenes. Disabled scenes are displayed in gray. The Merge button lets you insert the current XRef Scene into the current scene. This button removes the scene from the list and acts the same way as the File ⇨ Merge command.

Updating an external scene

Automatic is a key option that can set any XRef Scene to be automatically updated. Enable this option by selecting a scene from the list and checking the Automatic option box; thereafter, the scene is updated any time the source file is updated. This option can slow down the system if the external scene is updated frequently, but the benefit is that you can work with the latest update.

The Update Now button is for manually updating the XRef Scene. Click this button to update the external scene to the latest saved version.

External scene appearance

Other options let you decide how the scene is displayed in the viewports. You can choose to make the external scene invisible or to display it as a box. Making an external scene invisible removes it only from the viewports, but the scene is still included in the rendered output. To remove a scene from the rendered output, deselect the Enabled option.

The Ignore section lists objects such as lights, cameras, shapes, helpers, and animation; selecting them causes them to be ignored and to have no effect in the scene. If an external scene's animation is ignored, then the scene appears as it does in frame 0.

Positioning an external scene

Positioning an external scene is accomplished by binding the scene to an object in the current scene (a dummy object, for example). The XRef Scenes dialog box is modeless, so you can select the object to bind to without closing the dialog box. After a binding object is selected, the external scene transforms to the binding object's pivot point. The name of the parent object is also displayed in the XRef Scene dialog box.

Transforming the object that the scene is bound to can control how the external scene is repositioned. To unbind an object, click the Unbind button in the XRef Scenes dialog box. Unbound scenes are positioned at the World origin for the current scene.

Working with XRef Scenes

You can't edit XRef Scenes in the current scene. Their objects are not visible in the Select by Name dialog box or in the Track and Schematic Views. You also cannot access the Modifier Stack of external scenes' objects. However, you can make use of external scene objects in other ways. For example, you can change a viewport to show the view from any camera or light in the external scene. External scene objects are included in the Summary Info dialog box.

Tip

Another way to use XRef Scenes is to create a scene with lights and/or cameras positioned at regular intervals around the scene. You can then use the XRef Scenes dialog box to turn these lights on and off or to select from a number of different views without creating new cameras.

You can also nest XRef Scenes within each other, so you can have one XRef Scene for the distant mountains that includes another XRef for a castle.

Note If a gmax file is loaded with XRef files that cannot be located, a warning dialog box appears, enabling you to browse to the file's new location. If you click OK or Cancel, the scene still loads, but the external scenes are missing.

Tutorial: Adding an XRef Scene

As an example of a project that would benefit from XRefs, I've created a maze environment. I will open a new gmax file and animate a diamond moving through this maze that will be opened as an XRef Scene.

To set up an XRef Scene, follow these steps:

1. Create a new gmax file by choosing File ➪ New.

2. Choose File ➪ XRef Scenes to open the XRef Scenes dialog box.

3. Click the Add button, locate the Maze.gmax file from the Chap 04 directory on the CD-ROM, and click Open to add it to the XRef Scene dialog box list.

Tip You can add several XRef Scenes by clicking the Add button again. You can also add a scene to the XRef Scene dialog box by dragging a .gmax file from Windows Explorer or from the Asset Manager window.

4. In the new scene, open the Create panel, select the Helpers category, and click the Dummy Object button. Then create a simple dummy object in the scene.

5. In the XRef Scenes dialog box, click the Bind button and select the dummy object.

   This will enable you to reposition the XRef Scene as needed.

6. Select the Automatic update option, and then click the Close button to exit the dialog box.

7. Now animate objects moving through the maze.

Figure 4-13 shows the Maze.gmax scene included in the current gmax file as an XRef.

Tip With the diamond animated, you can replace it at a later time with a detailed model of a mouse using the File ➪ Replace command.

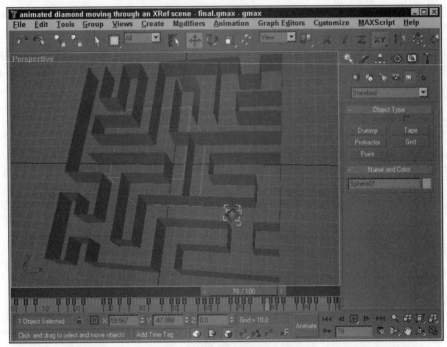

Figure 4-13: The maze.gmax file loaded into the current file as an XRef Scene

Using XRef Objects

XRef Objects are slightly different from XRef Scenes. They are objects that appear in a scene that you can transform and animate, but the original object's structure and Modifier Stack cannot be changed.

An innovative way to use this feature is to create a library of objects that you can load on the fly as needed. For example, if you had a furniture library, you could load several different styles until you got just the look you wanted.

You can also use XRef Objects to load low-resolution proxies of complex models in order to lighten the system load during a gmax session. This method increases the viewport refresh rate.

Many of the options in the XRef Objects dialog box, shown in Figure 4-14, are the same as in the XRef Scenes dialog box.

The left side of the XRef Objects dialog box is divided into two sections. The top section displays the externally referenced files, and the lower section displays the objects selected from that file. A file must be selected in order for you to see its objects.

The Convert Selected button works the same as in the XRef Scenes dialog box. It enables you to save the selected objects in the current scene to a separate file just like the File ➪ Save Selected command.

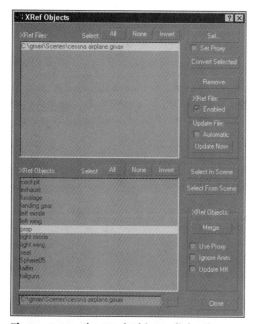

Figure 4-14: The XRef Objects dialog box lets you choose which files to look in for external objects.

In the XRef Objects dialog box, you can choose to automatically update the external referenced objects or use the Update Now button. You can also Enable and Disable all objects in a file.

The Select In Scene and Select From Scene buttons are useful for seeing which objects in the scene are related to which items in the XRef Objects dialog box list.

You have several options for controlling how the XRef Objects are displayed:

✦ **Use Proxy:** Lets you choose between displaying the proxy and displaying the actual object.

✦ **Ignore Animation:** Turns off any Modifier Stack animations associated with the object.

✦ **Update Materials:** Enables the object's materials to update as the source gets updated.

Using proxies

If the Use Proxy option is selected, then you can open a low-resolution proxy object in place of a more complex object. This feature saves memory by not requiring the more complex object to be kept in memory. You can also select to render the proxy, update its materials, or ignore its animation.

If an object in the lower section of the XRefs Objects dialog box is selected, then the Add button changes to a Set button. The Set button lets you choose a file and object to use as a proxy. The proxy is displayed in place of the actual referenced object.

Tip The real benefit of using proxies is to replace complex referenced objects with simpler objects that update quickly. When creating a complex object, remember to also create a low-resolution version to use as a proxy.

Tutorial: Using an XRef proxy

To set up an XRef proxy, follow these steps:

1. Open the Post Box with XRef Tree.gmax file from the Chap 04 directory on the CD-ROM.

   This file includes the post box model produced by Zygote Media.

2. Open the XRef Objects dialog box by choosing File ➪ XRef Objects.

3. Click the Add button, and locate the Park Bench under a Tree.gmax file from the Chap 04 directory on the CD-ROM.

   This file includes the old tree and park bench models made by Zygote Media. The XRef Merge dialog box, shown in Figure 4-15, automatically opens and displays a list of all the objects in the file just added.

Figure 4-15: The XRef Merge dialog box lets you choose specific objects from a scene.

4. Select the Tree object to add to the current scene, and click OK. (Hold down the Ctrl key to select several objects.) Use the Filter and Sort options to locate specific objects.

Note   If an object you've selected has the same name as an object that is currently in the scene, the Duplicate Name dialog box appears to let you rename the object, merge it anyway, skip the new object, or delete the old version.

5. Select the Tree object in the lower pane, and click the Set button with the Set Proxy option selected.

The Open File dialog box appears.

6. Select the Tree Lo-Res.gmax file from the Chap 04 directory on the CD-ROM.

The Merge dialog box opens.

7. Select the Cylinder01 object, and click OK.

Caution   If the proxy object has a different offset than the original object, a warning dialog box appears instructing you to use the Reset XForm utility to reset the transform of the objects.

8. With the Tree object selected in the lower pane, select the Use Proxy option to see the proxy object and deselect it to see the actual object.

XRef Objects that you add to a scene instantly appear in the current scene as you add them. Figure 4-16 shows the Post Box with the actual tree object. The XRef Objects dialog box lets you switch to the proxy object at any time.

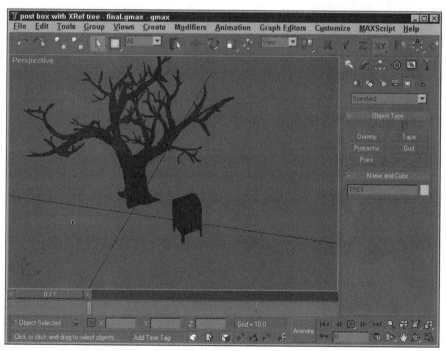

Figure 4-16: The tree object is an XRef from another scene. Its proxy is a simple cylinder.

XRef Objects in the Modifier Stack

XRef Objects appear and act like any other object in the scene. You'll see a difference only if you open the Modifier Stack. The Stack displays "XRef Object" as its only entry.

When you select the XRef Object item in the Modifier Stack, a rollout, shown in Figure 4-17, appears. The rollout includes many of the same controls displayed in the XRef Objects dialog box discussed earlier. These controls include the XRef File Name, Object Name, Proxy File Name, and Proxy Object Name.

Figure 4-17: The XRef Object rollout in the Modify panel lets you choose which objects from which files to include as external references.

Configuring XRef paths

The Configure Paths dialog box includes an XRefs tab for setting the paths for XRef Scenes and Objects, shown in Figure 4-18. Choose Customize ➪ Configure Paths to open the Configure Paths dialog box and click the XRefs panel.

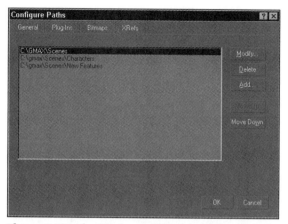

Figure 4-18: The XRefs panel in the Configure Paths dialog box lets you specify paths to be searched when an XRef cannot be located.

gmax keeps track of the path of any XRefs used in a scene, but if it cannot find them, it looks at the paths designated in the XRefs panel of the Configure Paths dialog box. For projects that use lots of XRefs, populating this list with potential paths is a good idea. Paths are scanned in the order they are listed, so place the most likely paths at the top of the list.

To add a new path to the panel, click the Add button. You can also modify or delete paths in this panel with the Modify and Delete buttons.

Using the File Utilities

With all these various files floating around, gmax has included several utilities that make working with them easier. The Utilities panel of the Command Panel includes several useful utilities for working with files. You can access these utilities by clicking the utility button; you can access its rollouts in the bottom of the Utilities panel.

Using the Asset Browser utility

The Asset Browser utility is the first default button in the Utility panel. Clicking this button opens the Asset Browser window. The Asset Browser resembles Windows Explorer, except that it displays thumbnail images of all the supported formats contained within the current directory. Using this window, shown in Figure 4-19, you can browse through directory files and see thumbnails of images and scenes.

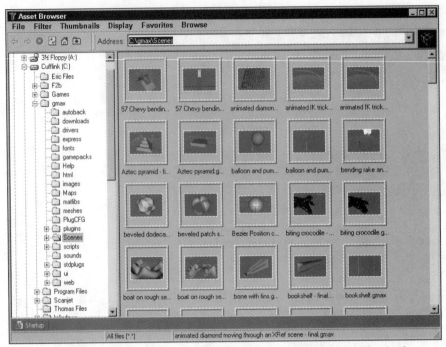

Figure 4-19: The Asset Browser window displays thumbnails of the files in the current directory.

The supported file types include BMP, JPEG, PNG, PSD, TGA, and TIF. These types are the same ones that the File ⇨ View File command can open. All files with these extensions are viewable within the Asset Browser. You can select to view only a certain type of file using the Filter menu. In addition to these formats, you can see the thumbnails of all gmax and 3ds max files.

Tip   Open and display the Asset Manager within a viewport by right-clicking the viewport title and choosing Views ⇨ Extended ⇨ Asset Manager from the pop-up menu.

You can also drag and drop files from the Asset Browser window to gmax. Drag a scene file, and drop it on gmax's title bar to merge the scene file within gmax. If you drop it onto one of the viewports, a small pop-up menu offers you the option to Open, Merge, or XRef the file. You can drop image files onto the map buttons in the Material Editor window to make the image a map or drop an image file onto a viewport to make it a viewport background.

The Asset Browser window is modeless, so you can work with the gmax interface while the Asset Browser window is open. Double-clicking an image opens it full size in the Virtual Frame Buffer window.

The Asset Browser can also act as a Web browser to look at content online. When the Asset Browser first opens, a dialog box reminds you that online content may be copyrighted and cannot be used without consent from the owner.

The Display menu includes three panes that you can select. The Thumbnail pane shows the files as thumbnails. You can change the size of these thumbnails using the Thumbnails menu. The Explorer pane displays the files as icons the same as you would see in Windows Explorer. The Web pane displays the Web page for the site listed in the Address field.

To view Web sites, you need to be connected to the Internet. The Asset Browser can remember your favorite Web sites using the Favorites menu. The Asset Browser window also includes the standard Web browser navigation buttons, such as Back, Forward, Home, Refresh, and Stop. You can also find these commands in the Browse menu.

gmax keeps thumbnails of all the images you access in its cache. The cache is a directory that holds thumbnails of all the recently accessed images. Each thumbnail image points to the actual directory where the image is located. In the Asset Browser, choose File ➪ Preferences to open the Preference dialog box, in which you can specify where you want the cache directory to be located. Its default location is the abcache directory located where gmax is installed. To view the cached files, choose Filter ➪ All in Cache.

Choose File ➪ Print to print the selected image.

Caution There is a nasty bug with the Asset Browser that scatters thumbnails all over the computer screen. This seems to happen only when viewing a directory of gmax files. You can get around this bug by maximizing and then restoring the Asset Browser window.

Finding files with the gmax File Finder utility

Another useful utility for locating files is the gmax File Finder utility, which is the second button in the Utilities panel. When you select this utility, a rollout with a Start button appears in the Utility panel. Clicking this button opens the gmaxFinder dialog box. Using gmaxFinder, you can search for scene files by any of the information listed in the File Properties dialog box.

You can use the Browse button to specify the root directory to search. You can select to have the search also examine any subfolders. Figure 4-20 shows the gmaxFinder dialog box locating all the scene files that include the word *blue*.

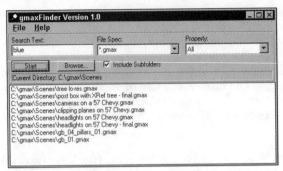

Figure 4-20: You can use the gmaxFinder utility to
search for scene files by property.

Collecting files with the Resource Collector utility

When a scene is created, image and object files can be pulled from several different
locations. The Resource Collector utility helps you consolidate all these files into
one location. The settings for this utility appear in the Parameters rollout in the
Utility panel, as shown in Figure 4-21. The Output Path is the location where the
files are collected. You can change this location using the Browse button.

Caution   The Resource Collector fails to gather Environment and Projector maps used on
lights. You also should double-check any scripts that are included in the scene.

Figure 4-21: The Resource Collector utility can compile
all referenced files into a single location.

The utility includes options to Collect Bitmaps, to Include the gmax scene file, and to Compress the files into a compressed WinZip file. The Copy option makes copies of the files, and the Move option moves the actual file into the directory specified in the Output Path field. The Update Materials option updates all material paths in the Material Editor. When you're comfortable with the settings, click the Begin button located at the bottom of the Parameters rollout to start the collecting.

Using the Map Path Utility

After you have all your maps in place, losing them can really make life troublesome. However, gmax includes a utility that helps you determine which maps are missing and lets you edit the path to them to quickly and easily locate them. The Bitmap Path Editor utility is available in the Utility panel.

When opened, the Path Editor rollout includes the Edit Bitmaps button that opens the Bitmap Path Editor window, shown in Figure 4-22. The rollout also provides two options for displaying the Materials Editor and Material Library bitmap paths. The Close button closes the rollout.

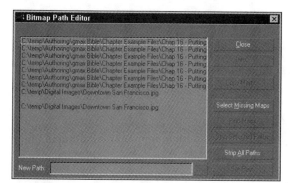

Figure 4-22: The Bitmap Path Editor window lets you alter map paths.

The Info button in the Bitmap Path Editor dialog box lists all the nodes that use the selected map. The Copy Maps button opens a File dialog where you can select the destination where you want to copy the selected map. The Select Missing Maps button selects any maps in the list that can't be located. The Find Maps button lists the maps in the current selection that can be located and the number that are missing. Stripping paths removes the path information and leaves only the map name. The New Path field lets you enter the path information to apply to the selected maps. The button with three dots, to the right of the New Path field, lets you browse for a path. The Set Path button applies the path designated in the New Path field to the selected maps.

Accessing File Information

As you work with files, several dialog boxes in gmax supply you with extra information about your scene. Using this information to your advantage can help you keep track of files and record valuable statistics about a scene.

Displaying scene information

If you like to keep statistics on your files (to see whether you've broken the company record for the model with the greatest number of faces), you'll find the Summary Info dialog box useful. Use File ➪ Summary Info to open a dialog box that displays all the relevant details about the current scene, such as the number of objects, lights, and cameras; the total number of vertices and faces; and various model settings, as well as a Description field where you can describe the scene. Figure 4-23 shows the Summary Info dialog box.

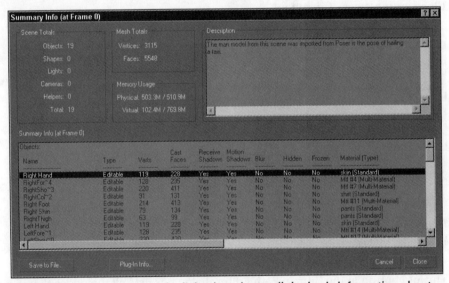

Figure 4-23: The Summary Info dialog box shows all the basic information about the current scene.

The Plug-In Info button in the Summary Info dialog box displays a list of all the plug-ins currently installed on your system. Even without any external plug-ins installed, the list is fairly long because many of the core features in gmax are implemented as plug-ins. The Summary Info dialog box also includes a Save to File button for saving the scene summary information as a text file.

Viewing file properties

As the number of files that you have on your system increases, you'll be wishing you had a card catalog to keep track of them all. gmax has an interface that you can use to attach keywords and other descriptive information about the scene to the file. Use File ⇨ File Properties to open the File Properties dialog box. This dialog box includes three panels: Summary, Contents, and Custom. The Summary and Custom panels are shown in Figure 4-24. The Summary panel holds information such as the Title, Subject, and Author of the gmax file and can be useful for managing a collaborative project. The Contents panel holds information about the scene such as the total number of objects and much more. Much of this information is also found in the Summary Info dialog box. The Custom panel includes a way to enter a custom list of properties such as client information, language, and so on.

Note   You can also view the Properties dialog box information while working in Windows Explorer by right-clicking the file and selecting Properties. Two unique tabs are visible — Summary and Statistics. The Summary tab holds the file identification information, including the Author, Keywords, Comments, Title, Subject, and Template. The Statistics tab displays the creation and modification dates, the name of the user who last saved the file, a revision number, and any descriptive information.

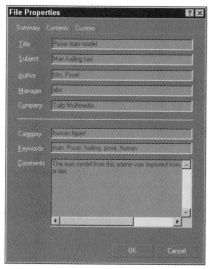

Figure 4-24: The File Properties dialog box contains workflow information such as the scene author, comments, and revision dates.

Viewing files

Sometimes, looking at the thumbnail of an image isn't enough to help you decide whether you have the right image. For these cases, you can quickly load the image in question into a viewer to look at it closely. Choose File ⇨ View Image File to open the View File dialog box, as shown in Figure 4-25. This dialog box lets you load and view graphics and animation files using the Virtual Frame Buffer or the default Media Player for your system.

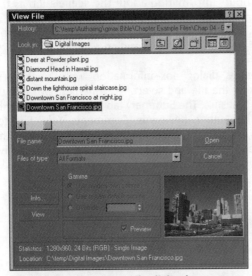

Figure 4-25: The View File dialog box can open an assortment of image and animation formats.

The View File dialog box includes several controls for viewing files. The Info button lets you view detailed information about the selected file. The View button opens the file for viewing while keeping the View File dialog box open. The Open button closes the dialog box. At the bottom of the View File dialog box, the statistics and path of the current file are displayed.

Note   The View File dialog box can open many types of files, including bitmap images (BMP), JPEG images (JPG), PNG images, Adobe Photoshop images (PSD), Targa images (TGA), and tagged image file format images (TIF).

You use the Gamma area on the View File dialog box to specify whether an image uses its own gamma settings or the system's default setting, or whether an override value should be used.

Using the Virtual Frame Buffer

The Virtual Frame Buffer is a temporary window that can be used to view images. It is especially useful for maps because it can display color and alpha channels. The Virtual Frame Buffer, shown in Figure 4-26, enables you to view images without leaving the gmax interface.

Figure 4-26: The Virtual Frame Buffer displays images. These images can be panned and zoomed within this interface.

You can view images from a local hard drive or a network drive in the Virtual Frame Buffer using the File ↔ View Image File menu command or by clicking on the View button within the gmax Material Editor. Several Virtual Frame Buffer windows can be opened at the same time.

To zoom in on the buffer, hold down the Ctrl key and click the buffer. To zoom out, click the right mouse button while holding down the Ctrl key. The Shift key enables you to pan the buffer image. You can also use the mouse wheel (if you have a scrolling mouse) to zoom and pan within the frame buffer. Scrolling the mouse wheel zooms in and out of the image, and holding the mouse wheel button down lets you pan about the image.

At the top of the frame buffer dialog box are several icon buttons. The first four buttons enable the red, green, blue, and alpha channels. The alpha channel holds any transparency information for the image. The alpha channel is a grayscale map, with black showing the transparent areas and white showing the opaque areas. Next to the Display Alpha Channel button is the Monochrome button, which displays the image as a grayscale image.

The Clear button erases the image from the window.

The Channel Display drop-down list lets you select the channel to display. The color swatch at the right shows the color of the currently selected pixel. You can select new pixels by right-clicking and holding on the image. This temporarily displays a small dialog box with the image dimensions and the RGB value of the pixel directly under the cursor. The color in the color swatch can then be dragged and dropped in other dialog boxes such as the Material Editor.

Summary

Working with files will let you save your work, share it with others, and collaborate across teams. This chapter covered these basics:

✦ Creating, saving, opening, merging, and archiving files

✦ Understanding the various import and export types

✦ Importing models from other programs, such as Poser

✦ Using externally referenced scenes and objects to work on the same project at the same time as your fellow team members without interfering with their work (or they with yours)

✦ Configuring XRef paths to help gmax track your XRef Scenes and Objects

✦ Working with the file utilities, such as the Asset Browser, File Finder, Resource Collector and MapPath Editor

✦ Using the Summary Info and File Properties dialog box to keep track of scene files

Now that you've got working with files down, we'll move onto objects and how to select them.

✦   ✦   ✦

Choosing Your Poison – Selecting Objects

C H A P T E R

◆ ◆ ◆ ◆

In This Chapter

Selecting objects using toolbars and menus

Using named selection sets

Setting object properties

Hiding and freezing objects

◆ ◆ ◆ ◆

Now that you know how to import objects into gmax, you're probably staring at a collection of objects wondering what to do next. (If not, you can play with the Create menu to add some objects to the scene.) Well, the first thing you need to know is how to select an object.

To eliminate, move, or change the look of any object, you first have to know how to select the object. Doing so can be tricky if the viewports are all full of objects lying on top of one another. Luckily, gmax offers several selection features that make looking for a needle in a haystack easier.

gmax offers many different ways to select objects. You can select by name, color, type, and even material. You can also use selection filters to make only certain types of objects selectable. And after you've found all the objects you need, you can make a selection set, which will allow you to quickly select a set of objects by name. Now where is that needle?

All objects have properties that define their physical characteristics, such as shape, radius, and smoothness, but objects also have properties that control where they are located in the scene, how they are displayed and rendered, and what their parent objects are. These properties have a major impact on how you work with objects; understanding them can make objects in a scene easier to work with.

Selecting Objects

gmax includes several methods for selecting objects — the easiest being simply clicking on the object in one of the viewports. It is easy to identify the selected object or objects because they turn white and are enclosed in brackets called *selection brackets*.

Several additional options are available to identify the current selection. You can find these options in the Viewport Configuration dialog box (which you access with the Customize ⇨ Viewport Configuration menu command). These options include selection brackets (which can be turned on and off with the J keyboard shortcut) and edged faces (which are toggled with the F4 key). There is also an option to Shade Selected Faces, which shades the selected faces red when selected in subobject mode. Selection Brackets and Edged Faces are shown in Figure 5-1. Another way to identify the selected object is to look for the object's axes, which always appear at the object's pivot point for the selected object.

 Caution   The Viewport Configuration dialog box also includes an option to Shade Selected Faces (F2), but this option shades only selected sub-object faces.

Figure 5-1: Selected objects can be highlighted with selection brackets (left), edged faces (middle), or both (right).

With many objects in a scene, clicking directly on a single object (free from the others) can be difficult, but persistence can pay off. If you continue to click an object that is already selected, the object directly behind the object you clicked is selected. For example, if you have a row of spheres lined up, you can select the third sphere by clicking three times on the first object.

 Tip   In complicated scenes, finding objects is often much easier if they have a relevant name. Be sure to name your new objects using the Name and Color rollout.

Working with selection filters

Before examining the selection commands in the Edit menu, you need to know about Selection Filters. With a complex scene that includes geometry, lights, cameras, shapes, and so on, selecting the exact object that you want can be difficult. Selection filters can simplify this task.

Note If you ever find yourself unable to select an object that is right in front of you simply by clicking it, check the object filter drop-down list.

A selection filter specifies which types of objects can be selected. The Selection Filter drop-down list is located on the main toolbar (the leftmost drop-down list). Selecting Shapes, for example, makes only shape objects available for selection. Clicking a geometry object with the Shape Selection Filter enabled does nothing.

The available filters include All, Geometry, Shapes, Lights, Cameras, and Helpers.

The Combos option opens the Filter Combinations dialog box, shown in Figure 5-2. From this dialog box, you can select combinations of objects to filter. These new filter combinations are added to the bottom of the drop-down list. For example, to create a filter combination for lights and cameras, open the Filter Combinations dialog box, select Lights and Cameras, and click Add. The combination is listed as LC in the Current Combinations section, and the LC option is added to the drop-down list.

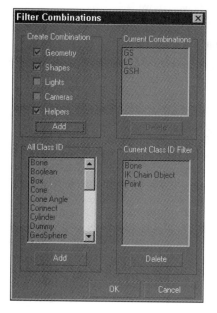

Figure 5-2: The Filter Combinations dialog box enables you to create a custom selection filter.

The Filter Combinations dialog box also includes a list of Class IDs. Using these IDs, you can filter very specific object types, such as a Boolean object or a Box primitive. In fact, the Bone, IK Chain Object, and Point filters are Class IDs.

Using the select buttons

On the main toolbar are four buttons used to select objects. These buttons are shown in Table 5-1. The Select Object button looks like the arrow cursor. The other three buttons select and transform objects. They are Select and Move, Select and Rotate, and Select and Scale. You can use any of these buttons to select objects.

Cross-Reference   See Chapter 7, "Moving, Rotating and Scaling Objects — Return of the –ings" for more details on the Select and Transform buttons.

	Table 5-1 Select Buttons	
Button Icon	**Name**	**Description**
↖	Select Objects	Click an object in one of the viewports to select it.
✥	Select and Move	Click an object in one of the viewports to select it, and then drag to move.
↻	Select and Rotate	Click an object in one of the viewports to select it, and then drag to rotate.
▪	Select and Scale	Click an object in one of the viewports to select it, and then drag to scale.

You can easily tell which selection button is enabled (if any) by looking for the orange highlighted button. If you right-click in one of the viewports, the most recently used selection button will be selected again.

Selecting with the Edit menu

The Edit menu includes several convenient selection commands. The Edit ➪ Select All menu command does just what you would think it does. It selects all objects in the current scene of the type defined by the selection filter. The Edit ➪ Select None menu command deselects all objects. You can also simulate this command by clicking in any viewport away from all objects. The Edit ➪ Select Invert menu command selects all objects defined by the selection filter that are currently not selected and deselects all currently selected objects.

Choosing Edit ➪ Select By ➪ Color lets you click a single object in any of the viewports. All objects with the same object (not material) color as the one you selected will be selected.

Note Even if you already have an object of that color selected, you still must select an object of the desired color.

This command, of course, will not work on any objects without an associated color, such as cameras.

Select by Name

Choosing Edit ➪ Select By ➪ Name (H) opens the Select Objects dialog box, as shown in Figure 5-3. Clicking the Select by Name button on the main toolbar, positioned to the right of the Selection Filter drop-down list, or pressing the keyboard shortcut H, can also open this dialog box.

Figure 5-3: The Select Objects dialog box displays all objects in the current scene by name.

You select objects by clicking their names in the list and then clicking the Select button. To pick and choose several objects, hold down the Ctrl key while selecting. Holding down the Shift key selects a range of objects. The All, None, and Invert buttons select all of the listed objects, none of the listed objects, or the inverse of the selected objects.

Note An identical version of the Select Objects dialog box works in a modeless state and enables you to interact with the viewports behind the dialog box. This dialog box is called the Selection Floater, and you can access it by choosing Tools ➪ Selection Floater.

You can also type an object name in the field above the name list. All objects that match the typed characters will be selected. The Sort options affect how the list is displayed. Objects can be sorted Alphabetically, By Type, By Color, and By Size. Selecting the Sort by Size option sorts the objects by the number of faces. This is an easy way to find the most complex object in the scene.

Tip   Within the Select by Name text field, you can use wildcards to locate objects. Acceptable wildcards include an asterisk (*) for multiple characters in a row and a question mark (?) for single characters. For example, an entry of **hedra*** will select all objects beginning with "hedra" regardless of the ending.

The Display Subtree option includes all child objects in the list. By enabling the Select Subtree option, you select all child objects along with their parent objects. The Select Dependents option automatically selects all instances and references. The Case Sensitive option checks the case of the letters typed in the name search field. If this option is not selected, then capital letters are the same as their lowercase counterparts.

The Select Object dialog box isn't subject to the selection filter because the object types can be selected in the dialog box. Selection sets (which are a predefined selected group of objects) are also accessible from the Select Objects dialog box.

Select by Region

The Edit ⇨ Region command lets you select from one of two different methods for selecting objects in the viewport using the mouse. First, make sure you're in select mode, click away from any of the objects, and drag over the objects to select. The first method for selecting objects is Window Selection. This method selects all objects that are contained completely within the dragged outline. The Crossing Selection method selects any objects that are inside or overlapping the dragged outline. You can also access these two selection methods via the Window Selection buttons on the main toolbar—Window and Crossing.

You can also change the shape of the selection outline. The Selection Region button on the main toolbar (to the left of the Selection Filter drop-down list) includes fly-out buttons for Rectangular, Circular, and Fence Selection Regions.

The Rectangular selection method lets you select objects by dragging a rectangular section (from corner to corner) over a viewport. The Circular selection method selects objects within a circle that grows from the center outward. The Fence method lets you draw a polygon-shaped selection area by clicking at each corner. Simply double-click to finish the fenced selection.

The Ctrl+F keyboard shortcut lets you cycle through the available selection methods. Figure 5-4 shows each of the selection methods.

 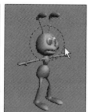 

Figure 5-4: The ant's head is selected using the Rectangular, Circular, and Fence selection methods.

Selecting multiple objects

As you work with objects in gmax, there will be times when you'll want to apply a modification to or transform several objects at once. You can select multiple objects in several ways. With the Select by Name dialog box open, you can choose several objects from the list using the standard Ctrl and Shift keys. Holding down the Ctrl key selects or deselects multiple list items, but holding down the Shift key selects all consecutive list items between the first selected and the second selected items.

The Ctrl key also works when selecting objects in the viewport using one of the main toolbar Select buttons. If you hold down the Ctrl key and click an object, then the object is added to the current selection set. If you click an item that is already selected, then it is deselected. If you drag over multiple objects while holding down the Ctrl key, then all items in the dragged selection are added to the current selection set.

The Alt key deselects objects from the current selection set, which is opposite of what the Ctrl key does.

If you drag over several objects while holding down the Shift key, then the selection set will be inverted. Each item that is selected will be deselected and vice versa.

Object hierarchies are established using the Link button on the main toolbar. You can select an entire hierarchy of objects by double-clicking on its parent object. You can also select multiple objects within the hierarchy. When you double-click an object, any children of that object will also be selected. When an object with a hierarchy is selected, the Page Up and Page Down keys select the next object up or down the hierarchy.

Grouping and linking several objects together will make working with the entire model easier. Another way to organize the model is to link all the various model parts to a single object. Then the parts will move along with this single object.

Cross-
Reference

You can learn more about linking objects and creating hierarchies in Chapter 6, "Cloning, Grouping, and Linking Objects, and other –ings."

Tutorial: Selecting objects

One of the most enjoyable parts of creating a new game level is to populate the level with all sorts of new challenges. These challenges can come in many forms, such as a hideous steel-eyed dragon that we'll use in this next example.

Note

The deer model used in this example has been modified from a model created by Viewpoint Datalabs.

To select objects, follow these steps:

1. Open the Steel-eyed dragon.gmax file from the Chap 05 directory on the CD-ROM.

2. Click the Select Object button on the main toolbar, and click the dragon's body in one of the viewports.

   The dragon's body will be highlighted in white in the Top, Front, and Left viewports and surrounded with brackets in the Perspective viewport. In the Command Panel, the name for this object, "body," will be displayed in the Name and Color rollout.

3. Click the Select and Move button, and then click the dragon's body and drag in the Perspective viewport to the right.

   As you can see, the deer's head and body form an object independent of the other parts of the deer object. Moving it separates it from the rest of the model's parts.

4. Choose Edit ⇨ Undo Move (or press Ctrl+Z) to undo the move and piece the deer back together again.

5. With the Select and Move tool still selected, drag an outline around the entire dragon in the Top view to select all the dragon parts, and then click and drag the entire dragon again.

   This time, the entire dragon moves as one entity, and the name field displays "Multiple Selected."

6. Open the Select Objects dialog box by clicking the Select by Name button on the main toolbar (or by pressing the H key).

   All the individual parts that make up this model are listed.

7. Double-click the "wings" object listed in the dialog box.

   The dialog box automatically closes, and the wings become selected in the viewports. Figure 5-5 shows our new challenge with just its wings selected. Notice that the name of the selected object in the Name and Color rollout says "wings."

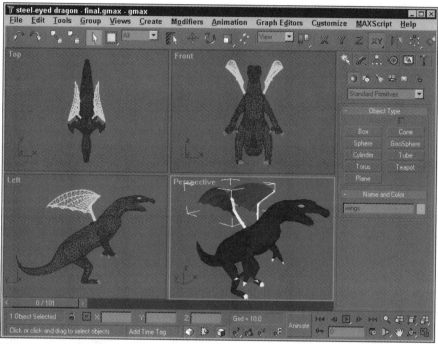

Figure 5-5: A dragon character with its white selected wings.

Locking selection sets

If you've finally selected the exact objects that you want to work with, you can disable any other selections using the Selection Lock Toggle button on the Status Bar (it looks like a lock). When this button is enabled, it is colored yellow, and clicking objects in the viewports won't have any effect on the current selection. The keyboard shortcut toggle for this command is the Spacebar.

Using named selection sets

With a group of objects selected, you can establish a selection set by typing a name into the Named Selection Set drop-down list on the main toolbar (the rightmost drop-down). After it is established as a selection set, you can recall this group of selected objects at any time by selecting its name from the Named Selection Set drop-down list, or by opening the Edit Named Selections dialog box, shown in Figure 5-6. You can access this dialog box by selecting the Edit ➪ Edit Named Selections menu command.

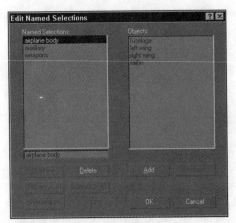

Figure 5-6: The Edit Named Selections dialog box lets you view and manage selection sets.

After you've created several named selection sets, you can use the Edit Named Selections dialog box to manage the selection sets. The dialog box includes two list panes. The left pane lists the current named selection sets, and the right pane displays the objects available in the selected set. The buttons beneath the panes let you create and delete sets, or add or remove objects from a set.

If several sets are selected in the left pane, then the Combine, Subtract, and Intersection buttons become enabled. These buttons let you combine objects from several sets into one, subtract objects found in both sets from one of the sets, or build a set of objects that includes only objects found in both sets.

You can also set named selection sets for subobject selections. Be aware that these subobject selection sets are only available when you're in subobject edit mode and only for the currently selected object.

Isolating the current selection

The Tools ⇨ Isolate menu command hides all objects except for the selected object. It also zooms to extents on the object in the active viewport. It also opens a simple dialog box with an Exit Isolation button in it. Clicking this button or selecting the Isolate command again exits isolation mode and displays all the objects again.

Tip

This feature is great if you want to work on a single object without affecting any of its surrounding objects.

Selecting objects in other interfaces

In addition to selecting objects in the viewports, you can also use some of the other interfaces and dialog boxes to select objects. For example, the Material Editor includes a button (in the upper-right corner that looks like a checkered cube with an arrow cursor) that selects all objects in a scene with the same material applied. The Select By Material button opens the Select Object dialog box, shown in Figure 5-7, with all objects that use the selected material highlighted.

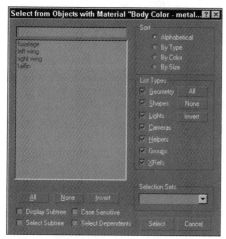

Figure 5-7: The Select By Material button in the Material Editor opens yet another variant of the Select Objects dialog box.

Another way to select objects is in the Track View. To view all the objects, click the + sign to the left of the Objects track. You can identify the Objects track by a small yellow cube icon. A hierarchy of all the objects in a scene will be displayed, as shown in Figure 5-8. At the bottom-left corner of the Track View window is the Select By Name text field. Typing an object name in this field automatically selects the object's track in the editor's window, but not in the viewport. Clicking the yellow cube icon to the left of the track name selects the object in the viewport.

Cross-Reference

The Material Editor is covered in detail in Chapter 16, "Putting on the Ritz with the gmax Material Editor," and the Track View interface is covered in Chapter 20, "Graphing Animations with the Track View."

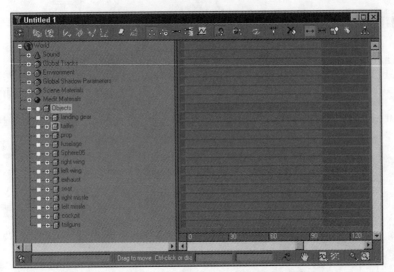

Figure 5-8: The Track View can also be used to select objects.

Setting Object Properties

Each object has properties that can be accessed using the Object Properties dialog box. These properties include details about the object, such as its dimensions. The dialog box also includes display options you can set that affect how the object is viewed in the viewports.

After you select an object or multiple objects, you can view their object properties by choosing Edit ⇨ Object Properties. Alternatively, you can right-click the object and select Properties from the pop-up quadmenu. Figure 5-9 shows the Object Properties dialog box. This dialog box includes two panels — General and User Defined.

Viewing object information

For a single object, the General panel of the Object Properties dialog box lists details about the object in the Object Information section. These details include the object's name, color, origin dimensions, and number of vertices and faces, as well as who the object's parent is, its Material Name, the number of children attached to the object, and the object's group name if it's part of a group. All of this information (except for its name and color) is for display only and cannot be changed.

Note   The two fields underneath the Vertices and Faces are used only when the properties for a Shape are displayed. These fields show the number of Shape Vertices and Shape Curves.

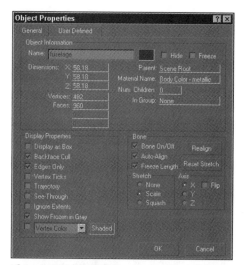

Figure 5-9: The Object Properties dialog box displays valuable information about a selected object.

If the properties for multiple objects are to be displayed, the Object Properties dialog box places the text, "Multiple Selected," in the Name field. The properties that are common to all these objects are displayed. With multiple objects selected, you can set their properties all at once.

The Object Properties dialog box can be displayed for all geometric objects and shapes, as well as for lights, cameras, and helper objects. Not all properties are available for all objects.

You can also Hide and Freeze objects using the appropriate check boxes. These options are covered later in this chapter.

Setting Display properties

Display properties don't affect how the object is displayed in the viewports. These options can speed up or slow down the viewport refresh rates. For example, Display as Box increases the viewport update rate dramatically for complex scenes, but at the expense of any detail. It displays the object as a simple box. This setting can be useful to see how the objects generally fit in comparison to one another.

Note You can also find and set the same Display properties that are listed in the Object Properties dialog box in the Display Properties rollout of the Display panel in the Command Panel.

When turned on, the Backface Cull option causes the faces on the backside of the object to be hidden. gmax considers the direction that each normal is pointing and doesn't display a face whose normal is pointing away from the view. This is important when you're looking at the inside portion of an object.

The Edges Only option displays only the edges of each face when the viewport is set to Wireframe mode. When Edges Only is not selected, a dashed line indicates polygon faces. The Vertex Ticks option displays all object vertices as blue plus signs.

The Trajectory option displays any animated motions as paths.

I describe using animated motion paths in more detail in Chapter 19, "Getting the Prop to Spin—Animation Basics."

The See-Through option causes shaded objects to appear transparent. This option is useful if you have several objects stacked on top of one another, because it allows you to see the obscured objects. This option really doesn't help in Wireframe mode.

The Ignore Extents option causes an object to be ignored when you are using the Zoom Extents button in the Viewport Navigation controls. For example, if you have a camera or light positioned at a distance from the objects in the scene and you use the Zoom Extents All button, all objects (including the distant camera or light) are shown in the viewport, making the objects so small that you can't see them. If you set the Ignore Extents option for the camera or light, then the Zoom Extents All button zooms in on just the geometry objects.

When objects are frozen, they appear dark gray, but if the Show Frozen in Gray option is disabled, then the object appears as it normally does in the viewport. I like to keep this option enabled because it provides a visual clue that reminds me when objects are frozen.

The Vertex Color option displays the colors of any Editable Mesh vertices that have been assigned colors. You can select to use Vertex Color, Vertex Illumination, or Vertex Alpha. The Shaded button causes the meshes to be shaded by the vertex colors. You can only assign vertex colors to editable meshes.

I talk about vertex colors in Chapter 11, "Moving On with Marvelous Meshes."

Using the User-Defined panel

The User-Defined panel contains a simple text window. In this window, you can enter any type of information. This information will be saved with the scene and can be referred to as notes about an object.

Hiding and freezing objects

You can hide or freeze objects in a scene by selecting the Hide or Freeze option at the top of the General panel. You can also hide and freeze objects using the Display Floater dialog box, which you access by choosing Tools ⇨ Display Floater.

Tip   There are also several keyboard shortcuts used to hide specific objects. These shortcuts are toggles, so one press will make the objects disappear and another press will make them reappear. Object types that can be hidden with these short-cuts include cameras (Shift+C), grids (G), grids in all viewports (Shift+G), helpers (Shift+H), and lights (Shift+L).

The Hide option makes the selected object in the scene invisible, and the Freeze option turns the selected object dark gray (if the Show Frozen in Gray option is enabled in the Object Properties dialog box) and doesn't allow it to be transformed or selected. You cannot select hidden objects by clicking in the viewport. These controls are useful if you want to make sure that an object doesn't move.

Note   When you use the Zoom Extents button to resize the viewports around the current objects, hidden objects aren't included.

Using the Display Floater dialog box

The Display Floater dialog box includes two tabs: Hide/Freeze and Object Level. The Hide/Freeze tab splits the dialog box into two columns, one for Hide and one for Freeze. Both columns have similar buttons that let you hide or freeze Selected or Unselected objects, By Name or By Hit. The By Name button opens the Select Objects dialog box (which is labeled Hide or Freeze Objects). The By Hit option lets you click in one of the viewports to select an object to hide or freeze. Each column also has additional buttons to unhide or unfreeze All objects, By Name, or in the case of Freeze, By Hit. You can also select an option to Hide Frozen Objects.

Note   The same buttons found in the Display Floater are available in the Hide and Freeze rollouts of the Display tab of the Command Panel.

The Object Level panel of the Display Floater lets you hide objects by category such as All Lights or Cameras. You can also view and change many of the Display Properties that are listed in the Object Properties dialog box.

Figure 5-10 shows the Hide/Freeze and Object Level panels of the Display Floater dialog box.

Figure 5-10: The Display Floater dialog box includes two panels — Hide/Freeze and Object Level.

Using the Display panel

If you were to take many of the features of the Display Floater and the Object Properties dialog box and mix them together with some new features, the result would be the Display panel. You access this panel by clicking the fifth icon from the left in the Command Panel (the icon that looks like a monitor screen).

The first rollout in the Display panel, shown in Figure 5-11, is the Display Color rollout. This rollout includes options for setting whether Wireframe and Shaded objects in the viewports are displayed using the Object Color or the Material Color.

The Display panel also includes a Hide by Category rollout. Using this rollout, you can add new categories that will appear in the Object Level panel of the Display Floater. To add a new category, click the Add button of the Hide by Category rollout. The Add Display Filter list appears, as shown in Figure 5-12. From this list, you can choose specific object categories to add to the Hide by Category list.

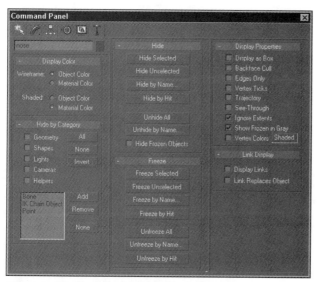

Figure 5-11: The Display panel includes many of the same features of the Display Floater and Object Properties dialog boxes.

Figure 5-12: From this dialog box, you can add new categories to the Hide by Category list.

The Display panel also includes Hide and Freeze rollouts that include the same buttons and features as the Hide/Freeze panel of the Display Floater. There is also a Display Properties rollout that is the same as the list found in the Display Floater's Object Level panel and the Object Properties dialog box.

The Link Display rollout at the bottom of the Display panel includes options for displaying links in the viewports. Links are displayed as lines that extend from the child to its parent object. Using the Link Replaces Object option, you can hide the objects in the viewport and see only the links.

Tutorial: Playing hide and seek

If you're reading this book, then you're into games, and for this example, I have one of the oldest games to play. It's the classic game of hide and seek with a new twist. The twist is that I've hidden and frozen several objects in this scene, and you need to find them.

To play hide and seek, follow these steps:

1. Open the hide and seek with crocodile teeth.gmax file found in the Chap 05 directory on the CD-ROM.

   This file includes a crocodile model created by Viewpoint Datalabs.

2. Locate the hidden object in the scene by opening the Display Floater (choose Tools ➪ Display Floater).

3. In the Display Floater, select the Hide/Freeze tab, and in the Unhide section click the By Name button.

   The Unhide Objects dialog box appears, which lists all the hidden objects in the scene.

4. Select the "upper teeth" object from the list, and click the Unhide button.

   The Unhide Objects dialog box closes, and the hidden objects become visible again.

 Note   Notice that the Display Floater is still open. That's because it's modeless. You don't need to close it in order to keep working.

   The "lower teeth" objects are grayed out, which means that they are frozen and you cannot select and move them.

5. To unfreeze these objects, you use the Freeze column in the Display Floater. In the Unfreeze section, click the By Hit button, and then unfreeze the lower teeth by clicking on them.

Figure 5-13 shows the Hide and Seek scene after locating all the teeth.

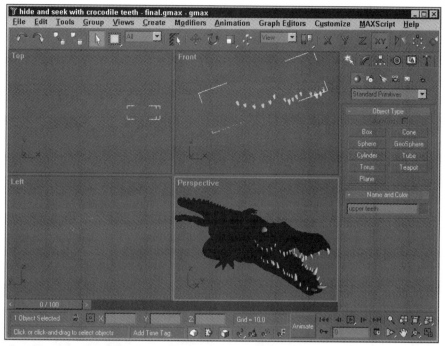

Figure 5-13: Our friendly crocodile, now with teeth

Summary

Selecting objects enables you to work with them, and gmax includes many different ways to select objects. In this chapter, you've done the following:

✦ Learned how to use selection filters

✦ Selected objects with the Edit menu by Name, Color, and Region

✦ Selected multiple objects and used a named selection set to find the set easily

✦ Selected objects using other interfaces

✦ Accessed the Object Properties dialog box to set Rendering and Display settings for an object

✦ Learned how to hide and freeze objects

In the next chapter, you work more with multiple objects by learning how to clone, group, and link objects. Using these techniques, you could very quickly have too many objects (and you were worried that you wouldn't have enough objects).

✦　　✦　　✦

Cloning, Grouping, and Linking Objects, and Other –ings

✦ ✦ ✦ ✦

In This Chapter

Cloning objects

Understanding copies, instances, and references

Using the Mirror and Snapshot tools

Spacing clones along a path with the Spacing tool

Creating object arrays

Using the Ring Array system

Grouping objects

Understanding root, parent, and child relationships

Linking and unlinking objects

✦ ✦ ✦ ✦

The only thing better than creating one perfect enemy for your game is two creating two perfect enemies and the weapon to destroy them. Cloning objects is the process of creating copies of objects. These copies can maintain an internal connection (called an Instance or a Reference) to the original object that allows them to be modified along with the original object. For example, if you create a school desk from a Box primitive and modify its parameters, the same resulting effect will be applied to all instances of the original.

An *array* is a discrete set of objects that are regularly ordered like a row of advancing zombie warriors. So, creating an array of objects involves cloning several copies of an object in a pattern, such as in rows and columns or in a circle. This would be great for creating trains, but all objects in the array will be the same (which would be a rather boring train).

After you've learned to clone objects, you will want to learn how to group objects together in an easily accessible form, especially as a scene becomes more complex. gmax's grouping features enable you to organize all the objects that you're dealing with, thereby making your workflow more efficient.

Another way of organizing objects is to build a linked hierarchy. A linked hierarchy attaches, or links, one object to another and makes it possible to transform the attached object by moving the one to which it is linked. For example, the arm is a classic example of a linked hierarchy — when the shoulder rotates, so do the elbow, wrist, and fingers. Establishing linked hierarchies can make moving, positioning, and animating many objects easy.

Cloning Objects

You can clone objects in gmax in a couple of ways (and luckily, it has nothing to do with DNA or gene splices). One method is to use the Edit ➪ Clone menu command, and another method is to transform an object while holding down the Shift key. And you won't need to worry about these clones attacking anyone (unlike *Star Wars: Episode II*).

Using the Clone command

You can create a duplicate object by choosing the Edit ➪ Clone menu command. You must select an object before the Clone command becomes active. Selecting this command opens the Clone Options dialog box, shown in Figure 6-1, where you can give the clone a name and specify it as a Copy, Instance, or Reference. You can also copy any controllers associated with the object as a Copy or an Instance.

Caution

The Edit menu doesn't include the common cut, copy, and paste commands because many objects and subobjects cannot be easily cut and pasted into a different place. However, you will find a Clone command, which can duplicate a selected object.

Figure 6-1: The Clone Options dialog box defines the new object as a Copy, Instance, or Reference.

A copy has the same geometry as the original, but all links to the original are cut. An instance maintains a link to the original and mirrors the changes of the original object as the original is modified. A reference lies somewhere between a copy and an instance, in that only some of the modifications applied to the original affect the reference. I cover more on copies, instances, and references later in this chapter.

When a clone is created with the Clone menu, it is positioned directly on top of the original, making distinguishing it from the original difficult. To verify that it has been created, open the Select by Name dialog box by pressing H and look for the cloned object (it will have the same name but an incremented number). To see both objects, click the Select and Move button on the main toolbar and move one of the objects away from the other.

Using the Shift-clone method

Another, and easier, way to create clones is with the Shift key. You can use the Shift key when objects are transformed using the Select and Move, Select and Rotate, and Select and Scale commands. Holding down the Shift key while you use any of these commands on an object clones the object and opens the Clone Options dialog box. This Clone Options dialog box is identical to the dialog box previously shown, except it includes a spinner to specify the Number of Copies.

Performing a transformation with the Shift key held down defines an offset that is applied repeatedly to each copy. For example, holding down the Shift key while moving an object 5 units to the left (with the Number of Copies set to 5) places the first cloned object 5 units away from the original, the second cloned object 10 units away from the original object, and so on.

Tutorial: Cloning cows

The scientific world has been in an uproar lately with the successful cloning of various animals. It started with a sheep named "Dolly," but I think they just cloned a rabbit (at least they're cloning furry animals instead of less desirable creatures like earwigs or slugs). With gmax, we can perform similar experiments on our own, but we'll be using a cow named "Rolly." Viewpoint Datalabs created this cow model. Cloning cows comes in handy when you need to populate an empty pasture for a Flight Simulator mod.

To investigate cloning objects, follow these steps:

1. Open the rolly cow.gmax file found in the Chap 06 directory of the CD-ROM.
2. Select the cow group by clicking it in one of the viewports.
3. With the cow model selected, choose Edit ➪ Clone.

   The Clone Options dialog box appears.
4. Name the clone Polly, select the Copy option, and click OK.
5. Click the Select and Move button on the main toolbar; then in the Left viewport, click and drag the cow model to the right.

   As you move the model, the original model beneath it is revealed.
6. Select each model in turn, and notice the name change in the Create panel's Name field; notice that the clone is even the same color as the original.
7. With the Select and Move button still active, hold down the Shift key, click the cloned cow in the Left viewport, and move it to the right again.
8. In the Clone Options dialog box that appears, select the Copy option, set the Number of Copies to 3, and click OK.

9. Click the Zoom Extents All button (or press Shift+Ctrl+Z) in the lower-right corner to view all the new cows.

Three additional cows have appeared, equally spaced from each other. The spacing was determined by the distance that you moved the second clone before releasing the mouse. Figure 6-2 shows the results of our cow cloning experiment. (It's starting to feel like a dairy.)

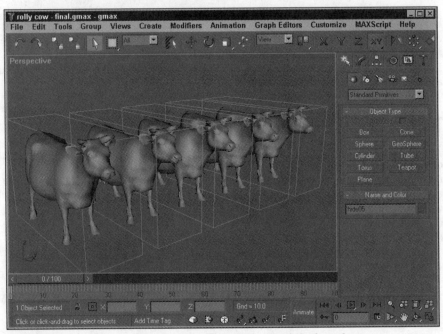

Figure 6-2: Cloning multiple objects is easy with the Shift-clone feature.

Understanding Cloning Options

When cloning in gmax, you'll be offered the option to create the copy as a copy, an instance, or a reference. This is true not only for objects, but for materials, modifiers, and controllers as well.

Working with copies, instances, and references

When an object is cloned, the Clone Options dialog box appears. This dialog box enables you to select to make a copy, an instance, or a reference of the original object. Each of these clone types is unique and offers different capabilities.

A copy is just what it sounds like — an exact replica of the original object. The new copy maintains no ties to the original object and is a unique object in its own right. Any changes to the copy will not affect the original object or vice versa.

Instances are different from copies in that they maintain strong ties to the original object. All instances of an object are interconnected, so that any geometry modifications (done with modifiers) to any single instance changes all other instances. For example, if you create several instances of a sphere and then use a modifier on one of the spheres, all instances will also be modified. Note that transformations (moving, rotating, or scaling) to an instance do not affect the other instances.

References are objects that inherit modifier changes from their parent objects but do not affect the parent when modified. At any time, you can break the tie between objects with the Make Unique button in the Modifier Stack.

Note   Instances and references can have different object colors and materials.

When an object is selected, all its instances and references will be surrounded with an orange-colored bounding box.

Tutorial: Copied, instanced, and referenced Genie's lamps

Learning how the different clone options work will save you lots of future modifications. To investigate these options, let's leave the farm and visit a deep dark cave where lies a magical Genie's lamp. Rather than wishing for more wishes, we'll just clone the genie lamp several times. To clone the Genie's lamp, follow these steps:

1. Open the Genie lamp.gmax file from the Chap 06 directory on the CD-ROM.
2. Click on the lamp object to select it.
3. With the lamp model selected, click the Select and Move.
4. Hold down the Shift key, and in the Top viewport, move the lamp to the right.
5. In the Clone Options dialog box, select the Copy option, set the Number of Copies to 1, name the new bear **Genie's Copy**, and click OK.
6. Click the Zoom Extents All button to widen your view.
7. Select the original lamp again and repeat Steps 3 through 6, but this time select the Instance option from the Clone Options dialog box and name the newly cloned bear **Genie's Instance**.
8. Select the original lamp again and repeat Steps 3 through 6 again, but this time select the Reference option from the Clone Options dialog box and name the new cloned bear **Genie's Reference**.

   You should now see four lamps.

Note   Be sure to select the original lamp each time you make a clone, or you'll accidentally make a reference of an instance.

9. Select the original lamp again. From the main menu, choose Modifiers ⇨
Parametric Deformers ⇨ Skew.

10. In the Parameters rollout of the Command Panel, enter **0.1** in the Amount field
and select the Y Skew Axis.

This will skew the lamp and surround it with an orange box (which is the
modifier's gizmo).

Note   If you have trouble locating the original lamp, click the Select by Name button on
the main toolbar (or press the H key) to open the Select Objects dialog box, select
lamp from the objects listed, and click the Select button.

11. Notice how the instanced and referenced objects (but not the copy) were
modified along with the original, as shown in Figure 6-3.

Original object | Instanced object
Copied object   Referenced object

Figure 6-3: Modifying an original object also modifies any instanced or referenced
clones.

Cross-Reference You can use modifiers to alter geometry. You can learn about using modifiers in Chapter 14, "Controlled Destruction with Modifiers."

If you were to return to this file and apply another modifier to Genie's Reference, then only the reference, and not the original, would be changed. Understanding how these various copy types work will enable you to create duplicates of objects and modify them without taking the time to change each one individually.

Mirroring Objects

Have you ever held the edge of a mirror up to your face to see half your head in the mirror? Many objects have a natural symmetry that you can exploit to require that only half an object be modeled. The human face is a good example. You can clone symmetrical parts using the Mirror command. Other good examples of things you can create using the Mirror command are planes for Flight Simulator, trains, weapons, characters, and just about everything you encounter in games.

Using the Mirror command

The Mirror command creates a clone (or No Clone if you so choose) of the selected object about the current coordinate system. To open the Mirror dialog box, shown in Figure 6-4, choose Tools ➪ Mirror, or click the Mirror button located on the main toolbar. You can access the Mirror dialog box only if an object is selected.

Figure 6-4: The Mirror dialog box can create an inverted clone of an object.

Within the Mirror dialog box, you can specify an axis or plane about which to mirror the selected object. You can also define an offset value. As with the other clone commands, you can specify whether the clone is to be a Copy, an Instance, or a

Reference, or you can choose No Clone, which will flip the object around the axis you specify. The dialog box also lets you mirror Inverse Kinematics Limits, which reduces the number of IK parameters that need to be set.

Cross-Reference   I talk about Inverse Kinematics in Chapter 15, "Skeletons Rule: Building with Bones and IK."

Tutorial: Mirroring a broadsword

Most simple weapons are easy to model using the Mirror command. The rough outline of a broadsword, for example, can be easily and quickly created. Then you mirror half of it as an Instance, so that any changes you make to one side are automatically applied to the opposite side.

Tip   It is often easier to build the entire model, rather than build only half a model. The best technique I've found is to build the entire model, select which side you like best (the better half), and use the Slice modifier to cut off the unneeded half. Then you can use the Mirror feature to create a perfectly symmetrical object.

To mirror a simple broadsword, follow these steps:

1. Open the half a broadsword.gmax file from the Chap 06 directory on the CD-ROM.

   This half was created using the Line tool to draw the outline of the sword. Then the Extrude modifier was used to give it some thickness.

2. With the half a sword selected, choose Tools ⇨ Mirror to open the Mirror: World Coordinates dialog box or click the Mirror button on the main toolbar.

3. In the Mirror: World Coordinates dialog box, select X as the Mirror Axis and Instance as the Clone Selection; then drag the Offset value until the sword is complete at a value of around –8.2.

   Any changes made to the dialog box are immediately shown in the viewports.

4. Click OK to close the dialog box.

Note   By making the clone selection an instance, you can ensure that any future modifications to the right half of the figure will be automatically applied to the left half.

Figure 6-5 shows the resulting figure — our broadsword with its split personalities combined.

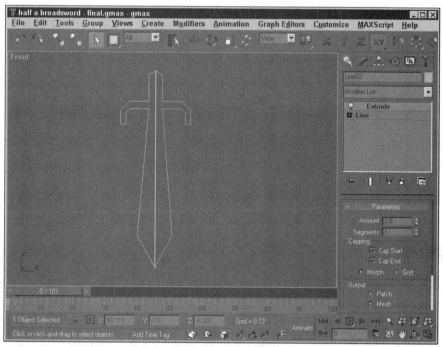

Figure 6-5: A perfectly symmetrical broadsword, compliments of the Mirror tool

Cloning Over Time

Another useful way to create multiple copies of an object is to have them appear at different times in an animation. This cloning over time is accomplished with the Snapshot feature.

Using the Snapshot command

The Snapshot command creates copies, instances, references, or even meshes of a selected object as it is transformed over time. For example, you could create a series of stairs by positioning the bottom stair at frame 1 and the top stair at frame 100, and then choose Tools ➪ Snapshot and enter the number of steps to appear between these two in the Snapshot dialog box. Be aware that the Snapshot command will only work with objects that have an animation path defined.

You can open the Snapshot dialog box by choosing Tools ➪ Snapshot or by clicking the Snapshot button (under the Array flyout). Snapshot is the second button in the flyout. In the Snapshot dialog box, shown in Figure 6-6, you can choose to produce a single clone or a range of clones over a given number of frames. Selecting Single creates a single clone at the current frame.

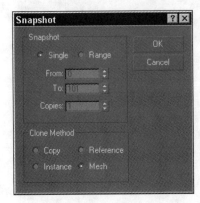

Figure 6-6: The Snapshot dialog box lets you clone a Copy, Instance, Reference, or Mesh.

Tip   Use the Snapshot command with the Snow Particle System to make snow pile up.

Tutorial: Following a mouse through a maze

A fine example of the Snapshot tool is to trace an object as it moves through the scene. For this example, you'll use the Snapshot tool to follow a mouse as it moves through a maze.

To use the Snapshot tool to create clones at individual frames, follow these steps:

1. Open the mouse in a maze.gmax file from the Chap 06 directory on the CD-ROM.

   The Perspective viewport is maximized. This file has an animation sequence defined that moves the mouse through the maze.

2. To take a snapshot of the mouse as it moves through the maze, select the mouse object and then choose Tools ➪ Snapshot or select the Snapshot flyout button.

3. In the Snapshot dialog box, select the Range option from frame 0 to frame 100 and specify 30 copies; then click the OK button.

Figure 6-7 shows the maze after the Snapshot tool cloned the mouse during his journey.

Figure 6-7: The Snapshot tool helps identify how the mouse traversed the maze.

Spacing Cloned Objects

The Snapshot tool offers a convenient way to clone objects along an animation path, but what if you want to clone objects along a path that isn't animated? The solution is the Spacing tool. The Spacing tool can position clones at regular intervals along a path by either selecting a path and the number of cloned objects or by picking points along the path.

Using the Spacing tool

You access the Spacing tool by clicking the last button in the flyout under the Array button. You can also access it using the Tools ⇨ Spacing Tool (Shift+I) menu command. When accessed, it opens the Spacing Tool dialog box, shown in Figure 6-8. At the top of this dialog box are two buttons — Pick Path and Pick Points.

You can also specify Count, Spacing, Start Offset, and End Offset values. The drop-down list offers several preset options, including Divide Evenly, Centered, End Offset, and more. These values and preset options are used to define the number and spacing of the objects. The Lock icons next to the Start and End Offset values will not require that an object be placed at the end of the path or point if enabled (the background of the Lock icon is white when enabled).

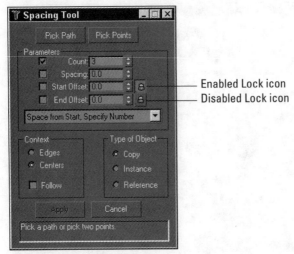

Figure 6-8: The Spacing Tool dialog box lets you select how to position clones along a path.

Before you can use either the Pick Path or Pick Points buttons, you must select the object to be cloned. Using the Pick Path button, you can select a spline path in the scene, and cloned objects will be regularly spaced according the values you selected. The Pick Points method lets you click in the viewport where the start and end points are, and the cloned objects will be spaced in a straight line between the two points.

The two options for determining the spacing width are Edges and Centers. The Edges option spaces objects from the edge of its bounding box to the edge of the adjacent bounding box, and the Centers option spaces objects based on their centers. The Follow option aligns the object with the path if the path is selected. Each object can be a copy, instance, or reference of the original. The text field at the bottom of the dialog box specifies the number of objects and the spacing value between each.

You can continue to modify the Spacing Tool dialog box's values while the dialog box is open, but the objects will not be added to the scene until you click the Apply button.

Tutorial: Building a roller coaster

To create a roller coaster, we need a path and a single cart. Then we can use the Spacing tool to clone this cart along the path.

To create a line of roller coaster carts by using the Spacing tool, follow these steps:

1. Open the roller coaster.gmax file from the Chap 06 directory on the CD-ROM.

   The Perspective viewport is maximized. This file includes a path and a single roller coaster cart.

2. Select the roller coaster cart, and open the Spacing tool by selecting the flyout button under the Array button (or by pressing Shift+I).

3. In the Spacing Tool dialog box, click the Pick Path button and select the wavy roller coaster path.

   The path name appears on the Pick Path button.

4. From the drop-down list in the Parameters section of the Spacing Tool dialog box, choose Start Offset, Divide Evenly. Enter a Count value of **8** and a Start Offset of **100**.

5. Select the Edges context option, check the Follow check box, and make all clones Instances.

6. When the result looks right, click Apply to close the Spacing Tool dialog box.

Figure 6-9 shows the simple results. The Spacing Tool dialog box remains open until you click the Close button.

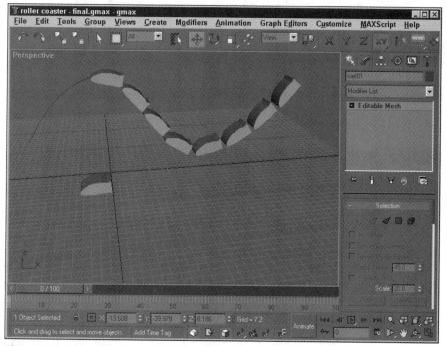

Figure 6-9: This roller coaster was created using the Spacing tool.

Creating Arrays of Objects

After you've figured out how to create objects, the Array command multiplies the fun by making it easy to create many copies instantaneously. The Array dialog box lets you specify the array dimensions, offsets, type of object, and transformation values. These parameters enable you to create an array of objects easily.

Access the Array dialog box by selecting an object and choosing Tools ➪ Array or by clicking the Array button. Figure 6-10 shows the Array dialog box. The top of the Array dialog box displays the coordinate system and the center about which the transformations are performed.

The Array dialog box is persistent, meaning that, after being applied, the settings remain until they are changed. You can reset all the values at once by clicking the Reset All Parameters button.

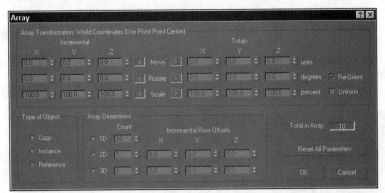

Figure 6-10: The Array dialog box defines the number of elements and transformation offsets in an array.

Linear arrays

Linear arrays are arrays where the objects form straight lines, such as rows and columns. Using the Array dialog box, you can specify an offset along the X, Y, and Z axes at the top of the dialog box and define this offset as an incremental amount or as a total amount. To change between incremental values and total values, click the arrows to the left and right of the Move, Rotate, and Scale labels. For example, an array with 10 elements and an incremental value of 5 would position each successive object a distance of 5 units from the previous one. An array with 5 elements and a total value of 100 would position each element a distance of 20 units from the previous one.

The Move row values represent units as specified in the Units Setup dialog box. The Rotate row values represent degrees, and the Scale row values are a percentage of the selected object. All values can be either positive or negative values.

Clicking the Re-Orient check box causes the coordinate system to be reoriented after each rotation is made. If this check box isn't enabled, then the objects in the array will not successively rotate. Clicking the Uniform check box to the right of the Scale row values disables the Y and Z Scale value columns and forces the scaling transformations to be uniform. To perform non-uniform scaling, simply deselect the Uniform check box.

The Type of Object section lets you define whether the new objects are copies, instances, or references. If you plan on modeling all the objects in a similar manner, then you will want to select the Instance option.

In the Array Dimensions section, you can specify the number of objects to copy along three different dimensions. You can also define incremental offsets for each individual row.

Caution   You can use the Array dialog box to create a large number of objects. If your array of objects is too large, your system may crash.

Tutorial: Building a white picket fence

To start with a simple example, we'll create a white picket fence. Because a fence repeats, we only need to create a single slat and use the Array command to duplicate it consistently.

To create a picket fence, follow these steps:

1. Open the white picket fence.gmax file from the Chap 06 directory on the CD-ROM.

2. With the single fence board selected, choose Tools ⇨ Array or click on the Array button to open the Array dialog box.

3. In the Array dialog box, click the Reset All Parameters button to start with a clean slate.

4. Then enter a value of **50** in the X column's Move row under the Incremental section.

    (This is the incremental value for spacing each successive picket.)

5. Next, enter **20** in the Array Dimensions section next to the 1D radio button.

    (This is the number of objects to include in the array.)

6. Click OK to create the objects.

Note   Don't worry if you don't get the values right the first time. The most recent values you entered into the Array dialog box will stay around until you exit gmax.

7. Click the Zoom Extents All button (or press Shift+Ctrl+Z) in the lower-right corner of the gmax window to see the entire fence in the viewports.

Figure 6-11 shows the completed fence.

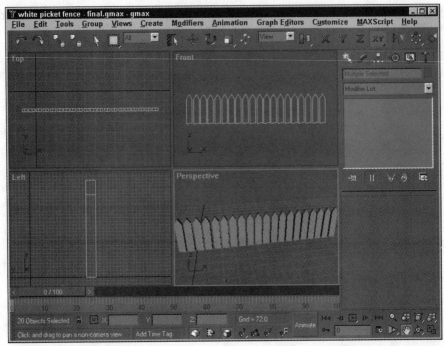

Figure 6-11: Tom Sawyer would be pleased to see this white picket fence created easily with the Array dialog box.

Circular arrays

You can use the Array dialog box for creating more than just linear arrays. For the last example, all transformations were done around the pivot point center. Notice in the previous figure that World Coordinates (Use Pivot Point Center) are listed at the top of the Array dialog box. In the next tutorial, you'll see how changing the transform center can create circular arrays.

All transformations are done relative to a center point. You can change the center point about which transformations are performed using the Use Selection Center button on the main toolbar. The three flyout options are Use Pivot Point Center, Use Selection Center, and Use Transform Coordinate Center.

Cross-Reference   For more about how these settings affect transformations, see Chapter 7, "Moving, Rotating, and Scaling Objects — The Return of the –ings."

Tutorial: Building a Ferris wheel

Ferris wheels, like most of the rides at the fair, entertain by going around and around, with the riders seated in chairs spaced around the Ferris wheel's central point. The Array dialog box can also create objects around a central point. In this example, you use the Rotate transformation along with the Use Transform Coordinate Center button to create a circular array.

To create a circular array, follow these steps:

1. Open the Ferris wheel.gmax file from the Chap 06 directory on the CD-ROM.

   This file has the Front viewport maximized to show the profile of the Ferris wheel.

2. Select the Use Selection Center button on the main toolbar and drag down to the last icon, which is the Use Transform Coordinate Center button.

   The Use Transform Coordinate Center button becomes active. This button causes all transformations to take place about the axes in the center of the screen.

3. Select the light blue chair object, and open the Array dialog box by choosing Tools ⇨ Array or by clicking the Array button.

4. Before entering any values into the Array dialog box, click the Reset All Parameters button.

5. In-between the Incremental and Totals sections are the labels Move, Rotate, and Scale; click the arrow button to the right of the Rotate label.

6. Set the Z column value of the Rotate row to **360** degrees, and make sure that the Re-Orient option is disabled.

   A value of 360 degrees defines one complete revolution. Disabling the Re-Orient option will keep each chair object from gradually turning upside down.

7. In the Array Dimensions section, set the 1D spinner Count value to **8** and click the OK button to create the array.

8. Next, select the green strut, and open the Array dialog box again with the Tools ⇨ Array command.

9. Select the Re-Orient option, and leave the rest of the settings as they are.

10. Click the OK button to create the array.

Figure 6-12 shows the resulting Ferris wheel. You can click the Min/Max toggle in the lower-right corner to view all four viewports again.

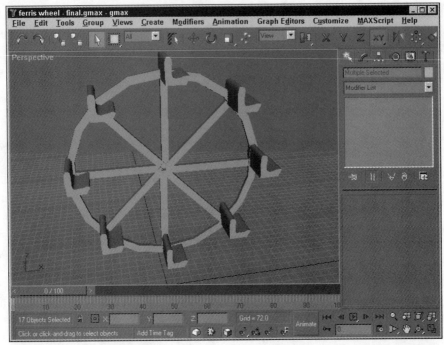

Figure 6-12: This circular array was created by rotating objects about the Transform Coordinate Center.

Spiral arrays

Before leaving arrays, there is one more special case to examine: spiral arrays. A spiral array results from moving and rotating objects along the same axis. Combinations of transforms in the Array dialog box can produce many interesting modeling possibilities.

Tutorial: Building a spiral staircase

To create a spiral staircase, we first need to create a simple rectangular box that can be used for the steps. Because a spiral staircase winds about a center pole, we need our transform's center to be located at one end of the stair object.

To create a spiral staircase, follow these steps:

1. Open the Spiral Staircase.gmax file from the Chap 06 directory on the CD-ROM.

   This file has the Top viewport maximized, which is the easiest view to use to create the spiral staircase.

2. Select the Use Transform Coordinate Center flyout from the Use Center button on the main toolbar.

   This setting transforms the selected object about the center of the active viewport. You should notice the axes are relocated to the center of the viewport.

3. Select the single stair, and open the Array dialog box by choosing Tools ⇨ Array or by clicking the Array button on the main toolbar.

4. Before entering any values into the Array dialog box, click the Reset All Parameters button.

5. In the Incremental section, enter the value of **2.5** in the Z column of the Move row and **45** in the Z column of the Rotate row.

6. Set the 1D Count spinner to 10, and click the OK button to create the array.

Figure 6-13 shows the results of the spiral array in the Perspective viewport.

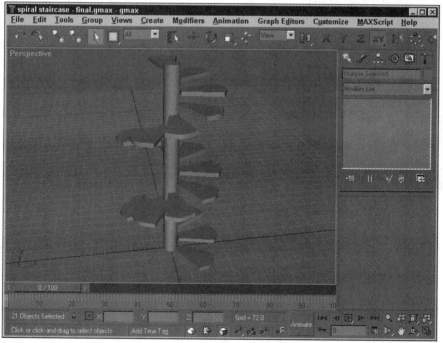

Figure 6-13: Getting fancy with the Array feature produced this spiral staircase.

Working with a ring array

You can find the Ring Array system by opening the Create panel and selecting the Systems category. Doing so makes two buttons appear for Bones and Ring Array. Clicking the Ring Array button opens a Parameters rollout, shown in Figure 6-14. In this rollout are parameters for the ring's Radius, Amplitude, Cycles, Phase, and the Number of elements to include.

You create the actual array by clicking and dragging in one of the viewports. Initially, all elements are simple box objects surrounding a green dummy object.

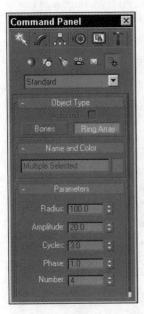

Figure 6-14: The Parameters rollout of the Ring Array system can create an oscillating circular array of objects.

Cross-Reference   You can change the boxes that appear as part of the ring array to another object using the Track View. To do so, you need to locate the copy object's track and paste it where the ring array's boxes are. Chapter 20, "Graphing Animations with the Track View," explains the Track View in more detail.

The Amplitude, Cycles, and Phase values define the sinusoidal nature of the circle. The Amplitude is the maximum distance that you can position the objects from the center axis. If the Amplitude is set to 0, then all objects lie in the same plane. The Cycles value is the number of waves that occur around the entire circle. The Phase determines which position along the circle starts in the up position.

For example, Figure 6-15 shows a ring array with 20 elements, a Radius of 100, an Amplitude of 25, a Cycles value of 2, and a Phase of 0. The dummy object in the middle lets you control the entire ring's position and orientation.

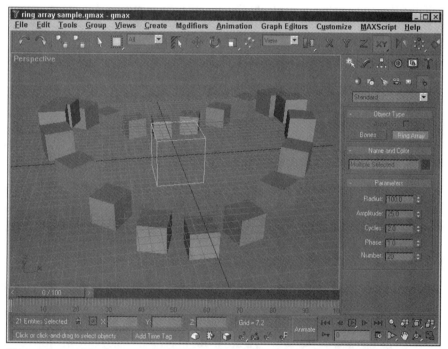

Figure 6-15: This ring array has only two cycles.

Tutorial: Using a ring array to create a carousel

Continuing with the theme park attractions motif, this example creates a carousel. The horse model comes from Poser but was simplified for this example. Ring arrays could be used to create a helicopter landing pad for Flight Simulator or a ring of mushrooms in an enchanted level for Dungeon Siege.

To use a Ring Array system to create a carousel, follow these steps.

1. Open the Carousel.gmax file from the Chap 06 directory on the CD-ROM.

   This file includes a carousel structure made from primitives along with a carousel horse.

2. Open the Create panel, select the Systems category, and click on the Ring Array button.

3. Drag in the Top viewport from the center of the carousel to create a ring array; then enter a Radius value of 250, an Amplitude of 20, a Cycles value of 3, and a Number value of 6.

4. Select the dummy object in the Left viewport, and drag it upward with the Select and Move tool until all the box objects are positioned between the carousel base and the top cone.

5. SelectGraph Editors ⇨ Track View ⇨ Open Track View.

6. Click on the plus sign to the left of the Object track, and then click on the plus sign next to the Horse object; locate the Object (Editable Mesh) object, and select it.

7. Then click the Copy Object button on the Track View toolbar.

8. Locate the Box01 track under the Objects ⇨ Dummy01.

9. Select the Object (Box) track and click the Paste Object button on the Track View toolbar.

   This opens the Paste dialog, shown in Figure 6-16.

10. Select Instance and the Replace All Instances option, and click OK; then close the Track View.

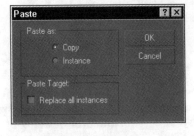

Figure 6-16: This Paste dialog box lets you replace all instances.

Figure 6-17 shows the finished carousel. Notice how each horse is at a different height.

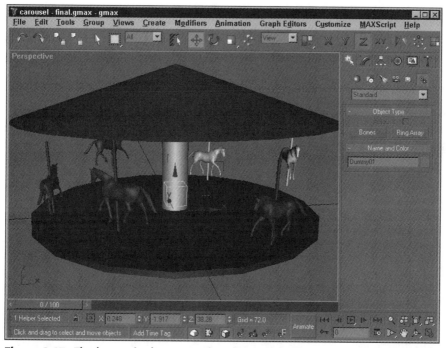

Figure 6-17: The horses in the carousel were created using a ring array system.

Working with Groups

Grouping objects organizes them and makes them easier to select and transform. Groups are different from selection sets in that groups exist like one object. Selecting any object in the group selects the entire group, whereas selecting an object in a selection set selects only that object and not the selection set. You can open groups to add, delete, or reposition objects within the group. Groups can also contain other groups. This is called nesting groups.

Creating groups

The Group command enables you to create a group. To do so, simply select the desired objects and choose Group ➪ Group. A simple Name Group dialog box opens and enables you to give the group a name. The newly created group displays a new bounding box that encompasses all the objects in the group. You can also create or nest groups within groups.

Tip   You can always identify groups in the Select by Name dialog box because they are surrounded by square brackets.

Ungrouping objects

The Ungroup command enables you to break up a group (kind of like a poor music album). To do so, simply select the desired group and choose Group ⇨ Ungroup. This menu command dissolves the group, and all the objects within the group revert to separate objects. The Ungroup command breaks up only the currently selected group. All nested groups within a group stay intact.

The easiest way to dissolve an entire group, including any nested groups, is with the Explode command. This command eliminates the group and the groups within the group, and makes each object separate.

Opening and closing groups

The Open command enables you to access the objects within a group. Grouped objects move, scale, and rotate as a unit when transformed, but individual objects within a group can be transformed independently after you open a group with the Open command.

To move an individual object in a group, select the group and choose Group ⇨ Open. The white bounding box changes to dark red. Select an object within the group, and move it with the Select and Move button. Choose Group ⇨ Close to reinstate the group.

Attaching and detaching objects

The Attach and Detach commands enable you to insert or remove objects from an opened group without dissolving the group. To do so, select an object in the opened group and choose Group ⇨ Attach or Detach. Remember to close the group when finished.

Tutorial: Grouping the deer parts together

Positioning objects relative to one another takes careful and precise work. After spending the time to place the eyes, ears, and nose of a face exactly where they need to be, transforming these objects can spell disaster (unless your name is Picasso). By grouping all the objects together, you can move all the objects at once.

With this tutorial, you can get some practice grouping all the parts of the deer character together. Follow these steps:

1. Open the Cartoon deer.gmax file from the Chap 06 directory on the CD-ROM.

    This file includes a cartoon deer model created by Hou Soon Ming.

2. Click the Select by Name button on the main toolbar (or press the H key) to open the Select by Name dialog box.

   In this dialog box, notice all the different deer character parts.

3. Click the All button to select all the separate objects, and click the Select button to close the dialog box.

4. With all the objects selected, choose Group ⇨ Group to open the Group dialog box.

5. Give the group the name **Deer**, and click OK.

6. Click the Select and Move button, and click and drag the deer.

   The entire group now moves together.

Figure 6-18 shows the deer grouped as one unit. Notice how only one set of brackets is around the deer in the Perspective viewport. The group name is displayed in the Name field of the Command Panel instead of saying Multiple Selected.

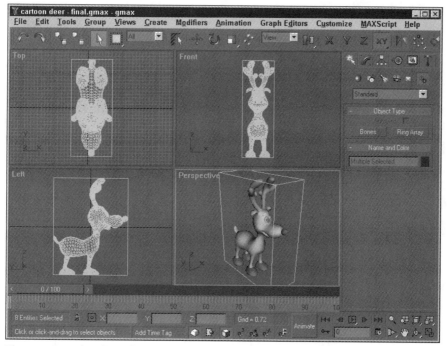

Figure 6-18: The deer character moves as one unit after its objects are grouped.

Understanding Parent, Child, and Root Relationships

gmax uses several terms to describe the relationships between objects. A parent object is an object that controls any secondary, or child, objects linked to it. A child object is an object that is linked to and controlled by a parent. A parent object can have many children, but a child can have only one parent. Additionally, an object can be both a parent and a child at the same time.

A hierarchy is the complete set of linked objects that includes these types of relationships. Ancestors are all the parents above a child object. Descendants are all the children below a parent object. The root object is the top parent object that has no parent and controls the entire hierarchy.

Each hierarchy can have several branches or subtrees. Any parent with two or more children represents the start of a new branch.

All objects in a scene, whether linked or not, belong to a hierarchy. An object that isn't linked to any other object is, by default, a child of the world object, which is an imaginary object that holds all objects.

Note   You can view the world object, labeled Objects, in the Track View. Individual objects are listed under the Objects track by their object name.

You have several ways to establish hierarchies using gmax. The simplest method is to use the Link and Unlink buttons found on the main toolbar. You can also find these buttons in the Schematic View window. The Hierarchy panel in the Command Panel provides access to valuable controls and information about established hierarchies. When creating complex hierarchies, the bones system can help.

Building Links between Objects

The main toolbar includes two buttons that you can use to build a hierarchy: Link and Unlink. The order of selection defines which object becomes the parent and which becomes the child.

Linking objects

The Link button always links children to parents. To remind you of this order, remember that a parent can have many children but a child can't have more than one parent.

To link two objects, click the Link button. This places you in Link mode, which continues until you turn it off by selecting another button, such as the Select button or one of the Transform buttons. When you're in Link mode, the Link button is highlighted dark yellow.

With the Link button highlighted, click an object, which will be the child, and drag a line to the target parent object. The cursor arrow changes to the link icon when it is over a potential parent. When you release the mouse button, the parent object flashes once, and the link is established. If you drag the same child object to a different parent, the link to the previous parent is replaced by the link to the new parent.

Once linked, all transformations applied to the parent are applied equally to its children about the parent's pivot point. A *pivot point* is the center about which the object rotates.

Unlinking objects

The Unlink button is used to destroy links, but only to the parent. For example, if a selected object has both children and a parent, clicking the Unlink button destroys the link to the parent of the selected object, but not the links to its children.

To eliminate all links for an entire hierarchy, double-click an object to select its entire hierarchy and click the Unlink button.

Tutorial: Creating a solar system

Because the planets in the solar system all rotate about the sun, a solar system is a good model to show the benefits of linking. After you link all planets to the sun, you can reposition the entire system simply by moving the sun.

To create a solar system of spheres that are linked together, follow these steps:

1. Open the Linked Solar System.gmax file from the Chap 06 directory on the CD-ROM.

   This file includes spheres that represent all the planets in the solar system.

2. Click the Link button in the main toolbar, and drag a line from each planet to the sun object.

3. Click the Select and Rotate button, and rotate the sun.

   Notice how all the planets rotate with the sun.

Figure 6-19 shows the planets as they orbit about the sun. The Link button made it possible to rotate all the planets simply by rotating their parent.

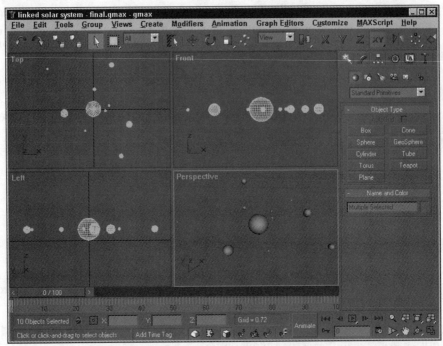

Figure 6-19: Linked child planets inherit transformations from their parent sun.

Displaying Links and Hierarchies

The Display panel includes a rollout that lets you display all the links in the viewports.

After links have been established, you can see linked objects listed as a hierarchy in several places. The Select Objects dialog box, opened with the Select by Name button (or with the H key), can display objects in this manner, as well as the Schematic and Track Views.

Displaying links in the viewport

You can see links between objects in the viewports by selecting the Display Links option in the Link Display rollout of the Display panel. The Display Links option shows links as lines that run between the pivot points of the objects with a diamond-shaped marker at the end of each line; these lines and markers are the same color as the object.

The Link Display rollout also offers the Link Replaces Object option, which removes the objects and displays only the link structure. This feature removes the complexity of the objects from the viewports and lets you work with the links directly. Although the objects disappear, you can still transform the objects using the link markers.

Figure 6-20 shows the solar system we created in the previous tutorial with the Display Links option enabled for all links.

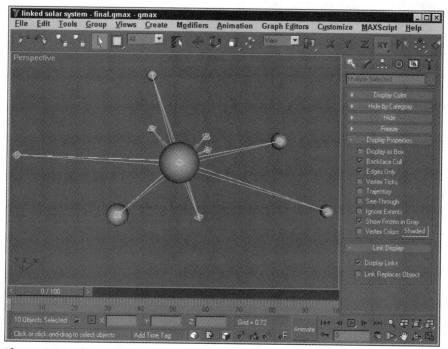

Figure 6-20: The solar system example with all links visible

Viewing hierarchies

The Select Objects dialog box and the Track View can display the hierarchy of objects in a scene as an ordered list, with child objects indented under parent objects.

Clicking the Select by Name button (H) on the main toolbar opens the Select Objects dialog box; click the Display Subtree option to see all the children under the selected object. Figure 6-21 shows the Select Objects dialog box with the Display Subtree option selected.

Figure 6-21: The Select Objects dialog box indents all child objects under their parent.

The Track View (opened with the Graph Editors ⇨ Open Track View menu command) displays lots of scene details in addition to the object hierarchy. In the Track View, you can easily expand and contract the hierarchy to focus on just the section you want to see or select.

Cross-Reference   For more information on using the Track View, see Chapter 20, "Graphing Animations with the Track View."

Working with Linked Objects

If you link some objects together and set some animation keys, and then the magical Play button starts sending objects hurtling off into space, chances are good that you have a linked object that you didn't know about. Understanding object hierarchies and being able to transform those hierarchies are the keys to efficient animation sequences.

All transformations are done about an object's pivot point. You can move and reorient these pivot points as needed by clicking the Pivot button under the Hierarchy panel.

Several additional settings for controlling links are available under the Hierarchy panel of the Command Panel (the Hierarchy panel tab looks like a mini-org chart). Just click the Link Info button. This button opens two rollouts if a linked object is selected. You can use the Locks and Inherit rollouts to limit an object's transformations and specify the transformations it inherits.

 Cross-Reference I present more information on object transformations in Chapter 7, "Moving, Rotating, and Scaling Objects–The Return of the –ings."

Selecting hierarchies

You need to select a hierarchy before you can transform it, and you have several ways to do so. The easiest method is to simply double-click an object. Double-clicking the root object selects the entire hierarchy, and double-clicking an object within the hierarchy selects it and all of its children.

After you select an object in a hierarchy, pressing the Page Up and Page Down keyboard shortcuts selects its parent or child objects.

Linking to dummies

Dummy objects are useful as root objects for controlling the motion of hierarchies. By linking the parent object of a hierarchy to a dummy object, you can control all the objects by moving the dummy.

To create a dummy object, open the Create panel and click the Helpers category button. (This button looks like a small tape measure.) Within the Object Type rollout is the Dummy button; click it, and then click in the viewport where you want the dummy object to be positioned. Dummy objects look like wireframe box objects in the viewports, but dummy objects are not rendered.

Tutorial: Creating the two-cars-in-a-sphere stunt

Have you ever seen the circus act where two motorcycles race around the inside of a wire sphere without colliding? Well, we're going to do that stunt one better — we're going to do it with cars.

To perform this stunt, we'll create two dummy objects in the center of the sphere, link a car model to each, and rotate the dummy objects. The car we'll be using is the '57 Chevy model created by Viewpoint Datalabs. This tutorial involves transforming and animating objects, which I cover in later chapters.

Cross-Reference Translating objects is covered in Chapter 7, "Moving, Rotating, and Scaling Objects — The Return of the –ings," and the basics of animation are covered in Chapter 19, "Getting the Prop to Spin — Animation Basics."

To link and transform objects using a dummy object, follow these steps:

1. Open the Two cars in a sphere stunt.gmax file found in the Chap 06 directory on the CD-ROM.

   This file includes a transparent wireframe sphere with two grouped car objects inside of it.

2. Open the Create panel, click the Helpers category button, and click the Dummy button; then create two dummy objects in the center of the sphere, and make them different sizes so that they are easier to select.

3. To make the cars move consistently around the sphere, you need to align the center of the sphere with the centers of the two dummy objects, so select the two dummy objects, and choose Tools ➪ Align (or press Alt+A).

4. Select the sphere object to open the Align Selection dialog box.

5. Select the X, Y, and Z Position options and the Center options for both the Current and Target Objects, and then click OK.

6. Because both the cars and the dummy objects are inside the sphere, creating the link between them can be difficult; to simplify this process, select and right-click the sphere object, select Properties from the pop-up menu, and select the Hide option in the Object Properties dialog box.

   This hides the sphere so that you can create the links between the cars and the dummy objects.

7. Click the Link button on the main toolbar, and drag a line from one of the cars to one of the dummy objects; then drag a line from the second car to the second dummy object.

8. Click the Select and Rotate button on the main toolbar, and select one of the dummy objects; then rotate the dummy object, and notice how the linked car also rotates along the inner surface of the sphere.

9. Open the Display Floater with the Tools ➪ Display Floater menu command, and click on the Unhide All button to make the sphere visible again.

By linking the cars to dummy objects, you don't have to worry about moving the individual cars' pivot points. Figure 6-22 shows a frame from the final scene.

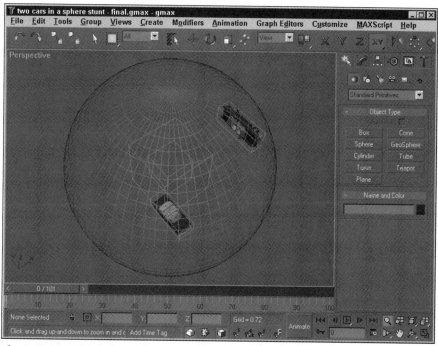

Figure 6-22: With links to dummy objects, animating these cars is easy.

Summary

Many ways exist to clone an object. You could use the Clone command under the Edit menu or the Shift-clone feature for quickly creating numerous clones. Clones can be copies, instances, or references. Each differs in how it retains links to the original object. You can also clone using the Mirror, Snapshot, and Spacing tools.

Arrays are another means of cloning. You can use the Array dialog box to produce clones in three different dimensions, and you can specify the offset transformations.

As scenes become more complex, the name of the game is organization. You can organize objects within the scene in several ways, including grouping, linking, and using the Schematic View window.

This chapter covered the following cloning topics:

✦ Cloning objects and Shift-cloning

✦ Understanding copies, instances, and references

✦ Using the Mirror, Snapshot, and Spacing tools

✦ Building linear, circular, and spiral arrays of objects

✦ Using the Ring Array system

✦ Grouping objects using the Group menu, and working with groups

✦ Understanding parent, child, and root relationships

✦ Creating a hierarchy of objects using the Link and Unlink features

✦ Viewing links in the viewport

In the next chapter, you learn to transform objects using the move, rotate, and scale features — finally, some motion for our static scenes.

✦   ✦   ✦

Moving, Rotating, and Scaling Objects – Return of the –ings

◆   ◆   ◆   ◆

In This Chapter

Transforming objects

Controlling transformations with the Transform Gizmo, the Transform Type-Ins, and the Transform Managers

Working with pivot points and axis constraints

Aligning objects with the align tools

Using grids and snapping objects to common points

◆   ◆   ◆   ◆

Although a transformation sounds like something that would happen during the climax of a superhero film or during the final boss of Quake, transformation is simply the process of "repositioning" or changing an object's position, rotation, and scale. So moving an object from here to there is a transformation. Superman would be so jealous.

Transformations occur when you select an object or objects, click one of the transformation buttons located on the main toolbar, and then drag in the viewport to apply the transformation. gmax includes various tools to help in the transformation of objects, including the Transform Gizmos, the Transform Type-In dialog box, and the Transform Managers.

This chapter covers these tools and several others that make transformations more automatic, such as the alignment, grid, and snap features.

Moving, Rotating, and Scaling Objects

So you have an object created, and it's just sitting there—sitting and waiting. Waiting for what? Waiting to be transformed, to be moved a little to the left or to be rotated to show its good side or to be scaled down a little smaller. These actions are called *transformations* because they transform the object to a different state. Transformations are different from modifications. Modifications change the object's geometry, but transformations do not affect the object's geometry at all.

The three different types of transformations are translation (which is a fancy word for moving objects), rotation, and scaling.

Moving objects

The first transformation type is *translation* or moving objects. You can move objects in any of the three axes. You can move objects to an absolute coordinate location or move them to a certain offset distance from their current location.

To move objects, click the Select and Move button on the main toolbar, select the object to move, and drag the object in the viewport to the desired location. Translations are measured in the defined system units for the scene, which may be inches, centimeters, meters, and so on.

Rotating objects

Rotation is the process of spinning the object about its Transform Center point. To rotate objects, click the Select and Rotate button on the main toolbar, select an object to rotate, and drag it in a viewport. Rotations are measured in degrees where 360 degrees is a full rotation.

Scaling objects

Scaling increases or decreases the overall size of an object. Most scaling operations are uniform, or equal in all directions. All scaling is done about the Transform Center point.

To scale objects uniformly, click the Select and Uniform Scale button on the main toolbar, select an object to scale, and drag it in a viewport. Scalings are measured as a percentage of the original. For example, a cube that is scaled to a value of 200 percent will be twice as big as the original.

Non-uniform scaling

The Select and Scale button includes two flyout buttons for scaling objects non-uniformly, allowing objects to be scaled unequally in different dimensions. The two additional tools are Select and Non-Uniform Scale, and Select and Squash, shown in Table 7-1. With Select and Non-Uniform Scale, resizing a basketball using this tool could result in a ball that is taller than it is wide. Scaling is done about the axis or axes that have been constrained (or limited) using the Restrict Axes buttons on the Axis Constraints toolbar.

	Table 7-1
	Non-Uniform Scale Flyout Buttons

Button	Description
	Select and Non-Uniform Scale
	Select and Squash

Squashing objects

The Squash option is a specialized type of non-uniform scaling. This scaling causes the constrained axis to be scaled at the same time the opposite axes are scaled in the opposite direction. For example, if you push down on the basketball by scaling the Z-axis, the sides, or the X- and Y-axes, it will bulge outward. This simulates the actual results of such materials as rubber and plastic.

Figure 7-1 shows a basketball that has been scaled using uniform scaling, non-uniform scaling, and squash modes.

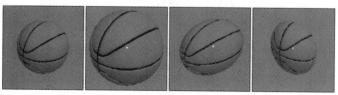

Figure 7-1: These basketballs have been scaled using uniform, non-uniform, and squash modes.

Using the transform buttons

The three transform buttons located on the main toolbar are Select and Move, Select and Rotate, and Select and Uniform Scale, as shown in Table 7-2. Using these buttons, you can select objects and transform them by dragging in one of the viewports with the mouse.

	Table 7-2 **Transform Buttons**	
Toolbar Button	**Name**	**Description**
✥	Select and Move	Enters move mode, in which clicking and dragging an object moves it.
↺	Select and Rotate	Enters rotate mode, in which clicking and dragging an object rotates it.
◻ ◹ ◺	Select and Uniform Scale, Select and Non-Uniform Scale, Select and Squash	Enters scale mode, in which clicking and dragging an object scales it.

Transformation Tools

To help in your transformations, you can use several tools to transform objects (and you don't even need a phone booth). These tools include the Transform Gizmo, the Transform Type-In dialog box (F12), Status Bar fields, and the Transform Managers.

Working with the Transform Gizmos

The Transform Gizmo appears at the center of the selected object (actually at the object's pivot point) when you click one of the transform buttons. The gizmo includes three color-coded arrows, circles, and lines representing the X-, Y-, and Z-axes. The X-axis is colored red, the Y-axis is colored green, and the Z-axis is colored blue. Figure 7-2 shows the gizmo at the center of an ice cream cone.

If the Transform Gizmo is not visible, you can enable it by choosing Views ➪ Show Transform Gizmo or by pressing the X key to toggle it on and off. You can use the – (minus) and = (equals) keys to decrease or increase the gizmo's size.

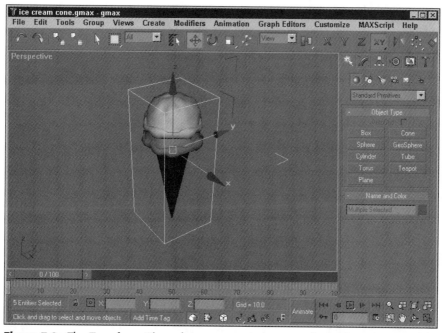

Figure 7-2: The Transform Gizmo lets you constrain a transformation to a single axis or a plane.

Using the interactive gizmo

Moving the cursor over the top of one of the Transform Gizmo's axes in the active viewport selects the axis, which changes to light orange. Dragging the selected axis restricts the transformation to that axis only. For example, selecting the red X-axis on the Move Gizmo and dragging will move the selected object along only the X-axis.

In addition to the arrows for each axis, in each corner of the Move Gizmo are two perpendicular lines for each plane. These lines let you transform along a plane (two axes simultaneously). The colors of these lines match the various colors used for the axes. For example, in the Perspective view, dragging on a red and blue corner would constrain the movement to the XZ plane. Selecting one of these planes highlights it. At the center of the Move Gizmo is a Center Box that marks the pivot point's origin.

Setting gizmo preferences

For the Transform Gizmo, you can set the preferences using the Viewports panel in the Preference Settings dialog box, shown in Figure 7-3. In this panel, you can turn the Transform Gizmo on or off, set to Show Labels, Use Center Box, Use Planes and set the Size of the gizmo's axes.

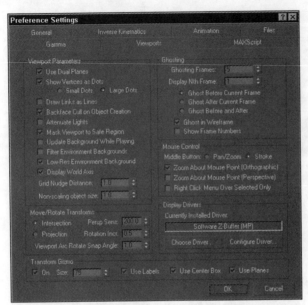

Figure 7-3: The Viewports panel in the Preference Settings dialog box lets you control how the Transform Gizmo looks.

Using the Transform Type-In dialog box

The Transform Type-In dialog box (F12) lets you input precise values for moving, rotating, and scaling objects. This command provides more exact control over the placement of objects than dragging with the mouse.

The Transform Type-In dialog box allows you to enter numerical coordinates or offsets that can be used for precise transformations. Open this dialog box by choosing Tools ➪ Transform Type-In, or by pressing the F12 key.

Tip   Right-clicking any of the transform buttons opens the Transform Type-In dialog box, but the dialog box will open for whichever button is enabled, regardless of which button you right-click.

The Transform Type-In dialog box is modeless and allows you to select new objects as needed, or switch between the various transforms. When the dialog box appears, it displays the coordinate locations for the current selection in the Absolute: World column.

Within the Transform Type-In dialog box are two columns. The first column displays the current Absolute coordinates. Updating these coordinates will transform the selected object in the viewport. The second column displays the Offset values. These values are all set to 0.0 when the dialog box is first opened, but changing these values will transform the object. Figure 7-4 shows the Transform Type-In dialog box for the Move Transform.

Note
The name of this dialog box changes depending on the type of transformation taking place and the coordinate system. If the Select and Move button is selected along with the world coordinate system, the Transform Type-In dialog box is labeled Move Transform Type-In and the column titles will indicate the coordinate system.

Figure 7-4: The Transform Type-In dialog box displays the current Absolute coordinates and Offset values.

Using the status bar Type-In fields

The status bar includes three fields labeled X, Y, and Z for displaying transformation coordinates. When you move, rotate, or scale an object, the X, Y, and Z offset values appear in these fields. The values depend on the type of transformation taking place. Translation shows the unit distances, rotation displays the angle in degrees, and scaling shows a percentage value of the original size.

When you click the Select Objects button, these fields show the absolute position of the cursor in world coordinates based on the active viewport.

You can also use these fields to enter values, like with the Transform Type-In dialog box. The type of transform depends on which transform button you select. The values that you enter can be either absolute coordinates or offset values, depending on the setting of the Transform Type-In toggle button that appears to the left of the transform fields. This toggle button lets you switch between Absolute and Offset modes, shown in Table 7-3.

| Table 7-3 | |
| **Transform Type-In Mode Buttons** | |
Button	**Description**
	Absolute
	Offset

Understanding the Transform Managers

The Transform Managers are three different types of controls that help you define the system about which objects are transformed. These controls, found on the main toolbar, directly affect your transformations. They include the following:

✦ **Reference Coordinate System:** Defines the coordinate system about which the transformations take place.

✦ **Transform Center settings:** Include the Pivot Point Center, the Selection Center, and the Transform Coordinate Center. These settings specify the center about which the transformations take place.

✦ **Axis Constraint settings:** Allow the transformation to happen using only one axis or plane. These buttons are on the Axis Constraints toolbar.

Understanding coordinate systems

gmax supports several different coordinate systems, and knowing which coordinate system you are working with as you transform an object is important. Using the wrong coordinate system can produce unexpected transformations.

To understand the concept of coordinate systems, imagine that you're visiting the Grand Canyon and standing precariously on the edge of a lookout. To nervous onlookers calling the park rangers, the description of your position would vary from viewpoint to viewpoint. A person standing by you would say you are next to him. A person on the other side of the canyon would say that you're across from her. A person at the floor of the canyon would say you're above him. And a person in an airplane would describe you as being on the east side of the canyon. Each person would have a different viewpoint of you (the object), even though you have not moved.

The coordinate systems that gmax recognizes include the following:

✦ **View Coordinate System:** A coordinate system based on the viewports; X points right, Y points up, and Z points out of the screen (toward you). The views are fixed, making this perhaps the most intuitive coordinate system to work with.

✦ **Screen Coordinate System:** Identical to the View Coordinate System, except the active viewport determines the coordinate system axes, whereas the inactive viewports show the axes as defined by the active viewport.

✦ **World Coordinate System:** Specifies X pointing to the right, Z pointing up, and Y pointing into the screen (away from you). The coordinate axes remain fixed regardless of any transformations applied to an object.

✦ **Parent Coordinate System:** Uses the coordinate system applied to a linked object's parent and maintains consistency between hierarchical transformations. If an object doesn't have a parent, then the world is its parent and the system is set to the World Coordinate System.

✦ **Local Coordinate System:** Sets the coordinate system based on the selected object. The axes are located at the pivot point for the object. You can reorient and move the pivot point using the Pivot button in the Hierarchy panel.

✦ **Grid Coordinate System:** Uses the coordinate system for the active grid.

✦ **Pick Coordinate System:** Lets you select an object about which to transform. The Coordinate System list keeps the last four picked objects as coordinate system options.

All transforms occur relative to the current coordinate system as selected in the Referenced Coordinate System drop-down list found on the main toolbar.

Each of the three basic transforms can have a different coordinate system specified, or you can set it to change uniformly when a new coordinate system is selected. To do this, open the General panel in the Preference Settings dialog box, and select the Constant option in the Reference Coordinate System section.

Using a transform center

All transforms are done about a center point. When transforming an object, you must know what the object's current center point is, as well as the coordinate system that you're working in.

The Transform Center flyout consists of three buttons: Use Pivot Point Center, Use Selection Center, and Use Transform Coordinate Center, shown in Table 7-4. Each of these buttons alters how the transformations are done. The origin of the Transform Gizmo is always positioned at the center point specified by these buttons.

Table 7-4
Transform Center Flyout Buttons

Button	Description
	Use Pivot Point Center
	Use Selection Center
	Use Transform Coordinate Center

Pivot Point Center

Pivot points are typically set to the center of an object when the object is first created, but they can be relocated anywhere within the scene, including outside of the object. Relocating the pivot point allows you to change the point about which objects are rotated. For example, if you have a car model that you want to position along an incline, moving the pivot point to the bottom of one of the tires will allow you to easily line up the car with the incline.

Selection Center

The Use Selection Center button sets the transform center to the center of the selected object or objects, regardless of the individual object's pivot point. If multiple objects are selected, then the center will be computed to be in the middle of a bounding box that surrounds all the objects.

Transform Coordinate Center

The Transform Coordinate Center button uses the center of the Local Coordinate System. If View Coordinate System is selected, then all objects are transformed about the center of the viewport. If an object is selected as the coordinate system using the Pick option, then all transformations will be transformed about that object's center.

When you select the Local Coordinate System, the Use Transform Center button is ignored, and objects are transformed about their local axes. If you select multiple objects, then they all transform individually about their local axes. Grouped objects transform about the group axes.

Figure 7-5 shows the ice cream cone and firecracker object using the different transform center modes. The left image shows the Pivot Point Center mode, the middle image shows the Selection Center mode with both objects selected, and the right image shows the Transform Coordinate Center mode. For each mode, notice that the Move Gizmo is in a different location.

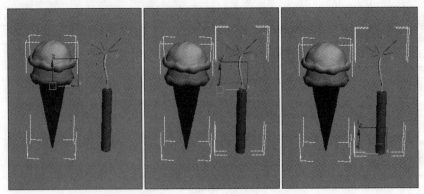

Figure 7-5: The Move Gizmo is located in different places depending on the selected Transform Center mode.

Selecting axis constraints

Three-dimensional space consists of three basic directions defined by three axes: X, Y, and Z. If you were to stand on each axis and look at a scene, you would see three separate planes: the XY plane, the YZ plane, and the ZX plane. These planes show only two dimensions at a time and restrict any transformations to the two axes.

By default, the Top, Side, and Front viewports show only a single plane and thereby restrict transformations to that single plane. The Top view constrains movement to the XY plane, the Left or Right side view constrains movement to the YZ plane, and the Front view constrains movement to the ZX plane. This setting is adequate for most modeling purposes, but sometimes you might need to limit the transformations in all the viewports to a single plane. In gmax, you can restrict movement to specific transform axes using the Restrict Axes buttons in the main toolbar.

The four Restrict Axes buttons are Restrict to X (F5), Restrict to Y (F6), Restrict to Z (F7), and the flyout buttons, Restrict to XY, YZ, and ZX Plane (F8). The effect of selecting one of the Restrict Axes buttons is based on the coordinate system selected. For example, if you click the Restrict to X button and the coordinate system is set to View, then the object is always transformed to the right because, in the View coordinate system, the X-axis is always to the right. If you click the Restrict to X button and the coordinate system is set to Local, the axes are attached to the object, so transformations along the X-axis will be consistent in all viewports. (With this setting, the object will not move in the Left view because it only shows the YZ plane.)

 Caution   If the axis constraints don't seem to be working, check the Preference Settings dialog box and look at the General panel to make sure that the Reference Coordinate System option is set to Constant.

Additionally, you can restrict movement to a single plane with the Restrict to Plane flyouts consisting of Restrict to XY, Restrict to YZ, and Restrict to ZX. (Use the F8 key to quickly cycle through the various planes.) If the Transform Gizmo is enabled, then the available axis or axes are displayed in yellow.

Locking axes and inheriting transformations

To lock an object's transformation axes on a more permanent basis, go to the Command Panel and select the Hierarchy tab. Click the Link Info button to open the Locks rollout, shown in Figure 7-6. The rollout displays each axis for the three types of transformations: Move, Rotate, and Scale. Make sure the object is selected, and then click the transformation axes you want to lock. Be aware that if all Move axes are selected, you won't be able to move the object until you de-select the axes.

Locking axes is helpful if you want to prevent accidental scaling of an object or restrict a vehicle's movement to a plane that makes up a road.

Figure 7-6: The Locks and Inherit rollouts can prevent any transforms along an axis and specify which transformations are inherited.

The Locks rollout displays unselected X, Y, and Z check boxes for the Move, Rotate, and Scale transformations. By selecting the check boxes, you limit the axes about which the object can be transformed. For example, if you check the X and Y boxes under the Move transformation, the object can move only in the Z direction of the Local Coordinate System.

Note   These locks work regardless of the axis constraint settings in the main toolbar.

The Inherit rollout, like the Locks rollout, includes check boxes for each axis and each transformation, except that all the transformations are selected by default. By de-selecting a check box, you specify which transformations an object does not inherit from its parent. The Inherit rollout appears only if the selected object is part of a hierarchy.

For example, suppose a child object is created and linked to a parent, and the X Move Inherit check box is de-selected. As the parent is moved in the Y or Z direction, the child follows, but if the parent is moved in the X direction, the child does not follow. If a parent doesn't inherit a transformation, then its children don't either.

Using the Link Inheritance utility

The Link Inheritance utility works in the same way as the Inherit rollout of the Hierarchy panel, except that you can apply it to multiple objects at the same time. To use this utility, open the Utility panel, and click the More button. In the Utilities dialog box, select the Link Inheritance utility, and click OK. The rollout for this utility is identical to the Inherit rollout discussed in the previous section.

Tutorial: Re-creating a chess game

Chess is a great game, and every time I get a book to help me become a better player, I am presented with example after example of the great matches throughout history that have been re-created using this strange notation that is completely foreign and difficult to follow. This is obviously a case where 3D graphics, which is all about visualization, would help.

To re-create a chess game for this tutorial, I could model a chess set and a board, or I could borrow a model from my friends at Viewpoint Datalabs. The tutorial deals with transforming objects and not with modeling, so I chose the latter option.

With the pieces in place, I can re-create the game by moving the pieces. (Now, all I need is help understanding chess game notation.)

To re-create a chess game, follow these steps:

1. Open the Chess game.gmax file from the Chap 07 directory on the CD-ROM.

2. To prevent any extraneous movements, restrict any movement of the board itself by locking the transformation axes. Select the board by clicking it (be sure to get the border also). Open the Hierarchy panel and click the Link Info button. Then in the Locks rollout, select all nine boxes to restrict all transformations.

3. Back in the Top viewport, click the Select and Move button and try to drag the board in the viewport.

   It won't move because all of its transformations are now locked.

Note Another way to keep the chessboard from moving is to use the Freeze option. To freeze an object, open the Display panel and in the Freeze rollout, select Freeze Selected. You can also choose Edit ⇨ Properties to open the Object Properties dialog box. In the Object Information section, click the Freeze option.

4. The next step is to restrict all pieces to move only in the XY plane. For this to happen, the coordinate system needs to change. Select the World Coordinate System from the Reference Coordinate System drop-down list on the main toolbar.

5. On the main toolbar, click the Restrict to XY Plane button (or you can cycle through the constrain planes using the F8 key). Select and move an object in the scene, and notice how its movements stay within the XY plane.

   You can also restrict movement to the XY plane by moving only objects in the Top viewport.

6. Before you make your first move, click the Animate button in the Lower Interface Bar (or press the N key) and go to the next animation frame by clicking the Next Frame button in the Time Controls (or press the . key).

7. Select and Move a chess piece, repositioning the object in the Top view. Then click the large Animate button to record the transformation.

8. Continue clicking the Next Frame button and moving the pieces frame by frame until the game is finished.

9. After you finish the game, click the Go to Start button in the Time Controls (or press the Home key) and click repeatedly on the Next Frame button to see the game unfold.

Figure 7-7 shows the chess game in progress.

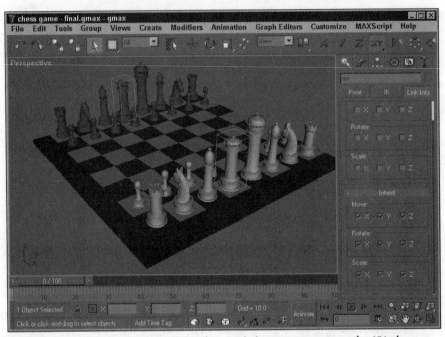

Figure 7-7: Re-creating a chess game by restricting movements to the XY plane

Tutorial: Setting the dining room table

Using gmax, the age-old chore of setting the table for dinner becomes easy (still not fun, but easy). Now, you could just move the dishes into place, but learning to rotate them will make it easier for the diners. In this tutorial, you'll start with a dining room table model provided by Zygote Media from their Sampler CD-ROM.

To set the table, follow these steps:

1. Open the Dining Room.gmax file from the Chap 07 directory on the CD-ROM.

2. Clone the set of dishes by selecting the Dishes group and choosing Edit ⇨ Clone (or you can hold down the Shift key while moving the object).

3. Select the World Coordinate System and Restrict to XY Plane (F8) to ensure that the dishes stay on the table plane.

4. Select and Move the cloned dishes across the table.

5. With the cloned dishes still selected, click the Select and Rotate button. Then right-click the Select and Rotate button to open the Rotate Transform Type-In dialog box.

6. In the Rotate Transform Type-In dialog box (F12), enter **180** degrees for the Z-axis and press the Enter key; then close the dialog box.

This step reorients the dishes correctly.

7. Hold down the Ctrl key while selecting both sets of dishes. Select the Use Selection Center flyout. Then choose Edit ➪ Clone to create the last two sets of dishes.

8. With the second set of cloned dishes still selected, right-click the Select and Rotate button to open the Rotate Transform Type-In dialog box again. This time, enter **90** in the Z offset field and press the Enter key; then close the dialog box.

9. Select and Move each individual place setting to its final place. Figure 7-8 shows the table all set and ready for dinner.

Figure 7-8: Setting the table is accomplished by moving and rotating cloned copies of the dishes.

Now you've done some translation and some rotation. In the next example, you'll scale some sphere objects to build a snowman.

Tutorial: Building a snowman

A snowman is a fine example of symmetrical body parts. First, you start with a base, then duplicate the base, only smaller, and finally create the head, which is even smaller. This sounds like a good place to use the Scale transformation.

To build a snowman, follow these steps:

1. Open the Create panel in the Command Panel and click the Sphere button.

2. Create a sphere object by dragging in the Top viewport.

    This will be the base of your snowman.

3. Snowman parts are never perfectly round, so let's squash the sphere by click-ing the Select and Squash flyout button under the Select and Scale button. When the non-uniform scaling warning dialog box appears, click Yes.

    We won't be applying any modifiers to these squashed spheres, so clicking Yes to close the warning dialog box isn't a problem.

4. Set the coordinate system to Local, and click the Restrict to Z-Axis button (or press F7). Now, drag the sphere downward in the Top viewport to squash it slightly.

5. Select the Select and Uniform Scale flyout, and clone the sphere by holding down the Shift key while dragging on the sphere. Enter **2** in the Clone Options dialog box to create two clones at the same time (one for the upper torso and one for the head).

    Each successive clone will be scaled by the same offset between the original and first cloned spheres.

6. Click the Select and Move button, and position the new cloned spheres on top of the original sphere.

Note   If you have any problems moving the spheres, check your coordinate system set-ting. It should be set to Local.

7. To complete the snowman, add some primitive objects for coal eyes, a mouth, a carrot nose, and a top hat.

Figure 7-9 shows the finished snowman produced by scaling spheres.

Figure 7-9: A simple snowman model composed of scaled spheres

Using Pivot Points

An object's pivot point is the center about which the object is rotated and scaled and about which most modifiers are applied. Pivot points are created by default when an object is created and are usually created at the center or base of an object. You can move and orient a pivot point in any direction, but repositioning the pivot cannot be animated. Pivot points exist for all objects, whether or not they are part of a hierarchy.

Caution
Try to set your pivot points before animating any objects in your scene. If you relocate the pivot point after animation keys have been placed, all transformations are modified to use the new pivot point.

Positioning pivot points

To move and orient a pivot point, open the Hierarchy panel in the Command Panel and click the Pivot button, shown in Figure 7-10. At the top of the Adjust Pivot rollout are three buttons; each button represents a different mode. The Affect Pivot

Only mode makes the transformation buttons affect only the pivot point of the current selection. The object will not move. The Affect Object Only mode causes the object to be transformed, but not the pivot point; and the Affect Hierarchy Only mode allows an object's links to be moved.

Figure 7-10: The Pivot button under the Hierarchy panel includes controls for affecting the pivot point.

Using the Scale transformation while one of these modes is selected alters the selected object but has no effect on the pivot point or the link.

Aligning pivot points

Below the mode buttons are three more buttons that are used to align the pivot points. These buttons are active only when a mode is selected. These buttons are Center to Object/Pivot, Align to Object/Pivot, and Align to World. The first two buttons switch between Object and Pivot, depending on the mode that is selected. You may select only one mode at a time. The button turns light gray when selected.

The Center to Object/Pivot button moves the object or the pivot point so that its centers are aligned. The Align to Object/Pivot button rotates the object or pivot point until the object's Local Coordinate System and the pivot point are aligned. The Align to World button rotates either to the World Coordinate system. For example, if the Affect Object Only mode is selected and the object is separated from the pivot point, clicking the Center to Pivot button will move the object so that its center is on the pivot point.

Under these three alignment buttons is another button labeled Reset Pivot, which you use to reset the pivot point to its original location.

Transform adjustments

The Hierarchy panel of the Command Panel includes another useful rollout labeled Adjust Transform. This rollout, also shown in Figure 7-10, includes another mode that you can use with hierarchies of objects. Clicking the Don't Affect Children button places you in a mode where any transformations of a linked hierarchy will not affect the children. Typically, transformations are applied to all linked children of a hierarchy, but this mode disables that feature.

The Adjust Transform rollout also includes two buttons that allow you to reset the Local Coordinate System and scale percentage. These buttons set the current orientation of an object as the World coordinate or as the 100 percent standard. For example, if you select an object and move it 30 units to the left and scale it to 200 percent, these values will be displayed in the coordinate fields on the status bar. Clicking the Reset Transform and Reset Scale buttons resets these values to 0 and 100 percent.

You use the Reset Scale button to reset the scale values for an object that has been scaled using non-uniform scaling. Non-uniform scaling can cause problems for child objects that inherit this type of scaling such as shortening the links, and the Reset Scale button can remedy these problems by resetting the parent's scaling values. When the scale is reset, there is no visible change to the object, but if you open the Scale Transform Type-In dialog box while the scale is being reset, you see the absolute local values being set back to 100 each.

 Tip

If you are using an object that has been non-uniformly scaled, using Reset Scale before the item is linked will save you some headaches if you plan on using modifiers.

Using the Reset XForm utility

You can also reset transform values using the Reset XForm utility. To use this utility, open the Utility panel and click the Reset XForm button, which is one of the default buttons. The benefit of this utility is that you can reset the transform values for multiple objects simultaneously. The rollout for this utility includes only a single button labeled Reset Selected.

Using the Align Commands

The Align commands are an easy way to automatically transform objects. You can use these commands to line up object centers or edges, align normals and highlights, align to views and grids, and even line up cameras.

Aligning objects

Any object that you can transform, you can align, including lights, cameras, and Space Warps. After selecting the object to be aligned, click the Align flyout button on the main toolbar or choose Tools ➪ Align (or press Alt+A). The cursor changes to the Align icon; now click a target object with which you want to align all the selected objects. Clicking the target object opens the Align Selection dialog box with the target object's name displayed in the dialog box's title, as shown in Figure 7-11.

Figure 7-11: The Align Selection dialog box can align objects along any axes by their Minimum, Center, Pivot, or Maximum points.

The Align Selection dialog box includes settings for the X, Y, and Z positions to line up the Minimum, Center, Pivot Point, or Maximum dimensions for the selected or target object's Bounding Box. As you change the settings in the dialog box, the objects reposition themselves, but the actual transformations don't take place until you click the Apply button or the OK button.

Aligning normals

You can use the Normal Align command to line up points of the surface of two objects. A Normal vector is a projected line that extends from the center of a polygon face exactly perpendicular to the surface. When two Normal vectors are aligned, the objects are perfectly adjacent to one another. If the two objects are spheres, then they will touch at only one point.

To align normals, you need to first select the object to move (this is the source object). Then choose Tools ➪ Normal Align, or click the Normal Align flyout button under the Align button on the main toolbar (or press Alt+N). The cursor will change to the Normal Align icon. Drag the cursor across the surface of the source object, and a blue arrow pointing out from the face center appears. Release the mouse when you've correctly pinpointed the position to align.

Next, click the target object, and drag the mouse to locate the target object's align point. This is displayed as a green arrow. When you release the mouse, the source object moves to align the two points and the Normal Align dialog box appears, as shown in Figure 7-12.

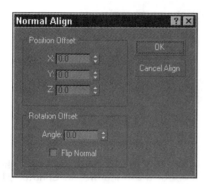

Figure 7-12: The Normal Align dialog box allows you to define offset values when aligning normals.

When the objects are aligned, the two points match up exactly. The Normal Align dialog box lets you specify offset values that you can use to keep a distance between the two objects. You can also specify an Angle Offset, which is used to deviate the parallelism of the normals. The Flip Normal option aligns the objects so that their selected normals point in the same direction.

Objects without any faces, like Point Helper objects and Space Warps, use a vector between the origin and the Z-axis for normal alignment.

Tutorial: Aligning a kissing couple

Aligning normals positions two faces directly opposite one another, so what better way to practice this tool than to align two faces.

To connect the kissing couple using the Normal Align command, follow these steps:

1. Open the Kissing couple.gmax file from the Chap 07 directory on the CD-ROM. This file includes two extruded shapes of a boy and a girl. The extruded shapes give us a flat face that is easy to align.

2. Select the girl shape, and choose the Tools ⇨ Align Normals menu command (or press Alt+N). Then drag the cursor over the extruded shape until the blue vector points out from the front of the lips, as shown in Figure 7-13.

3. Then drag the cursor over the boy shape until the green vector points out from the front of the lips. Release the mouse, and the Normal Align dialog box appears. Enter a value of **5** in the Z-Axis Offset field, and click OK.

Figure 7-13 shows the resulting couple with normal aligned faces.

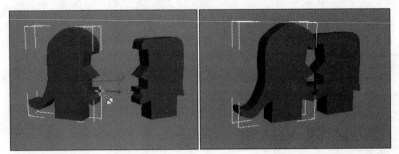

Figure 7-13: Using the Normal Align feature, you can align object faces.

Cross-Reference

In the Align button flyout are two other common ways to align objects — Align Camera and Place Highlight (Ctrl+H). I talk about these features in Chapter 21, "Controlling Cameras," and Chapter 22, "Working with Lights," respectively.

Aligning to a view

The Align to View command provides an easy and quick way to reposition objects to one of the axes. To use this command, select an object and then choose Tools ➪ Align to View. The Align to View dialog box appears, as shown in Figure 7-14. Changing the settings in this dialog box displays the results in the viewports. You can use the Flip command for altering the direction of the object points. If no object is selected, then the Align to View command cannot be used.

Figure 7-14: The Align to View dialog box is a quick way to line up objects with the axes.

The Align to View command is especially useful for fixing the orientation of objects when you create them in the wrong view. All alignments are completed relative to the object's Local Coordinate System. If several objects are selected, each object is reoriented according to its Local Coordinate System.

Note

Using the Align to View command on symmetrical objects like spheres doesn't produce any noticeable difference in the viewports.

Using Grids

When gmax is started, the one element that is visible is the Home Grid. This grid is there to give you a reference point for creating objects in 3D space. At the center of each grid are two darker lines. These lines meet at the origin point for the World Coordinate System where the coordinates for X, Y, and Z are all 0.0. This point is where all objects are placed by default.

In addition to the Home Grid, you can create and place new grids in the scene. These grids are not rendered, but you can use them to help you locate and align objects in 3D space.

The Home Grid

You can turn the Home Grid on or off by choosing Views ➪ Grid ➪ Show Home Grid (you can also turn the Home Grid on and off for the selected viewport using the G key or for all viewports at once with the Shift+G keyboard shortcut). If the Home Grid is the only grid in the scene, then by default it is also the construction grid where new objects are positioned when created.

You can access the Home Grid parameters (shown in Figure 7-15) by choosing Customize ➪ Grid and Snap Settings. You can also access this dialog box by right-clicking the Snap, Angle Snap, or Percent Snap Toggle buttons located on the main toolbar.

In the Home Grid panel of the Grid and Snap Settings dialog box, you can set how often Major Lines appear, as well as set the Grid Spacing. (The Spacing value for the active grid is displayed on the status bar.) You can also specify to dynamically update the grid view in all viewports or just in the active one.

The User Grids panel lets you activate any new grids when created.

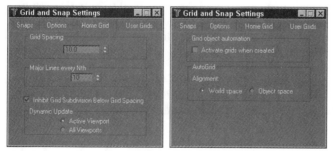

Figure 7-15: The Home Grid and User Grids panels of the Grid and Snap Settings dialog box let you define the grid spacing.

Creating and activating new grids

In addition to the Home Grid, you can create new grids. To create a new Grid object, open the Create panel, select the Helpers category, and click the Grid button. In the Parameters rollout are settings for specifying the new grid object's dimensions, spacing, and color, as well as which coordinate plane to display (XY, YZ, or ZX).

You can designate any newly created grid as the default active grid. To activate a grid, make sure it is selected and choose Views ➪ Grids ➪ Activate Grid Object. Keep in mind that only one grid may be active at a time, and the default Home Grid cannot be selected. You can also activate a grid by right-clicking the grid object and selecting Activate Grid from the pop-up menu. To deactivate the new grid and reactivate the Home Grid, choose Views ➪ Grids ➪ Activate Home Grid, or right-click the grid object and choose Activate Grid ➪ Home Grid from the pop-up quadmenu.

You can find further grid settings for new grids in the Grid and Snap Settings dialog box on the User Grids panel. The settings include automatically activating the grid when created, and an option for aligning an AutoGrid using World space or Object space coordinates.

Using AutoGrid

You can use the AutoGrid feature to create a new construction plane perpendicular to a face normal. This feature provides an easy way to create and align objects directly next to one another without manually lining them up or using the Align features.

The AutoGrid feature shows up as a check box at the top of the Object Type rollout for every category in the Create panel. It becomes active only when you're in Create Object mode.

To use AutoGrid, click the AutoGrid option after selecting an object type to create. If no objects are in the scene, then the object is created as usual. If an object is in the scene, then the cursor moves around on the surface of the object with its coordinate axes perpendicular to the surface that the cursor is over. Clicking and dragging creates the new object based on the precise location of the object under the mouse.

The AutoGrid option stays active for all new objects you create until you turn off the AutoGrid option by unchecking the box. Holding down the Alt key before creating the object makes the AutoGrid stay around after the object is created.

Using Snap Options

Often when an object is being transformed, you know exactly where you want to put it. The Snap feature can be the means whereby objects get to the precise place they should be. For example, if you are constructing a set of stairs from box primitives, you could enable the edge snap feature to make each adjacent step be aligned precisely along the edge of the previous step. With the snap feature enabled, an object automatically moves (or snaps) to the specified snap position when you place it close enough. If you enable the Snap features, they will affect any transformations that you make in a scene.

Snap points are defined in the Grid and Snap Settings dialog box that you can open by choosing Customize ⇨ Grid and Snap Settings or by right-clicking any of the first three Snap buttons on the main toolbar (these Snap buttons have a small magnet icon in them). Figure 7-16 shows the Snaps panel of the Grid and Snap Settings dialog box for Standard objects.

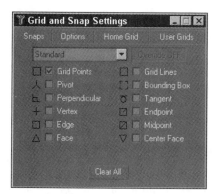

Figure 7-16: The Snaps panel includes many different points to snap to, depending on the object type.

After snap points have been defined, the Snap buttons on the main toolbar activate the Snaps feature. The first Snaps button consists of a flyout with three buttons: 3D Snap Toggle, 2.5D Snap Toggle, and 2D Snap Toggle. The 2D Snap Toggle button limits all snaps to the active construction grid. The 2.5D Snap Toggle button snaps to points on the construction grid as well as projected points from objects in the scene. The 3D Snap Toggle button can snap to any points in 3D space.

Tip

Right-clicking the snap toggles opens the Grid and Snap Settings dialog box, except for the Spinner Snap Toggle, which opens the Preference Settings dialog box.

These Snap buttons control the snapping for translations. To the right are two other buttons: Angle Snap Toggle and Percent Snap. These buttons control the snapping of rotations and scalings.

Note   The keyboard shortcut for turning the Snaps feature on and off is the S key.

With the Snaps feature enabled, the cursor becomes blue crosshairs wherever a snap point is located.

Setting snap points

The Snap panel in the Grid and Snap Settings dialog box has many different points that can be snapped to in two different categories: Standard and NURBS. The Standard snap points (previously shown in Figure 7-16) include the following:

✦ **Grid Points:** Snaps to the Grid intersection points

✦ **Grid Lines:** Snaps only to positions located on the Grid lines

✦ **Pivot:** Snaps to an object's pivot point

✦ **Bounding Box:** Snaps to one of the corners of a bounding box

✦ **Perpendicular:** Snaps to a spline's next perpendicular point

✦ **Tangent:** Snaps to a spline's next tangent point

✦ **Vertex:** Snaps to polygon vertices

✦ **Endpoint:** Snaps to a spline's end point or the end of a polygon edge

✦ **Edge:** Snaps to positions only on an edge

✦ **Midpoint:** Snaps to a spline's midpoint or the middle of a polygon edge

✦ **Face:** Snaps to any point on the surface of a face

✦ **Center Face:** Snaps to the center of a face

Setting snap options

The Grid and Snap Settings dialog box holds a panel of Options, shown in Figure 7-17, in which you can set whether markers display, the size of the markers, and their color. If you click on the color swatch, a Color Selector dialog box opens and enables you to select a new color. The Snap Strength setting determines how close the cursor must be to a snap point before it snaps to it. The Angle and Percent values are the strengths for any rotate and scale transformations, respectively. You can also cause translations to be affected by the designated axis constraints with the Use Axis Constraints option.

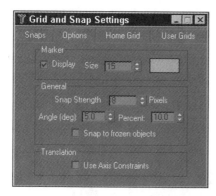

Figure 7-17: The Options panel includes settings for marker size and color and the Snap Strength value.

Within any viewport, holding down the Shift key and right-clicking in the viewport can access a pop-up menu of grid points and options. This pop-up quadmenu lets you quickly add or reset all the current snap points and change snap options, such as Transformed Constraints and Snap to Frozen.

Tutorial: Creating a lattice for a methane molecule

Many molecules are represented by a lattice of spheres. Trying to line up the exact positions of the spheres by hand could be extremely frustrating, but using the Snap feature makes this challenge, well . . . a snap.

One of the simpler molecules is methane, which is composed of one carbon atom surrounded by four smaller hydrogen atoms. To reproduce this molecule as a lattice, we will first create a tetrahedron primitive and snap spheres to each of its corners.

To create a lattice of the methane molecule, follow these steps:

1. Open the Methane Molecule.gmax file from the Chap 07 directory on the CD-ROM.

   This file includes a simple tetrahedron object created with the Hedra Extended Primitive surrounded by a sphere.

2. Open the Grid and Snap Settings dialog box by right-clicking the 3D Snap Toggle button at the bottom of the interface. In the Snaps panel, click the Clear All button to de-select any previous selections, and then select the Vertex option. Close the dialog box.

3. Enable the Snap feature by clicking the 3D Snap Toggle button (or press the S key).

4. In the Create panel drop-down list, select the Standard Primitives category, and then click the Sphere button.

5. Now create four hydrogen atoms. In the Top viewport, move the cursor over the tetrahedron. Move the cursor over each of the four corners of the tetrahedron until a blue vertex appears. Click and drag to create a sphere; in the Parameters rollout, enter a Radius value of **30**. Do this procedure for each of the spheres placed at a vertex.

6. When you've completed the molecule, you can delete the tetrahedron by selecting it from the Select by Name dialog box (the name is Hedra01).

Figure 7-18 shows the finished methane molecule.

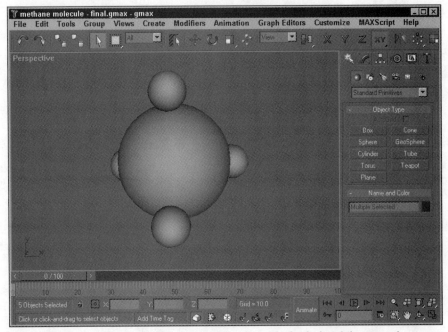

Figure 7-18: A methane molecule lattice drawn with the help of the Snap feature

Summary

Transforming objects in gmax is one of the fundamental actions. The three basic ways to transform objects are moving, rotating, and scaling. gmax includes many helpful features to enable these transformations to take place quickly and easily. In this chapter, we covered many of these features, including

✦ Using the Move, Rotate, and Scale buttons and the Transform Gizmos

✦ Transforming objects precisely with the Transform Type-In dialog box and status bar fields

✦ Using Transform Managers to change coordinate systems and lock axes

✦ Aligning objects with the Align dialog box, aligning normals, and aligning to views

✦ Manipulating pivot points

✦ Working with grids

✦ Setting up snap points

✦ Snapping objects to snap points

In the next chapter, we investigate the MAXScript features that enable you to automate mundane tasks in gmax.

✦　　✦　　✦

Placing gmax on Autopilot with MAXScript

C H A P T E R
8

◆ ◆ ◆ ◆

In This Chapter

Getting acquainted with MAXScript

Learning the MAXScript tools

Working with the MAXScript editor and Listener windows

Recording scripts with the Macro Recorder

Discovering the various script types

Writing your own scripts

Understanding the Visual MaxScript editor interface

Building a custom rollout with the Visual MAXScript editor

◆ ◆ ◆ ◆

The gmax designers went to great lengths to make sure that you are limited only by your imagination in terms of what you can do in gmax. They've packed in so many different features and so many different ways to use those features that you could use gmax for years and still learn new ways of doing things.

Despite gmax's wide range of capabilities, there may come a time when you want a new gmax feature. With MAXScript, you can actually extend gmax to meet your needs, customize it to work the way you want, and even have it do some of the more monotonous tasks for you.

What Is MAXScript?

In this chapter, we look at MAXScript — what it's for and why in the world you would ever want to use it. But before we get into the nitty-gritty details, let's start with a brief overview.

Simply put, MAXScript is a tool that you can use to expand the functionality of gmax. You can use it to add new features or to customize how gmax behaves, so that it's tailored to your needs and style. You can also use MAXScript as a sort of VCR — it can record your actions so you can play them back later, eliminating repetitive tasks.

You can use MAXScript to "talk" to gmax about a scene and tell it what you want to happen, either by having gmax watch what you do or by typing in a list of instructions that you want gmax to execute.

The beauty of MAXScript lies in its flexibility and simplicity: It is easy to use and was designed from the ground up to be an integral part of gmax. But don't let its simplicity fool you—MAXScript as a language is rich enough to let you control just about anything.

In fact, you have already used MAXScript without even knowing it. Some of the buttons and rollouts use bits of MAXScript to carry out your commands. And after you've created a new feature with MAXScript, you can integrate it into gmax transparently and use it just as easily as any other gmax feature.

MAXScript is a fully functional and very powerful computer language, but you don't have to be a computer programmer or even need any previous programming experience to benefit from MAXScript. In the next few sections, we look at some simple ways to use MAXScript. For now, just think of a script in gmax as you would a script in a movie or play—it tells what's going to happen, who's going to do what, and when it's going to happen. With your scene acting as the stage, a script directs gmax to put on a performance for you.

One final note before we dive in: MAXScript is so powerful that an entire book could be written about it and every last feature it supports, but that is not the purpose here. This chapter is organized to give you an introduction to the world of MAXScript and to teach you the basic skills you need to get some mileage out of it. What is given here is a foundation that you can build upon according to your own interests and needs.

Using MAXScript Tools

MAXScript is pervasive and can be found in many different places. This section looks at the MAXScript tools and how different scripts are created and used.

Let's take a look at some of the tools used in working with MAXScript. gmax has several tools that make creating and using scripts as simple as possible.

The MAXScript menu

The MAXScript menu includes commands that you can use to create a new script, open and run scripts, open the MAXScript Listener window (keyboard shortcut F11), or enable the Macro Recorder.

The New Script command opens a MAXScript editor window, a simple text editor in which you write your MAXScript. See the "MAXScript editor windows" section later in this chapter for more on this editor window. The Open Script command opens a file dialog box that you can use to locate a MAXScript file. When you use this dialog box, the script file is opened in a MAXScript editor window, as shown in Figure 8-1. MAXScript files have a .ms or a .mcr extension. The Run Script command also opens a file dialog box where you can select a script to be executed.

Note   When you use Run Script, some scripts do something right away, whereas others install themselves as new tools.

```
SphereArray.ms - MAXScript                    _ □ ×
File   Edit   Search   Help
utility sphereArray "Sphere Array"
(
spinner objCount "Object count:" range:[1,100,20] type:#integer
spinner radius "Radius:" range:[1,1000,50]

button go "Go!"

on go pressed do
(
  a = selection[1]
  if a != undefined do
  (
    c = objCount.value
    r = radius.value
    for i = 1 to c do
    (
      someObj = copy a
      someObj.position.x = someObj.position.x + r
      about selection rotate someObj (random 0 359) x_axis
      about selection rotate someObj (random 0 359) y_axis
      about selection rotate someObj (random 0 359) z_axis
    )
  )
)
)
```

Figure 8-1: MAXScript is written using standard syntax in a simple text editor window.

The MAXScript Listener command opens the MAXScript Listener window. You can also open this window by pressing the F11 keyboard shortcut. The Macro Recorder command starts recording a MAXScript macro. I cover the MAXScript Listener and recording macros later in this chapter.

The MAXScript Utility rollout

You access the MaxScript Utility rollout, shown in Figure 8-2, by opening the Utilities panel in the Command Panel and clicking the MAXScript button. This opens a rollout in which you can do many of the same commands as the MAXScript menu.

The MAXScript rollout also includes a Utilities drop-down list, which holds any installed scripted utilities. Each scripted utility acts as a new feature for you to use. The parameters for these utilities are displayed in a new rollout that appears below the MAXScript rollout.

Figure 8-2: The MAXScript rollout on the Utilities panel is a great place to start working with MAXScript.

Tutorial: Using the SphereArray script

Here's a chance for you to play around a little and get some experience with MAXScript in the process. In the Chap 08 directory of the CD-ROM is a simple script called SphereArray.ms. It's similar to the Array command found in the Tools menu, except that SphereArray creates copies of an object and randomly positions them in a spherical pattern.

To load and use the SphereArray script, follow these steps:

1. Open the SphereArray.gmax file from the Chap 08 directory on the CD-ROM.

   This file contains a single box object.

2. Select the box object, open the Utilities panel in the Command Panel (click the hammer icon), and click the MAXScript button.

   The MAXScript rollout appears.

3. Click the Run Script button in the MAXScript rollout to open the Choose Editor file dialog box, locate the SphereArray.ms file from the Chap 08 directory on the CD-ROM, and click Open.

   The SphereArray utility installs and appears in the Utilities drop-down list. (Because SphereArray is a scripted utility, running it only installs it.)

4. Choose SphereArray from the Utilities drop-down list. Make sure that the box object is selected.

5. In the Sphere Array rollout, enter **20** in the Object Count field and **50** for the Radius field. Now click the Go! button to run the script.

The script adds 20 copies of your box to the scene and randomly positions them two units away from the box's position.

Figure 8-3 shows the results of the SphereArray MAXScript utility. Notice how the SphereArray script looks much like any other function or tool in gmax.

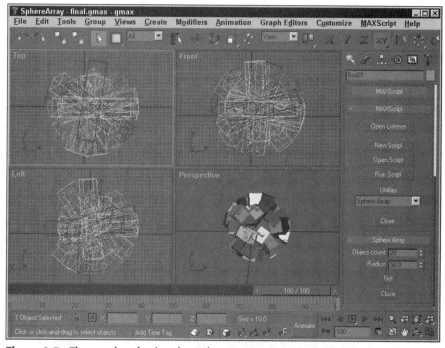

Figure 8-3: The results of using the SphereArray MAXScript utility

The MAXScript Listener window

Figure 8-4 shows the MAXScript Listener window (keyboard shortcut F11), which lets you work interactively with the part of gmax that interprets MAXScript commands. The top pane of the Listener window (the pink area) lets you enter MAXScript commands; the results are reported in the bottom pane (the white area) of the Listener window. You can also type MAXScript commands in the bottom pane, but typing them in the top pane keeps the commands separated from the results.

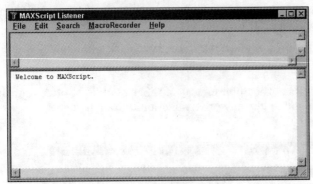

Figure 8-4: The MAXScript Listener window interprets your commands.

When you type commands into either pane and press Enter, the MAXScript interpreter evaluates the command and responds with the results. For example, if you type a simple mathematical expression such as **2+2** and press Enter, then the result of 4 is displayed in blue on the next line. Most results appear in blue, but the results display in red for any errors that occur. For example, if you enter the command **hello there**, then a Type error result appears in red because the MAXScript interpreter doesn't understand the command.

Caution   The MAXScript interpreter is very fickle. A misspelling generates an error, but MAXScript is *case-insensitive*, which means that uppercase and lowercase letters are the same as far as gmax is concerned. Thus, you can type **sphere, Sphere,** or **SPHERE,** and gmax sees no difference.

The Listener window has these menus:

✦ **File:** You can use this menu to close the window (Ctrl+W), run scripts (Ctrl+R), open a script for editing (Ctrl+O), or create a new script from scratch (Ctrl+N).

Note   The MAXScript Listener window provides no way to save scripts, so if you wish to save a script, you should copy and paste it to an editor window and save it from there.

✦ **Edit:** This menu is where you access all the common editing functions you'll need, such as cutting, pasting, and undoing.

✦ **Search:** You use this menu for searching through the window to find specific text (Ctrl+F), find the next instance (Ctrl+G), or replace text (Ctrl+H).

✦ **MacroRecorder:** This menu lets you set various options for the MAXScript Macro Recorder.

✦ **Help:** This menu provides access to the MAXScript Reference (F1).

Tutorial: Talking to the MAXScript interpreter

This tutorial gives you a little experience in working with the MAXScript Listener window and a chance to try some basic MAXScript commands.

To start using MAXScript, follow these steps:

1. Choose File ➪ Reset to reset gmax.

2. Choose MAXScript ➪ MAXScript Listener, or press F11 to open the MAXScript Listener window.

3. Click anywhere in the bottom pane of the Listener window, type the following, and press Enter:

   ```
   sphere()
   ```

   A sphere object with default parameters is created.

4. Next, enter the following in the lower pane, and press the Enter key:

   ```
   torus radius1:50 radius2:5
   ```

   gmax creates a torus and adds it to your scene. As you specified in your MAXScript, the outer radius (radius1) is 50, and the radius of the torus itself (radius2) is 5. The output tells you that gmax created a new torus at the origin of the coordinate system and gave that torus a name: Torus01.

5. Now use MAXScript to move the torus. In the Listener window, type the following:

   ```
   $Torus01.position.x = 20
   ```

   After you press Enter, you see the torus move along the positive X-axis. Each object in gmax has certain properties or attributes that describe it, and you have accessed one of these properties programmatically instead of by using the rollout or the mouse. In this case, you're telling gmax, "Torus01 has a position property. Set the X-coordinate of that position to 20."

Note The $ symbol identifies a named object. You can use it to refer to any named object.

6. To see a list of some of the properties specific to a torus, type the following:

   ```
   Showproperties $Torus01
   ```

   A list of the Torus01 properties appears in the window, as shown in Figure 8-5.

Figure 8-5 shows the MAXScript Listener window with all the associated commands and results. Figure 8-6 shows the objects completed in the gmax window.

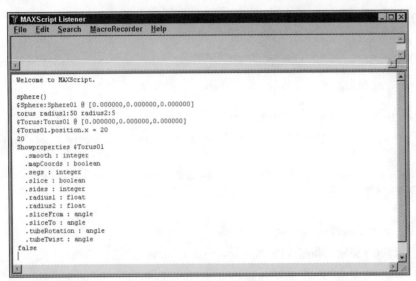

Figure 8-5: Use the MAXScript Listener window to query gmax about an object's properties.

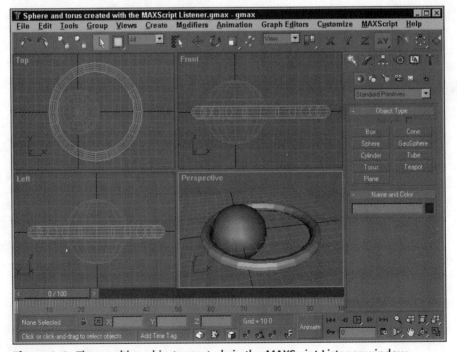

Figure 8-6: The resulting objects created via the MAXScript Listener window

An important thing to understand from this tutorial is that you can do almost anything with MAXScript. Any property of any object that you can access via a rollout is also available via MAXScript. You could go so far as to create entire scenes using just MAXScript, although the real power comes from using MAXScript to do things for you automatically.

Tip

gmax remembers the value of the last MAXScript command that it executed, and you can access that value through a special variable: ? (a question mark). For example, if you type **5 + 5** in the Listener window, gmax displays the result, 10. You can then use that result in your next MAXScript command by using the question mark variable. For example, you can type **$Torus01.radius2 = ?,** and gmax internally substitutes the question mark with the number 10.

At the left end of the status bar, you can access the MAXScript Mini Listener control by dragging the left edge of the status bar to the right. By right-clicking in this control, you can open a Listener window and view all the current commands recorded by the Listener. Figure 8-7 shows this control.

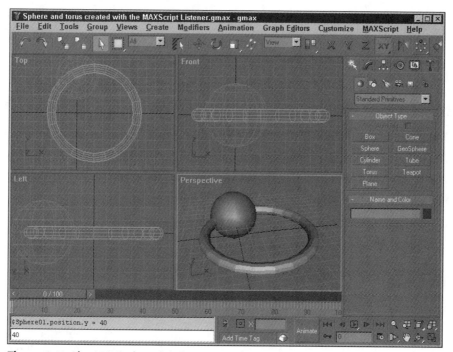

Figure 8-7: The MAXScript Mini Listener on the status bar provides quick access.

MAXScript editor windows

The MAXScript Editor window enables you to open and edit any type of text file, although its most common use is for editing MAXScript files. Although you can have only one Listener window open, you can open as many editor windows as you want.

To open a new MaxScript editor window, you can choose MAXScript ⇨ New Script from the menu bar, choose File ⇨ New from the MAXScript Listener window, or click the New Script button in the MAXScript rollout in the Utility panel. You can also use MAXScript editor windows to edit existing scripts.

For creating a new script, opening both an editor window and the Listener window is usually best. Then you can try out things in the Listener window, and when the pieces of the MAXScript work, you can cut and paste them into the main editor window. Then you can return to the Listener window, work on the next new thing, and continue creating, cutting, and pasting until the script is finished.

 Tip   You can also send text back to the Listener window for gmax to evaluate. Just select some text with the cursor or mouse, and press Shift+Enter (or just Enter on the numeric keypad). gmax copies the selected text to the Listener window and evaluates it for you.

The File, Search, and Help menus in the MAXScript editor window are the same as those used for the Listener window, with the exception of the Evaluate All command. This command (choose File ⇨ Evaluate All to access it or you can use the Ctrl+E keyboard shortcut) is a fast way of having gmax evaluate your entire script. The result is the same as if you had manually selected the entire text, copied it to the Listener window, and pressed Enter.

The Edit menu includes commands to Undo (Ctrl+Z), Cut (Ctrl+X), Copy (Ctrl+C), Paste (Ctrl+V), or Delete (Delete) text. It also includes access to the Visual MAXScript window with the New Rollout and Edit Rollout (F2) menu commands. The pop-up menu also includes a command to Select All (Ctrl+A). You can also access this menu as a pop-up menu by right-clicking in the window.

The Macro Recorder

The MAXScript Macro Recorder is a tool that records your actions and creates a MAXScript that can be recalled to duplicate those actions. Using the Macro Recorder is not only a quick and easy way to write entire scripts, but it is also a great way to make a working version of a script that you can then refine. After the Macro Recorder has created a MAXScript from your recorded actions, you can edit the script using a MAXScript editor window to make any changes you want.

You can turn the Macro Recorder on and off either by choosing MAXScript ⇨ Macro Recorder or by choosing Macro Recorder ⇨ Enable in the MAXScript Listener window. The check mark next to the Macro Recorder command on the MAXScript menu indicates that the Macro Recorder is turned on.

When the Macro Recorder is on, every action is converted to MAXScript and sent to the MAXScript Listener window's top pane. You can then take the MAXScript output and save it to a file or copy it to a MAXScript editor window for additional editing. The Macro Recorder continues to monitor your actions until you turn it off, which is done in the same way as turning it on.

The MacroRecorder menu in the MAXScript Listener window includes several options for customizing the macro recorder including

✦ **Enable:** This option turns the Macro Recorder on or off.

✦ **Explicit scene object names:** With this option, the Macro Recorder writes the MAXScript using the names of the objects you modify so that the script always modifies those exact same objects, regardless of what object you have selected when you run the script again. For example, if the Macro Recorder watches you move a pyramid named $Pyramid01 in your scene, then the resulting MAXScript always and only operates on the scene object named $Pyramid01.

✦ **Selection-relative scene object names:** With this option, the Macro Recorder writes MAXScript that operates on whatever object is currently selected. So if (when you recorded your script) you moved the pyramid named $Pyramid01, you can later select a different object and run your script, and the new object moves instead.

Note

To decide which of these options to use, ask yourself, "Do I want the script to always manipulate this particular object, or do I want the script to manipulate whatever I have selected?"

✦ **Absolute transform assignments:** This tells the Macro Recorder that any transformations you make are not relative to an object's current position or orientation. For example, if you move a sphere from (0,0,0) to (10,0,0), the Macro Recorder writes MAXScript that says, "Move the object to (10,0,0)."

✦ **Relative transforms operations:** Use this option to have the Macro Recorder apply transformations relative to an object's current state. For example, if you move a sphere from (0,0,0) to (10,0,0), the Macro Recorder says, "Move the object +10 units in the X-direction from its current location."

✦ **Explicit subobject sets:** If you choose this option and then record a script that manipulates a set of subobjects, running the script again always manipulates those same subobjects, even if you have other subobjects selected when you run the script again.

✦ **Selection-relative subobject sets:** This tells the Macro Recorder that you want the script to operate on whatever subobjects are selected when you run the script.

✦ **Show command panel switchings:** This option tells the Macro Recorder whether or not to write MAXScript for actions that take place on the Command Panel.

✦ **Show tool selections:** If this option is selected, the Macro Recorder records MAXScript to change to different tools.

✦ **Show menu item selections:** This option tells the Macro Recorder whether or not you want it to generate MAXScript for menu items you select while recording your script.

Tutorial: Recording a simple script

If you plan on using some actions over and over, recording the actions and saving them as a script that can be reused as needed makes good sense. In this tutorial, we'll record a simple script that slices an object in half and separates the halves.

To create a script using the Macro Recorder, follow these steps:

1. Open the slicing soda and firecracker.gmax file from the Chap 08 directory on the CD-ROM.

   This file includes two objects created by Zygote Media—a soda can and a firecracker.

2. With the soda can object selected, choose MAXScript ➪ MAXScript Listener (or press F11) to open the MAXScript Listener window.

3. In the Listener window, open the MacroRecorder menu and make sure that all the options are set to the relative and not the absolute object settings, thereby telling the script to work on any object that is selected instead of always modifying the same object.

4. Returning to the MacroRecorder menu, select Enable.

   The Macro Recorder is now on and ready to start writing MAXScript.

5. Minimize the Macro Recorder window (or at least move it out of the way so you can see the other viewports).

6. Select the Modifiers ➪ Parametric Deformers ➪ Slice to apply the slice modifier to the soda can. In the Slice Parameters rollout, select the Remove Top option.

7. Select the Edit ➪ Clone option to create a copy of the soda can. Accept the defaults in the Copy Object dialog box that appears.

8. Click the Select and Move button on the main toolbar, and drag the cloned soda can to the left.

9. For the cloned soda can object, enable the Remove Bottom option in the Modify panel.

10. The script is done, so in the MAXScript Listener window, choose MacroRecorder ➪ Enable to turn off the Macro Recorder.

11. Now it's time to try out your first MAXScript effort. Select the firecracker object.

12. In the top pane of the MAXScript Listener window, select all the text (an easy way to do so is by pressing Ctrl+A), and then press Shift+Enter to tell gmax to execute the MAXScript.

In Figure 8-8, you can see the script that has been recorded in the MAXScript Listener window.

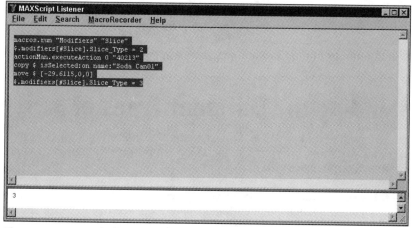

Figure 8-8: Recorded commands for the "slice and separate" script

Figure 8-9 shows the resulting objects sliced and separated. As a final step, the recorded script was copied to a new script window and saved as "Slice and separate.ms." This file can be recalled easily and used as needed.

Figure 8-9: The results of the "slice and separate" script on two different objects

Understanding the Different Types of Scripts

All scripts are not created equal, and gmax categorizes different scripts based on how they work. For more information, the MAXScript online help provides exhaustive information on their various options.

The main thing to consider when deciding what type of script to create is the user interface. Ask yourself what the most logical user interface would be for the type of tool you're creating, and this will give you a hint as to which type of script is well suited for the task.

Macro scripts

Macro scripts are scripts created with the Macro Recorder. Any script that is associated with a toolbar button is considered a Macro script. gmax organizes Macro scripts by their category, which you can change by editing the script file. To call a Macro script from another script, you can use the `macros` command. For example,

```
macros.run "objects" "sphere"
```

runs the "sphere" script in the "objects" category.

Macro scripts are generally scripts that require no other user input; you just click a button and the script works its magic.

Scripted utilities

A scripted utility is a MAXScript that has its own custom rollout in the Utilities panel, like the SphereArray example. This type of script is particularly useful when your script has parameters that the user needs to enter, such as the radius in the SphereArray script. Scripted utilities are easy to build using the Visual MAXScript editor, which is covered later in this chapter.

Scripted right-click menus

When you right-click an object in your scene, gmax opens a pop-up menu of options for you to choose from, much like a quadmenu. Scripted right-click menus let you append your own menu items to the right-click menu. If you create a script that modifies some property of an object, making the script available through the right-click menu makes it easily accessible.

Scripted mouse tools

You can use scripted mouse tools to create scripts that handle mouse input in the viewports. These scripts listen for commands from the mouse, such as clicking the mouse buttons and clicking and dragging the cursor. For example, you would use this type of MAXScript if you were making a new primitive object type so that users could create the new objects just like they would a sphere or a box.

Writing Your Own MAXScripts

This section presents the basics of the MAXScript language and shows you how to use the various parts of MAXScript in your own scripts. You can test any of these scripting commands using the MAXScript Listener window.

 Much of the discussion that follows will sound familiar if you've already read the chapter on expressions – Chapter 22, "Creating Automatic Actions with Controllers." Expressions use many of the same constructs as MAXScript.

Variables and data types

A *variable* in MAXScript is sort of like a variable in algebra. It represents some other value, and when you mention a variable in an equation you're actually talking about the value that the variable holds. You can think of variables in MAXScript as containers that you can put stuff into and take it out of later. Unlike variables in algebra, however, variables in MAXScript can "hold" other things besides numbers, as we'll soon see.

To put a value into a variable, you use the equal sign. For example, if you type

```
X = 5 * 3
```

in the MAXScript Listener window, gmax evaluates the expression on the right side of the equal sign and stores the result in the variable named X. In this case, gmax multiplies 5 by 3 and stores the result (15) into X. You can then see what is in X by just typing **X** in the Listener window and pressing Enter. gmax then displays the value stored in X, or 15.

You can name your variables whatever you want, and naming them something that helps you remember what the variable is for is a good idea. For example, if you want a variable that keeps track of how many objects you're going to manipulate, the name "objCount" is better than something like "Z."

Note   Variable names can be just about anything you want, but you must start a variable name with a letter. Also, the variable name can't have any special characters in it, like spaces, commas, or quotation marks. You can, however, use the underscore character and any normal alphabetic characters.

Variables can also hold strings, which are groups of characters. For example,

```
badDay = "Monday"
```

stores the word "Monday" in the variable `badDay`. You can attach two strings together using the plus sign, like this:

```
grouchy = "My least favorite day is" + badDay
```

Now the variable `grouchy` holds the value "My least favorite day is Monday."

Try this:

```
wontWork = 5 + "cheese"
```

gmax prints an error because it's confused—you're asking it to add a number to a string. The problem is that "5" and "cheese" are two different data types. Data types are different classes of values that you can store in variables. You can almost always mix values of the same data type, but values of different types usually don't make sense together.

Note To see the data type of a variable, use the `classof` command. Using the previous example, you could type **classof grouchy** and gmax would in turn print `String`.

Another very common data type is Point3, which represents a three-dimensional point. Following are a few examples of using points, with explanatory comments:

```
Pos = [5,3,2]          -- Marks a point at (5,3,2)
Pos.x = 7              -- Changes the x-coordinate to 7
                       -- Now the point is at (7,3,2)
Pos = Pos + (1,2,5)    -- Takes the old value for Pos,
                       -- moves it by (1,2,5) to (8,5,7)
                       -- and stores the new value in Pos
```

In addition to these basic data types, each object in your scene has its own data type. For example, if you use `classof` on a sphere object, gmax prints `Sphere`. Data types for scene objects are actually complex data types or structures, which means that they are groups of other data types in a single unit. The pieces of data inside a larger object are called *members* or *properties*. Most scene objects have a member called Name, which is of type String. The Name member tells the specific name of that object. Another common property is Position, a Point3 variable that tells the object's position.

gmax has a special built-in variable that represents whatever object is currently selected. This variable is $ (the dollar sign), which is used in the following tutorial.

Tutorial: Using variables

In this tutorial, you learn more about variables in MAXScript by using them to manipulate an object in your scene.

To use variables to manipulate scene objects, follow these steps:

1. Open the Teapot.gmax file from the Chap 08 directory on the CD-ROM.

   This file has a simple teapot object.

2. Right-click on the title for the Left viewport, and choose Views ⇨ Extended ⇨ MAXScript Listener to open the MAXScript Listener window in the Left viewport.

3. Select the teapot, type **$,** and press Enter.

   gmax displays information about the teapot. (Your numbers may be different, depending on where you placed your teapot.)

4. Type the following lines one at a time to see the property values stored as part of the teapot object:

```
$.position
$.wirecolor
$.radius
$.name
$.lid
```

5. Now type these lines, one at a time, to set the property values of the teapot object:

```
$.lid = false
$.segs = 5
```

Figure 8-10 shows the commands and their results in the MAXScript Listener window and also the resulting teapot object.

Figure 8-10: The script commands entered in the MAXScript Listener affect the objects in the viewports.

Program flow and comments

In general, when gmax begins executing a script, it starts with the first line of the script, processes it, and then moves on to the next line. Execution of the script continues until no more lines are in the script file. (Later, we look at some MAXScript keywords that let you change the flow of script execution.)

gmax lets you embed comments or notes in your script file to help explain what is happening. To insert a comment, precede it with two hyphens (--). When gmax encounters the double hyphen, it skips the comment and everything else on that line and moves to the next line of the script. For example, in this line of MAXScript

```
$Torus01.pos = [0,0,0]    -- Moves it back to the origin
```

gmax processes the first part of the line (and moves the object to the origin) and then moves on to the next line after it reaches the comment.

Using comments in your MAXScript files is very important because after your scripts start to become complex, figuring out what is happening can get difficult. Also, when you come back a few months later to improve your script, comments will refresh your memory and help keep you from repeating the same mistakes you made the first time around.

Note Because gmax ignores anything after the double hyphen, you can use comments to temporarily remove MAXScript lines from your script. If something isn't working right, you can *comment out* the lines that you want gmax to skip. Later, when you want to add them back in, you don't have to retype them. You can just remove the comment marks, and your script is back to normal.

Expressions

An *expression* is what gmax uses to make decisions. An expression compares two things and draws a simple conclusion based on that comparison.

Cross-Reference These same expressions can be used within the Expression controller. You can find details on this controller in Chapter 22, "Creating Automatic Actions with Controllers."

Simple expressions

The expression

```
1 < 2
```

is a simple expression that asks the question, "Is 1 less than 2?" Expressions always ask yes/no type questions. When you type an expression in the MAXScript Listener window (or inside of a script), gmax evaluates the expression and prints `true` if the expression is valid (like the preceding example) and `false` if it isn't. Try the following expressions in the Listener window; gmax prints the results as shown in Figure 8-11 (you don't have to type the comments):

```
1 < 2              -- 1 IS less than 2, so expression is true
1 > 2              -- 1 is NOT greater than 2, so false
2 + 2 == 4         -- '==' means "is equal to". 2 + 2 is
                   -- equal to 4, so true
2 + 2 == 5         -- 4 is NOT equal to 5, so false
3 * 3 == 5 + 4     -- 9 IS equal to 9, so true

3 * 3 != 5 + 4     -- '!=' means "not equal to". "9 is not
                   -- equal to 9" is a false statement, so
                   -- the expression is false

a = 23             -- store 23 in variable a
b = 14 + 9         -- store 23 in variable b
a == b             -- 23 IS equal to 23, so true
```

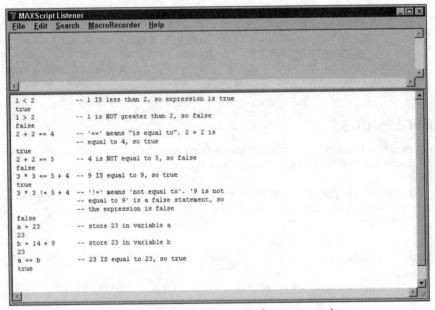

Figure 8-11: Using the MAXScript Listener to evaluate expressions

Play around with simple expressions until you're familiar with what they mean and have an intuitive feel for whether an expression is going to evaluate to true or false.

Complex expressions

Sometimes, you need an expression to decide on more than just two pieces of data. MAXScript has the and, or, and not operators to help you do this.

The and operator combines two expressions and asks the question, "Are both expressions true?" If both are true, then the entire expression evaluates to true. But if either is false, or if they are both false, then the entire expression is false. You can use parentheses to group expressions, so an expression with the and operator might look something like this:

```
(1 < 2) and (1 < 3)      -- true because (1 < 2) is true AND
                         -- (1 < 3) is true
```

The or operator is similar to and, except that an expression with or is true if either of the expressions is true or if both are true. Here are some examples:

```
(2 > 3) or (2 > 1)       -- even though (2 > 3) is false, the
                         -- entire expression is true because
                         -- (2 > 1) is true
(2 > 3) and (2 > 1)      -- false because both expressions are
                         -- not true
```

Try some of these complex expressions to make sure you understand how they work:

```
a = 3
b = 2
(a == b) or (a > b)      -- true because a IS greater than b
(a == b) and (b == 2)    -- false because both expressions are
                         -- not true
(a > b) or (a < b)       -- true because at least one IS true
(a != b) and (b == 3)    -- false because b is NOT equal to 3
```

The not operator negates or flips the value of an expression from true to false or vice versa. For example

```
(1 == 2)                 -- false because 1 is NOT equal to 2
not (1 == 2)             -- true. 'not' flips the false to true
```

Conditions

Conditions are one way in which you can control program flow in a script. Normally, gmax processes each line, no matter what, and then quits; but with *conditions*, gmax executes certain lines only if an expression is true.

For example, suppose you have a script with the following lines:

```
a = 4
If (a == 5) then
(
   b = 2
)
```

gmax would not execute the line b = 2 because the expression (a == 5) evaluates to false. Conditional statements, or "if" statements, basically say, "If this expression evaluates to true, then do the stuff inside the block of parentheses. If the expression evaluates to false, skip those lines of script."

Conditional statements follow this form:

```
If <expr> then <stuff>
```

where <expr> is an expression to evaluate and <stuff> is some MAXScript to execute if the expression evaluates to true. You can also use the keyword else to specify what happens if the expression evaluates to false, as shown in the following example:

```
a = 4
if (a == 5) then
(
  b = 2
)
else
(
  b = 3
)
```

After this block of MAXScript, the variable b would have the value of 3 because the expression (a == 5) evaluated to false. Consequently, gmax executed the MAXScript in the else section of the statement.

Collections and arrays

MAXScript has some very useful features to help you manipulate groups of objects. A group of objects is called a *collection*. You can think of a collection as a bag that holds a bunch of objects or variables. The things in the bag are in no particular order; they're just grouped together.

You can use collections to work with groups of a particular type of object. For example, the MAXScript

```
a = $pokey*
a.wirecolor = red
```

creates a collection that contains every object in your scene whose name starts with "Pokey" and makes every object in that collection turn red.

MAXScript has several built-in collections that you might find useful, such as cameras and lights, containing all the cameras and lights in your scene. So

```
delete lights
```

removes all the light objects from your scene (which may or may not be a good idea).

An *array* is a type of collection in which all the objects are in a fixed order, and you can access each member of the array by an index. For example

```
a = #()      -- creates an empty array to use
a[1] = 5
a[2] = 10
a[5] = 12
a
```

After the last line, gmax prints the current value for the array:

```
#(5, 10, undefined, undefined, 12)
```

Notice that gmax makes the array big enough to hold as many elements as we want to put in it, and that if we don't put anything in one of the positions, gmax automatically inserts undefined, which simply means that array location has no value at all.

One last useful trick is that gmax lets you use the as keyword to convert from a collection to an array:

```
LightArray = (lights as array)
```

gmax takes the built-in collection of lights, converts it to an array, and names the array LightArray.

The members of an array or a collection don't all have to have the same data type, so it's completely valid to have an array with numbers, strings, and objects, like this:

```
A = #(5,"Mr. Nutty",box radius:5)
```

Note   You can use the as MAXScript keyword to convert between data types. For example, (5 as string) converts the number 5 to the string "5," and (5 as float) converts the whole number 5 to the floating-point number 5.0.

Loops

A *loop* is a MAXScript construct that lets you override the normal flow of execution. Instead of processing each line in your script once and then quitting, gmax can use loops to do something several times.

For example,

```
j = 0
for i = 1 to 5 do
(
  j = j + i
)
```

This MAXScript uses two variables — i and j — but you can use any variables you want in your loops. The script sets the variable j to 0 and then uses the variable i to count from 1 to 5. gmax repeats the code between the parentheses five times, and each time the variable i is incremented by 1. Inside the loop, gmax adds the current value of i to j. Can you figure out what the value of j is at the end of the script? If you guessed 15, you're right. To see why, look at the value of each variable as the script is running:

```
When                    j    i
----------------------------
First line              0    0
Start of loop           0    1
After first loop        1    1
Start of second loop    1    2
After second loop       3    2
Start of third loop     3    3
After third loop        6    3
Start of fourth loop    6    4
After fourth loop       10   4
Start of fifth loop     10   5
After fifth loop        15   5
```

A loop is also useful for processing each member of an array or collection. The following MAXScript shows one way to turn every teapot in a scene blue:

```
teapots = $teapot*          -- gets the collection of teapots
for singleTeapot in teapots do
(
  singleTeapot.wirecolor = blue
)
```

You can use a for loop to create a bunch of objects for you. Try this MAXScript:

```
for I = 1 to 10 collect
  (
  sphere radius:15
  )
```

The `collect` keyword tells gmax to create a collection with the results of the MAXScript in the block of code inside the parentheses. The line

```
sphere radius:15
```

tells gmax to create a sphere with a radius of 15, so the entire script created 10 spheres and added them to your scene. Unfortunately, gmax puts them all in the same spot, so let's move them around a bit so we can see them:

```
i = -50
For s in spheres do
(
  s.position = [i,i,i]
  i = i + 10
)
```

Study this script to make sure you understand what's going on. We use a `for` loop to process each sphere in our collection of spheres. For each one, we set its position to [i,i,i], and then we change the value of i so that the next sphere will be at a different location.

Functions

The last feature of basic MAXScript that we look at here is the *function*. Functions are small chunks of MAXScript that act like program building blocks. For example, suppose you need to compute the average of a collection of numbers many times during a script you're writing. The MAXScript to do this might be

```
Total = 0
Count = 0
For n in numbers do
(
  total = total + n
  count = count + 1
)
average = total / (count as float)
```

Given a collection of numbers called `numbers`, this MAXScript computes the average. Unfortunately, every time you need to compute the average, you have to type all that MAXScript again. Or you might be smart and just cut and paste it each time you need it. Still, your script is quickly becoming large and ugly, and you always have to change the script to match the name of the collection you're averaging.

A function solves your problem. At the beginning of your script, you can define an average function like this:

```
Function average numbers =
( -- Function to average the numbers in a collection
  local Total = 0
  local Count = 0
```

```
For n in numbers do
(
total = total + n
count = count + 1
)
total / (count as float)
)
```

Now, any time you need to average any collection of numbers in your script, you could just use this to take all the numbers in the collection called num and store their average in a variable called Ave:

```
Ave = average num        -- assuming num is a collection
```

Not only does this make your script much shorter if you need to average numbers often, but it makes it much more readable, too. It's very clear to the casual reader that you're going to average some numbers. Also, if you later realize that you wrote the average function incorrectly, you can just fix it at the top of the script. If you weren't using functions, you would have to go through your script and find every case where you averaged numbers and then fix the problem. (What a headache!)

Let's take another look at the function definition. The first line

```
Function average numbers =
```

tells gmax that you're creating a new function called average. It also tells gmax that, to use this function, you have to pass in one piece of data and that, inside the function, you'll refer to that data using a variable called numbers. It doesn't matter what the name of the actual variable was when the function was called; inside the function, you can simply refer to it as numbers.

Creating functions that use multiple pieces of data is also easy. For example,

```
Function multEm a b c = (a * b * c)
```

creates a function that multiplies three numbers together. To use this function to multiply three numbers and store the result in a variable called B, you would simply enter

```
B = multEm 2 3 4
```

The next two lines

```
local Total = 0
local Count = 0
```

create two variables and set them both to 0. The local keyword tells gmax that the variable belongs to this function. No part of the script outside of the function can see this variable, and if there is a variable outside the function with the same name, changing the variable inside this function won't affect that variable outside the function. That way, you never have to worry about what other variables are in use when someone calls average; even if variables are in use that are named Total or Count, they won't be affected.

The last line

```
total / (count as float)
```

uses the Total and Count values to compute the average. How does that value get sent back to whoever called the function? gmax evaluates all the MAXScript inside the function and returns the result. Because the last line is the last thing to be evaluated, gmax uses the result of that calculation as the result of the entire function.

Tutorial: Creating a school of fish

Let's look at an example that puts into practice some of the things you've been learning in this chapter. In this multipart tutorial, we use MAXScript to create a small school of fish that follows the dummy object around the path.

Part 1: Making the fish follow a path

In this part of the tutorial, we use MAXScript to move one of the fish along a path in the scene. To do this, follow these steps:

1. Open the Fish scene.gmax file from the Chap 08 directory on the CD-ROM.

   This scene consists of two fish and a dummy object that follows a path. We need to use MAXScript to create a small school of fish that follows the dummy object around the path.

2. Press F11 to open the MAXScript Listener window. In the window, choose File ➪ New Script to open the MAXScript editor window, and type the following script:

```
pathObj = $Dummy01
fishObj = $Fish1/FishBody
relPos = [5075,0]    -- How close the fish is to the path

animate on
(
  for t = 1 to 100 do at time t
  (
  fishObj.position = pathObj.position + relPos
  )
)
```

3. Choose File ➪ Evaluate All (or press Ctrl+E) to evaluate all the MAXScript in the editor window, right-click the Camera01 viewport to activate it, and click the Play Animation button.

   The fish rigidly follows the dummy object's path. Figure 8-12 shows one frame of this animation.

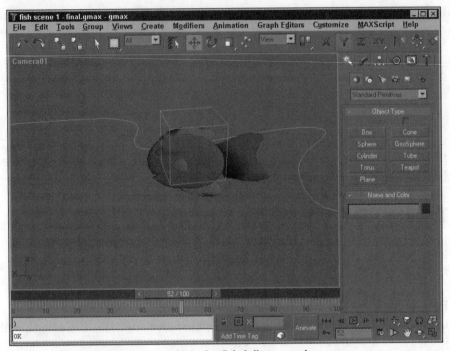

Figure 8-12: First attempt at making the fish follow a path

Now, let me explain the MAXScript entered in the previous tutorial. The first few lines create some variables that the rest of the script uses. pathObj tells the name of the object that the fish will follow, and fishObj is the name of the fish's body. (Notice that we can reference parts of the group hierarchy by using the object name, a forward slash, and then a child part.) Why bother creating a variable for the fish object? After we get this first fish working, we want to apply the same script to another fish. All we'll have to do is rename Fish1 as Fish2, re-execute the script, and we're finished!

The script also creates a variable called relPos, which we use to refer to the relative position of the fish with respect to the dummy object. If we have several fish in the scene, we don't want them all in the exact same spot, so this is an easy way to position each one.

The next block of MAXScript is new: We're using the animate on construct. This tells gmax to generate key frames for our animation. It's the same as if we had pressed gmax's Animation button, run our script, and then shut Animation off. So, any MAXScript inside the animate on parentheses creates animation key frames. These parentheses define a section of the script that we call a block.

Inside the animation block, we have a loop that counts from 1 to 100 (corresponding to each frame of our animation). On the end of the loop line we have at time t, which tells gmax that for each time through the loop, we want all the variables to have whatever values they'll have at that time. For example, if we want the fish to follow the dummy object, we have to know the position of the object at each point in time instead of just at the beginning, so each time through the loop, gmax figures out for us where the dummy object is.

Inside the loop, we set the fish's object to be that of the dummy object (at that point in time) and then adjust the fish's position by relPos.

Part 2: Adding body rotation

Let's make that fish look a little more lifelike by rotating its body to actually follow the path. Also, we'll add a little unpredictability to its motion so that when we add other fish, they won't be exact copies of each other.

To improve the fish's animation, follow these steps:

1. Type the revised version of the script (the new lines are in bold):

```
pathObj = $Dummy01
fishObj = $Fish1/FishBody
fishTail = $Fish1/FishBody/FishTail
relPos = [0,-150,-50]  -- How close the fish is to the path

zadd = 4                    -- vertical movement at each step
animate on
(
 for t = 0 to 100 do at time t
 (
  fishObj.position = pathObj.position + relPos
  fishObj.position.z = relPos.z
  relPos.z += zadd

  -- let's say that there's a 10% chance that the fish
  -- will change directions vertically
  if ((random 1 100) > 90) then
  (
   zadd = -zadd
  )

    oldRt = fishObj.rotation.z_rotation
 newRt = (in coordsys pathObj pathObj.rotation.z_rotation)

  if ((random 1 100) > 85) then
  (
   fishObj.rotation.z_rotation += (newRt - oldRt) *
   (random 0.5 1.5)
  )
 )
)
```

2. Save your script (File ⇨ Save), and then press Ctrl+E to evaluate the script again.

This script is saved in the Chap 08 directory as FishPath2.ms.

3. Make the Camera01 viewport active, and click Play Animation.

Figure 8-13 shows another frame of the animation. As you can see, the fish is heading in the right direction this time, and the tail is flapping wildly.

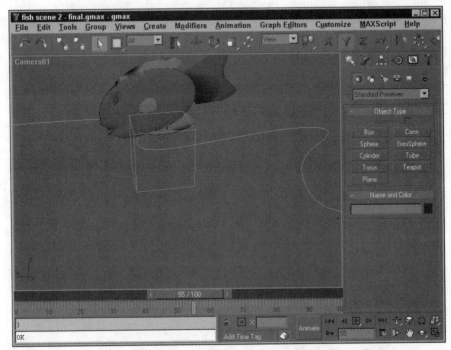

Figure 8-13: A fish that faces the right direction as it follows the path

Okay, let's look at what changed. First, we created some more variables. We use zadd to tell gmax how much to move the fish in the Z direction at each step (we don't want our fish to always swim at the same level).

Inside the for loop, notice that we've overridden the fish's Z-position and replaced it with just the relative Z-position, so that each fish will swim at its own depth and not the dummy object's depth. Then, at each step we add zadd to the Z-position so that the fish changes depth slowly. We have to be careful, or our fish will continue to climb out of the scene or run into the ground, so at each step we also choose a random number between 1 and 100 with the function (random 1 100). If the random number that gmax picks is greater than 90, we flip the sign of zadd so that the fish starts moving in the other direction. This is a fancy way of saying, "There's a 90 percent chance that the fish will continue moving in the same direction and a 10 percent chance that it will switch directions."

The only thing left for us to do is to make the fish "follow" the path; that is, rotate its body so that it's facing the direction it's moving. The simplest way to do this is to use the following MAXScript (split into two lines to make it easier to read):

```
newRt = (in coordsys pathObj pathObj.rotation.z_rotation)
fishObj.rotation.z_rotation = newRt
```

The `in coordsys` construct tells gmax to give us a value from the point of view of a particular coordinate system. Instead of `pathObj`, we could have asked for the Z-rotation in the world, local, screen, or parent coordinate system, too. In this case, we want to rotate the fish in the same coordinate system as the dummy object. In order to randomize the direction of the fish a little, we've made the rotation a little more complex:

```
oldRt = fishObj.rotation.z_rotation
newRt = (in coordsys pathObj pathObj.rotation.z_rotation)

if ((random 1 100) > 85) then
(
  fishObj.rotation.z_rotation += (newRt - oldRt) *
                                  (random 0.5 1.5)
)
```

First, we save the old Z-rotation in `oldRt`, and then we put the new rotation in `newRt`. Again we pick a random number to decide whether we'll do something; in this case we're saying, "There's an 85 percent chance we won't change directions at all." If our random number does fall in that other 15 percent, however, we adjust the fish's rotation a little. We take the difference between the new rotation and the old rotation and multiply it by a random number between 0.5 and 1.5, which means we'll adjust the rotation by anywhere from 50 percent to 150 percent of the difference between the two rotations. So any fish will basically follow the same path, but with a little variation here and there.

Note gmax lets you use shorthand when adjusting the values of variables. Instead of saying `a = a + b`, you can just say `a += b`. Both have the same effect.

Part 3: Animating the second fish

This scene actually has two fish in it (the other one has been sitting patiently off to the side), so for the final part of this tutorial, we'll get both fish involved in the animation. To animate the second fish alongside the first one, follow these steps:

1. At the top of the script, change these three lines (what changed is bolded):

```
pathObj = $Dummy01
fishObj = $Fish2/FishBody
relPos = [0,-150,-50]    -- How close the fish is to the path
```

2. Choose File ⇨ Evaluate All (or press Ctrl+E) to run the script again, and then animate it.

Figure 8-14 shows both fish swimming merrily.

This script generates key frames for the second fish because we changed the fishObj and fishTail variables to refer to the second fish. We've also moved the second fish's relative position so that the two don't run into each other.

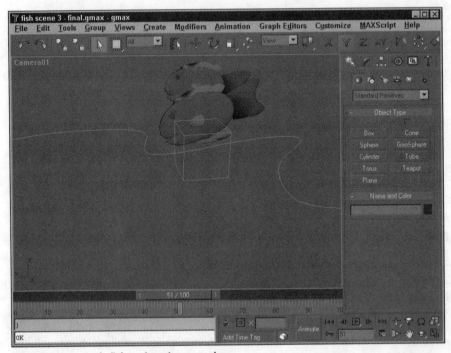

Figure 8-14: Both fish swimming together

Using the Visual MAXScript Editor

Building scripts can be complicated, and piecing together a rollout for a scripted utility can be especially time-consuming and frustrating when done by hand. To help create such custom rollouts, Max includes the Visual MAXScript editor. Using this editor, you can drag and drop rollout elements and automatically create a code skeleton for certain events.

Working with textual commands can be time-consuming. In order for the script to work, you need to enter the commands exactly. This can be especially tricky when you're trying to lay out the controls for a rollout. Max includes a tool that speeds up the creation of rollouts called the Visual MAXScript editor.

To access the Visual MAXScript window, shown in Figure 8-15, open the Utility panel in the Command Panel and click the More button. Then select the Visual MAXScript option from the list of utilities, and click OK. Another way to access this window is to select Edit ➪ New Rollout or Edit Rollout (F2) in the MAXScript editor window.

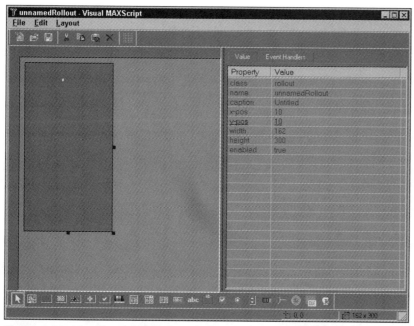

Figure 8-15: The Visual MAXScript window makes building rollouts easy.

Layouts for a rollout created in the Visual MAXScript window can be saved as files with the .vms extension using the File menu. If you access the window from a MAXScript editor window, the Save menu automatically updates the editor window.

The editor interface

The editor window includes two major panes. The left pane is where the various rollout elements are assembled, and the right pane holds the Value and Event Handlers tabbed panels. The Value panel lists all the properties and their associated values for the selected element. You can change the property values by clicking on them and entering a new value. For example, if you select a Button element in the left panel, then the properties for that control are presented in the Value panel. If you click the Caption Property, its value becomes highlighted; you can type a new caption, and the new caption appears on the button.

The Event Handlers panel lists all the available events that can be associated with the selected element. Clicking the check box to the left of an event can enable the event. For a button element, you can enable the pressed event. With this event enabled, the code includes a function where you can define what happens when this event is fired.

The menus and the main toolbar

At the top of the interface are some menu options and a main toolbar. The File menu also lets you create a new layout (Ctrl+N), save (Ctrl+S) layouts to a file, and open saved layouts (Ctrl+O). The Edit menu allows you to cut (Ctrl+X), copy (Ctrl+C), and paste (Ctrl+V) form elements. You can find these same features as buttons on the top toolbar.

The Layout menu includes options for aligning elements left (Ctrl+left arrow), right (Ctrl+right arrow), top (Ctrl+up arrow), bottom (Ctrl+down arrow), vertical center (F9), and horizontal center (Shift+F9); to space elements evenly across (Alt+right arrow) or down (Alt+up arrow); make elements the same size by width, height, or both; center vertically (Ctrl+F9) or horizontally (Ctrl+Shift+F9) in the dialog box; and flip. You can use the Layout ⇨ Guide Settings menu command to specify grid snapping and spacing. Grids are enabled using the Toggle Grid/Snap button on the right end of the main toolbar.

You can also access these commands using a right-click pop-up menu when clicking on the left pane.

Toolbar elements

The toolbar along the bottom of the window contains the form elements that you can drop on the form. These buttons and elements include those shown in Table 8-1.

<table>
<tr><td colspan="3" align="center">Table 8-1
Visual MAXScript Form Elements</td></tr>
<tr><td>*Button*</td><td>*Element*</td><td>*Description*</td></tr>
<tr><td></td><td>Bitmap</td><td>Lets you add bitmap images to a rollout</td></tr>
<tr><td></td><td>Button</td><td>Adds a simple button</td></tr>
<tr><td></td><td>Map Button</td><td>Adds a mapping button that opens the Material/Map Browser</td></tr>
<tr><td></td><td>Material Button</td><td>Adds a material button that also opens the Material/Map Browser</td></tr>
</table>

Button	Element	Description
	Pick Button	Adds a button that lets you pick an object in a viewport
	Check Button	Adds a button that can be toggled on and off
	Color Picker	Adds a color swatch that opens the Color Picker dialog box when clicked
	Combo Box	Adds a list with several items
	Drop-Down List	Adds a list with one item displayed
	List Box	Adds a list with several items displayed
	Edit Box	Adds a text field that can be modified
	Label	Adds a text label
	Group Box	Adds a grouping outline to surround several controls
	Check Box	Adds a check box control that can be toggled on or off
	Radio Buttons	Adds a set of buttons where only one can be selected
	Spinner	Adds an up and down set of arrows that can modify a value field
	Progress Bar	Adds a bar that highlights from left to right as a function is completed
	Slider	Adds a slider control that can move from a minimum to a maximum value
	Timer	Adds a timer that counts time intervals
	ActiveX Control	Adds a generic ActiveX control created by a separate vendor
	Custom	Adds a custom control that can be defined as needed

At the bottom right of the window are two text fields that display the coordinates of the current mouse cursor position and the size of the rollout. The default size of the rollout is 162×300, which is the size needed to fit perfectly in the Command Panel.

Laying out a rollout

The rollout space, which appears gray in the left pane, can be selected and resized by dragging the black square handles at the edges of the form. As you change its size, its dimensions are displayed in the lower-right corner of the interface. With the rollout space correctly sized, you are ready to add elements to the space.

To add one of these elements to the form, click the element button on the toolbar and drag on the form. The element appears and is selected. The selected element is easy to identify by the black handles that surround it. Dragging on these handles resizes the element, and clicking and dragging on the center of the element repositions it within the rollout space.

The Value and Events panels are automatically updated to show the values and events for the selected element. Values such as width and x-pos are automatically updated if you drag an element or drag its handles to resize it.

Aligning and spacing elements

Although only a single element can be surrounded by black handles at a time, you can actually drag an outline in the rollout space to select multiple elements at once. With several elements selected, you can align them all to the left (Ctlr+left arrow), right (Ctrl+right arrow), top (Ctrl+up arrow), or bottom (Ctrl+down arrow), or you can vertically center (F9) or horizontally center (Shift+F9) all the selected items.

Multiple elements can also be spaced across (Alt+right arrow) or down (Alt+up arrow). To make several elements the same width, height, or both, use Layout ⇨ Make Same Size. The Center in Dialog menu aligns elements to the center of the dialog either vertically (Ctrl+F9) or horizontally (Ctrl+Shift+F9). The Flip command reverses the position of the selected elements.

Figure 8-16 shows a form with several aligned elements added to it.

Tutorial: Building a custom rollout with the Visual MAXScript editor

Now it's time for some practice using this powerful tool. In this example, you'll use the Visual MAXScript window to lay out a rollout and code the script to make it work.

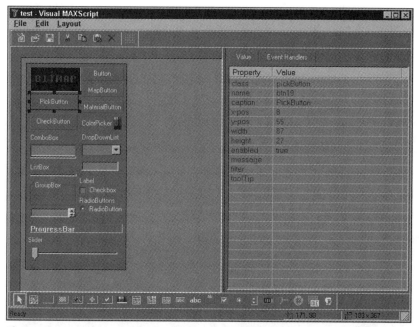

Figure 8-16: You can add control elements to the form in the Visual MAXScript window.

To create a custom rollout using the Visual MAXScript editor, follow these steps:

1. Open the BuildCube.gmax file from the Chap 08 directory on the CD-ROM.

   This file includes a simple sphere object.

2. Choose MAXScript ➪ New Script to open the MAXScript editor window. In the editor window, enter the following:

```
utility buildCube "Build Cube" ( )
```

   This line creates a utility named buildCube. The rollout name will be Build Cube. Make sure to include a space in between the parentheses.

3. Choose Edit ➪ New Rollout from the window menu (or press the F2 key). The Visual MAXScript window opens. The properties for this rollout are displayed in the Properties panel. Drag the lower-right black square handle to resize the rollout form.

4. Click the spinner button on the bottom toolbar, and drag in the rollout form to create a spinner element. In the Properties panel, set the name to SideNum, set the caption value to No. of Side Objects, select the #integer for the type, and set the range to [1,100,5]. The range values set the lower, upper, and default values for the spinner. Then drag on the element handles to resize the element to fit in the form.

5. Click the spinner button again, and drag in the rollout form to create another spinner element. In the Properties panel, set the name to length, set the caption value to Side Length, select the #integer for the type, and set the range to [1,1000,50]. Then drag on the element handles to resize the element to fit in the form.

6. Click the button icon on the bottom toolbar, and drag in the rollout form to create a button below the spinners. In the Properties panel, set the name to **createCube** and the caption value to **Create Cube**. Then drag on the element handles to resize the button so the text fits on the button. Open the Events panel, and select the Pressed check box.

7. Drag over the top of both the spinners to select them both, and choose Layout ➪ Align ➪ Right (or press Ctrl+right arrow) to align the spinners.

Figure 8-17 shows how the rollout layout looks.

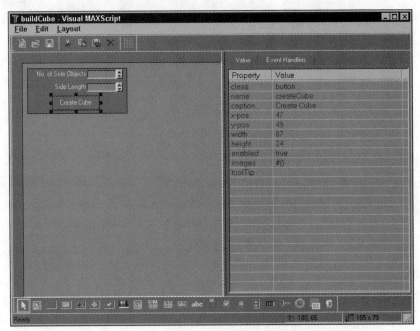

Figure 8-17: The rollout as laid out in the Visual MAXScript window

8. With the layout complete, choose File ➪ Save (or press Ctrl+S) to save the layout and then close the Visual MAXScript window. The script code associated with the layout is placed in the editor window automatically.

9. Complete the script by entering the script commands immediately after the open parenthesis that appears on the line following the `on createCube pressed do` event, as shown in Figure 8-18.

Refer to the BuildCube.ms file from the Chap 08 directory on the CD-ROM to see the entire script.

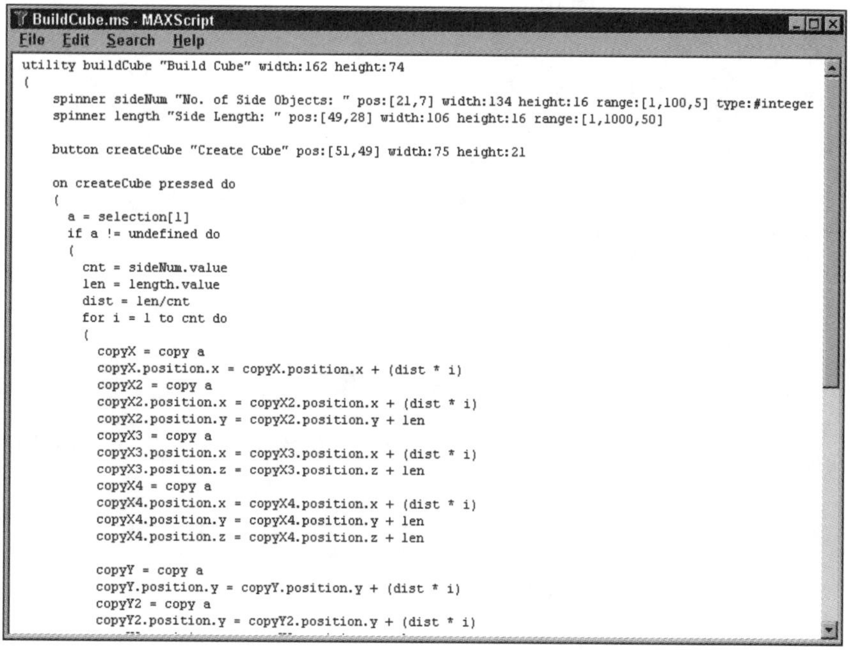

```
BuildCube.ms - MAXScript                                    _ □ ✕
File   Edit   Search   Help

utility buildCube "Build Cube" width:162 height:74
(
    spinner sideNum "No. of Side Objects: " pos:[21,7] width:134 height:16 range:[1,100,5] type:#integer
    spinner length "Side Length: " pos:[49,28] width:106 height:16 range:[1,1000,50]

    button createCube "Create Cube" pos:[51,49] width:75 height:21

    on createCube pressed do
    (
      a = selection[1]
      if a != undefined do
      (
        cnt = sideNum.value
        len = length.value
        dist = len/cnt
        for i = 1 to cnt do
        (
          copyX = copy a
          copyX.position.x = copyX.position.x + (dist * i)
          copyX2 = copy a
          copyX2.position.x = copyX2.position.x + (dist * i)
          copyX2.position.y = copyX2.position.y + len
          copyX3 = copy a
          copyX3.position.x = copyX3.position.x + (dist * i)
          copyX3.position.z = copyX3.position.z + len
          copyX4 = copy a
          copyX4.position.x = copyX4.position.x + (dist * i)
          copyX4.position.y = copyX4.position.y + len
          copyX4.position.z = copyX4.position.z + len

          copyY = copy a
          copyY.position.y = copyY.position.y + (dist * i)
          copyY2 = copy a
          copyY2.position.y = copyY2.position.y + (dist * i)
```

Figure 8-18: The MAXScript editor window is updated with the code from the Visual MAXScript window.

10. Open the Utilities panel, and click the MAXScript button. Then click the Run Script button, and select the BuildCube.ms file from the Chap 08 directory on the CD-ROM.

    The utility installs and appears in the Utility drop-down list in the MAXScript rollout.

11. Select the BuildCube utility from the drop-down list in the MAXScript rollout, and scroll down the Command Panel to see the Build Cube rollout. Select the sphere object, and click the Create Cube button.

    The script executes, and a cube of spheres is created.

Figure 8-19 shows the results of the BuildCube.ms script. You can use this script with any selected object.

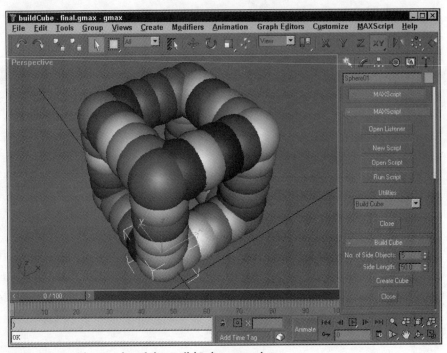

Figure 8-19: The results of the BuildCube.ms script

Summary

This chapter gave you a brief introduction to MAXScript, gmax's powerful, built-in scripting language. Besides describing the different types of scripts you can create, the chapter covered these topics:

✦ Understanding the basics of MAXScript

✦ Using the MAXScript tools such as the MAXScript editor and Listener windows

✦ Using the Macro Recorder to create scripts

✦ Understanding the different script types

✦ Writing your own scripts

✦ Exploring the Visual MAXScript editor interface

✦ Learning the features of each rollout element

✦ Discovering how to create scripted utilities with custom rollouts

The next chapter begins a journey into the world of modeling with gmax. The first stop on this journey is the primitive objects.

✦   ✦   ✦

Building an Empire of Objects

✦ ✦ ✦ ✦

In This Part

Chapter 9
Beginning with the
Basic Building Blocks

Chapter 10
Starting with Simple
Splines and Shapes

Chapter 11
Moving on with
Marvelous Meshes

Chapter 12
Performing with
Perfect Patches

Chapter 13
Continuing with
Crazy Compound
Objects

✦ ✦ ✦ ✦

Beginning with the Basic Building Blocks

In This Chapter

Understanding the modeling types

Working with subobjects and soft selections

Creating primitive objects

Naming objects and setting object colors

Using different creation methods

Setting object parameters

Exploring the various primitive types

Using helper objects

Modeling is the process of pure creation. Whether it is sculpting, building with blocks, construction work, carving, architecture, or advanced injection molding, many different ways exist for creating objects. gmax includes many different model types and even more ways to work with these model types.

This chapter gives you the scoop on modeling and introduces you to many utilities and helpers that, well, help as you begin to model objects.

So what exactly did the Romans use to build their civilization? The answer is lots and lots of basic blocks. The basic building blocks in gmax are primitives. You can use these basic primitives to start any modeling job. I cover bending, stretching, smashing, and cutting these primitives to create new objects in later chapters, but primitives have many uses in their default shape.

This chapter covers the basics of primitive object types and introduces you to the various primitive objects, including how to accurately create and control them. The Ancient Romans would be jealous.

Exploring the Modeling Types

There are many ways to climb a mountain and many ways to model one. You could make a mountain model out of primitive objects like blocks, cubes, and spheres, or you could create one as a polygon mesh. As your experience grows, you'll discover that some objects are easier to model using one method and some are easier using another. gmax offers several different modeling types to handle various modeling situations.

gmax includes the following modeling types:

✦ **Primitives:** Basic parametric shapes such as cubes, spheres, and pyramids.

✦ **Shapes and splines:** Simple vector shapes such as circles, stars, arcs, and text, and splines such as a Helix. These objects can also be made visible to the game engine.

✦ **Meshes:** Complex models created from many polygon faces that are smoothed together when the object is rendered in the game engine.

✦ **Polys:** Objects composed of polygon faces, similar to mesh objects with unique features.

✦ **Patches:** Based on spline curves; patches can be modified using control points.

✦ **Compound objects:** A miscellaneous group of modeling types, including objects such as Boolean, and loft objects.

Shapes and splines are covered in Chapter 10, "Starting with Simple Splines and Shapes," and mesh and poly objects are covered in Chapter 11, "Moving On with Marvelous Meshes." Patches are the topic of Chapter 12, "Performing with Perfect Patches." I cover compound objects in Chapter 13, "Continuing with Crazy Compound Objects."

Converting objects

The Create menu includes submenus for creating primitives and shape objects, and the Create panel includes subcategories and buttons for creating primitives, splines, compound objects, and patches. But you won't find any menus or subcategories for creating mesh or poly objects.

To create one of these object types, you'll need to convert it from another object type. You can convert objects by right-clicking on the object in the viewport and selecting the Convert To submenu from the pop-up quadmenu, or by right-clicking on the object in the Modifier Stack and selecting the object type to convert to in the pop-up menu. Once converted, all the editing features of the selected type will be available in the Modify panel, but the object will no longer be parametric.

Parametric vs. non-parametric

All geometric primitives in gmax are parametric. *Parametric* means that the geometry of the object is controlled by variables called parameters. Modifying these parameters modifies the geometry of the object. This powerful concept gives parametric objects unlimited flexibility. For example, the sphere object has a parameter called Radius. Changing this parameter changes the size of the sphere.

Non-parametric objects do not have this flexibility. After you've created a non-parametric object, you cannot modify it by changing parameters. The editable objects (Editable Spline, Mesh, Poly, or Patch) in gmax are non-parametric and don't have parameters; they rely on modifiers or subobject edits to change their geometry.

When a primitive object is converted to a different object type like an Editable Mesh, it loses its parametric nature and can no longer be changed by altering its parameters. Editable objects do have their advantages, though. You can edit subobjects such as vertices, edges, and faces of meshes — all things that you cannot edit for a parametric object. Each editable object type has a host of functions that are specific to its type. I discuss these functions in the coming chapters.

Note   Several modifiers enable you to edit subobjects while maintaining the parametric nature of an object. These include Edit Patch, Edit Mesh, and Edit Spline.

Working with Subobjects

Most of the editable modeling types offer the ability to work with subobjects. Subobjects are the elements that make up the model and can include vertices, edges, polygons, and elements. These individual subobjects can be selected and transformed just like normal objects using the transformation tools located on the main toolbar. But before you can transform these subobjects, you'll need to select them. You can select subobjects only when you're in a particular subobject mode.

If you expand the object's hierarchy in the Modifier Stack (by clicking on the small plus sign to the left of the object's name), all subobjects for an object are displayed, as shown in Figure 9-1. Selecting a subobject in the Modifier Stack will place you in subobject mode for that subobject type. You can also enter subobject mode by clicking on the subobject icons located at the top of the Selection rollout. When you're in subobject mode, the subobject title is highlighted blue and the icon in the Selection rollout is highlighted yellow. You can work with the selected subobjects only while in subobject mode. To transform the entire object again, you'll need to exit subobject mode, which you can do by clicking either the subobject title or the subobject icon.

Tip   While in subobject mode, you can move between the various subobjects using the 1 through 5 keyboard shortcuts.

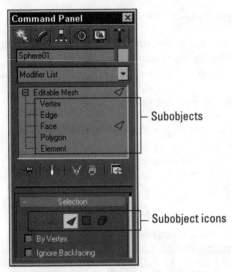

Figure 9-1: Expanding an editable object in the Modifier Stack reveals its subobjects.

Using Soft Selection

When working with mesh, poly, patches, or splines, the Soft Selection rollout, shown in Figure 9-2, becomes available in subobject mode. Soft Selection selects all the subobjects surrounding the current selection and applies transformations to them to a lesser extent. For example, if a face is selected and moved a distance of 2, then with linear Soft Selection, the neighboring faces within the soft selection range will move a distance of 1. The overall effect is a smoother transition.

The Use Soft Selection parameter enables or disables the Soft Selection feature. The Edge Distance option sets the range (the number of edges in the current selection) that Soft Selection will affect. The Affect Backfacing option applies the Soft Selection to selected subobjects on the backside of an object.

The Soft Selection Curve shows a graphical representation of how the Soft Selection is applied. The Falloff value defines the spherical region where the Soft Selection has an effect. The Pinch button sharpens the point at the top of the curve. The Bubble button has an opposite effect and widens the curve. Figure 9-3 shows several sample values and the resulting curve.

Figure 9-2: The Soft Selection rollout is available only in subobject mode.

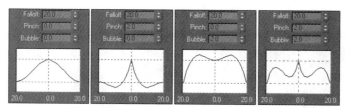

Figure 9-3: The Soft Selection curve is affected by the Falloff, Pinch, and Bubble values.

Tutorial: Soft selecting a heart from a plane

Soft Selection enables a smooth transition between subobjects, but sometimes you'll want the abrupt edge. This tutorial looks at moving some subobject vertices in a plane object with and without Soft Selection enabled.

To move subobject vertices with and without Soft Selection, follow these steps:

1. Open the Soft Selection heart.gmax file from the Chap 09 directory on the CD-ROM.

   This file contains two simple plane objects that have been converted to Editable Meshes. Several vertices in the shape of a heart are selected. The vertices on the first plane object are already selected (or you can select them using a named selection set).

2. In Vertex subobject mode, click the Select and Move button, move the cursor over the selected vertices, and drag upward in the Left viewport away from the plane.

3. Exit subobject mode, select the second plane object, and enter Vertex subobject mode.

   The same vertices will again be selected.

4. Open the Soft Selection rollout, enable the Use Soft Selection option, and set the Falloff value to 40.

5. Click the Select and Move button (or press the W key), and move the selected vertices upward. Notice the difference that Soft Selection makes.

Figure 9-4 shows the two resulting plane objects with the heart selections.

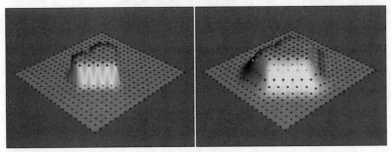

Figure 9-4: Soft Selection makes a smooth transition between the subobjects that are moved and those that are not.

When you select subobjects, they turn red. Non-selected subobjects are blue, and soft selected subobjects are colored a gradient from orange to yellow depending on their distance from the selected subobjects. This visual clue provides valuable feedback on how Soft Selection impacts the subobjects. Figure 9-5 shows the selected vertices from the previous tutorial with Falloff values of 0, 20, 40, 60, and 80.

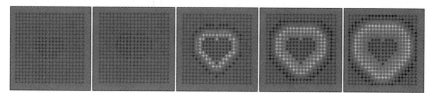

Figure 9-5: A gradient of colors shows the transition zone for soft selected subobjects.

Creating Primitive Objects

In addition to the complex modeling types just mentioned, gmax also includes many simple, default geometric objects called *primitives* that you can use as a starting point. Creating these primitive objects can be as easy as clicking a menu or button and dragging in a viewport.

Using the Create panel

The creation of all default gmax objects, such as primitive spheres, shapes, lights, and cameras, starts with the Create panel. This panel is the first panel in the Command Panel with an icon of an arrow pointing to a star.

Of all the panels in the Command Panel, only the Create panel (shown in Figure 9-6) includes both categories and subcategories. After you click the Create tab in the Command Panel, six category icons are displayed. From left to right, they are Geometry, Shapes, Lights, Cameras, Helpers, and Systems.

When you select the Geometry button (which has an icon of a sphere on it), a drop-down list with several subcategories appears directly below the category icons. The first available subcategory is Standard Primitives. When you select this subcategory, several text buttons appear that enable you to create some simple primitive objects.

As an example, click the button labeled Sphere (not to be confused with the Geometry category, which has a sphere icon). Several rollouts appear at the bottom of the Command Panel. The rollouts for the Sphere primitive object include Name and Color, Creation Method, Keyboard Entry, and Parameters. The rollouts for each primitive are slightly different, as are the parameters within each rollout.

If you want to ignore these rollouts and just create a sphere, simply click and drag within one of the viewports, and a sphere object appears. Figure 9-7 shows the new sphere and its parameters.

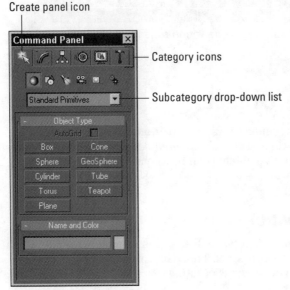

Figure 9-6: The Create panel includes categories and subcategories.

When an object button, such as the Sphere button, is selected, it turns orange. This color change reminds you that you are in creation mode. Clicking within any viewport window creates an additional sphere. While in creation mode, you can create many spheres by clicking and dragging several times in one of the viewports. To get out of creation mode, click the Select Object button or one of the transform buttons on the main toolbar, or right-click in the active viewport.

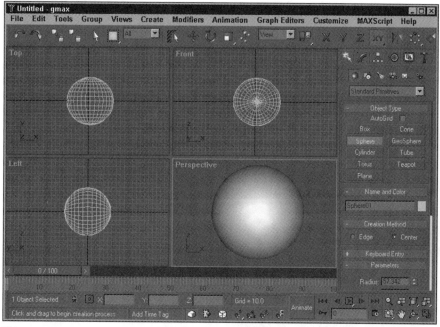

Figure 9-7: You can create primitive spheres easily by dragging in a viewport.

Using the Create menu

The Create menu offers quick access to the buttons in the Create panel. Most of the objects that you can create using the Create panel (including Standard Primitives, Shapes, and Lights) can be accessed using the Create menu. Selecting an object from the Create menu opens the Create panel and automatically selects the matching button. However, you still need to click and drag in the viewport to create the object.

Naming objects, renaming objects, and assigning colors

Every object in the scene can have both a name and color assigned to it. Each object is given a default name and random color when first created. The default name is the type of object followed by a number. For example, when you create a sphere object, gmax labels it "Sphere01." These default names aren't very exciting and can be confusing if you have many objects. You can change the object's name at any time by modifying the Name field in the Name and Color rollout of the Command Panel.

Cross-Reference   Names and colors are useful for locating and selecting objects, as you find out in Chapter 5, "Choosing Your Poison—Selecting Objects."

The object color is shown in the color swatch to the right of the object name. This color is the color that is used to display the object within the viewports. To change an object's color, just click the color swatch next to the Name field to make the Object Color dialog box appear. This dialog box, shown in Figure 9-8, lets you select a different color or create a custom color.

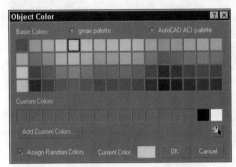

Figure 9-8: You use the Object Color dialog box to define the color of objects displayed in the viewports.

The Object Color dialog box includes the standard gmax palette and the AutoCAD ACI palette. The AutoCAD palette has many more colors than the gmax palette, but the gmax palette allows a row of custom colors. Above the Cancel button is the Select by Color button. Click this button to open the Select Objects dialog box where you can select all the objects that have a certain color.

With the Object Color dialog box, if the Assign Random Colors option is selected, then a random color from the palette is chosen every time a new object is created. If this option is not selected, the color of all new objects is the same until you choose a different object color. Making objects different colors makes distinguishing between the two objects easier for selection and transformation.

You can select custom colors by clicking the Add Custom Colors button. This button opens a Color Selector: Add Color dialog box, shown in Figure 9-9.

The Color Selector: Add Color dialog box defines colors using the RGB (red, green, and blue) and HSV (hue, saturation, and value) color systems. Another way to select colors is to drag the cursor around the rainbow palette on the left. After you find the perfect custom color to add to the Object Color dialog box, click the Add Color button. This custom color will then be available wherever the Object Color dialog box is opened.

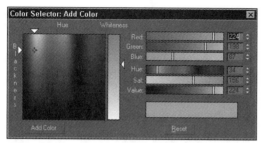

Figure 9-9: The Color Selector: Add Color dialog box lets you choose new custom colors.

If no material has been applied to an object, then the object will be rendered in the game engine using the object color.

Object colors are also important because you can use them to select and filter objects. For example, the Selection Floater (open by choosing Tools ➪ Selection Floater) includes a Sort by Color setting. You can also choose Edit ➪ Select by ➪ Color menu (or click the Select by Color button) to select only objects that match a selected color.

You can set objects to display an object's default color or its Material Color. These options are in the Display Color rollout under the Display panel (the fifth tab from the left in the Command Panel with an icon of a monitor). You can set them differently for Wireframe and Shaded views.

Using different creation methods

You actually have a couple of ways to create primitive objects by dragging in a viewport. With the first method, the first place you click sets the object's initial position. You then need to drag the mouse to define the object's first dimension and then click again to set each additional dimension, if needed. Primitive objects with a different number of dimensions require a different number of clicks and drags.

For example, a sphere is one of the simplest objects to create. To create a sphere, click in a viewport to set the location of the sphere's center, then drag the mouse to the desired radius and release the mouse button to complete. A Box object, on the other hand, requires a click and drag move to define the base (width and depth), then another drag and click again to set the height. If you ever get lost when defining these dimensions, check the Prompt Line to see what dimension the interface is expecting next.

When you click a primitive object button, the Creation Method rollout appears and offers different methods for creating the primitives. For example, click the Sphere button, and the Creation Method rollout displays two options: Edge and Center.

When you choose the Edge method, the first viewport click sets one edge of the sphere, and dragging and clicking again sets the diameter of the sphere. The default Center creation method defines the sphere's center location; dragging sets the sphere's radius. The creation method for each primitive can be different. For example, the Box primitive object has a creation method for creating perfect cubes. Table 5-1 shows the number of clicks required to create an object and the creation methods for each primitive object.

Table 9-1
Primitive Object Creation Methods

Primitive Object	Number of Viewport Clicks to Create	Default Creation Method	Other Creation Method
Box	2	Box	Cube
Sphere	1	Center	Edge
Cylinder	2	Center	Edge
Torus	2	Center	Edge
Plane	1	Rectangle	Square
Cone	3	Center	Edge
GeoSphere	1	Center	Diameter
Tube	3	Center	Edge
Teapot	1	Center	Edge

Using the Keyboard Entry rollout for precise dimensions

When creating a primitive object, you can define its location and dimensions by clicking in a viewport and dragging, or you can enter precise values in the Keyboard Entry rollout, located in the Create panel. Within this rollout, you can enter the offset XYZ values for positioning the origin of the primitive and the dimensions of the object. The offset values are defined relative to the active construction plane that is usually the Home Grid.

When all the dimension fields are set, click the Create button to create the actual primitive. You can create multiple objects by clicking the Create button several times. After a primitive is created, altering the fields in the Keyboard Entry rollout has no effect on the current object, but you can always use the Undo feature to try again.

Altering object parameters

The final rollout for all primitive objects is the Parameters rollout. This rollout holds all the various settings for the object. Compared to the Keyboard Entry rollout, which you can use only when creating the primitive, you can use the Parameters rollout to alter the primitive's parameters before or after the creation of the object. For example, increasing the Radius value after creating an object makes an existing sphere larger.

The parameters are different for each primitive object, but you can generally use them to control the dimensions, the number of segments that make up the object, and whether the object is sliced into sections. You can also select the Generate Mapping Coordinates option (which automatically creates material mapping coordinates that are used to position maps).

Note After you deselect an object, the Parameters rollout disappears from the Create tab and moves to the Modify tab. You can make future parameter adjustments by selecting an object and clicking the Modify tab.

Recovering from mistakes and deleting objects

Before going any further, you need to learn how to undo the last action with the Undo menu command. The Undo (Ctrl+Z) menu command will undo the last action whether it's creating an object or changing a parameter. The Redo (Ctrl+Y) menu command lets you redo an action that was undone.

Caution Many operations such as applying or deleting modifiers and changing parameters cannot be undone.

You can set the levels of undo in the Preference Settings dialog box. If you right-click on either the Undo or the Redo button on the main toolbar, a list of recent actions is displayed. You can select any action from this list to be undone.

The Edit ⇨ Delete menu command removes the selected object (or objects) from the scene. (The keyboard shortcut for this command is, luckily, the Delete key, as anything else would be confusing.)

Primitive Object Types

In the Create panel, all the geometric primitives are contained within the Standard Primitives subcategory. These primitives include several simple objects from simple boxes and spheres to cones and cylinders. You can create all of these primitives from the Create panel.

Standard Primitives

The Standard Primitives include many of the most basic and most used objects, including boxes, spheres, and cylinders. Figure 9-10 shows all the Standard Primitives.

Figure 9-10: The Standard Primitives: Box, Sphere, Cylinder, Torus, Plane, Cone, GeoSphere, Tube, and Teapot

Box

You can use the Box primitive to create regular cubes and boxes of any width, length, and height. Holding down the Ctrl key while dragging the box base creates a perfect square for the base. To create a cube, select the Cube option in the Creation Method rollout. A single click and drag completes the cube.

The Length, Width, and Height Segment values indicate how many polygons make up each dimension. The default is only one segment.

Sphere

Spheres appear everywhere from sports balls to planets in space. Spheres are also among the easiest primitives to create. After clicking the Sphere button, simply click and drag in a viewport.

In the Parameters rollout, the Segments value specifies the number of polygons that make up the sphere. The higher the number of segments, the smoother the sphere will be. The default value of 32 produces a smooth sphere, and a value of 4 actually produces a diamond-shaped object. The Smooth option lets you make the sphere smooth or faceted. Faceted spheres are useful for identifying faces for modifications. Figure 9-11 shows five spheres. The one on the left has a Segments value of 32 and the Smooth option turned on. The remaining spheres have the Smooth option disabled with Segment values of 32, 16, 8, and 4.

Figure 9-11: Sphere primitives of various Segment values with the Smooth option on and off

The Parameters rollout also lets you create hemispheres. The hemisphere shape is set by the Hemisphere value, which can range from 0.0 to 1.0, with 0 being a full sphere and 1 being nothing at all. (A value of 0.5 would be a perfect hemisphere.) With the Hemisphere value specified, you now have two options for dealing with the unused polygons that make up the originating sphere: the Chop option, which removes the unused polygons, and the Squash option, which retains the polygons but "squashes" them to fit in the hemisphere shape.

Figure 9-12 shows two hemispheres with Hemisphere values of 0.5. The Edged Faces option was enabled in the Viewport Configuration dialog box so you could see the polygon faces. The left hemisphere was created using the Chop option and the right hemisphere was created with the Squash option. Notice how many extra polygons are included in the right hemisphere.

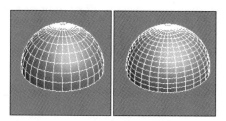

Figure 9-12: Creating hemispheres with the Chop and Squash options

The Slice option enables you to dissect the sphere into slices (like segmenting an orange). The Slice From and Slice To fields accept values ranging from 0 to 360 degrees. Figure 9-13 shows three spheres that have been sliced. Because the Segments value hasn't changed, all slices have the same number of faces.

Note   You can use the Slice feature on several primitives, including the sphere, cylinder, torus, cone, tube, oiltank, spindle, chamfercyl, and capsule.

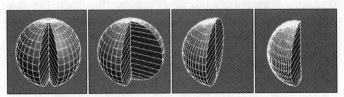

Figure 9-13: Using the Slice option to create sphere slices

The Base to Pivot parameter determines whether the position of the pivot point will be at the bottom of the sphere or at the center. The default (with the Base to Pivot setting not enabled) sets the pivot point for the sphere at the center of the sphere.

Cylinder

You can use a cylinder in many places — for example, as a pillar in front of a home or as a car driveshaft. To create one, first specify a base circle and then a height. The default number of sides is 18, which produces a smooth cylinder. Height and Cap Segments values define the number of polygons that make up the cylinder sides and caps. The Smooth and Slice options work the same as they do with a sphere (see the preceding section).

Tip   If you don't plan to modify the ends of the cylinder, make the Cap Segments equal to 1 to keep the model complexity down.

Torus

A Torus (which is the mathematical name for a "doughnut") is a ring with a circular cross section. To create a Torus, you need to specify two radii values. The first is the value from the center of the Torus to the center of the ring; the second is the radius of the circular cross section. The default settings create a Torus with 24 segments and 12 sides. The Rotation and Twist options cause the sides to twist a specified value as the ring is circumnavigated.

Figure 9-14 shows some sample Toruses with a Smooth setting of None. The first three have Segments values of 24, 12, and 6. The last two have Twist values of 90 and 360. The higher the number of segments, the rounder the Torus looks when viewed from above. The default of 24 is sufficient to create a smooth Torus. The number of sides defines the circular smoothness of the cross section.

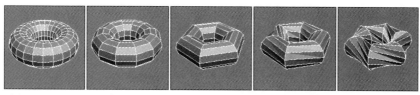

Figure 9-14: Using the Segments and Twist options on a Torus

The Parameters rollout includes settings for four different Smooth options. The All option smoothes all edges, and the None option displays all polygons as faceted. The Sides option smoothes edges between sides, resulting in a Torus with banded sides. The Segment option smoothes between segment edges, resulting in separate smooth sections around the Torus.

The Slice options work with a Torus the same way as they do with the sphere and cylinder objects (see the section "Sphere" earlier in this chapter).

Plane

The Plane object enables you to model the Great Plains (good pun, eh?). The Plane primitive creates a simple plane that looks like a rectangle.

The Plane primitive includes two creation methods: Rectangle and Square. The Square method creates a perfect square in the viewport when dragged. You can also define the Length and Width Segments.

Cone

The Cone object, whether used to create ice cream cones or megaphones, is created exactly like the cylinder object, except that the second cap can have a radius different from that of the first. You create it by clicking and dragging to specify the base circle, dragging to specify the cone's height, and then dragging again for the second cap to create a Cone.

In addition to the two cap radii and the Height, parameter options include the number of Height and Cap Segments, the number of Sides, and the Smooth and Slice options.

GeoSphere

The GeoSphere object is a sphere that is created using fewer polygon faces than the standard Sphere object. This type of sphere spreads the polygon faces, which are all equal in size, around the object, instead of concentrating them on either end like the normal Sphere object. This makes the GeoSphere object easier to model while using less memory. One reason for this is that a GeoSphere uses triangle faces instead of square faces.

In the Parameters rollout are several Geodesic Base Type options, including Tetra, Octa, and Icosa. The Tetra type is based on a 4-sided tetrahedron, the Octa type is based on an 8-sided Octahedron, and the Icosa type is based on the 20-sided Icosahedron. Setting the Segment value to 1 produces each of these Hedron shapes. Each type aligns the triangle faces differently.

GeoSpheres also have the same Smooth, Hemisphere, and Base-to-Pivot options as the Sphere primitive. Selecting the Hemisphere option changes the GeoSphere into a hemisphere, but there are no additional options like Chop and Squash. Also, GeoSpheres cannot be sliced.

Tutorial: Comparing Spheres and GeoSpheres

To prove that GeoSpheres are more efficient than Sphere objects, follow these steps:

1. Create a normal Sphere, and set its Segment value to 4.

2. Next to the Sphere object, create a GeoSphere object with a Tetra Base Type and the number of Segments set to 4.

3. Create another GeoSphere object with the Octa Base Type and 4 Segments.

4. Finally, create a GeoSphere with the Icosa Base Type and 4 Segments.

Figure 9-15 shows these spheres as a comparison. The normal sphere, shown to the left, looks like a diamond, but the GeoSpheres still resemble spheres. Notice how the Icosa type GeoSphere, shown at the right, produces the smoothest sphere.

Figure 9-15: Even with a similar number of segments, GeoSpheres are much more spherical.

Tube

The Tube primitive is useful for any time you need a pipe object. You can also use it to create ring-shaped objects that have rectangular cross sections. Creating a Tube object is very similar to the Cylinder and Cone objects. Tube parameters include two radii for the inner and outer tube wall. Tubes also have the Smooth and Slice options.

Teapot

Okay, let's all sing together, "I'm a little teapot, short and stout. . . ." The teapot is another object that, like the sphere, is easy to create. Within the Parameters roll-out, you can specify the number of Segments, whether the surface is smooth or faceted, and which parts to display, including Body, Handle, Spout, and Lid.

> **Note**   You may recognize most of these primitives as standard shapes, with the exception of the teapot. The teapot has a special place in computer graphics. In early computer graphics development labs, the teapot was chosen as the test model for many early algorithms. It is still included as a valuable benchmark for computer graphics programmers.

Modifying object parameters

Primitive objects provide a good starting point for many of the other modeling types. They also provide a good way to show off parameter-based modeling.

All objects have parameters. These parameters help define how the object looks. For example, consider the primitive objects. The primitive objects contained in gmax are parametric. Parametric objects are mathematically defined, and you can change them by modifying their parameters. The easiest object modifications to make are simply changing these parameters. For example, a sphere with a radius of 4 can be made into a sphere with a radius of 10 by simply typing "10" in the Radius field. The viewports display these changes automatically when you press the Enter key.

> **Note**   When an object is first created, its parameters are displayed in the Parameters roll-out of the Create panel. As long as the object remains the current object, you can modify its parameters using this rollout. After you select a different tool or object, the Parameters rollout is no longer accessible from the Create panel. It can be found from then on under the Modify panel.

Tutorial: Filling a treasure chest with gems

I haven't found many treasure chests lately, but if I remember correctly, they are normally filled with bright, sparkling gems. In this tutorial, we'll fill the chest with a number of primitive objects and alter the object properties in the Modify panel to create a diverse offering of gems.

To create a treasure chest with many unique gems, follow these steps:

1. Open the Treasure chest of gems.gmax file from the Chap 09 directory on the CD-ROM.

   This file includes a simple treasure chest model.

2. Click the Create panel, and select the Standard Primitives subcategory; then click the GeoSphere button.

3. Create a single GeoSphere object.

4. In the Parameters rollout, set the Segments value to 1, select the Octa option, and disable the Smooth option to produce a nice gem.

5. Create several more gems by clicking and dragging within the center of the chest.

6. Select all the gems, and move them all to the top of the chest.

Figure 9-16 shows the resulting chest with a variety of gems.

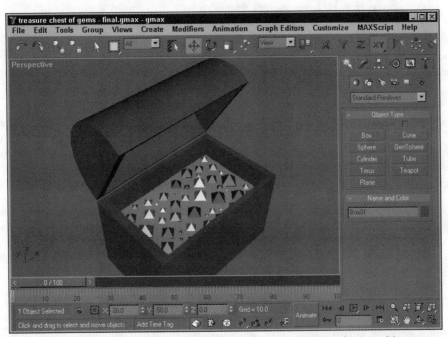

Figure 9-16: A treasure chest full of gems is quickly created by altering object parameters.

Every modeling type, whether it is an Editable Spline, a Compound Boolean object, or a primitive sphere, has parameters. These parameters, which you can modify, appear in rollouts using the Modify panel.

Modeling Helpers

In the Create panel is a category of miscellaneous objects called Helpers (the icon looks like a tape measure). These objects are useful in positioning objects and measuring dimensions. The buttons in the Helper category include Dummy, Point, Protractor, Grid, and Tape.

Using Dummy and Point objects

The Dummy object is a useful object for controlling complex object hierarchies. This object is a simple cube with a pivot point at its center that doesn't render and has no parameters. It is used only as an object about which to transform objects. For example, you could create a Dummy object that the camera could follow through an animation sequence. Dummy objects will be used in many examples throughout the remainder of the book.

The Point object is very similar to the Dummy object in that it is not rendered and has only two modifiable parameters. A Point object defines a point in space and is identified by an axis tripod. This tripod and its length are the only parameters that you can alter under the Parameters rollout in the Command Panel. The main purpose for the Point object is to mark positions within the scene.

 Caution Point objects are difficult to see and easy to lose. If you use a point object, but sure to name it so it is easy to find in the Select by Name dialog box.

Measuring coordinate distances

The Helpers category also includes handy utilities for measuring dimensions and directions. These are the Tape and Protractor objects. The units are all based on the current selected system units.

Using the Tape helper

You use the Tape object to measure distances. To use it, simply drag the distance that you would like to measure and view the resulting dimension in the Parameters rollout. You can also set the length of the Tape object using the Specify Length option. You can move and reposition the endpoints of the Tape object with the Select and Move button, but the Rotate and Scale buttons have no effect.

Using the Protractor helper

The Protractor object works in a manner similar to the Tape object, but it measures the angle between two objects. To use the Protractor object, click in a viewport to position the Protractor object. (The Protractor object looks like two pyramids aligned point to point and represents the origin of the angle.) Click the Pick Object

1 button, and select an object in the scene. A line is drawn from the Protractor object to the selected object. Next, click the Pick Object 2 button. The angle-formed objects and the Protractor object is displayed in the Parameters rollout. The value changes when either of the selected objects or the Protractor is moved.

Note   All measurement values are presented in gray fields within the Parameters rollout. This gray field indicates that the value cannot be modified.

Tutorial: Testing the Pythagorean Theorem

I always trusted my teachers in school to tell me the truth, but maybe they were just making it all up, especially my math teacher. (He did have shifty eyes, after all.) For my peace of mind, I would like to test one of the mathematical principles he taught us — the Pythagorean Theorem. (What kind of name is that anyway?)

If I remember the theorem correctly, it says that the sum of squares of the sides of a right triangle equals the sum of the hypotenuse squared. So, according to my calculations, a right triangle with a side of 3 and a side of 4 would have a hypotenuse of 5. Because gmax is proficient at drawing shapes such as this one, we'll test the theorem by creating a box with a width of 40 and a height of 30 and then measuring the diagonal.

To test the Pythagorean Theorem, follow these steps:

1. Open the Testing Pythagoras.gmax file from the Chap 09 directory on the CD-ROM.

   This file includes a simple box with the dimensions: 40×30×10.

2. Right-click on any of the Snap buttons at the bottom of the interface to open the Snap and Grid Settings dialog box, select the Snaps panel, and set the Snap feature to snap to vertices by selecting the Vertex option. Close the Grid and Snap Settings dialog box, and enable the 3D Snap feature.

3. Open the Create panel, and select the Helper category; then click the Tape object.

4. In the viewport, move the cursor over the upper-left corner of the object and click on the blue vertex that appears. Then drag down to the lower-right corner, and click the next blue vertex that appears. Note the measurement in the Parameters rollout.

Well, I guess my math teacher didn't lie about this theorem, but I wonder whether he was correct about all those multiplication tables. Figure 9-17 shows the resulting box and measurement value.

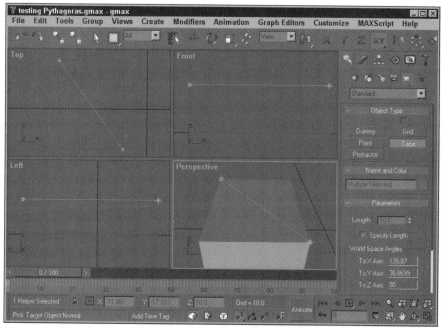

Figure 9-17: I guess old Pythagoras was right. (Good thing I have gmax to help me check.)

Summary

Understanding the basics of modeling will help you as you build scenes. In this chapter, you've seen several different object types that are available in gmax. Many of these types will have similar features, such as Soft Selection. There are also several helper objects that can assist as well.

Primitives are the most basic shapes and often provide a starting point for more ambitious modeling projects. The primitive objects provide a host of possible objects. This chapter covered

✦ Understanding parametric objects and the various modeling types

✦ Using subobjects and soft selections

✦ Understanding the basics of creating primitives by both dragging and entering keyboard values

✦ Discovering how to name objects and set and change the object color

✦ Learning the various creation methods for all the primitive objects

✦ Exploring all the various primitives in the Standard subcategory

✦ Understanding the possible parameters for each of the primitive objects

✦ Using Helper objects

Now that you have the basics covered, you're ready to dive into the various modeling types, and the first modeling type on the list is splines and shapes, which I cover next.

✦   ✦   ✦

Starting with Simple Splines and Shapes

✦ ✦ ✦ ✦

In This Chapter

Working with shape
primitives

Editing splines and
shapes

Using spline
modifiers

✦ ✦ ✦ ✦

Many game modeling projects start from the ground
up, and you can't get much lower to the ground than
2D. "But my games deal with 3D," you say? "What place is
there for 2D shapes?" Within the 3D world, you frequently
encounter flat surfaces — the side of a building, the top of a
table, a billboard, and so on. All these objects have flat 2D surfaces. Understanding how objects are composed of 2D surfaces will help as you start to build objects in 3D. This chapter
examines the 2D elements of 3D objects and covers the tools
needed to work with them.

Working in 2D in gmax, you'll work with two general objects —
splines and shapes. A *spline* is a special type of line that
curves according to mathematical principles. In gmax, splines
are used to create all sorts of shapes such as circles, ellipses,
and rectangles.

You can create splines and shapes using the Shapes category
on the Create panel, and just as with the other categories,
there are several spline-based shape primitives. Spline shapes
can be rendered, but they are normally used to create more
advanced 3D geometric objects by extruding or lathing the
spline. You can use splines to create animation paths as well
as Loft and NURBS objects, and you will find that splines and
shapes are used frequently in gmax.

Drawing in 2D

Shapes in gmax are unique from other objects because they
are drawn in 2D, which confines them to a single plane. That
plane is defined by the viewport used to create the shape. For

example, drawing a shape in the Top view constrains the shape to the XY plane, whereas drawing the shape in the Front view constrains it to the ZX plane. Even shapes drawn in the Perspective view are constrained to a plane such as the Home Grid.

You usually produce 2D shapes in a drawing package like Adobe Illustrator or CorelDRAW. gmax supports importing line drawings using the 3D Studio Shape (SHP) format.

Whereas newly created or imported shapes are 2D and are confined to a single plane, splines can exist in 3D space. The Helix shape, for example, exists in 3D, having height as well as width values. Animation paths in particular need to move into 3D space.

Working with shape primitives

The shape primitives that are displayed in the Object Type rollout of the Create panel when the Shapes category is selected include many basic shapes, including Line, Circle, Arc, NGon (a polygon for which you can set the number of sides), Text, Rectangle, Ellipse, Donut, Star, and Helix, as shown in Figure 10-1. Clicking any of these shape buttons lets you create the shape by dragging in one of the viewports. You can also use the Create ⇨ Shapes menu to select a shape to create. After a shape is created, several new rollouts appear.

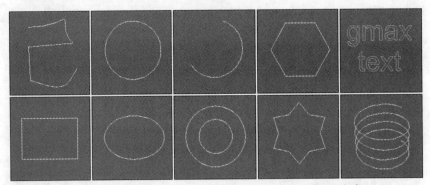

Figure 10-1: These shape primitives in all their 2D glory: Line, Circle, Arc, NGon, Text, Rectangle, Ellipse, Donut, Star, and Helix

Above the Shape buttons are two check boxes: AutoGrid and Start New Shape. AutoGrid creates a temporary grid, which you can use to align the shape with the surface of the nearest object under the mouse at the time of creation. This feature is helpful for starting a new spline on the surface of an object.

I discuss AutoGrid in more detail in Chapter 7, "Moving, Rotating, and Scaling Objects — Return of the –ings."

The Start New Shape option creates a new object with every new shape drawn in a viewport. Leaving this option unchecked lets you create compound shapes, which consist of several shapes used to create one object. Because compound shapes consist of several shapes, you cannot edit them using the Parameters rollout. For example, if you want to write out your name using splines, keep the Start New Shape option unselected to make all the letters part of the same object.

Just as with the Geometric primitives, every shape that is created is given a name and a color. You can change either of these in the Name and Color rollout.

Most of the shape primitives have several common rollouts — Mesh Settings, Interpolation, Creation Method, Keyboard Entry, and Parameters (for some shapes), as shown in Figure 10-2. I cover these rollouts initially and then present the individual shape primitives.

Figure 10-2: These rollouts are common for most of the shape primitives.

Mesh Settings rollout

The Mesh Settings rollout includes options for giving a spline some breadth so it will be visible to the game engine. Adding breadth converts the spline into a 3D object that you can view in the viewport and in the game engine. Without a thickness, the spline wouldn't be visible in the game.

For spline objects, you can specify values for Thickness, the number of Sides, and the Angle. The Thickness is the diameter of the visible spline. The number of Sides sets the number of sides that make up the cross-section of the renderable spline. The lowest value possible is 3, which would create a triangle cross-section. The Angle value determines where the corners of the cross-section sides start, so you could set a three-sided spline to have either a corner pointing up or an edge.

Note   By default, a spline that is made visible has a 12-sided circle as its cross-section.

The Mesh Settings rollout also includes the Generate Mapping Coordinates option. These coordinates are automatically generated when this option is selected and are used to mark where a material map is placed.

Cross-Reference   I talk about mapping coordinates in Chapter 16, "Putting on the Ritz with the gmax Material Editor."

Visible splines appear as normal splines in the viewport unless the Display Mesh option is selected. To view the mesh spline in the viewport, select the Display Mesh option.

Interpolation rollout

In the Interpolation rollout, you can define the number of interpolation steps or segments that make up the shape. The Interpolation Steps value determines how many segments to include between vertices. For example, a circle shape with a Steps value of 0 has only four segments and looks like a diamond. Increasing the Steps value to 1 makes a circle out of eight segments. For shapes composed of straight lines (like the Rectangle and simple NGons), the Steps value isn't an issue, but for a shape with many sides (like a Circle, Ellipse, or Helix), it can have a big effect. Larger step values result in smoother curves. The Adaptive option automatically sets the number of steps to produce a smooth curve and sets the number of steps for straight segments to 0. The Optimize option attempts to reduce the number of steps to produce a simpler spline by eliminating all the extra vertices and segments associated with the shape.

Note   The Helix shape primitive has no Interpolation rollout.

Creation Method and Keyboard Entry rollouts

Most shape primitives also include Creation Method and Keyboard Entry rollouts (Text and Star are the exceptions). The Creation Method rollout offers options for specifying different ways to create the spline by dragging in a viewport, such as from edge to edge or from the center out. Table 10-1 lists the various creation method options for each of the shapes.

Table 10-1
Shape Primitive Creation Methods

Primitive Object	Number of Viewport Clicks to Create	Default Creation Method	Other Creation Method
Line	2 to Infinite	Corner Initial, Bézier Drag	Smooth, Initial, Corner, or Smooth Drag
Circle	1	Center	Edge
Arc	2	End-End-Middle	Center-End-End
NGon	1	Center	Edge
Text	1	None	None
Rectangle	1	Edge	Center
Ellipse	1	Edge	Center
Donut	2	Center	Edge
Star	2	None	None
Helix	3	Center	Edge

The Keyboard Entry rollout offers a way to enter exact position and dimension values. After you enter the values, click the Create button to create the spline or shape in the active viewport. The settings are different for each shape.

The Parameters rollout includes such basic settings for the primitive as Radius, Length, and Width. You can alter these settings immediately after an object is created. However, after you deselect an object, the Parameters rollout moves to the Modify panel, and you must make any alterations to the shape there.

Line

The Line primitive includes several creation method settings, enabling you to create hard, sharp corners or smooth corners. You can set the Initial Type option to either Corner or Smooth to create a sharp or smooth corner for the first point created.

After clicking where the initial point is located, you can add points by clicking in the viewport. Dragging while creating a new point can make a point either a Corner, Smooth, or Bézier based on the Drag Type option selected in the Creation Method rollout. The curvature created by the Smooth option is determined by the distance between adjacent vertices, whereas you can control the curvature created by the Bézier option by dragging with the mouse a desired distance after the point is created. Bézier corners have control handles associated with them, enabling you to change their curvature.

Tip   Holding down the Shift key while clicking creates points that are vertically or horizontally in line with the previous point. Holding down the Ctrl key snaps new points at an angle from the last segment, as determined by the Angle Snap setting.

After creating all the points, you exit line mode by clicking the right mouse button. If the last point is on top of the first point, then a dialog box asks whether you want to close the spline. Click Yes to create a closed spline or No to continue adding points. Even after creating a closed spline, you can add more points to the current selection to create a compound shape if the Start New Shape option isn't selected. If the first and last points don't correspond, then an open spline will be created.

Figure 10-3 shows several splines created using the various creation method settings. The left spline was created with all the options set to Corner, and the second spline with all the options set to Smooth. The third spline uses the Corner Initial type and shows where dragging has smoothed many of the points. The last spline was created using the Bézier option.

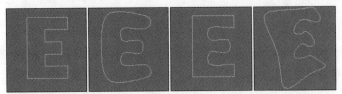

Figure 10-3: The Line shape can create various combinations of shapes with smooth and sharp corners.

In the Keyboard Entry rollout, you can add points by entering their X, Y, and Z dimensions and clicking the Add Point button. You can close the spline at any time by clicking the Close button or keep it open by clicking the Finish button.

Circle

The Circle button creates — you guessed it — circles. The only adjustable parameter in the Parameters rollout is the Radius. All other rollouts are the same, as explained earlier.

Arc

The Arc primitive has two creation methods. Use the End-End-Middle method to create an arc shape by clicking and dragging to specify the two end points and then dragging to complete the shape. Use the Center-End-End method to create an arc shape by clicking and dragging from the center to one of the end points and then dragging the arc length to the second end point.

Other parameters include the Radius and the From and To settings where you can enter the value in degrees for the start and end of the arc. The Pie Slice option connects the end points of the arc to its center to create a pie-sliced shape, as shown in Figure 10-4. The Reverse option lets you reverse the arc's direction.

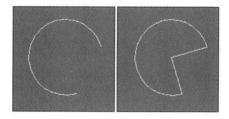

Figure 10-4: Enabling the Pie Slice option connects the arc ends with the center of the circle.

NGon

The NGon shape lets you create regular polygons by specifying the Number of Sides and the Corner Radius. You can also specify whether the NGon is Inscribed or Circumscribed, as shown in Figure 10-5. Inscribed polygons are positioned within a circle that touches all the polygon's vertices. Circumscribed polygons are positioned outside of a circle that touches the midpoint of each polygon edge. The Circular option changes the polygon to a circle that inscribes the polygon.

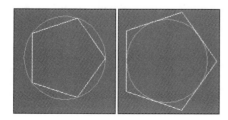

Figure 10-5: An inscribed pentagon and a circumscribed pentagon

Text

You can use the Text primitive to add outlined text to the scene. In the Parameters rollout, you can specify a Font by choosing one from the drop-down list at the top of the Parameters rollout. Under the Font drop-down list are six icons, shown in Table 10-2. The left two icons are for the Italics and Underline styles. Selecting either of these styles applies the style to all the text. The right four icons are for aligning the text to the left, centered, right, or justified.

Table 10-2 Text Primitive Parameters	
Icon	*Description*
I	Italics
U	Underline
≣	Left
≣	Centered
≣	Right
≣	Justified

Note The list of available fonts includes only the Windows TrueType fonts and Type 1 PostScript fonts installed on your system and any extra fonts located in the font path listed in the Configure Paths dialog box.

The size of the text is determined by the Size value. The Kerning (which is the space between adjacent characters) and Leading (which is the space between adjacent lines of text) values can actually be negative. Setting the Kerning value to a large negative number actually displays the text backwards.

There is also a text area where you can type the text to be created. You can cut, copy, and paste text into this text area from an external application. After setting the parameters and typing the text, the text appears as soon as you click in one of the viewports. The Text is automatically updated when any of the parameters (including the text) is changed. To turn off automatic updating, select the Manual Update toggle. You can then update with the Update button.

Figure 10-6 shows an example of some text and an example of kerning values in the gmax interface.

Figure 10-6: The Text shape can create text with several settings such as font, justification, and style.

Rectangle

The Rectangle shape produces simple rectangles. In the Parameters rollout, you can specify the Length and Width and also a Corner Radius.

Ellipse

Ellipses are simple variations of the Circle shape. You define them by Length and Width values.

Donut

As another variation of the Circle shape, the Donut shape consists of two concentric circles; you create it by dragging once to specify the outer circle and again to specify the inner circle. The parameters for this object are simply two radii.

Star

The Star shape also includes two radii values—the larger Radius value defines the distance of the outer points of the Star shape from its center, and the smaller Radius value is the distance from the center of the star to the inner points. The Point setting indicates the number of points. This value can range from 3 to 100. The Distortion value causes the inner points to rotate relative to the outer points and can be used to create some interesting new star types. The Fillet Radius 1 and Fillet Radius 2 values adjust the Fillet for the inner and outer points. Figure 10-7 shows a sampling of what is possible with the Star shapes.

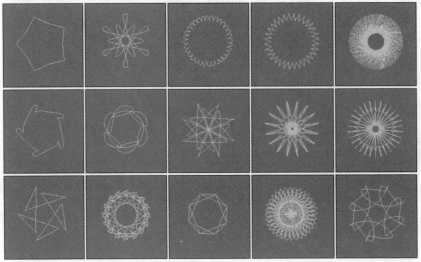

Figure 10-7: The Star primitive can be changed to create some amazing shapes.

Helix

A Helix is like a spring coil shape, and it is the one shape of all the Shape primitives that exists in 3D. Helix parameters include two radii for specifying the inner radius and the outer radius. These two values can be equal to create a coil or unequal to create a spiral. Parameters also exist for the Height and number of Turns. The Bias parameter causes the Helix turns to be gathered all together at the top or bottom of the shape. The CW and CCW options let you specify whether the Helix turns clockwise or counterclockwise. Figure 10-8 shows a sampling of Helix shapes: The first Helix has equal radii values, the second one has a smaller second radius, the third Helix spirals to a second radius value of 0, and the last two Helix objects have Bias values of 0.8 and –0.8.

Figure 10-8: The Helix shape can be straight or spiral shaped.

Tutorial: Drawing a company logo

One common place to use 2D splines and shapes is in creating logos and signs that appear on billboards or on the sides of buildings. In this example, we'll design and create a simple logo using the Shape tools for the fictitious company named "Expeditions South." This logo can then be plastered on billboards for a Flight or Train Simulator world.

To use the Shape tools to design and create a company logo, follow these steps:

1. Start by creating a four-pointed star. Click the Star button, and drag in the Top view to create a shape. Change the parameters for this star as follows: Radius1 = 60, Radius2 = 20, and Points = 4.

2. Select and move the star shape to the left side of the viewport.

3. Now, click the Text button. Change the font to Impact and the Size to 50. In the Text area, type **Expeditions South** and include a line return and several spaces between the two words so they are offset. Click in the Top viewport to place the text.

4. Use the Select and Move button to reposition the text next to the Star shape.

5. Click the Line button and create several short highlighting lines around the bottom point of the star.

The finished logo is now ready to extrude and animate. Figure 10-9 shows the results.

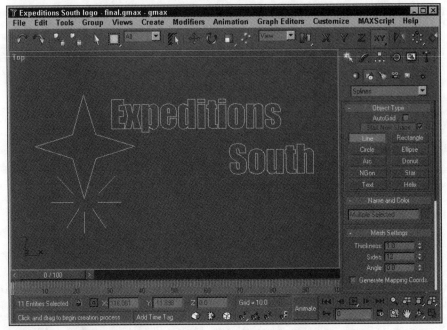

Figure 10-9: A company logo created entirely in gmax using shapes

Editing Splines

After you create a shape primitive, you can edit it by modifying its parameters, but
the parameters for the shape primitives are fairly limited. For example, the only
parameter for the Circle shape is Radius. All shapes can be converted to Editable
Splines or could have the Edit Spline modifier applied to them. Doing either enables
a host of editing features. Before you can use these editing features, you must convert the shape primitive to an Editable Spline (except for the Line shape, which is
editable by default).

You can convert any shape to an Editable Spline by right-clicking the spline shape in
the viewport and choosing Convert to ⇨ Convert to Editable Spline from the pop-up
quadmenu. Another way to enable these features is to apply the Edit Spline modifier.

Cross-Reference   Chapter 14, "Controlled Destruction with Modifiers," explains how to apply and
use modifiers.

Editable Splines versus the Edit Spline modifier

After you convert the spline to an Editable Spline, you can edit individual sub-objects within the spline, including Vertices, Segments, and Splines. There is a subtle difference in applying the Edit Spline modifier and converting the shape to an Editable Spline. Applying the Edit Spline modifier maintains the shape parameters and enables the editing features found in the Geometry rollout. However, an Editable Spline loses the ability to change the base parameters associated with the spline shape.

 When you create an object that contains two or more splines (such as when you create splines with the Start New Shape option disabled), all the splines in the object are automatically converted into Editable Splines.

Another difference is that the shape primitive name is listed along with the Edit Spline modifier in the Modifier Stack. Selecting the shape primitive name makes the Rendering, Interpolation, and Parameters rollouts visible, and the Selection, Soft Selection, and Geometry rollouts are made visible by selecting the Edit Spline modifier in the Modifier Stack. For Editable Splines, only a single name is visible in the Modifier Stack and all rollouts are accessible under it.

Selecting spline subobjects

When editing splines, you must choose the subobject level to work on. For example, when editing splines, you can work with Vertex, Segment, or Spline subobjects. Before you can edit spline subobjects, you must select them. To select the sub-object type, click the small plus sign icon to the left of the Editable Spline object in the Modifier Stack. A list of all the subobjects available for this object appears. Click the subobject in the Modifier Stack to select it. Alternatively, you can click the red-colored icons under the Selection rollout, shown in Figure 10-10. When you select a subobject, the selection in the Modifier Stack and the associated icon in the Selection rollout turn yellow.

 The Sub-Object button turns yellow when selected to remind you that you are in subobject edit mode. Remember that you must exit this mode before you can select another object.

You can select many subobjects at once by dragging an outline over them in the viewports. You can also select and deselect vertices by holding down the Ctrl key while clicking them. Holding down the Alt key removes any selected vertices from the selection set.

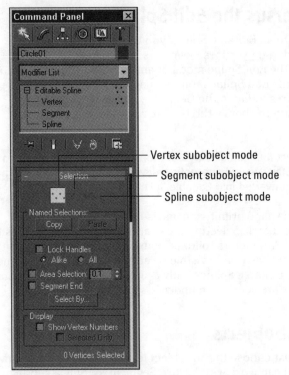

Figure 10-10: The Selection rollout provides icons for entering the various subobject modes.

After selecting several vertices, you can create a named selection set by typing a name in the Name Selection Sets drop-down list in the main toolbar. You can then copy and paste these selection sets onto other shapes using the buttons in the Selection rollout. The Lock Handles option causes the angle between the Bézier handles of the selected vertices to be locked and unchangeable. With the Lock Handles and the All options selected, all selected handles will move together. The Alike option causes all handles on one side to move together. The Area Selection option selects all the vertices within a defined radius.

The Segment End option, when enabled, allows you to select a vertex by clicking the segment. The closest vertex to the segment that you clicked is selected. This feature is useful when you are trying to select a vertex that lies near other vertices. The Select By button opens a dialog box with Segment and Spline buttons on it. These buttons allow you to select all the vertices on either a spline or segment that you choose.

The Selection rollout also has the Show Vertex Numbers option to display all the vertex numbers of a spline or to show the numbers of only the selected vertices. This can be convenient for understanding how a spline is put together and to help you find noncritical vertices.

Figure 10-11 shows a simple star shape that was converted to an Editable Spline. The left image shows the spline in Vertex subobject mode. All the vertices are marked with a small plus sign and the end point is marked with a small square. The middle image has the Show Vertex Numbers option enabled. For the right image, the vertex numbers are shown after the Reverse button was used (in Spline subobject mode).

Spline end point

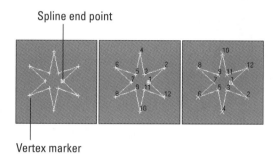

Vertex marker

Figure 10-11: Several spline shapes displayed with vertex numbering turned on

At the bottom of the Selection rollout, the Selection Information is displayed. This information tells you the number of selected items and whether a spline is closed.

 The Soft Selection rollout allows you to alter adjacent non-selected subobjects (to a lesser extent) when selected subobjects are moved, creating a smooth transition. See Chapter 9, "Beginning with the Basic Building Blocks" for the details on this rollout.

Controlling spline geometry

Much of the power of editing splines is contained within the Geometry rollout, shown in Figure 10-12, including the ability to add new splines, attach objects to the spline, weld vertices, use Boolean operations such as Trim and Extend, and many more. Some Geometry buttons may be disabled, depending on the subobject type that you've selected. Many of the features in the Geometry rollout can be used in all subobject modes. Some of these features do not even require that you be in a subobject mode. These features will be covered first.

Figure 10-12: For Editable Splines, the Geometry rollout holds most of the features.

Create line

While editing splines, you can add new lines to a spline by clicking the Create Line button and then clicking in one of the viewports. You can add several lines at the same time. Right-click in the viewport to exit this mode. Any new lines will be their own spline, but you can weld them to the existing splines.

Break

Clicking the Break button and then clicking a vertex breaks the segment at that location by creating two separate end points. You can use the Break button in the Geometry rollout to add another vertex along a segment, thereby breaking the segment into two. You can exit Break mode by right-clicking in the viewport or by clicking the Break button again. You can use the Break button in Vertex and Segment subobject modes.

Attach and Attach Mult.

The Attach button lets you attach any existing splines to the currently selected spline. The cursor changes when you're over the top of a spline that can be attached. Clicking an unselected object makes it part of the current object. The Reorient option aligns the coordinate system of the spline being attached with the selected spline's coordinate system.

For example, using the Boolean button requires that objects be part of the same object. You can use the Attach button to attach several splines into the same object.

The Attach Mult. button enables several splines to be attached at once. When you click the Attach Mult. button, the Attach Multiple dialog box (which looks a lot like the Select by Name dialog box) opens. Use this dialog box to select the objects that you want to attach to the current selection. Click the Attach button in the dialog box when you're finished. A right-click in the viewport or another click of the Attach Mult. button exits Attach mode. You can use both the Attach and Attach Mult. buttons in all three subobject modes.

Insert

Insert adds vertices to a selected spline. Click the Insert button and then click the spline to place the new vertex. At this point, you can reposition the new vertex and its attached segments — click again to set it in place. A single click adds a Corner type vertex, and a click-and-drag adds a Bézier type vertex.

After positioning the new vertex, you can add another vertex next to the first vertex by dragging the mouse and clicking. To add vertices to a different segment, right-click to release the currently selected segment but stay in Insert mode. To exit Insert mode, right-click in the viewport or click the Insert button to deselect it.

Refine

The Refine button adds vertices to a spline without changing the curvature, giving you more control over the details of the spline. The Connect option makes a new spline out of the added vertices. When the Connect option is enabled, the Linear, Closed, Bind First, and Bind Last options become enabled. The Linear option creates Corner type vertices resulting in linear segments. The Closed option closes the spline by connecting the first and last vertices. The Bind First and Bind Last options bind the first and last vertices to the center of the selected segment. Refine is available only for Vertex and Segment subobject modes.

Hide/Unhide All

The Hide and Unhide All buttons hide spline subobjects. They can be used in any subobject mode. To hide a subobject, select the subobject and click the Hide button. To Unhide the hidden subobjects, click the Unhide All button.

Delete and Detach

The Delete button deletes the selected subobject. You can use it to delete vertices, segments, or splines. This button is available in all subobject modes.

The Detach button separates the selected subobjects from the rest of the object (opposite of the Attach button). When you click this button, the Detach dialog box opens, enabling you to name the new detached subobject. When segments are detached, you can select the Same Shape option to keep them as part of the original object. The Reorient option realigns the new detached subobject to match the position and orientation of the current active grid. The Copy option creates a new copy of the detached subobject.

You can use Detach on either selected Spline or Segment subobjects.

Show Selected Segs

The Show Selected Segs option causes any selected segments to continue to be highlighted in Vertex subobject mode as well as Segment subobject mode. This feature helps you keep track of the segments that you are working on when moving vertices.

Editing vertices

To edit a vertex, click the Vertex subobject in the Modifier Stack or select the vertex icon from the Selection rollout. After the Vertex subobject type is selected, you can use the Select and Move button on the main toolbar to move vertices. Moving a vertex around causes the associated spline segments to follow.

With a vertex selected, you can change its type from Corner, Smooth, Bézier, or Corner Bézier by right-clicking and selecting the type from the pop-up quadmenu. Clicking the Bézier type vertex reveals two green-colored handles on either side of the vertex. Dragging these handles away from the vertex alters the curvature of the segment. Bézier type vertices have both handles in the same line, but Corner Bézier type vertices do not. This allows them to create sharp angles.

Note   Holding down the Shift key while clicking and dragging on a handle causes it to move independently of the other handle, turning it into a Bézier Corner type vertex instead of a plain Bézier. You can use it to create sharp corner points.

Weld and Fuse

When two vertices are selected and are within the specified Weld Threshold, they can be welded into one vertex using the Weld button. Several vertices can be welded simultaneously. Another way to weld vertices is to move one vertex on top of another. If they are within the threshold distance, a dialog box asks whether you want them to be welded. Click the Yes button to weld them. The Fuse button is similar to the Weld command, except it doesn't delete any vertices.

In Figure 10-13, the left image shows a star shape with its lower vertices selected. The middle image is the same star shape after the selected vertices have been welded together, and the right image shows the star shape with the selected vertices fused. The Selection rollout shows five selected vertices for the fused version.

You can use the Fuse button to move the selected vertices to a single location. This is accomplished by selecting all the vertices to relocate and clicking the Fuse button. The average point between all the selected vertices becomes the new location. You can combine these vertices into one after they've been fused by clicking the Weld button. The difference between the Weld and Fuse functions is that Weld reduces the number of vertices to 1 and Fuse does not reduce the number of vertices.

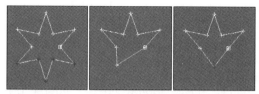

Figure 10-13: Using the Fuse and Weld buttons, several vertices in our star shape have been combined.

Connect

The Connect button lets you connect end vertices to each other to create a new line. This works only on end vertices and not on connected points within a spline. To connect the ends, click the Connect button and drag the cursor from one end point to another (the cursor changes to a plus sign when it is over a valid end point) and release. To exit Connect mode, click the Connect button again or right-click anywhere in the viewport. The left image in Figure 10-14 shows an incomplete star drawn with the Line primitive, the middle image shows a line being drawn between the end points (notice the cursor), and the right image is the resulting star.

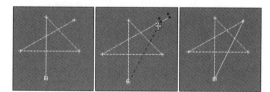

Figure 10-14: You can use the Connect button to connect end points of shapes.

Make First

The Show Vertex Numbers option displays the number of each vertex. The first vertex is identified with a square around it. The Make First button lets you change which vertex you want to be the first vertex in the spline. To do this, select a single vertex and click the Make First button. If more than one vertex is selected, gmax ignores the command. If the selected spline is an open spline, an end point must be selected.

Note   The vertex number is important because it determines the first key for path animations and where Loft objects start.

Cycle

If a single vertex is selected, the Cycle button causes the next vertex in the Vertex Number order to be selected. The Cycle button can be used on open and closed splines and can be repeated around the spline. The exact vertex number is shown at the bottom of the Selection rollout. This is very useful in locating individual vertices in groups that are close together, such as groups that have been fused.

CrossInsert

If two splines that are part of the same object overlap, you can use the CrossInsert button to create a vertex on each spline at the location where they intersect. The distance between the two splines must be closer than the Threshold value for this to work. Note that this button does not join the two splines; it merely creates a vertex on each spline. Use the Weld button to join the splines. To exit this mode, right-click in the viewport or click the CrossInsert button again. Figure 10-15 shows how you can use the CrossInsert button to add vertices at the intersection points of two elliptical splines. Notice how each ellipse now has eight vertices.

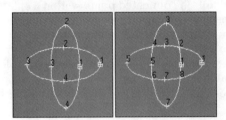

Figure 10-15: The CrossInsert button can add vertices to any overlapping splines of the same object.

Fillet

The Fillet button is used to round the corners of a spline where two edges meet. To use the Fillet command, click the Fillet button and then drag on a corner vertex in the viewport. The more you drag, the larger the Fillet. You can also enter a Fillet value in the Fillet spinner for the vertices that are selected. The Fillet has a maximum value based on the geometry of the spline. To exit Fillet mode, right-click in the viewport or click the Fillet button again. Figure 10-16 shows the Fillet command applied to an eight-pointed star with values of 10, 15, and 20. Notice how each selected vertex has split into two.

Note   You can fillet several vertices at once by selecting them and then clicking the Fillet button and dragging the Fillet distance.

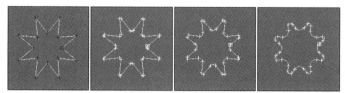

Figure 10-16: The Fillet button can round the corners of a shape.

Chamfer

The Chamfer button works much like the Fillet button, except the corners are replaced with straight-line segments instead of smooth curves. This keeps the resulting shape simpler and maintains hard corners. To use the Chamfer command, click the Chamfer button and drag on a vertex to create the Chamfer. You can also enter a Chamfer value in the rollout. To exit Chamfer mode, right-click in the viewport or click the Chamfer button again. Figure 10-17 shows chamfers applied to the same eight-pointed shape with the same values of 10, 15, and 20.

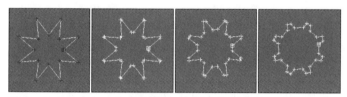

Figure 10-17: Chamfers alter the look of spline corners.

Bind/Unbind

The Bind button attaches an end vertex to a segment. The bound vertex then cannot be moved independently, but only as part of the bound segment. The Unbind button removes the binding on the vertex and lets it move independently again. To bind a vertex, click the Bind button and then drag from the vertex to the segment to which you want to bind. To exit Bind mode, right-click in the viewport or click the Bind button again.

For Figure 10-18, a circle shape is created and converted to an Editable Spline object. The right vertex is selected and then separated from the circle with the Break button. Then by clicking the Bind button and dragging the vertex to the opposite line segment, the vertex is bound to the segment. Any movement of the spline keeps this vertex bound to the segment.

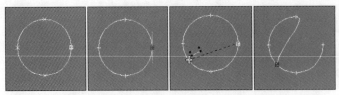

Figure 10-18: The Bind button attaches one end of the circle shape to a segment.

Tutorial: Making a ninja star

If you're involved with fighting games, either creating or playing them, then chances are good that when you look at the Star primitive, you think, "Wow, this is perfect for creating a ninja star weapon." If not, then just pretend.

To create a ninja star using splines, follow these steps:

1. Open the Ninja star.gmax file from the Chap 10 directory on the CD-ROM.

   This file includes a 10-pointed star shape with a circle in its center. Both of these shapes have already been converted to Editable Splines.

2. Select the circle shape, click the Modify tab in the Command Panel, and click the Vertex icon in the Selection rollout to enter Vertex subobject mode.

3. Click the Create Line button in the Geometry rollout, click the circle's top vertex and bottom vertex, right-click to end the line, and then right-click again to exit Create Line mode.

4. Select the top vertex of the line that you just created (be careful not to select the circle's top vertex; you can use the Cycle button to find the correct vertex). Right-click the vertex, and select the Bézier vertex type from the quad-menu. Then drag its lower handle until it is on top of the circle's left vertex. Repeat this step for the bottom vertex, and drag its handle to the circle's right vertex to create a ying-yang symbol in the center of the ninja star.

5. Exit Vertex subobject mode, and select the Star shape, select Vertex subobject mode again, and while holding down the Ctrl key, click on all the inner vertices of the star shape. Click the Chamfer button, enter a value of **15** in the Chamfer field, and press the Enter key.

Figure 10-19 shows the resulting ninja star.

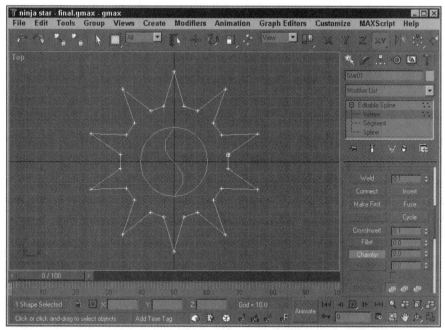

Figure 10-19: The completed ninja star, ready for action (or extruding)

Editing segments

To edit a segment, click the Segment subobject in the Modifier Stack or select the segment icon from the Selection rollout to enter segment subobject mode. Clicking again on either exits this mode. Segments are the lines or edges that run between two vertices. Many of the editing options work in the same way as when editing Vertex subobjects. You can select multiple segments by holding down the Ctrl key while clicking the segments, or you can hold down the Alt key to remove selected segments from the selection set. You can also copy segments when they're being transformed by holding down the Shift key. The cloned segments break away from the original spline while still remaining attached to it.

You can change segments from straight lines to curves by right-clicking the segment and selecting Line or Curve from the pop-up quadmenu. Line segments created with the Corner type vertex option cannot be changed to Curves, but lines created with Smooth and Bézier type vertex options can be switched back and forth.

Several Geometry rollout buttons work on more than one subobject type.

When you select a segment, the Divide button becomes active. This button adds the number of vertices specified to the selected segment or segments. Figure 10-20 shows the hexagon shape (second row, second from right) after all four segments are selected, a value of 1 is entered into the spinner, and the Divide button is clicked.

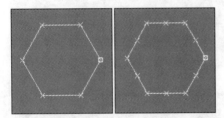

Figure 10-20: The Divide button adds segments to the spline.

Editing spline subobjects

To edit a spline, click Spline subobject in the Modifier Stack or select the spline icon from the Selection rollout. Transforming a spline object containing only one spline works the same way in subobject mode as it does in a normal transformation. Working in spline subobject mode on a spline object containing several splines lets you transform individual splines. Right-clicking a spline in subobject mode opens a pop-up quadmenu that lets you convert it between Curve and Line types. The Curve type option changes all vertices to Bézier type, and the Line type option makes all vertices Corner type. Spline subobject mode includes many of the buttons previously discussed, as well as some new ones in the Geometry rollout.

Reverse

The Reverse button is available only for Spline subobjects. It reverses the order of the vertex numbers. For example, a circle that is numbered clockwise from 1 to 4 would be numbered counterclockwise after using the Reverse button. The vertex order is important for splines that are used for animation paths or loft compound objects.

Outline

The Outline button creates a spline that is identical to the one selected and is offset based upon an amount specified by dragging or specified in the Offset value. The Center option creates an outline on either side of the selected spline, centered on the original spline. When the Center option is not selected, then an outline is created by offsetting a duplicate of the spline on only one side of the original spline. To exit Outline mode, click the Outline button again or right-click in the viewport. Figure 10-21 shows an arc that has had the Outline feature applied. The right image was created with the Center option enabled.

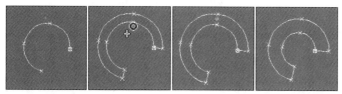

Figure 10-21: The Outline button creates a duplicate copy of the original spline and offsets it.

Boolean

Boolean operations work with two or more splines that overlap one another. There are three different operations that can happen — you could combine the splines to create a single spline (*union*), you could subtract the overlapping area from one of the splines (*subtract*), or you could throw away everything except the overlapping area (*intersection*).

Cross-Reference

You can also use Booleans to combine or subtract 3D volumes, which are covered in Chapter 13, "Continuing with Crazy Compound Objects."

The Boolean button works on overlapping closed splines and has three different options: Union, Subtraction, and Intersection, shown in Table 10-3. The splines must all be part of the same object. The Union option combines the areas of both splines, the Subtraction option removes the second spline's area from the first, and the Intersection option keeps only the areas that overlap.

Table 10-3
Shape Boolean Operations in gmax

Button	Description
	Union
	Subtraction
	Intersection

To use the Boolean feature, select one of the splines and select one of the Boolean operation options. Then click the Boolean button, and select the second spline. Depending on which Boolean operation you chose, the overlapping area is deleted, the second spline acts to cut away the overlapping area on the first, or only the overlapping area remains. To exit Boolean mode, right-click in the viewport.

Note   Boolean operations can be performed only on closed splines.

Figure 10-22 shows the results of applying the Spline Boolean operators on a circle and star shape. The second image illustrates the Union feature, the third (circle selected first) and fourth (star selected first) show the results of the Subtraction feature, and the fifth image illustrates the Intersection feature.

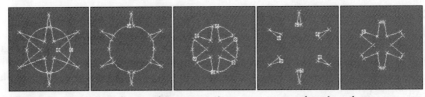

Figure 10-22: Using the Boolean operations on two overlapping shapes

Mirror

You can use the Mirror button to mirror a spline object horizontally, vertically, or along both axes. To use this feature, select a spline object to mirror and then locate the Mirror button. To the right of the Mirror button are three smaller buttons, indicating directions: Mirror Horizontally, Mirror Vertically, and Mirror Both, shown in Table 10-4. Select a direction, and then click the Mirror button. If the Copy option is selected, a new spline is created and mirrored. The About Pivot option causes the mirroring to be completed about the pivot point axes.

Table 10-4 Mirror Button Features	
Button	**Description**
▮▯	Mirror Horizontally
▱	Mirror Vertically
◈	Mirror Both

Figure 10-23 shows a little Pacman critter that has been mirrored horizontally, vertically, and both. The right image was horizontally mirrored with the About Pivot option disabled. Notice how the eye spline was mirrored about its own pivot.

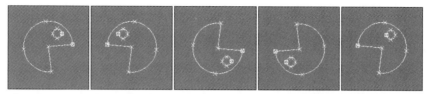

Figure 10-23: Mirroring a shape is as simple as selecting a direction and clicking the Mirror button.

Trim and Extend

The Trim button cuts off any extending portion between two overlapping splines. The splines must be part of the same object. To use the Trim feature, select the spline that you want to keep, click the Trim button, and then click the segment to trim. The spline you click is trimmed back to the nearest intersecting point of the selected object. To exit Trim mode, right-click in the viewport or click the Trim button again. This button works only in Spline subobject mode.

Figure 10-24 shows a circle intersected by two ellipse shapes. The Trim button was used to cut away the center sections of the ellipse shapes.

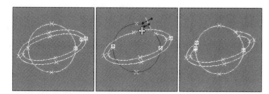

Figure 10-24: You can use the Trim button to cut away the excess of a spline.

The Extend button works in the reverse manner compared to the Trim button. The Extend button lengthens the end of a spline until it encounters an intersection. (There must be a spline segment to intersect.) To use the Extend command, click the Extend button and then click the segment to extend. The spline you click is extended. To exit Extend mode, right-click in the viewport or click the Extend button again.

The Infinite Bounds option works for both the Trim and Extend buttons. When enabled, it treats all open splines as if they were infinite for the purpose of locating an intersecting point.

Close

The Close button completes an open spline and creates a closed spline by attaching a segment between the first and last vertices. You can check which vertex is first by enabling the Show Vertex Numbers in the Selection rollout. This is similar to the Connect feature (accessible in Vertex subobject mode), but the Connect feature can connect the end point of one spline to the end point of another as long as they are part of the same Editable Spline object. The Close feature works only in Spline subobject mode and connects only the end points of each given spline.

Explode

The Explode button performs the Detach command on all subobject splines at once. It separates each segment into a separate spline.

 Cross-Reference The final rollout available for Editable Splines is the Surface Properties rollout. This rollout lets you assign a Material ID to a spline. You can find information on Material IDs in Chapter 19, "Creating and Applying Materials."

Tutorial: Spinning a spider's web

Now that you're familiar with the many aspects of editing splines, let's try to mimic one of the best spline producers in the world—the spider. The spider is an expert at connecting lines together to create an intricate pattern. (Luckily, unlike the spider who depends on its web for food, we won't go hungry if this example fails.)

To create a spider web from splines, follow these steps:

1. Open the Spider web.gmax file from the Chap 10 directory on the CD-ROM.

   This file includes a circle shape that represents the edges of the web. (We'll pretend that the spider is building this web inside a tire swing.) The circle shape has already been converted to an Editable Spline.

2. Open the Modify panel, and select the Spline subobject in the Modifier Stack to enter Spline subobject mode.

3. Click the Create Line button in the Geometry rollout, and then click in the center of the circle and again outside the circle to create a line. Then right-click to end the line. Repeat this step until 12 or so radial lines extend from the center of the circle outward.

4. While you're still in Create Line mode, click on the circle's center and create lines in a spiral pattern by clicking on each radial line that you intersect. Right-click to end the line when you finally reach the edge of the circle. Then right-click again to exit Create Line mode.

5. Select the circle shape, and click the Trim button. Then click on each line segment on the portion that extends beyond the circle. This trims the radial lines to the edge of the circle. Right click to exit Trim mode.

6. Change to Vertex subobject mode by clicking Vertex in the Modifier Stack. Then select all the vertices in the center of the circle, and click the Fuse and Weld buttons.

Figure 10-25 shows the finished spider web. (I have a new respect for spiders.)

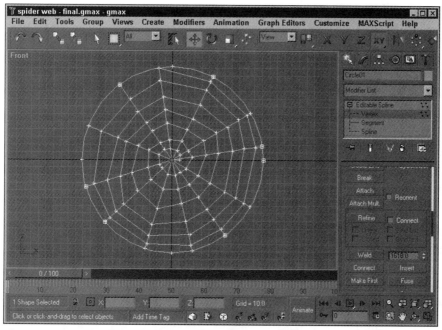

Figure 10-25: A spider web made from Editable Splines

Using Spline Modifiers

Modifiers are used to change the geometry of objects, but they can also be used on splines. In fact, there are several modifiers that can be used only on splines. You can find these modifiers in the Modifiers ➪ Patch/Spline Editing menu.

Cross-Reference Chapter 14, "Controlled Destruction with Modifiers," covers the ins and outs of modifiers in more detail.

Spline-specific modifiers

Of the modifiers that work only on splines, several of these duplicate functionality that is available for Editable Splines, such as the Fillet/Chamfer modifier. Applying these features as modifiers gives you better control over the results because you can remove them using the Modifier Stack at any time.

Edit Spline modifier

The Edit Spline modifier (mentioned at the start of the chapter) makes spline objects so they can be edited. It has all the same features as the Editable Spline object. The Edit Spline modifier isn't really a modifier, but an Object type. It shows up in the Modifier Stack above the base object. The key benefit of the Edit Spline modifier is that it enables you to edit spline subobjects while maintaining the parametric nature of the primitive object.

Spline Select modifier

This modifier enables you to select spline subobjects, including Vertex, Segment, and Spline. You can copy and paste named selection sets. The selection can then be passed up the Stack to the next modifier. The Spline Select modifier provides a way to apply a modifier to a subobject selection.

Delete Spline modifier

You can use the Delete Spline modifier to delete spline subobjects. Another good use of this modifier is to hide splines that are used for other purposes. For example, when creating an animation path, you could apply this modifier to the path to hide it, but by removing this modifier, you can get back to the base spline at any time.

Normalize Spline modifier

The Normalize Spline modifier adds new points to the spline. These points are spaced regularly based on the Segment Length value. This provides a quick way to optimize a spline. Figure 10-26 shows a simple flower shape with the Spline Select modifier applied so you can see the vertices. The Normalize Spline modifier was then applied with Segment Length values of 1, 5, 10, and 15. Notice how the shape is changing with fewer vertices.

Figure 10-26: The Normalize Spline modifier relaxes the shape by removing vertices.

Moving Splines to 3D

Although splines can be made visible, the real benefit of splines in gmax is to use them to create 3D objects and for animation paths. You can model 3D objects in several ways, including using Loft objects and modifiers. One way to use splines to make 3D objects is with modifiers.

Using splines to create an animation path is covered in Chapter 19, "Getting the Prop to Spin—Animation Basics," and Loft objects are covered in Chapter 13, "Continuing with Crazy Compound Objects." General information on working with modifiers is covered in Chapter 14, "Controlled Destruction with Modifiers."

Extruding splines

Because splines are drawn in a 2D plane, they already include two of the three dimensions. By adding a Height value to the shape, you can create a simple 3D object. The process of adding Height to a shape is called extruding.

To extrude a shape, you'll need to apply the Extrude modifier. To do so, select a spline object and choose Modifiers ➪ Mesh Editing ➪ Extrude, or select the Extrude modifier from the Modifier Stack drop-down list. In the Parameters rollout, you can specify an Amount (which is the height value of the extrusion), the number of Segments, and the Capping options (caps fill in the surface at each end of the Extruded shape). You can also specify the final Output to be a Patch, Mesh, or NURBS object. Figure 10-27 shows our capital Es that modeled the various vertex types extruded to a depth of 10.0.

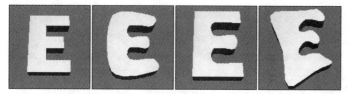

Figure 10-27: Extruding simple shapes adds depth to the spline.

Tutorial: Routing a custom shelf

In Woodshop 101, you use a router to add a designer edge to doorframes, window frames, and shelving of all sorts. In Woodshop 3D, the Boolean tools work nicely as we customize a bookshelf, which easily can be added to a Dungeon Siege room.

To create a custom bookshelf using spline Boolean operations, follow these steps:

1. Open the Bookshelf.gmax file from the Chap 10 directory on the CD-ROM.

   This file includes a triangle shape drawn with the Line primitive that is over-lapped by three circles. All these shapes have been converted to Editable Splines.

2. With the shape selected, open the Modify panel and select the Spline subob-ject mode, then select the triangle shape.

3. Select the Subtraction Boolean operation (the middle icon) in the Geometry rollout, and click the Boolean button. Then select each of the circles. Right-click in the viewport to exit Boolean mode, and click Spline in the Modifier Stack again to exit subobject mode.

4. Back in the Modify panel, select the Extrude modifier from the Modifier drop-down list and enter an Amount of **1000**. Select Zoom Extents All to resize your viewports, and view your bookshelf.

Figure 10-28 shows the finished bookshelf in the Perspective viewport ready to hang on the wall.

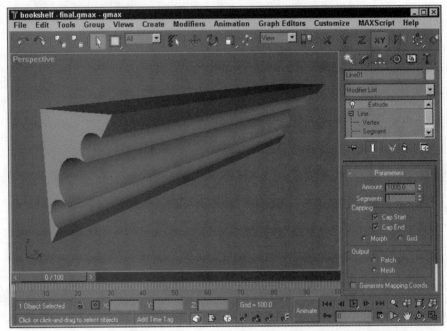

Figure 10-28: The finished bookshelf created with spline Boolean operations and the Extrude modifier

Lathing splines

Another useful modifier for 2D splines is the Lathe. This modifier rotates the spline about an axis to create an object with a circular cross-section (such as a baseball bat). In the Parameters rollout, you can specify the Degrees to rotate (a value of 360 makes a full rotation) and Cappings, which add ends to the resulting mesh. Additional options include Weld Core, which causes all vertices at the center of the lathe to be welded together, and Flip Normals, which realigns all the normals.

The Direction option determines the axis about which the rotation takes place. The rotation takes place about the object's pivot point.

Caution   If your shape is created in the Top view, then lathing about the screen Z-axis produces a thin disc with no depth.

Tutorial: Lathing a crucible

As an example of the Lathe modifier, we'll create a simple crucible, suitable for adorning a potion master's table, although we could produce any object that has a circular cross-section. A crucible is a thick porcelain cup used to melt chemicals. I chose this as an example because it is simple (and saying "crucible" sounds much more scientific than "cup").

To create a crucible using the Lathe modifier, follow these steps:

1. Open the Crucible.gmax file from the Chap 10 directory on the CD-ROM.

   This file includes a rough profile cross-section line of the crucible that has been converted to an Editable Spline, and the line's pivot point has been moved to its right edge.

2. Select the line, and then select the Modifiers ⇨ Patch/Spline Editing ⇨ Lathe menu command. Set the Degrees value in the Parameters rollout to 360.

   Because you'll lathe a full revolution, you don't need to check the Cap options.

3. In the Direction section, select the Y button (the Y-axis), and you're finished.

Figure 10-29 shows the finished product. You can easily make this into a coffee mug by adding a handle. To make a handle, simply loft an ellipse along a curved path.

CrossSection modifier

The CrossSection modifier is one of two modifiers that collectively are referred to as the surface tools. The surface tools provide a way to cover a series of connected cross-sections with a surface. It connects the vertices of several cross-sectional splines together with additional splines in preparation for the Surface modifier. These cross-sectional splines can have different numbers of vertices. Parameters include different spline types, such as Linear, Smooth, Bézier, and Bézier Corner.

Cross-Reference   The Surface modifier is the other half of the surface tools. You can find this modifier and an example in Chapter 12, "Performing with Perfect Patches." The surface tools are similar in many ways to the Loft compound object, which I cover in Chapter 13, "Continuing with Crazy Compound Objects."

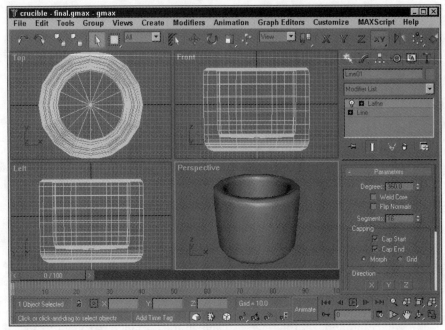

Figure 10-29: Lathing a simple profile can create a circular object.

Summary

As this chapter has shown, there is much more to splines than just points, lines, and control handles. Splines in gmax are one of the fundamental building elements and are especially useful as the basis for creating models using modifiers such as Extrude and Lathe.

This chapter covered the following spline topics:

✦ Understanding the various shape primitives

✦ Editing splines

✦ Working with the various spline subobjects

✦ Applying modifiers to splines

The next chapter continues our voyage down the modeling pathway with perhaps the most common modeling type—meshes.

✦   ✦   ✦

Moving On with Marvelous Meshes

✦   ✦   ✦   ✦

In This Chapter

Creating Editable Mesh and Poly objects

Working with the mesh and poly subobject modes

Editing meshes and polys

Modeling in Low-Res

✦   ✦   ✦   ✦

Meshes, or more specifically — polygon meshes, are perhaps the most popular and the default model type for most 3D programs. You create them by placing polygonal faces next to one another so the edges are joined. The polygons can then be smoothed from face to face during the rendering process. Using meshes, you can create almost any 3D object including simple primitives such as a cube converted to a mesh or a realistic dinosaur.

Meshes have lots of advantages. They are common, intuitive to work with, and supported by a large number of 3D software packages. In this chapter, you'll learn how to create and edit mesh and poly objects, and you'll also get experience using some mesh object modifiers.

Creating Editable Mesh and Poly Objects

The Create panel does not include a method for making mesh objects — mesh objects need to be converted from another object type or produced as the result of a modifier. Object types that you can convert include shapes, primitives, Booleans, and patches. Many models that are imported will appear as mesh objects. Most 3D formats, including 3DS and DXF, import as mesh objects.

Note

You can even convert spline shapes to editable meshes, whether they are open or closed. Closed splines are filled with a polygon, whereas open splines are only a single edge and can be hard to see.

Before you can use many of the mesh editing functions discussed in this chapter, you'll need to convert the object to an Editable Mesh or an Editable Poly object, collapse an object with modifiers applied, or apply the Edit Mesh modifier.

Converting objects

To convert an object into an Editable Mesh or an Editable Poly object, right-click on the object and choose Convert To ➪ Convert to Editable Mesh or Convert to Editable Poly from the pop-up quadmenu. You can also convert an object by right-clicking on the object within the Modifier Stack and selecting one of the convert options from the pop-up menu.

Collapsing to a mesh object

When an object is collapsed, it loses its parametric nature and the parameters associated with any applied modifiers. Only objects that have had modifiers applied to them can be collapsed. Objects are made into an Editable Mesh object when you use the Collapse To option available from the right-click pop-up menu in the Modifier Stack or when you use the Collapse utility.

Most objects will collapse to an Editable Mesh object, but objects with the Select Poly modifier applied will collapse to an Editable Poly object.

Applying the Edit Mesh modifier

Another way to enable the mesh editing features is to apply the Edit Mesh modifier to an object. You apply this modifier by selecting the object and choosing Modifiers ➪ Mesh Editing ➪ Edit Mesh, or selecting Edit Mesh from the Modifier drop-down list in the Modify panel.

The Edit Mesh modifier is different from the Editable Mesh object in that as an applied modifier, it maintains the parametric nature of the original object. For example, you cannot change the Radius value of a sphere object that has been converted to an Editable Mesh, but you could if the Edit Mesh modifier were applied.

 Note   There is no Edit Poly modifier.

Editable Mesh versus Editable Poly objects

Editable Mesh objects split all polygons up into triangular faces, but the Editable Poly object maintains four-sided polygon faces. Another key difference is found in the subobjects. Editable Meshes can work with Vertex, Edge, Face, Polygon, and Element subobjects; Editable Poly objects can work with Vertex, Edge, Border, Polygon, and Element subobjects.

The majority of features are the same for both Editable Mesh and Editable Poly objects, but some features are available for only one of these. These differences will be pointed out in the sections to follow.

Editing Mesh and Poly Objects

After an object has been converted to an Editable Mesh or an Editable Poly, you can alter its shape by applying modifiers, or you can work with the mesh subobjects. In the Modify panel are many tools for controlling meshes and working with their individual subobjects.

Note Open spline objects that have been converted to an Editable Mesh have only the Vertex subobject mode available because they don't have any edges or faces.

Editable Mesh subobjects modes

Before you can edit Mesh subobjects, you must select them. To select a Subobject mode, select Editable Mesh in the Modifier Stack and click the small plus sign to its left to display a hierarchy of subobjects, then click the subobject type that you want to work with. Another way to select a subobject type is to click on the appropriate subobject button in the Selection rollout. The subobject button in the Selection rollout turns bright yellow when selected, and the subobject listed in the Modifier Stack is highlighted blue. When a subobject mode is selected, you can also type a number 1–5 to switch among the different subobject modes: 1 is for Vertex, 2 is for Edge, 3 is for Face, 4 is for Polygon, and 5 is for Element.

To exit subobject edit mode, click the subobject button (displayed in yellow) again. Remember, you must exit this mode before you can select another object.

Note Selected subobject edges appear in the viewports in red to distinguish them from edges of the selected object, which appear white when displayed as wireframes.

After you're in a subobject mode, you can click an object (or drag over an area to select multiple subobjects) to select it and edit the subobject using the transformation buttons on the main toolbar. You can transform subobjects just like other objects.

Cross-Reference For more information on transforming objects, see Chapter 7, "Moving, Rotating, and Scaling Objects — The Return of the –ings."

You can select multiple subobjects at the same time by dragging an outline over them. You can also select multiple subobjects by holding down the Ctrl key while clicking them. The Ctrl key can also deselect selected subobjects while maintaining the rest of the selection. Holding down the Alt key removes any selected vertices from the current selection set.

With the Select and Move button selected, hold down the Shift key while clicking and dragging on a subobject to clone it. During cloning, the Clone Part of the Mesh dialog box appears enabling you to Clone to Object or Clone to Element. Using the Clone to Object option makes the selection an entirely new object, and you will be able to give the new object a name. If the Clone to Element option is selected, the clone remains part of the existing object but is a new element within that object.

Editable Poly subobject modes

The subobject modes for the Editable Poly are a little different. They include Vertex, Edge, Border, Polygon, and Element. The Border subobject mode selects all the edges around a polygon face, which may be more than three. The various subobject modes can be selected in the same manner as the Editable Mesh.

Before you can edit Mesh or Poly subobjects, you must select them. To select a Subobject mode, select the hierarchy element under the Editable Poly object and then click one of the subobject buttons in the Selection rollout.

Caution   The 1–5 keyboard shortcuts to switch between subobject modes for Editable Meshes don't work for Editable Poly objects.

Selection rollout

The Selection rollout includes options for selecting subobjects. The By Vertex option is available in all but the Vertex subobject mode. It requires that you click a vertex in order to select an edge, face, polygon, or element. It selects all edges and faces that are connected to a vertex when the vertex is selected. The Ignore Backfacing option selects only those subobjects with normals pointing toward the current viewport. For example, if you are trying to select some faces on a sphere, only the faces on the side closest to you are selected. If this option is off, then faces on both sides of the sphere are selected. This option is helpful if many subobjects are on top of one another in the viewport.

The Ignore Visible Edges option is active only in Polygon subobject mode. This button enables you to select all the polygons within a plane, as determined by the Planar Threshold value. If the Ignore Visible Edges option is not selected, the selection is limited to the edges of the polygon that is clicked. For example, if you click a sphere toward one end with a Planar Threshold of 10, all the polygons within a single ring around the sphere are selected.

In all subobject modes except Edge, you can select to Show Normals and set a Scale value. Normals are vectors that extend outward perpendicular to the surface of an object. Using this option, you can determine which way a subobject is facing, which could affect how the object is smoothed. Figure 11-1 shows a sphere object that has been converted to an Editable Mesh with all faces selected in Face subobject mode with the Show Normals option selected.

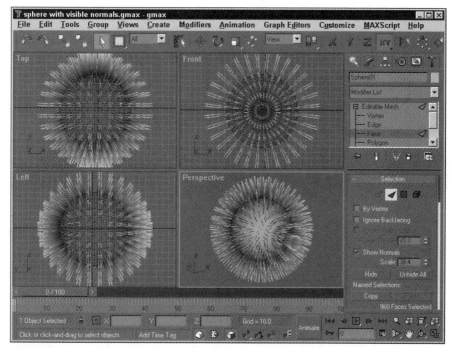

Figure 11-1: The Show Normals option shows the normal vectors for each face in a sphere.

The Hide button hides the selected subobjects. You can make hidden objects visible again with the Unhide All button.

After selecting several subobjects, you can create a named selection set by typing a name in the Name Selection Sets drop-down list in the main toolbar. You can then copy and paste these selection sets onto other mesh objects.

At the bottom of the Selection rollout is the Selection Information, which is a text line that automatically displays the number and type of selected items.

Cross-
Reference

The Soft Selection rollout allows you to alter adjacent non-selected subobjects when selected subobjects are moved, creating a smooth transition. For the details on this rollout, see Chapter 9, "Beginning with the Basic Building Blocks."

Edit Geometry rollout

Much of the power of editing meshes is contained within the Edit Geometry rollout. Features contained here include, among many others, the ability to create new subobjects, attach subobjects to the mesh, weld vertices, chamfer vertices, slice, explode, and align. Some Edit Geometry buttons are disabled depending on the subobject mode that you've selected. The following buttons are enabled before you enter a subobject mode.

Attach

The Attach button is available with all subobject modes and even when you are not in subobject mode. When no subobject mode is selected, the Detach button (to the right) changes to an Attach List button for mesh objects. Clicking the Attach List button opens the Attach List dialog box where you can select from a list of all the objects to attach. The list contains only objects that you can attach.

Use the Attach button to add objects to the current Editable Mesh (or Editable Poly) objects. You can add primitives, splines, patch objects, and other mesh objects. Any object that is attached to a mesh object is automatically converted into an editable mesh. Any objects that are added to a mesh object can be selected using the Element subobject mode.

To use this feature, select the main object and click the Attach button. Move the mouse over the object to be attached — the cursor changes to a plus sign over any acceptable objects. Click the object to select it. Click the Attach button again or right-click in the viewport to exit Attach mode.

Explode

The Explode button can also be used outside of all subobject modes and with the Face, Polygon, and Element subobject modes. It is the opposite of the Attach button and can be used to separate all selected faces or polygons into individual objects or elements. The spinner to the right sets the angle value of the faces to include in this operation. If the Objects option is selected, the Explode to Objects dialog box appears, enabling you to name the object.

Remove Isolated Vertices

The Remove Isolated Vertices button can be used at any time and in any subobject mode. It automatically deletes all isolated vertices associated with a mesh object, selected or not. Isolated vertices can result from deleting a face, or they could be inserted with the Create button and never connected. This helpful feature cleans up a mesh before applying any modifiers. Some modifiers cannot be applied if isolated vertices are part of the mesh.

View and Grid Align

The View and Grid Align buttons move and orient all selected vertices to the current active viewport or to the current construction grid. These buttons can also be used in all subobject modes.

Editing vertices

When working with Editable Mesh and Poly objects, after you select Vertex subobject mode and select vertices, you can transform them using the transform buttons on the main toolbar. When you move the vertices around, the mesh edges follow.

Create

The Create button lets you add new vertices to a mesh object. To create a new vertex, click the Create button to enter Create mode. You can then click where you want the new vertex to be located. Click the Create button again or right-click in the viewport to exit Create mode.

Create mode works for all mesh subobject types except edges. Be aware that creating a vertex doesn't add it to any of the edges, but the Create button in Edge subobject mode can connect edges to these isolated vertices.

Delete

The Delete button lets you delete the selected vertices. To use this button, select a vertex or vertices to delete and click the Delete button. This button works for all the subobject types.

Caution   Deleting a vertex also deletes all faces and their edges connected to that vertex. This deletion can cause holes in the geometry and cause problems with many modifiers.

Figure 11-2 shows an Editable Mesh sphere object with several deleted vertices. The deleted vertices have created a hole in the geometry. You cannot see the back inside of the sphere because the Force 2-Sided option was disabled in the Viewport Configuration dialog box.

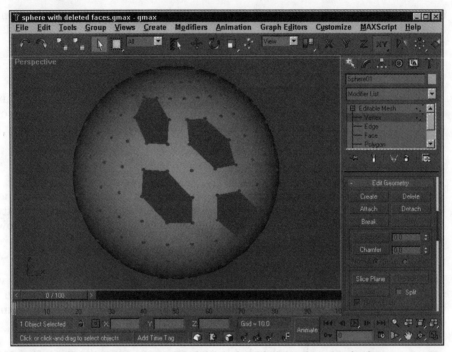

Figure 11-2: Deleting vertices also deletes the adjoining faces and edges.

Detach

Use the Detach button to separate the selected subobjects from the rest of the object. To use this button, select the subobject and click the Detach button. The Detach dialog box opens, enabling you to name the new detached subobject. You also have the options to Detach to Element or to Detach as Clone. All subobject modes except Edge have a Detach option. This button appears in place of the Attach List button in all subobject modes.

Break

You use the Break button to create a separate vertex for adjoining faces that are connected by a single vertex.

In a normal mesh, faces are all connected by vertices — moving one vertex changes the position of all adjoining faces. The Break button enables you to move the vertex associated with each face independent of the others. The button is available only in Vertex subobject mode.

Figure 11-3 shows a hexagon shape with polygon faces that were joined at the center. The Break button was used to separate the center vertex into separate vertices for each face. The faces can be manipulated independently, as the figure shows.

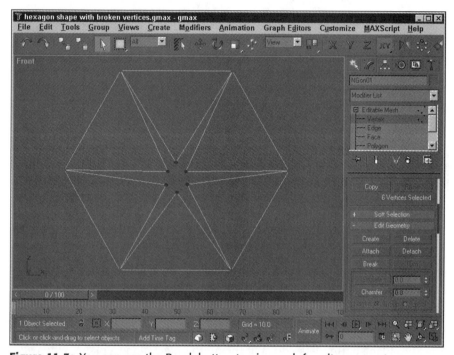

Figure 11-3: You can use the Break button to give each face its own vertex.

Chamfer

The Chamfer button, which is enabled in Vertex, Edge, and Border subobject modes, lets you cut the edge off a corner and replace it with a face. This existing corner vertex is deleted and automatically replaced with a face as well as vertices for each edge that was connected to the original corner vertex. The Chamfer amount is the distance the new face vertices move along the edge away from the original vertex position.

To use this feature, click the Chamfer button, and then click and drag the vertex to be chamfered or select a vertex and enter a value in the Chamfer spinner. If multiple vertices are selected, they all are chamfered equal amounts. If you click and drag on an unselected vertex, then the current selection is dropped and the new selection is chamfered.

Figure 11-4 shows the results of chamfering all the vertices of a cube at the same time.

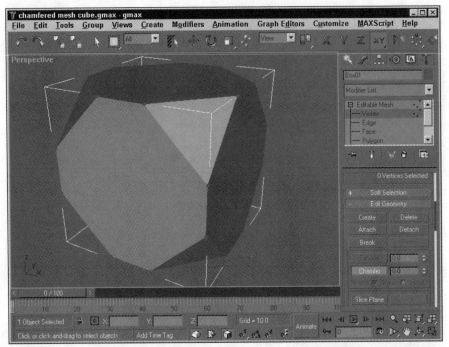

Figure 11-4: You use the Chamfer button to replace all vertices with faces.

Slice

The Slice Plane button lets you split the mesh object along a plane. When you click the Slice Plane button, a yellow slice plane gizmo appears on the selected object. You can move, rotate, and scale this gizmo using the transform buttons. After you properly position the plane and set all options, click the Slice button to finish slicing the mesh. All intersected faces split in two and new vertices and edges are added to the mesh where the Slice Plane intersects the original mesh.

The Slice Plane mode stays active until you deselect the Slice Plane button or until you right-click in the viewport; this feature enables you to make several slices in one session. The Slice Plane button is enabled for all subobject modes. For the Editable Poly object, a Reset Plane button is located next to the Slice Plane button. Use this button to reset the slice plane to its original location.

You use the Split option to double the number of vertices along the Slice Plane. Choosing the Refine Ends option causes open ends on adjacent faces to be connected to avoid discontinuities in the surface.

Weld Selected and Weld Target

The Weld Selected button works like the Weld function for splines. To use this feature, select two or more vertices and click the Weld button. If the vertices are within the threshold value specified by the spinner to the right of the button, they are welded into one vertex. If no vertices are within the threshold, an alert box opens and notifies you of this situation.

Tip   If you run into trouble with the Weld button and its Threshold value, try using the Collapse button.

The Weld Target button lets you select a vertex and drag and drop it on top of another vertex. If the target vertex is within the number of pixels specified by the Target value, the vertices are welded into one vertex. To exit Weld Target mode, click the Target button again or right-click in the viewport.

These buttons are available only in Vertex subobject mode.

Make Planar

A single vertex or two vertices don't define a plane, but three or more vertices do. If three or more vertices are selected, you can use the Make Planar button to make these vertices coplanar (which means that all vertices are on the same plane). Doing so positions the selected vertices so they lie in the same plane. This is helpful if you want to build a new polygon face. Polygonal faces need to be coplanar. This button works in all subobject modes.

Collapse

The Collapse button is used to collapse all the selected subobjects to a single subobject located at the averaged center of the selection. This button is similar to the Weld button, except that the selected vertices don't need to be within a Threshold value to be combined. This button works in all subobject modes.

Vertex Surface properties

The Surface Properties rollout in Vertex subobject mode lets you define the Weight, Color, and Illumination of object vertices. In Vertex mode, this rollout lets you give selected vertices a Weight. Vertices with higher weight have a greater pull, like the gravity of a larger planet. Several modifiers (such as MeshSmooth) use this weight setting.

Also within this rollout are several color swatches, which enable you to select Color and Illumination colors for the selected vertices. Vertex colors are useful for game engines because they provide an efficient way to color objects without the overhead of a texture map.

The Alpha value sets the amount of transparency for the vertices. After you assign colors, you can then recall vertices with the same color by selecting a color (or illumination color) in the Select Vertices By section and clicking the Select button. The RGB values match all colors within the Range defined by these values. For example, if the RGB Range values are all set to 255, then every vertex is selected.

Tutorial: Modeling a clown head

Now that all the editable mesh features have been covered, let's use them to actually get some work done. In this example, you'll quickly deform a mesh sphere to create a clown face by selecting, moving, and working with some vertices.

To create a clown head by moving vertices, follow these steps:

1. Open the Mesh clown head.gmax file from the Chap 11 directory on the CD-ROM.

   This file includes a simple sphere that has been converted to an Editable Mesh object.

2. Open the Modify panel. Now make a long, pointy nose by pulling a vertex outward from the sphere object. Click the small plus (+) sign to the left of the Editable Mesh object in the Modifier Stack, and select Vertex in the hierarchy.

   This activates the Vertex subobject mode.

3. Select the single vertex at the top of the sphere. Make sure the Select and Move button is selected, and in the Top viewport, drag the vertex along the Y-axis until it projects from the sphere.

4. Next, create the mouth by selecting and indenting a row of vertices. For this selection, open the Soft Selection rollout, and click the Use Soft Selection option. Under the nose, select several vertices in a circular arc to make a smile and press the Spacebar to lock the selection. Then move the selected vertices along the negative Y-axis.

5. Unlock the mouth selection. For the eyes, select two sets of three vertices above the nose and lock the selection. With the Soft Selection still enabled, move the eye vertices in the Y-axis, but not as far as the nose.

6. Unlock the eye selections. Select each eye set of vertices independently, and click the Weld Selected button. (If the vertices aren't within the threshold, increase the threshold and try again.)

7. Select both sets of eye vertices, and click the Chamfer button. Then drag in the viewport an intermediate distance back to the surface of the sphere.

This clown head is just a simple example of what is possible by editing subobjects. Figure 11-5 shows the clown head in a shaded view.

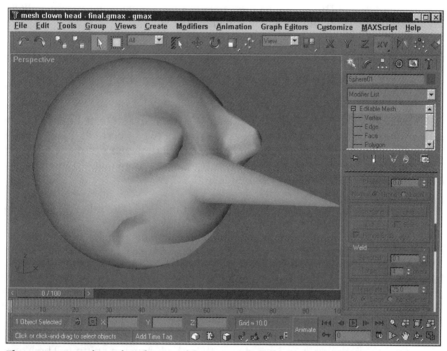

Figure 11-5: A clown head created from an editable mesh by selecting and moving vertices

Editing edges

Edges are the lines that run between two vertices. Edges can be closed (which means that each side of the edge is connected to a face) or open (which means that only one face connects to the edge). Mesh edges, such as in the interior of a shape that has been converted to a mesh, can also be invisible.

You can select multiple edges by holding down either the Ctrl key while clicking the edges, or the Alt key to remove selected edges from the selection set. You can also copy edges using the Shift key while transforming the edge. The cloned edge maintains connections to its vertices by creating new edges.

Many of the Edge subobject options work in the same way as the Vertex subobject options.

Divide

The Divide button adds a new vertex at the middle of the edge and splits the edge into two equal sections. When in Edge, Face, Border, Polygon, or Element subobject mode, the Divide button replaces the Break button. To exit Divide mode, click the Divide button again or right-click in the viewport.

This button works in all subobject modes except Vertex.

Turn

The Turn button rotates the hidden edges that break up the polygon into triangles (all polygonal faces include these hidden edges). For example, if a quadrilateral (four-sided) face has a hidden edge, which runs between vertices 1 and 3, then the Turn button would change this hidden edge to run between 2 and 4. This affects how the surface is smoothed when the polygon is not coplanar. To exit Turn mode, click the Turn button again or right-click in the viewport.

This button is available only in Edge subobject mode for the Editable Mesh object.

Extrude

The Extrude button adds depth to an edge by extending it and creating a new face behind the extruded edge. For example, a square extruded from a patch grid would form a box with no lid. To use this feature, select an edge or edges and click the Extrude button; then drag in a viewport. The edges interactively show the extrude depth. Release the button when you've reached the desired distance.

Alternatively, you can set an extrude depth in the Extrusion spinner. The Normal Group option extrudes all selected edges along the normal for the group (the normal runs perpendicular to the face), and the Normal Local option moves each individual edge along its local normal. To exit Extrude mode, click the Extrude button again or right-click in the viewport.

The Extrude button is enabled for Face, Polygon, and Element subobject modes for the Editable Mesh object.

Cut

The Cut button enables you to split an edge into two by cutting an existing edge. To use this feature, click the Cut button. The cursor changes to a plus sign when over an edge. You can then click on an edge and drag across the edges you want to cut. If you drag across several faces, a new vertex and edge are created at each intersection. You can make several successive cuts at one time. To exit cutting mode, right-click. Then right-click again to disable the Cut button.

The Split option creates two vertices at every junction, enabling these faces to be easily separated. The Refine Edges option maintains the continuous surface of the mesh by adding additional vertices to all adjacent faces to the cut. The Cut button is available for Editable Mesh objects in all subobject modes except Vertex.

Select Open Edges and Create Shape from Edges options

The Select Open Edges button locates and selects all open edges. Using this button is a good way to find any holes in the geometry. This feature is another one that helps eliminate potential problems with a mesh object. The Create Shape from Edges button creates a new spline shape from selected edges. The Create Shape dialog box appears, enabling you to give the new shape a name. You can also select options for Smooth or Linear shape types and to Ignore Hidden Edges.

Edge Surface properties

The Surface Properties rollout for the Editable Mesh object in the Edge subobject mode includes Visible and Invisible buttons that you can use to make invisible edges between polygons visible. The Auto Edge button automatically makes invisible all selected edges less than the Threshold value if the Set and Clear Edge Vis option is selected. The Set option makes invisible edges visible, and the Clear option makes visible edges invisible.

Editing Face, Border, Polygon, and Element subobjects

Editable Mesh objects include two different types of faces: Face and Polygon subobjects. Face subobjects have only three edges. This polygon is the simplest possible, and all other polygons can be broken down into this type of face. Polygon subobjects are any faces with more than three vertices. A Polygon subobject includes two or more faces. A dashed line contained within the polygon designates these faces.

Editable Poly objects do not need the Face subobject because they support polygon faces. Instead, they have a Border subobject. A Border subobject is a polygon with no face but with edges on all sides that is actually a hole within the geometry.

Transforming a face or polygon object works the same way in subobject mode as in normal transformations. The Edit Geometry rollout includes many of the same buttons previously covered in the "Editing vertices" and "Editing edges" sections, but includes some additional features that apply only to Face, Border, and Polygon subobjects.

A mesh object can also contain several elements. The Element subobject mode includes all the same commands as the Face, Border, and Polygon subobject modes.

Create

You can use the Create button to create new faces and/or polygons based on new or existing vertices. To create a new face, click the Create button — all vertices in the selected mesh are highlighted. Next, click a vertex to start the face — after clicking two more vertices, a new face is created. You can also create a new vertex not based on any existing vertices by holding down the Shift key while clicking.

Polygons aren't limited to three vertices. You can click as many times as you want to add additional vertices to the polygon. Click the first vertex, or double-click to complete the polygon. Figure 11-6 shows a simple shape that has been supplemented with additional polygon faces.

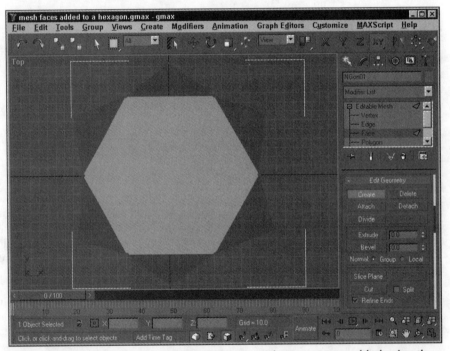

Figure 11-6: All the triangles exterior to the center hexagon were added using the Create button in Face subobject mode.

Bevel

The Bevel button appears in place of the Chamfer button for Face, Polygon, and Element subobject modes. It extrudes the Face or Polygon subobject selection and then lets you bevel the edges. To use this feature, select a face or polygon and click the Bevel button; then drag up or down in a viewport to the Extrusion depth and release the button. Drag again to specify the Bevel amount. The Bevel amount determines the relative size of the extruded face.

The Normal Group option extrudes all selected faces or polygons along the normal for the group, and the Normal Local option moves each individual face or polygon along its local normal. For Editable Poly objects, you can also use the Bevel By Polygon option. To exit Bevel mode, click the Bevel button again or right-click in the viewport. The Bevel button is enabled for all subobject modes except Vertex, Edge, and Border.

Figure 11-7 displays a poly dodecahedron. Each face has been locally extruded with a value of 20 and then locally beveled with a value of –10.

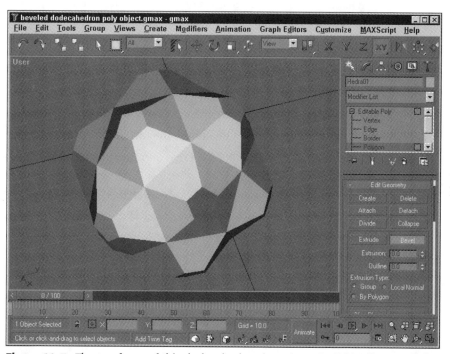

Figure 11-7: The top faces of this dodecahedron have been individually extruded and beveled.

Tutorial: Building a beveled pyramid

The Egyptians were pyramid masters, but modeling a pyramid is too easy because it can be easily created using the primitives. Instead, we'll look to the Aztec civilization for a pyramid example that has several flat terraces on the way to the top. This gives you a chance to practice working with an Editable Poly object.

To create a multi-stage pyramid from an Editable Poly object, follow these steps:

1. Open the Aztec pyramid.gmax file from the Chap 11 directory on the CD-ROM.

   This file includes a simple box primitive that has been converted to an Editable Poly.

2. Open the Modify panel. In the Selection rollout, click the Polygon subobject button and enable the Ignore Backfacing option. Click the Select Objects button on the main toolbar, and then click on the box object in the Top viewport to select the topmost polygon.

   Notice at the bottom of the Selection rollout that only one polygon is mentioned as being selected.

3. In the Edit Polygon rollout, click the Bevel button and enter a value of –5 in the Outline field.

   This makes the top polygon smaller than the bottom polygon.

4. Click again on the Select Objects button on the main toolbar to exit this mode.

5. In the Edit Geometry rollout, select the Edge option and click the Tessellate button three times.

   This divides the top polygon into 64 separate polygons.

6. While still in Polygon subobject mode, drag over all the internal polygons to select them.

   The bottom of the Selection rollout lists 36 polygons selected.

7. Click on the Bevel button in the Edit Geometry rollout again, and enter **20** for the Extrusion value and **–5** for the Outline value.

8. Repeat Steps 6 and 7 two more times to complete the pyramid.

Figure 11-8 shows the completed pyramid.

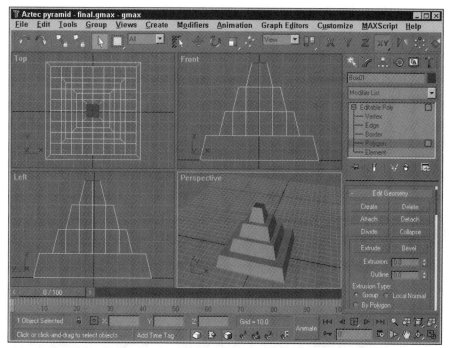

Figure 11-8: This pyramid was created from an Editable Poly object.

Tessellate

You can use the Tessellate button to increase the resolution of a mesh by splitting a face or polygon into several faces or polygons. You have two options to do this: Edge and Face-Center.

The Edge method splits each edge at its midpoint. For example, a triangular face would be split into three smaller triangles. The Tension spinner to the right of the Tessellate button specifies a value that is used to make the tessellated face concave or convex.

The Face-Center option creates a vertex in the center of the face and also creates three new edges that extend from the center vertex to each original vertex. For a square polygon, this option would create six new triangular faces. (Remember that a square polygon is actually composed of two triangular faces.)

Figure 11-9 shows the faces of a cube that has been tessellated once using the Edge option and then again using the Face-Center option.

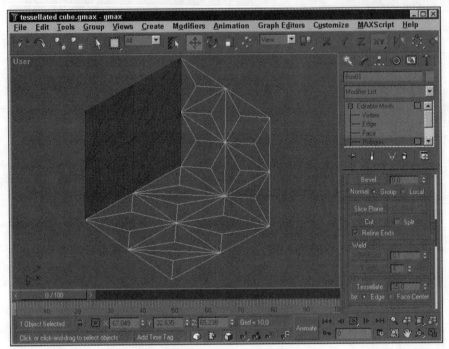

Figure 11-9: A cube tessellated twice using each option

Subdivide rollout

Another key difference between Editable Mesh and Editable Poly objects is that Editable Poly objects include a Subdivide rollout. Within this rollout are options to MeshSmooth and Tessellate subobject selections.

The MeshSmooth button can help create smoother edges and higher resolution areas. This button can be used several times on the same object. The Smoothness value determines which vertices are used to smooth the object. The higher the value, the more vertices are included and the smoother the result. You can also select that the smoothing is separated by Smoothing Groups or by Materials. Figure 11-10 shows the result of clicking the MeshSmooth button four times to smooth a simple cube. Notice how the size of the object has been reduced as it has been smoothed.

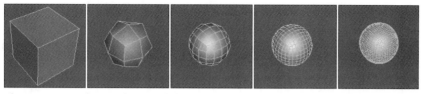

Figure 11-10: The MeshSmooth button can smooth sharp edges of an object.

Tip

If you plan on using the MeshSmooth button, use the Tessellate button first to increase its resolution. This prevents a dramatic change in the structure of the object.

Tessellation subdivides the number of faces to increase higher resolution. If you plan on working with subobjects to edit an object, you'll probably want a higher resolution. Subdividing using tessellation can be done using Edges or Faces, and the Tension setting controls how tight the adjacent faces are. Figure 11-11 shows a cube that has been repeatedly tessellated using the Edge method.

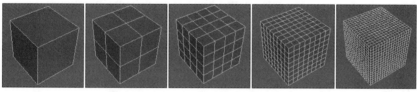

Figure 11-11: The Tessellate button increases the number of faces for an object.

Without a subobject mode selected, the Surface Properties rollout includes an option to enable NURMS Subdivision. NURMS stands for Non-Uniform Rational MeshSmooth. NURMS can weight each control point. It works by smoothing the entire surface of an object by applying a chamfer function to both vertices and edges at the same time. It has the greatest effect on sharp corners and edges.

There are also settings for the number of Iterations to run, a Smoothness value and whether to apply the smoothing within Smoothing Group boundaries and/or Materials. Update Options can be set to Always and Manually using the Update button.

Caution

Increasing the Iterations value can very quickly increase the total number of faces to an unruly number, which take a long time to update. You can press the Escape key to halt the calculations.

Face, Polygon, and Element Surface properties

For Face, Polygon, and Element subobjects, the Surface Properties rollout includes Flip, Unify, and Flip Normal Mode buttons to control the direction of the normal vectors. Flip reverses the direction of the normals of each selected face; Unify makes all normals face the same direction based on the majority. The Flip Normal Mode button activates a mode in which you can click individual faces and flip their normals. This mode stays active until you click the Flip Normal Mode button again or right-click in the viewport. These buttons are available only for the Editable Mesh object.

For the Editable Poly object, the Edge, Border, Polygon, and Element subobjects include the Edit Triangulation button. This button lets you change the internal edges of the polygon by dragging from one vertex to another. The Retriangulate button automatically computes all the internal edges for you, and the Flip Normals button flips the normal vectors for the selected subobjects.

The Surface Properties rollout also includes Material IDs and Smoothing Groups options.

The Material IDs option settings are used by the Multi/Sub-Object material type to apply different materials to faces or polygons within an object. By selecting a polygon subobject, you can use these option settings to apply a unique material to the selected polygon. The Select By ID button opens a simple dialog box in which you can enter a Material ID. Clicking OK selects all subobjects that have the specific material ID applied.

You can find more information on the Multi/Sub-Object material type in Chapter 16, "Putting On the Ritz with the gmax Material Editor."

You use the Smoothing Group option to assign a subobject to a unique smoothing group. To do this, select a subobject and click a Smoothing Group number. The Select By SG button, like the Select By ID button, opens a dialog box in which you can enter a smoothing group number, and all subobjects with that number are selected. The Clear All button clears all smoothing group number assignments, and the Auto Smooth button automatically assigns smoothing group numbers based on the angle between faces as set by the value to the right of the Auto Smooth button.

Tutorial: Cleaning up imported meshes

Almost all 3D formats are mesh formats, and importing mesh objects can sometimes create problems. By collapsing an imported model to an editable mesh, you can take advantage of several of the editable mesh features to clean up these problems.

Figure 11-12 shows a model that was exported from Poser using the 3ds format. Notice that the model's waist is the same color as the background. It appears this way only because the normals for this object are pointing in the wrong direction. This problem is common for imported meshes, and we'll fix it in this tutorial.

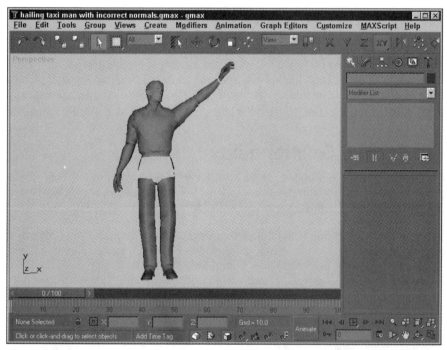

Figure 11-12: This mesh suffers from objects with flipped normals, which makes them invisible.

To fix the normals on an imported mesh model, follow these steps:

1. Open the Hailing taxi man with incorrect normals.gmax file from the Chap 11 directory on the CD-ROM.

2. Select the problem object — the waist. Open the object hierarchy by clicking the plus (+) sign to the left of the Editable Mesh object in the Modifier Stack, and select Element subobject mode.

3. In the Selection rollout, select the Show Normals option and set the Scale value to a small number such as 0.1, and then select the waist subobject.

   The normals will be visible. Notice how some of them point outward and some inward.

4. With the element subobject still selected, click the Unify button in the Surface Properties rollout and then click the Flip button until all normals are pointing outward.

This problem is now fixed, and the waist object is now a visible part of the mesh. The fixed mesh looks just like the original mesh without the ugly black shorts.

Creating Low-Res Models

Many 3D games require fast real-time scene updates, and one of the first lessons you need to learn as you begin to create game content is that low-polygon count models render faster than high-polygon count models. For these types of games, low-resolution models are necessary, so you'd better get used to counting polygons. gmax includes several tools that aid in developing low-res versions of complex models.

The Polygon Counter utility

For game worlds, the polygon count is important when figuring out how quickly a scene will load. For example, a model with 2,000 polygons takes roughly twice the amount of time to display as a model with 1,000 polygons.

To accurately determine the number of polygons in a scene, use the Polygon Counter utility. This simple utility, displayed in Figure 11-13, enables you to set a Budget value for the Selected Objects and for All Objects. It also displays the number of polygons and a graph for each. This utility is located in the Utilities panel.

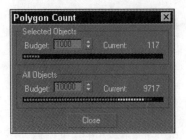

Figure 11-13: The Polygon Counter utility helps you understand how complex an object or scene is.

Using the Optimize modifier

The Optimize modifier (Modifiers ➪ Mesh Editing ➪ Optimize) does the opposite of the Tessellation button. It simplifies models by reducing the number of faces, edges, and vertices. The Level of Detail can be set for the Viewports. The text field at the bottom of the rollout displays the number of vertices and faces for the current optimization.

Cross-Reference You can learn about modifiers and how to use them in Chapter 14, "Controlled Destruction with Modifiers."

Figure 11-14 shows a cow model that has been optimized. Notice the dramatic reduction in the number of faces from the left to the right. Viewpoint Datalabs, known for producing high-resolution models, created this model. At the bottom of the Modify panel, the number of faces has been reduced from 4,326 to 670 faces by setting the Face Threshold to 20. (I guess that would be considered "lean beef.")

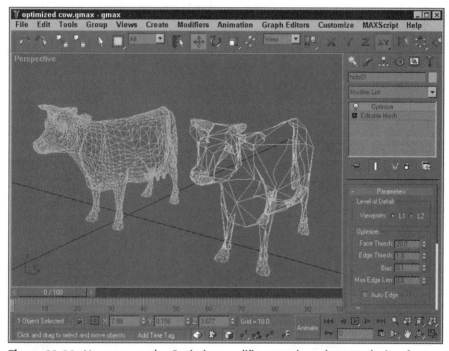

Figure 11-14: You can use the Optimize modifier to reduce the complexity of a model.

Caution Applying the Optimize modifier reduces the overall number of polygons, but it also reduces the detail of the model. Be careful when using this modifier repeatedly because it could increase the number of polygons to an unhealthy number.

Summary

Meshes are probably the most common 3D modeling type. You can create them by converting objects to Editable Meshes or Editable Poly objects or by collapsing the Stack. Editable Meshes and Editable Poly objects in gmax have a host of features for editing meshes, as you learned in this chapter.

More specifically, this chapter covered these topics:

✦ Creating Editable Mesh and Editable Poly objects by converting other objects or applying the Edit Mesh modifier

✦ Discovering the features of the Editable Mesh and Editable Poly objects

✦ Learning to select and use the various mesh subobject modes

✦ Using the Polygon Counter utility and the Optimize modifier to create low-res models

The next chapter covers modeling and working with patch objects.

✦   ✦   ✦

Performing with Perfect Patches

✦ ✦ ✦ ✦

In This Chapter

Creating patch grids

Editing patches

Working with patch subobjects

✦ ✦ ✦ ✦

Patches are a modeling type that combine the power of meshes with the flexibility of splines. They are essentially polygon surfaces stretched along a closed spline. Modifying the spline alters the surface of the patch.

In many ways, patches have advantages over the more common mesh objects. They take less memory to store, are easier to edit at the edges, and are easy to join to one another.

Introducing Patch Grids

Because patches have splines along their edges, a patch can be deformed in ways that a normal polygon cannot. For example, a polygon always needs to be coplanar, meaning that if you look at it on edge, it appears as a line. A patch doesn't have this requirement and can actually bend, which permits greater control over the surface and makes it better for modeling things like clothes and natural objects like leaves.

Another key advantage of Patch objects is that they efficiently represent the object geometry. If you examine a mesh object, you will notice that it contains a discrete vertex at the intersection of every edge at the corner of every face. Patch grids, on the other hand, have a vertex only at the corner of every patch. Each patch can consist of several faces. This reduction of vertices makes patches much cleaner and less cumbersome objects to work with.

Creating a patch grid

Patches are named according to the number of vertices at their edges; for example, a Tri Patch has three vertices, a Quad Patch has four vertices, and so on. The default Quad Patch is made up of 36 visible rectangular faces, and the default Tri Patch has 72 triangular faces. Both are shown in Figure 12-1.

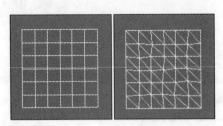

Figure 12-1: A Quad Patch and a Tri Patch

To create patches, open the Create panel and select the Geometry category. In the Object-Type drop-down list, select Patch Grids. Under the Object Type rollout, two buttons appear: Quad Patch and Tri Patch. To create a patch grid, click a button, click in a viewport, and drag to specify the dimensions of the grid.

You can also use the Keyboard Entry rollout to create patch grids with precise dimensions. To use this rollout, enter the grid's position coordinates and its dimensions, and then click the Create button. The X, Y, and Z coordinates define the location of the center of the grid.

The Patch Grid Parameters rollout includes Length and Width values and values for the number of Segments for each dimension (but only for the Quad Patch). A Segment value of 1 creates six rows or columns of segments, so the total number of polygons for a Quad Patch never drops below 36. Tri Patches do not have a Segments parameter. You can also select to automatically Generate Mapping Coordinates. Newly created patches are always flat.

Caution

If you increase the number of segments in a Quad Patch, it doesn't take a very high value to completely overwhelm your system. A segment value of 30 is enough to make the patch so dense that you can't see the individual faces unless you zoom in. A segment value of 100 really slows down your system.

Tutorial: Creating a checkerboard

In this tutorial, we'll create a simple checkerboard. To keep the white squares separate from the black squares, we'll use Quad and Tri Patches.

To create a checkerboard from patch surfaces, follow these steps:

1. Open the Create panel, and click the Geometry category. Select Patch Grids from the subcategory drop-down list.

2. Click the Quad Patch button in the Command Panel, and in the Top view, create a perfect square using the grid. Click the color swatch in the Name and Color rollout, and select the color black.

3. In the Command Panel, click the Tri Patch button and drag in the Top view to create an equally sized patch to the right of the first object. Select the Tri Patch, click its color swatch, and change its object color to white.

Caution With the Tri Patch's object color set to white, telling when it is selected can be difficult.

4. Repeat Steps 2 and 3, alternating which color comes first until the complete 8×8 checkerboard is complete.

Tip An easier way to accomplish the checkerboard is to create the first two squares and then to use the Array dialog box to create the rest. Find out more about the Array dialog box in Chapter 6, "Cloning, Grouping, and Linking Objects, and Other –ings."

Figure 12-2 shows the completed checkerboard.

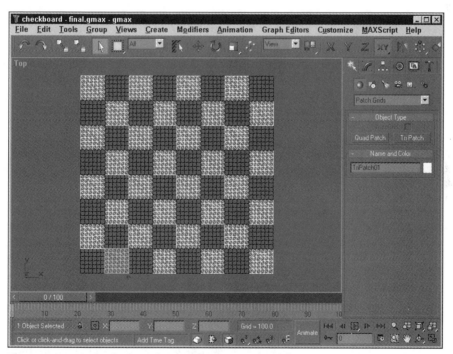

Figure 12-2: A checkerboard created using patch grids

Editing Patches

Creating and working with patches is easy, but because they are always flat, they have limited functionality. The key to making patches really useful is to convert the object into an Editable Patch object. Any type of geometric object can be converted to an Editable Patch object. Even patch grids created with the Quad Patch and Tri Patch buttons described earlier need to be converted before they can be edited at the subobject level.

You have several ways to convert an object to an Editable Patch. One way is to right-click a selected object and choose Convert To ⇨ Convert to Editable Patch from the pop-up quadmenu. Another way is to apply the Edit Patch modifier by selecting it from the Modifier List in the Modifier Stack, or by choosing Modifiers ⇨ Patch/Spline Editing ⇨ Edit Patch. These two methods create slightly different Editable Patches.

Editable patches versus the Edit Patch modifier

The differences between Editable Patches and objects with the Edit Patch modifier applied are subtle. The main difference between these two appears in the Modifier Stack. Editable Patch objects have the type Editable Patch displayed in the Stack. Patch grids with the Edit Patch modifier applied maintain their creation parameters, and the Edit Patch modifier is displayed in the Stack above the object type, where you can move or remove it at any time.

The other big difference is that the transformation of an Editable Patch subobject can be animated, whereas patch grids with the Edit Patch modifier cannot.

Editable patches and patch grids with the Edit Patch modifier applied both access subobjects and their parameters in the same way. These are covered in the next section.

Note   The Editable Patch object actually requires less memory than using the Edit Patch modifier and is the recommended method.

Selecting patch subobjects

Editable patches and the Edit Patch modifier both make patch subobjects accessible. The subobjects for patches include Vertex, Edge, Patch, and Element. Before you can edit patch subobjects, you must select them. To select a subobject type, click the small plus (+) sign to the left of the Editable Patch object in the Modifier Stack. Alternatively, you can click the red-colored icons under the Selection rollout. When selected, the subobject button and hierarchy turn yellow.

Note As you progress through this chapter, you should get a strange sense of déjà vu if you've already read Chapter 11. This is because many of the features available for editing meshes work exactly the same as those for editing patches.

Clicking either the subobject button or the hierarchy object again exits subobject mode. Remember that you must exit this mode before you can select another object. This is called Top Level in the quadmenu.

To select many subobjects at once, drag an outline over them. You can also select and deselect many subobjects by holding down the Ctrl key while clicking them. Hold down the Alt key to remove any selected vertices from the current selection set.

With subobjects selected, the options in the Selection rollout become enabled. Using these controls enables you to more easily select the desired subobjects. Figure 12-3 shows the Selection and Soft Selection rollouts.

Figure 12-3: The Selection rollout includes icon buttons for selecting the various subobject modes.

After selecting several subobjects, you can create a named selection set by typing a name in the Name Selection Sets drop-down list on the main toolbar. You can then copy and paste these selection sets onto other patch objects using the Copy and

Paste buttons in the Selection rollout. In Vertex subobject mode, the Selection rollout lets you see, when selected, just Vertices or just Vectors or both. The Lock Handles option causes all selected Bézier handles to move together when one handle is moved.

The By Vertex option is available in all but the Vertex subobject mode. It requires that you click a vertex in order to select an Edge, Face, Polygon, or Element. It selects all edges and faces that are connected to a vertex when the vertex is selected. This is handy because selecting a vertex is often easier than selecting numerous faces or edges.

The Ignore Backfacing option selects only those subobjects with normals pointing toward the current viewport. This option is helpful if many subobjects are on top of one another in the viewport. For example, if a sphere object were converted into an Editable Patch, you could enable the Ignore Backfacing option, and then selecting subobjects on the front of the sphere would not select the subobjects on the back of the sphere at the same time.

The Select Open Edges option is active only in Edge subobject mode. This button lets you select all the edges in the patch that are connected only to one face. This provides an easy way to quickly locate all the holes in your current model.

At the bottom of the Selection rollout is some information on the current selection. This lists the current subobject type and number selected.

The Soft Selection rollout allows you to alter (to a lesser extent) adjacent non-selected subobjects when selected subobjects are moved, creating a smooth transition. Check out the details of this rollout in Chapter 11, "Moving On with Marvelous Meshes."

Working with Patch Geometry

Much of the power of editing patches is contained within the Geometry rollout, shown in Figure 12-4. You can use this rollout to attach new patches, to weld and delete vertices, and to bind and hide elements. Some Geometry rollout buttons may be disabled in the various subobject modes but are enabled in one of the other subobject editing modes.

Editing vertices

After you select Vertex subobject mode, you can transform selected vertices using the transform buttons on the main toolbar, and you can distort the faces around the selected vertex by transforming the handles, shown as small green squares. Dragging these handles changes the surface of the patch as shown in Figure 12-5. The first patch shows the handles before being moved, the second patch shows the effect of moving the handles with the Lock Handles option enabled, the third patch shows a single handle moved, and the fourth patch shows where both handles have been moved.

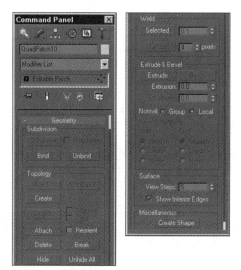

Figure 12-4: The Geometry rollout (shown in two parts) includes controls for editing patches.

Selected vertex

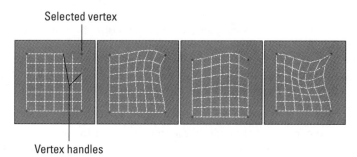

Vertex handles

Figure 12-5: Moving the Vertex handles alters the adjacent faces.

Patch vertices can be either of two types: coplanar or corner. Coplanar vertices maintain a smooth transition from vertex to vertex because their handles are locked. This causes the handles to always move so as to prevent any surface discontinuities. You can drag the handles of corner vertices to create gaps and seams in the surface.

You can switch between these vertex types by right-clicking a vertex while in vertex subobject mode and selecting the desired type from the pop-up quadmenu.

Note   Holding down the Shift key while clicking and dragging on a handle unlocks the handles and automatically changes the vertex type to corner.

Bind and Unbind

You can use the Bind button to connect edge vertices of one patch to an edge of another patch, which is useful for connecting edges with a different number of vertices. Be aware that the two patches must be part of the same object (you can make them part of the same object using the Attach button) and that the corner vertices must be welded together first. If you try to bind a vertex before welding the corner vertices, then the Bind action won't work. To use the Bind feature, click the Bind button and then drag a line from a vertex to the edge where it should join.

The Bind button attaches vertices to edges; to attach vertices to vertices, use one of the Weld buttons. When binding vertices, the point of contact between the two patches is seamless and the vertex becomes part of the interior. To exit Bind mode, click the Bind button again or right-click in a viewport.

You use the Unbind button to detach vertices that have been connected using the Bind button.

Create

You can use the Create button in the Vertex subobject mode to create patch vertices by clicking in the viewport. Use the Create button in Patch or Element subobject mode to connect the created vertices into three- or four-sided patches. Right-click in the viewport or click again on the Create button to exit Create mode.

The order in which you click on the vertices determines the direction of the normal vector, which determines the visibility of the patch in the viewports (unless the Force 2-Sided display option is enabled). If you click on the vertices in a clockwise direction, then the normal vector points away from the current viewport. The counterclockwise order points the normal vector out toward the user (which makes it visible).

Tip   An easy way to determine the direction of the normal vector is to curl the fingers on your right hand in the direction that the vertices were clicked. Your thumb points toward the direction of the normal vector. This is called the right-hand rule.

Attach

The Attach button enables you to connect separate objects to the patch object so that you can edit them all at once. It is available in all subobject modes and also when no subobject mode is selected. All objects that are attached to the current patch object are also converted into patch objects. These attached objects become separate elements in the Editable Patch.Spline objects cannot be attached to a patch object. Most Editable Patch features like weld work only if all the involved patch pieces are attached as part of the same patch object.

To use the Attach feature, select an object, click the Attach button, and move the mouse over the object to attach. The cursor changes to a plus sign when it is positioned over objects that can be attached. Click the object to be attached. Click the Attach button again or right-click in the viewport to exit Attach mode. The Reorient option aligns the attached object's local coordinate system with the local coordinate system of the patch that it is being attached to.

Converting mesh objects to patch objects results in objects with many vertices.

Delete

The Delete button (or pressing the Delete key) deletes the selected vertices. This button works for all the subobject types.

Deleting a vertex also deletes all faces and edges connected to that vertex. For example, deleting a single (top) vertex from a sphere that has been converted to an Editable Patch object leaves only a hemisphere.

Break

Click the Break button to create a separate vertex for adjoining faces that are connected by a single vertex.

Patches are all connected by vertices — moving one vertex changes the position of all adjoining patches. The Break button enables you to move the vertex associated with each patch independent of the others. The button is available only in Vertex subobject mode.

Hide and Unhide All

The Hide and Unhide All buttons hide and unhide selected vertices. They can be used in any subobject mode. To hide a subobject, select the subobject and click the Hide button. To Unhide the hidden subobjects, click the Unhide All button. Clicking the Unhide All button makes all subobjects, regardless of type, visible.

Weld Selected and Weld Target

The Weld button enables you to weld two or more vertices into one vertex. To use this feature, move the vertices close to one another, drag an outline over them to select them, and then click the Weld button. You can tell whether the weld has been successful by looking at the number of vertices selected at the bottom of the Selection rollout. If the Weld was unsuccessful, increase the Weld Threshold specified by the spinner and try again.

The Weld Target button is a little different from the Weld button. Using it, you can select and drag a vertex to another vertex. If the target vertex is within the number of pixels specified by the Target value, the vertices are welded into one vertex. To exit Weld Target mode, click the Target button again or right-click in the viewport.

Figure 12-6 shows two inverted sloping patches that have been combined. The resolution of the patch on the right is twice that of the patch on the left. The Bind button was used to attach the center vertex to the edge of the other patch. Notice that the seam between the two patches is smooth.

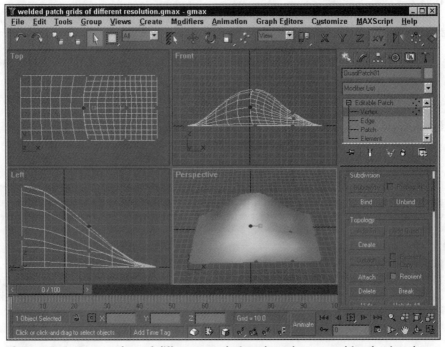

Figure 12-6: Two patches of different resolutions have been combined using the Weld and Bind buttons.

Surface settings

The View Steps value determines the resolution of the patch grid that is displayed in the viewport. You can change this resolution for rendering using the Render Steps value. You can turn off the Interior Edges altogether using the Show Interior Edges option.

A Quad Patch with a View Steps value of 0 is a simple square. Figure 12-7 shows four spheres that have all been cloned from one, converted to Editable Patches, and set with different View Steps. From left to right, the View Steps values are 0, 2, 4, 6, and 10.

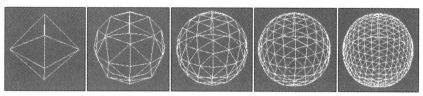

Figure 12-7: The only difference among these patch spheres is the View Steps value.

Vertex surface properties

In Vertex subobject mode, the Surface Properties rollout appears to let you color the object by assigning colors to its vertices. For each vertex, you can also specify an Illumination color and an Alpha value, which sets the transparency. You can also specify vertex colors in Patch and Element subobject modes.

Cross-Reference You can find more information on vertex colors in Chapter 16, "Putting on the Ritz with the gmax Material Editor."

After you assign vertex colors, you can use the Select Vertices By option to recall all vertices with the same color. The RGB values match all colors within the Range defined by these values. For example, if the R Range value is set to 255 and the G and B values are set to 0, then all vertices that are red will be selected.

Editing edges

Edges are the lines that run between two vertices. You can select multiple edges by holding down the Ctrl key while clicking the edges or by holding down the Alt key to remove selected edges from the current selection set.

Many of the features in the Geometry rollout work in the same way as the Vertex subobjects, but the Geometry rollout also includes some features that are enabled in Edge subobject mode, like the ones in the following sections.

Subdivide

You use the Subdivide button to increase the resolution of a patch. This is done by splitting an edge into two separate edges divided at the original edge's center. To use this feature, select an edge or edges and click the Subdivide button. The Propagate option causes the edges or neighboring patches to also be subdivided. Using Subdivide without the Propagate option enabled can cause cracks to appear in the patch. The Subdivide button also works in Patch subobject mode.

In Figure 12-8, I've subdivided a Quad Patch edge three times after selecting the upper-right corner edges.

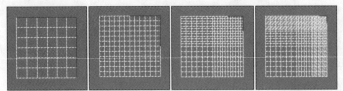

Figure 12-8: By subdividing edge subobjects, you can control where the greatest resolution is located.

Add Tri and Add Quad

You can add Quad and Tri Patches to any open edge of a patch. To do this, select the open edge or edges and click the Add Tri or Add Quad button. You can locate all open edges using the Select Open Edges button in the Selection rollout. The new patch extends along the current curvature of the patch. To add a patch to a closed surface, like a box, you'll first need to detach one of the patches to create an open edge. This feature provides a way to extend the current patch.

Figure 12-9 shows a simple quad patch that was subdivided and then added to using the Add Quad button. This provides an easy way to very quickly create a rough outline of an object that you want to model.

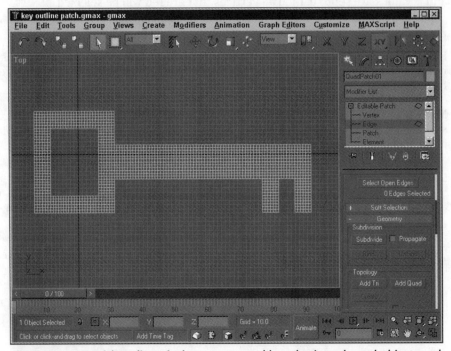

Figure 12-9: A quick outline of a key was created by selecting edge subobjects and adding Quad patches.

Create Shape

You can use the Create Shape button that appears at the bottom of the Geometry rollout in Edge subobject mode to create spline shapes from all the selected edges. To use this button, select several edge subobjects and click the button. A dialog box appears that allows you to name the new shape. You can then use the Select by Name dialog box (keyboard shortcut H) to select the newly created shape.

Editing Patch and Element subobjects

Transforming a patch object containing only one patch works the same way in sub-object mode as it works for normal transformations. Working with the Patch subobject on an object that contains several patches lets you transform individual patches. A key advantage of working with the patch subobjects is controlling their geometry using the buttons in the Geometry rollout. The following sections discuss the additional features available in Patch subobject mode.

Detach

The Detach button separates the selected patch or element subobjects from the rest of the object. Using this button opens the Detach dialog box, which enables you to name the detached subobject. The Reorient option realigns the detached subobject patch to match the position and orientation of the current active patch. The Copy option creates a new copy of the detached subobject.

Note This feature is different from Delete. Detach maintains the subobject and gives it a separate name, but the Delete function eliminates the subobject.

Extrude

The Extrude button adds depth to a patch by replicating a patch surface and creating sides to connect the new patch surface to the original. For example, a square patch grid that is extruded forms a cube. To use this feature, select a patch, click the Extrude button, and then drag in a viewport — the patch interactively shows the extrude depth. Release the button when you've reached the desired distance.

Alternatively, you can specify an extrude depth in the Extrusion spinner. The Outlining value lets you resize the extruded patch. Positive outlining values cause the extrusion to get larger, whereas negative values reduce its size. The Normal Group option extrudes all selected patches along the normal for the group, and the Normal Local option moves each individual patch along its local normal. To exit extrude mode, click the Extrude button again or right-click in the viewport.

Tip One place to use this function is to add arms to the torso of a character. If you've created a torso model out of patches, you can add arms by detaching a patch and extruding the area where the arms go.

Figure 12-10 shows the key-shaped patch that has been extruded using the Extrude button.

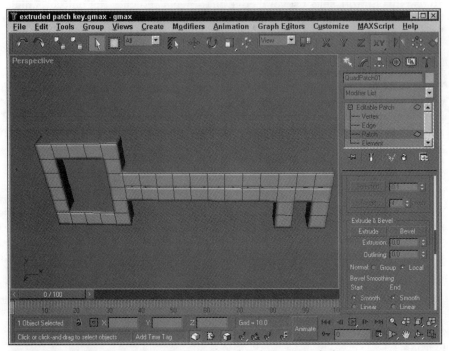

Figure 12-10: The simple key-shaped patch has been extruded.

Bevel

The Bevel button extrudes a patch and then lets you bevel the edges. To use this feature, select a patch, click the Bevel button, and then drag in a viewport to the Extrusion depth and release the button. Then drag again to specify the Outlining amount.

You can use the same options for the Bevel button as for the Extrude button described previously. In addition, the Bevel button includes Smoothing options for the bevel. Set the Start and End Smoothing options to Smooth, Linear, or None.

Figure 12-11 displays a sphere that has been converted to an Editable Patch object. Each corner of the sphere object was selected and beveled with an Extrusion value of 20.

Patch and element surface properties

If either the patch or element subobject modes are selected, the Surface Properties rollout appears. You can use this rollout to control Normal vectors and assign Material IDs and Smoothing groups.

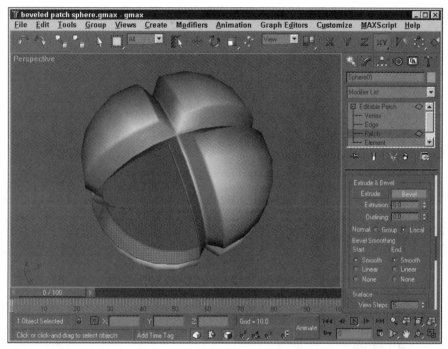

Figure 12-11: A patch sphere with corner patches that have been beveled

The Surface Properties rollout includes three buttons for working with normals. The Flip button reverses the direction of the normals of each selected face and the Unify button makes all normals face the same direction based on the majority. The Flip Normal Mode button activates a mode in which you can click individual faces and flip their normals one by one. This mode stays active until you click the Flip Normal Mode button again or right-click in the viewport.

Material IDs are used by the Multi/Sub-Object materials to apply different materials to different patches within an object. By selecting a patch subobject, you can use this control to apply a unique material to each patch.

Cross-Reference

You can find more information on the Multi/Sub-Object material in Chapter 16, "Putting On the Ritz with the gmax Material Editor."

You can also assign a patch to a unique Smoothing group. To do this, select a patch and click a Smoothing Group number.

Relaxing a patch

When the Editable Patch object is selected without any subobject modes, the Surface Properties rollout includes an option to Relax the patch. Enabling this option moves slightly apart vertices that are too close to neighboring vertices. The net result is to smooth the areas of tension, making the entire patch more continuous and less abrupt.

With the Relax option enabled, the other options in the rollout become available. The Relax Value determines how far the vertices will move. The Iterations value sets how many times the relax function is performed. The Keep Boundary Points Fixed and Save Outer Corners options can be used to maintain the exterior profile of the patch and to prevent edges and corners from being relaxed.

Tutorial: Modeling a shell

Now that you've seen all the various tools, let's try some of them. A Patch object can be used to create a common beach shell, as we'll do in this tutorial.

To model a shell using a patch, follow these steps:

1. Open the Patch seashell.gmax file from the Chap 12 directory on the CD-ROM.

    This file includes a simple disk that has been converted to an Editable Patch object.

2. Select the extruded circle, and open the Modify panel. Click the small plus (+) icon to the left of the Editable Patch object in the Modifier Stack, and select Vertex from the hierarchy.

    You are now in Vertex subobject mode.

3. Click the Select and Move button on the main toolbar. Then while holding down the Ctrl key, select all the vertices in the lower half of the circle in the Front viewport and move them close to the main vertex to form a fan-shaped patch.

4. After the neighboring vertices have been positioned, select them all (including the main vertices to which all the edges are connected) and click the Weld button. If the vertices fail to weld, increase the Weld Threshold and try again.

5. Click Edge in the Modifier Stack hierarchy to enter Edge subobject mode. Then select every other interior set of edges in the Front viewport along the top of the circle while holding down the Ctrl key.

    Make sure that you select both the front and back edges. The Info line at the bottom of the Selection rollout tells you what is selected.

6. When you have the edges selected, press the Spacebar to lock the selection.

7. Click the Select and Move button, and move the edges upward in the Top view.

    A zigzag pattern appears on the surface of the patch.

Figure 12-12 shows the completed shell.

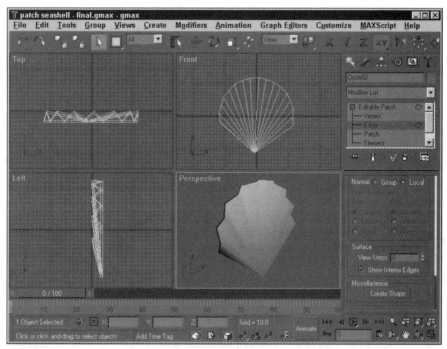

Figure 12-12: This shell is an Editable Patch created by moving every other interior edge.

Tutorial: Creating a maple leaf from patches

Because patches are a good modeling type for organic objects, let's put it to the test by trying to create a maple leaf. Because of the symmetry of the leaf, we really need to create only half of the leaf. We can then use the Mirror tool to create the other half.

To model a maple leaf using patches, follow these steps:

1. Open the Maple leaf.gmax file from the Chap 12 directory on the CD-ROM.

   This file includes a background image of a real maple leaf loaded into the Front viewport.

2. Open the Create panel, and select the Patch Grids subcategory. Click on the Tri Patch button, and drag in the Front viewport to create a square patch grid from the base where the stem is to the upper-left interior area of the leaf.

   The right edge of the patch should run about halfway up along the midline of the leaf.

3. In the Modify panel, right-click on the Tri Patch name and select Convert to Editable Patch from the pop-up menu.

4. In the Modifier Stack, select the Element subobject mode, select the patch element, and with the Propagate option selected, click the Subdivide button.

5. Select the Edge subobject mode, and select one of the edges that is completely within the interior area of the background leaf image. Then press the Add Tri button to extend the patch. Repeat this step until you have added a patch for each point around the outer perimeter of the leaf.

6. Select Vertex subobject mode, and with the Select and Move button on the main toolbar, select and drag the edge vertices so they align with the corners of the background leaf. Move all internal vertices so they lie within the leaf area. Select each vertex that lies along the outer edge of the leaf, and move its handles so the patch edge aligns with the background leaf's border. If the handles move together, hold down the Shift key to move them individually.

7. Deselect the Vertex subobject mode. In the Surface Properties rollout, enable all the options and set the Relax Value to 1.0 and the Iterations to 50.

This smoothes out the wrinkles in the patch.

Figure 12-13 shows the completed maple leaf patch (half of it, anyway). To complete this leaf, use the Mirror tool and add a spline object for the stem.

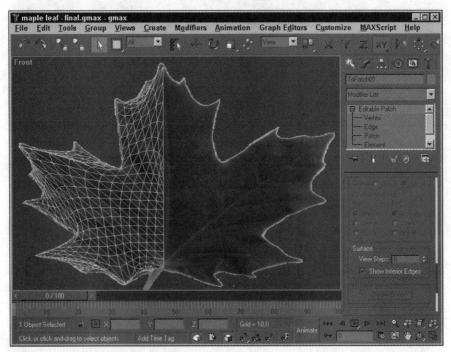

Figure 12-13: By repositioning the vertex handles, you can make the patch object match the leaf's edges precisely.

Summary

Patches are better optimized than mesh objects. Editable Patch objects include a huge list of tools that you can use to edit and modify them. In this chapter, you learned how to create and edit patches.

More specifically, this chapter covered

✦ Learning to create Quad and Tri Patch grids

✦ Discovering the features of an Editable Patch object

✦ Working with the Editable Patch subobjects

Now that splines, meshes, and patches have been covered, we'll take the escalator to the next floor, which covers those crazy complex objects, including a wide assortment of modeling coolness.

✦   ✦   ✦

Continuing with Crazy Compound Objects

✦ ✦ ✦ ✦

In This Chapter

Understanding compound objects

Morphing objects

Using the Connect and ShapeMerge compound objects

Creating Boolean objects

Lofting objects

Deforming lofted objects

✦ ✦ ✦ ✦

So far, we have covered a variety of different modeling types, including primitives, shapes, meshes, polys, and patches. The Compound Objects subcategory includes several additional modeling types that don't seem to fit anywhere else. As you will see in this chapter, these modeling types provide several new and unique ways to model objects.

Understanding Compound Object Types

The Compound Objects subcategory includes several unique object types. You can access these object types by clicking the Geometry category button in the Create panel and by selecting Compound Objects in the subcategory drop-down list. All the object types included in the Compound Object subcategory are displayed as buttons at the top of the Create panel. They include the following:

✦ **Morph:** Consists of two or more objects with the same number of vertices. The vertices are interpolated from one object to the other over several frames.

✦ **Connect:** Connects two objects with open faces by joining the holes with additional faces.

✦ **Loft:** Sweeps a cross-section shape along a spline path.

✦ **ShapeMerge:** Lets you embed a spline into a mesh object or subtract the area of a spline from a mesh object.

✦ **Boolean:** Created by performing Boolean operations on two or more overlapping objects. The operations include Union, Subtraction, Intersection, and Cut.

Morphing Objects

Morph objects are used to create a Morph animation by interpolating the vertices in one object to the vertex positions of a second object over time. The original object is called the Base object, and the second object is called the Target object. The Base and Target objects must have the same number of vertices. One Base object can be morphed into several targets.

Caution   To ensure that the Base and Target objects have the same number of vertices, create a copy of one object and modify it to be a target. Be sure to avoid such modifiers as Tessellate and Optimize, which change the number of vertices.

To morph a Base object into a Target, select the Base object and open the Create panel. Select the Compound Objects subcategory, and click the Morph button. Then click the Pick Target button in the Pick Targets rollout, shown in Figure 13-1, and select a Target object in the viewport. The cursor changes to a plus (+) sign when it is over an acceptable object. Unavailable objects (that have a different number of vertices) cannot be selected. Pick Target options include Copy, Instance, Reference, and Move. (The Move option deletes the original object that is selected.) The Target object appears under the Current Targets rollout in the Morph Targets list.

Figure 13-1: A Morph rollout lets you pick targets and create morph keys.

Each Morph object can have several Target objects. You can use the Pick Target button to select several targets, and the order in which these targets appear in the list is the order in which they are morphed. To delete a Target object, select it from the list and click the Delete Morph Target button. Beneath the list is a Name field where you can change the name of the selected Target object.

Creating Morph keys

With a Target object name selected in the Morph Targets list, you can drag the Time Slider to a frame and set a Morph key by clicking the Create Morph Key button found at the bottom of the rollout. This option sets the number of frames used to interpolate among the different morph states.

Note   If the Morph object changes dramatically, set the Morph Keys to include enough frames to interpolate smoothly.

If a frame other than 0 is selected when a Target object is picked, a Morph Key is automatically created.

Morph objects versus the Morpher modifier

gmax includes two different ways to morph an object. You can create a Morph object or apply the Morpher modifier to an existing object. The Morph object is different from the Morpher modifier, but the results are the same; however, some subtle differences exist between these two.

A Morph object can include multiple Morph targets, but it can be created only once. Each target can have several Morph keys, which makes it easy to control. For example, you could set an object to morph to a different shape and return to its original form with only two Morph keys.

The Morpher modifier, on the other hand, can be applied multiple times and works well with other modifiers, but the control for each modifier is buried in the Stack. The Parameters rollout options available for the Morpher modifier are much more extensive than for the Morph object, and they include channels.

For the best of both worlds, apply the Morpher modifier to a Morph object.

Tutorial: Morphing an alien head

In my virtual intergalactic travels, I've encountered many different types of aliens. One interesting alien had a head that would change when the alien got angry. Using the Morph compound object, I can show what it looked like.

To morph an alien head, follow these steps:

1. Open the Morphing alien head.gmax file from the Chap 13 directory on the CD-ROM.

    This file includes a simple alien head created using primitives. The eyes and mouth have been animated with keys.

2. Open the Create panel, click the Geometry category button, and select Compound Objects from the subcategory drop-down list.

3. With the Alien helmet start object selected, click the Morph button.

4. In the Pick Targets rollout, select the Move option and click the Pick Target button. Then click the Alien helmet object, or press the H key and select it from the Select Objects dialog box. (Actually, it is the only object that you can select.) Click the Pick Target button again to disable Pick mode.

5. In the Morph Targets list, select the Alien helmet start object and click the Create Morph Target button. Then drag the Time Slider (below the viewports) to frame 100, select the Alien helmet object, and press the Morph Target button again.

6. Click the Play button (in the Time Controls section at the bottom of the gmax window) to see the morph.

The Alien helmet object morphs.

Figure 13-2 shows different stages of the morph object.

Figure 13-2: A simple alien head being morphed

Creating Connect Objects

A Connect object is useful for building a connecting bridge between two separate objects. Each object must have an open face or hole that specifies where the two objects are to be connected.

To use this object, delete a face on two Editable Mesh objects and then position the holes across from each other. Select one of the objects. In the Create panel, select the Compound Objects subcategory from the drop-down list. Click the Connect button, click the Pick Operand button, and select the second object. The parameters for the Connect object are shown in Figure 13-3. The Connect object builds the additional faces required to connect the two holes.

Filling object holes

If multiple holes exist between the objects, the Connect object attempts to patch them all. You can also use the button several times to connect a single object to multiple objects.

Figure 13-4 shows a normal Connect object with no smoothing options.

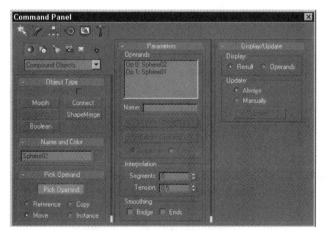

Figure 13-3: The Parameters rollout for the Connect compound object can specify smoothing and interpolation options.

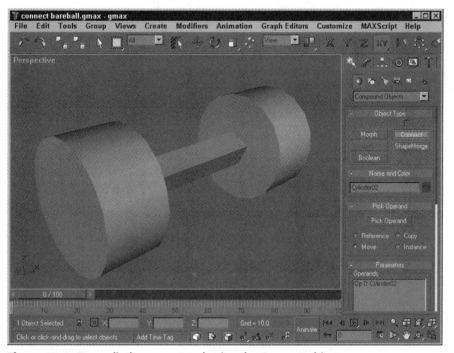

Figure 13-4: Two cylinders connected using the Connect object

The Parameters rollout includes a list of all the operands or objects involved in the connection. You can delete any of these with the Delete Operand button. The Extract Operand button lets you separate the Operand object from the Connect object.

In the Interpolation section, the Segments value is the number of segments used to create the bridge section, and the Tension value is the amount of curvature to use in an attempt to smooth the connected bridge.

The Bridge Smoothing option smoothes the faces of the bridge, and the Ends option smoothes where the bridge and the original objects connect.

Tutorial: Creating a park bench

The Connect object is best used between two symmetrical copies of an object that need to be attached, as with a table or bridge. For this tutorial, we'll use the Connect object to create a park bench between two end pieces.

To connect two ends of a park bench, follow these steps:

1. Open the Park bench.gmax file from the Chap 13 directory on the CD-ROM.

   This file includes symmetrical ends of the park bench. Each end was created by extruding a spline shape and using the ShapeMerge tool to cut the holes. The Mirror tool was then used to create and rotate the symmetrical clone.

2. Select one end of the park bench, open the Create panel, select the Compound Objects subcategory, and click the Connect button.

3. In the Pick Operand rollout, click the Pick Operand button, select the Move option, and click on the opposite side of the park bench.

   The two end pieces connect.

4. In the Parameters rollout, select the Smoothing: Bridge option to smooth the seat of the bench.

Figure 13-5 shows the resulting park bench.

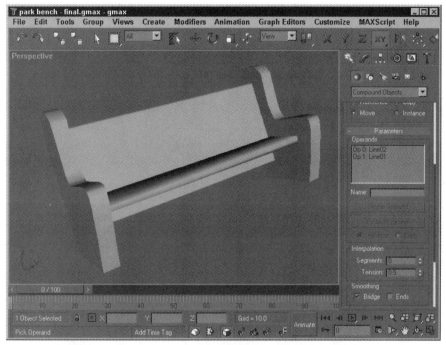

Figure 13-5: A Connect compound object can join two open holes in separate objects.

Creating a ShapeMerge Object

The ShapeMerge compound object enables you to use a spline shape as a cookie cutter to extract a portion of a mesh object. This button is enabled only if a mesh object and a spline exist in the scene. To use this object, select a mesh object, click the Pick Shape button in the Pick Operand rollout, and then select a spline shape. The shape can be a Reference, Move, Instance, or Copy.

The spline shape is always projected toward its negative Z-axis. By rotating and positioning the spline before selecting it, you can apply it to different sides of an object. You can apply multiple shapes to the same mesh object.

The Parameters rollout, shown in Figure 13-6, displays each mesh and shape object in a list. You can also rename either object using the Name field. The Extract Operand button lets you separate either object as an Instance or a Copy.

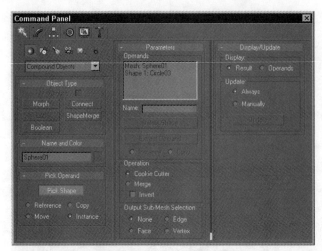

Figure 13-6: Use the Parameters rollout for the ShapeMerge compound object to cookie cutter or merge a shape.

Cookie Cutter and Merge options

The Operations group includes options for cutting the mesh, including Cookie Cutter and Merge. The Cookie Cutter option cuts the shape out of the mesh surface, and the Merge option combines the spline with the mesh. You can also Invert the operation to remove the inside or outside of the selected area.

Like the Boolean Subtraction operations, the Cookie Cutter option can remove sections of the mesh, but it uses the area defined by a spline instead of a volume defined by a mesh object. The Merge option is useful for marking an area for selection. Figure 13-7 shows a ShapeMerge object with the Cookie Cutter option selected.

Note   You can use the Merge option to create a precise face object that can be used with the Connect object.

The Output Sub-Mesh Selection option lets you pass the selection up the Stack for additional modifiers. Options include None, Face, Edge, and Vertex.

Note   To see the backsides of the faces, right-click the object, select Properties from the pop-up menu, and disable the Backface Cull option.

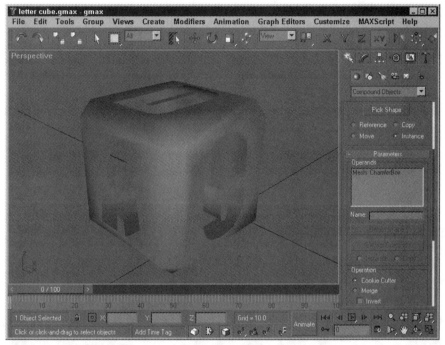

Figure 13-7: A ShapeMerge object using the Cookie Cutter option

Tutorial: Using the ShapeMerge compound object

When outlined text is imported into gmax, it typically contains letters that have shapes within shapes. For example, the letter *p*, when outlined, includes the outline of the letter *p* and a circle shape to denote the interior section of the letter. When outline text like this is converted to a mesh object, both the letter outline and its interior section are covered, making the text illegible. You can use the ShapeMerge compound object to remedy this tricky situation.

To use the ShapeMerge object to remove the center area from an extrusion, follow these steps:

1. Open the Bugs Head Software logo.gmax file from the Chap 13 directory on the CD-ROM.

2. Click away from the objects to deselect all the objects, and select (while holding down the Ctrl key) the two interior splines of the letter *B* that make up the bug's left eye. Open the Display Floater by choosing Tools ➪ Display Floater, and click the Selected button under the Hide column to hide the interior portions of this letter.

3. Select the bug's head shape. Then open the Create panel, select the Compound Objects subcategory, and click the ShapeMerge button.

4. Set the Operation to Cookie Cutter, and click the Pick Shape button in the Pick Operand rollout. Select the mouth and the letters used for the eyes and nose. Click the Pick Shape button again to exit Pick mode. Click away from the objects in the viewport to deselect the bug's head.

5. Now select the letter *B* in the logo name, and click the ShapeMerge button again. Use the Pick Shape button and the Cookie Cutter operation option to remove the centers of this letter. Click the Select Object button on the main toolbar to exit ShapeMerge mode. Repeat this step for each letter that has an interior portion, including the *g, e, a, d, o, a,* and *e* letters.

6. Open the Display panel again, and in the Hide rollout, click Unhide All to redisplay the interior splines of the letter *B* that make up the bug's left eye. Hold down the Ctrl key, select all the remaining splines, and choose Modifiers ⇨ Mesh Editing ⇨ Face Extrude.

Figure 13-8 shows the finished logo. Notice that the letters have the interior sections removed.

Figure 13-8: The logo with the interior centers removed from extruded letters using the ShapeMerge object

Modeling with Boolean Objects

When two objects overlap, you can perform different Boolean operations on them to create a unique object. The Boolean operations include Union, Subtraction, Intersection, and Cut, as found in the Parameters rollout shown in Figure 13-9.

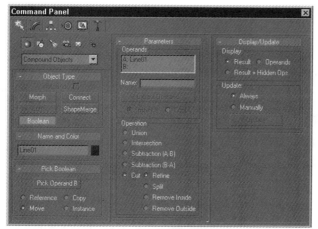

Figure 13-9: The Parameters rollout lets you select the type of Boolean operation to apply.

The Union operation combines two objects into one. The Subtraction operation subtracts the overlapping portions of one object from another. The Intersection operation retains only the overlapping sections of two objects, and the Cut operation can cut an object like the Subtraction operator does, while letting the cut piece remain. Figure 13-10 shows each of the possible Boolean operators.

Note Unlike many CAD packages that deal with solid objects, gmax's Booleans are applied to surfaces, so if the surfaces of the two objects don't overlap, the Boolean operation has no effect.

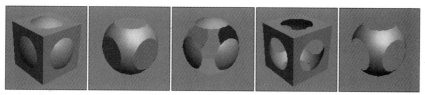

Figure 13-10: Boolean operations: Union, Intersection, Subtraction (A-B), Subtraction (B-A), and Cut: Remove Inside

All Boolean operations are layered in the Stack. You can revisit an operation at any time and make changes to it.

Cross-Reference   You can also apply Boolean operations to shapes using the Boolean operators available for Editable Splines in the Geometry rollout. Chapter 10, "Starting with Simple Splines and Shapes," covers these 2D Boolean operators.

Union

The Union operation combines two objects into one. To Union two objects, select an object and click the Boolean button. Under the Parameters rollout, the selected object is referred to as Operand A. In the Pick Operand rollout, click the Pick Operand B button and select a second object in the viewport. (Operand B can be a Copy, Instance, Reference, or Move object.) To apply the Boolean operation, click the Union option.

Intersection

The Intersection operation creates an object from the overlapping sections of two objects. For this operation, like the Union operator, which object is A and which is B isn't important.

Subtraction

The Subtraction operation subtracts the overlapping portions of one object from the other. For this operation, the order in which the objects are selected is important. Subtracting object A from object B gives you a different object than you get when you subtract object B from object A.

Cut

The Cut operation is similar to the Slice modifier, except it uses another object instead of a slice plane gizmo and only Operand A is modified in the process. The Cut operation has several options, including Refine, Split, Remove Inside, and Remove Outside.

The Refine option marks the selected object with new edges where it intersects Operand B. The Split option actually divides the mesh object into separate elements.

The Remove Inside and Remove Outside options are variations of the Split option. They remove the inner or outer portion of the object. These options work like the Subtraction and Intersection options, except the Cut operation leaves holes in the base geometry.

Tips for working with Booleans

Working with Boolean objects can be difficult. If you try to perform a Boolean operation on an ill-suited object, the results could end up being erratic. As you prepare objects for Boolean operations, keep the following points in mind:

✦ Avoid meshes with long, skinny polygon faces. All faces should have roughly equal lengths and widths. The ratio of edge length to width should be less than 4 to 1.

✦ Avoid curved lines where possible. Curved lines have the potential of folding back on themselves, which causes problems. If you need to use a curve, try not to intersect it with another curve; keep the curvature to a minimum.

✦ Unlink any objects not involved in the Boolean operation. Linked objects, even if they don't intersect, can cause problems.

✦ If you're having difficulty getting a Boolean operation to work, try applying the XForm modifier (found in the Modifiers List) to combine all the transformations into one. Then collapse the Stack, and convert the objects to Editable Mesh objects. This technique removes any modifier dependencies.

✦ Make sure that your objects are completely closed surfaces with no holes, overlapping faces, or unwelded vertices.

✦ Make sure that all surface normals are consistent — inconsistent normals will cause unexpected results. You can use the Normal modifier to unify and flip all normals on an object. The Show Normals option in the viewport can also help.

✦ Collapsing the Stack after all Boolean operations have been performed eliminates dependencies on the previous object types.

Tutorial: Creating a Lincoln Log set

In the household where I grew up, we had sets of Legos and a lesser-known construction set known as Lincoln Logs that let you to create buildings using notched logs that fit together. Using a Subtraction operation, you can create your own virtual set of Lincoln Logs.

This tutorial transforms objects and uses the Array dialog box. You can find information about transforming objects in Chapter 6, "Cloning, Grouping, and Linking Objects, and Other –ings."

To use Boolean objects to create a log cabin, follow these steps:

1. Open the Lincoln logs booleans.gmax from the Chap 13 directory on the CD-ROM.

   This file contains some simple primitives including four Box objects positioned at each end of the log at a distance of 10 from the end.

2. Select the Cylinder object, select the Compound Objects subcategory from the drop-down list in the Create panel, and click the Boolean button. In the Operation section, select the Subtraction (A–B) option. Then in the Pick Boolean rollout, click the Pick Operand B button and select one of the Box objects.

3. Repeat the Subtraction operation on the other three boxes by clicking the Select button and performing Step 3 again.

   When finished, you should have a cylinder with four notches.

Note   If you simply click the Pick Operand B button again, the first notch is replaced by the second operation.

4. Clone the single log by choosing Edit ⇨ Clone and then selecting the Copy option. Move the cloned log along the negative Y-axis a distance of 160. The easiest way to do this is to right-click the Select and Move button to open the Move Transform Type-In dialog box. In the Absolute World field, enter **–160** as the Y-axis value.

   This step positions two logs next to one another to form the bottom layer of the house.

5. Select both logs, and open the Array dialog box by choosing Tools ⇨ Array. In the Incremental Move row, enter **10** for the Z-axis. In the Incremental Rotate row, enter **90** for the Z-axis. In the Array Dimensions section, enter a Count value of **16**. Click the OK button.

   This step stacks several layers of logs.

6. Select one log, and use the right-click pop-up menu to convert that log to an Editable Mesh. Open the Modify panel, click the Attach List button, click the All button to select all the cylinder objects, and then click the Attach button to combine them all into a single object.

7. In the Create panel, click the Geometry category button, select the Box button, and create a Box object with the following dimensions: Length of 40, Width of 40, and Height of 80. Then position the Box where the front door should be.

8. Return to the Compound Objects subcategory, select the logs, and click the Boolean button. Then click the Pick Operand B button again, and select the Box.

   The rollout remembers and retains the last options selected, including the Subtraction (A–B) operation.

Figure 13-11 shows our Boolean log cabin — ready for the virtual pioneers (after you add a roof).

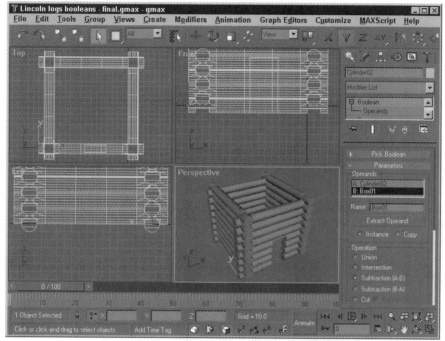

Figure 13-11: A log cabin built using Boolean objects

Creating a Loft Object

Lofting is a term that comes from the shipbuilding industry. It describes a method for building ships that creates and positions the cross sections and then attaches a surface or skin along the length of the cross sections.

To create a Loft object, you need to have at least two spline shapes: one shape that defines the path of the Loft and a second shape that defines its cross section. After the shapes are created, open the Create panel, click the Geometry category button, and select Compound Objects from the subcategory drop-down list. A Loft button is enabled if two or more splines are present in the viewport.

Using the Get Shape and Get Path buttons

After you click the Loft button, the Creation Method rollout, shown in Figure 13-12, displays the Get Path and Get Shape buttons, which you use to specify which spline is the path and which spline is the cross section. Select a spline, and then click either the Get Path button or the Get Shape button. If you click the Get Shape button, the selected spline is the path and the next spline shape you select is the cross section. If you click the Get Path button, the selected spline is the shape and the next spline shape you select is the path.

Note After you click the Get Path or Get Spline button, although the cursor changes when you're over a valid spline, not all spline shapes can be used to create Loft objects. For example, you cannot use a spline created with the Donut button as a path.

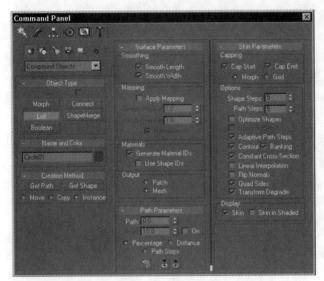

Figure 13-12: The Loft compound object rollouts

When creating a Loft object with the Get Shape and Get Path buttons, you can specify either to Move the spline shape, or to create a Copy or an Instance of it. The Move option replaces both splines with a Loft object. The Copy option leaves both splines in the viewport and creates a new Loft object. The Instance maintains a link between the spline and the Loft object. This link enables you to modify the original spline. The Loft object is updated automatically.

The vertex order of the path spline is important. The Loft object is created starting at the vertex numbered 1.

Note You can tell which vertex is the first by enabling Vertex Numbering in the Selection rollout of an editable spline.

Controlling surface parameters

All Loft objects include the Surface Parameters rollout. Using this rollout, you can set the smoothing of the Loft object with two different options: Smooth Length and Smooth Width. You can use the Mapping options to control the mapping of textures by setting values for the number of times the map repeats over the Length or Width of the Loft. The Normalize option applies the map to the surface evenly or proportionately according to the shape's vertex spacing. You can set the Loft object to automatically generate Material and Shape IDs, and you can specify the output of the Loft to be either a Patch or Mesh.

Changing path parameters

The Path Parameters rollout lets you position several different cross-sectional shapes at different positions along the Loft path. The Path value indicates either the Distance or Percentage along the path where this new shape should be located. The Snap option, if turned on, enables you to snap to consistent distances along the path. The Path Steps option enables you to place new shapes at steps along the path where the vertices are located. Each path has a different number of steps depending on its complexity.

The viewport displays a small yellow X at the location where the new cross-sectional shape will be inserted. At the bottom of the rollout are three buttons, which are illustrated and described in Table 13-1.

Table 13-1
Path Rollout Buttons

Toolbar Button	Name	Description
	Pick Shape	Selects a new cross-section spline to be inserted at the specified location
	Previous Shape	Moves to the previous cross-section shape along the Loft path
	Next Shape	Moves to the next cross-section shape along the Loft path

Setting skin parameters

The Skin Parameters rollout includes many options for determining the complexity of the Loft skin. You can specify whether to cap either end of the Loft using the Cap Start and/or Cap End options. The caps can be either Morph or Grid type.

This rollout also includes many options for controlling the look of the skin. These include the following:

✦ **Shape and Path Steps:** Sets the number of segments that appear in each vertex's cross-sectional shape and between each division along the path. The straight segments are ignored if the Optimize Path option is selected.

✦ **Optimize Shapes and Paths:** Reduces the Loft's complexity by deleting any unneeded edges or vertices.

✦ **Adaptive Path Steps:** Automatically determines the number of steps to use for the path.

✦ **Contour:** Determines how the cross-sectional shapes line up with the path. If this option is enabled, the cross section is aligned to be perpendicular to the path at all times. If disabled, this option causes the cross-sectional shapes to maintain their orientation as the path is traversed.

✦ **Banking:** Causes the cross-section shape to rotate as the path bends.

✦ **Constant Cross-Section:** Scales the cross-sectional shapes in order to maintain a uniform width along the path. Turning off this option causes the cross sections to pinch at any sharp angles along the path.

✦ **Linear Interpolation:** Causes straight linear edges to appear between different cross-sectional shapes. Turning off this option causes smooth curves to connect various shapes.

✦ **Flip Normals:** Used to correct difficulties that would appear with the normals. Often, the normals are flipped accidentally when the Loft is created.

✦ **Quad Sides:** Creates four-sided polygons to connect to adjacent cross-section shapes with the same number of sides.

✦ **Transform Degrade:** Makes the Loft skin disappear when subobjects are transformed. This feature can help you better visualize the cross-sectional area while it is being moved.

The Display options at the bottom of the Skin Parameters rollout give you the choice of displaying the skin in all viewports or displaying the Loft skin only in the viewports with shading turned on.

Tutorial: Designing a slip-proof hanger

As an example of creating a Loft object with different cross-sectional shapes, we'll design a new hanger that includes some rough edges along its bottom section to keep slacks from sliding off.

To design a hanger Loft object with different cross sections, follow these steps:

1. Open the Lofted slip-proof hanger.gmax from the Chap 13 directory on the CD-ROM.

   This file includes a spline outline of a hanger and two simple shapes.

2. Click the Geometry category button in the Create panel, select the Compound Objects subcategory from the drop-down list, and select the hanger spline. Click the Loft button.

3. In the Creation Method rollout, click the Get Shape button and then click the small circle shape (make sure the Copy option is selected).

This lofts the entire hanger with a circular cross section.

4. In the Path Parameters rollout, select the Path Steps option.

A dialog box appears warning that this may change the relocate shapes.

5. Click Yes to continue. Increment the Path value until the yellow X marker in the viewport is positioned at the beginning of the hanger's bottom bar (at Step 53 for this tutorial). Click the Get Shape button again, and click the small circular shape again. This extends the circular cross section from the start at Step 0 to Step 53.

6. Increment the Path value by 1 to Step 54, click the Get Shape button, and select the star shape.

This makes the remainder of the hanger use a star-shaped cross section.

7. Increment the Path value again to the end of the hanger's bottom bar (at Step 60), click the Get Shape button, and select the star shape again to end the star cross section.

Note If you forget to start and end a section with the same cross section, the loft blends between the two different cross sections.

8. Increment the Path value a final time to Step 61, click the Get Shape button, and click the circular shape. Click the Get Shape button at the bottom of the Path Parameters dialog box to change the cross section of the hanger to the end of the path. Right-click in the viewport to exit Get Shape mode.

Figure 13-13 shows the finished designer hanger.

Deforming Loft objects

When you select a Loft object and open the Modify panel, the Deformation rollout appears. This rollout includes five buttons that let you Scale, Twist, Teeter, Bevel, and Fit the cross-section shapes along the path. All five buttons open similar graph windows that include control points and a line that represents the amount of the effect to apply. Next to each button is a toggle button with a light bulb on it. This button enables or disables the respective effect.

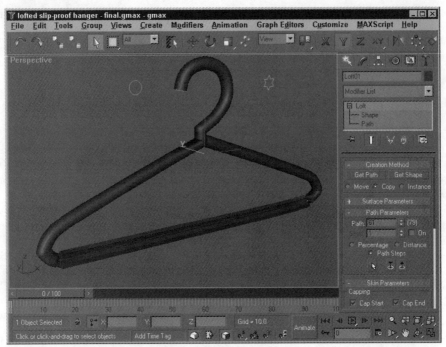

Figure 13-13: A lofted hanger created with two different cross-sectional shapes

The Deformation window interface

All five deformation options use the same basic window and controls. The lines within the window represent the length of the path. As an example of the Deformation window interface, Figure 13-14 shows the Scale Deformation window.

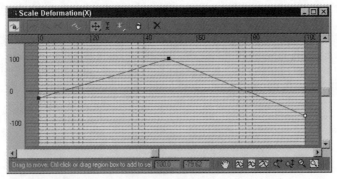

Figure 13-14: The Deformation dialog box interface lets you control the cross section over the length of the path.

Dragging the curve directly can modify the deformation curve. You can also insert control points at any location along the curve. These control points can be one of three different types: Corner, Bézier Corner, or Bézier Smooth. Bézier type points have handles for controlling the curvature at the point. To change the point type, select the point and right-click. Then make your selection from the pop-up menu. The end points must always be either Corner or Bézier Corner type.

To move a control point, select and drag it or enter a horizontal and/or vertical value in the fields at the bottom of the window.

Table 13-2 describes the buttons at the top of the Deformation window.

Table 13-2		
Deformation Dialog Box Buttons		
Toolbar Button	**Name**	**Description**
	Make Symmetrical	Links the two curves so that changes made to one curve are also made to the other
	Display X-Axis	Makes the line controlling the X-axis visible
	Display Y-Axis	Makes the line controlling the Y-axis visible
	Display XY Axes	Makes both lines visible
	Swap Deform Curves	Switches the lines
	Move Control Point	Enables you to move control points, and includes flyouts for horizontal and vertical movements
	Scale Control Point	Scales the selected control point
	Insert Corner Point, Insert Bézier Point	Inserts new points on a deformation curve
	Delete Control Point	Deletes the current control point
	Reset Curve	Returns to the original curve
	Pan	Pans the curve as the mouse is dragged
	Zoom Extents	Zooms to display the entire curve

Continued

Toolbar Button	Name	Description
	Zoom Extents Horizontal	Zooms to display the entire horizontal curve range
	Zoom Extents Vertical	Zooms to display the entire vertical curve range
	Zoom Horizontal	Zooms on the horizontal curve range
	Zoom Vertical	Zooms on the vertical curve range
	Zoom	Zooms in and out as the mouse is dragged
	Zoom Region	Zooms to the region specified by the mouse

Table 13-2 *(continued)*

Note Several buttons are disabled on the Twist and Bevel Deformation windows because these dialog boxes have only one deformation curve.

At the bottom of the Deformation dialog boxes are two value fields. The value fields display the X and Y coordinate values for the currently selected point. The navigation buttons enable you to pan and zoom within the dialog box.

Figure 13-15 and Figure 13-16 show each of the various deformation options applied to a lofted column.

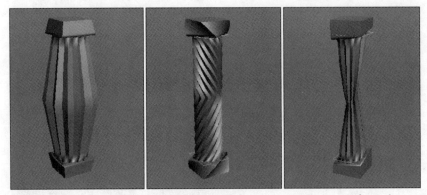

Figure 13-15: The Loft compound object deformation options: Scale, Twist, and Teeter

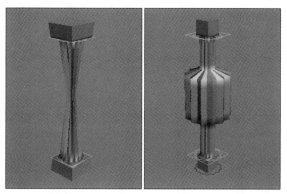

Figure 13-16: The Loft compound object deformation options: Bevel and Fit

Scale Deformation

The Scale Deformation window can alter the relative scale of the Loft object at any point along its path. This window includes two lines — one red and one green. The red line displays the X-axis scale, and the green line displays the Y-axis scale. By default, both lines are positioned equally at the 100 percent value. Specifying a value that is greater than 100 percent increases the scale, and specifying a value that is less than 100 percent has the opposite effect.

Twist Deformation

The Twist Deformation rotates one cross section relative to the others and can be used to create an object that spirals along its path. This option is similar to the Banking option, which can also produce rotations about the path.

The Twist Deformation window includes only one red line representing the rotation value. By default, this line is set to a 0-degree rotation value. Positive values result in counterclockwise rotations, and negative values have the opposite effect.

Teeter Deformation

Teeter Deformation rotates a cross section so that its outer edges move closer to the path. This is done by rotating the cross section about its local X- or Y-axis. The result is similar to that produced by the Contour option.

The Teeter Deformation window includes two lines — one red and one green. The red line displays the X-axis rotation, and the green line displays the Y-axis rotation. By default, both lines are positioned equally at the 0-degree value. Positive values result in counterclockwise rotations, and negative values have the opposite effect.

Bevel Deformation

Bevel Deformation bevels the cross-section shapes. The Bevel Deformation window includes only one red line representing the amount of bevel that is applied. By default, this line is set to a 0 value. Positive values increase the bevel amount, which equals a reduction in the shape area, and negative values have the opposite effect.

You can also use the Bevel Deformation window to select three different types of beveling: Normal, Adaptive Linear, and Adaptive Cubic. Table 13-3 shows and describes the buttons for these three beveling types. You can select them from a flyout at the right end of the window.

Table 13-3 Bevel Deformation Buttons		
Toolbar Button	**Name**	**Description**
	Normal Bevel	Produces a normal bevel with parallel edges, regardless of the path angle
LIN	Adaptive (Linear)	Alters the bevel linearly, based on the path angle
CUB	Adaptive (Cubic)	Alters the bevel using a cubic spline based on the path angle

Fit Deformation

The Fit Deformation window, shown in Figure 13-17, lets you specify a profile for the outer edges of the cross-section shapes to follow. This window includes two lines — one red and one green. The red line displays the X-axis scale, and the green line displays the Y-axis scale. By default, both lines are positioned equally at the 100-percent value. Specifying a value that is greater than 100 percent increases the scale, and specifying a value that is less than 100 percent has the opposite effect.

The Fit Deformation window includes ten buttons unique to it that are used to control the profile curves. These buttons are illustrated and described in Table 13-4.

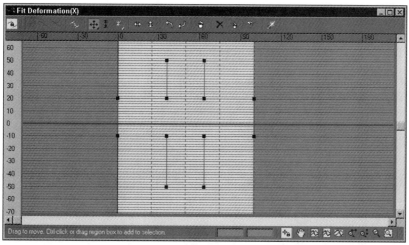

Figure 13-17: A Loft object with Fit Deformation applied

Table 13-4
Fit Deformation Dialog Box Buttons

Toolbar Button	Name	Description
⟷	Mirror Horizontally	Mirrors the selection horizontally
↕	Mirror Vertically	Mirrors the selection vertically
↶	Rotate 90 Degrees CCW	Rotates the selection 90 degrees counterclockwise
↵	Rotate 90 Degrees CW	Rotates the selection 90 degrees clockwise
⊖	Delete Control Point	Deletes the selected control point
✕	Reset Curve	Returns the curve to its original form
⊘	Delete Curve	Deletes the selected curve
⟲	Get Shape	Selects a separate spline to use as a profile
✂	Generate Path	Replaces the current path with a straight line
✛ₐ	Lock Aspect	Maintains the relationship between height and width

Modifying Loft subobjects

When you select a Loft object, you can work with its subobjects in the Modify panel. The subobjects for a Loft include Path and Shape. The Path subobject opens the Path Commands rollout. This rollout has only a single button, Put, for creating a copy of the Loft path. If you click this button, the Put To Scene dialog box appears, enabling you to give the path a name and to create it as a Copy or an Instance.

If your path is created as an Instance, you can edit the instance to control the Loft path.

The Shape subobject opens the Shape Commands rollout. This rollout also includes a Put button along with some additional controls. The Path Level value adjusts the shape's position on the path. The Compare button opens the Compare dialog box, which is discussed in the following section. The Reset button returns the shape to its former state before any rotation or scaling has taken place, and the Delete button deletes the shape entirely.

Note   You cannot delete a shape if it is the only shape in the Loft object.

The Shape Commands rollout also includes six Align buttons for aligning the shape to the Center, Default, Left, Right, Top, and Bottom. For the Loft object local coordinates, Left and Right move the shape along the X-axis, and Top and Bottom move it along the Y-axis.

Comparing shapes

The Compare dialog box superimposes selected cross-sectional shapes included in a Loft object on top of one another to check their center alignment. The button in the upper-left corner is the Pick Shape button. This button lets you select which shapes to display in the dialog box. The button to its right is the Delete Shape button, for removing a shape from the dialog box. Figure 13-18 shows the Compare dialog box with the two shapes from the pillar example selected. Notice that the first vertices on these two shapes are in different locations. This causes the strange twisting at both the top and bottom of the pillar.

Note   You can align these two vertices by subdividing the square shape in Edit Spline mode and selecting a new first vertex with the Make First button.

While the Compare dialog box is open, the Align buttons in the Shape Commands rollout are still active and can be used to move and position the shapes. The first vertex on each shape is shown as a small square. If these vertices aren't correctly aligned on top of one another, then the resulting Loft object will have skewed edges. The lower-right corner of the dialog box includes buttons to View Extents, Pan, Zoom, and Zoom Region.

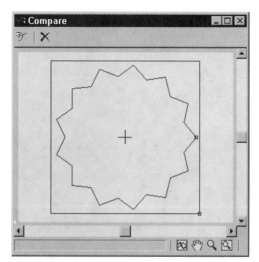

Figure 13-18: You can use the Compare dialog box to align shapes included in a Loft.

Editing Loft paths

The original shapes that were used to create the Loft object can be edited at any time. These updates also modify the Loft object. The shapes, if not visible, can be selected using the Select by Name button. The shapes maintain their base parameters, or they can be converted to an Editable Spline.

Tutorial: Creating drapes

Modeling home interiors is a task commonly performed by professional architects and interior designers, but creating the drapes can be tricky. In this tutorial, we'll create some simple drapes using a Loft object.

To create drapes using a Loft object, follow these steps:

1. Open the Lofted drapes.gmax file from the Chap 13 directory on the CD-ROM.

   This file contains two splines that can be used to create the loft.

2. Click the Geometry category button in the Create panel, and select the Compound Objects subcategory from the drop-down list. Select the straight line spline, and click the Loft button. In the Creation Method rollout, click the Get Shape button and then click the cross-section spline.

3. Open the Modify panel, and under the Skin Parameters rollout, turn off the Contour and Banking options.

4. Use the Deformation functions to add more control to the drapes, such as tying them together as shown in Figure 13-19.

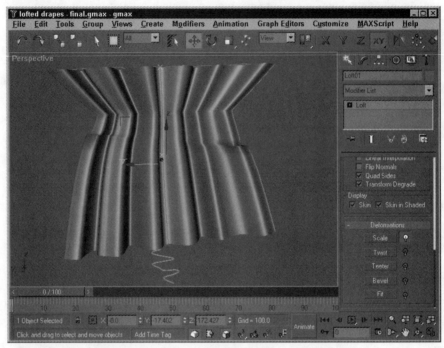

Figure 13-19: Drapes that have been modeled using a Loft object

Loft objects versus surface tools

You can create compound loft objects completely from 2D shape splines; one open spline is typically used as the Loft path, and other, closed splines are used as the cross sections. You can have several different cross sections, and these can change as you travel the path. Loft cross sections aren't required to have the same number of vertices, and you can modify the scale and rotation of the cross sections with the Deformation options.

Cross-Reference See Chapter 14, "Controlled Destruction with Modifiers," for more detail on the surface tools.

The surface tools, which include the CrossSection and Surface modifiers, provide another way to model that is similar to lofting. The CrossSection modifier takes several cross-section shapes and connects their vertices with additional splines to create a spline framework. You can then use the Surface modifier to cover this framework with a skin.

Although similar in nature, Loft objects and the surface tools have different subtleties and strengths.

One difference is that the CrossSection modifier connects spline cross sections according to their order. This can cause strange results if the order is incorrect. A Loft always follows a path, so the cross-section order isn't a problem.

Another difference is that surface tools give you more control over the surface of a created object. Because the underlying structure is a series of splines, you can add new branches and objects with little difficulty. This can be hard to do with Loft objects.

As a general guideline, Loft objects are better suited to modeling rigid objects with relatively uniform cross sections, whereas the surface tools are better for modeling more organic model types.

Summary

Compound objects provide several additional modeling types to our bulging modeling toolkit. From morph objects to complex deformed lofts, you can use these special-purpose types to model many different objects. This chapter covered the following topics:

- ✦ Understanding the various compound object types
- ✦ Morphing objects with the same number of vertices
- ✦ Using splines and mesh objects to create a ShapeMerge object
- ✦ Creating a Connect object to join two objects
- ✦ Modeling with Boolean objects
- ✦ Creating a Loft object
- ✦ Discovering how to control Loft parameters
- ✦ Using Loft deformations
- ✦ Modifying Loft subobjects
- ✦ Comparing the strengths of loft objects and surface tools

With all these different modeling types, you've probably started to create lots of different objects, but next is your chance to destroy . . . I mean, modify . . . your perfect objects.

✦   ✦   ✦

Changing Object Appearance Inside and Out

In This Part

Chapter 14
Controlled
Destruction with
Modifiers

Chapter 15
Skeletons Rule:
Building with
Bones and IK

Chapter 16
Putting on the Ritz
with the gmax
Material Editor

Controlled Destruction with Modifiers

✦ ✦ ✦ ✦

In This Chapter

Using the Modifier Stack to manage modifiers

Learning to work with modifier gizmos

Exploring the Select modifiers

Working with Patch, Spline, and Mesh modifiers

Using the animation modifiers

Smoothing objects with MeshSmooth

Deforming objects with the FFD and Parametric Deformer modifiers

✦ ✦ ✦ ✦

Think for a moment of a wood shop with all its various (and expensive) tools and machines. Some tools are simple like a screwdriver or a sander; others like a planer or router are more complex, but they all change the wood (or model) in different ways. In some ways, you can think of modifiers as these tools and machines that work on 3D objects.

Each woodshop tool has different parameters that control how it works, such as how hard you turn the screwdriver or the coarseness of the sandpaper. Likewise, each modifier has parameters that you can set that determine how it affects the 3D object.

Modifiers can be used to reshape objects, apply material mappings, deform an object's surface, and perform many other actions. Many different types of modifiers exist. This chapter introduces you to many different modifiers and, more importantly, teaches you how to use them.

Exploring the Modifier Stack

All modifiers that are applied to an object are listed together in a single location known as the Modifier Stack. This Stack is the manager for all modifiers applied to an object and can be found at the top of the Modify panel in the Command Panel. You can also use the Stack to apply and delete modifiers; cut, copy, and paste modifiers between objects; and reorder them.

Applying modifiers

An object can have several modifiers applied to it. Modifiers can be applied using the Modifiers menu or by selecting the modifier from the Modifier List drop-down list located at the top of the Modify panel directly under the object name. Selecting a modifier in the Modifiers menu or from the Modifier List applies the modifier to the current selected object. Modifiers can be applied to multiple objects if several objects are selected.

Note   Some modifiers aren't available for some types of objects. For example, the Extrude and Lathe modifiers are enabled only when a spline shape is selected.

Using the Modifier Stack

After a modifier is applied, its parameters appear in rollouts within the Command Panel. The Modifier Stack rollout, shown in Figure 14-1, lists the base object and all the modifiers that have been applied to an object. Any new modifiers applied to an object are placed at the top of the stack. By selecting a modifier from the list in the Modifier Stack, all the parameters for that specific modifier are displayed in rollouts.

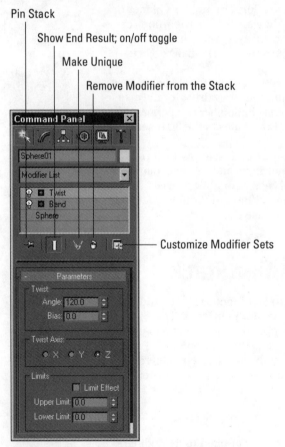

Figure 14-1: The Modifier Stack rollout displays all modifiers applied to an object.

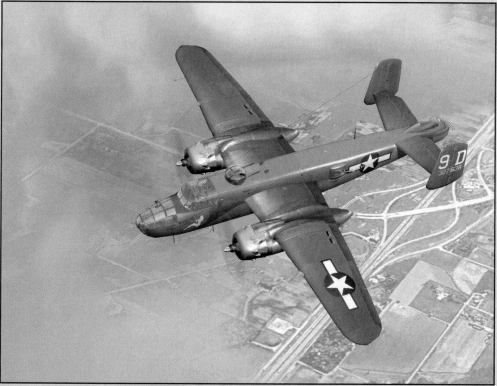

This North American B-25 aircraft was modeled after the Mid Atlantic Air Museum's (MAAM) meticulously restored B-25 by a Flight Simulator 2002 (FS2002) team consisting of Bill Rambow, Jan Visser, Fred Banting, and Rob Young. The model, created using gmax, features all-around photorealistic texturing inside as well as outside.

These images feature a MAAM-SIM Douglas R4D-6 NATS (Naval Air Transport Service) aircraft. All textures, including those used for the 2D panel, the gauge faces, virtual cockpit, and visual model, are photorealistic. Jan Visser created this model in gmax for Flight Simulator 2002.

The top image shows a view aboard the "virtual cockpit" of the MAAM-SIM gmax North American B-25J model for FS2002. The bottom image shows the view from the captain's seat of the MAAM-SIM gmax Douglas R4D-6 (DC-3) NATS model for Microsoft Flight Simulator 2002. Both images are by Jan Visser.

The possibilities for creating detailed models in gmax are apparent in Jan Visser's images of the Douglas R4D-6 aircraft.

The B-25 model as seen from the cockpit and from above. Both images are by Jan Visser.

These images are from a custom Quake III Arena deathmatch map titled "Japanese Castles," created by Mike "g1zm0" Burbidge. Notice the detailed texture map of a dragon applied to the door. Small additions like this can add greatly to the visual appeal of the map.

These images are from "Si'Metrik," a custom Quake III Arena deathmatch map created by Simon "sock" O'Callaghan. For this map, Simon has addressed a key playability issue by making sure there is no place to run and hide. One wrong step, and you're all wet.

The top image is a Quake III Arena level named "Laser Turkey Mouth," created by Dan "Inflict" Haigh and Robert "Sgt Hulka" Waring of Team Evolve (www.team-evolve.com). The lower image is named "Techwalk" and was created by Mike "Minty Fresh" Reed, also of Team Evolve.

These Quake III Arena levels named "Spear Point" and "The Lonely Graveyards of the Mind" were created by Team Evolve's Tim "ThinG" Smith.

Marco "Rox" Pantozzi created these Trainz images. In the top image, notice the graffiti on the wall and the train. The bottom image shows an amazing amount of detail including a white picket fence that lines the tracks.

Matthew Williams created this image of the BNSF 675 engine crossing the Illinois River and running the Clinchfield, Minnesota route. Andy Quaas and Mark Hoffman created the engine models. You can find more of Matthew's work at www.trainzproroutes.com and more of Andy and Mark's models at www.digitalroundhouse.com.

These two images show the diversity that is possible with Trainz and gmax, from the modern engine (top) created by Chris Caswell to the older steam locomotive (bottom) created by Peter Pardoe-Matthews.

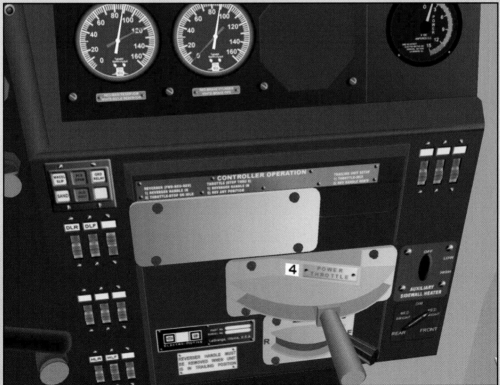

Andy Quaas created these images and their models. The lower image shows the console found inside the train engine. You can see more of Andy's work at www.digitalroundhouse.com.

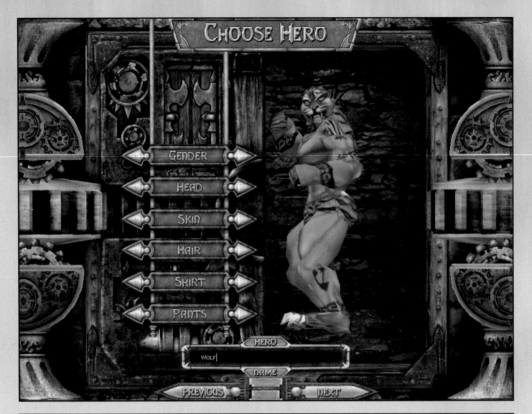

These Dungeon Siege images show a new player character created by Team Elemental that will appear in their custom adventure. This character is half-tiger wielding a Falcata weapon.

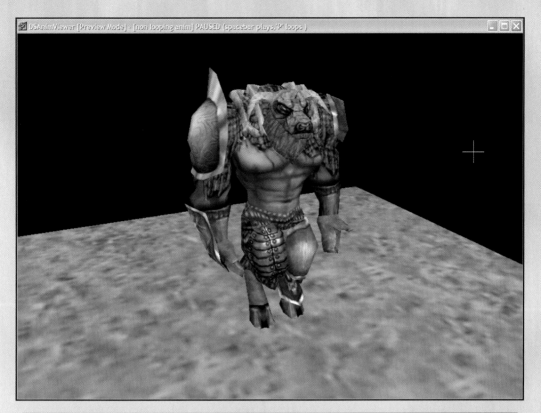

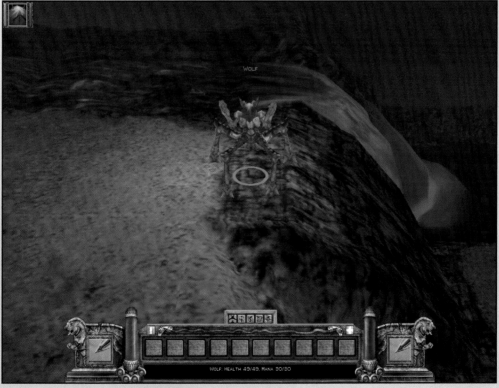

The Elemental Siegelet includes other characters such as Anakim, shown in the Animation Previewer tool, and Mantis, another player character race.

The Dungeon Siege tools enable you to create new places such as Jericho and this snowy mountain scene. Team Elemental created these images.

Tip   You can increase or decrease the size of the Modifier Stack by dragging the horizontal bar beneath the Modifier Stack buttons.

Beneath the Modifier Stack are five buttons that affect the selected modifier. They are as follows:

✦ **Pin Stack button:** Makes the parameters for the selected modifier available for editing even if another object is selected (like taking a physical pin and sticking it into the screen so it won't move).

✦ **Show End Result on/off toggle button:** Shows the results of all the modifiers in the entire Stack when enabled and only the modifiers up to the current selected modifier if disabled.

✦ **Make Unique button:** Used to break any instance or reference links to the selected object. After you click this button, an object will no longer be modified along with the other objects for which it was an instance or reference.

✦ **Remove Modifier from the Stack button:** Used to delete a modifier from the Stack or unbind a Space Warp if one is selected. Deleting a modifier restores it to its same state that it was in before the modifier was applied.

✦ **Customize Modifier Sets button:** Opens a pop-up menu where you can select to show a set of modifiers as buttons above the Modifier Stack. You can also select which modifier set appears at the top of the list of modifiers. The pop-up menu also includes an option to configure and define the various sets of modifiers.

Cross-Reference   For more information on configuring modifier sets, see Chapter 3, "Making a Custom Face, er, Interface."

If you right-click on a modifier, a pop-up menu appears. This pop-up menu includes commands to rename the selected modifier, which you might want to do if the same modifier is applied to the same object multiple times. This pop-up menu also includes an option to delete the selected modifier.

Copying and pasting modifiers

The pop-up menu also includes options to Cut, Copy, Paste, and Paste Instance modifiers. The Cut command deletes the modifier from the current object but makes it available for pasting onto other objects. The Copy command retains the modifier for the current object and makes it available to paste onto another object. After you use the Cut or Copy command, you can use the Paste command to apply the modifier to another object. The Paste Instance command retains a link between the original modifier and the instanced modifier, so that any changes to either modifier affect the other instances.

Tip

The format of the modifier name indicates whether it is an instance or reference. Instanced objects appear in bold in the Modifier Stack, and instanced modifiers appear in italic. Referenced objects have a black bar above them.

You can also apply modifiers for the current object onto other objects by dragging the modifier from the Modifier Stack and dropping it on the other object (like the Copy and Paste commands). Holding down the Ctrl key while dropping a modifier onto an object applies the modifier as an instance (like the Paste Instance command). Holding down the Shift key removes the modifier from the current modifier and applies it to the object on which it is dropped (like the Cut and Paste commands).

Using instanced modifiers

When a single modifier is applied to several objects at the same time, the modifier shows up in the Modifier Stack for each object. These are instanced modifiers that maintain a connection to each other. If you change any of these instanced modifiers, the change is propagated to all other instances. This feature is very helpful for modifying large groups of objects.

When a modifier is copied between different objects, you can select to make the copy an instance.

To see all the objects that are linked to a particular modifier, choose Views ⇨ Show Dependencies. All objects with instanced modifiers that are connected to the current selection appear as bright pink.

At any time, you can break the link between a particular instanced modifier and the rest of the objects using the Make Unique button in the Modifier Stack rollout. After clicking this button, a dialog box appears that asks whether you are sure about this action. Click Yes to complete the action.

Disabling modifiers

Clicking the light bulb icon to the left of the modifier name toggles the modifier on and off. The right-click pop-up menu also offers options to turn the modifier off in the viewport or off for the renderer.

Reordering the Stack

The Stack order is important and can change the appearance of the object. gmax applies the modifiers starting with the lowest one in the Stack first and the topmost modifier last. You can change the order of the modifiers in the Stack by selecting a modifier and dragging it above or below the other modifiers. You cannot drag it below the object type.

Tutorial: Learning the effect of Stack order

To see the effect of the Stack order, you'll apply some simple modifiers to a cylinder object and then copy those modifiers to another object and reorient their order.

To learn how the Stack order can affect the resulting geometry, follow these steps:

1. Open the Cylinders showing modifier stack order.gmax file from the Chap 14 directory on the CD-ROM.

   This file includes two simple cylinders.

2. Select the cylinder on the left, and open the Modify panel. From the Modifier List drop-down list, select the Bend modifier, and in the Parameters rollout, set the Angle value to 60 and the Bend Axis to Z.

3. Next, apply the Skew modifier from the Modifier List drop-down list in the Modify panel. Set the Skew Amount to 30 and Skew Axis to Z in the Parameters rollout.

   These settings cause the cylinder to curve to the right.

4. In the Modifier Stack, select and drag the Bend modifier to the cylinder on the right. Then select and drag the Skew modifier also onto the right cylinder.

   Notice how the right cylinder now bends to the right just like the other cylinder.

5. Select the cylinder on the right, and in the Modify panel, select the Skew modifier in the Modifier Stack and drag it below the Bend modifier to reorder the modifiers.

   With the modifiers reordered, the cylinder on the right looks different from the one on the left.

Figure 14-2 shows the original cylinder (left), the cylinder with the Bend and Skew modifiers applied (middle), and the same cylinder with the order of the two modifiers reversed (right). The box surrounding the modified cylinders is the modifier gizmo that will be covered in the next section.

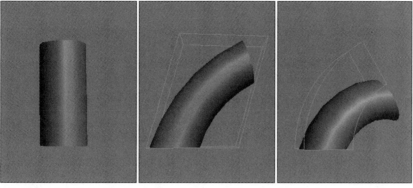

Figure 14-2: Changing the order of the modifiers in the Stack can affect the end result.

Collapsing the Stack

Collapsing the Stack removes its history and resets the modification history to a baseline. All the individual modifiers in the Stack are combined into one single modification. This feature eliminates the ability to change any modifier parameters, but it simplifies the object and conserves memory. The right-click pop-up menu also offers options to Collapse To and Collapse All. You can collapse the entire Stack with the Collapse All command, or you can collapse to the current selected modifier with the Collapse To command.

When you apply a collapse command, a warning dialog box appears, notifying you that this action will delete all the creation parameters. Click Yes to continue with the collapse.

Note   In addition to the Yes and No buttons, the warning dialog box includes a Hold/Yes button. This button saves the current state of the object to the Hold buffer and then applies the Collapse All function. If you have any problems, you can retrieve the object's previous state before the collapse was applied by choosing Edit ➪ Fetch (Alt+Ctrl+F).

Using gizmo subobjects

As you've worked with modifiers, you've probably noticed the orange wireframe box that surrounds the object in the viewports when you apply the modifier. These boxes are called modifier gizmos, and they provide a visual control for how the modifier changes the geometry. If you want, you can work directly with these gizmos.

Clicking the plus (+) sign to the left of the modifier name reveals any subobjects associated with the modifier. To select the modifier subobjects, simply click the subobject name. Many modifiers create gizmo subobjects. Gizmos have a center and can be transformed and controlled like regular objects using the transformation buttons on the main toolbar. Another common modifier subobject is Center, which controls the point about which the gizmo is transformed.

Modifying subobjects

In addition to being applied to complete objects, modifiers can also be applied and used to modify subobjects. Subobjects are defined as portions of an object. Subobjects can be vertices, edges, faces, or combinations of object parts.

Cross-Reference   To learn more about applying modifiers to subobject selections, see Chapter 9, "Beginning with the Basic Building Blocks."

To work in subobject selection mode, click the plus (+) sign to the left of the object name to see the subobjects. Several modifiers, including Mesh Select, Patch Select, Spline Select, and Volume Select, can select subobject areas for passing these selections up to the next modifier in the Stack. For example, you can use the Mesh Select modifier to select several faces on the front of a sphere and then apply the Face Extrude modifier to extrude just those faces.

Topology dependency warning

When you attempt to modify the parameters of a base object that has a modifier applied or when you collapse the stack, you often get a warning dialog box, like the one shown in Figure 14-3, telling you that the modifier depends on topology that may change or that the creation parameters will be removed. You can disable the warning by selecting the "Do not show this message again" option on the dialog box or by turning off the Warning options in the General panel of the Preference Settings dialog box. Disabling the warning will not make the potential problem go away; it only prevents the warning dialog box from appearing.

Figure 14-3: You can disable the Topology Dependence warning dialog box.

Holding and fetching a scene

Before going any farther, you need to know about an important feature in gmax that allows you to set a stopping point for the current scene. In the Edit menu, the Hold command saves the scene into a temporary buffer for easy recovery. After a scene is set with the Edit ⇨ Hold command (Alt+Ctrl+H), you can bring it back instantly with the Edit ⇨ Fetch command (Alt+Ctrl+F). These commands provide a quick way to backtrack on modifications to a scene or project without your having to save and reload the project. If you use these commands before applying or deleting modifiers, you can save some potential headaches.

Tip It is a good idea, along with saving your file often, to use the Hold command before applying any complex modifier to an object.

Exploring Modifier Types

To keep all the various modifiers straight, they have been grouped into several distinct modifier sets. The default modifier sets (as defined by right-clicking on the Modifier List in the Modify panel) include the following: Selection modifiers, Patch/Spline Editing, Mesh Editing, Animation modifiers, UV Coordinates,

Subdivision Surfaces, Free Form Deformations, Parametric modifiers, Surface modifiers, and Conversion modifiers. These modifier sets are roughly the same as the submenus found in the Modifiers menu, except for some name changes.

 Cross-Reference This chapter covers almost all of the modifiers. The exceptions are the UV Coordinates and Surface modifiers, which are covered in Chapter 16, "Putting on the Ritz with the gmax Material Editor."

Selection modifiers

The first set of modifiers available in the Modifiers menu is the Selection modifiers. You can use these modifiers to select subobject sections for the various object types. You can then apply other modifiers to these subobject selections by selecting the Selection modifier and applying a new modifier.

Selection modifiers are available for every modeling type, including Mesh Select, Poly Select, Patch Select, Spline Select, and Volume Select. You can apply the Mesh Select, Poly Select, Patch Select, and Volume Select modifiers to any 3D object, but you can apply the Spline Select modifier only to spline and shape objects. Any modifiers that appear above one of these Selection modifiers in the Modifier Stack will be applied only to the selected subobjects.

Applying modifiers to subobject selections

Even if your object isn't an editable object with available subobjects, you still can apply a modifier using one of the specialized Select modifiers. These modifiers let you select a subobject and apply a modifier to it without having to convert it to a non-parametric object. These Select modifiers include Mesh Select, Poly Select, Patch Select, Spline Select, and Volume Select. You can find all these modifiers in the Modifiers ➪ Selection Modifiers submenu (except for Poly Select, which is available in the Modifier Stack drop-down list).

After you apply a Select modifier to an object, you can select subobjects in the normal manner using the hierarchy in the Modifier Stack or the subobject icons in the Parameters rollout. Any modifiers that you apply after the Select modifier (they appear above the Select modifier in the Modifier Stack) affect only the subobject selection.

Mesh, Patch, Poly, and Spline Select modifiers

These modifiers enable you to select subobjects. Each has a different set of subobjects that you can select. The Mesh Select modifier includes Vertex, Edge, Face, Polygon, and Element subobjects. The Patch Select modifier includes Vertex, Edge,

Patch, and Element subobjects. The Poly Select modifier includes the same sub-objects as the Mesh Select modifier except the Border replaced the Face subobject. The Spline Select modifier includes Vertex, Segment, and Spline subobjects. You can copy and paste named selection sets. The selection can then be passed up the Stack to the next modifier. These modifiers provide a way to apply a modifier to a subobject selection.

Tutorial: Building a superman logo

Applying modifiers to a subobject selection is accomplished by passing the subob-ject selection up the Stack. This means that the Select modifier needs to come below the other modifier in the Modifier Stack. To give you some practice, this example uses the Extrude modifier to build a Superman logo.

To apply the Extrude modifier to a subobject selection, follow these steps:

1. Open the Superman logo.gmax file from the Chap 14 directory on the CD-ROM.

   This file includes a simple extruded shape with the shape of a letter *S* in it.

2. With the S shape selected, choose Modifiers ➪ Selection Modifiers ➪ Spline Select.

   This command applies the Spline Select modifier to the object.

3. In the Modifier Stack, expand the Spline Select title and click the Spline subob-ject icon to enter spline subobject selection mode. Click the S shape to select it.

4. With the spline subobject still selected, choose Modifiers ➪ Mesh Editing ➪ Extrude to apply the Extrude modifier to the subobject selection. In the Parameters rollout, set the Amount to 10.

Figure 14-4 shows the resulting extruded S shape. The power of this example is that you can select the Text object in the Modifier Stack and change the letter *S* to a *B* (for Batman) or an *A* (for Aquaman), and the same modifier is applied to the new letter.

Volume Select modifier

Among the Selection modifiers, the Volume Select modifier is unique. It selects subobjects based on the area defined by the modifier's gizmo. In the Parameters rollout for the Volume Select modifier, shown in Figure 14-5, you can specify whether subobjects selected within a given volume should be Object, Vertex, or Face subobjects. Any new selection can Replace, be Added to, or be Subtracted from the current selection. An Invert option is also available, which you can use to select the subobjects outside of the current volume. You can also choose either a Window or Crossing Selection Type.

Figure 14-4: The Extrude modifier is applied only to the subobject selection.

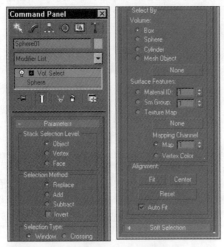

Figure 14-5: The Volume Select parameters let you select using different shaped volumes.

The actual shape of the gizmo can be a Box, a Sphere, a Cylinder, or a Mesh Object. To use a Mesh Object, click the button beneath the Mesh Object option and then click the object to use in a viewport. In addition to selecting by a gizmo-defined volume, you can select by Material IDs, Smoothing Groups, or a Texture Map.

The Alignment options can Fit or Center the volume on the current subobject selection. The Reset button moves the gizmo to its original position and orientation, which typically is the bounding box of the object.

Tutorial: Melting half an ice cream cone

Applying modifiers to a subobject selection is accomplished by passing the subobject selection up the Stack. This means that the select modifier needs to come below the other modifier in the Modifier Stack. To give you some practice, this example shows you how to use the Volume Select and Skew modifiers to melt only half of an ice cream cone.

To apply the Volume Select and Skew modifiers to a subobject selection, follow these steps:

1. Open the Melting ice cream cone.gmax file from the Chap 14 directory on the CD-ROM.

   This file includes an ice cream cone model created by Zygote Media.

2. With the top scoop object selected, choose Modifiers ➪ Selection Modifiers ➪ Volume Select.

   This command applies the Volume Select modifier to the top cone object.

3. In the Parameters rollout, select the Vertex option. Then click the Volume Select modifier in the Modifier Stack to select the gizmo subobject mode. With the Select and Move button on the main toolbar selected, drag in the Top viewport over the right half of the top scoop.

4. With the subobject still selected, choose Modifiers ➪ Parametric Deformers ➪ Skew to apply the Skew modifier to the subobject selection. In the Parameters rollout, set the Amount to 0.2 about the X-axis and enable the Limit Effect with an Upper Limit value of 0.2.

Figure 14-6 shows the resulting ice cream cone with half of the top scoop starting to melt.

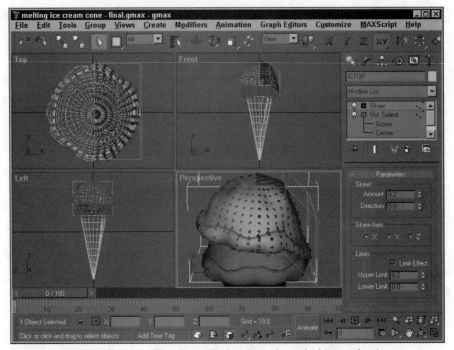

Figure 14-6: The Skew modifier is applied only to the subobject selection.

Using Modifiers on Patch and Spline Objects

Several modifiers work specifically on patch objects. Modifiers are used to change the geometry of objects, but they also can be used on splines. In fact, several modifiers can be used only on splines. The Modifiers ⇨ Patch/Spline Editing submenu contains most of these modifiers.

Tip Many other modifiers work on patch and spline objects. To see which modifiers work on which object types, select the object and check the Modifiers menu to see which modifiers are enabled.

Of the modifiers that work only on patches and splines, several of these duplicate functionality that is available for Editable Patches and Splines, such as the Fillet/Chamfer modifier. Applying these features as modifiers gives you better control over the results because you can remove them using the Modifier Stack at any time.

Edit Patch modifier

This modifier includes tools for editing patch objects. The features of this modifier are the same as those of the Editable Patch object. If you want to animate the features of an Editable Patch, use the Edit Patch modifier. You can even apply the Edit Patch modifier to an Editable Patch. The key benefit of the Edit Patch modifier is that it enables you to edit patch subobjects while maintaining the parametric nature of the object.

Edit Spline modifier

The Edit Spline modifier makes spline objects editable. This modifier has the same features as the Editable Spline object. The Edit Spline modifier isn't really a modifier but an Object type. It appears in the Modifier Stack above the base object. The key benefit of the Edit Spline modifier is that it enables you to edit spline subobjects while maintaining the parametric nature of the primitive object.

Using the surface tools

The surface tools, which include the CrossSection and Surface modifiers, provide a way to model that is similar to lofting. The CrossSection modifier takes several cross-section shapes and connects their vertices with additional splines to create a spline framework. You can then use the Surface modifier to cover this framework with a skin.

 Cross-Reference   Lofting is accomplished with the Loft compound object. For more information on it, see Chapter 13, "Continuing with Crazy Compound Objects."

CrossSection modifier

The CrossSection modifier is the first modifier that is used to create surfaces based on cross-sectional splines. This modifier and the Surface modifier are the key reason why the spline and patch modifiers have been combined into a single submenu.

The CrossSection modifier works only on spline objects, but without the Surface modifier, it isn't very useful. This modifier connects the vertices of several cross-sectional splines together with another spline that runs along their edges like a backbone. The various cross-sectional splines can have different numbers of vertices. Parameters include different spline types such as Linear, Smooth, Bézier, and Bézier Corner.

To apply this modifier, all the cross-section splines need to belong to the same Editable Spline object. You can connect them using the Attach button. The cross-section splines are attached in the order they exist. Figure 14-7 shows a spline network that has been created with the CrossSection modifier.

Surface modifier

The Surface modifier is the other part of the surface tools. It creates a surface from several combined splines. It can use any spline network but works best with structures created with the CrossSection modifier. The surface created with this modifier is a patch surface.

Parameters for this modifier include a Spline Threshold value and options to Flip Normals, to Remove Interior Patches, and to Use Only Selected Segments. You can also specify the steps used to create the patch topology. After the surface is created, you can apply the Edit Patch modifier to further edit and refine the patch surface.

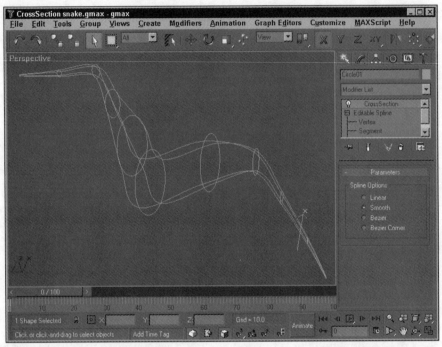

Figure 14-7: The CrossSection modifier joins several cross-section splines into a network of splines ready for a surface.

Figure 14-8 shows the spline structure illustrated in the previous figure with the Surface modifier applied.

Tutorial: Modeling the Mercury space capsule

One of the early space capsules used in the space race was the Mercury space capsule. Although lots of advanced technology was contained within the capsule, the exterior shape was relatively simple. Primitive shapes could be used to create the capsule, but in this tutorial, we'll create it using the surface tools.

To create a space capsule, follow these steps:

1. Open the Mercury space capsule.gmax file from the Chap 14 directory on the CD-ROM.

   This file includes all the cross-section splines needed to create the space capsule.

2. Select the top circle, open the Modify panel, click the Attach button, and then click each individual circle in order (the order is important for the CrossSection modifier).

   This step attaches all the circles together into one Editable Spline object.

Note   You can check the spline order by entering Spline subobject mode and selecting each spline. The spline number appears at the bottom of the Selection rollout.

   3. With the entire spline selected, choose Modifiers ⇨ Patch/Spline Editing ⇨ CrossSection to apply the CrossSection modifier to the spline object. Select the Linear option in the Parameters rollout.

   This command automatically connects all the splines in order by connecting their vertices.

   4. Choose Modifiers ⇨ Patch/Spline Editing ⇨ Surface to apply the Surface modifier. Then enable the Flip Normals option.

   This command creates a surface that covers the spline framework. The surface that is created is a patch object.

Figure 14-9 shows the completed Mercury space capsule. Using the surface tools to create patch objects results in objects that are easy to modify. You can change any patch subobject by applying the Edit Patch modifier and using the rollouts in the Modify panel.

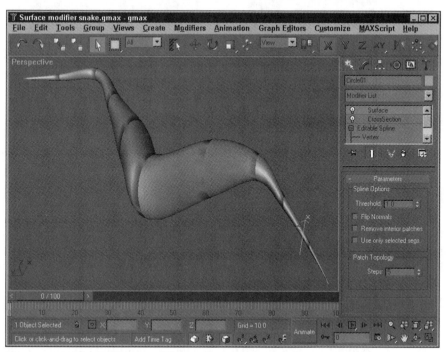

Figure 14-8: The Surface modifier applies a surface to the cross-section spline network.

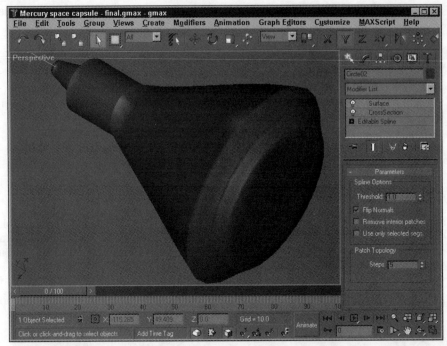

Figure 14-9: The Mercury space capsule, created using the CrossSection and Surface modifiers.

Delete Patch modifier

You can use the Delete Patch modifier to delete a patch subobject from a patch object. You use the Patch Select modifier to select the patch subobjects to delete, and you apply the Delete Patch modifier to the Patch Select modifier.

Delete Spline modifier

You can use the Delete Spline modifier to delete spline subobjects. Another good use of this modifier is to hide splines that are used for other purposes. For example, when creating an animation path, you could apply this modifier to the path to hide it, but by removing this modifier, you can get back to the base spline at any time.

Lathe modifier

The Lathe modifier rotates the spline about an axis to create an object with a circular cross section (such as a baseball bat). In the Parameters rollout, you can specify the Degrees to rotate (a value of 360 makes a full rotation) and Cappings, which add ends to the resulting mesh. Additional options include Weld Core, which causes all vertices at the center of the lathe to be welded together, and Flip Normals, which realigns all the normals.

Caution If your shape is created in the Top view, lathing about the screen Z-axis produces a thin disc with no depth.

The Direction option determines the axis about which the rotation takes place. The rotation takes place about the object's pivot point.

 Cross-Reference Chapter 10, "Starting with Simple Splines and Shapes," includes a good example of using the lathe modifier to create a crucible.

Normalize Spline modifier

The Normalize Spline modifier is used to add new points to (or subtract points from) the spline. These new points (or vertices) are spaced regularly based on the Segment Length value. This provides a quick way to optimize a spline.

 Caution Small Segment Length values result in a large number of vertices and large values destroy the original shape of the spline.

Using Mesh Editing Modifiers

The Editable Mesh and Editable Poly objects can have modifiers applied to them. The Modifiers menu includes a submenu of modifiers that are specific to mesh objects. These modifiers are found in the Mesh Editing submenu and can be used to enhance the features available for Editable Mesh objects.

Delete Mesh modifier

You use the Delete Mesh modifier to delete mesh subobjects. Subobjects that you can delete include Vertices, Edges, Faces, and Objects.

The Delete Mesh modifier deletes the current selection as defined by the Mesh Select (or Poly Select) modifier. It can be used to delete a selection of Vertices, Edges, Faces, Polygons, or even the entire mesh if there is no subobject selection. The Delete Mesh modifier has no parameters.

 Note Even if the entire mesh is deleted using the Delete Mesh modifier, the object still remains. To completely delete an object, use the Delete key.

Edit Mesh modifier

All mesh objects are by default Editable Mesh objects. This modifier enables objects to be modified using the Editable Mesh feature while maintaining their basic creation parameters.

 Caution Modifying an object's parameters after applying the Edit Mesh modifier or any modifier that alters the geometric topology of an object can cause erratic results.

When an object is converted to an Editable Mesh, its parametric nature is eliminated. However, if you use the Edit Mesh modifier, you can still retain the same object type and its parametric nature while having access to all the Editable Mesh features. For example, if you create a sphere and apply the Edit Mesh modifier and then extrude several faces, you can still change the radius of the sphere by selecting the Sphere object in the Modifier Stack and changing the Radius value in the Parameters rollout.

Note   There is no Edit Poly modifier.

Face Extrude modifier

The Face Extrude modifier extrudes the selected faces in the same direction as their normals. Face Extrude parameters include Amount and Scale values and an option to Extrude From Center. Figure 14-10 shows a mesh object with several extruded faces. The Mesh Select modifier was used to select the faces, and the extrude Amount was set to 30.

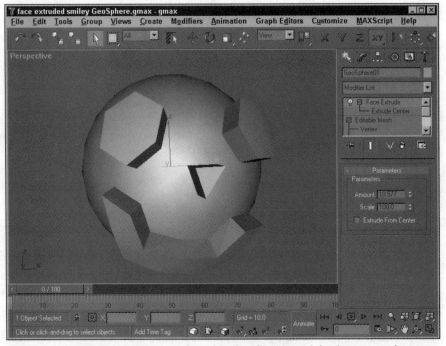

Figure 14-10: Extruded faces are moved in the direction of the face normal.

Extrude modifier

The Extrude modifier copies the selected subobject, moves it a given distance, and connects the two areas to form a 3D shape. Parameters for this modifier include an Amount value, which is the distance to extrude, and the number of segments to use to define the height. The Capping options let you specify a Start Cap and/or an End Cap. The Cap fills the spline area and can be made as a Patch or Mesh object. Only closed splines that are extruded can be capped. You can also have mapping coordinates and Material IDs generated automatically.

One common place to use the Extrude modifier is on closed splines. Closed splines (or shapes) can be extruded easily, making them full-fledged 3D objects.

 Chapter 10, "Starting with Simple Splines and Shapes," includes an example using the lathe modifier to create a bookshelf.

Normal modifier

The Normal modifier enables object normals to be flipped or unified. When some objects are imported, their normals can become erratic, producing holes in the geometry. By unifying and flipping the normals, you can restore an object's consistency. This modifier includes two options: Unify Normals and Flip Normals.

Smooth modifier

You use the Smooth modifier to auto-smooth an object. Smooth parameters include options for Auto Smooth and Prevent Indirect Smoothing along with a Threshold value. The Parameters rollout also includes a set of 32 Smoothing Groups buttons labeled 1 through 32.

Tessellate modifier

You use the Tessellate modifier to subdivide the selected faces for higher-resolution models. You can apply tessellation to either Triangle or Polygonal faces. The Edge option creates new faces by dividing the face from the face center to the middle of the edges. The Face-Center option divides each face from the face center to the corners of the face. The Tension setting determines whether the faces are convex or concave. The Iterations setting is the number of times the modifier is applied.

 Applying the Tessellate modifier to an object with a high Iterations value produces objects with many times the original number of faces.

Cap Holes modifier

The Cap Holes modifier patches any holes found in a geometry object. Sometimes when objects are imported, they are missing faces. This modifier can detect and eliminate these holes by creating a face along open edges.

For example, if a spline is extruded and you don't specify Caps, the Cap Holes modifier detects these holes and creates a Cap. Cap Holes parameters include Smooth New Faces, Smooth with Old Faces, and All New Edges Visible. Smooth with Old Faces applies the same smoothing group used on the bordering faces.

Vertex Paint modifier

A unique way to color objects is with the Vertex Paint modifier. This modifier lets you paint with different colors on an object. The colors are stored as a color value assigned to the closest vertex. If adjacent vertices have different colors assigned, then a gradient is created across the face. The benefit of this coloring option is that it is very efficient and requires almost no memory making it a good option to use for game models.

Chapter 16, "Putting on the Ritz with the gmax Material Editor," provides more details and an example of the Vertex Paint modifier in action.

The Vertex Paint modifier lets you specify a color and paint directly on the surface of an object by painting the vertices. The color is applied with a paintbrush-shaped cursor.

The Assign Vertex Color utility works a little differently. It converts any existing material colors to vertex colors. To use this utility, select an object, choose a Light Model (Scene Lights or Diffuse lighting), and click the Assign to Selected button.

The parameters for this modifier include a Paint button, an Opacity toggle, and a color swatch for selecting the color with which to paint. VertCol and Shaded toggles turn Vertex Shading and normal Shading on and off, and you can use a 16-color palette for quick color selection.

Correct display of the Vertex Paint modifier can be problematic in gmax depending on your video card and display driver. The modifier works, but often it isn't displayed correctly in the viewports. The Direct3D driver, in particular, does not correctly display vertex colors.

Optimize modifier

The Optimize modifier simplifies the mesh model by reducing the number of faces, edges, and vertices. The Level of Detail can be set for the viewports. Face and Edge Thresholds determine whether elements should be collapsed. Other options include Bias and Maximum Edge Length. Parameters can also be set to Preserve Material and Smoothing Boundaries. The Update button enables manual updating of the object, and the text field at the bottom of the rollout displays the number of vertices and faces for the current optimization.

You can see a figure of the Optimize modifier applied to a detailed cow model in Chapter 11, "Moving On with Marvelous Meshes."

Animation modifiers

Modifiers are used to deform and otherwise alter the geometry of objects in an automatic way. These alterations can include animated changes. The Modifiers menu includes a submenu that contains many such modifiers. These modifiers are unique in that each changes with time. They can be useful as an alternate to controllers, but their resulting effects are very specific.

 Cross-Reference I cover the Skin modifier in Chapter 15, "Skeletons Rule: Building with Bones and IK."

Morpher modifier

The Morpher modifier lets you change a shape from one form into another. You can apply this modifier only to objects with the same number of vertices.

 Cross-Reference In many ways, the Morph modifier is similar to the Morph compound object, which is covered in Chapter 13, "Continuing with Crazy Compound Objects."

The Morpher modifier can be very useful for creating facial expressions and character lip-synching. You can also use it to morph materials. There are 100 separate channels available for morph targets, and channels can be mixed. You can use the Morpher modifier in conjunction with the Morpher material. For example, you could use the Morpher material to make a character blush for an embarrassed expression.

 Tip When it comes to making facial expressions, a mirror and your own face can be the biggest help. Coworkers may look at you funny, but the facial expressions you create in gmax will benefit from the exercise.

The first task before using this modifier is to create all the different morph targets. Because the morph targets need to contain the same number of vertices as the base object, make a copy of the base object for each morph target that you are going to create. As you create these targets, be careful not to add or delete any vertices from the object.

After all your morph targets are created, select a channel in the Channel Parameters rollout, shown in Figure 14-11, and use the Pick Object from Scene button to select the morph target for that channel. The other option in that section is to Capture Current State. After a morph target has been added to a channel, you can view it in the Channel List rollout.

As you animate, you can specify the amount of each morph target to include in the frame using the value to the right of the channel name in the Channel List rollout. The slim color bar to the left of the channel name designates the status of the channel. You can find information on what each color represents in the Channel Color Legend rollout.

Figure 14-11: The Morph modifier's rollouts

Tutorial: Morphing facial expressions

The Morph modifier is very helpful when you're trying to morph facial expressions such as those to make a character talk. With the various sounds added to the different channels, you can quickly morph between them. In this example, we'll use the Morph modifier to change the facial expressions of the general character.

Tip   When creating facial expressions, be sure to enable the Soft Selection features, which makes modifying the face meshes much easier.

To change facial expressions using the Morph modifier, follow these steps:

1. Open the Morphing facial expressions.gmax file from the Chap 14 directory on the CD-ROM.

   This file includes the General's head model created by Viewpoint Datalabs. The model has been copied twice, and the morph targets have already been created by modifying the subobjects around the mouth.

2. Select the face on the left where the General is snarling, and choose Modifiers ➪ Animation Modifiers ➪ Morpher to apply the Morpher modifier.

3. In the Channel Parameters rollout, select channel 1, click the Pick Object from Scene button (or you can right click on the channel button and select the Pick from Scene option), select the middle face object, and name it Closed lips. Then repeat this step for the smiling face and name it Smile.

   If you look in the Channel List rollout, you'll see Closed lips in Channel 1 and Smile in Channel 2.

4. Click the Animate button (or press the N key), drag the Time Slider to frame 50 and then increase the Closed lips channel in the Channel List rollout to 100. Drag the Time Slider to frame 100, and increase the Smile channel to 100 and the Closed lips channel to 0.

5. Click the Play Animation button in the Time Controls to see the resulting animation.

Figure 14-12 shows the three facial expressions. The Morpher modifier is applied to the left face.

 Tip   Be sure to keep the morph target objects around. You can hide them in the scene or select them and save them to a separate file with File ➪ Save Selected.

Linked XForm modifier

The Linked XForm modifier passes all transformations of one object onto another, but not vice versa. The object that controls the transformation is designated as the Control Object and is selected via the Pick Control Object button (which is the only control in the Parameters rollout for this modifier). After the Control Object is selected, it controls the selected object's transforms, but the object that is being controlled can move independent of the Control Object without affecting the Control Object.

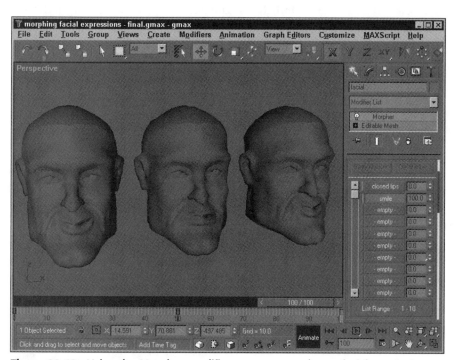

Figure 14-12: Using the Morpher modifier, you can morph one facial expression into another.

PatchDeform modifiers

Among the animation modifiers are several modifiers that are similar in function, but they work on different types of objects. The PatchDeform modifier uses patches, and the PathDeform modifier deforms an object according to a spline path.

In the Parameters rollout for each of these modifiers is a Pick Patch button that lets you select an object to use in the deformation process. After the object is selected, you can enter the Percent and Stretch values for the U and V directions, along with a Rotation value.

Tutorial: Deforming a car going over a hill

Have you seen those commercials that use rubber cars to follow the curvature of the road? In this tutorial, we'll use the PatchDeform modifier to bend a car over a hill made from a patch.

To deform a car according to a patch surface, follow these steps:

1. Open the 57 Chevy bending over a hill.gmax file from the Chap 14 directory on the CD-ROM.

   This file contains a simple hill made from patch objects and a '57 Chevy model created by Viewpoint Datalabs.

2. Select the car model, and choose the PatchDeform modifier from the Modifier List drop-down list in the Modifier Stack of the Modify panel.

   This applies the PatchDeform modifier to the car object.

3. In the Parameters rollout, click the Pick Patch button and select the hill object.

   This makes the car deform around the patch hill object.

4. Set the U Percent value to 75, the V Percent value to 20, and the U and V Stretch values to 1.0.

   I've set the Deform Plane to the XY plane.

Figure 14-13 shows the results of this tutorial.

PathDeform modifier

The PathDeform modifier uses a spline path to deform an object. The Pick Path button lets you select a spline to use in the deformation process. You can select either an open or closed spline. The Parameters rollout also includes spinners for controlling the Percent, Stretch, Rotation, and Twist of the object. The Percent value is the distance the object moves along the path.

Figure 14-14 shows some text wrapped around a spline path.

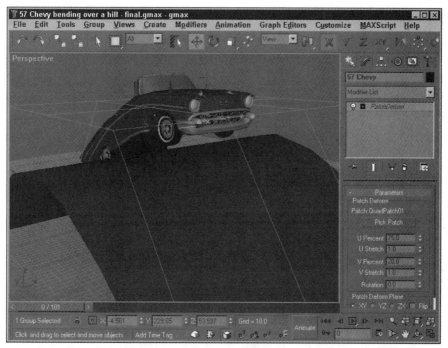

Figure 14-13: Our '57 Chevy hugs the road thanks to the PatchDeform modifier.

Cross-Reference

The modifiers found in the UV Coordinates submenu are discussed in Chapter 16, "Putting on the Ritz with the gmax Material Editor."

Subdivision Surface modifiers

The Modifiers menu also includes a submenu of modifiers for subdividing surfaces. This submenu includes only a single modifier — MeshSmooth. You can use this modifier to smooth and subdivide the surface of an object. Subdividing a surface increases the resolution of the object, allowing for more detailed modeling.

MeshSmooth modifier

The MeshSmooth modifier smoothes the entire surface of an object by applying a chamfer function to both vertices and edges at the same time. This modifier has the greatest effect on sharp corners and edges. With this modifier, you can create a NURMS object. NURMS stands for Non-Uniform Rational MeshSmooth. NURMS can weight each control point. The Parameters rollout includes three MeshSmooth types: Classic, NURMS, and Quad Output. You can set it to operate on triangular or polygonal faces. Smoothing parameters include Strength and Relax values.

There are also settings for the number of Subdivision Iterations to run and controls for weighting selected control points. Update Options can be set to Always, and Manually using the Update button.

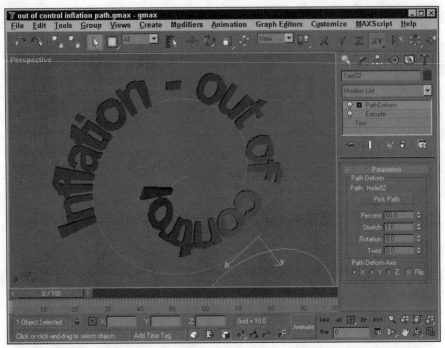

Figure 14-14: The text in this example has been deformed around a spline path using the PathDeform modifier.

Caution The maximum number of supported iterations is 10. To complete 10 iterations on a simple patch terrain that I created would take over 2 million megabytes of memory, as shown in a warning dialog box that appears. You'll want to keep the number of iterations well below 10.

You can also select and work with either Vertex or Edge subobjects. These subobjects give you local control over the MeshSmooth object. Included within the Local Control rollout is a Crease value, which is available in Edge subobject mode. Selecting an Edge subobject and applying a 1.0 value causes a hard edge to be retained while the rest of the object is smoothed. The MeshSmooth modifier also makes the Soft Selection rollout available. The Reset rollout is included to quickly reset any crease and weight values.

Tutorial: Creating a heart-shaped NURMS

You'll never know when your game will need a heart-shaped object, and here's an example just for Valentine's Day. Create a spline heart, extrude it, and then convert it to a NURMS object using the MeshSmooth modifier.

To create a heart-shaped NURMS object, follow these steps:

1. Open the Heart Shaped NURMS.gmax file from the Chap 14 directory on the CD-ROM.

   This file includes a simple extruded heart shape.

2. With the heart shape selected, choose Modifiers ➪ Subdivision Surfaces ➪ MeshSmooth to apply the MeshSmooth modifier. In the Parameters rollout, select the NURMS option in the Subdivision Method drop-down list (if it isn't already selected).

3. In the Local Control rollout, select the Edge subobject icon and click in the Front viewport on the single edge at the center of the heart shape. Then set the Crease value to 1.0. Click again on the Edge subobject to exit subobject mode.

4. To apply the smoothing option to the entire object, select an Iterations value of 1 in the Subdivision Amount rollout.

   The entire heart will be smoothed with the exception of the crease located at the center of the heart. If you click the vertex icon in the Local Control rollout, you can use the transform buttons on the main toolbar to edit selected vertices. Changing the weight of its vertices also alters a NURMS object.

5. In the Local Control rollout, select the Display Control Mesh option, select the two vertices at the heart's top (the bottom of the crease), and increase the Weight value to 100.

   The faces gravitate toward the selected vertices.

Figure 14-15 shows the NURMS heart.

Free Form Deformer modifiers

The Free Form Deformers category of modifiers causes a lattice to appear around an object. This lattice is bound to the object, and you can alter the object's surface by moving the lattice control points. Modifiers include FFD (Free Form Deformation) and FFD (Box/Cyl).

FFD (Free Form Deformation) modifier

The Free Form Deformation modifiers create a lattice of control points around the object. The object's surface can deform the object when you move the control points. The object is deformed only if the object is within the volume of the FFD lattice. The three different resolutions of FFDs are 2×2, 3×3, and 4×4. The Set Number of Points button enables you to specify the number of points to be included in the FFD lattice.

You can also select to display the lattice or the source volume, or both. If the Lattice option is disabled, only the control points are visible. The Source Volume option shows the original lattice before any vertices were moved.

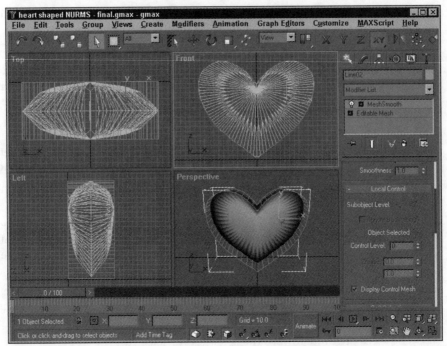

Figure 14-15: A NURMS heart created with the MeshSmooth modifier

The two deform options are Only In Volume and All Vertices. The Only In Volume option limits the vertices that can be moved to the interior vertices only. If the All Vertices option is selected, the Falloff value determines the point at which vertices are no longer affected by the FFD. Falloff values can range between 0 and 1. The Tension and Continuity values control how tight the lines of the lattice are when moved.

The three buttons at the bottom of the FFD Parameters rollout help in the selection of control points. If the All X button is selected, then when a single control point is selected, all the adjacent control points along the X-axis are also selected. This feature makes selecting an entire line of control points easier. The All Y and All Z buttons work in a similar manner in the other dimensions.

Use the Reset button to return the volume to its original shape if you make a mistake. The Conform to Shape button sets the offset of the Control Points with Inside Points, Outside Points, and Offset options.

To move the control points, select the Control Points subobject. This enables you to alter the control points individually.

FFD (Box/Cyl) modifier

The FFD (Box) and FFD (Cyl) modifiers can create a box- or cylinder-shaped lattice of control points for deforming objects. Figure 14-16 shows how you can use the

FFD modifier to distort the hammer by selecting the control point's subobjects. The left hammer is distorted using a 2×2×2 FFD, the middle hammer has a 4×4×4 FFD, and the right hammer is surrounded with an FFD (Cyl) modifier.

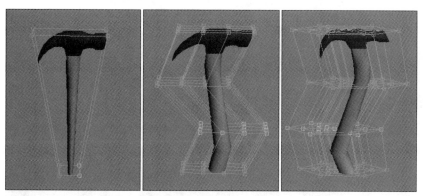

Figure 14-16: The FFD modifier changes the shape of an object by moving the lattice of control points that surround it.

Tutorial: Modeling hyperspace deformation

Why is it that whenever a person (or object) travels through a hyperspace portal, he (or it) deforms before disappearing? It must have something to do with compressing the molecules. (Anyway, it looks like it hurts. I prefer the *Star Trek* method where you just twinkle and you're gone.) In this tutorial, we'll re-create this hyperspace deformation using an FFD modifier. The object I'm transporting is a television created by Zygote Media. (Perhaps the *Enterprise* crew wants to watch some old episodes.)

To simulate the hyperspace deformation effect, follow these steps:

1. Open the TV – hyperspace deformation.gmax file from the Chap 14 directory on the CD-ROM.

   This file includes a television object that is animated to move through a set of semi-transparent rings to represent the hyperspace portal.

2. With the television selected, choose Modifiers ⇨ Free Form Deformers ⇨ FFD 3×3×3.

   A lattice gizmo appears around the television.

3. Move the Time Slide to frame 100 (or press the End key) and click the Animate button (or press the N key).

4. Click the FFD name in the Modifier Stack and select the Control Points subobject from the hierarchy list. Then select the upper row of Control Points and move them to the right.

Figure 14-17 shows our television being deformed as it travels through the hyperspace transporter.

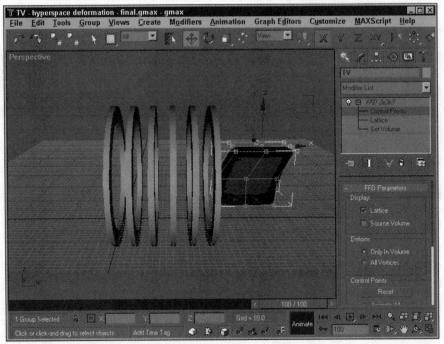

Figure 14-17: This television is being deformed via an FFD modifier.

Parametric Deformer modifiers

Perhaps the most representative group of modifiers is the Parametric Deformers. These modifiers affect the geometry of objects by pulling, pushing, and stretching them. They all can be applied to any of the modeling types, including primitive objects.

Note You might start to get sick of seeing the hammer model used over and over again, but using the same model enables you to more easily compare the effects of the various modifiers.

Bend modifier

The Bend modifier can bend an object along any axis. Bend parameters include Bend Angle and Direction, Bend Axis, and Limits. The hammer in Figure 14-18 shows several bending options. Limit settings are the boundaries beyond which the modifier has no effect. You can set Upper and Lower Limits. The left hammer shows a bend value of 75 degrees around the Z-axis, the middle hammer also has a Direction value of 60, and the right hammer has an Upper Limit of 8. Limits are useful if you want the modifier applied to only one half of the object.

Note   Several modifiers have the option to impose limits on the modifier including upper and lower limit values.

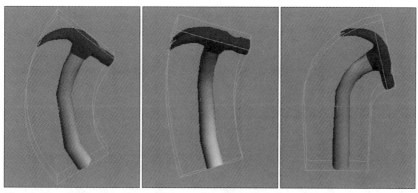

Figure 14-18: The Bend modifier can bend objects about any axis.

Taper modifier

The Taper modifier scales only one end of an object. Taper parameters include the Amount and Curve, Primary and Effect Axes, and Limits. The Curve value tapes the object along a curve. You can also select a Symmetry option to taper both ends equally. The left hammer in Figure 14-19 shows a taper of 1.0 about the Z-axis, the middle hammer also has a Curve value of –2, and the right hammer has the Symmetry option selected.

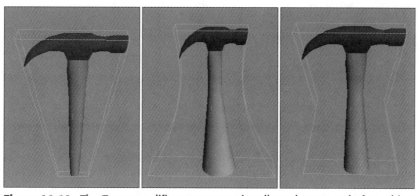

Figure 14-19: The Taper modifier can proportionally scale one end of an object.

Twist modifier

The Twist modifier deforms an object by rotating one end of an axis in one direction and the other end in the opposite direction. Twist parameters include Angle and Bias values, Twist Axis, and Limits. The Bias value determines how much of the twist is completed; a value of 0 is the full twist, and 100 keeps the object in its original state. The Bias value makes it easy to animate the twisting of the object. The left hammer in Figure 14-20 shows a twist angle of 120 about the Z-axis, the middle hammer shows a Bias value of 20, and the right hammer has an Upper Limit value of 8.

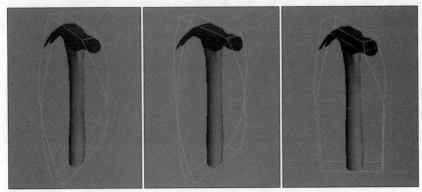

Figure 14-20: The Twist modifiers can twist an object about an axis.

Tutorial: Twisting a bridge

Do you remember back in science class seeing the short film on the collapse of the Tacoma Narrows Bridge caused by resonate winds through a canyon? We can re-create this scenario using the Twist modifier.

To use the Twist modifier on a bridge model, follow these steps:

1. Open the Twisting bridge.gmax file from the Chap 14 directory on the CD-ROM.

   This file includes a simple bridge spanning a canyon.

2. Select the bridge object, and apply the Twist modifier by choosing Modifiers ➪ Parametric Deformers ➪ Twist.

3. Click the Animate button (or press the N key), and drag the Time Slider to frame 30. Enter an Angle value of **−15** in the Parameters rollout, and select the Y Twist Axis option. Drag the Time Slider to frame 60, and enter an Angle value of **0**. Drag the slider to frame 90, and enter **15**. At frame 100, enter a value of **0** again.

4. Click the Play Animation button to see the brief animation.

This example shows how all modifiers can be animated. Figure 14-21 includes a frame from this simple animation.

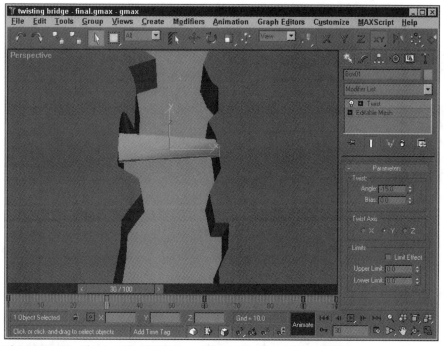

Figure 14-21: The twisting bridge modified with the Twist modifier.

Noise modifier

The Noise modifier randomly varies the position of object vertices. Noise parameters include Seed and Scale values, a Fractal option with Roughness and Iterations settings, Strength about each axis, and Animation settings. The Seed value sets the randomness of the noise. Two objects with the same Seed value will have the noise effect applied to them. The Scale value determines the size of the position changes, so larger Scale values result in a smoother, less rough shape. For the Animation settings, the Frequency controls how quickly the object's noise changes and the Phase setting determines where the noise wave starts and will set keys when changed.

Figure 14-22 shows the Noise modifier applied to several sphere objects. These spheres make the Noise modifier easier to see than on the hammer object. The left sphere has Seed, Scale, and Strength values along all three axes set to 1.0, the middle sphere has increased the Strength values to 2.0, and the right sphere has enabled the Fractal option with a Roughness value of 1.0 and an Iterations value of 6.0.

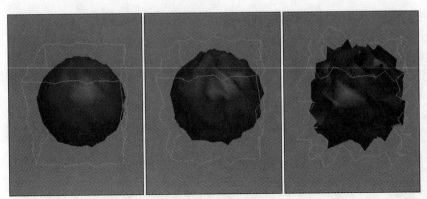

Figure 14-22: The Noise modifier can apply a smooth or wild look to your objects.

Tutorial: Creating a terrain

As a simple example of applying a modifier to a patch grid, we'll create a terrain. Using a patch grid and the Noise modifier, we can quickly create a hilly or jagged terrain.

To create a terrain, follow these steps:

1. In the Create panel, click the Geometry category button and select the Patch Grids subcategory from the subcategory drop-down list.

2. Click the Quad Patch button, and create a patch in the Top view. In the Parameters rollout, change the Length and Width Segments to 20 each.

   These settings supply ample resolution for the terrain.

3. Choose Modifiers ➪ Parametric Deformations ➪ Noise to apply the Noise modifier. In the Parameters rollout, enter a Z Strength value of **200** for smooth, rolling hills, or click the Fractal option for more rough and jagged peaks.

Figure 14-23 shows a sample terrain with gently rolling hills.

Push modifier

The Push modifier pushes an object's vertices inward or outward as if they were being filled with air. The Push modifier also has one parameter: the Push Value. This value is the distance to move with respect to the object's center. Figure 14-24 shows the hammer pushed with 0.05, 0.1, and 0.15 values.

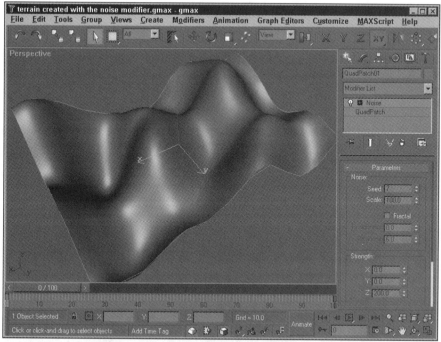

Figure 14-23: A terrain created from a patch grid and the Noise modifier

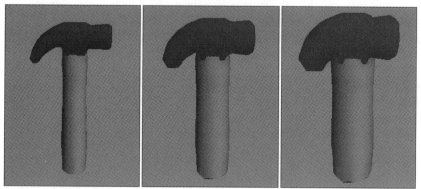

Figure 14-24: The Push modifier can increase the volume of an object.

Relax modifier

The Relax modifier tends to smooth the overall geometry by separating vertices that lie closer than an average distance. Parameters include a Relax Value that is the percentage of the distance that the vertices move. Values can range between 1.0 and –1.0. A value of 0 has no effect on the object. Positive values relax an object; negative values have the opposite effect, causing an object to become tighter and more distorted.

The Iterations value determines how many times this calculation is computed. The Keep Boundary Points Fixed option removes any points that are next to an open hole. Save Outer Corners maintains the vertex position of corners of an object. The left and middle hammers of Figure 14-25 have Relax values of 1.0 and Iteration values of 1 and 3. The right hammer has a Relax value of –1.0 and an Iteration value of 1.

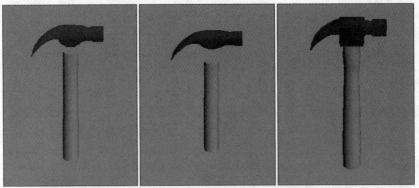

Figure 14-25: The Relax modifier can simplify the number of vertices in an object.

Ripple modifier

The Ripple modifier creates ripples across the surface of an object. This modifier is best used on a single object; if several objects need a ripple effect, use the Ripple Space Warp. The ripple is applied via a gizmo that you can control. Parameters for this modifier include two Amplitude values and values for the Wave Length, Phase, and Decay of the ripple. The two amplitude values cause an increase in the height of the ripples opposite one another. Figure 14-26 shows the Ripple modifier applied to a simple Quad Patch with values of 10 for Amplitude 1 and a Wave Length value of 50. The right Quad Patch also has an Amplitude 2 value of 20.

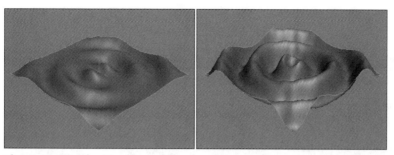

Figure 14-26: The Ripple modifier can make small waves appear over the surface of an object.

Wave modifier

The Wave modifier produces a wave-like effect across the surface of the object. All the parameters of the Wave Parameter are identical to the Ripple modifier parameters. The difference is that the waves produced by the Wave modifier are parallel, and they propagate in a straight line. Figure 14-27 shows the Wave modifier applied to a simple Quad Patch with values of 5 for Amplitude 1 and a Wave Length value of 50. The right Quad Patch also has an Amplitude 2 value of 20.

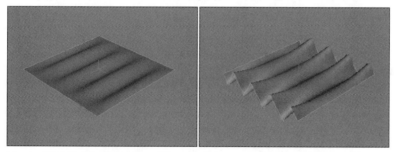

Figure 14-27: The Wave modifier produces parallel waves across the surface of an object.

Skew modifier

The Skew modifier changes the tilt of an object by moving its top portion while keeping the bottom half fixed. Skew parameters include Amount and Direction values, Skew Axis, and Limits. Figure 14-28 shows the hammer with a Skew value of 2.0, the middle hammer has a Skew value of 5.0, and the right hammer has an Upper Limit of 8.0.

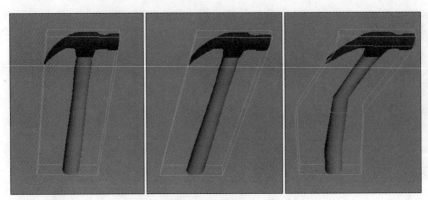

Figure 14-28: You can use the Skew modifier to tilt objects.

Slice modifier

You can use the Slice modifier to divide an object into two separate objects. Applying the Slice modifier creates a Slice gizmo. This gizmo looks like a simple plane and can be transformed and positioned to define the slice location. To transform the gizmo, you need to select it from the Stack hierarchy.

Note   You can use the Slice modifier to make objects slowly disappear a layer at a time.

The Slice parameters include four slice type options. Refine Mesh simply adds new vertices and edges where the gizmo intersects the object. The Split Mesh option creates two separate objects. The Remove Top and Remove Bottom options delete all faces and vertices above or below the gizmo intersection plane.

Using the Faces or Polygon buttons, you can also specify whether the faces are divided. Figure 14-29 shows the top and bottom halves of a hammer object. The right hammer is sliced at an angle.

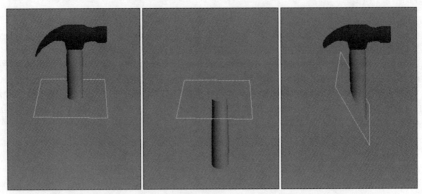

Figure 14-29: The Slice modifier can cut objects into two separate pieces.

Note Editable Meshes also have a Slice tool that can produce similar results. The difference is that the Slice modifier can work on any type of object, not only on meshes.

Affect Region modifier

The Affect Region modifier can cause a local surface region to bubble up or be indented. Affect Region parameters include Falloff, Pinch, and Bubble values. The Falloff value sets the size of the area that is affected. The Pinch value makes the region tall and thin, and the Bubble value rounds the affected region. You can also select the Ignore Back Facing option. Figure 14-30 shows the Affect Region modifier applied to a Quad Patch with a Falloff value of 80 on the left and a Bubble value of 1.0 on the right. The height and direction of the region is determined by the position of the modifier gizmo, which is a line connected by two points.

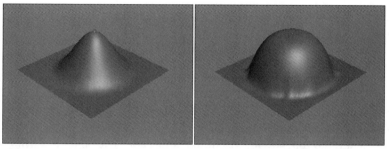

Figure 14-30: The Affect Region modifier can raise or lower the surface region of an object.

Mirror modifier

You can use the Mirror modifier to create a mirrored copy of an object or subobject. The Parameters rollout lets you pick a mirror axis or plane and an Offset value. The Copy option creates a copy of the mirrored object and retains the original selection.

Displace modifier

The Displace modifier offers two unique sets of features. It can alter an object's geometry by displacing elements using a gizmo, or it can change the object's surface using a grayscale bitmap image. The Displace gizmo can have one of four different shapes: Planar, Cylindrical, Spherical, or Shrink Wrap. This gizmo can be placed exterior to an object or inside an object to push it from the inside.

The Displace modifier parameters include Strength and Decay values. You can also specify the dimensions of the gizmo. A cylindrical-shaped gizmo can be capped or uncapped. The alignment parameters let you align the gizmo to the X, Y, or Z axes, or you can align it to the current view. The rest of the parameters deal with displacing the surface using a bitmap image. Figure 14-31 shows a Quad Patch with the Plane-shaped gizmo applied with a Strength value of 25. To the right is a Quad Patch with the Sphere-shaped gizmo.

Figure 14-31: You can use the Displace modifier's gizmo as a modeling tool to change the surface of an object.

Tutorial: Creating an alien landscape

A Displacement map determines surface height based on the gradient value, making black pixels low and white pixels high. To illustrate this feature, we'll use a Displacement map to create an alien landscape.

To create a landscape using a Displacement map, follow these steps:

1. Open the Alien landscape.max file from the Chap 14 directory on the CD-ROM.

   This file includes a large patch object. The Chap 14 directory also includes a grayscale bitmap that will represent the landscape. The peaks are white and the valleys are black. The file is saved as Alien Landscape Grad.tif.

2. Select the patch grid and choose Modifiers ⇨ Parametric Deformers ⇨ Displace to apply the Displace modifier to the patch object.

3. In the Parameters rollout, click the None button under the Bitmap Image section and locate the Alien Landscape Grad.tif file from the Chap 14 directory on the CD-ROM and click OK.

4. Set the Strength value to 30 and the terrain appears.

Figure 14-32 shows the resulting rendered displacement.

XForm modifier

The XForm modifier enables you to apply transforms such as Move, Rotate, and Scale to objects and/or subobjects. This modifier is applied by means of a gizmo that can be transformed using the transform buttons on the main toolbar. The XForm modifier has no parameters.

Note   XForm is short for the word *transform*.

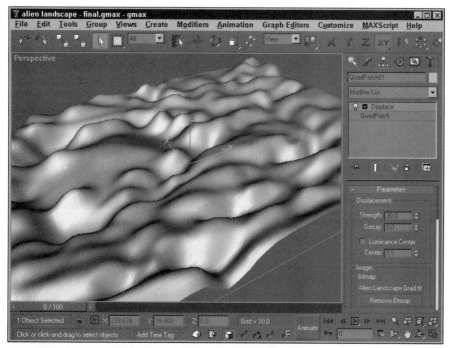

Figure 14-32: Using the Displace modifier, you can modify geometry based on a bitmap.

Preserve modifier

The Preserve modifier works to maintain Edge Lengths, Face Angles, and Volume as an object is deformed and edited. Before an object is modified, make an additional copy. Then edit one of the copies. To apply the Preserve modifier, click the Pick Original button, then click the unmodified object, and finally, click the modified object. The object will be modified to preserve the Edge Lengths, Face Angles, and Volume as defined in the Weight values. This helps prevent the topology of the modified object from becoming too irregular.

The Iterations option determines the number of times the process is applied. You can also specify to apply to the Whole Mesh, to Selected Vertices Only, or to an Inverted Selection.

Cross-Reference

The final submenu in the Modifiers menu is Surface, which includes a modifier called Material. This modifier is used to apply Material IDs to objects or subobjects and is discussed in Chapter 16, "Putting On the Ritz with the gmax Material Editor."

Summary

With the modifiers contained in the Modify panel, you can alter objects in a vast number of ways. Modifiers can work with every aspect of an object, including geometric deformations, materials, and general object maintenance. In this chapter, we've taken a look at the Modifier Stack and how modifiers are applied, and we have examined several useful modifier sets. The topics covered in this chapter included

✦ Working with the Modifier Stack to apply, reorder, and collapse modifiers

✦ Exploring the Select modifiers

✦ Using modifiers to alter patches, splines, and meshes

✦ Controlling motion with the Animation modifiers

✦ Smoothing objects with the MeshSmooth modifier

✦ Using the FFD and Parametric Deformer modifiers

Now that we've got the wanton destruction out of our system, it's time for something creepy—the next chapter deals with bones, skin, and the horrors of Inverse Kinematics.

✦   ✦   ✦

Skeletons Rule: Building with Bones and IK

✦ ✦ ✦ ✦

In This Chapter

Building a bones
system

Setting bone
parameters and IK
Solvers

Making linked
objects into a bones
system

Using the Skin
modifier

Understanding
forward and inverse
kinematics

Using interactive and
applied IK methods

Setting thresholds in
the IK panel of the
Preference Settings
dialog box

Learning to work with
the IK Limb solver

✦ ✦ ✦ ✦

A linked hierarchy attaches, or links, one object to
another and makes transforming the attached object by
moving the one it is linked to possible. For example, the arm
is a classic example of a linked hierarchy — when the shoulder
rotates, so do the elbow, wrist, and fingers. Establishing linked
hierarchies can make moving, positioning, and animating
many objects easy.

A bones system is a unique case of a linked hierarchy that has a
specific structure. You can create a structure of bones from an
existing hierarchy, or you can create a bones system and attach
objects to it. A key advantage of a bones system is that you can
use IK Solvers to manipulate and animate the structure.

Kinematics is a branch of mechanics that deals with the
motions of a system of objects, so inverse kinematics should
be its evil twin brother that deals with the non-motion of a
system of objects. Well, not exactly.

In gmax, a system of objects is a bunch of objects that are
linked together such as a bone system. After a system is built
and the parameters of the links are defined, the motions of all
the pieces below the parent object can be determined as the
parent moves, using kinematic formulas.

Inverse kinematics (IK) is similar except that it determines all
the motions of objects in a system when the last object in the
hierarchy chain is moved. The position of the last object, such
as a finger or a foot, is typically the one you're concerned
with. Using IK, you can then use these solutions to animate
the system of objects by moving the last object in the system.

After you've created a system of bones and applied an IK solution, you can cover the bones with objects that have the Skin modifier applied. This modifier lets the covering object move and bend with the bone structure underneath.

Building a Bones System

In some instances, establishing a hierarchy of objects before linking objects together is easier. By building the hierarchy first, you can be sure of the links between objects. One way to build this hierarchy is to use a bones system. A bones system consists of many bone objects that are linked together. These bone objects are normally not rendered in the game engine, but you can set them to be visible, like splines. You can also assign an IK Solver to the bones system for controlling their motion.

To create a bones system, open the Create panel, click the Systems category button, and then click the Bones button. Now click in a viewport to create a root bone, then click a short distance away to create another bone, and repeat this a few more times. Each subsequent click creates another bone linked to the previous one. When you're finished adding bones, right-click to exit bone-creation mode. In this manner, you can create a long chain of bone objects all linked together.

These bones are actually linked joints. Moving one bone pulls its neighbors in the chain along with it. Bones can also be rotated, scaled, and stretched. Scaling a bones system affects the distance between the bones.

To branch the hierarchy of bones, simply click the bone where you want the branch to start while still in Bones creation mode. A new branching bone is created automatically. Click the Bones button again to create a new bone. Then continue to click to add new bones to the branch.

Figure 15-1 shows the rollouts that are available for creating bones.

Assigning an IK Solver

In the IK Chain Assignment rollout, you can select the single available IK Solver — IK Limb. You can assign this solver to the children bones and to the root bone using the available options. You must select both the Assign to Children and the Assign to Root options to assign the IK Controller to all bones in the system. If the Assign to Children option is deselected, then the Assign to Root option is disabled.

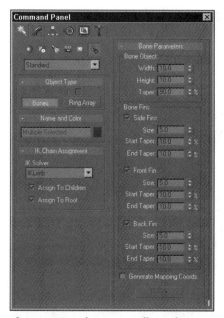

Figure 15-1: The Bone rollouts let you specify which bones get assigned an IK Controller.

Setting bone parameters

The Bone Parameters rollout includes parameters for setting the size of each individual bone, including its Width and Height. You can also set the percentage of Taper applied to the bone.

Fins can be displayed on the front, back, and/or sides of each bone. For each fin, you can specify its size and start and end taper values. Including fins on your bones makes correctly positioning and rotating the bone objects easier. Figure 15-2 shows two simple bone systems with and without fins.

At the bottom of the Bone Parameters rollout is an option to Generate Mapping Coordinates. Bones are renderable objects, so this option lets you apply texture maps to them.

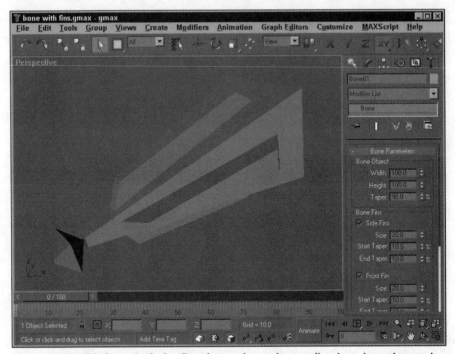

Figure 15-2: This bone includes fins that make understanding its orientation easier.

Refining bones

As you start to work with a bones system that you've created, you may discover that the one long bone for the backbone of your monster is too long to allow the monster to move like you want. If this happens, you can refine individual bones using the Refine button. This button appears at the bottom of the Bone Parameters rollout.

Clicking the Refine button enables you to select bones in the viewport. Every bone that you select is broken into two bones at the location where you click. Click the Refine button again to exit Refine mode.

Tutorial: Making a simple puppet using bones

Starting simply, a good example is a puppet. The bones system for the puppet can be built first. If you specify the IK Solver before building the bones, then you'll be ready to animate the puppet after it is ready.

To create a simple puppet out of bones, follow these steps:

1. Open the Create panel, select the Systems category, and click the Bones button. In the IK Chain Assignment rollout, select IK Limb from the IK Solver drop-down list. To be able to see the orientation of each bone, enable the Side Fins.

2. In the Front viewport, click where you want the head bone to start and click again where the neck will be; continue to click to form the spine, pelvis, right thigh, lower right leg, and foot bones. Then right-click to end the bones chain.

3. While still in Bones mode, move the cursor over the pelvis bone (the cursor changes to crosshairs), click in the Front viewport, and drag to the left to form the left thigh bone. Continue to click to form the lower left leg and left foot bones. Right-click to end the chain.

4. Form the right arm bones by clicking the head bone and clicking consecutively to form the right shoulder, right upper arm, lower right arm, and hand bones. Right-click to end the chain.

5. Repeat Step 4 for the left arm.

6. Click the Select Objects button on the main toolbar to exit Bones mode, and select and name each bone object so it can be easily identified later.

Figure 15-3 shows the completed bones system for the puppet. You can select the bones at the end of each chain and move them to see how the inverse kinematics solution works.

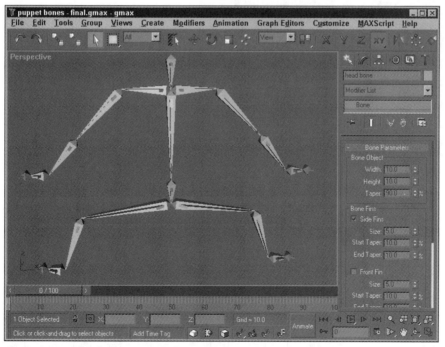

Figure 15-3: This bones system for a puppet was easy to create.

Making objects into bones

You can make any object act like a bone. To make an object into a bone, you need to open the Edit ➪ Object Properties dialog box. This dialog box, shown in Figure 15-4, includes a setting for Bone On/Off. If enabled, the object acts like a bone. When the Bone On/Off option is enabled, then the remaining Bone controls become available.

The Auto-Align option causes the pivot points of adjacent bones to be aligned automatically. The Freeze Length option causes a bone to keep its length as the bone system is moved. If the Freeze Length is disabled, you can specify a Stretch type. None prevents any stretching from occurring, and Scale changes the size along one axis, but Squash causes the bone to get wider as its length is decreased and thinner as it is elongated. You can also select a stretch axis and whether to Flip the axis.

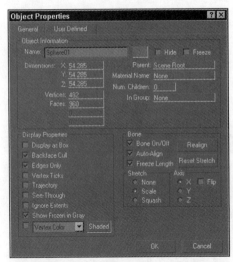

Figure 15-4: Use the Object Properties dialog box to make any object act like a bone.

You can use the Realign button to realign a bone; click the Reset Stretch button to normalize the stretch value to its current value.

Tutorial: Making a linked teddy bear into a bones system

Models such as vehicles and life forms have a natural link order and often come already linked. By making a linked model into bone objects, the model inherits the benefits of a bones system. In this tutorial, we'll import a teddy bear model created by Viewpoint Datalabs.

To make the teddy bear model a bones system, follow these steps:

1. Open the Teddy bear.gmax file in the Chap 15 directory on the CD-ROM.

   This file includes the Teddy Bear model.

2. Click the Select and Link button on the main toolbar. Drag from the left leg to the body to make the leg a child link to the body. Repeat the linking for the other leg, the arms, and the head. Link the nose to the head object.

3. With all the objects linked, choose Edit ⇨ Object Properties to open the Object Properties dialog box.

4. Select all the objects, and in the Object Properties dialog box, select the Bone On/Off and Auto-Align options. Also select the Squash option.

5. In the Link Display rollout of the Display panel, click the Display Links check box to see the links between the bones.

Figure 15-5 shows the bear with its bone links. Bones are created at the pivot point of each child object. To see the difference between the bones system and no bones, click the Select and Move button and try to move the head object off the bear. As a bone object, it cannot move away from the body. You can also select the See Through option in the Object Properties dialog box to see the links.

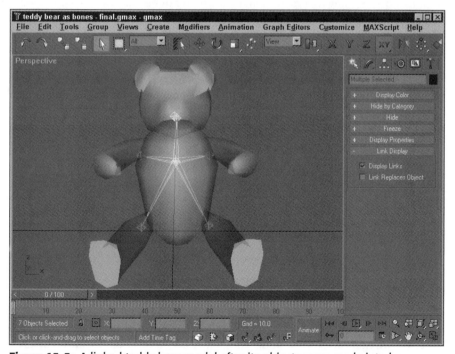

Figure 15-5: A linked teddy bear model after its objects were made into bones

Using the Skin Modifier

Unless you like working with skeletons, a bone system typically will have a skin attached to it. Any mesh can be made into a skin using the Skin modifier. With a skin attached to a bone system, you can move the bone system and the skin follows. The key advantage of working with a bone system is the Skin modifier.

To work with the Skin modifier, you need two important pieces — a mesh and a bone system. The bone system typically is placed inside of the mesh object, but it doesn't have to be. Each bone in the system is then added to the Skin modifier using the buttons in the Parameters rollout.

 Note   Actually, bone objects can be attached to meshes, patches, other bones, or even splines.

Each bone object with the Skin modifier applied gets a capsule-shaped envelope attached to it. These envelopes define which portion of the mesh moves when the underlying bone is moved. When two envelopes overlap, their surfaces blend together like skin around a bone joint. Once completed, you can control your character by simply moving the bones and the skin will follow.

The Skin modifier is one of the keys to character animation. The ability to control a system of bones using Inverse Kinematics would not be very beneficial without the ability to cover the bones with a skin. You can apply the Skin modifier to an object or a group of objects using the Modifier List or Modifiers ➪ Animation Modifiers ➪ Skin.

Each bone to which the modifier is applied is listed in the Parameters rollout. You can Add and Remove Bones, Add and Remove Bone Cross Sections, and control the position and size of the Envelopes. There are also settings to weight the various vertices. The Skin modifier also includes three unique deformer gizmos that can be used to control how the skin bends at the joint, bulges, and morphs over an animation sequence.

Skin subobjects

The single subobject available for the Skin modifier is Envelope. An Envelope is an area that surrounds the bone that defines which vertices of the Skin object are to be moved with the bone. In Envelope subobject mode, you can edit the size and influence of the envelope.

Editing envelopes

The Parameters rollout of the Skin modifier includes an Edit Envelopes button that places you in a special mode that lets you change the size of the envelope for each bone. Within Edit Envelopes mode, the object is colored blue to show the areas where the envelope is within the object and is colored red where the envelope is outside of the object. Using these visual clues, you can easily edit the envelopes to the desired effect. Once edited, you can copy and paste envelopes to other bones.

The Parameters rollout also includes a list of bones that are assigned to the Skin modifier. You can add and remove bones from this list using the Add Bone and Remove Bone buttons below the list. The Edit Envelope button works the same as clicking on the Envelope subobject in the Modifier Stack.

Figure 15-6 shows a simple arm object surrounding four bone objects with a Skin modifier applied. The Add Bone button was used to include the four bones within the Skin modifier list. The first bone was selected within the list, and the Edit Envelope button was clicked, revealing the envelope for the first bone.

For each envelope, you can add a cross section using the Add Cross Section button. This button lets you select a cross-section shape within the viewports. The Remove Cross Section button removes an added cross section from the envelope.

When the envelope is visible within the viewport, the envelope consists of two capsule-shaped areas within each other. At either end of these areas are four small square handles that can be dragged to change the cross-section radius. The cross-section area changes to pink when selected. The radius of the selected cross section is displayed in the Radius field within the Envelope Properties section of the Parameters rollout.

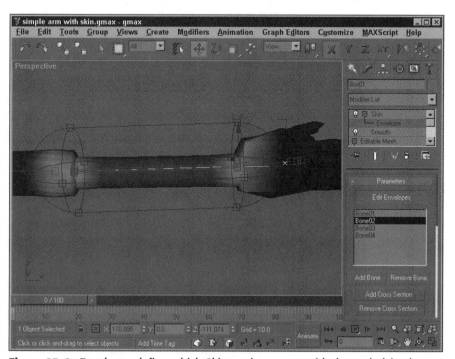

Figure 15-6: Envelopes define which Skin vertices move with the underlying bone.

The Envelope Properties section of the Parameters rollout includes five icon buttons, shown in Table 15-1. The first toggles between Absolute and Relative. All vertices that fall within the outer envelope are fully weighted when the Absolute toggle is set, but only those within both envelopes are fully weighted when the Relative toggle is selected.

	Table 15-1 Envelope Properties	
Button	**Description**	
A	Toggles between Absolute and Relative	
/	Makes envelopes visible even when not selected	
/	Sets Falloff curve	
	Copies envelope settings	
	Pastes envelope settings	

The second icon button enables envelopes to be visible even when not selected. This helps you see how adjacent bones overlap. The third icon button sets the Falloff curve for the envelopes. The options within this flyout are Fast Out, Slow Out, Linear, and Sinual. The last two icon buttons can be used to Copy and Paste envelope settings to other bones. The flyout options for the Paste button include Paste (to a single bone), Paste to All Bones, and Paste to Multiple Bones (which opens a selection dialog box).

When you select the Squash option in the Object Properties dialog box, you can set a Squash value, which determines the amount of squash applied to the object. This reduces one dimension as the other is stretched, as is common when you push or pull on a balloon.

Working with weights

Working with the various envelopes and all their controls can be tricky. The Filters section can limit the controls that you can select. Filter options include Vertices, Envelopes, and Cross Sections.

The Absolute Effect field lets you specify a weight value for the selected bone or vertices.

The Include and Exclude Vertices buttons lets you remove the selected vertices from those being affected by the selected bone. The Select Exclude Verts button selects all excluded vertices.

Painting weights

Another way to assign whether vertices in the skin move with the bone is to assign weights to the vertices. Using the Paint Weights button, you can paint with a brush over the surface of the skin object. The Paint Strength value sets the value of each brush stroke. This value can be positive (up to 1.0) for vertices that move with the bone or negative (to –1.0) for vertices that don't move with the bone. The Radius and Feather settings define the size and softness of the brush.

Tip   The Skin Paint Strength value can only be positive, but you can paint a negative value by holding down the Alt key while painting.

Display and Advanced settings

The Display rollout controls that features are visible within the viewports. Options include Color Vertices Weights, Draw All Envelopes, Show All Vertices, Show All Gizmos, Cross Sections on Top, and Envelopes on Top.

The Advanced Parameters rollout includes an option to Always Deform. This option lets you move the control points without having the skin mesh move when it is not enabled. The Rigid Vertices and Rigid Patch Handles options set the vertices to be controlled by only one bone. This rollout also includes buttons for resetting vertices and bones. It also includes buttons for saving and loading envelopes. The envelopes are saved as files with the .env extension.

Tutorial: Applying the Skin modifier to a flamingo

The flamingo is perhaps one of the best examples of a character that needs a bone system because its legs are practically nothing but bones. Viewpoint Datalabs provided this flamingo model that we can practice with.

To apply the Skin modifier to a flamingo model, follow these steps:

1. Open the Flamingo skin.gmax file from the Chap 15 directory on the CD-ROM.

   This file includes a flamingo model with all its parts linked together. The leg parts have all been attached into a single object.

2. The first step is to create a bones system for the flamingo's raised leg. In the Create panel, select the Systems category and click the Bones button. Click on the flamingo where the upper leg connects to the body, click again on each joint to the foot, and right-click the complete bone system. I created five bones in the system — one to anchor the leg to the body, three for the leg, and the last one to end the bone system.

Tip   With a complex model, it can be tricky to position the bones. It is easier to create a bone system for an existing model if you first hide all the objects that don't need bones.

3. Use the Select and Move button on the main toolbar to align the bones within the upper leg objects. Keep in mind that the pivot point for each bone is located at the start of the bone.

Caution   Be careful when rotating bones because the bones are no longer connected.

4. Select the left leg (the one that is raised) and choose Modifiers ➪ Animation Modifiers ➪ Skin to apply the Skin modifier to the leg.

5. In the Parameters rollout, click the Add Bone button; the Select Bones dialog box opens. Select the middle three bones and click the Select button.

   The first and last bones don't affect the model and don't need to be selected.

6. In the Parameters rollout, select the first bone in the list and click the Edit Envelopes button. Use the Zoom Region button in the Viewport Navigation button in the lower right to zoom in on the bones in the viewports. Select the cross-section handles for this bone, and set the Radius values to 0.3 (near the body) and 0.2 for each end. Select the second bone in the list, and set the Radius values to 0.5 and 0.6. Then select the last bone, and set the Radius values to 0.8 and 2.0. Figure 15-7 shows the results.

Using deformers

Below the Advanced Parameters rollout is the Gizmos rollout. You use this rollout to apply deformers to selected skin object vertices. Three different deformers are available in the Gizmos rollout including a Joint Angle Deformer, a Bulge Angle Deformer, and a Morph Angle Deformer.

Each of these deformers is unique. They include the following features:

✦ **Joint Angle Deformer:** Deforms the vertices around the joint between two bones where the skin can bunch up and cause problems. This deformer moves vertices on both the parent and child bones.

✦ **Bulge Angle Deformer:** Moves vertices away from the bone to simulate a bulging muscle. This deformer only works on the parent bone.

✦ **Morph Angle Deformer:** Can be used on vertices for both the parent and child bones to move the vertices to a morph position.

All deformers added to a skin object are listed in the Gizmo rollout. You can add deformers to and remove deformers from this list using the Add and Remove Gizmo buttons. You can also Copy and Paste the deformers to other sets of vertices. Before a deformer gizmo can be applied, you need to select vertices within the skin object. To select vertices, enable the Vertices check box of the Parameters rollout and drag over the vertices in the viewport to select the vertices.

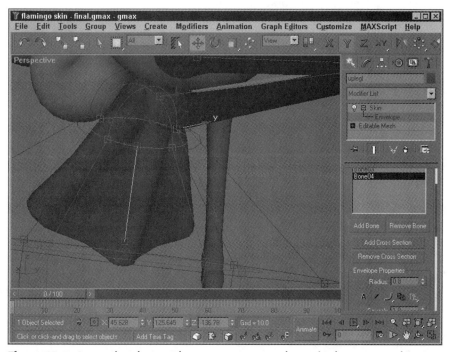

Figure 15-7: Increasing the envelope to encompass the entire leg ensures that the entire leg moves with the bones.

The parameters for the deformer selected in the Gizmo rollout's list appear when the deformer is selected in the Deformer Parameters rollout. This rollout lists the Parent and Child bones for the selected vertices and the Angle between them. This rollout changes depending on the type of deformer selected.

For the Joint and Bulge Angle Deformers, the Gizmo Parameters rollout includes buttons to edit the control Lattice and to edit the deformer Key Curves. The Edit Lattice button lets you move the lattice control points in the viewports. The Edit Angle Keys Curves opens a Graph window that displays the transformation curves for the deformation.

Forward versus Inverse Kinematics

Before you can understand Inverse Kinematics (IK), you need to realize that another type of kinematics exists — forward kinematics. Kinematic solutions work only on a kinematic chain, which you can create by linking children objects to their parents.

Cross-Reference Chapter 6, "Cloning, Grouping, and Linking Objects, and Other –ings," covers linking objects and creating kinematic chains.

Forward kinematics causes objects at the bottom of a linked structure to move along with their parents. For example, consider the linked structure of an arm, where the upper arm is connected to a forearm, which is connected to a hand and finally to some fingers. Using forward kinematics, the lower arm, hand, and fingers all move when the upper arm is moved.

Having the linked children move with their parent is what you would expect and want, but suppose the actual object that you wanted to place is the hand. Inverse kinematics (IK) enables child objects to control their parent objects. So, using inverse kinematics, you can drag the hand to the exact position you want, and all other parts in the system follow.

Forward kinematics in gmax involves simply transforming linked hierarchies. Anytime you move, rotate, or scale a linked hierarchy, the children move with the parent, but the child object can also be transformed independent of its parent.

Creating an Inverse Kinematics System

Before you can animate an inverse kinematics system, you'll need to build and link the system, define joints by positioning pivot points, and define any joint constraints you want.

Building and linking a system

The first step in creating an inverse kinematics system is to create and link several objects together. You can create links using the Link button on the main toolbar.

With the linked system created, position the child object's pivot point at the center of the joint between it and its parent. For example, the joint between an upper and lower arm would be at the elbow, so this is where the pivot point for the lower arm should be located.

After you create the linked system and correctly position your pivot points, open the Hierarchy panel and click the IK button. Several rollouts open that let you control the IK system, including the Object Parameters rollout shown in Figure 15-8.

Selecting a terminator

Because child objects in an inverse kinematics system can cause their parents to move, moving a child could cause unwanted movements all the way up the system to the root object. For example, pulling on the little finger of a human model could actually move the head. To prevent this, you can select an object in the system to be a terminator.

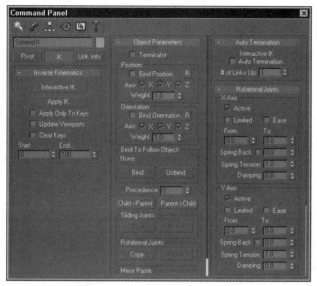

Figure 15-8: The IK rollouts let you control the binding of an IK system.

A terminator is the last object in the IK system that is affected by the child's movement. Making the upper arm a terminator would prevent the finger's movement from affecting any objects above the arm.

To set a terminator, select an object and then enable the Terminator option in the Object Parameters rollout.

For Interactive IK mode, you can also enable the Auto Termination option included in the Auto Termination rollout. The Number of Links Up value sets the terminator a specified number of links above the current selection.

Defining joint constraints

The next step is to define the joint constraints, which you specify in the Sliding Joints and the Rotational Joints rollouts. By default, each joint has six degrees of freedom, meaning that the two objects that make up the joint can each move or rotate along the X-, Y-, or Z-axes. The axis settings for all other sliding and rotational joints are identical. Defining joint constraints enables you to constrain these motions to prevent unnatural motions, such as an elbow bending backward. To constrain an axis, select the object that includes the pivot point for the joint, and in the appropriate rollout, locate the section for the axis that you want to restrict and deselect the Active option. If an axis's Active option is deselected, the axis is constrained. You can also limit the motion of joints by selecting the Limited option.

When the Limited option is selected, the object can move only within the bounds set by the From and To values. The Ease option causes the motion of the object to slow as it approaches either limit. The Spring Back option lets you set a rest position for the object — the object returns to this position when pulled away. The Spring Tension sets the amount of force that the object uses to resist being moved from its rest position. The Damping value sets the friction in the joint, which is the value with which the object resists any motion.

Note   As you enter values in the From and To fields, the object moves to that value to show visually the location specified. You can also hold down the mouse on the From and To values to cause the object to move temporally to its limits. These settings are based on the current Reference Coordinate system.

Copying, pasting, and mirroring joints

Defining joint constraints can be work — work that you don't want to duplicate if you don't have to. The Copy and Paste buttons in the Object Parameters rollout enable you to copy Sliding Joints or Rotational Joints constraints from one IK joint to another.

To use these buttons, select an IK system and click the Copy button; then select each of the joints to be constrained in a similar manner, and click the Paste button. You can also mirror the joints about an axis. This is useful for duplicating an IK system for opposite arms or legs of a human or animal model.

Binding objects

When using applied IK, you need to bind an object in the IK system to a follow object. The IK joint that is bound to the follow object then follows the follow object around the scene. The bind controls are located in the Hierarchy panel under the Object Properties rollout. To bind an object to a follow object, click the Bind button in the Object Properties rollout and select the follow object.

In addition to binding to a follow object, IK joints can also be bound to the world for each axis by position and orientation. This causes the object to be locked in its current position so it won't move or rotate along the axis that is selected. You can also assign a Weight value. When the IK computations determine that two objects need to move in opposite directions, the solution favors the object with the largest Weight value.

The Unbind button eliminates the binding.

Understanding precedence

When gmax computes an IK solution, the order in which the joints are solved determines the end result. The Precedence value (located in the Object Parameters rollout) lets you set the order in which joints are solved. To set the precedence for an object, select the object and enter a value in the Precedence value setting. gmax computes the object with a higher precedence value first.

The default joint precedence for all objects is 0. This assumes that the objects farthest down the linkage will move the most. The Object Parameters rollout also includes two default precedence settings. The Child to Parent button sets the precedence value for the root object to 0 and increments the precedence of each level under the root by 10. The Parent to Child button sets the opposite precedence, with the root object having a value of 0 and the precedence value of each successive object decreasing by 10.

Tutorial: Building an extensible arm linkage

As an example of a kinematics system, we'll design a simple arm linkage composed of six struts. To the end of this linkage, we'll attach a rubber spider on a string. (This contraption will be perfect for surprising your coworkers in the office.)

To create an inverse kinematics system for an extensible arm, follow these steps:

1. Open the Extensible arm with spider.gmax file from the Chap 15 directory on the CD-ROM.

   This file includes a spider model on the end of a string with several strut objects. The pivot points for the positioned objects have been moved already. The spider was created by Zygote Media.

2. Click the Select and Link button on the main toolbar, and link the spider to the string object by selecting the spider and dragging from the spider to the cylinder. The spider then becomes the child to the string object. Next link the string to the last strut and so on back to the first strut.

3. Next, we need to define the joint constraints for the system. Open the Hierarchy panel, and click the IK button. In the Object Parameters rollout, select the first strut and enable the Terminator, Bind Position, and Bind Orientation options.

   Doing so prevents the first strut from moving anywhere.

4. In the Sliding and Rotational Joint rollouts, deactivate all the axes except for the Rotational Z-axis.

   When this is done, the Active box for the Rotational Z-axis is the only one selected.

5. Then click the Copy buttons for both joint types in the Object Parameters rollout, select the other struts, and click both Paste buttons.

   This copies the joint constraints from the first strut to the other strut objects.

6. For the string object, make all Rotational Joint axes active.

7. To test the system, select the Interactive IK button in the Inverse Kinematics rollout and select and move the spider.

All the struts rotate together as the spider moves.

Figure 15-9 shows the struts bending to follow the spider as it is moved downward. Notice for this system that the first strut doesn't move or rotate and that all the struts can be rotated only along the Z-axis, but that the spider can move freely within the range of the string. With the Interactive IK mode disabled, any object can be moved and/or rotated and only the links are enforced.

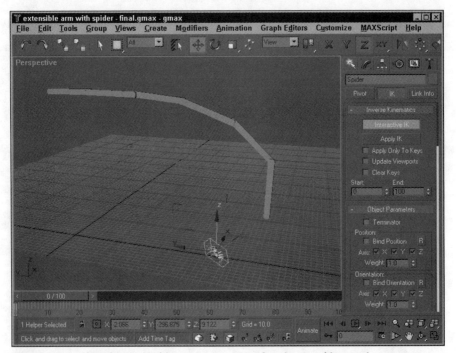

Figure 15-9: The objects in this scene are part of an inverse kinematics system.

Using the Inverse Kinematics Methods

After you create a linked hierarchy chain, you need to apply an IK method to the chain before you can animate it. gmax includes several methods for animating using inverse kinematics — the traditional methods of Interactive and Applied IK and an IK Limb Solver. The Interactive and Applied IK methods are applied using the Hierarchy panel; the IK Limb Solver can be applied to a bones system, or you can use the Animation ➪ IK Limb Solver menu.

An IK solver is a specialized controller that computes an inverse kinematic solution. This solution is used to automatically set all the required keys needed for the animation. gmax offers a single IK solver — the IK Limb Solver.

Interactive IK

Interactive IK is the method that lets you position a linked hierarchy of objects at different frames. gmax then interpolates all the keyframes between the various keys. This method isn't as precise, but it uses a minimum number of keys and is useful for an animation sequence involving many frames. Interactive IK interpolates positions between the two different keys, whereas Applied IK computes positions for every key. Because the motions are simple interpolations between two keys, the result may not be accurate, but the motion is smooth.

After your IK system is established, animating using the Interactive IK method is simple. First, you need to enable the Auto Key button and select the Interactive IK button in the Inverse Kinematics rollout of the Hierarchy panel. Enabling this button places you in Interactive IK mode, causing the system to move together as a hierarchy. Then reposition the system in a different frame, and gmax automatically interpolates between the two positions and creates the animation keys. To exit Interactive IK mode, simply click the Interactive IK button again.

The Inverse Kinematics rollout includes several options. The Apply Only to Keys option forces gmax to solve IK positions for only those frames that currently have keys. The Update Viewports option shows the animation solutions in the viewports as it progresses, and the Clear Keys option removes any existing keys as the solution is calculated. The Start and End values mark the frames to include in the solution.

IK Preference settings

The required accuracy of the IK solution can be set using the Inverse Kinematics panel in the Preference Settings dialog box, shown in Figure 15-10. You can open this dialog box by choosing Customize ➪ Preferences. For the Interactive and Applied IK methods, you can set Position and Rotation Thresholds. These Threshold values determine how close the moving object must be to the defined position for the solution to be valid.

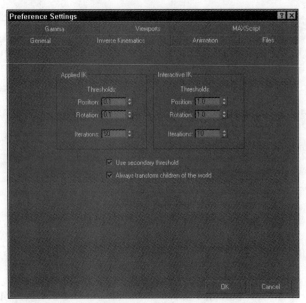

Figure 15-10: The Inverse Kinematics panel of the Preference Settings dialog box lets you set the global Threshold values.

Note Because the Applied IK method is more accurate, you'll want to set its Threshold values lower than those of the Interactive IK method.

You can also set an Iterations limit for both methods. The Iterations value is the maximum number of times the calculations are performed. This value limits the time that gmax spends looking for a valid solution. The Iterations settings control the speed and accuracy of each IK solution.

Note If the Iterations value is reached without a valid solution, gmax uses the last calculated iteration.

The Use Secondary Threshold option provides a backup method to determine whether gmax should continue to look for a valid solution. This method should be used if you want gmax to bail out of a particularly difficult solution rather than to continue to try to find a solution. If you are working with very small thresholds, you want to enable this option.

The Always Transform Children of the World option enables you to move the root object when it is selected by itself, but constrains its movement when any of its children are moved.

Tutorial: Animating a simple IK propeller system

Machines are good examples of a kinematics system. In this example, you'll animate a simple gear-and-propeller system using the Applied IK method.

To animate an inverse kinematics system with a propeller, follow these steps:

1. Open the Gear and prop.gmax file from the Chap 15 directory on the CD-ROM.

    This file includes a simple handle and prop system.

2. The first task is to link the model. Click the Select and Link button on the main toolbar. Then drag from each child object to its parent. Connect the propeller to the shaft, the shaft to the gear, and the gear to the handle.

3. Open the Hierarchy panel, and click the IK button. Next, we'll constrain the motions of the parts by selecting the handle object. All Sliding Joints can be deactivated, and only the Z-axis Rotational Joint needs to be activated. To do this, make sure a check mark is next to the Active option. When this is set for the handle object, click the Copy button for both joint types, select the gear object, and click Paste to copy these constraints. Then select the shaft object, click both Paste buttons again, and repeat this process for the propeller.

4. Finally, enable the Animate button (or press the N key), drag the Time Slider to frame 100 (or press the End key), and click the Interactive IK button in the Inverse Kinematics rollout of the Hierarchy panel. Then select the Select and Rotate button, and drag in the Left viewport to rotate the handle about its X-axis.

Figure 15-11 shows the propeller system.

Applied IK

Applied IK applies a solution over a range of frames, computing the keys for every frame. This task is accomplished by binding the IK system to an object that it follows. This method is more precise than the interactive IK method, but it creates lots of keys. Because keys are set for every object and every transform, this solution sets lots of keys, which increases the size and complexity of the scene. Each frame has its own set of keys, which can result in jerky and non-smooth results.

To animate using the Applied IK method, you need to bind one or more parts of the system to a follow object, which can be a dummy object or an object in the scene. You do so by clicking the Bind button in the Object Parameters rollout of the Hierarchy panel and selecting an object in one of the viewports.

Caution   There seems to be a problem with the Bind button in gmax. When you click on the Bind button and select a follow object, the cursor changes into a plus sign when it is over an object that you can bind to, but gmax doesn't seem to recognize the follow object.

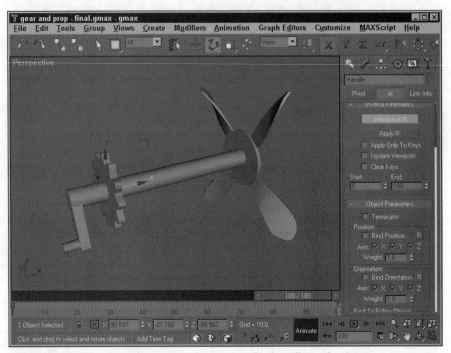

Figure 15-11: The propeller rotates by turning the handle and using inverse kinematics.

After the system has a bound follow object, select an object in the system. Open the Hierarchy panel, and in the Inverse Kinematics rollout, click the Apply IK button. gmax then computes the keys for every frame between the Start and End frames specified in the rollout. Click the Apply IK button to start the computation process that sets all the animation keys for the range of frames indicated.

Tip   If you plan to use the Applied IK method, set the Threshold values in the Inverse Kinematics panel of the Preference Settings dialog box to small values to ensure accurate results.

IK Limb Solver

The IK Limb Solver was specifically created to work with limbs such as arms and legs. It is used on chains of three bones such as a hip, upper leg, and lower leg. Only two of the bones in the chain actually move. The goal for these three joints is located at the pivot point for the third bone.

This solver works by considering the first joint as being a spherical joint that can rotate along three different axes, like a hip or shoulder joint. The second joint can bend in only one direction, such as an elbow or knee joint.

You can apply the IK Limb solver to any hierarchy of objects. The IK Limb solver is applied automatically to a bones system when you create the system. You also can choose Animation ⇨ IK Solvers to select the IK Limb solver.

When you choose Animation ⇨ IK Solvers ⇨ IK Limb Solver, a dotted line appears from the selected object. You can drag this line within a viewport and click another object within the hierarchy to be the end joint. A white line is drawn between the beginning and ending joints. The pivot point of the end joint is the goal for the IK solver. A blue cross marks the goal of the IK solver. Several rollouts within the Hierarchy panel also appear. These rollouts let you set the parameters for the IK Limb solver.

The first rollout is the IK Solver rollout, shown in Figure 15-12. The Enabled button lets you disable the solver. By disabling the solver, you can use forward kinematics to move the objects. To return to the IK solution, simply click the Enabled button again. The IK for FK Pose option enables IK control even if the IK solver is disabled. This lets you manipulate the hierarchy of objects using forward kinematics while still working with the IK solution. If both the IK for FK Pose and the Enabled buttons are disabled, then the goal can move without affecting the hierarchy of objects.

If the goal ever gets moved away from the end link, clicking the IK/FK Snap button automatically moves the goal to match the end links position. Auto Snap automatically keeps the goal and the end link together. The Set as Preferred Angle button remembers the angles for the IK system. These angles can be recalled at any time using the Assume Preferred Angle button.

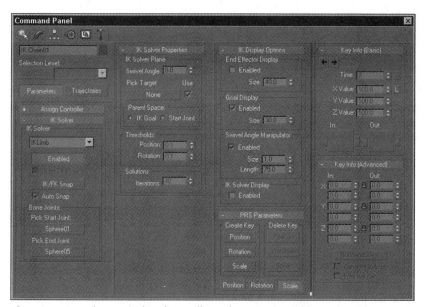

Figure 15-12: The IK Limb solver rollouts let you control how the solver works.

When you choose Animation ⇨ IK Solvers ⇨ IK Limb Solver, the start joint is the selected object, and the end joint is the object that you drag the dotted line to. If you want to change these objects, click the Pick Start Joint or Pick End Joint buttons.

Tip   The best way to select an object using the Pick Start or End Joint buttons is to open the Select by Name dialog box by pressing the H key. Using this dialog box, you can select an exact object without having to miss selecting it in a complex viewport.

Caution   If you select a child as the start joint and an object above the child as the end joint, moving the goal has no effect on the IK chain.

Defining a swivel angle

The IK Solver Properties rollout includes the Swivel Angle value. The swivel angle defines the plane that includes the joint objects and the line that connects the starting and ending joints. This plane is key because it defines the direction that the joint moves when bent.

The Swivel Angle value can change during an animation. Using the Pick Target button, you also can select a Target object to control the swivel angle. The Use button turns the target on and off. The Parent Space group defines whether the IK Goal or the Start Joint's parent object is used to define the plane. Having an option lets you select two different parent objects that control the swivel plane if two or more IK solvers are applied to a single IK chain.

You also can change the Swivel Angle value by using a manipulator. To view the manipulator, click the Select and Manipulate button on the main toolbar. This manipulator is a green line with a square on the end. Dragging this manipulator in the viewports changes the swivel angle.

To understand the swivel angle, try holding your arm straight out to the side. If you bend your elbow, you can move your hand forward. The Swivel Angle (90 degrees) for your arm allows your arm to bend in this way. If the Swivel Angle for your arm were reversed (180 degrees), your hand would move backwards when you bend your elbow and you could easily touch the back of your head. Using the Swivel Angle, you can control how your character's limbs move—without having to break their arms.

The IK Solver Properties rollout also includes Threshold values. These values determine how close the end joint and the goal must be before the solution is pronounced valid. You can set thresholds for Position and Rotation. The Iterations value sets the number of times the solution will be tried.

Tip Setting the Iterations value to a higher number results in smoother — less jerky — results, but it increases the time required to find a solution.

Displaying IK controls

The IK Display Options rollouts can enable, disable, and set the size of the gizmos used when working with IK solvers. Using this rollout, you can Enable the End Effector, the Goal, the Swivel Angle Manipulator, and the IK solver (which is the line connecting the start and end joints).

Tutorial: Animating a flamingo's leg with the IK Limb Solver

As an example of the IK Limb Solver, we should probably animate a limb, and the flamingo model produced by Viewpoint Datalabs fits the bill (although the limb bends backward). This tutorial continues the example earlier in this chapter in which a Skin modifier was applied to the flamingo's leg.

To animate the flamingo's leg using the IK Limb Solver, follow these steps:

1. Open the Flamingo leg.gmax file from the Chap 15 directory on the CD-ROM.

   This file includes a flamingo model created by Viewpoint Datalabs. This file is the result of the previous flamingo example.

2. Click the Select by Name button on the main toolbar (or press the H key) to open the Select Objects dialog box. Double-click on the Bone02 object to select the upper leg bone object.

3. With the upper leg bone selected, choose Animation ➪ IK Solvers ➪ IK Limb Solver.

   A dotted line appears in the viewport.

4. Press the H key again to open the Pick Object dialog box, and double-click on the Bone04 object to select it.

   This bone corresponds to the foot bone, which is the end of the limb hierarchy.

5. With the IK Chain01 object selected, click the Animate button (or press the N key) and drag the Time Slider to frame 100 (or press the End key). With the Select and Move button, move the IK chain in the viewport.

   The arm chain bends as you move the third bone.

Figure 15-13 shows the flamingo's leg being moved via the IK Limb Solver.

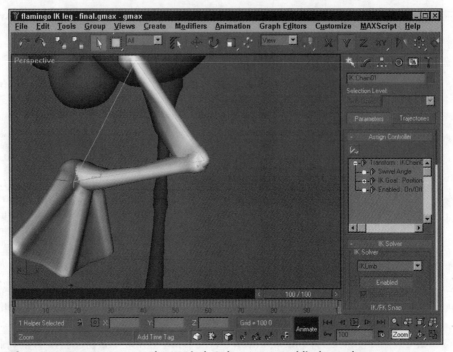

Figure 15-13: You can use the IK Limb Solver to control limbs such as legs and arms.

Summary

The benefit of a bones system becomes obvious when it is combined with the Skin modifier and an IK system. In this chapter, you learned how to create and work with bones systems, the skin modifier, and Inverse Kinematics. This chapter covered these topics:

✦ Creating bones systems

✦ Setting bone parameters

✦ Making objects into bones systems

✦ Working with the Skin modifier

✦ Learning the basic concepts behind inverse kinematics

✦ Exploring the difference between interactive and applied IK methods

✦ Creating and animating an inverse kinematics system

✦ Using the IK settings in the Preference Settings dialog box

✦ Learning how to use the IK Limb solver

In the next chapter, you'll get a chance to dress up your objects with materials and maps.

✦   ✦   ✦

Putting on the Ritz with the gmax Material Editor

In This Chapter

Understanding
material properties

Working with the
gmax Material Editor

Using the gmax
Material Navigator

Using standard and
Multi-Materials

Using material IDs to
apply multiple
materials

Understanding
mapping

Using the Maps
rollout

Working with
material modifiers
such as UVW Map
and Unwrap UVW

Removing materials

Materials are used to dress, color, and paint objects. Just as materials in real life can be described as scaly, soft, smooth, opaque, or blue, materials applied to 3D objects can mimic properties such as color, texture, transparency, shininess, and so on. In this chapter, you'll learn the basics of working with materials and all the features of the gmax Material Editor.

Understanding Material Properties

Before jumping into the gmax Material Editor, let's take a close look at the type of material properties that you can deal with. Understanding these properties will help you as you begin to create new materials.

Up until now, the only material property that has been applied to an object has been the default object color, randomly assigned by gmax. The gmax Material Editor can add a whole new level of realism using materials that simulate many different types of physical properties, such as the ones discussed in the following sections.

 Note   Many of these material properties are not visible until the scene is loaded and rendered in the game engine.

Colors

Color is probably the simplest material property and the easiest to identify. However, unlike the object color defined in the Create and Modify panels, there isn't a single color swatch that controls an object's color.

Consider a basket of shiny red apples. When you shine a bright blue spotlight on them, all the apples turn purple. So, even if the apples are assigned a red material, the final color in the image may be very different.

Within the gmax Material Editor are several color swatches that control different aspects of the object's color. The following list describes the types of color swatches that are available:

✦ **Ambient:** Defines an overall background lighting that affects all objects in the scene, including the color of the object when it is in the shadows. This color can often be locked to the Diffuse color so that they are changed together.

✦ **Diffuse:** The surface color of the object surface in normal, full white light. The normal color of an object is typically defined by its Diffuse color.

✦ **Specular:** The color of the highlights where the light is focused on the surface of a shiny material.

✦ **Self-Illumination:** The color that the object glows from within. This color takes over any shadows on the object.

If you ask someone the color of an object, he or she would respond by identifying the Diffuse color, but all these properties play an important part in bringing a sense of realism to the material. Try applying very different, bright materials to each of these color swatches and notice the results. The object will look unique, but not very realistic.

Tip   For realistic materials, your choice of colors depends on the scene lights. Indoor lights have a result different from an outdoor light like the sun. You can simulate objects in direct sunlight by giving their Specular color a yellow tint and their Ambient color a complementary, dark, almost black or purple color. For indoor objects, make the Specular color bright white and use an Ambient color that is the same as the Diffuse color, only much darker.

Opacity and transparency

Opaque objects are objects that you cannot see through, such as rocks and trees. Transparent objects, on the other hand, are objects that you can see through, like glass and clear plastic. gmax's materials include a control for adjusting the Opacity property.

Opacity is the amount that an object refuses to allow light to pass through it. It is the opposite of transparency and is typically measured as a percentage. An object with 0 percent opacity is completely transparent, and an object with an opacity of 100 percent doesn't let any light through.

Transparency is the amount of light that is allowed to pass through an object. Because this is the opposite of opacity, transparency can be defined by the opacity value.

Reflection and refraction

A reflection is what you see when you look in the mirror. Shiny objects reflect their surroundings. By defining a material's reflection values, you can control how much it reflects its surroundings. A mirror, for example, reflects everything, but a rock won't reflect at all. Refraction is the bending of light as it moves through a transparent material. You can simulate both reflection and refraction in gmax using material maps.

Shininess and specular highlights

Shiny objects, such as polished metal or clean windows, include highlights where the lights reflect off their surfaces. These highlights are called specular highlights and are determined by the Specular settings. These settings include Specular Level, Glossiness, and Soften values.

The Specular Level is a setting for the intensity of the highlight. The Glossiness determines the size of the highlight — higher values result in a smaller highlight. The Soften value thins the highlight by lowering its intensity and increasing its size.

A rough material has the opposite properties of a shiny material and almost no highlights. The Roughness property sets how quickly the Diffuse color blends with the Ambient color. Cloth and fabric materials have a high Roughness value, and plastic and metal Roughness values are small.

Working with the gmax Material Editor

The gmax Material Editor is the interface with which you define, create, and apply materials to objects. You can access the gmax Material Editor by clicking the gmax Material Editor button on the main toolbar (it's a large red sphere icon located at the right end of the main toolbar), or by using the M keyboard shortcut.

Note

The gmax Material Editor specifically includes the word gmax in front of it. This is on purpose because gmax's Material Editor is quite different from the Material Editor found in 3ds max.

At the top-left corner of the gmax Material Editor window is a single material sample slot that displays a preview sphere with the current material applied to it. To its right are six buttons for controlling what happens to the current material. Below the sample slot and the buttons are a Name field and several icon buttons. Figure 16-1 shows the gmax Material Editor as it first appears before any materials are created.

Figure 16-1: Use the gmax Material Editor window to create, store, and work with materials.

The button icons to the right of the name field are defined in Table 16-1.

Table 16-1
gmax Material Editor Buttons

Button	Name	Description
	Show Map in Viewport	Displays 2D material maps on objects in the viewports.
	Go to Parent	Moves up one level for the current material. This applies only to compound objects with several levels.
	Go Forward to Sibling	Selects the next maps or material at the same level.
	Background	Displays a checkered background image (or a custom background) behind the material, helpful when displaying a transparent material.
	gmax Material Navigator	Opens the gmax Material Navigator where saved materials can be accessed.

Note   Before proceeding, you need to understand the difference between a material and a map. A *material* is an effect that permeates the 3D object, but most *maps* are 2D images (although procedural 3D maps also exist) that can be wrapped on top of the object. Materials can contain maps, and maps can be made up of several materials. In the gmax Material Editor, materials appear shaded in the sample slot. You usually can tell whether you're working with a material or a map by looking at the default name. Maps show up in the name drop-down list as Map and a number (Map #1) and materials are named with a number and Default (7- Default).

Creating a new material

The first button, labeled New lets you create a new material. When this button is clicked, a small dialog box, shown in Figure 16-2, appears allowing you to create a Standard material or a Multi-Material. Each of these material types is covered shortly.

Figure 16-2: The New Material dialog box lets you select to create a Standard material or a Multi-Material.

After a material type is selected, a sphere object appears in the sample slot, the material's name is listed in the Name field, and three rollouts appear within the gmax Material Editor, as shown in Figure 16-3.

Figure 16-3: After a new material is created, the gmax Material Editor window includes several rollouts for defining the material.

Using the sample slot

The gmax Material Editor includes a single sample slot that displays the current material or map. The sample slot is only a temporary placeholder for the current material or map. An actual scene can have hundreds of materials. By loading a material into the sample slot, you can change its parameters or apply it to other objects.

Dragging materials

When you right-click the active sample slot, a pop-up menu appears. From this menu, you can select several commands. The Drag/Copy command is a toggle setting. This option also lets you drag and drop a material or map from the sample slot to the gmax Material Navigator. This option also allows you to drag a material to an object in the viewports. Dropping a material onto an object automatically assigns the material to that object.

The Drag/Rotate pop-up menu command lets you rotate the material object in the sample slot when you drag with the mouse. Dragging on the object rotates it about its X- and Y-axes, and dragging from the corner of the sample slot rotates it about its Z-axis. This feature is useful for looking at how maps are applied. Holding down the Shift key constrains the rotation about a single axis. The Reset Rotation pop-up menu command resets the material's rotation to its original orientation.

You can also drag materials from the sample slots back and forth among the Asset Manager Utility, any rollouts where you can specify maps, such as the Environment Map button (found in the Environment dialog box accessed via Rendering ⇨ Environment), and the Projector and Shadow Map buttons (found in the rollouts for a selected light).

Rendering maps

The Render Map pop-up menu command opens the Render Map dialog box, shown in Figure 16-4. This option is available only if the current material in the sample slot has a map applied. The Render Map dialog box lets you select the Range of frames to include and the Dimensions of the rendered image. You can click the Files button to open a file dialog box where you can name the render map and specify the file type. The Render button renders the current map as a bitmap or an animation to the Virtual Frame Buffer and to the file (if selected).

Cross-Reference

The Virtual Frame Buffer is used to display images from within gmax. It is covered in Chapter 4, "Getting Files In and Out of gmax."

Figure 16-4: The Render Map dialog box lets you render and save a map applied to a material.

Note You can save render maps as BMP, JPEG, PNG, TGA, and TIF files.

Magnifying the sample slot

Right-clicking on the sample slot opens a pop-up menu where you can define the actions of the sample slot. The Magnify menu command opens the material in a magnified window. You can also open this window by double-clicking the sample slot. You can resize the window to view the material at any size, and you can set it to automatically update when changes are made. If the Auto option is disabled, you can update the material by clicking the Update button. Figure 16-5 shows the magnified window. This window is great for seeing the intricate details of a material.

Figure 16-5: You can open materials in a magnified window by double-clicking them.

Naming materials

Every material has a name that appears below the sample slot in a drop-down list. This same name appears in the gmax Material Editor's title bar. You can rename a material by typing a new name in the name field. This name appears in the gmax Material Navigator dialog box and in the Track View.

Assigning materials to objects

To apply the current material to the selected object in the viewports, you need only to click the Apply button. Alternatively, you can drag a material from its sample slot and drop it on an object. If several objects are selected and you try to drag and drop a material onto one of the objects, a simple dialog box appears asking you whether to apply the material to the selection or to the object on which the material was dropped.

When you assign a material to an object in the scene, the material becomes "Hot." A *Hot material* is automatically updated in the scene when the material parameters change. You can "cool" a material by clicking the Copy button. This detaches the sample slot from the material in the scene to which it is applied, so that any changes to the material aren't applied to the object. The name also changes to show that you are working on a material copy.

Whenever a material is applied to an object in the scene, the material is added to a special library of materials that get saved with the scene. You can also load materials into the scene library that aren't applied to an object using the gmax Material Navigator. You can see all the materials included in the scene library in the gmax Material Navigator by selecting one of the Scene radio buttons.

Picking materials from a scene

Another useful option is obtaining a material from an object in the scene. Clicking the Pick button changes the cursor to an eyedropper. You can then click an object in one of the viewports, and the object's material is loaded into the sample slot. Only an object with materials applied to it can be picked from the viewports.

Resetting a material

The Reset button lets you reset the selected material to its default settings. If you apply the selected material to a material in the scene, then a dialog box, shown in Figure 16-6, appears that lets you reset just the sample slots or both the sample slots and the material applied to objects in the scene.

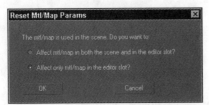

Figure 16-6: When resetting a material, you have the option to reset the material in the scene and the editor or just in the gmax Material Editor.

Removing materials and maps

If you accidentally apply an unwanted material to an object, you can replace the material with another material by dragging the new material onto the object. If you want to view the object color within the viewport, then open the Display panel and in the Display Color rollout, select the Object color option for Wireframe and Shaded. The Material Color options display the material color in the viewports.

If you apply a material or map to an object that doesn't look just right and tweaking it won't help, you can always return to square one by removing the material or any mappings that have been applied to the object. The Delete button removes the current material or map from the gmax Material Editor and from the scene.

Tutorial: Coloring Easter eggs

Everyone loves spring with its bright colors and newness of life. One of the highlights of the season is the tradition of coloring Easter eggs. In this tutorial, we'll use virtual eggs — no messy dyes and no egg salad sandwiches for the next two weeks.

To create our virtual Easter eggs and apply different colors to them, follow these steps:

1. Open the Easter eggs.gmax file from the Chap 16 directory on the CD-ROM.

   This file contains several egg-shaped objects.

2. Open the gmax Material Editor by pressing the M key.

3. Create a new material by clicking the New button and selecting Standard from the New Material dialog box.

4. Click the Diffuse color swatch in the Blinn Basic Parameters rollout. From the Color Selector that appears, drag the cursor around the color palette until you find the color you want, and then click Close.

5. In any viewport, select an egg and then click the Apply button in the gmax Material Editor, or you could simply drag the material from its sample slot to the viewport object.

6. Repeat Steps 4 and 5 for all the eggs.

Figure 16-7 shows the assortment of eggs we just created.

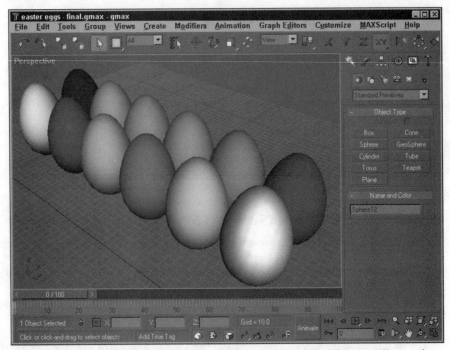

Figure 16-7: These eggs have been assigned materials with different Diffuse colors.

Using the gmax Material Navigator

The gmax Material Navigator, shown in Figure 16-8, is the place where all your materials are stored. They are stored in sets called libraries. These libraries are saved along with the scene file. The gmax Material Navigator opens whenever you choose a new map or click the gmax Material Navigator button in the Material Editor or on the main toolbar. Materials are indicated with red and blue sphere icons, and maps have a green parallelogram next to them.

Caution

The gmax Material Navigator holds materials and maps. If you select a material map, a 2D map is loaded into the sample slot. 2D maps cannot be applied directly to an object in the viewport. You can tell the difference between a map and material because maps are flat 2D bitmaps and materials are shown on an object like a sphere.

The Find material text field in the upper-left corner of the gmax Material Navigator is useful for locating materials within a library. If you type in the name of a material, it is selected automatically in the navigator.

Find material   Library name

Material name   Apply material to selected object

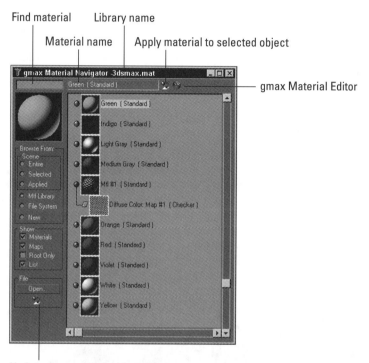

gmax Material Editor

Update scene materials from library

Figure 16-8: The gmax Material Navigator lets you select new materials from a library of materials.

The gmax Material Navigator includes several browse options accessible as radio buttons on the left of the dialog box. The browse options include three Scene options — Entire, Selected, and Applied. These options display all the materials in the scene (Entire), just the material for the selected object or objects (Selected), or just the applied materials (Applied).

The other browse options are Material Library, File System, and New. The Material Library option lists all the materials available in the open material library. The current library set is listed in the title bar of the gmax Material Navigator. The File System option displays the Asset Browser in the gmax Material Navigator. The New option lists all the available material types and maps. For gmax, these include None, Multi-Material, and Standard for materials, and None, Bitmap, and Checker for maps.

Cross-
Reference

Chapter 4, "Getting Files In and Out of gmax," covers the Asset Browser in more detail.

You can also limit the material list to show only materials, only maps, or both, and you can specify to see all the pieces that make up a material or only the base material with the Root Only option. The List option displays the materials along with their material names when enabled. If disabled, only the material preview icons are visible. Figure 16-9 shows the gmax Material Navigator with the List option enabled and disabled.

Getting new materials

To load new materials into the gmax Material Editor sample slot, you simply need to double click on the material in the gmax Material Navigator. If you drag the material from the gmax Material Navigator and drop it on the sample slot in the gmax Material Editor, a dialog box appears that lets you make the new material an Instance or a Copy.

Caution   If the current sample slot is blank, you need to create a new material before you can drop a material from the navigator.

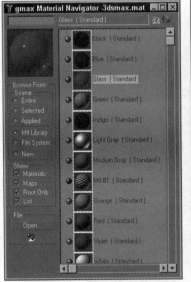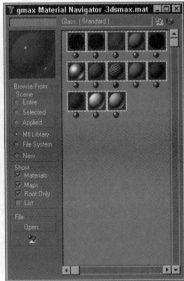

Figure 16-9: The gmax Material Navigator lets you select to see materials with or without names.

Working with libraries

When you adjust a material or map parameter, a new material is created, and the material's sample slot is updated. Although newly created materials are saved along with the scene file, you can reuse materials by opening the gmax file or library that contains them.

Note   gmax ships with several material libraries, including Backgrounds, Bricks, Concrete, Fabric, Ground, Metal, RayTraced, ReflectionMaps, Skys, Space, Stones, and Wood. You can find all these libraries in the matlibs directory.

You can add materials to the default material library by dragging the created material from the Material Editor to the Material Library in the navigator. To see which library is current, open the gmax Material Navigator and select the Mtl Library option in the Browse From section. The library name is shown in the title bar. The File section includes a button for opening other material libraries.

Tutorial: Loading a custom material library

To practice loading a material library, I've created a custom library of materials using various textures created with Kai's Power Tools.

To load a custom material library, follow these steps:

1. Click the gmax Material Navigator button at the right end of the main toolbar to open the gmax Material Navigator.

2. In the Browse From section, select the Mtl Library option and click the Open button.

3. Select and open the KPT samples.mat file from the Chap 16 directory on the CD-ROM.

   The library loads into the gmax Material Navigator.

4. In the selection field (above the sample slot), type **Bug** to locate and select the bug eyes material.

Figure 16-10 shows the gmax Material Navigator with the custom material library open.

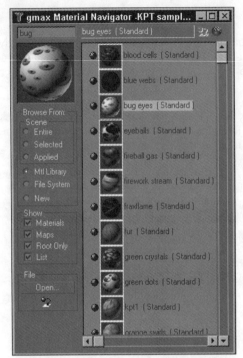

Figure 16-10: The gmax Material Navigator also lets you work with custom material libraries.

Understanding Material/Map Hierarchies

Each material can consist of several submaterials. For example, anytime a map is added to a material, it becomes a submaterial. A single material can consist of many submaterials, which may be maps or materials. You can edit each submaterial by accessing the rollouts associated with it. The trick is being able to locate the various submaterials.

The gmax Material Navigator, shown in Figure 16-11, shows all the submaterials that make up a material in a hierarchy list. Double-clicking a submaterial opens the submaterial and all of its associated rollouts in the gmax Material Editor.

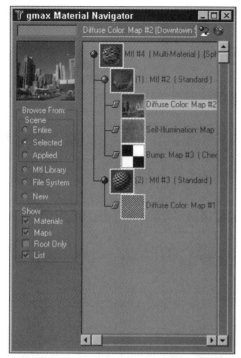

Figure 16-11: The Material/Map Navigator shows the layered material as a hierarchy.

The Go to Parent and Go Forward to Sibling buttons in the gmax Material Editor become active when you select a submaterial. These buttons, shown in Table 16-2, enable you to navigate the submaterial hierarchy. The Go Forward to Sibling button moves to the next adjacent submaterial on the same level. The Go to Parent button selects the submaterial's parent.

Table 16-2
Submaterial Buttons

Button	Description
	Go Forward to Sibling
	Go to Parent

If the submaterial is itself a material, such as one of the submaterials for the Multi-Material, then you can separate the submaterial from the base material using the Copy button.

Using the Standard Material

Standard materials are the default gmax material type. They provide a single, uniform color determined by the Ambient, Diffuse, and Specular color swatches. Standard materials can use any one of several different shaders. *Shaders* are algorithms used to compute how the material should look, given its parameters.

Standard materials also have parameters for controlling highlights, opacity, and self-illumination. These materials include the following rollouts: Shader Basic Parameters, Basic Parameters (based on the shader type), and Maps. By modifying these parameters, you can create really unique materials. With all the various rollouts, even a standard material has an infinite number of possibilities.

Using shading types

gmax includes several different shader types. These shaders are available in a drop-down list in the Shader Basic Parameters rollout. Each shader type displays different options in its respective Basic Parameters rollout. The three available shaders in gmax are Blinn, Metal, and Phong.

The Shader Basic Parameters rollout also includes a 2-Sided option, which makes the material appear on both sides of the face and is typically enabled on objects where the interior of the object is visible, such as partially transparent objects.

Blinn shader

This shader is the default. It renders simple circular highlights and smoothes adjacent faces.

The Blinn shader includes color swatches for setting Ambient, Diffuse, Specular, and Self-Illumination colors. To change the color, click the color swatch and select a new color in the Color Selector dialog box.

Note You can drag colors among the various color swatches. When you do so, the Copy or Swap Colors dialog box appears that enables you to copy or swap the colors.

You can use the Lock buttons to the left of the color swatches to lock the colors together so that a change to one automatically changes the other. You can lock Ambient to Diffuse and Diffuse to Specular.

The small square buttons to the right of the Diffuse, Specular, Self-Illumination, Opacity, Specular Level, and Glossiness controls are shortcut buttons for adding a map in place of the respective parameter. Clicking these buttons opens the gmax Material Navigator where you can select the map type. You can also lock the Ambient and Diffuse maps together with the lock icon to the right of the map buttons.

When a map is loaded and active, it appears in the Maps rollout and an uppercase letter *M* appears on its shortcut button. When a map is loaded but inactive, a lower-case *m* appears. After you apply a map, these buttons open to make the map the active level and display its parameters in the rollout. Figure 16-12 shows these map buttons.

Self-Illumination can use a color if the Color option is enabled. If this option is disabled, a spinner appears that enables you to adjust the amount of default color used for illumination. Materials with a Self-Illumination value of 100 or a bright color like white lose all shadows and highlights and appear to glow from within. To remove the effect of Self-Illumination, set the spinner to 0 or the color to black. Figure 16-13 shows a sphere with Self-Illumination values from left to right of 0, 25, 50, 75, and 100.

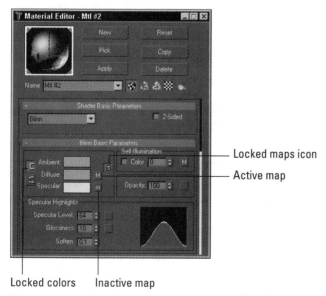

Locked maps icon

Active map

Locked colors   Inactive map

Figure 16-12: The Blinn Basic Parameters rollout lets you select and control properties for the Blinn shader.

Figure 16-13: Increasing the Self-Illumination value reduces the shadows in an object.

The Opacity spinner sets the level of transparency of an object. A value of 100 makes a material completely opaque, while a value of 0 makes the material completely transparent. Use the Background button to enable a patterned background image to make it easier to view the effects of the Opacity setting. Figure 16-14 shows materials with Opacity values of 10, 25, 50, 75, and 90.

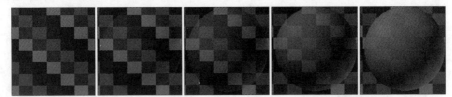

Figure 16-14: The Opacity value sets how transparent a material is.

Specular Highlights are the bright points on the surface where the light is reflected at a maximum value. The Specular Level value determines how bright the highlight is. Its values can range from 0, where there is no highlight, to 100, where the highlight is at a maximum. The graph to the right of the values displays the intensity per distance for a cross section of the highlight. The Specular Level defines the height of the curve or the value at the center of the highlight where it is the brightest. This value can be overloaded to accept numbers greater than 100. Overloaded values create a larger, wider highlight.

The Glossiness value determines the size of the highlight. A value of 100 produces a pinpoint highlight, and a value of 0 increases the highlight to the edges of the graph. The Soften value doesn't affect the graph, but it spreads the highlight across the area defined by the Glossiness value. It can range between 0 (wider) and 1 (thinner). Figure 16-15 shows a sampling of materials with Specular Highlights. The left image has a Specular Level of 20 and a Glossiness of 10, the second image has the

Specular Level increased to 80, the third image has the Specular Level overloaded with a value of 150, and the last two images have the Glossiness value increased to 50 and 80.

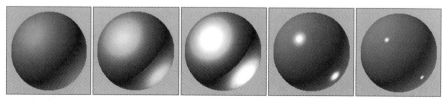

Figure 16-15: Control Specular Highlights by altering brightness and size.

Metal shader

The Metal shader simulates the luster of metallic surfaces. The Highlight curve has a shape that is different from those of the other shaders. It is rounder at the top and doesn't include a Soften value. It can also accept a much higher Specular Level value (up to 999) than the other shaders can. You also cannot specify a Specular color. All other parameters are similar to those of the Blinn shader. Figure 16-16 shows several materials with the Metal shader applied. These materials differ in Specular Level values, which are 50, 100, 200, 400, and 800.

Figure 16-16: A material with a Metal shader applied generates its own highlights.

Phong shader

The Phong shader creates smooth surfaces like Blinn without the quality highlights, but it renders more quickly than the Blinn shader does. The parameters for the Phong shader are identical to those for the Blinn shader. The differences between Blinn and Phong are very subtle, but Blinn can produce highlights for lights at low angles to the surface, and its highlights are generally softer.

Maps rollout

A *map* is a bitmap image that is pasted on an image. The Maps rollout includes a list of the maps that you can apply to an object. Using this rollout, you can enable or disable maps, specify the intensity of the map in the Amount field, and load maps. Clicking the Map button (originally labeled as None) opens the gmax Material Navigator where you can select the map type. When a map file is loaded, the name of the bitmap file appears on the button.

Tutorial: Coloring a dolphin

As a quick example of applying materials, we'll take a dolphin model created by Zygote Media and position it over a watery plane. We'll then apply custom materials to both objects.

To add materials to a dolphin, follow these steps:

1. Open the Dolphin.gmax file from the Chap 16 directory on the CD-ROM.

   This file contains a simple plane object and a dolphin mesh.

2. Open the gmax Material Editor by clicking the gmax Material Editor button on the main toolbar (or by pressing the M key).

3. In the gmax Material Editor, click the New button and select the Standard material type. In the Name field, rename the material Dolphin Skin. Click the Diffuse color swatch, and select a light gray color. Then click the Specular color swatch, and select a light yellow color. Click the Close button to exit the Color Selector. In the Specular Highlights section, increase the Specular Level to 45.

4. Click the Copy button, and name the material Ocean Surface. Click the Diffuse color swatch, and select a light blue color. Set the Specular Level and Opacity values to 80. In the Maps rollout, click the None button to the right of the Bump selection. When the gmax Material Navigator opens, double-click the Bitmap type and select the Noise.tif file from the Chap 16 directory on CD-ROM.

5. Drag the Ocean Surface material onto the plane object in the Top viewport. Then drag the Dolphin Skin material onto the dolphin model.

Note   This model also includes separate objects for the eyes, mouth, and tongue. These objects could have different materials applied to them, but they are so small in this image that we won't worry about them.

Figure 16-17 shows the resulting rendered image.

Figure 16-17: A dolphin over the water with applied materials

Using Multi-Materials

Multi-Material is the other available material type in gmax. This material type combines several different materials into one. You can select this material type by clicking the New button and then selecting the material type from the New Material dialog box.

You can use the Multi-Material to assign several different materials to a single object via the material IDs. You can use the Mesh Select modifier to select each sub-object area to receive the different materials.

Multi-Material rollouts

At the top of the Multi/Sub-Object Basic Parameters rollout, shown in Figure 16-18, is a Set Number button that lets you select the number of subobject materials to include. This number is displayed in a text field to the left of the button. Each sub-material is displayed as a separate area on the sample object in the sample slots. Using the Add and Delete buttons, you can selectively add or delete submaterials from the list.

Figure 16-18: The Multi-Material defines materials according to material IDs.

Each submaterial includes a sample preview of the submaterial and an index number listed to the right, a Name field where you can type the name of the submaterial, a button for selecting the material, a color swatch for creating solid color materials, and a check box for enabling or disabling the submaterial. You can sort the submaterials by clicking on the ID, Name, or Sub-Material buttons at the top of each column.

After you apply a Multi-Material to an object, use the Mesh Select modifier to make a subobject selection. In the Material rollout for this subobject selection, choose a material ID to associate with a submaterial ID.

If you click on the material's name, you can edit the individual materials that make up the Multi-Material. With a particular material selected, you can move to the next material in the list with the Go Forward to Sibling button or you can return to the parent material with the Go to Parent button.

Tutorial: Creating a patchwork quilt

When I think of patches, I think of a 3D gmax object type, but for many people, "patches" would instead bring to mind small scraps of cloth used to make a quilt. Because they share the same name, maybe we can use gmax patches to create a quilt. We can then use the Multi-Material to appropriately color the various patches.

To create a quilt using patches, follow these steps:

1. Open the Patch quilt.gmax file from the Chap 16 directory on the CD-ROM.

   This file contains a quilt made of patch objects that have been combined into one object.

2. Open the gmax Material Editor by pressing the M key. Click the New button, and select the Multi-Material type.

   The Multi-Material loads into the sample slot, and the Multi/Sub-Object Basic Parameters rollout displays in the gmax Material Editor.

3. In the Multi/Sub-Object Basic Parameters rollout, click the Set Number button and set the number of submaterials to 8. Then click the color swatches to the right of the Material button to open the Color Selector. Select different colors for each of the material ID slots.

4. Drag the Multi-Material from its sample slot in the gmax Material Editor and onto the quilt object. The quilt object turns a single color. Close the gmax Material Editor.

5. In the Modify panel, select the Element subobject and scroll to the bottom of the Modify panel to the Surface Properties rollout.

6. Assign each patch a separate material ID by clicking a patch and changing the ID number in the rollout field.

Figure 16-19 shows the finished quilt. Because it's a patch, you'll be able to drape it over objects easily.

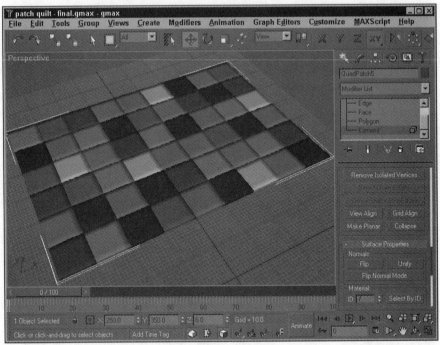

Figure 16-19: A quilt composed of patches and colored using the Multi/Sub-Object material

Applying Multiple Materials

Most complex models are divided into multiple parts, each distinguished by the material type that is applied to it. For example, a car model is separated into windows, tires, and the body, so that each part could have a unique material applied to it.

Using material IDs

You'll probably want to apply multiple materials to a single part at some time. Selecting subobject areas and using material IDs can help you accomplish this task.

Many of the standard primitives have material IDs automatically assigned— spheres get a single material ID, whereas boxes get six (one for each side) and cylinders get three (one for the cylinder and one for each end cap). In addition to the standard primitives, you can assign material IDs to Editable Mesh objects. These material IDs correspond to the various materials specified in the Multi-Material.

Tutorial: Mapping die faces

As an example of mapping multiple materials to a single object, consider a die. Splitting the cube object that makes up the die into several parts wouldn't make sense, so we'll use the Multi-Material instead.

To create a die model, follow these steps:

1. Open the Pair of dice.gmax file from the Chap 16 directory on the CD-ROM.

   This file contains two simple cube primitives that represent a pair of dice. I also used Adobe Photoshop and created six images with the dots of a die on them. All of these images are the same size.

2. Open the gmax Material Editor by pressing the M key. Click the New button, and select the Multi-Material type. Name the material **Die Faces**.

3. In the Multi/Sub-Object Basic Parameters rollout, click the Set Number button and enter a value of **6**.

4. Name the first material **face 1**, and click the material button to open the parameter rollouts for the first material. Then click the map button to the right of the Diffuse color swatch to open the gmax Material Navigator and double-click the Bitmap map. In the Select Bitmap Image File dialog box, choose the dieface1.tif image from the Chap 16 directory on the CD-ROM and click Open.

5. Back in the gmax Material Editor, click the Go to Parent button twice to return to the Multi Sub-Object Basic Parameters rollout and repeat Step 4 for each of the die faces.

6. When the Multi-Material is defined, select the cube object and click the Apply button.

Note

Because the cube object used in this example is a box primitive, we didn't need to assign the material IDs to different subobject selections. The box primitive automatically assigned a different material ID to each face of the cube. When material IDs do need to be assigned, you can specify them in the Surface Properties rollout for editable meshes.

Figure 16-20 shows a rendered image of two dice being rolled.

Caution

The Multi-Material is not visible in the viewport and can be seen only in the rendered image. You can use the ActiveShade window to view the results before rendering the final image.

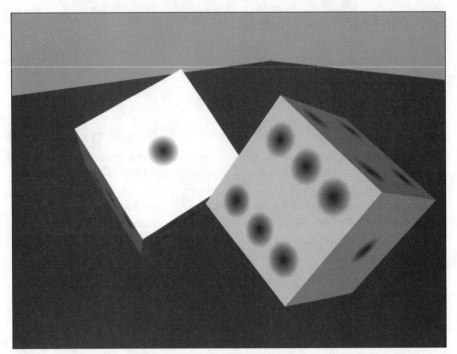

Figure 16-20: These dice have different bitmaps applied to each face.

Understanding Maps

In addition to using materials, another way to enhance an object is to use a map — but not a roadmap; these maps are closer to bitmaps, with patterns that can be applied to the surface of an object. Some maps wrap an image onto objects, but others, such as displacement and bump maps, modify the surface based on the map's intensity. For example, you can use a diffuse map to add a label to a soup can or a bump map to add some texture to the surface of an orange.

To understand a material map, think of this example. Cut the label off of a soup can, scan it into the computer, and save the image as a bitmap. You could then create a cylinder with roughly the same dimensions as the can, load the scanned label image as a material map, and apply it to the cylinder object to simulate the original soup can.

Different types of maps exist. Some maps wrap images about objects, while others define areas to be modified by comparing the intensity of the pixels in the map. An example of this is a bump map. A standard bump map is a grayscale image — when mapped onto an object, lighter color sections are raised to a maximum of pure white and darker sections are indented to a minimum of black. This enables you to easily create surface textures, such as an orange rind, without having to model them.

Still other uses for maps include projection maps that are used with lights.

Cross-Reference For information on projection maps, see Chapter 17, "Creating Ambiance and Mood with Lights."

Maps that are used to create materials are applied using the gmax Material Editor. The gmax Material Navigator lists the two available maps — Bitmap and Checker.

Tip In the gmax Material Editor, you can enable maps in the Viewport by clicking the Show Map in Viewport button. But this can slow the display, so Views ➪ Deactivate All Maps can be used to turn off all maps to speed the display.

Maps are typically used along with materials. You can open the material maps from the gmax Material Navigator. To open the gmax Material Navigator, click any of the map buttons found throughout the gmax Material Editor, including those found in the Maps rollout. Figure 16-21 shows this browser filtered to display the available default map types.

To load a material into the gmax Material Editor, simply either double-click it or select it and click OK.

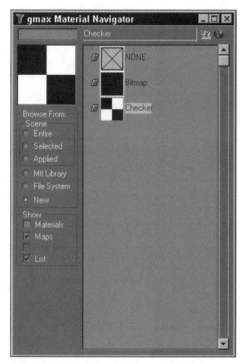

Figure 16-21: Use the gmax Material Navigator to list the default map types available for assigning to materials.

Using the Bitmap Map

A two-dimensional map can be wrapped onto the surface of an object. Because they have no depth, 2D maps appear only on the surface. The Bitmap map is perhaps the most common 2D map. It enables you to load any image, which can be wrapped around an object's surface in a number of ways.

The Bitmap and Checker maps have several rollouts in common. These include Coordinates and Noise. In addition to these rollouts, each individual map type has its own parameters rollout.

The Coordinates rollout

Every map that is applied to an object needs to have mapping coordinates that define how the map lines up with the object. For example, with the soup can label example mentioned earlier, you'll probably want to align the top edge of the label with the top edge of the can, but you could position the top edge at the middle of the can. Mapping coordinates define where the map's upper-right corner is located on the object.

All map coordinates are based on a UVW coordinate system that equates to the familiar XYZ coordinate system, except that it is named uniquely so as not to be confused with transformation coordinates. These coordinates are required for every object to which a map is applied. In most cases, you can generate these coordinates automatically when you create an object by selecting the Generate Mapping Coordinates option in the object's Parameter rollout.

Note   Editable meshes don't have any default mapping coordinates, but you can generate mapping coordinates using the UVW Map modifier.

In the Coordinates rollout for 2D Maps, shown in Figure 16-22, you can specify whether the map is a texture map or an environment map. The Texture option applies the map to the surface of an object as a texture. This texture moves with the object as the object moves. The Environ option creates an environment map. Environment maps are locked to the world and not to an object. Moving an object with an environment map applied to it scrolls the map across the surface of the object.

Different mapping types are available for both the Texture and Environ options. Mapping types for the Texture option include Explicit Map Channel, Vertex Color Channel, Planar from Object XYZ, and Planar from World XYZ. The Explicit Map Channel option is the default. It applies the map using the designated Map Channel. The Vertex Color Channel uses specified vertex colors as its channel. The two planar mapping types place the map in a plane based on the Local or World coordinate systems.

Figure 16-22: The Coordinates and Noise rollouts let you offset and tile a map and apply noise to the texture.

The Environ option includes Spherical Environment, Cylindrical Environment, Shrink-Wrap Environment, and Screen mapping types. The Spherical Environment mapping type is applied as if the entire scene were contained within a giant sphere. The same applies for the Cylindrical Environment mapping type except the shape is a cylinder. The Shrink-Wrap Environment plasters the map directly on the scene as if it were covering it like a blanket. The Screen mapping type just projects the map flatly on the background.

The Show Map on Back option causes planar maps to project through the object and be rendered on the object's back.

The U and V coordinates define the X and Y positions for the map. For each coordinate, you can specify an Offset value, which is the distance from the origin. The Tiling value is the number of times to repeat the image and is used only if the Tile option is selected. The Mirror option inverts the map. The UV, VW, and WU options apply the map onto different planes.

Tiling is the process of placing a copy of the applied map next to the current one and so on until the entire surface is covered with the map placed edge to edge. You will often want to use tiled images that are seamless, or that repeat from edge to edge.

Figure 16-23 shows an image tile that is seamless. The horizontal and vertical seams line up. Below the tile, three more tiles have been positioned next to each another. This tile was created using Fractal Design Painter 3D. Notice how the image repeats itself over and over.

Figure 16-23: Seamless image tiles are a useful way to cover an entire surface with a small map.

You can also rotate the map about each of the U, V, and W axes by entering values in the respective fields, or by clicking the Rotate button, which opens the Rotate Mapping Coordinates dialog box, shown in Figure 16-24. Using this dialog box, you can drag the mouse to rotate the mapping coordinates. Dragging within the circle rotates about all three coordinates, and dragging outside the circle rotates the mapping coordinates about their center point.

The Blur and Blur Offset values affect the blurriness of the image. The Blur value blurs the image based on its distance from the view, whereas the Blur Offset value blurs the image regardless of its distance.

Tip   You can use the Blur setting to help make tile seams less noticeable.

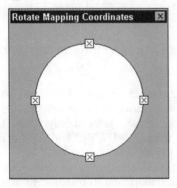

Figure 16-24: The Rotate Mapping Coordinates dialog box appears when you click the Rotate button in the Coordinates rollout.

The Noise rollout

The Noise rollout, also shown in Figure 16-22, adds noise to the map. Noise is similar to the static that you may see on the television added to a bitmap. This feature is helpful for making textures more grainy, which is useful for certain materials.

The Amount value is the strength of the noise function that is applied; the value ranges from 0 for no noise through 100 for maximum noise. You can disable this noise function at any time, using the On option.

The Levels value defines the number of times the noise function is applied. The Size value determines the extent of the noise function based on the geometry. You can also Animate the noise. The Phase value controls how quickly the noise changes over time.

Bitmap map

Selecting the Bitmap map from the gmax Material Navigator opens the Select Bitmap Image File dialog box, shown in Figure 16-25, where you can locate an image file. Various image and animation formats are supported; these include BMP, JPEG, PNG, PSD, TGA, and TIF.

The name of the current bitmap file is displayed on the button in the Bitmap Parameters rollout, shown in Figure 16-26. If you need to change the bitmap file, click the Bitmap button and select the new file. Use the Reload button to update the bitmap if you've made changes to the bitmap image by an external program.

Figure 16-25: The Select Bitmap Image File dialog box lets you preview images before opening them.

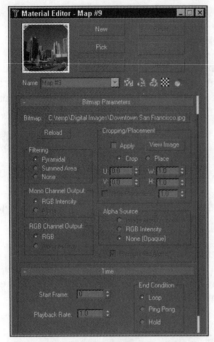

Figure 16-26: The Bitmap Parameters rollout offers several settings for controlling a bitmap map.

The Bitmap Parameters rollout includes three Filtering options: Pyramidal, Summed Area, and None. These methods perform a pixel averaging operation to anti-alias the image. The Summed Area option requires more memory but produces better results.

You can also specify the output for a mono channel or for an RGB channel. For maps that only use the monochrome information in the image (such as an opacity map), the Mono Channel as RGB Intensity or Alpha option can be used. For maps that use color information (for example, a diffuse map), the RGB Channel can be RGB (full color) or Alpha as Gray.

The Cropping/Placement controls enable you to crop or place the image. Cropping is the process of cutting out a portion of the image, and Placing is resizing the image while maintaining the entire image.

Caution If the gmax Material Navigator is open when you try to crop or place an image, the Cropping/Placement window will close randomly without warning.

The View Image button opens the image in a Cropping/Placement dialog box, shown in Figure 16-27. The rectangle is available within the image when Crop mode is selected. You can move the handles of this rectangle to specify the crop region.

Note When the Crop option is selected, a UV button is displayed in the upper right of the Cropping/Placement dialog box. Clicking this button changes the U and V values to X and Y pixels.

You can also adjust the U and V parameters, which define the upper-left corner of the cropping rectangle, and the W and H parameters, which define the crop or placement width and height. The Jitter Placement option works with the Place option to randomly place and size the image.

Note The U and V values are a percentage of the total image. For example, a U value of 0.25 positions the image's left edge at a location that is 25 percent of the distance of the total width from the left edge of the original image.

If the bitmap has an alpha channel, you can specify whether it is to be used with the Image Alpha option, or you can define the alpha values as RGB Intensity or as None. You can also select to use Premultiplied Alphas, which are alpha channels that have already been multiplied by each separate RGB channel. By premultiplying, you won't need to multiply the channels when compositing the image.

Figure 16-27: Viewing an image in the Cropping/Placement dialog box enables you to set the crop marks.

The Time rollout

Maps, such as bitmaps, that can load animations also include a Time rollout for controlling animation files. In this rollout, also shown in Figure 16-26, you can choose a Start Frame and the Playback Rate. The default Playback Rate is 1.0— higher values run the animation faster, and lower values run it slower. You can also set the animation to Loop, Ping Pong, or Hold the last frame.

The Output rollout

The Output rollout includes settings for controlling the final look of the map. The Invert option creates a negative version of the image. The Clamp option prevents any colors from exceeding a value of 1.0 and prevents maps from becoming self-illu-minating if the brightness is increased.

The Alpha From RGB Intensity option generates an alpha channel based on the Intensity of the map. Black areas become transparent and white areas opaque.

Note   For materials that don't include an Output rollout, you can apply an Output map, which accepts a submaterial.

The Output Amount value controls how much of the map should be mixed when it is part of a composite material. You use the RGB Offset value to increase or decrease the map's tonal values. Use the RGB Level value to increase or decrease the saturation level of the map. The Bump Amount value is used only if the map is being used as a bump map; it determines the height of the bumps.

The Enable Color Map option enables the Color Map graph at the bottom of the Output rollout. This graph displays the tonal range of the map. Adjusting this graph affects the highlights, midtones, and shadows of the map. Figure 16-28 shows a Color Map graph.

The left end of the graph equates to the shadows, and the right end is for the high-lights. The RGB and Mono options let you display the graphs as independent red, green, and blue curves or as a single monocolor curve. The Copy CurvePoints option copies any existing points from Mono mode over to RGB mode and vice versa. The buttons across the top of the graph are used to manage the graph points.

The buttons above the graph include Move (with flyout buttons for Move Horizontally and Move Vertically), Scale Point, Add Point (with a flyout button for adding a point with handles), Delete Point, and Reset Curves. Along the bottom of the graph are buttons for managing the graph view. The two fields on the left con-tain the horizontal and vertical values for the current selected point. The other but-tons are to Pan and Zoom the graph.

Figure 16-28: The Color Map graph enables you to adjust the highlights, midtones, and shadows of a map.

Checker map

The Checker map creates a checkerboard image with two colors. The Checker Parameters rollout, shown in Figure 16-29, includes two color swatches for changing the checker colors. You can also load maps in place of each color. Use the Swap button to switch the position of the two colors and the Soften value to blur the edges between the two colors.

Figure 16-30 shows three Checker maps with Tiling values of 2 for the U and V directions and Soften values of 0, 0.2, and 0.5.

Figure 16-29: The Checker Parameters rollout lets you select the colors to use in the checker pattern.

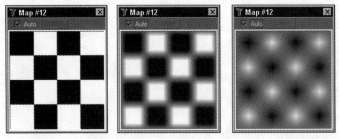

Figure 16-30: The Checker map can be softened as these three maps are with Soften values of 0, 0.2, and 0.5.

Using the Maps Rollout

Now that you've seen the two available types of maps, we'll revisit the Maps rollout, shown in Figure 16-31, and cover it in more detail.

The Maps rollout is where you apply maps to the various materials. To use a map, click the Map button—this opens the gmax Material Navigator where you can select the map to use. The Amount spinner sets the intensity of the map, and there is an option to enable or disable the map. For example, a white material with a red Diffuse map set at 50 percent Intensity results in a pink material.

The available maps in the Maps rollout depend on the type of material and the Shader that you are using. Raytrace materials have many more available maps than the standard material. Some of the common mapping types found in the Maps rollout are discussed in this section.

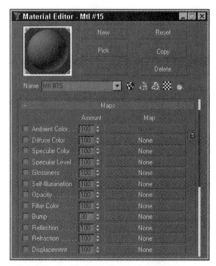

Figure 16-31: The Maps rollout can turn maps on or off.

Ambient mapping

Ambient mapping replaces the ambient color component of the base material. You can use this feature to make an object's shadow appear as a map. Diffuse mapping (discussed next) also affects the Ambient color. A lock button in the Maps rollout enables you to lock these two mappings together.

Diffuse mapping

Diffuse mapping replaces the diffuse color component of the base material. This is the main color used for the object. When you select a map such as Wood, the object appears to be created out of wood. As mentioned previously, diffuse mapping can also affect the Ambient color if the lock button is selected.

Specular mapping

Specular mapping replaces the specular color component of the base material. This option enables you to include a different color or image in place of the specular color. It is different from the Specular Level and Glossiness mappings, which also affect the specular highlights.

Specular Level mapping

Specular Level mapping controls the intensity of the specular highlights from 0, where the map is black, to 1, where the map is white. For the best effect, apply this mapping along with the Glossiness mapping.

Note   The Specular Level map isn't available if the Metal shader is selected.

Glossiness mapping

Glossiness mapping defines where the specular highlights appear. You can use this option to make an object appear older by diminishing certain areas. Black areas on the map show the non-glossy areas, and white areas are where the glossiness is at a maximum.

Self-Illumination mapping

Self-Illumination mapping makes certain areas of an object glow, and, because they glow, they won't receive any lighting effects, such as highlights or shadows. Black areas represent areas that have no self-illumination, and white areas receive full self-illumination.

Opacity mapping

Opacity mapping determines which areas are visible and which are transparent. Black areas for this map are transparent, and white areas are opaque. This mapping works in conjunction with the Opacity value in the Basic Parameters rollout. Transparent areas, even if perfectly transparent, still receive specular highlights.

Filter color mapping

Filter color mapping is used to color transparent areas for creating materials such as colored glass. White light that is cast through an object using filter color mapping is colored with the filter color.

Bump mapping

Bump mapping uses the intensity of the bitmap to raise or indent the surface of an object. The white areas of the map are raised, and darker areas are lowered. Although bump mapping appears to alter the geometry, it actually doesn't affect the surface geometry.

Reflection mapping

Reflection mapping reflects images off the surface as a mirror does. Reflection mapping doesn't need mapping coordinates because the coordinates are based on world coordinates and not on object coordinates. Therefore, the map appears different if the object is moved — which is how reflections work in the real world.

Refraction mapping

Refraction mapping bends light and displays images through a transparent object, in the same way that a room appears through a glass of water. The amount of this effect is controlled by a value called the Index of Refraction. This value is set in the parent material's Extended Parameters rollout.

Displacement mapping

You can use displacement mapping, unlike bump mapping, to change the geometry of an object. The white areas of the map are pushed outward, and the dark areas are pushed in. The amount of the surface that is displaced is based on a percentage of the diagonal that makes up the bounding box of the object. Displacement mapping can be applied only to patches and Editable Mesh objects.

Mapping Modifiers

Several of the modifiers found in the Modifiers menu are specific to material and maps. These modifiers are found in the UV Coordinates and Surface submenus and the UVW Map, UVW XForm, Unwrap UVW and Material modifiers.

One other modifier works closely with materials — the Vertex Paint modifier. The Vertex Paint modifier is found in the Mesh Editing submenu.

UVW Map modifier

The UVW Map modifier lets you specify the mapping coordinates for an object. Primitives and Loft Objects can generate their own mapping coordinates, but you need to use this modifier to apply mapping coordinates to mesh objects and patches.

Note　　Objects that create their own mapping coordinates apply them to Map Channel 1. If you apply the UVW Map modifier to Map Channel 1 of an object that already has mapping coordinates, then the applied coordinates overwrite the existing ones.

You can apply the UVW Map modifier to different map channels. Applying this modifier places a map gizmo on the object. You can move, scale, or rotate this gizmo. To transform a UVW Map gizmo, you must select it from the subobject list. Gizmos that are scaled smaller than the object can be tiled.

There are many different types of mappings, and the parameter rollout for this modifier lets you select which one to use. The Length, Width, and Height values are the dimensions for the UVW Map gizmo. You can also set tiling values in all directions.

The Alignment section offers eight buttons for controlling the alignment of the gizmo. The Fit button fits the gizmo to the edges of the object. The Center button aligns the gizmo center with the object's center. The Bitmap Fit button opens a File dialog box where you can align the gizmo to the resolution of the selected bitmaps. The Normal Align button lets you drag on the surface of the object, and when you release the mouse button, the gizmo origin is aligned with the normal. The View Align button aligns the gizmo to match the current viewport. The Region Fit button lets you drag a region in the viewport and match the gizmo to this region. The Reset button moves the gizmo to its original location. The Acquire button aligns the gizmo with the same coordinates as another object.

Figure 16-32 displays a brick map applied to an umbrella using spherical mapping.

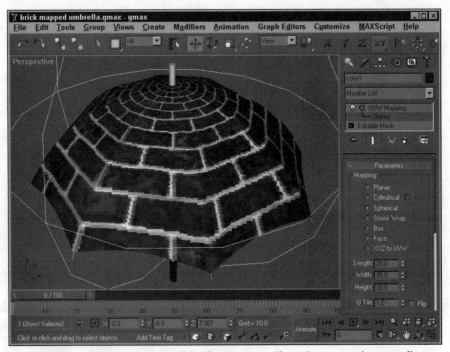

Figure 16-32: The UVW Map modifier lets you specify various mapping coordinates for material maps.

Tutorial: Using the UVW Map modifier to apply decals

After mapping coordinates have been applied either automatically or with the UVW Map modifier, you can use the UVW XForm modifier to move, rotate, and scale the mapping coordinates.

Most objects can automatically generate mapping coordinates — with the exception of meshes. For meshes, you need to use the UVW Map modifier. The UVW Map modifier includes seven mapping options. Each mapping option wraps the map in a different way. The options include Planar, Cylindrical, Spherical, Shrink Wrap, Box, Face, and XYZ to UVW.

In this tutorial, we use the UVW Map modifier to apply a decal to a rocket model. Zygote Media created the rocket model.

To use the UVW Map modifier, follow these steps:

1. Open the Nasa decal on rocket.gmax file from the Chap 16 directory on the CD-ROM.

   This file includes a model of a rocket with the appropriate materials applied. The Chap 16 directory on the CD-ROM also includes a 300×600 image of the word NASA in black capital letters on a white background. The image was saved as a .TIF file.

2. Open the gmax Material Editor (or press the M key), click the New button, and name the material **NASA Logo**. Click the Diffuse color swatch, and select a white color. Then click the map button to the right of the Diffuse color swatch, and from the gmax Material Navigator, double-click the Bitmap map. Locate the NASA image from the Chap 16 directory on the CD-ROM, and click Open.

   The bitmap image loads, and the Bitmap parameters display in the rollouts.

3. In the Coordinates rollout, enter a value of **–90** in the W Angle field. The letters rotate vertically.

4. Select the lower white section of the rocket in the viewport, and open the Modify panel. At the top of the Modify panel, click the Modifier List and select the UVW Map modifier. Select the Cylindrical Mapping option, but don't select the Cap option in the Parameters rollout.

5. With the cylinder section selected, open the gmax Material Editor again, select the first sample slot, and click the Apply button. Then click on the Show Map in Viewport button to see the map within the viewport.

Tip   When a bitmap is applied to an object using the UVW Map modifier, you can change the length, width, and tiling of the bitmap using the UVW Map manipulator. Enable the Select and Manipulate button on the main toolbar, and the manipulator appears as green lines. When you move the mouse over the top of these green lines, they turn red, and you can drag them to alter the map dimensions. Use the small green circles at the edges of the map to change the tiling values. As you use the manipulator, the map is updated in real time within the viewports if you enabled the Show Map in Viewport option in the gmax Material Editor.

Figure 16-33 shows the resulting rendered image.

UVW XForm modifier

The UVW XForm modifier enables you to adjust mapping coordinates. It can be applied to mapping coordinates that are automatically created or to mapping coordinates created with the UVW Map modifier. The parameter rollout includes values for the UVW Tile and UVW Offsets. You can also select the Map Channel to use.

Figure 16-33: You can use the UVW Map modifier to apply decals to objects.

Unwrap UVW modifier

The Unwrap UVW modifier lets you control how a map is applied to an object. Using this modifier, you can place all the graphics details for the texture map in a single image file and then map the coordinates to specific coordinates on the image map. You accomplish this task by creating planar maps for various sides of an object and then editing the mapping coordinates in the Edit UVWs dialog box, shown in Figure 16-34. You can open this dialog box by applying the Unwrap UVW modifier to an object and clicking the Edit button in the Parameters rollout of the Modify panel.

You can also load and save the edited mapping coordinates. Saved mapping coordinate files have the .UVW extension. The buttons in the Edit UVWs dialog box are shown and described in Table 16-3.

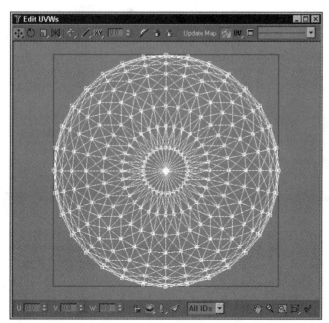

Figure 16-34: The Edit UVWs dialog box lets you control how different planar maps line up with the model.

Table 16-3
Edit UVW Dialog Box Buttons

Button	Name	Description
	Move, Move Horizontal, Move Vertical	These buttons move the selected vertices when dragged.
	Rotate	This button rotates the selected vertices when dragged.
	Scale, Scale Horizontal, Scale Vertical	These buttons scale the selected vertices when dragged.
	Mirror Horizontal, Mirror Vertical, Flip Horizontal, Flip Vertical	These buttons mirror (or flip) the selected vertices about the center of the selection.
	Expand Selection, Contract Selection	These buttons add or subtract all adjacent vertices to the current selection.
	Falloff Type	This button enables you to select a falloff type, including Linear, Sinusoidal, Slow Out, and Fast Out.
	World Falloff Space, Texture Falloff Space	These buttons set the falloff coordinate system.
	Falloff Distance	This field determines the distance before the color changes.
	Break Selected Vertices	This button splits the selected vertices into two.
	Target Weld	This button enables you to drag selected vertices to a single vertex for welding.
	Weld Selected	This button welds all the selected vertices together.
	Update Map	This button updates the map in the viewport.
	Show Map	This button toggles the display of the map in the dialog box.
	Coordinates	This button displays the vertices for the UV, UW, and WU axes.
	Unwrap Options	This button opens the Unwrap Options dialog box for setting preferences.
	Pick Texture	This field displays a drop-down list of all the maps applied to this object. You can display new maps by using the Pick Texture option.

Button	Name	Description
	U, V, W values	These fields display the coordinates of the selected vertex. You can use these values to move a vertex.
	Lock Selected Vertices	This button locks the selected vertices and prevents additional vertices from being selected.
	Hide, Unhide	This toggle button hides or unhides the selected vertices.
	Freeze, Unfreeze	This toggle button freezes or unfreezes the selected vertices.
	Filter Selected Faces	This button displays vertices for only the selected faces.
All IDs	All IDs	This field filters selected material IDs.

The buttons in the lower-right corner of the Edit UVWs dialog box work just like the Viewport Navigation buttons described in earlier chapters.

The Unwrap Options dialog box, shown in Figure 16-35, lets you set the Line and Selection Colors as well as the preferences for the Edit UVWs dialog box. You can set the map resolution or use the Use Bitmap Resolution option. Also available are a setting for the Weld Threshold and options to constantly update, show selected vertices in the viewport, and snap to the map's pixels.

Tip   The default color for lines and unselected vertices is white, so if your texture map has a white background, it can be difficult to see the vertices. In the Unwrap Options dialog box, you can change the default line and vertex colors to make them easier to see.

Creating Planar Maps

If you open the Edit UVWs dialog box for a fairly complex model, you'll see a mess of lines and vertices. Locating the specific faces can be a challenge, but many of the features of the Edit UVWs dialog box can help.

One of the easiest ways to work with the various faces of an object is to use the default Material IDs applied as mapping coordinates. All default primitive objects have an option to Generate Mapping Coordinates. If this option is enabled, then Material IDs and mapping coordinates are applied automatically. For example, a Box primitive assigned a separate ID to each face. With the Edit UVWs dialog box, you can access these Material IDs using the ID drop-down list at the bottom of the Edit UVWs dialog box.

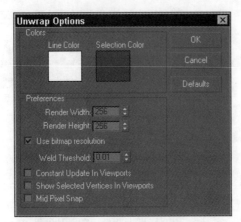

Figure 16-35: In the Unwrap Options dialog box, you can set the preferences for the Edit UVWs dialog box.

Another easy way to identify these separate faces is with the Planar Map button found in the Parameters rollout in the Modify panel. If you select the Select Face subobject mode under the Unwrap UVW modifier, you can select individual faces on the model. Clicking the Planar Map button creates a named selected set for the selected face. You can then filter these selected faces in the Edit UVWs dialog box using the Filter Selected Faces button also on the lower toolbar of the Edit UVWs dialog box.

To select a Planar Map, you can use the X, Y or Z axis options or the Average Normals option, which selects the planar map based on the average of all the normals for the selected faces.

Tutorial: Mapping a house

For many of the games, scenery is a common element that you can customize. Whether it's Flight Simulator or Trainz, an everyday house is a good detail to be able to create. By mapping the details, you can use very simple box primitives as the 3D model and let the texture map hold all the details. In this example, we'll use the Unwrap UVW modifier to map some details onto a very simple house.

To control how planar maps are applied to a house, follow these steps:

1. Open the Simple house.gmax file from the Chap 16 directory on the CD-ROM.

   This file includes a simple house made from a primitive. The UVW Mapping and Unwrap UVW modifiers have been applied to this object. The Chap 16 directory also includes a 256×256 image of some simple house details created in PhotoShop. The file is saved as House details map.tif.

2. Press the M key to open the Material Editor, click the New button and select the Standard material type and name the material **House Details**. Then click the map button to the right of the Diffuse color button to open the gmax Material Navigator, and double-click the Bitmap map type. In the Select Bitmap Image File dialog box, locate the House Details Map.tif file from the Chap 16 directory on the CD-ROM and click OK. Then drag this material to the house object to apply this material.

Tip   Enable the Show Map in Viewport button to see the bitmap image on the house object.

3. Select the house object, open the Modify panel and in the Modifier Stack, select the Select Face subobject mode under the Unwrap UVW modifier. Then select the front face of the house and, with the Averaged Normals option selected, click the Planar Map button. This creates a named selection for the face that in the Named Selection drop-down list on the main toolbar. Continue to select all four sides of the house and the two faces that make up the roof and create a Planar Map selection for each face.

4. In the Parameters rollout, click the Edit button to open the Edit UVWs dialog box, as shown in Figure 16-36. In the lower toolbar of the Edit UVWs dialog box, enable the Filter Selected Faces button (to the left of the All IDs drop-down list).

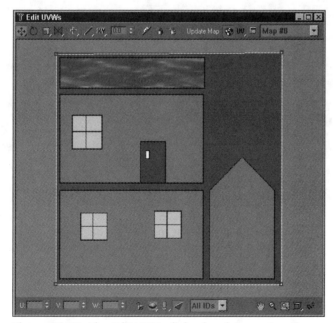

Figure 16-36: The Edit UVWs dialog box lets you transform the mapping coordinates by moving the vertices.

5. With the Filter Selected Faces button enabled, you can select the Named Selections from the main toolbar and the vertices for each selected face will appear. Select the first named selected titled, "PlanarMap1." This face is associated with the front of the house. In the Edit UVWs dialog box, drag the mouse over the upper right vertex and with the Move button selected on the Edit UVWs toolbar, drag the vertex so it matches the upper right corner for the house on the texture map. Then match the other vertices for this face.

These vertices turn red when selected and you'll be able to see the map updated in the Perspective viewport.

6. Select the next named selection set and move its vertices to correspond to the texture map. Repeat this process for each face.

Figure 16-37 shows the results of the new mapping coordinates.

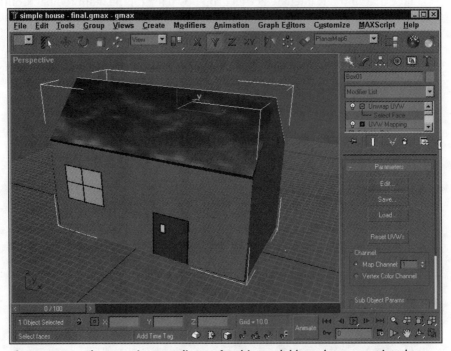

Figure 16-37: The mapping coordinates for this model have been associated to different portions of the texture using the Unwrap UVW modifier.

Material modifier

The Material modifier is the only modifier available in the Surface modifiers sub-menu. It lets you change the material ID of an object. The only parameter for this modifier is the Material ID. When you select a subobject and apply this modifier, the material ID is applied to only the subobject selection. This modifier is used in conjunction with the Multi Material type to create a single object with multiple materials.

Vertex Paint modifier

A unique way to color objects is with the Vertex Paint modifier. This modifier lets you paint on an object by specifying a color for each vertex. If adjacent vertices have different colors assigned, a gradient is created across the face. The benefit of this coloring option is that it is very efficient and requires almost no memory.

 Note The Assign Vertex Color utility works a little differently. It converts any existing material colors to vertex colors. To use this utility, select an object, choose a Light Model (Scene Lights or Diffuse lighting), and click the Assign to Selected button.

The Vertex Paint modifier lets you specify a color and paint directly on the surface of an object by painting the vertices. The color is applied with a paintbrush-shaped cursor. If several vertices of one face have different colors, then the color is applied as a gradient across the face.

The parameters for this modifier include a Paint button, an Opacity toggle, and a color swatch for selecting the color to paint with. VertCol and Shaded toggles turn Vertex Shading and normal Shading on and off, and you can use a 16-color palette for quick color selection.

Caution Once vertex colors are painted on an object, you need to enable the VertCol and Shaded button in order to see the colors. Vertex color displays cannot be seen if the Direct3D driver is selected, but are clearly visible if the Heidi or OpenGL drivers are used.

Figure 16-38 shows an umbrella with the Vertex Paint modifier applied.

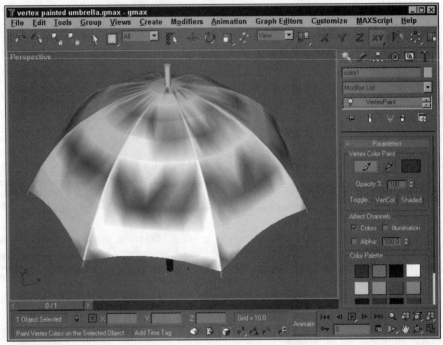

Figure 16-38: The Vertex Paint modifier lets you paint on object surfaces by coloring vertices.

Tutorial: Marking heart tension

As an example of using the Vertex Paint modifier, imagine a doctor who has a 3D model of the human heart. While discussing the results of the latest test with a patient, the doctor can color parts of the heart model to illustrate the various points.

To color on a human heart using the Vertex Paint modifier, follow these steps:

1. Open the Vertex Paint on Heart.gmax file from the Chap 16 directory on the CD-ROM.

   This file includes a heart mesh created by Viewpoint Datalabs.

2. Select a portion of the heart model and open the Modify panel. Select the Vertex Paint modifier from the Modifier List.

3. In the Parameters rollout, select the red color, select both the VertCol and Shaded buttons, and click the Paint button. Then drag the mouse over the surface of the model in the Perspective view.

Figure 16-39 shows the resulting color.

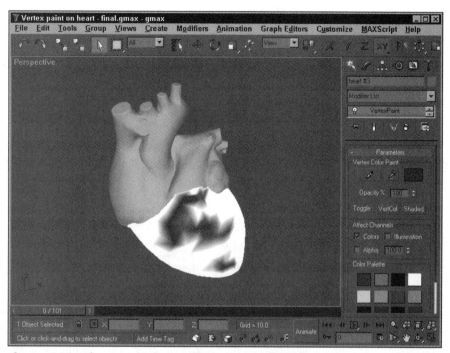

Figure 16-39: The Vertex Paint modifier can apply color to an object by assigning a color to its vertices.

Removing Materials and Maps

If you apply a material or map to an object that doesn't look just right and tweaking it won't help, you can always return to square one by removing the material or any mappings that have been applied to the object. The tool to remove materials and maps is the UVW Remove utility. You can access this utility by clicking the UVW Remove button from the list of Utilities.

Caution The Remove UVW utility does not work on patch objects.

This utility includes a single rollout that lists the number of objects selected. It also includes two buttons. The UVW button removes any mapping coordinates from the selected objects, and the Materials button removes any materials from the selected objects. This button restores the original object color to the selected objects. Alternatively, you can select the Set Gray option that makes the selected object gray when the materials are removed.

Summary

Materials can add much to the realism of your models. Learning to use the gmax Material Editor and the gmax Material Navigator enables you to work with materials.

In this chapter, you've learned some tricks to help you unravel the complexities of working with materials and maps. Materials can add lots of realism to your models. This chapter presented the various material and maps and explained how to use them.

This chapter covered these topics:

✦ Learning about various material properties

✦ Working with the gmax Material Editor and the gmax Material Navigator

✦ Using the Standard and Multi-Materials

✦ Applying multiple materials to an object with material IDs

✦ Understanding the basics of mapping coordinates and tiling

✦ Discovering the various mapping possibilities provided in the Maps rollout

✦ Using mapping modifiers

✦ Controlling mapping coordinates with the Unwrap UVW modifier

✦ Removing maps with the Remove UVW utility

The next chapter adds lights to the scene, which are important for some game packs in setting mood.

✦   ✦   ✦

Lights, Camera, Action

◆   ◆   ◆   ◆

In This Part

Chapter 17
Creating Ambiance
and Mood with Lights

Chapter 18
If You Could See
What I See —
Controlling Cameras

Chapter 19
Getting the
Prop to Spin —
Animation Basics

Chapter 20
Graphing Animations
with the Track View

Chapter 21
Whoa, Betty!
Constraining Motion

Chapter 22
Creating Automatic
Actions with
Controllers

◆   ◆   ◆   ◆

Creating Ambiance and Mood with Lights

◆ ◆ ◆ ◆

In This Chapter

Understanding
lighting basics

Understanding
gmax's light types

Creating and
positioning light
objects

Viewing a scene from
a light

Altering light
parameters

Using projector maps
and raytraced
shadows

◆ ◆ ◆ ◆

Lights play an important part in the visual process. Have you ever looked at a blank page and been told it was a picture of a polar bear in a snow blizzard or looked at a completely black image and been told it was a rendering of a black spider crawling down a chimney covered in soot? The point of these two examples is that with too much or too little light, you really can't see anything.

Light in the gaming world plays an important part in the equation. Quake, for example, uses low-level lighting that projects an eerie, scary feel, but Flight Simulator during the day uses lots of light. If you build game levels with the wrong amount of lighting, the feel and mood of the game play will be off. This chapter covers creating and controlling lights in your scene.

Understanding the Basics of Lighting

Lighting plays a critical part of any gmax scene. Understanding the basics of lighting can make a big difference in the overall feeling and mood of your game levels. Most gmax scenes typically use one of two types of lighting: natural light or artificial light. Natural light is used for outside scenes and uses the sun and moon for its light source. Artificial light is usually reserved for indoor scenes where light bulbs provide the light. However, when working with lights, there will be cases where natural light is used indoors, such as sunlight streaming through a window, or where artificial light is used outdoors, such as a streetlight.

Natural and artificial light

Natural light is best created using lights that have parallel light rays coming from a single direction—you can create this type of light using a Direct Light. The intensity of natural light is also dependent on the time, date, and location of the sun.

The weather can also make a difference in the light color. In clear weather, the color of sunlight is pale yellow; in clouds, sunlight has a blue tint; and in dark, stormy weather, sunlight is dark gray. The colors of light at sunrise and sunset are more orange and red. Moonlight is typically white.

Artificial light is typically produced with multiple lights of lower intensity. The Omni light is usually a good choice for indoor lighting because it casts light rays in all directions from a single source. Standard white fluorescent lights usually have a light green or light blue tint.

 Note   Most game engines have their own lighting method for natural light, but you have lots of control over the secondary lights.

The final type of light to keep in mind is ambient light. Ambient light is not from a direct source but is created by light that is deflected off walls and objects. It provides overall lighting to the entire scene and keeps shadows from becoming completely black.

Shadows

Shadows are the areas behind an object where the light is obscured. gmax supports two types of shadows: shadow maps and raytraced shadows. Shadow maps are actual bitmaps that the game engine loads and combines with the finished scene to produce an image. These maps can have different resolutions, but higher resolutions require more memory. Shadow maps typically create shadows that are softer and more realistic.

gmax calculates raytraced shadows by following the path of every light ray striking a scene. This process takes a significant amount of processing cycles but can produce very accurate, hard-edged shadows. Raytracing enables you to create shadows for objects that shadow maps can't, such as transparent glass.

Figure 17-1 shows several images rendered with the different shadow types. The image in the upper left includes no shadows. The upper-right image uses a shadow map set to a Size of 512. The lower-left image uses a shadow map set to a Size of 4096, and the lower-right image uses raytraced shadows. The last two images took considerably longer to create. Viewpoint Datalabs created the pelican model shown in this figure.

Figure 17-1: Images rendered with different shadow types, including no shadow (upper left), a 512 shadow map (upper right), a 4096 shadow map (lower left), and raytraced shadows (lower right)

Getting to Know the Light Types

gmax includes several different types of lights. The main difference in these types is how the light rays are cast into the scene. Light can come from the default lights that are present when no other lights have been added to the scene. Light can also come from ambient light, which is light that bounces off other objects. gmax also includes Omni, Direct, and Spotlights, each having its own characteristics. Understanding these sources of light will help you to know where to look to control the lighting.

Default lighting

So, you get gmax installed, and you eagerly start the application, throw some objects in a scene, and send it out to your game engine . . . and you'll be disappointed in the output, because you forgot to put lights in the scene. Right? Wrong! gmax is smart enough to place default lighting in a scene that does not have any lights.

The default lighting disappears as soon as a light is created in a scene (even if the light is turned off). When all the lights in a scene are deleted, default lighting magically reappears. So you can always be sure that your objects will always have some light to make them visible. Default lighting actually consists of two lights — the first light is positioned above and to the left, and the second light is positioned below and to the right.

The Viewport Configuration dialog box has an option to enable default lighting for any viewport or to set the default lighting to use only one light. You can open this dialog box by choosing Customize ⇨ Viewport Configuration or by right-clicking the viewport title and selecting Configuration from the pop-up menu.

If the Default Lighting and 2 Lights options are enabled, then a menu appears in the Views menu to add the default lights to the scene. The Views ⇨ Add Default Lights to Scene command makes a simple dialog box appear, as shown in Figure 17-2. In the Add Default Lights to Scene dialog box, you can select which of the two lights to include and the Distance Scaling, which is the distance from the origin at which the lights are placed. The Distance Scaling value of 1.0 places them in the same location as the default lights; higher values move them further away. After they are created, the two lights are listed as DefaultKeyLight and DefaultFillLight.

Figure 17-2: The Add Default Lights to Scene dialog box converts the default lights into actual objects that you can control.

Ambient light

Ambient light is general lighting that uniformly illuminates the entire scene. It is caused by light that bounces off other objects. In the Viewport Background dialog box (Alt+B), you can set the ambient light color using a color swatch. You can also set the default ambient light color in the Global Settings panel of the Light Lister dialog box (which is accessed using the Tools menu). This color is the darkest color that can appear in the scene, generally in the shadows.

In addition to these global ambient settings, each material can have an ambient color selected in the Material Editor.

Caution

Don't rely on ambient light to fill in unlit sections of your scene. If you use a heavy dose of ambient light instead of placing secondary lights, your scene objects will appear flat, and you won't get the needed contrast to make your objects stand out. Your game engine also will not like a bright ambient color.

Omni light

The Omni light is like a light bulb — it casts light rays in all directions. The two default lights are Omni lights.

Spot light

Spotlights are directional — they can be pointed and sized. The two different spotlights available in gmax are a Target Spot and a Free Spot. A Target Spot light consists of a light object and a target marker at which the spotlight points. A Free Spot light has no target, which enables it to be rotated in any direction using the Select and Rotate transform button. Spotlights always are displayed in the viewport as a cone with the light positioned at the cone apex.

Cross-Reference

Both Target Spot and Target Direct lights are very similar in functionality to the Target Camera object, which you learn about in Chapter 18, "If You Could See What I See — Controlling Cameras."

Direct light

Direct lights cast parallel light rays in a single direction, like the sun. Just like spotlights, direct lights come in two types: a Target Direct light and a Free Direct light. The position of the Target Direct light always points toward the target, which you can move within the scene using the Select and Move button. A Free Direct light can be rotated to determine where it points. Direct lights are always displayed in the viewport as cylinders.

Creating and Positioning Light Objects

gmax, in its default setup, can create many different types of light. Each has different properties and features. To create a light, just open the Create panel and click the Lights category button. Then click the button for the type of light you want to create, and drag in a viewport to create it. The five standard light types are Target Spot, Target Direct, Omni, Free Spot, and Free Direct. Omni and Free lights are created with a single click, but you create Target lights by clicking at the light's position and dragging to the position of the target. Spotlights are identified by a cone, and direct lights are identified by a cylinder shape.

Transforming lights

Lights can be transformed just like other geometric objects; however, not all transformations are available for all the light types. An Omni light, for example, cannot be scaled, and rotating an Omni light has no effect on the scene. To transform a light, click one of the transformation buttons and select and drag the light.

Target lights can have the light and the target transformed independently, or you can select both the light and target by clicking the line that connects them. Target lights can be rotated and scaled only if the light and target are selected together. Scaling a Target light increases its cone or cylinder. Scaling a Target Direct light with only the light selected increases the diameter of the light's beam, but if the light and target are selected, then the diameter and distance are scaled.

An easy way to select or deselect the target is to right-click the light and choose Select Target from the pop-up menu. All transformations work on free lights.

Listing lights

The Tools ⇨ Light Lister menu command opens the Light Lister dialog box, shown in Figure 17-3, where you can see at a quick glance all the details for all the lights in the scene. It includes two rollouts: Global Settings and Lights.

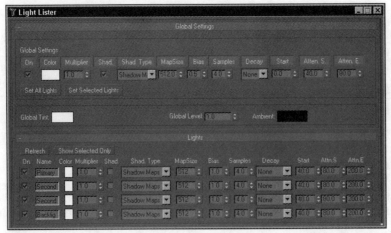

Figure 17-3: The Light Lister dialog box includes a comprehensive list of light settings in one place.

The Global Settings rollout includes settings for Multiplier, Color, Shadows, Map Size, and so on. You can apply these changes to all the Selected Lights or to All Lights. The Light Lister provides an easy way to change the parameters of many lights at once.

The Lights rollout lists the settings for each individual light. Using this rollout, you can change the settings for any of the listed lights. The light settings are covered later in the chapter.

Placing highlights

The Place Highlight (Ctrl+H) feature enables you to control the position and orientation of a light in order to achieve a highlight in a precise location. To use this feature, you must select a light object in the scene and then choose Tools ➪ Place Highlight or click the Place Highlight button (which is a flyout under the Align button) on the toolbar. The cursor changes to the Place Highlight icon. Click a point on the object in the scene where you want the highlight to be positioned, and the selected light repositions itself to create a specular highlight at the exact location where you clicked. The light's position is determined by the Angle of Incidence between the highlight point and the light.

Tutorial: Lighting the snowman's face

You can use the Place Highlight feature to position a light for our snowman. To place a highlight, follow these steps:

1. Open the Snowman highlight.gmax file from the Chap 17 directory on the CD-ROM.

   This file contains a simple snowman created using primitive objects.

2. Open the Create panel, select the Lights category, click the Target Spot button, and position it below and to the left of the Snowman model.

3. To place the highlight so it shows the Snowman's face, select the Spot light and then choose Tools ➪ Place Highlight (or press Ctrl+H). Then click the Snowman's face where the highlight should be located, just above his right eye.

4. With the light still selected, right-click on the Perspective viewport title and select Views ➪ Spot01 from the pop-up menu (or press the Shift+4 key) to see the snowman from the light's perspective.

Figure 17-4 shows the results.

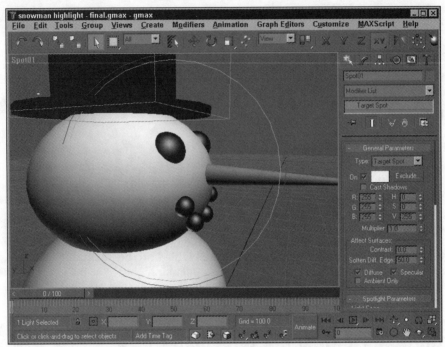

Figure 17-4: The snowman, after the lights have been automatically repositioned using the Place Highlights command

Viewing a Scene from a Light

You can configure viewports to display the view from any light, with the exception of an Omni light. To do so, right-click the viewport title and select Views and the light name at the top of the pop-up menu.

Note The keyboard shortcut for making the active viewport a Light view is the $ (the dollar sign is the shift of the 4) key. If more than one light exists, then the Select Light dialog box appears and lets you select which light to use. This can be used only on spotlights and direct lights.

Light viewport controls

When a viewport is changed to show a light view, the Viewport Navigation buttons in the lower-right corner of the screen change into Light Navigation controls. Table 17-1 describes these controls.

Note Many of these controls are identical for viewports displaying lights or cameras.

Table 17-1
Light Navigation Control Buttons

Toolbar Button	Name	Description
	Dolly, Target, Both	Moves the light, its target, or both the light and its target closer to or farther away from the scene in the direction it is pointing.
	Light Hotspot	Adjusts the angle of the light's hotspot, which is displayed as a blue cone.
	Roll Light	Spins the light about its local Z-axis.
	Zoom Extents All, Zoom Extents All Selected	Zooms in on all objects or the selected objects until they fill the viewport.
	Light Falloff	Changes the angle of the light's falloff cone.
	Truck Light	Moves the light perpendicular to the line of sight.
	Orbit, Pan Light	The Orbit button rotates the light around the target, whereas the Pan Light button rotates the target around the light.
	Min/Max Toggle	Makes the current viewport fill the screen. Clicking this button a second time returns the display to several viewports.

If you hold down the Ctrl key while using the Light Hotspot or Falloff buttons, gmax maintains the distance between the hotspot and falloff cones. The Hotspot cone cannot grow any larger than the Falloff cone.

You can constrain any light movements to a single axis by holding down the Shift key. The Ctrl key causes the movements to increase rapidly.

For Free lights, an invisible target is determined by the distance computed from the other light properties. You can use the Shift key to constrain rotations to be vertical or horizontal.

Note You can undo changes in the normal viewports using the Views ⇨ Undo command (Shift+Z), but you undo light viewport changes with the regular Edit ⇨ Undo command.

Tutorial: Lighting a lamp

To practice using lights, let's try to get a lamp model to work as it should.

To add a light to a lamp model, follow these steps:

1. Open the Lamp.gmax file from the Chap 17 directory on the CD-ROM.

   This file includes a lamp mesh surrounded by some plane objects used to create the walls and floor. The lamp model was created by Zygote Media. It looks like a standard living room lamp that you could buy in any department store.

2. Create an Omni light by opening the Create panel and clicking the Lights category. Click the Omni button, and click again in any viewport.

3. Use the Select and Move transform button to position the light object inside the lamp's light bulb.

The resulting image is shown in Figure 17-5. Notice how the light intensity is greater at places closer to the light.

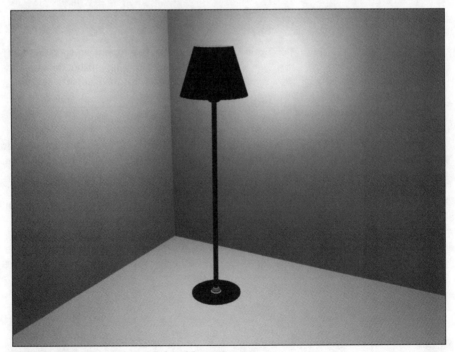

Figure 17-5: The rendered lighted-lamp image

Altering Light Parameters

Lights affect every object in a scene and can really make or break a game, so it shouldn't be surprising that each light comes with many controls and parameters. Several different rollouts work with lights, as shown in Figure 17-6.

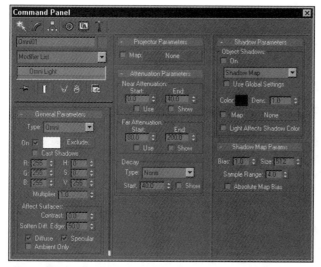

Figure 17-6: The various light rollouts control parameters and shadows.

General parameters

If you're looking for a light switch to turn lights on and off, look no further than the Modify panel. When a light is selected, the General Parameters rollout appears. The options contained in this rollout enable you to turn the lights on and off, select a light color and intensity, and determine how a light affects object surfaces.

The Type drop-down list lets you change the type of light instantly, so that you can switch from Omni light to Spot light without lots of work. This feature provides an easy way to look at the results of using a different type of light. When you change the type of light, you lose the settings for the previous light.

To the right of the on/off switch is a color swatch. Clicking this swatch opens a color selector where you can choose a new light color. The RGB and HSV values provide an alternative method for selecting a light color.

The Exclude button opens the Exclude/Include dialog box, where you can select objects to be included or excluded from illumination and/or shadows. The pane on the left includes a list of all the current objects in the scene. To exclude objects from being lit, select the Exclude option, select the objects to be excluded from the pane on the left, and click the double-arrow icon pointing to the right to move the objects to the pane on the right.

Figure 17-7 shows the Exclude/Include dialog box. This dialog box also recognizes any Selection Sets you've previously defined. They can be selected from the Selection Sets drop-down list.

Figure 17-7: The Exclude/Include dialog box lets you set which objects are included or excluded from being illuminated.

Back in the light's General Parameters rollout, the Multiplier value is the light intensity. A light with a Multiplier set to 2 is twice as bright as a light with its Multiplier set to 1.

Note   Higher Multiplier values make a light appear white regardless of the light color.

Options in the Affect Surface section control how light interacts with an object's surface. The Contrast value alters the contrast between the diffuse and the ambient surface areas. The Soften Diffuse Edge value blurs the edges between the diffuse and ambient areas of a surface. The Diffuse and Specular options let you disable these properties of an object's surface. When the Ambient Only option is turned on, the light affects only the ambient properties of the surface.

Attenuation parameters

Attenuation is a property that determines how light fades over distance. An example of this is a candle set in a room. The farther you get from the candle, the less the light shines.

You use three basic parameters to simulate realistic attenuation. These parameters are displayed in the Attenuation Parameters rollout. Near Attenuation sets the distance at which the light begins to fade, and Far Attenuation sets the distance at which the light falls to 0. These properties are ranges that include Start and End values. The third parameter sets the Decay value, which simulates attenuation using a mathematical formula to compute the drop in light intensity over time.

Selecting the Use option enables the Near and Far Attenuation values; each has a Start and End value that sets the range for this attenuation type. The Show option makes the attenuation distances and decay values visible in the viewports. The three types of decay from which you can choose are None, Inverse, and Inverse Square. The Inverse type decays linearly with the distance away from the light. The Inverse Square type decays exponentially with distance.

Note   The Inverse Square type approximates real lights the best, but it is often too dim for games. You can compensate for this by increasing the Multiplier value.

Spot and directional light parameters

The Spotlight Parameters rollout, shown in Figure 17-8, includes values to set the angular distance of both the Hot Spot and Falloff cones. The Show Cone option makes the Hotspot and Falloff cones visible in the viewport when the light is not selected. The Overshoot option makes the light shine in all directions like an Omni light, but projections and shadows occur only within the Falloff cone. You can also set the light shape to be circular or rectangular. For a rectangular-shaped spotlight, you can control the aspect ratio. You can use the Bitmap Fit button to make the aspect ratio match a particular bitmap.

The Directional Light Parameters rollout, which appears for Direct light types, is identical to the Spotlight Parameters rollout and also includes settings for the Hot Spot and Falloff values.

Projection maps

You can use any light as a projector; the location of this option depends on the type of light. For Spot and Direct lights, you can find this option in their respective rollouts. For Omni lights, you can use a Projector Parameters rollout. In any of these rollouts, selecting the Map option enables you to use the light as a projector. You can select a map to project by clicking the button to the right of the map option. You can drag a material map directly from the Material/Map Browser onto the Projector Map button.

Figure 17-8: The Spotlight Parameters rollout includes settings for the Hot Spot and Falloff cones.

Shadow parameters

All light types have a Shadow Parameters rollout. This rollout, just like the General Parameters rollout, has an On/Off switch. This switch lets you specify whether a light casts shadows.

You can also select from a drop-down list whether the shadows are created using a shadow map or raytraced shadows. If the Shadow Map option is selected in the Shadow Parameters rollout, the Shadow Map Params (Parameters) rollout appears below it. This rollout includes controls for the Bias, Size, and Sample Range of the map.

Note   Depending on the number of objects in your scene, shadows can take a long time to render. Enabling raytraced shadows for a complex scene can greatly increase the render time.

Back in the main Shadow Parameters rollout, you can defer to the global settings by selecting the Use Global Settings option. This option helps to maintain consistent settings across several lights. It applies the same settings to all lights, so that changing the value for one light changes that same value for all lights that have this option selected.

You can also select a shadow color by clicking the color swatch. The default color is black.

The "Dens" setting stands for density and controls how dark the shadow appears. Lower values produce light shadows, and higher values produce dark shadows. This value can also be negative.

The Map option, like the Projection Map, can be used to project a map along with the shadow color. The Light Affects Shadow Color option alters the Shadow Color by blending it with the light color, if selected.

Manipulating Hotspot and Falloff cones

When the Select and Manipulate mode is enabled in the main toolbar, the end of the Hotspot and Falloff cones appear green for a selected spotlight. When you move the mouse over these lines, the lines turn orange, allowing you to drag the lines and make the Hotspot and/or Falloff angle values greater. These manipulators provide visual feedback as you resize the spotlight cone.

Tutorial: Creating twinkling stars

Surely there is some poetry somewhere that speaks of dotting the sky with stars. In this tutorial, I'll be showing you how to do just that using a view full of Omni lights positioned close to a Plane object.

To create a background of controllable stars, follow these steps:

1. Open the Create panel, and select the Lights category. Then click the Omni button, and click in the Top viewport to create about 30 to 50 lights.

   Each light is a separate star.

2. Next, click the Geometry category and click the Plane button. Then drag in the Top view to create a simple plane object that fills the viewport. Change the Object Color swatch for the plane object to dark blue.

3. With the Select and Move button, select the Plane object and right-click the Select and Move button to access the Move Transform Type-In dialog box (F12). In this dialog box, enter **–1.0** in the Z-axis field.

   This step moves the Plane object barely underneath all the Omni lights.

4. Click the Select by Name button on the main toolbar (or press the H key), and in the Select Objects dialog box, select all the Omni lights. Then open the Modify panel, and click the Noise button. This applies the Noise Modifier to all the lights. In the Strength field for the Z-axis, enter **5** and select the Animate Noise option with a Frequency of 1.0.

5. When you render the animation, set the render viewport to the Top view.

Although a black-and-white figure doesn't really do the rendered image justice, Figure 17-9 shows the scene set up in gmax.

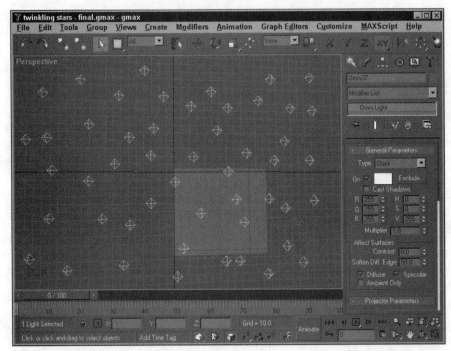

Figure 17-9: Countless Omni lights positioned close to a Plane object can create a realistic star field with animated twinkling stars.

Tutorial: Showing car headlights

One popular way to use lights is to display the headlights of cars, trains, or airplanes. For this tutorial, we're going to use the '57 Chevy model created by Viewpoint Datalabs.

To display the headlights of a car, follow these steps:

1. Open the Headlights on a 57 Chevy.gmax file from the Chap 17 directory on the CD-ROM.

   This file includes a model of a '57 Chevy.

2. In the Create panel, click the Lights category, and then click the Target Spot button and drag in the Left viewport to create a spotlight object. Select and

move the spotlight and the target to be positioned to look as if a light is shining out from the left headlight.

3. Open the Modify panel, and in the Spotlight Parameters rollout, set the Hotspot value to 20 and the Falloff to 25.

4. When a light is added to the scene, the default lights are automatically turned off. To provide any additional lighting, add some Omni lights above the car.

5. Now, create the second headlight. To do this, select both the first spotlight object and its target, and create a cloned copy by holding down the Shift key while moving it toward the right headlight. Position the second spotlight so that it shines outward from the right headlight.

6. Press the M key to open the Material Editor and click the Pick button. Then move the cursor over the headlight object and click to select the headlight's material. In the Phong Basic Parameters rollout, set the Self-Illumination value to 100. The light materials are automatically updated.

Figure 17-10 shows the car with its two headlights shining brightly.

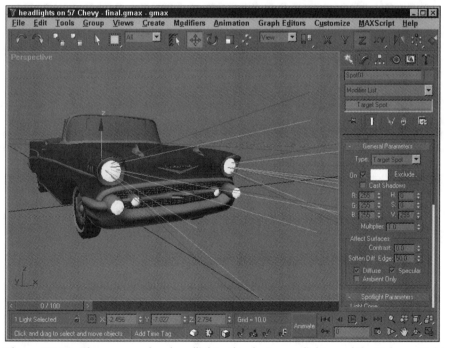

Figure 17-10: The car now has headlights, thanks to spotlights and the Volume Light effect.

Using projector maps and raytraced shadows

If a map is added to a light in the Parameters rollout, the light becomes a projector. Projector maps can be simple images, animated images, or black-and-white masks to cast shadows. To load a projector map, select a light, open the Modify panel, and under the Spotlight Parameters rollout, click the Projector Map button and select the map to use from the Material/Map Browser.

Raytraced shadows take longer to render than the Shadow Maps or Area Shadows option, but the shadows will always have a hard edge and be an accurate representation of the object.

 Note   You can create shadows for wire-frame objects only by using raytraced shadows.

In the Shadow Parameters rollout, you can select whether shadows are computed using shadow maps or raytraced shadows. Using the latter selection lets you project a transparent object's color onto the shadow.

Tutorial: Projecting a trumpet image onto a scene

As an example of a projector light, we'll create a musical scene with several musical notes and project the image of a trumpet onto them.

To project an image onto a rendered scene, follow these steps:

1. Open the Musical notes.gmax file from the Chap 17 directory on the CD-ROM.

   This file contains several musical notes created from primitive objects.

2. Open the Create panel, and select the Lights category. Click the Target Spot button, and drag to create two lights in the Top viewport. Position the first spotlight to be perpendicular to the scene and to shine down on it from above.

3. Open the Modify panel, and in the Spotlight Parameters rollout, enable the Map option, click the Projector Map button, and double-click Bitmap from the gmax Material Navigator. Locate and select the Trumpet Mask.tif file, and click Open. This projects the silhouette of a trumpet onto the scene. Use the second spotlight to light the music notes.

Figure 17-11 shows the musical notes with the trumpet projection map.

Tutorial: Creating a stained-glass window

When a light that uses raytraced shadows shines through an object with transparent materials, the Filter color of the material is projected onto objects behind. In this tutorial, we will create a stained-glass window and shine a light through it using raytraced shadows.

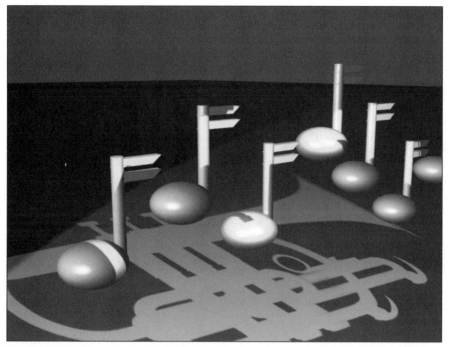

Figure 17-11: You can use Projection maps to project an image in the scene, like this trumpet.

To create a stained-glass window, follow these steps:

1. Open the Stained glass window.gmax file from the Chap 17 directory on the CD-ROM.

   This file includes a stained-glass window for a fish market (don't ask me why a fish market has stained-glass window).

2. In the Create panel, select the Lights category and click the Target Spot button. Then drag in the Left view from a position to the right of and above the window to the window — this creates a target spotlight that shines through the stained-glass window onto the floor behind it.

3. In the General Parameters rollout, make sure the Cast Shadows option is selected and select Ray Traced Shadows from the drop-down list. In the Shadow Parameters rollout, enable the On option.

Figure 17-12 shows the stained-glass window with the colored shadow cast on the scene floor.

Figure 17-12: A stained-glass window effect created with raytraced shadows

Summary

I hope you have found this chapter enlightening. (Sorry about the bad pun, but I need to work them in where I can.) There are many different lights in gmax, each with plenty of controls. Learning to master these controls can take you a long way toward increasing the realism of the scene. This chapter covered these topics:

✦ Learning the basics of lighting

✦ Discovering gmax's light types

✦ Creating and positioning light objects

✦ Learning to change the viewport view to a light

✦ Adding projection maps to lights

✦ Using raytraced shadows to create a stained-glass window

In the next chapter, we'll cover cameras and you'll find that they are easier to use than disposable cameras.

✦   ✦   ✦

If You Could See What I See – Controlling Cameras

In This Chapter

Understanding camera basics

Creating a camera object

Viewing a camera in a viewport

Controlling cameras with the viewport camera controls

Aiming a camera at objects

Altering camera parameters

Do you remember as a kid when you first got your own camera? After taking the usual pictures of your dog and the neighbor's fence, you quickly learned how much fun you could have with camera placement such as a picture of a flagpole from the top of the flagpole or your mom's timeless expression when she found you inside the dryer. Cameras in gmax can also offer all kinds of amusing views of your scene.

The benefit of cameras is that you can position them anywhere within a scene to offer a custom view. You can open camera views in a viewport, and you can use them to render images or animated sequences. Cameras in gmax can also be animated (without damaging the camera, even if your mischievous older brother turns on the dryer).

Working with Cameras

Cameras in the gaming world are unique because the viewpoint is mostly controlled by the game engine during game play. But in many instances, you want to control the viewpoint precisely. For example, in Dungeon Siege, you can zoom over the level as an intro section to an adventure, and in Flight Simulator, you can control the panning motion of the view sweeping over your plane.

If you're a photography hobbyist or like to take your video camera out and shoot your own footage, then many of the terms in this section will be familiar to you. The cameras used in gmax to get custom views of a scene behave in many respects just like real-world cameras.

gmax and real-world cameras both work with different lens settings, which are measured and defined in millimeters. You can select from a variety of preset stock lenses, including 35mm, 80mm, and even 200mm. gmax cameras also offer complete control over the camera's focal length, field of view, and perspective for wide-angle or telephoto shots. The big difference is that you never have to worry about focusing a lens, setting flashes, or loading film.

Light coming into a camera is bent through the camera lens and focused on the film, where the image is captured. The distance between the film and the lens is known as the focal length. This distance is measured in millimeters, and you can change it by switching to a different lens. On a camera that shoots 35mm film, a lens with a focal length of 50mm produces a view similar to what your eyes would see. A lens with a focal length less than 50mm is known as a wide-angle lens because it displays a wider view of the scene. A lens longer than 50mm is called a telephoto lens because it has the ability to give a closer view of objects for more detail, as a telescope does.

Field of view is directly related to focal length and is a measurement of how much of the scene is visible. It is measured in degrees. The shorter the focal length, the wider the field of view.

When we look at a scene, objects appear larger if they are up close than they would lying at a farther distance. This effect is referred to as *perspective* and helps us to interpret distances. As mentioned, a 50mm lens gives a perspective similar to what our eyes give. Images taken with a wide field of view look distorted because the effect of perspective is increased.

Creating a camera object

To create a camera object, you'll need to open the familiar Create panel and click the Cameras category button. The two different types of cameras that you can create are a Free camera and a Target camera.

Camera objects are visible as icons in the viewports, but they aren't rendered. The camera icon looks like a box with a smaller box in front of it, which represents the lens or front end of the camera. Both the Free and Target camera types can include a cone that shows where the camera is pointing.

Free camera

The Free camera object offers a view of the area that is directly in front of the camera and is the better choice if the camera will be animated. When a Free camera is initially created, it points at the negative Z-axis of the active viewport. The single parameter for Free cameras defines a Target Distance — the distance to an invisible target about which the camera can orbit.

Target camera

A Target camera always points at a controllable target point some distance in front of the camera. Target cameras are easy to aim and are useful for situations where the camera won't move. To create this type of camera, click a viewport to position the camera and drag to the location of its target. The target can be named along with the camera. When a target is created, gmax automatically names the target by attaching ".target" on the end of the camera name. You can change this default name by typing a different name in the Name field.

Creating a camera view

You can change any viewport to show a camera's viewpoint. To do so, right-click the viewport's title, and select View and the camera's name from the pop-up menu. Any movements done to the camera are reflected immediately in the viewport.

Another way to select a camera for a viewport is to press the C key. This keyboard shortcut makes the active viewport into a camera view. If several cameras exist in a scene, then the Select Camera dialog box appears, from which you can select a camera to use. Figure 18-1 shows two Target cameras pointing at a '57 Chevy. The two viewports on the right are the views from these cameras.

You can turn off the camera object icons using the Display panel. In the Display panel, under the Hide by Category rollout, select the Cameras option. When selected, the camera icons will not be visible in the viewports.

Note   Cameras are usually positioned at some distance away from the rest of the scene. Their distant position can make scene objects appear very small when the Zoom Extents button is used. If the visibility of the camera icons is turned off, the Zoom Extents does not include them in the zoom. You could also enable the Ignore Extents option in the camera's Object Properties dialog box.

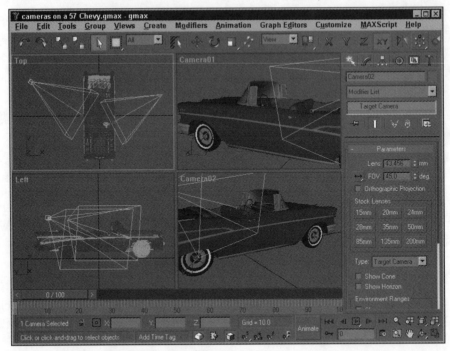

Figure 18-1: A car as seen by two different cameras

Tutorial: Setting up an opponent's view

There is no limit to the number of cameras that you can place in a scene. Chapter 9, "Transforming Objects," shows an example of re-creating a chess game, in which one camera shows the board from one player's perspective. Creating another camera and moving the camera target enables us to create a similar view from the opponent's perspective.

To create a new aligned view from the opponent's perspective, follow these steps:

1. Open the Chess game — Opponents View.gmax file from the Chap 18 directory on the CD-ROM.

2. Open the Create panel, select the Cameras category, and click the Target Camera button. Drag in the Top viewport to create the camera. Then give the new camera the name **Black Camera**.

3. Position the new target camera behind the opponent's pieces roughly symmetrical to the other camera.

4. With the new camera selected, drag the target point and position it on top of the other camera's target point somewhere below the center of the board.

To see the new camera view, right-click the Perspective viewport title and choose View ⇨ Black Camera (or select the camera and the Perspective viewport and press the C key). Figure 18-2 shows the view from this camera.

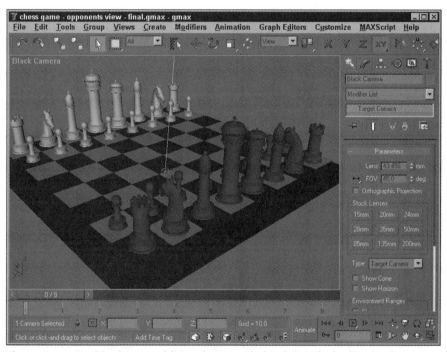

Figure 18-2: Positioning an additional camera behind the Black player's pieces offers the opponent's view.

Controlling a camera

I was once on a ride at Disneyland when a person behind me decided to blatantly disregard the signs not to take photographs. As he leaned over to snap another picture, I heard a fumbling noise, a faint, "Oh no," and then the distinct sound of his camera falling into the depths of the ride. (That was actually more enjoyable than the ride. It served him right.) As this example shows, controlling a camera can be difficult. This chapter offers many tips and tricks for dealing with the cameras in gmax, and you won't have to worry about dropping them.

You control the camera view in a viewport by means of the Camera Navigation controls located in the lower-right corner of the screen. These controls replace the viewport controls when a camera view is selected and are different from the normal Viewport Navigation controls. The Camera Navigation controls are identified and defined in Table 18-1.

Note   Many of these controls are identical to the controls for lights.

You can constrain the movements to a single axis by holding down the Shift key. The Ctrl key causes the movements to increase rapidly. For example, holding down the Ctrl key while dragging the Perspective tool magnifies the amount of perspective applied to the viewport.

You can undo changes in the normal viewports using the Views ⇨ Undo command, but you undo camera viewport changes with the regular Edit ⇨ Undo command.

Table 18-1 Camera Navigation Control Buttons		
Control Button	*Name*	*Description*
	Dolly Camera, Dolly Target, Dolly Camera + Target	Moves the camera, its target, or both the camera and its target closer to or farther away from the scene in the direction it is pointing.
	Perspective	Increases or decreases the viewport's perspective by dollying the camera and altering its field of view.
	Roll Camera	Spins the camera about its local Z-axis.
	Zoom Extents All, Zoom Extents All Selected	Zooms in on all objects or the selected objects by reducing the field of view until they fill the viewport.
	Field of View	Changes the width of the view, similar to changing the camera lens or zooming without moving the camera.

Control Button	Name	Description
	Truck Camera	Moves the camera perpendicular to the line of sight.
	Orbit, Pan Camera	The Orbit button rotates the camera around the target, and the Pan button rotates the target around the camera.
	Min/Max Toggle	Makes the current viewport fill the screen. Clicking this button a second time returns the display to several viewports.

Aiming a camera

In addition to the Camera Navigation buttons, you can use the Transformation buttons on the main toolbar to reposition the camera object. To move a camera, select the camera object, and click the Select and Move button. Then drag in the viewports to move the camera.

Using the Select and Rotate button changes the direction in which a camera points, but only Free cameras rotate in all directions. When applied to a Target camera, the rotate transformation spins the camera only about the axis pointing to the target. You aim Target cameras by moving their targets.

Note Don't try to rotate a Target camera so that it is pointing directly up or down, or the camera will flip.

Select the target for a Target camera by selecting its camera object, right-clicking to open the pop-up menu, and selecting Select Target.

Tutorial: Watching a rocket

Because cameras can be transformed like any other geometry, they can also be set to watch the movements of any other geometry. In this tutorial, we'll aim a camera at a distant rocket and watch it as it flies past us and on into the sky. Zygote Media created the rocket model used in this tutorial.

To aim a camera at a rocket as it hurtles into the sky, follow these steps:

1. Open the Following a rocket.gmax file from the Chap 18 directory on the CD-ROM.

   This file includes a rocket mesh and a camera.

2. Position the Target camera's target in the Left view about two-thirds of the way up along the rocket's path and to the right a distance, and set the Field of View value to 2.0 degrees.

   The corresponding Lens value is around 1031mm.

3. Click the Auto Key button (or press the N key), and position the camera's target on the rocket at its starting location. Then drag the Time slider to frame 100, and position the camera's target once again on top of the rocket at the top of the screen. Then turn off the Auto Key button.

4. To view the scene from the camera's viewpoint, right-click the Perspective viewport title and choose Views ⇨ Camera01 from the pop-up menu (or press the C button). Then click the Play Animation button to see how well the camera follows the target. If you need to, position the target on the rocket halfway through its motion at frame 50.

Figure 18-3 shows some frames from this animation.

Figure 18-3: Positioning the camera's target on the rocket enables the camera to follow the rocket's ascent.

Aligning cameras

 You may also align a camera using the Tools ➪ Align Camera menu command, or you may click on the Align Camera button on the main toolbar (under the Align flyout). After selecting this command, click an object face and hold down the mouse button; the normal to the object face that is currently under the cursor icon is displayed as a blue arrow. When you've located the precise location at which you want the camera to point, release the mouse button. The camera is repositioned to point directly at the selected location on the selected face along the normal. This works only if there is already a camera created in the scene.

Cross-Reference

The Align Camera command does the same thing for cameras that the Place Highlight command does for lights. I discuss the Place Highlight command in Chapter 17, "Creating Ambiance and Mood with Lights."

Cameras can be automatically positioned to match the Perspective view or a light or camera view. To do this, select a camera, activate the viewport with the view that you want to match, and choose Views ➪ Match Camera to View (Ctrl+C). The camera is moved to display this view.

Caution

If you use the Match Camera to View command while a camera view is the active viewport, the two cameras are positioned on top of each other.

Tutorial: Seeing the snowman's good side

Using the Align Camera tool, you can place a camera so that it points directly at an item or the face of an object, such as the snowman's good side. To align a camera with an object point, follow these steps:

1. Open the Snowman camera.gmax from the Chap 18 directory on the CD-ROM.

    This file includes a snowman modeled from primitive objects.

2. Open the Create panel, select the Cameras category, and then click the Free button. Click in any viewport to create a new Free camera in the scene.

3. With the camera selected, choose Tools ➪ Align Camera, or click the Align Camera flyout button on the main toolbar.

    The cursor changes to a small camera icon.

4. Click the cursor on the snowman's face just under its right eye.

    This location is where the camera will point.

5. To see the new camera view, right-click the viewport title and choose Views ➪ Camera01 (or press the C key). Although the camera is pointing at the selected object, you may need to change the field of view to correct the zoom ratios.

Figure 18-4 shows our snowman from the newly aligned camera.

The Align Camera command points a camera at an object only for the current frame. It does not follow an object if it moves during an animation. To have a camera follow an object, you need to use the Look At Controller.

Figure 18-4: This new camera view of the snowman shows his best side.

Setting Camera Parameters

When a camera is first created, you can modify the camera parameters directly in the Create panel as long as the new camera is selected. After the camera object has been deselected, you can make modifications in the Modify panel's Parameters rollout for the camera, shown in Figure 18-5.

Lens settings and field of view

The first parameter in the Parameters rollout sets the Lens value or more simply, the camera's focal length in millimeters.

The second parameter, FOV (which stands for field of view), sets the width of the area that the camera displays. The value is specified in degrees and can be set to represent a Horizontal, Vertical, or Diagonal distance using the flyout button to its left, as shown in Table 18-2.

Figure 18-5: The Parameters rollout (shown in two parts) lets you specify Lens values or choose from a selection of stock lenses.

Table 18-2
Field of View Settings

Button	Description
↔	Horizontal distance
↕	Vertical distance
↗	Diagonal distance

The Orthographic Projection option displays the camera view in a manner similar to any of the orthographic viewports such as Top, Left, or Front. This eliminates any perspective distortion of objects farther back in the scene and displays true dimensions for all edges in the scene.

Professional photographers and film crews use standard stock lenses in the course of their work. These lenses can be simulated in gmax by clicking one of the Stock Lens buttons. Preset stock lenses include 15, 20, 24, 28, 35, 50, 85, 135, and 200mm lengths. The Lens and FOV fields are automatically updated upon stock lens selection.

Camera type and display options

The Type option enables you to change a Free camera to a Target camera and back at any time.

The Show Cone option enables you to display the camera's cone, showing the boundaries of the camera view when the camera isn't selected (the camera cone is always visible when a camera is selected). The Show Horizon option sets a horizon line within the camera view, which is a dark gray line where the horizon is located.

Environment ranges and clipping planes

You use the Near and Far Range values to specify the volume within which the objects are visible. The Show option causes these limits to be displayed as yellow rectangles within the camera's cone.

You use clipping planes to designate the closest and farthest object that the camera can see. In gmax, they are displayed as red rectangles with crossing diagonals in the camera cone. The Clip Manually option lets you specify the Near Clip Plane to be something less than three units. Figure 18-6 shows a camera with Clipping Planes specified. The front Clipping Plane intersects the car and chops off its front end. The far Clipping Plane intersects the middle of the car and clips the back-end of the car as well as the construction grid.

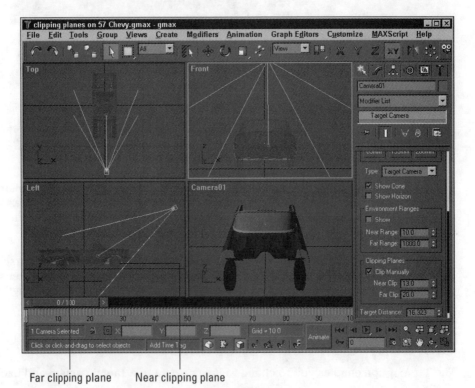

Far clipping plane   Near clipping plane

Figure 18-6: A camera cone displaying Clipping Planes

Summary

Cameras can offer a unique look at your scene. You can position and move them anywhere. In this chapter, you discovered how cameras work and how to control and aim them at objects.

This chapter has covered these topics:

✦ Learning the basics of cameras

✦ Creating a camera object and view

✦ Discovering how to control a camera

✦ Aiming a camera at objects

✦ Changing camera parameters

We're now two-thirds of the way through the director's famous line, "Lights, camera, action!" The next chapters will finally get us to some action.

✦   ✦   ✦

Getting the Prop to Spin – Animation Basics

✦   ✦   ✦   ✦

In This Chapter

Controlling time

Using the animation mode buttons to create keys

Using the Track Bar

Viewing and editing key values

Using the Motion panel and trajectories

Enabling ghosting

Merging animations

Creating custom parameters

Wiring parameters with manipulator helpers

✦   ✦   ✦   ✦

gmax can be used to create some really amazing gaming characters, but what good are cool characters that just stand there?

In this chapter, we'll start discussing what is probably one of the main reasons that you decided to learn gmax in the first place — animation. gmax includes many tools for creating animations. This chapter covers the easiest and most basic of these tools.

Using the Time Controls

Before jumping into animation, you need to understand the controls that make it possible. These controls collectively are called the Time Controls and can be found in the lower interface bar between the key controls and the Viewport Navigation Controls. The Time Controls also include the Time Slider found directly under the viewports.

The Time Slider provides an easy way to move through the frames of an animation. To do this, just drag the Time Slider button in either direction. The Time Slider button is labeled with the current frame number and the total number of frames. The arrow buttons on either side of this button work the same as the Previous and Next Frame (Key) buttons.

The Time Controls include buttons for jumping to the Start or End of the animation, or to step forward or back by a single frame. You can also jump to an exact frame by entering the frame number in the Current Frame Field. The Time Controls are presented in Table 19-1.

Table 19-1 Time Controls		
Toolbar Button	**Name**	**Description**
	Go to Start	Sets the time to frame 1.
	Previous Frame/Key	Decreases the time by one frame or selects the previous key.
	Play Animation, Play Selected	Cycles through the frames. This button becomes a Stop button when an animation is playing.
	Next Frame/Key	Advances the time by one frame, or selects the next key.
	Go to End	Sets the time to the final frame.
	Key Mode Toggle	Toggles between key and frame modes. With Key Mode on, the icon turns light blue and the Previous Frame and Next Frame buttons change to Previous Key and Next Key.
	Current Frame field	Indicates the current frame. A frame number can be typed in this field for more exact control than the Time Slider.
	Time Configuration	Opens the Time Configuration dialog box where settings like frame rate, time display, and animation length can be set.

The default scene starts with 100 frames, but this is seldom what you actually need. You can change the number of frames at any time by clicking the Time Configuration button, which is to the right of the frame number field. Clicking this button opens the Time Configuration dialog box, shown in Figure 19-1. You also can access this dialog box by right-clicking any of the Time Control buttons.

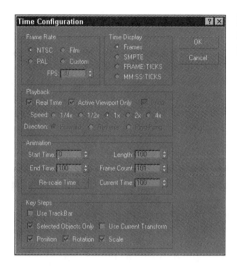

Figure 19-1: The Time Configuration dialog box lets you set the number of frames to include in a scene.

Setting frame rate

Within this dialog box, you can set several options, including the Frame Rate. Frame Rate provides the connection between the number of frames and time. It is measured in frames per second. The options include standard frame rates such as NTSC (National Television Standards Committee, around 30 frames per second), Film (around 24 frames per second), and PAL (Phase Alternate Line, used by European countries, around 25 frames per second), or you can select Custom and enter your own frame rate.

The Time Display section lets you set how time is displayed on the Time Slider. The options include Frames, SMPTE (Society of Motion Picture Technical Engineers), Frame:Ticks, and MM:SS:Ticks (Minutes and Seconds). SMPTE is a standard time measurement used in video and television. A Tick is ¼₈₀₀ of a second.

Setting speed and direction

The Playback section sets options for how the animation sequence is played back. The Real Time option skips frames to maintain the specified frame rate. The Active Viewport Only option causes the animation to play in a single viewport only, which speeds up the animation. The Loop option repeats the animation over and over. The Loop option is available only if the Real Time option is disabled. If the Loop option is set, then you can specify the Direction as Forward, Reverse, or Ping Pong (which will repeat playing forward and then reverse). The Speed setting can be ¼, ½, 1, 2, or 4 times normal.

The Time Configuration dialog box also lets you specify Start Time, End Time, Length, and Current Time values. These values are all interrelated, so setting the Length and Start Time, for example, automatically changes the End Time. These values can be changed at any time without destroying any keys. For example, if you have an animation of 500 frames and you set the Start Time to 30 and the End Time to 50, the Time Slider controls only those 21 frames. Keys before or after this time are still available and can be accessed by resetting the Start Time to 0 and the End Time to 500.

The Re-scale Time button fits all the keys into the active time segment by stretching or shrinking the number of frames between keys. You can use this feature to resize the animation to the number of frames defined by the Start and End Time values.

The Key Steps group lets you set which key objects are navigated using key mode. If you select Use TrackBar, key mode moves only through the keys on the TrackBar. If you select the Selected Objects Only option, key mode jumps only to the keys for the currently selected object. You also can filter to move among Position, Rotation, and Scale keys. The Use Current Transform option locates only those keys that are the same as the current selected transform button.

Using Time Tags

To the right of the Prompt Line is a field marked Add Time Tag. Clicking this field pops up a menu with options to Add or Edit a Time Tag. Time Tags can be set for each frame in the scene. Once set, the Time Tags are visible in the Time Tag field whenever that time is selected.

Working with Keys

It isn't just a coincidence that the largest button in the entire gmax interface has the word *Animate* on it. This button is used to create keys. Creating and working with keys is how animations are accomplished. Keys define a particular state of an object at a particular time. Animations are created as the object moves or changes between two different key states. Complex animations can be generated with only a handful of keys.

The Animate button can be enabled using the N keyboard shortcut. When this button is selected, the button turns bright red, and the border around the active viewport turns red to remind you that you are in animate mode.

Using the Animate button

With the Animate button enabled, every transformation or parameter change creates a key that defines where and how an object should look at that specific frame.

To create a key, enable the Animate button, drag the Time Slider to a frame where you want to create a key, and then move the selected object or change the parameter; a key is created automatically. You can tell by looking at the TrackBar that the key has been created; a small rectangular marker appears under the frame where the key was created.

When the first key is created, gmax automatically goes back and creates a key for frame 0 that holds the object's original position or parameter. Upon setting the key, gmax then interpolates all the positions and changes between the keys. The key is displayed in the TrackBar.

Each frame can hold several different keys, but only one for each type of transform and each parameter. For example, if you move, rotate, scale, and change the Radius parameter for a sphere object with the Animate button enabled, then a separate key is created for position, rotation, scaling, and a parameter change.

Tutorial: Rotating an airplane propeller

The best way to learn is to practice, and there is no better time to practice than now. For this quick example, you'll make an airplane prop spin (which is a good idea if you plan to fly an airplane). To animate a prop rotating, follow these steps:

1. Open the Spinning prop.gmax file from the Chap 19 directory on the CD-ROM.

   This file includes a simple propeller model.

2. Click the Animate button (or press the N key) at the bottom of the gmax window, and drag the Time Slider to frame 50. Then click the Select and Rotate button on the main toolbar.

3. With the prop object selected, click the Offset Mode Transfer Type-In button in the lower interface bar and type a value of **180** in the X coordinate field.

4. Drag the Time Slider to 100 and enter the value of **180** in the X coordinate field again.

5. Click the Animate button (or press the N key) again to disable animation mode.

6. Click the Play Animation button in the Time Controls (or press the / key) to see the animation.

Figure 19-2 shows frame 50 of this simple animation.

Figure 19-2: Frame 50 of this simple animation

Creating keys with the Time Slider

Another way to create keys is to select the object to be animated and right-click the Time Slider button that shows the frame number. This opens the Create Key dialog box, shown in Figure 19-3, where you can set Position, Rotation, and Scale keys for the currently selected object. You can use this method only to create transform keys.

Figure 19-3: The Create Key dialog box enables you to create a Position, Rotation, or Scale key quickly.

If a key already exists, you can clone it by dragging the selected key with the Shift key held down. Dragging the TrackBar with the Ctrl and Alt keys held down changes the active time segment.

Copying parameter animation keys

If a parameter is changed while the Animate button is enabled, then keys are set for that parameter. You can tell when a parameter has a key set because the arrows to the right of its spinner are outlined in red when the Time Slider is on the frame where the key is set. If you change the parameter value when the spinner is highlighted red, then the key value is changed (and the Animate button doesn't need to be enabled).

If you right-click on the spinner value, then a pop-up menu of options appears. Using this pop-up menu, you can Cut, Copy, Paste, and Delete the parameter value. You can also select Copy Animation, which copies all the keys associated with this parameter and lets you paste them to another parameter. Pasting the animation keys can be done as a Copy, an Instance, or a Wire. A Copy is independent, an Instance ties the animation keys to the original copy so that they both are changed when either is changed, and a Wire lets one parameter control some other parameter.

 Caution Right-clicking on the spinner arrows automatically sets the spinner value to its minimum value.

The right-click pop-up menu also includes commands to let you Edit a wired parameter, show the parameter in the Track View, or show the parameter in the Parameter Wiring dialog box.

 Cross-Reference Parameter wiring and the Parameter Wiring dialog box are discussed in more detail in the "Parameter Wiring" section later in this chapter.

Using the TrackBar

The gmax interface includes a simple way to work with keys: the TrackBar, which is situated directly under the Time Slider. The TrackBar displays a light blue rectangular marker for every key for the selected object.

The current frame is also shown in the TrackBar as a light transparent rectangle, as shown in Figure 19-4.

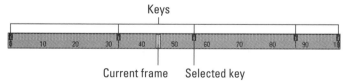

Figure 19-4: The TrackBar displays all keys for the selected object.

Using the TrackBar, you can move, copy, and delete keys. The TrackBar shows key markers only for the currently selected object or objects, and each marker can represent several different keys. When the mouse is moved over the top of these markers, the cursor changes to a plus (+) sign, and you can select it by clicking; selected markers turn green. Using the Ctrl key, you can select multiple keys at the same time. You can also select multiple key markers by clicking an area of the TrackBar that contains no keys and then dragging an outline over all the keys you want to select. If you move the cursor over the top of a selected key, the cursor is displayed as a set of arrows enabling you to drag the selected key to the left or right. Holding down the Shift key while dragging a key creates a copy of the key. Pressing the Delete key deletes the selected key.

Tip   If you drag a key off the end of the TrackBar, the frame number is displayed on the Prompt Line at the bottom of the interface and the key is not included in the current time range. If you ever want to remove a key without deleting it, you can drag it off the end of the TrackBar and recover it by resetting the time in the Time Configuration dialog box.

Because each marker can represent several keys, you can view all the keys associated with the marker in a pop-up menu by right-clicking the marker.

The marker pop-up menu also offers options for deleting selected keys or filtering the keys. In addition, there is a Goto Time command that automatically moves the Time Slider to the key's location when selected.

To delete a key marker with all of its keys, right-click to open the pop-up menu and choose Delete Key ⇨ All, or select the key marker and press the Delete key.

Viewing and Editing Key Values

At the top of the marker's right-click pop-up menu is a list of current keys for the selected object (or if there are too many keys for a marker, they are placed under the Key Properties menu in the pop-up menu). When you select one of these keys, a key information dialog box opens. This dialog box displays different controls depending on the type of key that is selected. Figure 19-5 shows the dialog box for the Position key. There are slight variations in this dialog box depending on the key type.

Note   You can also access key-specific dialog boxes in the Motion panel for a selected object by clicking the Parameters button.

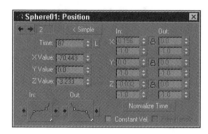

Figure 19-5: Key dialog boxes enable you to change the key parameters.

Within each of these key dialog boxes is a Time value that shows the current frame. Next to the Time value are two arrows that enable you to move easily to the other keys in the scene. The dialog box also includes several text fields, where you can change the key parameters.

Most of the key dialog boxes also include flyout buttons for selecting Key Tangents. Key Tangents determine how the animation moves into and out of the key. For example, if the In Key Tangent is set to Slow and the Out Key Tangent is set to Fast, the object approaches the key position slowly but accelerates as it leaves the key position. The arrow buttons on either side of the Key Tangent buttons can copy the current Key Tangent selection to the previous or next key.

The six different types of Tangents are detailed in Table 19-2.

Table 19-2 Key Tangents		
Toolbar Button	**Name**	**Description**
	Smooth	The default type that produces straight, smooth motion.
	Linear	Moves at a constant rate between keys.
	Step	Causes discontinuous motion between keys. It occurs only between matching In-Out pairs.
	Slow	Decelerates as you approach the key.
	Fast	Accelerates as you approach the key.
	Custom	Lets you control the Tangent handles in function curves mode.

Using the Motion Panel

And there is yet another way to create keys using the Motion panel. The Motion panel in the Command Panel includes settings and controls for animating objects. At the top of the Motion panel are two buttons: Parameters and Trajectories.

Setting parameters

The Parameters button on the Motion panel lets you assign controllers and create and delete keys. Controllers are custom key-creating algorithms that can be defined through the Parameters rollout, shown in Figure 19-6. These controllers are assigned by selecting the position, rotation, or scaling track and clicking the **Assign Controller** button to open a list of applicable controllers that you can select.

 For more information on controllers, see Chapter 22, "Creating Automatic Actions with Controllers."

Figure 19-6: The Parameters section of the Motion panel lets you assign controllers and create keys.

Below the Assign Controllers rollout is the PRS Parameters rollout, where you can create and delete Position, Rotation, and Scale keys. You can use this rollout to create keys whether or not the Animate or Set Key buttons are enabled.

Below the PRS Parameters rollout are two Key Info rollouts: Basic and Advanced. These rollouts include the same key-specific information that you can access using the right-click pop-up menu found in the TrackBar.

Using trajectories

A trajectory is the actual path that the animation follows. When you click the Trajectories button in the Motion panel, the animation trajectory is shown as a spline with each key displayed as a node and each frame shown as a white dot. You can then edit the trajectory and its nodes by clicking the Sub-Object button at the top of the Motion panel, shown in Figure 19-7. The only subobject available is Keys. With the Sub-Object button enabled, you can use the transform buttons to move and reposition the trajectory nodes. You can also add and delete keys with the Add Key and Delete Key buttons.

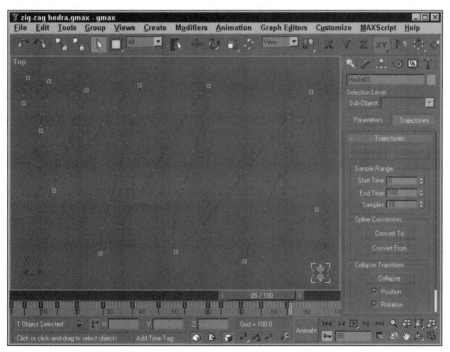

Figure 19-7: The Trajectories rollout in the Motion panel enables you to see the animation path as a spline.

For more control over the trajectory path, you can convert the trajectory path to a normal editable spline with the Convert To button. You can also convert an existing spline into a trajectory with the Convert From button.

To use the Convert From button, select an object, click the Convert From button, and then click a spline path in the scene. This creates a new trajectory path for the selected object. The first key of this path is the selected object's original position, and the second key is located at the spline's first vertex position. Additional keys are added as determined by the Samples value listed in the Sample Range group. All these new keys are equally spaced between the Start and End times. The selected spline is traversed from its initial vertex around the spline in order to the last vertex.

Click the Collapse button at the bottom of the Trajectories rollout to reduce all transform keys into a single editable path. You can select which transformations to collapse including Position, Rotation, and Scale using the options under the Collapse button. For example, an object with several Controllers assigned can be collapsed, thereby reducing the complexity of all the keys.

Note   If you collapse all keys, you cannot alter their parameters via the controller rollouts.

The Views menu includes an option to Show Key Times. Enabling this option causes the display of the frame numbers next to any key along a trajectory path.

Tutorial: Making an airplane follow a looping path

Airplanes that perform aerobatic stunts often follow paths that are smooth. You can see this clearly when watching a sky writer. In this example, I've created a simple looping path using the Line spline primitive. We'll use this path to make a plane complete a loop.

To make an airplane follow a looping path, follow these steps:

1. Open the Looping airplane.gmax file from the Chap 19 directory on the CD-ROM.

   This file includes a simple looping spline path and an airplane created by Viewpoint Datalabs.

2. With the airplane selected, open the Motion panel and click the Trajectories button. Then click the Convert From button in the Trajectories rollout, and select the path in the Front viewport.

3. If you drag the Time Slider, you'll notice that the plane moves along the path, but it doesn't rotate with the path. To fix this, Click the Key Mode Toggle

button in the Time Controls to easily move from key to key. Click the Animate button (or press the N key) to enter auto key creation mode.

4. Select the Select and Rotate button, rotate the plane in the Front viewport to match the path, and then click the Next Key button to move to the next key. Repeat this step until rotation keys have been set for the entire path.

5. Click the Animate button again to disable key creation, drag the Time Slider, and watch the airplane circle about the loop.

Figure 19-8 shows the plane's trajectory.

Figure 19-8: Using a spline path, the position keys are automatically set for this plane.

Using Ghosting

As you're trying to animate objects, using the ghosting feature can be very helpful. This feature displays a copy of the object being animated before and after its current position. To enable ghosting, choose Views ➪ Show Ghosting. This command uses the options set in the Preference Settings dialog box. Access this dialog box by choosing Customize ⇨ Preferences. In the Viewports panel of this dialog box is a Ghosting section.

You use this Ghosting section to set how many ghosted objects are to appear, whether the ghosted objects appear before, after, or both before and after the current frame, and whether frame numbers should be shown. You can also specify every *n*th frame to be displayed. There is also an option to display the ghost object in wireframe (they are displayed as shaded if this option is not enabled) and an option to Show Frame Numbers. Objects before the current frame are colored yellow and objects after are colored light blue.

Figure 19-9 shows a Hedra object that is animated to travel in a simple circle with ghosting enabled. The Preference settings are set to show three ghosting frames at every five frames before and after the current frame. The Trajectory path has also been enabled.

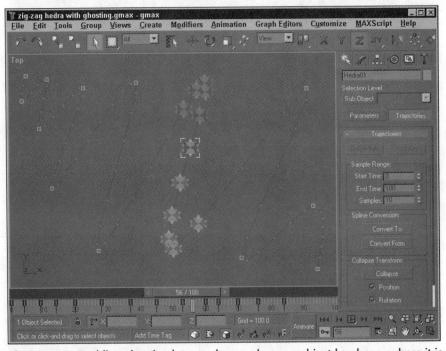

Figure 19-9: Enabling ghosting lets you know where an object has been, where it is, and where it's going.

Animating Objects

Many objects in gmax can be animated, including geometric objects, cameras, lights, and materials. In this section, we'll look at several types of objects and parameters that can be animated.

Animating cameras

You can animate cameras using the standard transform buttons found on the main toolbar. When animating a camera that actually moves in the scene, using a Free camera is best. A Target camera can be pointed by moving its target, but you risk having it flip over if the target is ever directly above the camera. If you want to use a Target camera, attach both the camera and its target to a Dummy object using the Link button and move the Dummy object.

Two useful constraints when animating cameras are the Path constraint and the Look At constraint. You can find both of these in the Animation ➪ Constraints menu. The Path constraint can make a camera follow a spline path, and the Look At constraint can direct the focus of a camera to follow an object as the camera or the object moves through the scene.

For more on constraints, including these two, see Chapter 21, "Whoa, Betty! Constraining Motion."

Animating lights

The process for animating lights includes many of the same techniques as that for animating cameras. For moving lights, use a Free spotlight or attach a Target spotlight to a Dummy object. You can also use the Look At and Path Controllers with lights.

To flash lights on and off, enable and disable the On parameter at different frames and assign a Step Tangent. To dim lights, just alter the Multiplier value over several frames.

Animating materials

You can animate materials by changing an object's parameters at different frames with the Animate button enabled. You can also control maps and their mapping coordinate systems in this manner.

Tutorial: Animating darts hitting a dartboard

As a simple example of animating objects using the Animate button, we'll animate several darts hitting a dartboard.

To animate darts hitting a dartboard, follow these steps:

1. Open the Dart and Dartboard.gmax file from the Chap 19 directory on the CD-ROM.

   This file includes a dart and dartboard objects created by Zygote Media.

2. Click the Animate button (or press the N key) to enable animation mode. Drag the Time Slider to frame 25, and click the Select and Move button on the main toolbar.

3. Select the first dart in the Left viewport, and drag it to the left until its tip just touches the dartboard.

   This step creates a key in the TrackBar for frames 0 and 25.

4. Click the Select and Rotate button on the main toolbar, set the reference coordinate system to Local, and constrain the rotation to the Y-axis. Then drag the selected dart in the Front viewport to rotate it about its local Y-axis.

   This step also sets a key in the TrackBar.

5. Select the second dart, and click the Select and Move button again. Right-click the Time Slider to make the Create Key dialog box appear. Make sure that the check boxes for Position and Rotation are selected, and click OK.

   This step creates a key that keeps the second dart from moving before it's ready.

6. With the second dart still selected, drag the Time Slider to frame 50 and move the dart to the dartboard as shown in Step 3. Then repeat Step 4 to set the rotation key for the second dart.

7. Repeat Steps 3, 4, and 5 for the last two darts.

8. Click the Animate button (or press the N key) again to disable animation mode, maximize the Perspective viewport, and click the Play Animation button to see the animation.

Figure 19-10 shows the darts as they're flying toward the dartboard.

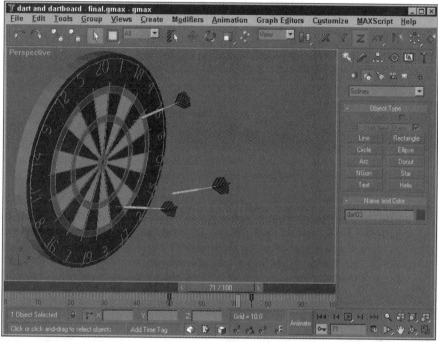

Figure 19-10: One frame of the dart animation

Merging Animations

After you've saved an animated sequence for an object, you can reuse it on other characters using File ⇨ Merge Animation. This command opens the Merge Animation dialog box, as shown in Figure 19-11. This dialog box includes settings for specifying the animation sequence and the destination object.

The Source Objects are displayed in a pane to the left. From the pane, you can select the object and its animation sequence to merge. This imports the keys from the source object, but not the model. You can also select to Replace Controllers used by the destination object. With this command, you can set up dummy controllers in an object and then merge the animation keys from another object.

Figure 19-11: The Merge Animation dialog box lets you combine animation sequences from other characters.

The Paste Time options include the source objects Start and End Times and a button to sync the first and last keys for smooth motion. You can also select where to insert the animation sequence.

The right group of options lets you import only specific animation keys including Transforms, Modifiers, Materials/Maps, Base Objects, and Visibility Tracks.

Wiring Parameters

Another useful way to expand the number of parameters is to create custom parameters. These custom parameters can define some aspect of the scene that makes sense to you. For example, if you create a model of the bicycle, you could define a custom parameter for the pedal rotation.

These custom parameters can then be wired to other objects using the Wiring Parameters feature. By wiring parameters, you can make the parameter of one object control the parameter of another object. For example, you can wire the On/Off parameter of a light to the movement of a switch. All parameters that can be animated can be wired.

Adding custom parameters

As if the standard parameters for the various modeling types weren't enough, you can also add your own custom parameters using the Add Parameter panel, shown in Figure 19-12. You can open this modeless panel by choosing Animation ⇨ Add Custom Attributes.

Figure 19-12: You can use the Add Parameter dialog box to create custom parameters.

The Parameter Type drop-down list lets you choose the parameter format. Possibilities include float (a decimal-point number), integer, Boolean (true or false), array, node, color, and texture map. The UI Type drop-down list defines how the parameter is displayed in the rollout. How the parameter looks depends on the type of parameter. Float and integer values can be spinners or sliders, Boolean values can be check boxes or radio buttons, array values are drop-down lists, nodes are pick buttons (which allow you to select an object in the viewport), color values are color pickers, and texture maps are map buttons. You can also name the parameter.

The Options rollout changes depending on which parameter type was selected. These rollouts contain settings for the interface's Width, value ranges, default values, Alignment (left, right, or center), and list items.

The Finish rollout determines to which rollout the custom attribute is added. From the Add Attribute to Type drop-down list, you can choose to add the attribute to the object's base level, to the selected modifier, or to the object material. The Add and Delete buttons can make the custom parameter appear or disappear in the rollout you specified. The Testing Attribute rollout shows what the interface element will look like.

The value of custom attributes becomes apparent when you start wiring parameters.

Using the Parameter Wiring dialog box

You can access the Parameter Wiring dialog box in several places. The Animation ⇨ Wire Parameters ⇨ Wire Parameters menu command makes a pop-up menu of parameters appear. Selecting a parameter from the menu changes the cursor to a dotted line (like the one used when linking objects). Click the object that you want to wire to, and another pop-up menu lets you choose the parameter to wire to. The Parameter Wiring dialog box appears with the parameter for each object selected from a hierarchy tree.

You can also wire parameters using the right-click quadmenu and selecting Wire Parameters. The Wire Parameters option is disabled if multiple objects are selected.

The Parameter Wiring dialog box, shown in Figure 19-13, displays two tree lists containing all the available parameters. This tree list looks very similar to the Track View and lets you connect parameters in either direction or to each other. If you used the Wire Parameters feature to open the Parameter Wiring dialog box, then the parameter for each object is already selected and highlighted in yellow.

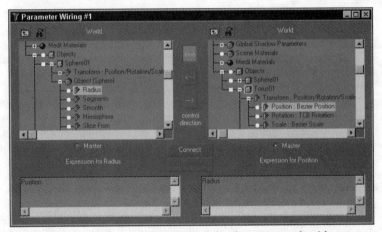

Figure 19-13: The Parameter Wiring dialog box can work with expressions.

The three arrow buttons between the two tree lists let you specify the connection direction. These buttons connect the parameter in one pane to the selected parameter in the opposite pane. The direction determines whether the parameter in the left pane controls the parameter in the right pane or vice versa. You can also select the top bidirectional button to make the parameters mutually affect each other.

Below each tree list is a text area where you can enter an expression. An *expression* is a mathematical statement that follows a specific syntax for defining how one parameter controls the other. These expressions can be any valid expression that is accepted in the Animation Controller dialog box or in MAXScript.

 Cross-Reference You can learn more about creating and using expressions in Chapter 22, "Creating Automatic Actions with Controllers."

After an expression is entered, click the Connect button to complete the wiring. Based on the connection direction, the Master radio button indicates which object controls the other. You can also use this dialog box to disconnect existing wired parameters. You can use the two icon buttons at the top of the dialog box, shown in Table 19-3, to Show All Tracks and to find the next wired parameter.

Table 19-3 Wiring Parameters	
Button	**Description**
📋	Show All Tracks
🔍	Next Wired Parameter

After the wiring is completed, the Parameter Wiring dialog box remains open. You can try out the wiring by moving the master object. If the results aren't what you wanted, you can edit the expression and click the Update button (the Connect button changes to an Update button).

If the expression contains an error, the track title displays in red and an error dialog box appears telling you what the error is. You need to correct the error and click the Update button before the wiring is in effect. If the wiring is successful, then the track title displays in green.

Manipulator helpers

To create general use controls that can be wired to control various properties, gmax includes three Manipulator Helpers. These helpers are Cone Angle, Plane Angle, and Slider. They are available as a subcategory under the Helpers category of the Create panel.

For the Cone Angle helper, you can set the Angle, Distance, and Aspect settings. The default cone is a circle, but you can make it a square. The Plane Angle helper includes settings for Angle, Distance, and Size.

You can name the Slider helper. This name will appear in the viewports above the slider object. You can also set a default value along with maximum and minimum values. To position the object, you can set the X Position, Y Position, and Width settings. You can also set a snap value for the slider.

Once created, you can use these manipulator helpers when the Select and Manipulate button on the main toolbar is enabled (this button must be disabled before the manipulator helpers can be created). The advantage of these helpers is in wiring parameters to be controlled using the helpers.

Tutorial: Controlling a crocodile's bite

One way to use manipulator helpers and wired parameters is to control within limits certain parameters that can be animated. This gives your animation team controls they can use to quickly build animation sequences. In this example, you'll use a slider to control a crocodile's jaw movement.

To create a slider to control a crocodile's bite, follow these steps:

1. Open the Biting crocodile.gmax file from the Chap 19 directory on the CD-ROM.

   This file includes a crocodile model created by Viewpoint Datalabs. For this model, the head, eyes, and upper teeth have been joined into a single object, and the pivot point for this object has been moved to where the jaw hinges.

2. Open the Create panel, select the Helpers category, and select the Manipulators subcategory from the drop-down list. Click the Slider button, and drag in the Perspective view above the crocodile. Name the slider **Croc Bite** and set the Maximum value to 60.

3. With the Slider selected, choose Animation ⇨ Wire Parameter ⇨ Wire Parameter to access the pop-up menu. Choose Object (Slider) ⇨ Value, drag the dotted line to the crocodile's head object, and click. Choose Transform ⇨ Rotation.

   The Parameter Wiring dialog box appears.

4. In the Parameter Wiring dialog box, click the direction arrow that points from the slider to the head. In the expression text area under the head object, enter the expression **angleaxis value [0,1,0]**, and click the Connect button. Then close the Parameter Wiring dialog box.

5. Click the Select and Manipulate button on the main toolbar, and drag the slider to the right.

The crocodile's mouth opens.

Figure 19-14 shows the crocodile biting using the slider control.

Figure 19-14: A slider control is wired to open the crocodile's mouth.

Summary

This chapter covered the basics of animating objects in gmax including working with time and keys. You've also learned about automatic key creation with the Animate key. There are a number of animation helps such as trajectories and ghosting. There are also several ways to automatically create keys like wiring parameters and animation modifiers. This chapter covered the following topics:

✦ Controlling time and working with keys

✦ Using the two key creation modes

✦ Working with the TrackBar and the Motion panel

✦ Viewing and editing key values

✦ Using trajectories and ghosting

✦ Reusing animation sequences with the Merge Animation dialog box

✦ Creating custom parameters and wire parameters, and using manipulator helpers

After this brief introduction to animation, you're ready to move on to the Track View, which offers the ability to control every aspect of an animation.

✦   ✦   ✦

Graphing Animations with the Track View

As you move objects around in a viewport, you'll often find yourself eyeballing the precise location of an object in the scene. If you've ever found yourself wishing that you could precisely see all the values behind the scene, then you need to find the Track View.

The Track View can display all the details of the current scene, including all the parameters and keys. This view lets you manage and control all these parameters and keys without having to look in several different places.

The Track Views also include additional features that enable you to edit key ranges, add and synchronize sound to your scene, and work with animation controllers using function curves.

Learning the Track View Interface

You can open the Track View window by choosing Graph Editors ➪ Track View ➪ Open Track View or by clicking the Open Track View button on the main toolbar. After the Track View opens, you can give a unique name to a particular view using the Name field at the right end of the Track View window toolbar (initially it is named "Untitled 1"). These named views are then listed in the Track View menu. Any Track Views that are named are saved along with the scene file.

You can view the Track View dialog box within any of the viewports by right-clicking the viewport title and choosing Views ➪ Track ➪ New or the name of one of the saved Track View views from the pop-up menu.

In This Chapter

Learning the Track View interface

Working with keys and time ranges

Adjusting function curves

Filtering tracks

Assigning controllers

Optimizing animation keys

Using out-of-range types

Adding notes to a track

Synching animation to a sound track

The Track View toolbar

No single dialog box in gmax uses more buttons than the Track View window, shown in Figure 20-1. This is because the Track View has numerous functions.

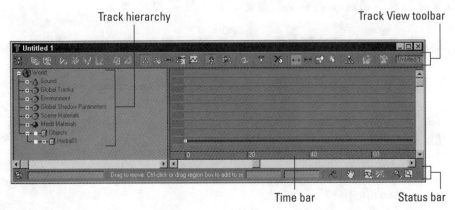

Figure 20-1: The Track View dialog box offers a complete hierarchical look at your scene.

The Track View toolbar contains two types of buttons: global and dynamic. The global buttons are described in Table 20-1. These buttons always stay the same. The dynamic buttons, on the other hand, change depending on the mode in which you are working; each of these buttons is discussed along with its corresponding mode in the "Track View Modes" section later in this chapter.

Table 20-1
Global Track View Toolbar Buttons

Toolbar Button	Name	Description
	Filters	Opens the Filter dialog box, where you can specify which tracks will appear
	Copy Controller	Copies the selected track for pasting elsewhere
	Paste Controller	Pastes the last copied track
	Assign Controller	Enables you to assign a controller to the selected track
	Delete Controller	Removes the current controller

Toolbar Button	Name	Description
	Make Controller Unique	Changes an instanced track to one that is unique
	Parameter Out-of-Range Types	Opens the Parameter Curve Out-of-Range Types dialog box, where you can make tracks loop and cycle
	Add Note Track	Adds a note track to the current track for recording information
	Delete Note Track	Deletes an associated note track
	Edit Keys	Enables edit keys mode
	Edit Time	Enables edit time mode
	Edit Ranges	Enables edit ranges mode
	Position Ranges	Enables position ranges mode
	Function Curves	Enables function curves mode
	Snap Frames	Causes moved tracks to snap to the nearest frame
	Lock Selection	Prevents any changes to the current selection
	Track View Utilities	Opens a dialog box of available Track View utilities (currently there are no utilities available in gmax)

Note Depending on the size of the Track View window, you may need to drag the toolbar to the left to see the buttons at the right end of the toolbar.

Tracks

Below the toolbar is a hierarchical list of all the tracks. The track names are listed in the pane on the left, while the pane on the right displays the time range, keys, or function curves, depending on the mode. You can pan the left pane by clicking and dragging on a blank section of the pane: The cursor changes to a hand to indicate when you can pan the pane.

Below the right pane is the Time Ruler, which displays the current time as specified in the Time Configuration dialog box.

Tip   You can drag the Time Ruler vertically in the right pane. You can also drag the sep-arator between the two panes.

Each track can include several subtracks. To display these subtracks, click the plus (+) sign to the left of the track name. To collapse a track, click the minus (–) sign.

Note   You can also select, expand, and collapse tracks using the right-click pop-up menu.

The hierarchy includes many different types of tracks. An icon appearing to the left of a track's name identifies its type. Table 20-2 describes the various track types and the icons that identify them.

	Table 20-2 Track Icons	
Icon	**Name**	**Description**
⬤	World	The root of the scene (which holds all tracks)
▲	Sound	Enables you to add sound to the scene
◉	Container	Can hold several different tracks
⬤	Materials	Indicates materials
▨	Maps	Indicates maps
▣	Objects	Indicates objects that are visible in the viewports
▷	Controllers	Indicates controllers
◆	Modifiers	Indicates modifiers
▷	Note Tracks	Marks note tracks

By default, every scene includes the following tracks: World, Sound, Global Tracks, Environment, Global Shadow Parameters, Scene Materials, Medit Materials (for materials in the Material Editor), and Objects.

The Shift, Ctrl, and Alt keys make selecting and deselecting multiple tracks possible. To select a contiguous range of tracks, select a single track, then select another track while holding down the Shift key. This selects the two tracks and all tracks in between. Hold down the Ctrl key while selecting tracks to select multiple tracks that are not contiguous. The Alt key removes selected items from the selection set.

Status bar

At the bottom edge of the Track View window is the status bar, which includes several fields and buttons for displaying information and navigating the window, as shown in Figure 20-2. Starting from the left is the Zoom Selected Object button. Next is the Select by Name field, in which you can type a name to locate any tracks with that name. To the right of the Select by Name field is the Prompt Line, which displays instructions about what is expected next.

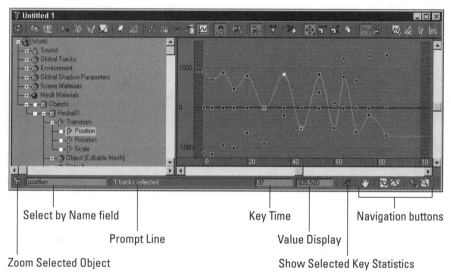

Figure 20-2: The Track View status bar includes buttons for navigating the window.

 Note   The Select by Name field can also use wildcard characters such as * (asterisk) and ? (question mark) to find several tracks at once.

The Key Time and Value Display fields display the current time and value. You can enter values in these fields to change the value for the current time. You can also enter an expression in these fields in which the variable n equals the key time or value. For example, to specify a key value that is 20 frames from the current frame, enter $n + 20$ (where you supply the current value in place of n). You can also include any function valid for the Expression controller, such as $\sin(\ )$ or $\log(\ )$.

Cross-Reference   The functions that are part of the Expression controller are presented in Chapter 22, "Creating Automatic Actions with Controllers."

Table 20-3 describes the status bar buttons.

	Table 20-3 Status Bar Buttons	
Button	**Name**	**Description**
	Zoom Selected Object	Places current selection at the top of the hierarchy
	Show Selected Key Statistics	Displays the frame number and values next to each key
	Pan	Pans the view
	Zoom Horizontal Extents, Zoom Horizontal Extents Keys	Displays the entire horizontal track or keys
	Zoom Value Extents	Displays the entire vertical track
	Zoom, Zoom Time, Zoom Values	Zooms in and out of the view
	Zoom Region	Zooms within a region selected by dragging the mouse

Track View Modes

The Track View includes five modes that enable you to work with keys, time, ranges, position ranges, and function curves. The mode is set using the buttons on the Track View toolbar.

Edit keys mode

The edit keys mode is the default mode when the Track View opens. It displays keys as small ovals and range bars for each track. Keys appear only within controller tracks.

You can use this mode to add, delete, move, align, slide, and scale the keys. You can also add and delete visibility tracks, which make an object visible or invisible, using edit keys mode. Figure 20-3 shows the Track View in edit keys mode.

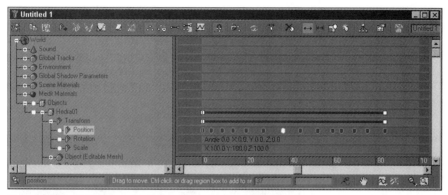

Figure 20-3: Edit keys mode lets you work with keys.

Although the edit keys mode is the default mode, you can return to this mode at any time by clicking on the Edit Keys button on the Track View toolbar. In edit keys mode, several new buttons appear on the Track View toolbar. These buttons are described in Table 20-4.

| | Table 20-4 | |
| | **Edit Keys Mode Buttons** | |
Button	*Name*	*Description*
	Add Visibility Track	Adds a track to an object for controlling its visibility
	Align Keys	Moves all selected keys to the same location
	Delete Keys	Deletes the selected keys
	Move Keys	Enables you to move the selected keys
	Slide Keys	Enables you to slide the selected keys
	Scale Keys	Enables you to scale the selected keys
	Add Keys	Enables you to add new keys to a track
	Modify Subtree	Causes changes to a parent to affect its children
	Properties	Displays a dialog box of properties associated with the track

Edit time mode

Edit time mode lets you work with time sections. Keys and range bars are also displayed but cannot be edited. Edit time mode lets you copy and paste time ranges between several different tracks, regardless of type. Figure 20-4 shows the Track View in edit time mode. I discuss the functions of this mode later in the chapter in the "Editing Time" section.

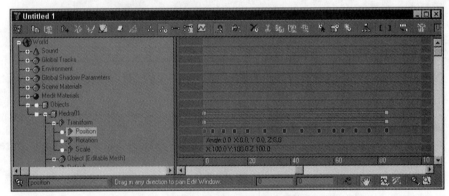

Figure 20-4: Edit time mode lets you work with blocks of time.

Clicking on the Edit Time button on the toolbar places you in edit time mode. In edit time mode, the buttons described in Table 20-5 become available.

	Table 20-5 Edit Time Mode Buttons	
Button	**Name**	**Description**
![Delete Time]	Delete Time	Deletes the selected block of time
![Cut Time]	Cut Time	Deletes the selected block of time, and places it on the clipboard for pasting
![Copy Time]	Copy Time	Makes a copy of the selected block of time on the clipboard for pasting
![Paste Time]	Paste Time	Inserts the current clipboard time selection
![Reverse Time]	Reverse Time	Reverses the order of the selected time block
![Select Time]	Select Time	Enables you to select a block of time by clicking and dragging

Button	Name	Description
	Scale Time	Scales the current time block
	Insert Time	Inserts an additional amount of time
	Modify Subtree	Causes changes to a parent to affect its children
[	Exclude Left End Point	Leaves the left end point out of the current time block
]	Exclude Right End Point	Leaves the right end point out of the current time block
	Reduce Keys	Optimizes the current time selection by eliminating unnecessary keys

Edit ranges mode

In edit ranges mode, all tracks appear as range bars. This makes scaling or sliding the track easy, but you can't edit the keys. Figure 20-5 shows the Track View in edit ranges mode. No new buttons are added to the toolbar in edit ranges mode, except the Modify Subtree button, which is explained earlier in this chapter.

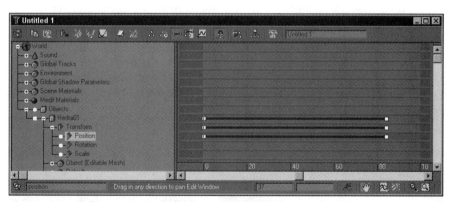

Figure 20-5: Edit ranges mode lets you work with ranges.

Position ranges mode

This mode also shows all tracks as range bars. In this mode, you can move and scale a range bar independently of its keys, ignoring any keys that are out of range. The Recouple Ranges button is added to the toolbar in this mode and can be used to line up the keys with the range again. The left end of the range aligns with the first key, and the right end aligns with the last key.

Figure 20-6 shows the Track View in position ranges mode. All other buttons for this mode are global and are covered earlier in the chapter.

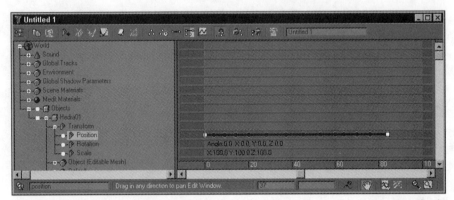

Figure 20-6: Position ranges mode lets you move the ranges without moving the keys.

Function curves mode

Function curves are graphs of a controller's value over time. In function curves mode, you can alter the shape of these curves. Each key represents a vertex on the curve. You can edit and add new keys to each curve. If a key is added to a track without any controller, a new controller is automatically assigned to the track. Figure 20-7 shows the Track View in function curves mode. The toolbar has been dragged to the left to show its far end.

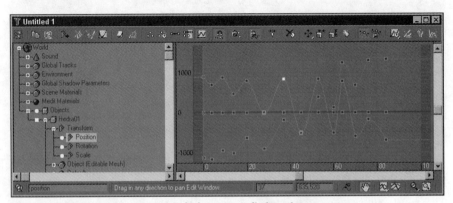

Figure 20-7: Function curves mode lets you edit function curves.

Function curves mode enables several new buttons, which Table 20-6 describes.

	Table 20-6	
	Function Curves Mode Buttons	
Button	**Name**	**Description**
	Freeze Nonselected Curves	Prevents editing of unselected curves
	Align Keys	Moves all selected keys to the same location
	Delete Keys	Deletes the selected keys
	Move Keys, Move Horizontal, Move Vertical	Moves the selected function curve point
	Scale Keys	Scales the selected keys' positions horizontally
	Scale Values	Scales the selected keys' values vertically
	Add Keys	Enables you to add keys to the function curve
	Show Tangents	Displays the Bézier curve handles
	Lock Tangents	Prevents the curve handles from moving
	Apply Ease Curve, Apply Multiplier Curve	Applies an ease or multiplier curve
	Delete Ease/Multiplier Curve	Removes the ease or multiplier curve
	Enable Ease/Multiplier Curve Toggle	Turns the ease or multiplier curve on or off
	Ease Curve Out-of-Range Types	Opens a dialog box in which you can select an out-of-range type
	Multiplier Curve Out-of-Range Types	Opens a dialog box in which you can select an out-of-range type
	Properties	Displays a dialog box of properties associated with the track

Working with Keys

Keys define the main animation points in an animation. gmax interpolates all the positions and values between the key points to generate the animation. Using the Track View and edit keys mode, you can edit these animation keys with precision. (The buttons that are used to edit keys are described in Table 20-4.)

Adding and deleting keys

With edit keys mode enabled and an animation track selected, you can add a key by clicking the Add Keys button and clicking the location where the new key should appear. Each new key is set with the interpolated value between the existing keys.

To delete keys, select the keys and click the Delete Keys button or press the Delete key on the keyboard. By selecting the track name and pressing the Delete key, you can delete all keys in a track.

Moving, sliding, and scaling keys

The Move Keys button lets you select and move a key to a new location. You can clone keys by holding down the Shift key while moving a key.

The Slide Keys button lets you select a key and move all adjacent keys in unison to the left or right. If the selected key is moved to the right, all keys from that key to the end of the animation slide to the right. If the key is moved to the left, then all keys to the beginning of the animation slide to the left.

The Scale Keys button lets you move a group of keys closer together or farther apart. The scale center is the current frame. You can use the Shift key to clone keys while dragging.

Aligning keys

You can move selected keys to the current time using the Align Keys button. This feature works in both edit keys and function curves modes.

Editing keys

To edit the key parameters for any controller, click the Properties button; this opens the Key Info dialog box for most controllers. You can also access this dialog box by right-clicking a key and selecting Properties from the pop-up menu.

Using visibility tracks

When an object track (a track within the Objects hierarchy that is identified with a yellow cube icon to the left of its name) is selected, you can add a visibility track using the Add Visibility Track button. This track enables you to make the object visible or invisible during a selected range of frames. The selected track is automatically assigned the Bézier controller, but you can change it to an On/Off controller if you want that type of control. You can use function curves mode to edit the visibility track.

Editing Time

In some cases, directly working with keys isn't what you want to do. For example, if you need to change the animation length from six seconds to five seconds, you'll want to work in Track View's edit time mode. To switch to this mode, click the Edit Time button on the Track View toolbar. (The buttons used in this mode are described in Table 20-5.)

Selecting time

Before you can scale, cut, copy, or paste time, you need to select a track and then select a time block. To select a section of time, click the Select Time button and drag the mouse over the time block.

Deleting, cutting, copying, and pasting time

After you select a block of time, you can delete it by clicking the Delete Time button. Another way to delete a block of time is to use the Cut Time button, which removes the selected time block but places a copy of it on the clipboard for pasting. The Copy Time button also adds the time block to the clipboard for pasting, but it leaves the selected time in the track.

After you copy a time block to the clipboard, you can paste it to a different location within the Track View. The track where you paste it must be of the same type as the one from which you copied it.

All keys within the time block are also pasted, and you can select whether they are pasted relatively or absolutely. *Absolute* pasting adds keys with the exact values as the ones on the clipboard. *Relative* pasting adds the key value to the current initial value at the place where the key is pasted.

You can enable the Exclude Left End Point and Exclude Right End Point buttons when pasting multiple sections next to each other. By excluding either end point, the time block loops seamlessly.

Reversing, inserting, and scaling time

The Reverse Time button flips the keys within the selected time block.

The Insert Time button lets you insert a section of time anywhere within the current track. To insert time, click and drag to specify the amount of time to insert; all keys beyond the current insertion point slide to accommodate the inserted time.

The Scale Time button scales the selected time block. This feature causes all keys to be pushed closer together or farther apart.

Reducing keys

The Reduce Keys button enables you to optimize the number of keys used in an animation. Several modifiers calculate keys for every frame in the scene, which can increase your file size greatly. By optimizing with the Reduce Keys button, you can reduce the file size and complexity of your animations.

Clicking the Reduce Keys button opens the Reduce Keys dialog box, shown in Figure 20-8. The threshold value determines how close to the actual position the solution must be to eliminate the key.

Figure 20-8: The Reduce Keys dialog box lets you optimize the number of keys in an animation.

Setting ranges

The position ranges mode enables you to move ranges without moving keys. For example, this mode lets you remove the first several frames of an animation without moving the keys.

Adjusting Function Curves

When an object is moving through a scene, estimating the exact point where its position changes direction can sometimes be difficult. Function curves provide this information by presenting a controller's value as a function of time. Each key is a vertex in the curve.

Function curves mode lets you edit and work with these curves for complete control over the animation parameters. (The buttons used with this mode are described in Table 20-6.)

Inserting new keys

Function curves with only two keys are always linear. You can add some curvature to the line with the addition of another point or key. To add another key, click the Add Keys button, and then click the curve where you want to place the key.

If the curve contains multiple curves, such as a curve for the RGB color values, then a point is added to each curve.

Moving keys

The Move Keys button enables you to move individual keys by dragging them. It also includes flyouts for constraining the key movement to a horizontal or vertical direction.

Scaling keys and values

The Scale Keys button moves the selected keys toward or away from the current time. This moves keys only horizontally.

The Scale Values button moves the selected keys toward or away from the zero value. This moves keys only vertically.

Working with tangents

Keys that have the Custom tangent type selected in the Key Info dialog box have tangents with connected handles when viewed in Function Curve mode if the Show Tangents button is enabled. If a key doesn't display these handles, you can right click on the key to open the Key Info dialog. From this dialog box, the Custom option is the last icon for the In and Out curves. These tangents are lines that extend from the key point with a handle on each end. By moving these handles, you can alter the curvature of the curve around the key.

The Key Info dialog box, which you can open by selecting a key and clicking the Properties button or by right-clicking the key, lets you specify two different types of tangent points: Continuous and Discontinuous. *Continuous* tangents are points with two handles that are on the same line. The curvature for continuous tangents is always smooth. *Discontinuous* tangents have any angle between the two handle lines. These tangents form a sharp point.

Tip   Holding down the Shift key while dragging a handle lets you drag it independently of the other handle.

The Lock Tangents button lets you change the handles of several keys at the same time. If this button is disabled, adjusting a tangent handle affects only the key of that handle.

Applying ease and multiplier curves

You can apply ease curves to smooth the timing of a function curve. You can apply multiplier curves to alter the scaling of a function curve. You can use ease and multiplier curves to automatically smooth or scale an animation's motion. Each of these buttons adds a new track and function curve underneath the selected controller track. Figure 20-9 shows the Track View after an ease curve have been applied.

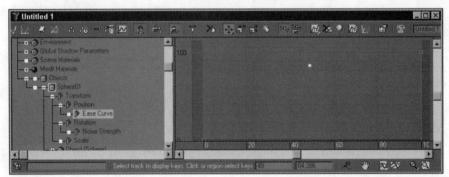

Figure 20-9: When ease and multiplier curves are added to a track, they become subtracks.

Note   Not all controllers can have an ease or multiplier curve applied.

You can delete these tracks and curves using the Delete Ease/Multiplier Curve button. It becomes enabled once you select the Ease Curve (or Multiplier Curve) track. You can also enable or disable these curves with the Enable Ease/Multiplier Curve Toggle button.

After you apply an ease or multiplier curve, you can assign the type of curve to use with the Ease Curve Out-of-Range Types button. This button opens the Ease Curve Out-of- Range Types dialog box, shown in Figure 20-10. The dialog box includes seven different ease curves. By clicking the buttons below the types, you can specify an ease curve for the beginning and end of the curve. The seven ease types include Constant, Cycle, Loop, Ping Pong, Linear, Relative, and Identity. For an explanation of these types, see the section "Using Out-of-Range Types" later in this chapter.

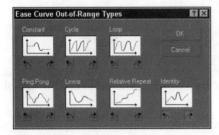

Figure 20-10: The Ease Curve Out-of-Range Types dialog box lets you select the type of ease curve to use.

Note In the Identity Curve Out-of-Range Types dialog box is an option that isn't present in the Parameter Curve Out-of-Range Types dialog box. The Identity option begins or ends the curve with a linear slope that produces a gradual, constant rate increase.

Tutorial: Animating a hyper pogo stick

As an example of working with function curves, we'll create a pogo stick that hops progressively higher.

To animate a hyper pogo stick using function curves, follow these steps:

1. Open the Hyper Pogo Stick.gmax file from the Chap 20 directory on the CD-ROM.

   This file contains a simple pogo stick model made from primitives.

2. Open the Track View, and locate the pogo stick group's Position track. (You can find this track under the Objects ⇨ Pogo Stick ⇨ Transform tracks.) Click the Assign Controller button to open the Assign Position Controller dialog box. Select the Bézier Position Controller, and click OK.

3. Click the Function Curves button to display the function curve for this track.

   Notice the three different curves: one red, one blue, and one green. These colors correspond to the default coordinate axes displayed in the lower-left corner of the viewport, so red is the X-axis, green is the Y-axis, and blue is the Z-axis.

4. Click the Add Keys button, and then click six different points along any one of the curves.

   Points are added on all three lines regardless of which line you click.

5. Next, click the Move Keys button, and drag the second, fourth, and sixth points for the Z-axis (blue line) upward at increasing heights to create three peaks. Also drag each point on the X-axis (red line) upward to form a straight line of increasing slope.

Note If you cannot see all the keys on a single screen, click the Zoom Value Extents button in the lower-right corner of the Track View.

These curves define the motions of the pogo stick, which bounces up and down along the Z-axis and gradually moves to the right along the X-axis. Figure 20-11 shows the function curves.

If you click the Play Animation button at this point, the motion may not be noticeable. This is because the values are so small. Notice how the values in Figure 20-11 range only between –100 and 100.

6. You can fix this by scaling the values. Click the Scale Values button, and select all the nonzero points on the X- and Z-axis curves by holding down the Ctrl key and dragging the points upward. Use the Zoom Value Extents button to resize the window, and continue to drag until the first peak is around 200.

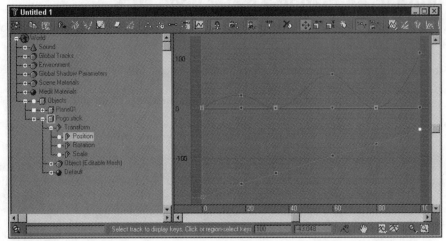

Figure 20-11: The function curves define the motions of the pogo stick object.

Figure 20-12 shows the results after scaling the values.

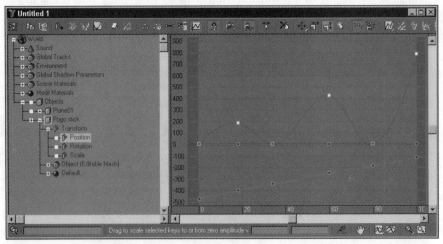

Figure 20-12: After you scale the values, the motions are visible in the viewports.

Figure 20-13 shows the pogo stick as it bounces along its way.

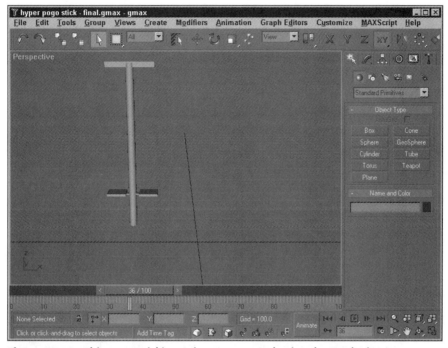

Figure 20-13: This pogo stick's motion was created using the Track View.

Filtering Tracks

With all the information included in the Track View, finding what you need can be difficult. The Filters button on the left end of the Track View window toolbar can help. Clicking this button opens the Filters dialog box, shown in Figure 20-14.

Tip Right-clicking the Filters button reveals a quick list of filter items.

Using this dialog box, you can limit the number of tracks that are displayed in the Track View. The Show section contains many display options. The Hide By Controller Type pane lists all the available controllers. Any controller types selected from this list do not show up in the Track View. You can also elect to not display objects by selecting Hide By Category.

The Show Only group includes options for displaying only the Animated Tracks, Selected Objects, Selected Tracks, Visible Objects, or any combination of these. For example, if you wanted to see the animation track for a selected object, select the Animated Tracks option and click the OK button, then open the Filters dialog box again, select Selected Objects, and click OK.

You can also specify whether the function curve display includes the Position, Rotation, and Scale components for each axis or the RGB color components.

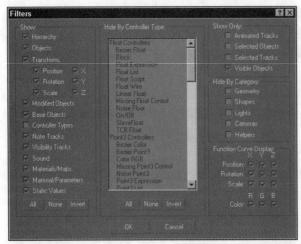

Figure 20-14: The Filters dialog box lets you focus on the specific tracks.

Working with Controllers

Controllers offer an alternative to manually positioning keys. Each controller can automatically control a key's position or a parameter's value. The Track View window toolbar includes three buttons for working with controllers. The Copy Controller and Paste Controller buttons let you move existing controllers between different tracks, and the Assign Controller button lets you add a new controller to a track.

Cross-Reference Chapter 22, "Creating Automatic Actions with Controllers," covers all the various controllers used to automate animated sequences.

Although the buttons are labeled Copy Controller and Paste Controller, they can be used to copy different tracks. Tracks can only be copied and pasted if they are of the same type. You can copy only one track at a time, but that single controller can be pasted to multiple tracks. A pasted track can be a copy or an instance, and you have the option to replace all instances. For example, if you have several objects that move together, using the Replace All Instances option when modifying the track for one object modifies the tracks for all objects that share the same motion.

All instanced copies of a track change when any instance of that track is modified. To break the linking between instances, you can use the Make Controller Unique button.

Clicking the Assign Controller button opens the Assign Controller dialog box, where you can select the controller to apply. If the controller types are similar, the keys are maintained, but a completely different controller replaces any existing keys in the track.

Using Out-of-Range Types

Using the edit ranges mode, you can make the range of a selected track smaller than the range of the whole animation. These tracks then go out of range at some point during the animation. The Ease/Multiplier Curve Out-of-Range Types buttons are used to tell the track how to handle its out-of-range time.

The Ease/Multiplier Curve Out-of-Range Types buttons open the Param Curve Out-of-Range Types dialog box, shown in Figure 20-15. You can access these buttons by selecting an Ease or Multiplier track in Function Curves mode. The appropriate button then becomes enabled.

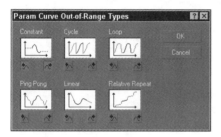

Figure 20-15: The Param Curve Out-of-Range Types dialog box lets you choose how to handle out-of-range values.

This dialog box includes six options:

✦ **Constant:** Holds the value constant for all out-of-range frames

✦ **Cycle:** Repeats the track values as soon as the range ends

✦ **Loop:** Repeats the range values, like the Cycle option, except the beginning and end points are interpolated to provide a smooth transition

✦ **Ping Pong:** Repeats the range values in reverse order after the range end is reached

✦ **Linear:** Projects the range values in a linear manner when out of range

✦ **Relative Repeat:** Repeats the range values offset by the distance between the start and end values

Adding Note Tracks

You can add note tracks to any track and use them to attach information about the track. The Add Note Track button is used to add a note track, which is marked with a yellow triangle and cannot be animated.

After a note track has been added in the left pane, use the Add Keys button in edit keys mode to position a note key in the track pane by clicking in the note track.

This adds a small note icon. Right-clicking the note icon opens the Notes dialog box, where you can enter the notes, as shown in Figure 20-16. Each note track can include several note keys.

The Notes dialog box includes arrow controls that you can use to move between the various notes. The field to the right of the arrows displays the current note key number. The Time value displays the frame where a selected note is located, and the Lock Key option locks the note to the frame so it can't be moved or scaled.

You can use the Delete Note Track button to delete a selected note track.

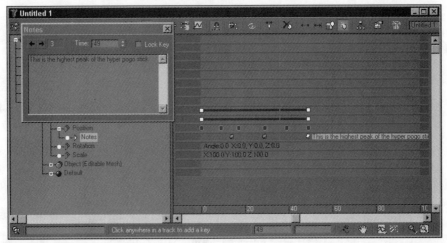

Figure 20-16: The Notes dialog box lets you enter notes and position them next to keys.

Synchronizing to a Sound Track

One of the default tracks for any scene is the sound track. Included in the Sound hierarchy is the metronome track. You can also set up a sound file using the Sound Options dialog box, shown in Figure 20-17. You can open this dialog box by right-clicking on the Metronome track and selecting Properties from the pop-up menu.

Figure 20-17: The Sound Options dialog box lets you select a sound to play during the animation.

You can make the sound track appear as a waveform curve underneath the Track Bar, which appears in the main interface under the Time Slider. This helps as you try to synchronize the sound to the movements in the viewports. To see this sound track, right-click the Track Bar and choose Configure ➪ Show Sound Track from the pop-up menu.

Using the Sound Options dialog box

You can use the Audio section of the Sound Options dialog box to load a sound or remove an existing sound. The Active option causes the sound file to play when the animation is played. The Choose Sound button can load AVI, WAV, and FLC file types. The dialog box also includes buttons to Remove Sound and Reload Sound. The Active option enables the sound file.

You can also set up a regular metronome beat with two tones. For a metronome, you can specify the beats per minute and the beats per measure. The first option sets how often the beats occur, and the second option determines how often a different tone is played. This dialog box also contains an Active option for turning the metronome on and off.

Tutorial: Adding sound to an animation

As an example of adding sound to an animation, we revisit the hyper pogo stick and synchronize its animation to a sound clip.

To synchronize an animation to a sound clip, follow these steps:

1. Open the Hyper Pogo Stick with Sound.gmax file from the Chap 20 directory on the CD-ROM.

2. In the Track View window, right-click one of the sound tracks and select Properties from the pop-up menu to open the Sound Options dialog box. In this dialog box, click the Choose Sound button. Then locate the boing.wav file from the Chap 20 directory on the CD-ROM, and click OK. Make sure the Active option is selected.

   The sound file appears as a waveform in the Track View, as shown in Figure 20-18.

 The Open Sound dialog box includes a play button that lets you play the sound before loading it.

3. Click the Edit Keys button, and move the keys to line up with the waveforms in the sound track.

4. Click the Play Animation button, and the sound file plays with the animation.

Figure 20-19 shows the sound track under the Track Bar for this example.

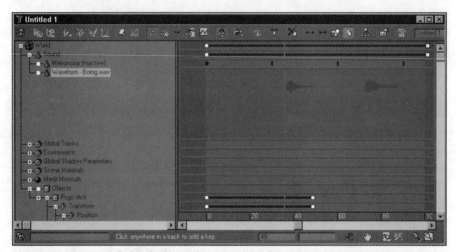

Figure 20-18: Sounds loaded into the sound track appear as waveforms.

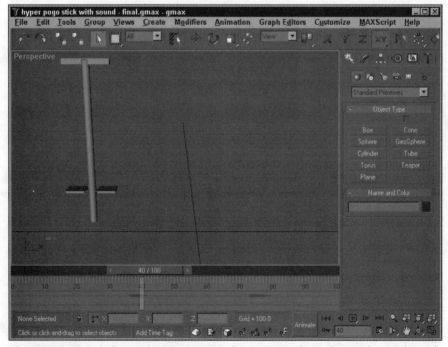

Figure 20-19: To help synchronize sound, the audio track can be made visible under the Track Bar.

Summary

Using the Track View, you have access to all the keys, parameters, and objects in a scene in one convenient location. Different features are available in the different layouts. This chapter covered the following topics:

- ✦ Learning the Track View interface elements
- ✦ Discovering how to work with keys, times, and ranges
- ✦ Controlling and adjusting function curves
- ✦ Selecting specific tracks using the Filter dialog box
- ✦ Assigning controllers
- ✦ Exploring the different out-of-range types
- ✦ Adding notes to a track
- ✦ Synchronizing animation to a sound track

The next chapter explores the various controllers that you can use to add all sorts of actions to your objects.

✦   ✦   ✦

Whoa, Betty! Constraining Motion

✦ ✦ ✦ ✦

In This Chapter

Using constraints

Attaching an object to the surface of an object

Making an object travel along a path with the Path constraint

Controlling the weighted position and orientation of objects

Shifting between two different controlling objects using the Link constraint

Following objects with the LookAt constraint

✦ ✦ ✦ ✦

The trick of animating an object is to make the object go where you want it to go. Animating objects deals not only with controlling the motion of the object, but controlling its lack of motion also. Constraints are a type of animation controller that you can use to restrict the motion of an object.

Using these constraints, you can force objects to stay attached to another object or follow a path. For example, the Attachment constraint can be used to make a robot's feet stay connected to a ground plane as it moves. The purpose of these constraints is to make animating your objects easier.

Using Constraints

You can apply constraints to selected objects using the Animation ⇨ Constraints menu. The constraints contained within this menu include Attachment, Surface, Path, Position, Link, LookAt, and Orientation.

After you select one of the constraints from the Animation ⇨ Constraints menu, a dotted link line extends from the current selected object to the mouse cursor. You can select a target object in any of the viewports to apply the constraint. The cursor changes to a plus sign when it is over a target object that can be selected. Selecting a constraint from the Constraints menu also opens the Motion panel where the settings of the constraint can be modified.

You can also apply constraints using the Assign Controller button found in the Motion panel and in the Track View window.

Find out more about Controllers in Chapter 22, "Creating Automatic Actions with Controllers," and more on the Track View window in Chapter 20, "Graphing Animations with the Track View."

Working with the Constraints

Each constraint is slightly different, but learning how to use these constraints will help you control the animated objects within a scene. You can apply several constraints to a single object. All constraints that are applied to an object are displayed in a list found in the Motion panel. From this list, you can select which constraint to make active and which to delete. You can also cut and paste constraints between objects.

Attachment constraint

The Attachment constraint determines an object's position by attaching it to the face of another object. This constraint lets you attach an object to the surface of another object. For example, you could animate the launch of a rocket ship with booster rockets that are attached with the Attachment constraint. The booster rockets would move along with the ship until the time when they are jettisoned.

The pivot point of the object that the constraint is applied to is attached to the target object. At the top of the Attachment Parameters rollout is a Pick Object button for selecting the target object to attach to. You can use this button to change the target object or to select the target object if the Animation ➪ Constraints menu wasn't used. There is also an option to align the object to the surface. The Update section enables you to manually or automatically update the attachment values.

The Attachment constraint shows up in the Position track of the Assign Controller rollout as the Position List controller. To minimize the effect of other controllers, set their Weight values in the Position List rollout to 0.

The Key Info section of the Attachment Parameters rollout displays the key number and lets you move between the various keys. The Time value is the current key value. In the Face field, you can specify the exact number of the face to attach to. To set this face, click the Set Position button and drag over the target object. The A and B values represent Barycentric coordinates for defining how the object lies on the face. You can change these coordinate values by entering values or by dragging the red cross-hairs in the box underneath the A and B values. The easiest way to position an object is to use the Set Position button to place the object and then to enhance its position with the A and B values. The Set Position button stays active until you click it again.

The TCB section sets the Tension, Continuity, and Bias values for the constraint. You can also set the Ease To and Ease From values.

Tutorial: Attaching a boat to the sea

One way to use the Attachment constraint is to attach characters or objects to the surface of a landscape object such as a terrain. In this example, you'll do just that by using the Attachment constraint to keep a boat object in contact with the rolling sea.

To constrain a sphere to a terrain object, follow these steps:

1. Open the Boat on rough seas.gmax file from the Chap 21 directory on the CD-ROM.

   This file includes a simple terrain plane and a boat object. The Pivot Point for the boat object has been moved to the base of the boat.

2. With the boat object selected, choose Animation ➪ Constraints ➪ Attachment Constraint. Then, while in pick object mode, select the terrain object.

   The boat becomes attached to the terrain object.

3. In the Attachment Parameters rollout, click the Set Position button and drag the object in the Perspective viewport until it is positioned on one of the terrain peaks.

Figure 21-1 shows the boat in its resulting position on the terrain peak.

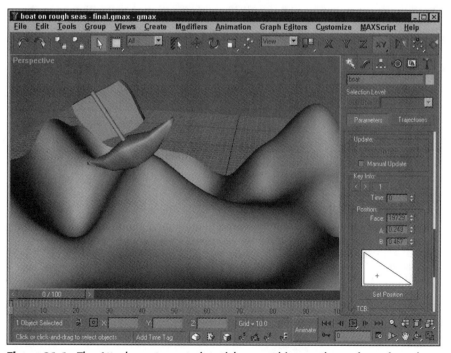

Figure 21-1: The Attachment constraint sticks one object to the surface of another.

Surface constraint

The Surface constraint moves an object so it is on the surface of another object. The object with Surface constraint applied to it is positioned so its pivot point is on the surface of the target object. You can use this constraint only on certain objects including Spheres, Cones, Cylinders, Toruses, Quad Patches, and Loft objects.

In the Surface Controller Parameters rollout is the name of the target object that was selected after the menu command. The Pick Surface button enables you to select a different surface to attach to. You can also select specific U and V Position values. Alignment options include No Alignment, Align to U, Align to V, and a Flip toggle.

Note   Don't be confused because the rollout is named Surface Controller Parameters instead of Surface Constraint Parameters. The developers at Discreet must have missed this one.

Tutorial: Rolling a tire down a hill with the Surface constraint

Moving a vehicle across a landscape can be a difficult procedure if you need to place every rotation and position key, but with the Surface constraint, it becomes easy. In this tutorial, we'll use the Surface constraint to roll a tire down a hill.

To roll a tire down a hill with the Surface Constraint, follow these steps:

1. Open the Tire rolling on a hill.gmax file from the Chap 21 directory on the CD-ROM.

    This file includes a cylinder hill and a wheel object made from primitives.

2. Create a dummy object from the Helpers category and position it so the dummy object's pivot point is at the base of the tire. Then link the tire object to the dummy object as a child—this causes the tire to move along with the dummy object.

3. Select the dummy object, choose Animation ➪ Constraints ➪ Surface Constraint, and select the hill object.

4. In the Surface Controller Parameters rollout, set the U Position value to 25 and the V Position value to 40 to move the tire down the hill.

5. Click the Animate button (or press the N key), drag the Time Slider to frame 100, and change the U Position to 40. Click the Animate button again to deactivate it, and click the Play Animation button to see the tire move down the hill.

Figure 21-2 shows the tire as it moves down the hill. In the Top view, you can see the function curves for this motion.

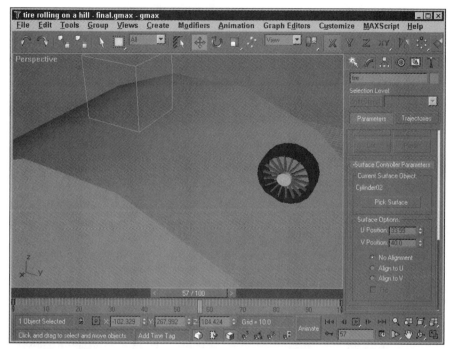

Figure 21-2: The Surface constraint can animate one object moving across the surface of another.

Path constraint

The Path constraint lets you select a spline path for the object to follow. The object will be locked to the path and will follow it even if the spline is changed. This is one of the most useful constraints because you can control the exact motion of an object using a spline. With gmax's spline features, you can control very precisely the motions of objects that are constrained with the Path constraint. A good example of this constraint is a train that is animated following a track. Using a spline to create the train tracks, the train is easily animated using the Path constraint.

When you choose the Animation ➪ Constraints ➪ Path Constraint menu command, you can select a single path for the object to follow. This path is added to a list of paths in the Path Parameters rollout.

The Path Parameters rollout also includes Add and Delete Path buttons for adding paths to and deleting paths from the list. If two paths are added to the list, then the object follows the position centered between these two paths. By adjusting the Weight value for each path, you can make the object favor a specific path.

The Path Options include a % Along Path value for defining the object's position along the path. This value ranges from 0 at one end to 100 at the other end. The Follow option causes the object to be aligned with the path as it moves, and the Bank option causes the object to rotate to simulate a banking motion.

The Bank Amount value sets the depth of the bank, and the Smoothness value determines how smooth the bank is. The Allow Upside Down option lets the object spin completely about the axis, and the Constant Velocity option keeps the speed regular. The Loop option returns the object to its original position for the last frame of the animation setting up a looping animation sequence. The Relative option lets the object maintain its current position and does not move the object to the start of the path. From its original position, it follows the path from its relative position. At the bottom of the Path Parameters rollout, you can select the axis to use.

Tutorial: Creating a dragonfly flight path

Another way to use splines is to create animation paths. As an example, we'll use a Helix spline to create an animation path. You can use splines in basically two ways for animation paths. One way is to create a spline and have an object follow it using either the Path constraint or the Path Follow Space Warp. The other way is to animate an object and then edit the Trajectory path.

In this tutorial, we'll use a simple Helix path and attach it to a Dragonfly model — the result will be a dizzy insect. The Dragonfly model was taken from the sampler CD-ROM provided by Zygote Media.

The Dragonfly model, along with many other Zygote models, is included on the CD-ROM provided with this book.

To attach an object to a spline path, follow these steps:

1. Open the Dizzy dragonfly.gmax file from the Chap 21 directory on the CD-ROM.

   This file contains the Dragonfly model and a Helix spline.

2. With the dragonfly selected, choose Animation ⇨ Constraints ⇨ Path Constraint. Then click the Helix spline to select it as the path to follow. Select the Follow option.

3. Click the Play Animation button in the Time Controls to see the dragonfly follow the path.

Figure 21-3 shows the dragonfly in its path up the spiral.

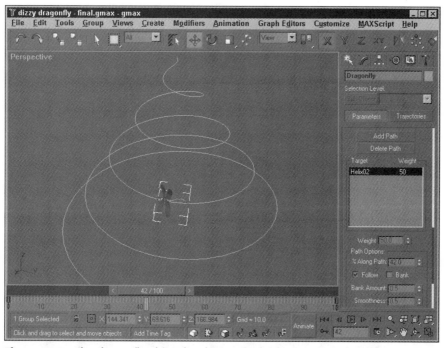

Figure 21-3: The dragonfly object has been attached to a spline path that it follows.

Position constraint

You can use the Position constraint to tie the position of an object to the weighted position of several target objects. For example, you could animate a formation of fighter jets by animating one of the jets and using Position constraints on all adjacent jets.

The Position constraint menu option lets you select a single target object, enabling you to place the pivot points of the two objects on top of one another. To add another target object, click the Add Position Target button in the Position Constraint rollout in the Motion panel. This button enables you to select another target object in the viewports; the target name appears within the target list in the rollout.

If you select a target name in the target list, you can assign a weight to the target. The constrained object is positioned close to the object with the higher weighted value. The Weight value provides a way to center objects between several other objects. The Keep Initial Offset option lets the object stay in its current location, but centers it relative to this position.

Figure 21-4 shows a sphere positioned between four diamond-shaped objects using the Position constraint. Notice how the weight of the left diamond object is weighted higher than the other targets, and the sphere is close to it.

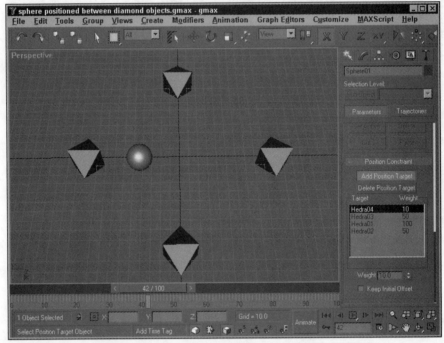

Figure 21-4: You can use the Position constraint to control the position of an object in relation to its targets.

Link constraint

The Link constraint can transfer hierarchical links between objects. This constraint can cause a child's link to be switched during an animation. Any time you animate a complex model with a dummy object, the Link constraint makes it possible to switch control from one dummy object to another during the animation sequence. This keeps the motions of the dummy objects simple.

The Link Parameters rollout includes Add Link, Link to World, and Delete Link buttons, a list of linked objects, and the Start Time field. To switch the link of an object, enter for the Start Time the frame where you want the link to switch, or drag the Time Slider and click the Add Link button. Then select the new parent object. The Link to World button includes a world link in the link list. The Delete key becomes active when you select a link in the list.

Note   If you create a link using the Link constraint, the object is not recognized as a child in any hierarchies.

All links are kept in a list in the Link Parameters rollout. You can add links to this list with the Add Link button or delete links with the Delete Link button. The Start Time field specifies when the selected object takes control of the link. The object listed in the list is the parent object, so the Start Time setting determines when each parent object takes control.

The Key Mode section lets you choose a No Key option. This option does not write any keyframes for the object. If you want to set keys, you can choose the Key Nodes options and set keys for the object itself (Child option) or for the entire hierarchy (Parent option). The Key Entire Hierarchy sets keys for the object and its parents (Child option) or for the object and its targets and their hierarchies (Parent option).

This constraint also includes the PRS Parameters and Key Info rollouts.

Caution   You cannot use Link constraints with inverse kinematics systems.

Tutorial: Skating a figure eight

For an animated object to switch its link from one parent to another halfway through an animation, you need to use the Link constraint. Rotating an object about a static point is easy enough — just link the object to a dummy object and rotate the dummy object. The figure-eight motion is more complex, but you can do it with the Link constraint.

To move an object in a figure eight, follow these steps:

1. Open the Figure skater skating a figure eight.gmax file from the Chap 21 directory on the CD-ROM.

This file includes a figure skater model imported from Poser and two dummy objects. The figure skater is linked to the first dummy object.

2. Click the Animate button (or press the N key), drag the Time Slider to frame 100, and rotate the first dummy object (the one closest to the figure skater) two full revolutions about its Z-axis in the Top viewport.

3. Select the second dummy object, and rotate it two full revolutions in the opposite direction, also about its Z-axis. Click the Animate button again to deactivate it.

4. With the figure skater selected, choose Animation ⇨ Constraints ⇨ Link Constraint. Then click the first dummy object (the top one in the Top viewport).

The Link constraint is assigned to the figure skater. This causes the figure skater to move from her origin. Use the Select and Move button to return her to her original position.

5. In the Link Parameters rollout, click the Add Link button. Click the first dummy object, and set the Start Time value to 0. Then click the second dummy object, and set the Start Time to 25. Finally, click the first dummy object again, and set the Start Time to 75.

6. Click the Play Animation button (or press the / key) to see the animation play.

Tip　Another way to accomplish this same motion is to create a spline of a figure eight and use the Path constraint.

Figure 21-5 shows the skater as she makes her path around the two dummy objects.

Figure 21-5: With the Link constraint, the figure skater can move in a figure eight by rotating about two dummy objects.

LookAt constraint

The LookAt constraint won't move an object, but it rotates the object so it is always orientated toward the target object. For example, you could use the LookAt constraint to animate the head of a character who is watching a flying bumblebee.

It is also very useful to apply to camera objects that follow a specific object throughout the animation.

After you select a target object, a single line extends from the object and points at the target object. This line, called the Viewline, is visible only within the viewports.

The LookAt Constraint rollout, like many of the other constraints, includes a list of targets. With the Add and Delete LookAt Target buttons, you can add and remove targets from the list. If several targets are on the list, the object is centered on a location between them. Using the Weight value, you can cause the various targets to have more of an influence over the orientation of the object. The Keep Initial Offset option prevents the object from reorienting itself when the constraint is applied. Any movement will be relative to it original position.

You can set the Viewline length, which is the distance that the Viewline extends from the object. The Viewline Length Absolute option draws the Viewline from the object to its target, ignoring the length value.

The Set Orientation button lets you change the offset orientation of the object using the Select and Rotation button on the main toolbar. If you get lost, Reset Orientation returns the orientation to its original position. You can select which local axis points at the target object.

The Upnode is an object that defines the up direction. If the LookAt axis ever lines up with the Upnode axis, then the object flips upside-down. To prevent this, you can select which local axis is used as the LookAt axis and which axis points at the Upnode. The World is the default Upnode object, but you can select any object as the Upnode object by deselecting the World object and clicking the button to its right.

To control the Upnode, you can select the LookAt option or the Axis Alignment option, which enables the Align to Upnode Axis option. Using this option, you can specify which axis points toward the Upnode.

Caution   The object using the LookAt constraint flips when the target point is positioned directly above or below the object's pivot point.

When you assign the LookAt constraint, the Create Key button for rotation changes to Roll. This is because the camera is locked to point at the assigned object and cannot rotate; it can only roll about the axis.

You can use the LookAt constraint to let cameras follow objects as they move around a scene. It is the default transform controller for Target camera objects.

Tutorial: Watching a dragonfly fly

Earlier in this chapter, I showed you an example of a dragonfly that was attached to a spiral path. To follow the dragonfly around his path, we could clone the original path and offset it so that it is slightly behind the dragonfly and then use a Path constraint to attach a camera to this cloned path. This method would create a camera that would follow the dragonfly on its spiral path, but it wouldn't be much different from the earlier example. Instead, in this tutorial, we'll use the LookAt constraint to watch the dragonfly as it circles about the spiral.

To have a camera watch the motions of an object with the LookAt constraint, follow these steps:

1. Open the Dizzy dragonfly and following camera.gmax file from the Chap 21 directory on the CD-ROM.

   This file is the same example that was used earlier, except I've added some cattails around the perimeter to give the scene some depth.

2. In the Create panel, click the Cameras category button and create a Free camera in any viewport. Position the camera in the center of the Helix.

3. With the camera selected, choose Animation ⇨ Constraints ⇨ LookAt Constraints. Click the dragonfly object to select it as the object to look at.

4. Move the camera up to the peak of the spiral and prepare to get really dizzy.

Figure 21-6 shows one frame of the dragonfly spinning along its path.

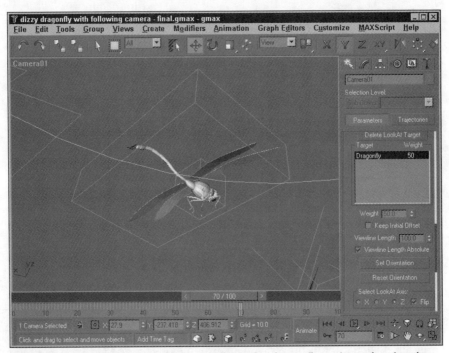

Figure 21-6: The camera in this scene follows the dragonfly on its path using the LookAt constraint.

Orientation constraint

You can use the Orientation constraint to lock the rotation of an object to another object. You can move and scale the objects independently, but the constrained object rotates along with the target object. A good example of an animation that uses this type of constraint is a satellite that orbits the Earth. You could offset the satellite and still constrain it to the Earth's surface. Then as the Earth moves, the satellite follows.

In the Orientation Constraint rollout, you can select several orientation targets and weight them in the same manner as with the Position constraint. The target with the greatest weight value has the most influence over the object's orientation. You can also constrain an object to the World object. The Keep Initial Offset option maintains the object's original orientation and rotates it relative to this original orientation. The Transform Rule setting determines whether the object rotates using the Local or World coordinate systems.

Summary

Using the Animation ⇨ Constraints menu, you can apply constraints to objects. This menu also lets you select a target object. You can use the various constraints to limit the motion of objects, which is helpful as you begin to animate. This chapter covered these topics:

✦ Learning to constrain an object to the surface of an object using the Attachment and Surface constraints

✦ Forcing an object to travel along a path with the Path constraint

✦ Controlling the position and orientation of objects with weighted Position and Orientation constraints

✦ Shifting between two different controlling objects using the Link constraint

✦ Following objects with the LookAt constraint

If you thought this chapter was cool, just wait until the next chapter, where I cover all the various controllers that are available in gmax.

✦　　✦　　✦

Creating Automatic Actions with Controllers

CHAPTER

22

✦ ✦ ✦ ✦

In This Chapter

Understanding the various controller types

Assigning controllers using the Motion panel and the Track View

Setting default controllers

Experimenting with controllers

Using the Numerical Expression Evaluator

Understanding the Expression controller interface

Learning about operators, variables, and functions

✦ ✦ ✦ ✦

When you first begin animating and working with keys, it seems amazing how easy it is to have gmax figure out all the frames between the start and end keys, especially if you've ever animated in 2D by drawing every frame. But soon you realize that animating with keys can be tough for complex realistic motions, and again, gmax comes to the rescue. You can use animation controllers to automate the creation of keys for certain types of motions.

Controllers store and manage the key values for all animations in gmax. When you animate an object using the Animate button, the default controller is automatically assigned. You can change the assigned controller or alter its parameters using the Motion panel or the Track View. This chapter explains how to work with controllers and examines all the various controllers that are available. For example, you can use the Noise controller to add random motion to a flag blowing in the wind or use the Waveform controller to produce regular repeating motions such as a sine or square wave.

Understanding Controller Types

Controllers are used to set the keys for animation sequences. Every object and parameter that is animated has a controller assigned, and almost every controller has parameters that you can alter to change its functionality. Some controllers present these parameters as rollouts in the Motion panel, and others use a Properties dialog box.

In gmax, there are five basic controller types that work with only a single parameter or track and one specialized controller type that manages several tracks at once (the Transform controllers). The type depends on the type of values the controller works with. The types include

✦ **Float controllers:** Used for all parameters with a single numeric value, such as Wind Strength and Sphere Radius

✦ **Point3 controllers:** Consist of color components for red, green, and blue, such as Diffuse and Background colors

✦ **Position controllers:** Control the position coordinates for objects, consisting of X, Y, and Z values

✦ **Rotation controllers:** Control the rotation values for objects along all three axes

✦ **Scale controllers:** Control the scale values for objects as percentages for each axis

✦ **Transform controllers:** A special controller type that applies to all transforms (position, rotation, and scale) at the same time, such as the Position, Rotation, Scale (PRS) controllers

Note   Understanding the different controller types is important. When you copy and paste controller parameters between different tracks, both tracks must have the same controller type.

Float controllers work with parameters that use float numbers, such as a sphere's Radius or a plane object's Scale Multiplier value. Float values are numbers with a decimal value, such as 2.3 or 10.99. A Float controller is assigned to any parameter that is animated. After it is assigned, you can access the function curves and keys for this controller in the Track View.

Assigning Controllers

Any object or parameter that is animated is automatically assigned a controller. The controller that is assigned is the default controller. The Animation panel in the Preference Settings dialog box lists and lets you change the default controllers. You can change this automatic default controller using the Track View window or the transformation tracks located in the Motion panel.

Automatically assigned controllers

The default controllers are automatically assigned for an object's transformation tracks when the object is created. For example, if you create a simple sphere and then open the Motion panel (which has the icon that looks like a wheel), you can find the transformation tracks in the Assign Controller rollout. The default Position controller is Bézier Position; the default Rotation controller is TCB Rotation; and the default Scale controller is the Bézier Scale controller, as shown in Figure 22-1.

Figure 22-1: The Motion panel displays all transform controllers applied to an object.

The default controller depends on the type of object. For example, the Barycentric Morph controller is automatically assigned when you create a morph compound object, and the Master Point controller is automatically assigned to any vertices or control point subobjects that are animated.

Note Because controllers are automatically assigned to animation tracks, they cannot be removed; they can only be changed to a different controller. There isn't a function to delete controllers.

Assigning controllers in the Motion panel

The top of the Motion panel includes two buttons: Parameters and Trajectories. Clicking the Parameters button makes the Assign Controller rollout available.

To change a transformation track's controller, select the track and click the Assign Controller button positioned directly above the list. An Assign Controller dialog box that is specific to the track you selected opens.

For example, Figure 22-2 shows the Assign Position Controller dialog box for selecting a controller for the Position track. The arrow mark (>) shows the current selected controller. At the bottom of the dialog box, the default controller type is listed. Select a new controller from the list, and click OK. This new controller now is listed in the track, and the controller's rollouts appear beneath the Assign Controller rollout.

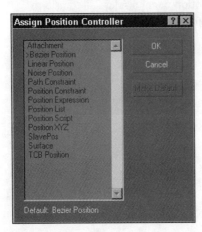

Figure 22-2: The Assign Position Controller dialog box lets you select a controller to assign.

Caution   You can assign controllers to other parameters for materials and modifiers, but you can assign controllers to the transformation tracks only using the Motion panel. All other controllers are assigned using the Track View.

For example, Figure 22-3 shows the Motion panel for a sphere object that has a Noise controller assigned to its Position track. Notice how the Noise Strength has become a subtrack under the Noise Position track.

Figure 22-3: The Motion panel displays all transform controllers applied to an object.

Assigning controllers in Track View

You can also use the Track View to assign controllers. To do this, locate and select the track to apply a controller to, and click the Assign Controller button in the Track View toolbar. An Assign Controller dialog box opens in which you can select the controller to use.

 Cross-Reference Chapter 20, "Graphing Animations with the Track View," covers the details of the Track View.

After a controller is assigned, you can also use the Copy Controller and Paste Controller buttons on the Track View toolbar to copy and paste controllers between tracks, but you can paste controllers only to similar types of tracks. When you paste controllers, the Paste dialog box, shown in Figure 22-4, lets you choose to paste the controller as a copy or as an instance. Changing an instanced controller's parameters changes the parameters for all instances. The Paste dialog box also includes an option to replace all instances. This option replaces all instances of the controller whether or not they are selected.

 Tip The Replace All Instances option in the Paste dialog box is very helpful when you have an array of objects. For example, if you create a jumping bean with a Noise controller assigned to it, then the Paste Controller button can be used to quickly paste the same Noise controller to all instances of the jumping bean in one operation.

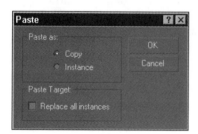

Figure 22-4: The Paste dialog box offers options for pasting controllers.

Setting Default Controllers

When you assign controllers using the Track View, the Assign Controller dialog box includes the option Make Default. With this option, the selected controller becomes the default for the selected track.

You can also set the global default controller for each type of track by choosing Customize ➪ Preferences, selecting the Animation panel, shown in Figure 22-5, and then clicking the Set Defaults button.

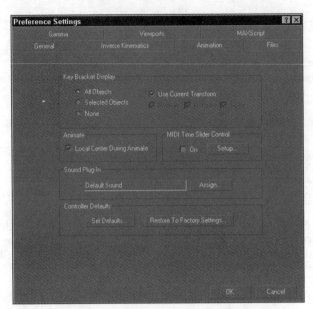

Figure 22-5: The Animation panel of the Preference Settings dialog box includes an option for setting the default controllers.

The Set Controller Defaults dialog box shown in Figure 22-6 opens, allowing you to set the default parameter settings, such as the In and Out curves or the default properties for the controller. To set the default controller, select a controller from the list and click the Set button to open a controller-specific dialog box where you can adjust the controller parameters. The Animation panel also includes a button to revert to the original settings.

Note Changing a default controller does not change any currently assigned controllers.

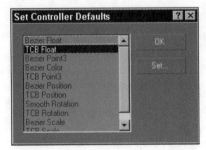

Figure 22-6: The Set Controller Defaults dialog box lists all the available default controllers.

Examining the Various Controllers

Now that you've learned how to assign a controller, let's take a look at the available controllers. gmax includes a vast assortment of controllers, and you can add more controllers as plug-ins.

Note The Constraints found in the Animation menu are also controllers. The menu for these controllers makes them easy to assign.

Earlier in the chapter, I mentioned six specific controller types. These types define the type of data with which the controller works. This section covers the various controllers according to the types of tracks with which they work.

Note Looking at the function curves for a controller provides a good idea of how you can control it, so many of the figures that follow show the various function curves for the different controllers.

Transform controllers

Multi-track transform controllers work with the Position, Rotation, and Scale tracks all at the same time. You access them by selecting the Transform track in the Motion panel and then clicking the Assign Controller button, or by choosing the Transform track in the Track View.

Note The Link Constraint can also be assigned to the Transform track.

Position/Rotation/Scale Transform controller

The Position/Rotation/Scale Transform controller is the default controller for all objects. This controller includes a Bézier controller for the Position and Scale tracks and the TCB Rotation controller for the Rotation track.

The PRS Parameters rollout, shown in Figure 22-7, lets you create and delete keys for Position, Rotation, and Scale transforms. The Position, Rotation, and Scale buttons control the fields that appear in the Key Info rollouts positioned below the PRS Parameters rollout.

Script controller

The Script controller is similar to the Expression controller, except that it can work with the MAXScript lines of code. Right-clicking a track with the Script controller assigned and selecting Properties opens the Script Controller dialog box, shown in Figure 22-8.

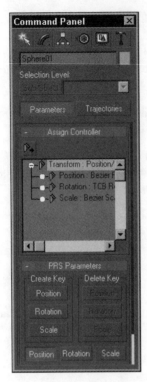

Figure 22-7: The PRS Parameters rollout is the default transform controller.

This dialog box includes a Script pane and a Results pane, along with buttons to Save and Load scripts. After a script loads, click the Evaluate button to execute the script.

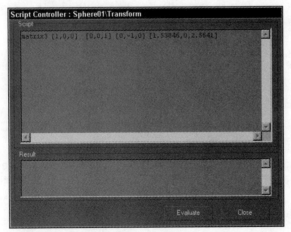

Figure 22-8: The Script Controller dialog box runs scripts to generate animation keys.

For more information on MAXScript, see Chapter 8, "Placing gmax on Autopilot with MAXScript."

Position track controllers

Position track controller types include some of the common default controllers and can be assigned to the Position track. They typically work with three unique values representing the X-, Y-, and Z-axes. These controllers can be assigned from the Motion panel and/or the Track View. Many of the controllers found in this menu are also found in the Rotation and Scale Controllers menu.

The Position, Rotation and Scale subtracks are only available if the PRS Transform controller is assigned to the Transform track.

Bézier controller

The Bézier controller is the default controller for many parameters. It enables you to interpolate between values using an adjustable Bézier spline. By dragging its tangent vertex handles, you can control the spline's curvature. Tangent handles produce a smooth transition when they lie on the same line, or you can create an angle between them for a sharp point. Figure 22-9 shows the Bézier controller assigned to a Position track.

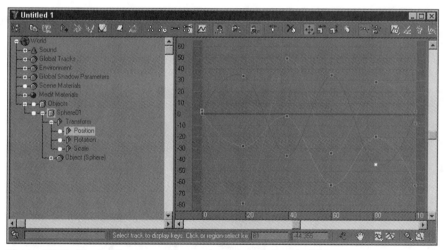

Figure 22-9: The Bézier controller produces smooth animation curves.

The Bézier controller parameters are displayed in the Motion panel under two rollouts: Key Info (Basic) and Key Info (Advanced).

At the top of the Key Info (Basic) rollout are two arrows and a field that shows the key number. The arrows let you move between the Previous and Next keys. Each vertex shown in the function curve represents a key. The Time field displays the frame number where the key is located. The Time Lock button next to the Time field can be set to prevent the key from being dragged in Track View. The value fields show the values for the selected track; the number of fields changes depending on the type of track that is selected.

At the bottom of the Key Info (Basic) rollout are two flyout buttons for specifying the In and Out curves for the key. The arrows to the sides of these buttons move between the various In/Out curve types. The curve types include Smooth, Linear, Step, Slow, Fast, Custom, and Tangent Copy.

Chapter 20, "Graphing Animations with the Track View," describes these various In/Out curve types.

The In and Out values in the Key Info (Advanced) rollout are enabled only when the Custom curve type is selected. These fields let you define the rate applied to each axis of the curve. The Lock button changes the two values by equal and opposite amounts. The Normalize Time button averages the positions of all keys. The Constant Velocity option interpolates the key between its neighboring keys to provide smoother motion.

Linear controller

The Linear controller interpolates between two values to create a straight line.

The Linear controller includes no parameters and can be applied to time or values. Figure 22-10 shows the function curves after the Linear controller is assigned; all curves are straight lines.

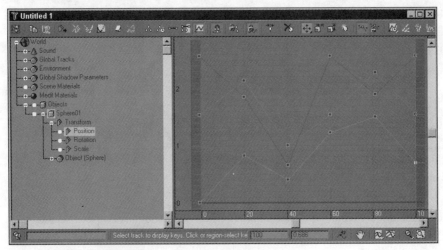

Figure 22-10: The Linear controller uses straight lines.

Noise controller

The Noise controller applies random variations in a track's values. In the Noise Controller dialog box shown in Figure 22-11, the Seed value determines the randomness of the noise, and the Frequency value determines how jagged the noise is. You can also set the Strength along each axis — the > (greater than) 0 option for each axis makes the noise values remain positive.

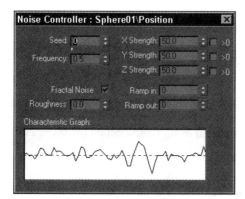

Figure 22-11: The Noise controller properties let you set the noise strength for each axis.

There is also an option to enable Fractal Noise with a Roughness setting.

The Ramp in and Ramp out values determine the length of time before or until the noise can reach full value. The Characteristic Graph gives a visual look at the noise over the range. Figure 22-12 shows the Noise controller assigned to the Position track.

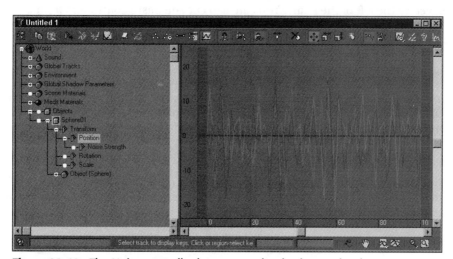

Figure 22-12: The Noise controller lets you randomly alter track values.

Expression controller

The Expression controller can define a mathematical expression that controls the track values. These expressions can use the values of other tracks and basic mathematical functions such as sines and logarithms to control animation keys.

The Expression controller is a complex controller that enables you to create detailed mathematical formulas for motions. It is discussed at the end of the chapter.

List controller

You can use the List controller to apply several controllers at once. This feature enables you to produce smaller, subtler deviations, such as adding some noise to a normal Bézier controller.

When the List controller is applied, the default track appears as a subtrack along with another subtrack labeled Available. By selecting the Available subtrack and clicking the Assign Controller button, you can assign additional controllers to the current track.

The List controller allows you to set Weights for each of its controllers. Using the Position List rollout, you can set the active controller and delete controllers from the list. You can also Cut and Paste controllers to other tracks.

All subtrack controllers are included in the List rollout of the Motion panel. You can also access this list by right-clicking the track and selecting Properties from the pop-up menu. The order of the list is important, because it defines which controllers are computed first.

The Set Active button lets you specify which controller you can interactively control in the viewport; the active controller is marked with an arrow, which is displayed to the left of the name. You can also cut and paste controllers from and to the list. Because you can use the same controller type multiple times, you can distinguish each one by entering a name in the Name field.

Figure 22-13 shows the List controller assigned to the Position track of a sphere. Listed are the Noise and Linear controllers and an Available track. The Linear controller was added by selecting the Available track and clicking the Assign Controller button. Notice in the function curves that the noise is secondary to the Linear motion.

Position XYZ controller

The Position XYZ controller splits position transforms into three separate tracks, one for each axis. Each axis has a Bézier controller applied to it, but each component track can be assigned a different controller. The Position XYZ Parameters rollout lets you switch between the component axes. Figure 22-14 shows the Position XYZ controller assigned to a Position track with a Noise controller assigned to the X position track, the Linear controller assigned to the Y position track, and the Bézier controller assigned to the Z position track.

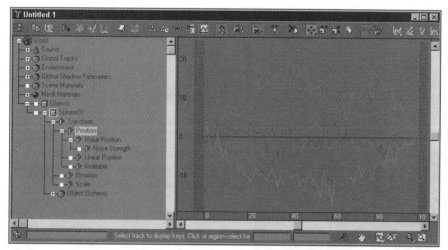

Figure 22-13: The List controller lets you assign multiple controllers to a single track.

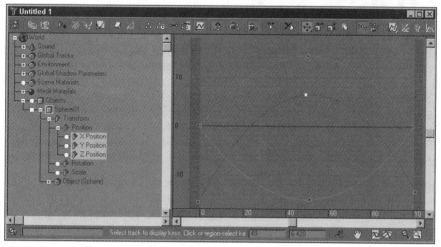

Figure 22-14: The Position XYZ controller splits each position axis into different components.

TCB controller

The TCB controller produces curved animation paths similar to the Bézier controller, except it uses the values for Tension, Continuity, and Bias to define their curvature.

The parameters for this controller are displayed in a single Key Info rollout. Like the Bézier controller rollouts, the TCB controller rollout includes arrows and Key, Time, and Value fields. It also includes a graph of the TCB values; the red plus (+) sign represents the current key's position while the rest of the graph shows the regular increments of time as black plus (+) signs. Changing the Tension, Continuity, and Bias values in the fields below the graph changes its shape. Right-clicking the track and selecting Properties from the pop-up menu opens the TCB graph dialog box, shown in Figure 22-15.

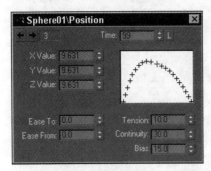

Figure 22-15: This dialog box shows and lets you control a curve defined by the Tension, Continuity, and Bias values.

The Tension value controls the amount of curvature: High Tension values produce a straight line leading into and away from the key, and low Tension values produce a round curve. The Continuity value controls how continuous, or smooth, the curve is around the key: The default value of 25 produces the smoothest curves, whereas high and low Continuity values produce sharp peaks from the top or bottom. The Bias value controls how the curve comes into and leaves the key point: High Bias values cause a bump to the right of the key, and low Bias values cause a bump to the left.

The Ease To and Ease From values control how quickly the key is approached or left.

Note   Enabling the trajectory path by clicking the Trajectory button in the Motion panel lets you see the changes to the path as they are made in the Key Info rollout.

Figure 22-16 shows three TCB curves assigned to the Position track of an object.

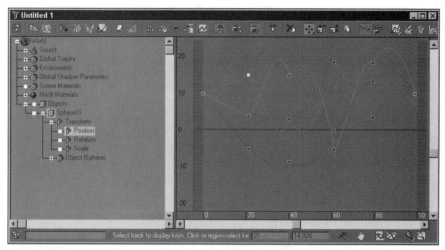

Figure 22-16: The TCB controller offers a different way to work with curves.

Rotation and Scale track controllers

The Rotation and Scale track controller types include some of the common default controllers and can be assigned to the Rotation and Scale tracks. They typically work with three unique values representing the X-, Y-, and Z-axes. These controllers can be assigned from both the Motion panel and the Track View. Many of the controllers found in this menu are also found in the Position Controllers menu. Only the controllers unique to the Rotation and Scale tracks are covered here.

Euler XYZ Rotation controller

The Euler XYZ Rotation controller lets you control the rotation angle along the X-, Y-, and Z-axes based on a single float value for each frame. Euler rotation is different from gmax's default rotation method (which is quaternion rotation and not as smooth).

The main difference is that Euler rotation gives you access to the function curves. Using these curves, you can smoothly define the rotation motion of the object.

Note   Euler XYZ Rotation values are in radians instead of degrees. Radians are much smaller values than degrees. A full revolution is 360 degrees or 2 times pi radians, so one degree equals about 0.0174 radians.

The Euler Parameters rollout lets you choose the Axis Order, the order in which the axes are calculated. You can also choose which axis to work with. Figure 22-17 shows all three Rotation tracks (with the Bézier controller applied to it) for the Euler XYZ controller.

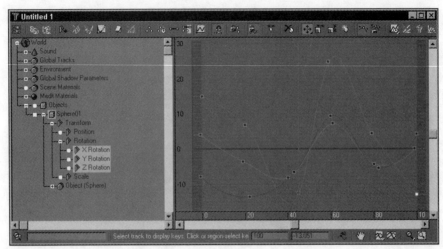

Figure 22-17: The Euler XYZ controller lets you assign separate float controllers to each axis.

Smooth Rotation controller

The Smooth Rotation controller automatically produces a smooth rotation. This controller doesn't add any new keys; it simply changes the timing of the existing keys to produce a smooth rotation. It has no parameters.

Scale XYZ controller

There is one controller that you can use only in Scale tracks. The Scale XYZ controller breaks scale transforms into three separate tracks, one for each axis. This feature enables you to precisely control the scaling of an object along separate axes. It is a better alternative to using Select and Non-Uniform Scale from the main toolbar because it is independent of the object geometry.

The Scale XYZ Parameters rollout lets you select an axis with which to work. This controller works the same way as the other position and rotation XYZ controllers.

Parameter controllers

Other types of controllers consist of miscellaneous collections that don't fit into the previous categories. Many of these controllers combine several controllers into one, such as the Block controller.

Most of these special-purpose controllers can be assigned only using the Track View window. The Motion panel contains only the tracks for transformations.

On/Off controller

The On/Off controller works on tracks that hold a binary value, such as the Visibility track; you can use it to turn the track on and off or to enable and disable options. In the Track View, each On section is displayed in blue, with keys alternating between on and off. No parameters exist for this controller. Figure 22-18 shows a Visibility track that has been added to a sphere object. This track was added using the Add Visibility Track button in Edit Keys mode. You can add keys with the Add Keys button. Each new key toggles the track on and off.

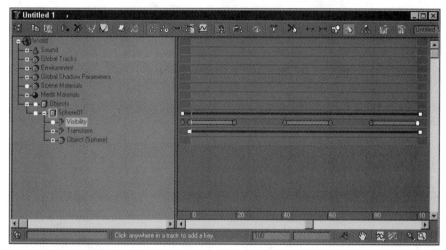

Figure 22-18: The On/Off controller lets you make objects appear and disappear.

Color RGB controller

You can use the Color RGB controller to animate colors. Color values are different from regular float values in that they include three values that represent the amounts of red, green, and blue (referred to as RGB values) that are present in the color. This data value type is known as Point3.

The Color RGB controller splits a track with color information into its component RGB tracks. You can use this controller to apply a different controller to each color component and also to animate any color swatch in gmax.

Figure 22-19 shows the function curves for the Color RGB controller assigned to the Diffuse Color track under the Material #1 track, including subtracks for Red, Green, and Blue. The figure shows the Bézier controller applied to the Red track, the Noise controller that is assigned to the Green track, and the Waveform controller with a triangle wave applied to the Blue track.

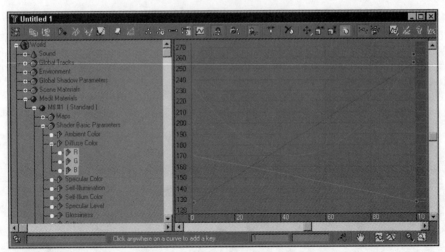

Figure 22-19: The Color RGB controller lets you assign different controllers to each color component.

Cubic Morph controller

You can assign the Cubic Morph controller to a morph compound object. You can find the track for this object under the Objects track. A subtrack of the morph object is the Morph track, which holds the morph keys.

The Cubic Morph controller uses Tension, Continuity, and Bias values to control how targets blend with one another. You can access these TCB values in the Key Info dialog box by right-clicking any morph key or by right-clicking the Morph track and selecting Properties from the pop-up menu.

 Note   You can also access the TCB values by right-clicking the keys in the Track Bar.

Barycentric Morph controller

The Barycentric Morph controller is automatically applied when a morph compound object is created. Keys are created for this controller based on the morph targets set in the Modify panel under the Current Targets rollout for the morph compound object. You can edit these keys using the Barycentric controller Key Info dialog box, which you can open by right-clicking a morph key in the Track View or in the Track Bar.

The main difference between the Cubic Morph controller and the Barycentric Morph controller is that the latter can have weights applied to the various morph keys.

The Barycentric Morph controller Key Info dialog box includes a list of morph targets. If a target is selected, its Percentage value sets the influence of the target. The Time value is the frame where this key is located. The TCB values and displayed curve control the Tension, Continuity, and Bias parameters for this controller. The Constrain to 100% option causes all weights to equal 100%; changing one value changes the other values proportionally if this option is selected.

Block controller

The Block controller combines several tracks into one block so you can handle them all together. This controller is located in the Global Tracks track. If a track is added to a Block controller, a Slave controller is placed in the track's original location.

To add a Block controller, select the Available track under the Block Control track under the Global Tracks track, and click the Assign Controller button. From the Assign Constant Controller dialog box that opens, select Master Block (Master Block is the only selection) and click OK. Right-click the Master Block track to open the Master Block Parameters dialog box, shown in Figure 22-20.

Figure 22-20: The Master Block Parameters dialog box lists all the tracks applied to a Block controller.

In the Master Block Parameters dialog box, you can add a track to the Block controller with the Add button. All tracks added are displayed in the list on the left. You can give each track a name by using the Name field. You can also use the Add Selected button to add any selected tracks. The Replace button lets you select a new controller to replace the currently selected track. The Load and Save buttons enable you to load or save blocks as separate files.

The Add button opens the Track View Pick dialog box, shown in Figure 22-21. This dialog box displays all valid tracks in a darker color to make them easier to see, while graying out invalid tracks.

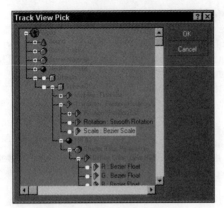

Figure 22-21: The Track View Pick dialog box lets you select the tracks you want to include in the Block controller.

Select the tracks that you want to include, and click the OK button. The Block Parameters dialog box shown in Figure 22-22 opens, in which you can name the block, specify Start and End frames, and choose a color. Click OK when you've finished with this dialog box.

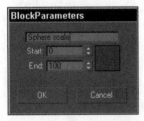

Figure 22-22: The Block Parameters dialog box lets you name a block.

Back in the Master Block Parameters dialog box, click the Load button to open a file dialog box where you can load a saved block of animation parameters. The saved block files have the .blk extension. After the parameters have loaded, the Attach Controls dialog box opens, as shown in Figure 22-23. This dialog box includes two panes. The Incoming Controls pane on the left lists all motions in the saved block. By clicking the Add button, you can add tracks from the current scene, to which you can copy the saved block motions.

Because the saved motions in the Incoming Controls pane match up with the Copy To entries in the right pane, the Add Null button adds a space in place of a specific track if you don't want a motion to be copied. The Match by Node button matches tracks by means of the Track View Pick dialog box.

Figure 22-24 shows a Block controller with several motions included. The MasterBlock track also includes a Blend subtrack for defining how the various tracks interact.

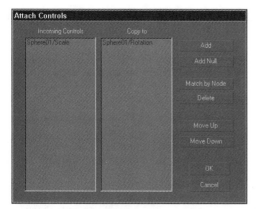

Figure 22-23: The Attach Controls dialog box lets you attach saved tracks to the Block controller.

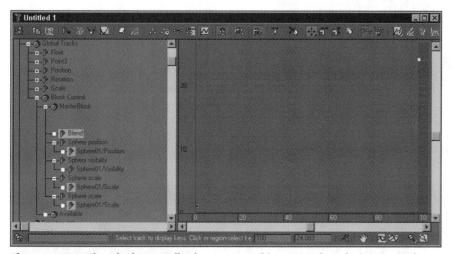

Figure 22-24: The Block controller lets you combine several tracks into a single global track.

Master Point controller

The Master Point controller controls the transforms of any point or vertex subobject selections. The Master Point controller gets added as a track to an object whose subobjects are transformed. Subtracks under this track are listed for each subobject. The keys in the Master track are colored green.

Right-clicking a green master key opens the Master Track Key Info dialog box, shown in Figure 22-25. This dialog box shows the Key number with arrows for selecting the previous or next key, a Time field that displays current the frame number, and a list of all the vertices. Selecting a vertex from the list displays its parameters at the bottom of the dialog box.

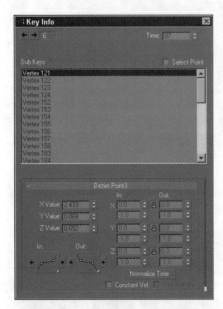

Figure 22-25: The Master Track Key Info dialog box lets you change the key values for each vertex.

Figure 22-26 shows the Master Point controller that was assigned automatically when a selection of vertex subobjects was moved with the Animate button enabled. A separate track is created for each vertex.

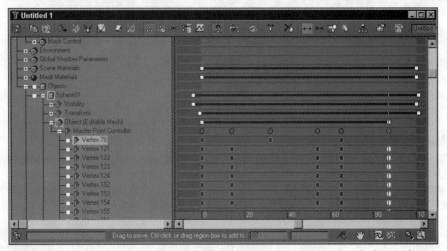

Figure 22-26: The Master Point controller defines tracks for each subobject element that is animated.

Working with Expressions in Spinners

Although much of this chapter focuses on using the expression controller, the Expression Controller Interface isn't the only place where you can play with expressions. Expressions can also be entered into spinner controls using the Numerical Expression Evaluator, shown in Figure 22-27. This simple dialog box is accessed by selecting a spinner field and pressing Ctrl+N.

 Cross-Reference Another common place that uses expressions is the Parameter Wiring dialog box. This dialog box is covered in Chapter 19, "Getting the Prop to Spin – Animation Basics."

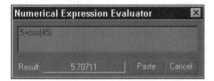

Figure 22-27: The Numerical Expression Evaluator dialog box lets you enter expressions for a spinner.

To use this evaluator, just type the expression in the field and the result is displayed in the result field. The result field is updated as you type the expression. If you make a mistake, the Result is blanked out. The Paste button places the result value in the spinner, and the Cancel button closes the dialog box without a change.

 Tip You can enter a relative value in a spinner by typing an R and a value. For example, if the Segments value of a sphere object is 32, then typing R20 changes the value to 52 and R-20 changes the value to 12.

Understanding the Expression Controller Interface

Expressions refer to mathematical expressions or simple formulas that compute a value based on other values. These expressions can be simple, as with moving a bicycle based on the rotation of the pedals, or complex, as with computing the sinusoidal translation of a boat on the sea as a function of the waves beneath it.

You can use almost any value as a variable in an expression, from object coordinates and modifier parameters, to light and material settings. The results of the expression are computed for every frame and used to affect various parameters in the scene. You can include the number of frames and time variables in the expression to cause the animation results to repeat for the entire sequence.

Of all the controllers that are available, the Expression controller has limitless possibilities that could fill an entire book. The following sections cover the basics of building expressions along with several examples.

The Expression controller enables you to define how the object is transformed by means of a mathematical formula or expression, which you can apply to any of the object's tracks. It shows up in the controller list, based on the type of track that it is assigned to, as a Position Expression, Rotation Expression, Scale Expression, Float Expression, or Point3 Expression controller.

Before you can use the Expression controller on a track, you must assign it to a track. You can assign controllers using the Motion panel or the Track View. After you assign it, the Expression Controller dialog box immediately opens up, or you can access this dialog box at any time by right-clicking the track and selecting Properties from the pop-up menu. For example, select an object in your scene, open the Motion panel, and select the Position track. Then click on the Assign Controller button at the top of the Assign Controller rollout, and select Position Expression from the list of Controllers. This causes the Expression Controller dialog box to appear.

You can use this dialog box to define variables and write expressions. The dialog box shown in Figure 22-28, includes four separate panes, which are used to display a list of Scalar and Vector variables, build an expression, and enter a description of the expression.

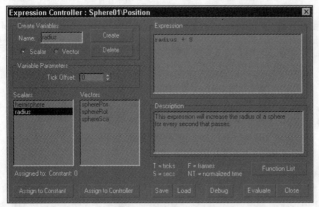

Figure 22-28: You can use the Expression controller to build expressions and define their results.

Defining variables

Variables are placeholders for different values. For example, creating a variable for a sphere's radius called "r" would simplify an expression for doubling its size from "take the sphere's radius and multiply it by two," to simply "r times 2."

To add Variables to the list panes in the Expression Controller dialog box, type a name in the Name field, select the Scalar or Vector option type, and click the Create button; the new variable appears in the Scalars or Vectors list. To delete a variable, select it from the list and click the Delete button. The Tick Offset value is the time added to the current time and can be used to delay variables.

You can assign any new variable either to a constant or to a controller. Assigning a variable to a constant does the same thing as typing the constant's value in the expression. Constant variables are simply for convenience in writing expressions. The Assign to Controller button opens the Track View Pick dialog box shown in Figure 22-29, where you can select the specific controller track for the variable such as the position of an object.

Assigning a variable to a controller enables you to animate the selected object based on other objects in the scene. To do this, create a variable and assign it to an animated track of another object. For example, if you create a Vector variable named boxPos and assign it to the Position track for a box object, then within the expression, you can use this variable to base the motion of the assigned object on the box's position.

Figure 22-29: The Track View Pick dialog box displays all the tracks for the scene. Tracks that you can select are displayed in black.

Building expressions

You can type expressions directly into the Expression pane of the Expression Controller dialog box. To use a named variable from one of the variable lists (Scalars or Vectors), type its name in the Expression pane. Predefined variables (presented later in the chapter) such as F and NT do not need to be defined in the variable panes. The Function List button opens a list of functions, shown in Figure 22-30, where you can view the functions that can be included in the expression. This list is for display only; you'll still need to type the function in the Expression pane.

Note

The Expression pane ignores any white space, so you can use line returns and spaces to make the expression easier to see and read.

Figure 22-30: The Function List dialog box lets you view all the available functions that you can use in an expression.

Debugging and evaluating expressions

After typing an expression in the Expression pane, you can check the values of all variables at any frame by clicking the Debug button. This opens the Expression Debug Window, shown in Figure 22-31. This window displays the values for all variables, as well as the return value. The values are automatically updated as you move the Time Slider.

The Evaluate button in the Expression Controller dialog box commits the results of the expression to the current frame segment. If there is an error in the expression, an alert dialog box warns you of the error. Replacing the controller with a different one can erase the animation resulting from an Expression controller.

Figure 22-31: The Expression Debug Window offers a way to test the expression before applying it.

Managing expressions

You can use the Save and Load button to save and recall expressions. Saved expressions are saved as files with an .XPR extension. Expression files do not save variable definitions.

Tutorial: Creating following eyes

As a quick example, we'll start with a simple expression. By setting the eye pupil objects to move along with the ball's motion, the expression controller is very useful. This same functionality can be accomplished using a manipulator and wiring the parameter, but we'll show it with the Float Expression controller.

To make eye pupil objects follow a moving ball object, follow these steps:

1. Open the Following eyes.gmax file from the Chap 22 directory on the CD-ROM.

   This file includes a face made from primitives along with a ball that is animated to rise and fall.

2. Select one of the eye pupil objects, and open the Motion panel. Select the Position track, and click the Assign Controller button. Select the Position Expression controller, and click Ok.

   The Expression Controller dialog box opens.

3. Create a new vector variable named **ballPos** by typing each name in the Name field, selecting the Vector option, and clicking the Create button.

4. With the ballPos variable selected, click the Assign to Controller button. In the Track View Pick dialog box, locate and select the Position track for the Sphere01 object, as shown in Figure 22-32, and click Ok.

Figure 22-32: Select the Position track for the Sphere01 object in the Track View Pick dialog box.

5. In the Expression pane, erase the existing expression and type the following:

```
[ 18, 0, ballPos.z/6 ]
```

Then click the Debug button. The Expression Debug Window appears, in which you can see the variable values change as items in the scene change. With the expression complete, you can drag the Time Slider back and forth and watch the pupil follow the ball up and down. If you're happy with the motion, click the Evaluate button and then the Close button to exit the interface.

6. With the pupil object still selected, open the Track View. Select the Position track for the selected pupil (Cylinder02) and click the Copy Controller button on the Track View toolbar. Locate the Position track for the other pupil (Cylinder03) and click the Paste Controller button on the toolbar.

7. Right-click the selected Position track, and select Properties.

This opens the Expression Controller interface again.

8. In the Expression pane, replace the first value of 18 to 75, and click the Debug button. Check the object motion, and click Evaluate and Close if it is okay.

Figure 22-33 shows the Expression Controller interface for this object.

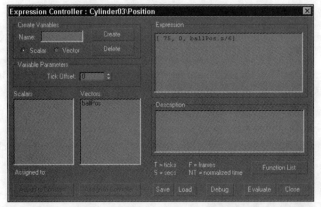

Figure 22-33: The Expression Controller interface is where you enter the expression and any variables to use.

This is a simple example, but it demonstrates what is possible. Figure 22-34 shows the resulting face.

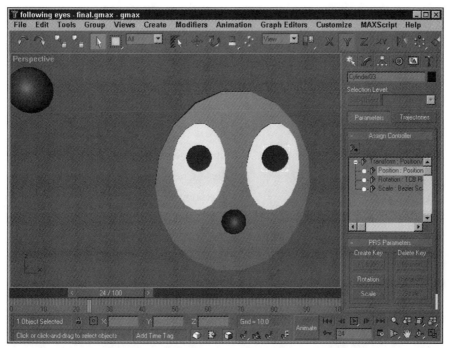

Figure 22-34: The Expression controller was used to animate the eyes' following the ball in this example.

Expression Elements

The key to making the Expression controller work is building expressions. Before you can build expressions, you need to understand the various elements that make up an expression. Expressions can consist of variables (including predefined variables), operators, and functions, so we'll start by explaining these. It is also important to understand what the expression returns and the various return types.

Predefined variables

gmax includes several predefined variables that have constant values. These predefined variables are defined in Table 22-1. They are case-sensitive and must be typed exactly as they appear in the Syntax column.

Table 22-1 Predefined Variables		
Variable	**Syntax**	**Value**
PI	Pi	3.14159
Natural Logarithm	E	2.71828
Ticks per Second	TPS	4800
Frame Number	F	Current frame number
Normalized Time	NT	The entire time of the active number of frames
Seconds	S	The number of seconds based on the frame rate
Ticks	T	The number of ticks based on the frame rate, where 4,800 ticks equal 1 second

In addition to these predefined variables, you can choose your own variables to use. These variables cannot contain spaces, and each variable must begin with a letter. After a variable is defined, you can assign it a constant value or have it pick up its value from a controller track.

Operators

An operator is the part of an expression that tells how to deal with the variables. One example of an operator is addition—it tells you to add a value to another value. These operators can be grouped as basic operators (which include the standard math functions such as addition and multiplication), logical operators (which compare two values and return a true or false result), and vector operators (which enable mathematical functions between vectors). Tables 22-2 through 22-4 identify the operators that are in each of these groups.

Tip

Although it isn't required, scalar variables are typically lowercase and vector variables are uppercase.

Table 22-2 Basic Operators		
Operator	**Syntax**	**Example**
Addition	+	i+j
Subtraction	-	i-j
Negation	-	-i

Operator	Syntax	Example
Multiplication	*	i*j
Division	/	i/j
Raise to the power	^ or **	i^j or i**j

Table 22-3
Logical Operators

Operator	Syntax	Example
Equal to	=	i=j
Less than	<	i<j
Greater than	>	i>j
Less than or equal to	<=	i<=j
Greater than or equal to	>=	i>=j
Logical Or (returns a 1 if either value is 1)	|	i|j
Logical And (returns a 1 if both values are 1)	&	i&j

Table 22-4
Vector Operators

Operator	Syntax	Example
Component (refers to the x component of vector V)	.	V.x
Vector Addition	+	V+W
Vector Subtraction	-	V-W
Scalar Multiplication	*	i*V
Scalar Division	/	V/i
Dot Product	*	V*W
Cross Product	X	VxW

The order in which the operators are applied is called operator precedence. The first equations to be calculated are the expressions contained inside of parentheses. If you're in doubt about which expression gets evaluated first, place each expression in separate parentheses. For example, the expression (2 + 3) * 4 equals 20 and 2 + (3 * 4) equals 14. If the equation doesn't contain any parentheses and only simple operators, then the precedence is from left to right with multiplication and division coming before addition and subtraction.

Functions

Functions are like mini-expressions that are given a parameter and return a value. For example, the trigonometric function for sine looks like this:

```
Sin()
```

It takes an angle, which is entered within the parentheses and returns a sine value. For example, if you open the Expression Controller dialog box and enter the expression

```
Sin(45)
```

and then open the Debug window, the Expression Value is 0.707, which is the sine value for 45 degrees.

Table 22-5 lists the functions that are used to create expressions.

 Tip   You can see a full list of all the possible functions with explanations by clicking the Function List button in the Expression Controller dialog box.

Table 22-5 Expression Functions		
Function	**Syntax**	**Description**
Sine	sin(i)	Computes the sine function for an angle
Cosine	cos(i)	Computes the cosine function for an angle
Tangent	tan(i)	Computes the tangent function for an angle
Arc Sine	asin(i)	Computes the arc sine function for an angle
Arc Cosine	acos(i)	Computes the arc cosine function for an angle
Arc Tangent	atan(i)	Computes the arc tangent function for an angle
Hyperbolic Sine	hsin(i)	Computes the hyperbolic sine function for an angle

Function	Syntax	Description
Hyperbolic Cosine	hcos(i)	Computes the hyperbolic cosine function for an angle
Hyperbolic Tangent	htan(i)	Computes the hyperbolic tangent function for an angle
Convert Radians degrees	radToDeg(i)	Converts an angle value from radians to to Degrees
Convert Degrees radians	degToRad(i)	Converts an angle value from degrees to to Radians
Ceiling	ceil(i)	Rounds floating values up to the next integer
Floor	floor(i)	Rounds floating values down to the next integer
Natural Logarithm (base e)	ln(i)	Computes the natural logarithm for a value
Common Logarithm (base 10)	log(i)	Computes the common logarithm for a value
Exponential Function	exp(i)	Computes the exponential for a value
Power	pow(i,j)	Raises i to the power of j
Square Root	sqrt(i)	Computes the square root for a value
Absolute Value	abs(i)	Changes negative numbers to positive
Minimum Value	min(i,j)	Returns the smaller of the two numbers
Maximum Value	max(i,j)	Returns the larger of the two numbers
Modulus Value	mod(i,j)	Returns the remainder of i divided by j
Conditional If	if(i,j,k)	Tests the value of i, and if it's not zero, then j is returned, or if it is zero then k is returned
Vector If	vif(i,V,W)	Same as the conditional if function, but works with vectors
Vector Length	length(V)	Computes the vector length
Vector Component	comp(V,i)	Returns the i component of vector V
Unit Vector	unit(V)	Returns a vector of length 1 that points in the same direction as V
Random Noise Position noise(i,j,k)		Returns a random position

Return types

A return type is the type of value that is expected to be returned to the track that was assigned the expression controller. For example, if you assign the Position Expression controller to the Position track of an object, then the return type is a vector, expecting coordinate values.

Tip

In the Expression Controller dialog box, the object and track that are assigned to the controller are displayed in the title bar.

These return types can be either a number (called a scalar), a collection of coordinates (called a vector), or a collection of color values (called a Point3). Scalars are used to control parameter values, vectors define actual coordinates in space, and the Point3 return type defines colors. Each one of these types has its own format that you need to know before you can use it in an expression.

Caution

Variables used in an expression need to match the return type. For example, if you have a Vector return type describing an object's position, it can use a scalar or vector variable, but the expression result needs to be a vector. A scalar return type (such as a sphere's Radius) cannot be multiplied by a vector; otherwise, an error appears.

Scalar return type

A scalar value is a single value typically used for an object parameter, such as a sphere's radius or the length of a Box object. This is used for tracks that have the Float Expression controller applied. Any resulting value from the expression is passed back to the assigned parameter. Scalars have no special format — only the number.

Vector return type

If a transform such as position is assigned, the Expression pane shows three values separated by commas and surrounded by brackets. These three values represent a vector, and each value is a different positional axis. You can refer to an individual axis value by placing a dot and the axis after the variable name. For example, if a vector variable named boxPosition exists, you could refer to the X-axis position component with the variable, boxPosition.x. Component values are actually scalars.

Point3 return type

Materials work with yet another return type called a Point3. This type includes three numbers separated by commas and surrounded by brackets. Each of these values, which can range between 0 and 255, represents the amount of red, green, or blue in a color.

Note

Any value that is out of range is automatically set to its nearest acceptable value. For example, if your expression returns a value of 500 for the green component, the color is shown as if green were simply 255.

Sample expressions

If you scan through your old physics and math books, you can find plenty of equations that you can use to create expressions. Following are some sample motions and their respective expressions.

For example, if the sphere object has the Float Expression controller applied to its Radius track, then a simple expression for increasing the radius from an initial radius value as the frame number increases would look like this:

```
initialRadius + F
```

You can use the trigonometric functions to produce a smooth curve from 0 to 360. Using the Sine function, you can cause the sphere's radius to increase to a maximum value of 50 and then decrease to its original radius. The expression would look like this:

```
50 * sin(360*NT)
```

To make our sphere example move in a zigzag path, we can use the mod function. This causes the position to increase slowly to a value and then reset. The expression looks like this:

```
[0, 10*mod(F,20), 10*F]
```

You can use the square root function to simulate ease in and ease out curves, causing the object to accelerate into or from a point. The expression would look like this:

```
[100*sqrt(NT*200), 10, 10]
```

Building complex expressions takes a little bit of math to accomplish, but it isn't difficult to do, and the more experience you get with expressions, the easier it becomes. To help get you started, Table 22-6 includes several pre-built expressions that can be entered into the Expression Controller Interface to get certain motions.

Table 22-6 Sample Expressions		
Motion	**Expression**	**Variable Description**
Circular	[Radius1 * cos(360*S), Radius1 * sin(360*S), 0]	Where Radius1 is the radius of the orbiting path
Elliptical	[Radius1 * cos(360*S),] Radius2 * sin(360*S), 0	Where Radius1 and Radius2 are theradii of the elliptical path

Continued

	Table 22-6 *(continued)*	
Motion	**Expression**	**Variable Description**
Rising Circular Coil	[Radius1 * cos(360*S), Radius1 * sin(360*S), S*AscentSpeed]	Where Radius1 is the radius of the orbiting path, and AscentSpeed is the speed at which the object rises
Back and Forth	[HalfDist * cos(360*S), 0, 0]	Where HalfDist is half the distance traveled
Zigzag	[0, ZigDist*mod(F,ZagFreq), AscentSpeed*F]	Where ZigDist is the distance the object moves before returning to the path, ZagFreq sets the frequency of the zigzag motion, and the AscentSpeed sets how quickly the object moves along the path
Accelerate Quickly	[Dist*sqrt(NT*Scale), 0, 0]	Where Dist is the distance that the object travels, and Scale is how long the acceleration takes
Y-Axis Rolling	BallPos.x/BallRadius	Where BallPos.x is the linear movement along the x-axis of the ball, and BallRadius is the radius of the ball object

Using Expression Controllers

You can use expressions to control the transforms of objects. You can access these transforms from the Track View or from the Motion panel. You can also use expressions to control object parameters such as a box's length or material properties such as the amount of illumination applied to a material. You can access all these parameters from the Track View.

Animating transforms with the Expression controller

After you assign a controller to a transform track, the Expression pane in the Expression Controller dialog box includes the current values of the selected object. Position transforms display the X, Y, and Z coordinates of the object. Rotation transforms display the rotation value in radians, and Scale transforms display values describing the relative scaling values for each axis.

Note

Radians are another way to measure angles. A full revolution equals 360 degrees, which equates to 2×pi radians. The Expression dialog box includes the degToRad and radToDeg functions to convert back and forth between these two measurement systems.

Animating parameters with the Float Expression controller

To assign the Float Expression controller, select an object with a parameter or a Modifier applied and open the Track View. Find the track for the parameter you want to change, and click the Assign Controller button. Select the Float Controller from the list, and click OK.

Note The actual controller type depends on the parameter selected. Many parameters use float expressions, but some use Transform controllers.

After you assign the Expression controller, the Expression Controller dialog box opens, or you can open it by right-clicking the track and selecting Properties from the pop-up menu to load the dialog box. Within this dialog box, the Expression pane includes the current value of the selected parameter.

Tutorial: Inflating a balloon

The Push Modifier mimics filling a balloon with air by pushing all its vertices outward. In this tutorial, we use a balloon model created by Zygote Media to demonstrate how you can use the Float Expression controller to control the parameters of a modifier.

To inflate a balloon using the Float Expression controller, follow these steps:

1. Open the Balloon and pump.gmax file from the Chap 22 directory on the CD-ROM.

   This file includes a pump created from primitives and the balloon model with the Push modifier applied.

2. Next, open the Track View by choosing Graph Editors ➪ Track View. Navigate the balloon object's tracks until you find the Push Value track (found in the Objects ➪ b3 ➪ Modified Object ➪ Push ➪ Push Value). Select the Push Value track, and click the Assign Controller button. From the list of controllers, select Float Expression and click OK.

   The Expression Controller dialog box opens.

3. In the Expression pane, you should see a single scalar value of 0. Modify the expression to read like this:

   ```
   2 * NT
   ```

4. Click the Debug button to see the value results. With the Expression Debug window open, drag the Time Slider and notice that the balloon inflates.

Note If you use a parameter such as Radius as part of an Expression, then the parameter is unavailable in the Modify panel if you try to change it by hand.

Figure 22-35 shows the balloon as it's being inflated.

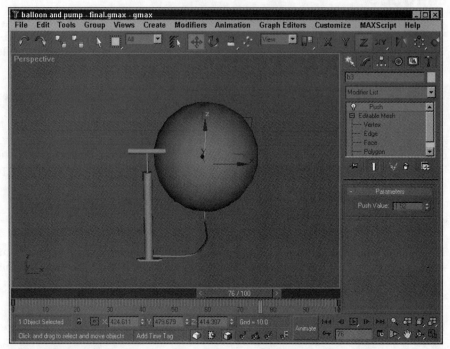

Figure 22-35: A balloon being inflated using an Expression controller to control the Push modifier

Animating materials with the Expression controller

You can locate the material's parameter in the Track View and assign the Expression controller to it to control material parameters. Some of these parameters are scalar values, but any material parameter set with a color swatch has a Point3 return type.

When using material parameters and color values, be sure not to combine them in expressions with vector values.

Tutorial: Controlling a stoplight

In this example, we use the if function to turn the colors of a sphere on and off to simulate a traffic light. We accomplish this task by applying the Expression controller to the Diffuse Color track. The goal is to show the color green for the first third of the animation, yellow for the second third, and red for the last third.

To change the colors of a stoplight sphere using the Expression controller, follow these steps:

1. Open the Stoplight.gmax file from the Chap 22 directory on the CD-ROM.

   This file includes a simple stoplight created using primitives. One of the spheres moves between the three light positions and has had a green material applied to it.

2. Open the Track View, and locate and select the Diffuse Color track, which you can find under Objects ➪ Sphere03 ➪ Material #1 ➪ Shader Basic Parameters tracks. Click the Assign Controller button, and double-click the Point3 Expression selection.

   This assigns the Point3 Expression controller to the Diffuse Color track. The Expression Controller dialog box opens automatically.

3. In the Expression pane, enter the following:

   ```
   [if(NT>=.33,255,0), if(NT<.66,255,0), 0]
   ```

4. Then click the Evaluate button, and close the Expression Controller dialog box.

   Click the Play Animation button to see the results.

Figure 22-36 shows the stoplight alongside the Dope Sheet for this stoplight.

Before leaving this example, let's examine the expression. The expression works with a Point3 number that includes the values of red, green, and blue. The first Point3 value represents red. Because yellow, in the RGB color system, is composed of equal parts of red and green, we want red to be visible for the last two-thirds of the time. To do this, we make the expression include the following statement:

```
if (NT >= .33, 255, 0)
```

This basically says that if the Normalized Time falls in the last two-thirds of the time, then set the red value to 255; if it does not, then set red to 0.

The second Point3 value is green, which appears for the first third of the animation and along with red for the second third to make yellow. So the following expression needs to go where the green value would be located:

```
if (NT < .66, 255, 0)
```

This expression says that if the Normalized Time is less than two-thirds of the time, then set the green value to its maximum; if it isn't, then set its value to 0.

The third Point3 value is for blue. Blue doesn't appear at all in green, yellow, or red, so its value is set to 0 for the entire animation.

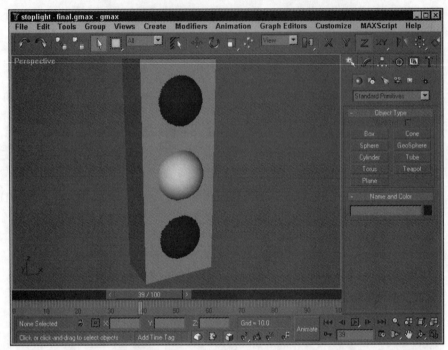

Figure 22-36: The Expression controller animates the diffuse color for this object.

The completed expression for the entire animation (which you entered in Step 4 of the tutorial) looks like this:

```
[if (NT >= .33, 255, 0), if (NT < .66, 255, 0), 0]
```

Summary

If you're an animator, you should thank your lucky stars for controllers. Controllers offer power flexibility for animating objects — and just think of all those keys that you don't have to set by hand.

Another thing to be thankful for is the Expression controller. Using mathematical formulas to control the animation of an object's transformation and parameters offers lots of power. You can also use the values of one object to control another object.

This chapter covered these topics:

✦ Learning about the various controller types

✦ Discovering how to assign controllers using the Motion panel and the Track View

✦ Setting default controllers in the Preference Settings dialog box

✦ Examining the various controllers in several different categories

✦ Viewing a few examples of using controllers

✦ Practicing building expressions in the Expression dialog box

✦ Learning about expressions and what they can do

✦ Reviewing the available operators, variables, and functions

✦ Working through examples of controlling object transformations and parameters

In the next chapter, we'll start looking at some specific game packs, so if you're a big Quake player, get ready for some serious fragging.

✦   ✦   ✦

Creating Mods with the gmax Game Packs

In This Part

Chapter 23
Making Worlds
with Tempest for
Quake III Arena

Chapter 24
Creating Custom
Content for Flight
Simulator 2002

Chapter 25
Creating Adventures
with Dungeon Siege®

Chapter 26
Creating New
Scenery for Trainz

◆   ◆   ◆   ◆

Making Worlds with Tempest for Quake III Arena

✦ ✦ ✦ ✦

In This Chapter

Installing and
configuring Tempest

Learning about
brushes, textures,
and entities

Controlling the
interface

Creating a Quake 3
Arena Map

Adding lights
and weapons

Building triggers
and doors

Learning advanced
texturing

Importing models

✦ ✦ ✦ ✦

Back in the early days of gmax, Discreet created the Tempest game pack for Quake III Arena as a proof-of-concept — a way for them to show the world that they were going to change the way gamers interact with their games. In this case, Tempest would allow gamers to create new levels and worlds for Quake III Arena that they could play in and pass around to their friends, giving everyone brand new arenas in which to engage in deathmatches (or where you can capture the enemy's flag, whichever you prefer).

Tempest is not bundled with Quake III Arena or gmax, so you'll have to visit Discreet's gmax Web site to download it (don't worry, it's a free download, and you'll find it here: http://www.discreet.com/products/gmax/).

The Tempest game pack is also available on the attached CD-ROM.

After you've installed it, you're ready to start constructing your own arenas. In this chapter, you'll create your very first map, learn how to texture it, and then add the fun stuff — weapons, items, and even a lava pit in which to fall.

As you use Tempest, keep in mind that it's currently in beta stage — that is, it's not a supported piece of software, and you may find a few bugs here and there. You'll find a few notes as you go through the tutorials dealing with bugs and workarounds.

Installing and Configuring Tempest for gmax

Because Tempest was created as a proof-of-concept, installing it isn't quite the simple process that it could be. But it's not difficult, and as long as you follow these steps, you'll have Tempest up and running in no time. You also need to download a copy of Q3Radiant, which is a free piece of software that contains the map compiler that Tempest uses. You'll find the latest version of Q3Radiant at http://www.qeradiant.com on the right side of the site under the link labeled "Files."

Level creation is a two-step process in Quake III Arena. First, the map must be created in Tempest. Next, the map must be *compiled*, or translated into a format that the game can understand. Any time you make a change to your map, you must compile it before you can play it and see the changes. You'll learn how to compile later in the chapter.

Follow these steps to properly install Tempest:

1. Make sure that you have Quake III Arena installed. Follow the installation instructions for the game if you don't already have it installed.

2. Install and run gmax at least once if you haven't done so already.

   Tempest needs gmax to initialize before it can be properly set up.

3. Double-click the tempestinstall.exe file that you downloaded from Discreet's Web site (or found on the book's CD-ROM) to install Tempest.

4. Open the Quake III Arena\baseq3 folder.

5. Find and open the pak0.pk3 file. This is a large file weighing in at about 470MB compressed and 670MB uncompressed, so make sure you have room for it.

 Note   If you have Team Arena (the Quake III Arena expansion pack) installed, you'll also find a pak0.pk3 file in the Quake III Arena\missionpack folder. In this chapter we only use Quake III Arena, so be sure to use the pak0.pk3 file found in Quake III Arena\baseq3.

   This is a special kind of compressed file, but you can use any program that opens compressed files — WinZip is a popular and reliable choice.

6. Extract the contents of the file into your Quake III Arena\baseq3 directory.

7. Install Q3Radiant.

   This puts the necessary compiler files into the Quake III Arena\baseq3\Tools directory.

8. Browse to the gmax\gamepacks\tempest\textures folder, and copy the Common directory into your Quake III Arena\baseq3\textures folder.

9. Browse to the gmax\gamepacks\tempest folder, and copy the file called leveltest.map into the Quake III Arena\baseq3\maps folder.

Setting up paths

Now that you've installed the compiler that Tempest needs and configured the directory structure, it's time to configure Tempest itself so that it knows where to find the Quake III Arena resources.

Follow these steps to properly configure Tempest:

1. Double-click the Tempest Desktop shortcut to start Tempest.

2. After you're prompted to choose a driver, choose the appropriate one, and click OK.

Note
Choosing the correct driver depends on what kind of video card you have, and not everyone has the same video card. Use this general rule in choosing the driver: if your card has an nVIDIA chipset, use the OpenGL driver. If your card is not nVIDIA, try the Direct3D driver. If you're not sure, you can choose the Heidi z-buffer driver, which should work regardless of which card you have.

If you need to change the display driver, you can do so in the Viewports panel of the Preference Setttings dialog box. The Preference Settings dialog box is covered in detail in Chapter 3, "Making a Custom Face, er, Interface."

Because this is the first time you've run Tempest, the Tempest Preferences dialog box, shown in Figure 23-1, appears. Enter or browse to the proper paths for the Tools folder in your Quake III Arena directory. This is most likely Quake III Arena\Tools.

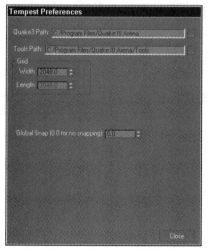

Figure 23-1: You can either enter the paths directly or browse to the folders to set the paths to the Quake III Arena directory and the Tools folder.

Testing it all out

After you've configured the paths, you should do a quick test to be sure you have it set up properly. A good way to do this is to look at the textures in Tempest and make sure that they display correctly.

Follow these steps to be sure the setup is accurate:

1. Click the Shader Nav button at the bottom left of the tool area.

2. Choose a texture category from the list.

   base_floor is a good choice.

3. Thumbnail images should appear in the window. If they do, Tempest is properly configured for textures. If they don't, check the steps for installing Tempest, and make sure the paths are set correctly.

Now the compiler needs to be tested, because if the path to the compiler is wrong, you won't be able to compile and play your map. To test that the compiler has been installed properly and all paths are correct, do the following:

1. Click the File ⇨ Open File menu (or press the Ctrl+O keyboard shortcut).

2. Open the file called leveltest.gmax.

   If your texture paths are set properly, you should see the textures load into the Shader Nav window at the left, as well as in the level itself in the Perspective viewport.

Cross-Reference   For help with textures, see the tutorial in this chapter on applying textures.

3. Click the Compile button in the tool area.

4. Click Quick Compile.

5. Tempest prompts you to save your file. Name it something simple for now, such as testmap.map.

Load it up!

If the compiler has been installed properly and the paths have been set correctly, your map should compile with no problems. Until you've gotten a handle on what the resulting text file produced by the compiler actually says, let's just try to load your map in Quake III Arena.

1. Load Quake III Arena.

2. Bring down the game console with the ~ key.

3. Type **/sv_pure 0** and press Enter.

4. Type **/map testmap** to load your map.

Your test map should now load, and you should be able to walk around and look at it.

After you've passed the test and determined that your paths are set correctly and Tempest is fully configured and ready to go, you'll want to jump right into creating some maps, right? Not exactly. You wouldn't start surgery on someone before you knew what the parts of the body were called first, right? Using that gruesome analogy, there are lots of terms unique to the world of level design. Let's first get a handle on some new terms you're going to see.

Brushes, Textures, and Entities: Learning Level-Speak

Talk to anyone who's made a level for Quake III Arena, and it can sound like they're speaking a different language. "Brushes," "textures," "entities" . . . what exactly are these things? Because making levels involves absorbing a few new words into your vocabulary, let's go over some new terms you'll be using.

Brushes

A brush is the generic term for "pieces of geometry that you create in a map." When you build a wall, some stairs, a floor, a ceiling—any kind of structure at all—in a map, you're doing it with brushes.

Textures

If a brush is a wall, a texture is the wallpaper. Textures are images designed to tile (in other words, their edges line up so that they repeat without any noticeable edges).

Shaders

Shaders are a special kind of dynamic texture. If you've seen moving flames behind a wall in Quake III Arena or the roving clouds in the sky, you've seen shaders. Shaders use alpha channels and small scripts to make specially created textures move, fade, shift, and perform other special effects. Although creating and editing shaders is outside the scope of gmax and Tempest, you can use the shaders that come with Quake III Arena to add special touches to your maps.

Entities

An entity is a very generic term in game programming—almost everything you see in Quake III Arena is an entity. For our purposes, an entity is something that is used or activated on the map. Weapons, ammo, items, jump pads—these are all examples of entities.

Triggers and functions

Triggers and functions are special kinds of entities, and I'm calling them out specifically because they do some particularly neat things in Quake III Arena maps, and we'll be using them in the tutorials. If you've catapulted off of a jump pad or fallen into an endless pit of fog, then you've experienced a trigger. Just like the word implies, a player's action triggers a particular response from the item the player touched. A function is something that usually requires some kind of movement in the world. A door that opens when the player gets near enough, for instance, is a use of the func_door entity. We'll learn more about these later in the tutorials.

Although you might come across a few more special terms as you become more experienced in creating Quake III Arena levels, these are the most common ones, and knowing them will help you navigate your way through Tempest. And how do we do that? Via the interface, of course.

Getting a Handle on the Tempest Interface

The first thing you might notice about Tempest's interface, shown in Figure 23-2, is how obvious everything is. Discreet created Tempest with the novice user in mind, so all the tools that you need to create a map are easy to find and easy to understand. Let's look through the main tool area at the bottom of Tempest and see what we have to work with. Table 23-1 describes the buttons on the Tempest toolbar.

	Table 23-1	
	The Tempest Toolbar	
Tool	**Name**	**Description**
	Shader Nav, Entity Editor, Compile	These three buttons on the left are used to bring up the navigation windows for textures, entities, and compiling.
	Select Tool	This button, highlighted green when enabled, lets you select objects to move and work with.

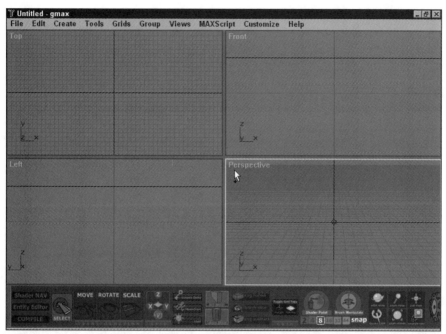

Figure 23-2: The Tempest work area. Tempest's toolbar sits below, while the upper area is the workspace where you'll create new levels.

Tool	Name	Description
	Transformation Tools	The Transformation tools: Move, Rotate, and Scale are used to — you guessed it — move, rotate, and scale pieces of your level.
	Axis	The Axis tool allows you to change the axis on which new brushes are created.
	Generic Entity	This button creates a generic entity in the world — after you've created it, you can use the Entity Editor to assign properties to it. For instance, you might turn it into a weapon or an item the player can pick up.
	Player Start	This tool adds the crucial Player Start to your level, the place on the map into which the player spawns when the level loads. No level can run without one.
	Light	This tool creates a light in the world that shines in all directions.

Continued

Table 23-1 *(continued)*

Tool	Name	Description
	Box Brush and Cylinder Brush	These create either a box-shaped brush or a cylindrical brush.
	CSG Hollow	CSG stands for "constructive solid geometry." This command turns the selected brush into a hollow box. This tool is useful for creating quick rooms out of single brushes.
	Brush Slice	This tool slices the selected brush along an axis that you choose and position.
	CSG Subtract	If two brushes intersect, this command subtracts the intersecting parts from the pieces (a fancier way of putting it is that the command performs a Boolean subtract on the selected brushes).
	Toggle Grid Type	This allows you to switch between the *height grid* and the *standard grid*. The standard grid is the simple grid pattern you see in the viewports. The height grid is a special grid with two sets of cross arms separated by a vertical bar. The height of the bar can be changed, allowing you to set the height of the next brush you create.
	Grid Divisions	These numbers set the divisions of your standard grid when selected. The smaller the division, the finer the control you have over placement and brushes.
snap	Snap	This tool toggles whether objects snap to the grid when you create them. You'll know that snap is enabled when you see light blue lines on your crosshair when mousing over the grid to place something.
	Shader Paint	When you apply a texture to a brush, the texture is applied by default to all sides of the brush. But sometimes, you want a different texture on each face. The shader paint tool allows you to apply different textures to different faces on a brush and to manipulate textures as well.
	Brush Manipulate	This tool gives you finer editing control on a brush than do the Transformation tools. Need to make the brush higher, but want to keep it the same width? This is where you would use Brush Manipulate.

Tool	Name	Description
	Camera Controls	The six tool buttons at the far right of the tool area control the display and camera movement in Tempest. For details on these buttons, see Table 23-2.
	Gears	At first, this might not look like a tool, but clicking it brings up an entire range of editing features that are very similar to what you see in gmax itself. These features give you much more editing control within Tempest.

Caution CSG Subtract is a tool best left unused in Tempest. When used, it can break up geometry in a way that actually creates more problems for Quake III Arena by adding more geometry than is necessary, bogging down the game. There is almost always a better way of doing what you need to do without using CSG Subtract.

The six tool buttons at the far right of the tool area in the Tempest toolbar control the display and camera movement. The cameras move your view when you click and hold the mouse button. Table 23-2 provides a quick overview of what each camera control does.

Table 23-2
Camera Controls

Name	Description
Orbit View	Rotates the camera around a central axis
Zoom View	Zooms in and out of the viewport
Pan View	Moves the world vertically or horizontally
Quake Cam	Allows you to move through your map using the standard Q3A keyboard and mouse configuration (WASD for moving forward, back, left, and right; the mouse for moving up and down and turning left and right)
Zoom Extents	Zooms in on a selected object to make the selected object fill the field of view
Maximize View	Maximizes the selected viewport

Tip   The Maximize View button does not work in the current version of Tempest. This is a known bug. To maximize a viewport, mouse over the central work area (where the corners of the viewports meet) until you see the crosshair arrows. Click and hold the left mouse button and drag the crosshairs to maximize any of the viewports.

Setting It Up: Getting Ready to Work

As with most things in life, you should do a little prep work before you dive in and make your first level. In our case, we'll want to set up our working space to make it as easy as possible to work with. When you open Tempest, you'll see four windows —these are the *viewports* (just like the viewports in gmax).

Each viewport looks at the level from a different angle, and you can see what that angle is by the label on the viewport located in the upper left of each viewport. The most useful of all four views is the lower right: the Perspective viewport. This viewport gives you the most "natural" view of your level – here, you'll see brushes, textures, and items as you would in-game, and you can move around the level in the Perspective viewport with your camera to navigate more naturally.

Doing most of your work is easiest—at least at first—in the Perspective viewport. Because you can resize each viewport, let's give Perspective the most screen real estate, as in Figure 23-3. Mouse over the upper-left corner of the viewport until you see the crosshair-style arrows, and then click and hold, dragging the viewport to the upper left to give it more space. Don't worry; you won't lose the other three viewports, and you can resize any of them to your liking as you work.

Tip   You can use the camera tools in each viewport without affecting the view of the other viewports. For example, you can zoom back in the Top viewport to see the whole level from a top-down perspective, without zooming out in any of the other viewports.

You can also change the view in each viewport to whichever view you prefer. To do this, right-click on the viewport label in the upper left of the viewport, choose Views, and then choose the view you want to see.

Cross-Reference   Chapter 2, "Using the In-Your-Face Interface," provides more details on using the gmax viewports.

Now that the workspace is set up, it's time to create your first level!

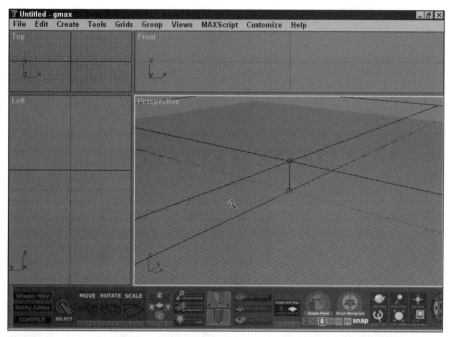

Figure 23-3: Setting up the workspace

Tutorial: Creating the building blocks

Creating a level is a lot like building a house: first you build the foundation and the frame, and then you start adding in more detail. And like any good builder, there are some basic things you need to do first when building a good level. The natural place to start is by constructing the walls. While you could create each wall individually, the easiest way to create the basic outer walls of your first room is to make a box and then hollow it out. Tempest allows you to do this easily with just a couple of operations.

If you haven't already done so, you should set up your Perspective viewport as described earlier. Then set up the view to make it easier to work in by following these steps:

1. Toggle the grid type to Height.

2. Rotate your view a little with the Orbit View tool so that you can see both arms of the height grid.

3. Zoom back so you can see the full grid in the viewport.

Now that you're set up, follow these steps to create the basic box that'll form your first room:

1. Mouse over the small circle at the center of the height grid — it should turn red, and the cursor should turn into a crosshair.

   Make sure that the circle is red and not the central line (we want to change the height of the grid, not move the entire grid, which is what moving that line would do).

Tip
If you see the red circle and the crosshair when you mouse over it, try right-clicking in the viewport and then mousing over it again.

2. Click and hold the left mouse button, and drag the circle up.

   You'll see the numbers in the description to its right change; you want to get it to a height of at least 256 units.

Tip
You'll probably need to zoom back as you raise the grid. Zoom back enough (click Zoom View, then left-click, hold the mouse button, and pull back) so that you can see the entire grid (edges and all) in the viewport.

3. Now, create the box. Select the Box Brush icon (in the center of the tool area). Make sure that you have snap enabled by clicking the Snap button (you'll know it's enabled when you see light blue marks on the crosshair as you position it on the grid). Click in one corner of the grid, and drag a box to the opposite corner as in Figure 23-4.

   It doesn't have to be exact, so don't worry about the box dimensions.

4. Set your grid size to 8 by clicking the number 8 in the strip on the toolbar.

   This will make sure that the walls are fairly thin.

5. Hollow the box by clicking the CSG Hollow button.

You've just taken a solid brush and made it a hollowed out box with walls that are eight grid units thick. Isn't that more convenient than creating each wall individually and matching the edges? This is a common way to build rooms in Q3A maps.

Tutorial: Applying textures

Just like our house analogy, your map won't be much to look at if you don't do a little decorating. And most decorating in maps is done through the use of textures, which are images that can be tiled (like wallpaper) and can be used on the surfaces of your level. Every surface in your level needs a texture; without it, all you see is an ugly default blue-and-black checkerboard pattern in-game that tells you a texture is missing.

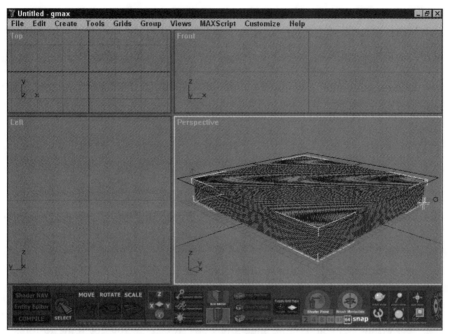

Figure 23-4: Making your first room with the CSG Hollow tool

Tip   If you have problems seeing your textures when you apply them, you're not alone. This is a common bug in Tempest. To fix it, you need to reinstall Tempest. The easiest way to do this is to go into your gmax folder and delete the Tempest folder (found under gmax\Gamepacks\). Remember to make copies in another folder of any levels you've saved up to this point! After you've deleted the folder, follow the installation instructions and run tempestinstall.exe again. You should now be able to see your textures.

To apply textures, follow these steps:

1. Click the Shader Nav button on the left of the tool area.

   This clears an area on the left and displays a drop-down box from which you can pick the textures you want to use.

2. Click the Quake Cam button.

   The Quake Cam puts you in the center of your new map.

Tip

The QuakeCam tool uses the traditional *WASD* setup to help you move around your map a little more naturally. *W* moves the camera forward, *S* moves it back, and *A* and *D* move the camera from side to side, exactly as if you were using those keys to strafe if you were playing the game. You can also pitch your view up and down or turn (rather than strafe) from side to side if you click and hold the left mouse button while QuakeCam in engaged. Most first-person shooter players are used to this configuration, so you'll probably find QuakeCam to be the most useful of all the camera tools if you've played any shooters.

Note

To use the keyboard in QuakeCam mode to move the camera, you must first move the camera by left-clicking and dragging it once.

3. Use the drop-down list in the Shader Nav to select a list of textures.

Choosing an item in the drop-down list displays the textures in that group.

4. Click the Select button. In your Perspective viewport, click the floor of your map, and then click a texture in the Shader Nav area.

You should see it applied to the floor.

Tip

Some texture groups contain lots of textures, and you can navigate your way through them in a couple of ways. If you look closely, you'll notice a very thin scroll bar on the right side of the shader nav box. You can scroll down the textures with that, or you can grab an area of the shader nav window (in a place where you won't select a texture) and use the Hand tool to pull the texture display up and down.

5. Repeat this process for the walls, using the camera tools to move your view.

Tip

To select multiple surfaces, hold down the Ctrl key while selecting.

6. To texture the ceiling, use a sky texture—this eliminates the need to add lights for now because sky textures cast their own light (you'll find the sky textures under the—surprise!—Sky group in the drop-down list).

Your finished room should look like Figure 23-5 when you're finished texturing.

Note

If you've been adventurous enough to browse through the Shader Nav window, you may have seen the Common set of textures and wondered why they didn't look like textures at all, but rather are just brightly colored images with words on them. These special textures assign properties to the brushes to which they're applied. You'll learn more about some of these special textures as you work through the tutorials.

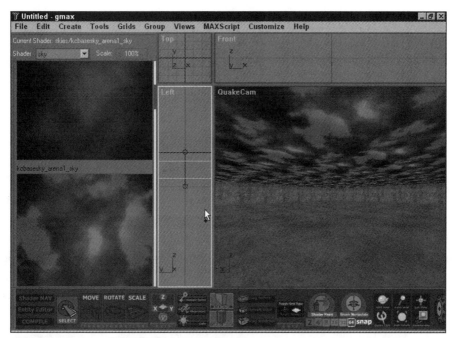

Figure 23-5: Your first textured room in Tempest

What Are Shaders?

You may wonder why the texture navigation window is called the Shader Nav. This is because many of the textures used in Quake III Arena are actually *shaders*, which are a special kind of texture. Shaders are dynamic textures; they often have movement or some kind of special effect on what they're applied to. The flames that flicker behind wall grates, the lava that flows under the floor in Arena Gate, and the sky in almost all of Quake III Arena's levels are examples of shaders.

Shaders are created using alpha channels, a special channel in the image file that allows the artist to specify which parts of the image are transparent to effects below. Creating shaders involves some scripting. We won't cover that in this book, but you can find lots of tutorials on the Web. See the section, "Enter the Arena: Finding Help in the Map Community," at the end of this chapter.

Tutorial: Adding the player start

You've built the walls and given them a new coat of paint; now your level is ready for you to walk around in to inspect your handiwork. We can't do that, though, until we add one very important item: the Player Start. This is a box placed in your level that tells the game where to place a player who's just spawned in, and every level must have one before it can load.

Add a Player Start by following these steps:

1. Adjust the height grid by right-clicking in the Perspective viewport and selecting Autoposition Grid Upper.

   This aligns the bottom of the height grid with the floor of your level for easy positioning.

2. Click the Player Start button in the center of the tool area.

3. Make sure that snap is set, and then in the Perspective viewport move the cursor to an area in your level and left-click.

   You should see a rectangular box appear in the map as in Figure 23-6. This is the Player Start.

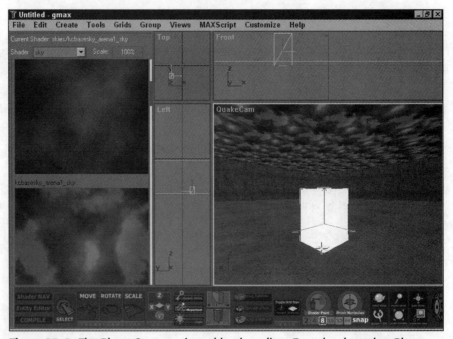

Figure 23-6: The Player Start, as viewed by the editor. Every level needs a Player Start, or it won't load.

Congratulations! You just created your first level. Sure, it's not much, but even the best level designers in the game industry had to start somewhere. These are only the most basic of basic items needed to create a level in which you can run around in Quake III Arena. We haven't gotten to the good stuff yet, like weapons and items. We'll leave those aside for now to learn how to compile the new level and then load it into Quake III Arena so you can check it out.

Tip If you try to load a map you've just created into Quake III Arena only to be booted back to Q3A's main menu, you may have forgotten to add a Player Start.

Tutorial: Compiling and loading a level

The compiling process takes your raw *.gmax level file and translates it into something that Quake III Arena can understand. Here's how to compile a level in Tempest:

1. Click the Compile button in the lower left of the tool area.

    You have three options: Quick Compile, Normal Compile, and Full Compile.

2. For now, choose Normal Compile.

3. You're asked to save your compiled map in a location and give it a name. Tempest automatically prompts you to save your .map file in your Maps folder under the Quake III Arena baseq3 folder. Give it a name, and click Save.

Note Tempest needs to create two files in the compile process: the .map file and the .bsp file. The .map file is created by the compiler from your .gmax file. This interim file type translates the .gmax data into something that the compiler can understand. The .bsp file is created from the .map file and is the actual, finished map that gets loaded into Quake III Arena.

You see a DOS window during the compile process. When the process is completed, a text file pops up with the full details of the compile process. Here, you can check for any errors during compiling that might prevent your map from running. Because we've got a simple map, we should encounter no errors and should be able to run our new map now.

To load the map in Quake III Arena, follow these steps:

1. Load Quake III Arena.

2. Pull down the console by pressing the ~ key.

3. Type **/sv_pure 0**.

    This sets the game server to unpure, allowing you to run non-standard maps.

4. Type **/map *<mapname>***, where *<mapname>* is the filename of your map. For example, if you named your file mylevel.map, you would type **/map mylevel**.

You can now spawn into your new map and check out the beautiful blue sky you see in Figure 23-7.

Figure 23-7: A cheerful blue sky. Okay, maybe not that cheerful.

Tip   After you make changes to your level, you must recompile it in order to see it in-game.

Adding the Good Stuff

Your new level has the bare minimum requirements to be called a level—technically. But it isn't much fun yet, is it? It's lacking the important things, like weapons to cause mass destruction to your enemies and fun things like lava and fog to fall into (or, preferably, for your enemies to fall into). The next few tutorials show you how to add all that cool stuff.

Which Compile Method?

Tempest allows you to choose among three methods of compiling your level. The compiling process itself is pretty complicated, and each method tells the compiler how to handle the lighting, visible geometry, and other factors. When compiling Q3A maps, the lighting is usually the most time-consuming operation. Here's a very quick and dirty guide to the three methods:

✦ **Quick Compile:** No lighting, fast VIS

This method does not compute any lighting at all. You jump into your map at what's called "fullbright," as if the entire level were lighted at maximum intensity. This method is usually used when you just want to quickly check something in your map — the placement of a couple of brushes. Fast VIS refers to how the compiler calculates visible geometry. Basically, it takes as many shortcuts as it can here.

✦ **Normal Compile:** Normal lighting, fast VIS

This compile method calculates the lighting in such a way that you can see how your final map will look, but it takes a few shortcuts that you won't notice in order to reduce compile time. You'll likely use this method the most, because as you build your level, you want an accurate view of how the final version will look without the lengthy compile times of the Full Compile.

✦ **Full Compile:** Extra lighting, full VIS

This method takes the longest to compile and is the method you want to use when you're absolutely sure that your level is finished and ready to release to the world. It fully calculates all the lighting and visible geometry and takes no shortcuts. Think of this method as the wrapping paper with a bow and nice label on your finished level. All finished maps should be compiled with Full Compile.

Tutorial: Adding lights

Sky textures are convenient in that they tend to add lots of light to a level. If parts of your level are indoors, however, you're going to have to add light to see your way around. Lighting your level can be done in many different ways — windows that look out into the sky and torches with bright, burning flames are just a couple of ways to shed some light on your map. The easiest way to light your level, however, is to add a simple light entity to your map. This light is a point source that radiates outward with an intensity that you specify.

Note   Lighting a level is almost an art form itself; just adding light entities to your map adds the necessary brightness so you can see, but without a careful marriage of light sources and architecture, your level may look like it has light sources coming from nothing. But don't worry; just practice lighting your levels by playing with light entities and matching them up with things like torch and lamp models. For now, adding point source lights to your first map will give you a feel for how to work with lighting.

Adding lights is a painless process in Tempest. Just follow these steps:

1. First, change the sky texture on the ceiling by selecting it and choosing another texture.

   We want to see what our lights look like in our level, so we have to change the sky texture to something else. Otherwise, the sky's brightness drowns out any lights we place.

2. Click the Light button in the center of the tool area.

3. Mouse over the area where the viewports meet, and then drag back and down a bit so you can see the other viewports more easily.

4. Look in the Top viewport, and find the red box. That's the Player Start that you placed in the preceding tutorial. Click in that viewport, and place the light somewhere near the box.

5. A small square appears near your Player Start in the Top viewport.

   It is also visible in the Front viewport, as shown in Figure 23-8.

   If you had snap enabled, however, it's probably on the floor. We want to move it up a little so it's closer to the ceiling.

6. Click the Move button in the toolbar.

7. In the other viewports, the square now has two arrows near it. Mousing over each arrow highlights it. If you click and hold the highlighted arrow, you can move the light in the direction of that arrow. In the Front viewport, move the square just a little farther away from the Player Start and the floor.

8. You can edit the light's intensity value if you so choose. The default value is 300, the maximum value it can have. To edit the light's intensity, click the Select button and then click the light in the Perspective viewport. Then click the Entity Editor button on the left.

9. Click Light (not "classname: light") in the Properties dialog box to bring it up in the key area.

10. Enter a value between 0 and 300 in the Value box, and click Close.

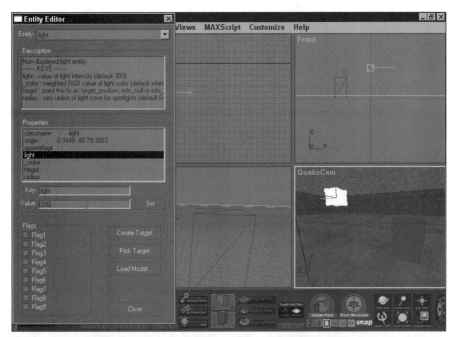

Figure 23-8: Adding a light is a simple process of adding the light entity and then entering the value in the Entity Editor.

You can check out your new light by recompiling your level and loading it in Quake III Arena. (Remember that you must recompile your map and reload it in Quake III Arena to see any changes you've made.) Add more lights so that your new level isn't so dark, and play with the values to see how they change the look of your level.

Tutorial: Adding a weapon

This is what you've been waiting for, right? Lights and textures are all well and good, but let's just come out and admit it: We want firepower on this map, and plenty of it. Weapons are the bread and butter of Quake III Arena, where the bread is a rocket launcher or a lightning gun , and the butter is plenty of ammo to get the job done (and that job, of course, is decimating your enemies). Adding weapons to your level is easy.

Note   Level designers love to talk about balance when creating their maps. *Balance* refers to the fairness in the distribution of weapons, powerups, and other items, and getting that right can be difficult even for the pros. Adding weapons to your map is part of achieving the right balance. You don't want to bunch all the powerful weapons into one area of the map, for instance, or not provide enough (or provide too much) ammo for some of them. Study some of the most popular maps created for Quake III Arena by the level designers at Id Software for tips on improving the balance of your own maps.

1. Click the Generic Entity button in the tool area.

2. Click somewhere in the level to place the entity. Use the Move tool to move it so that it rests on the floor of your level.

3. Click the Entity Editor button in the left tool area, so we can assign it properties that will turn it into the weapon you want.

4. In the drop-down list, scroll to the weapons at the and choose a weapon.

   I'm a rocket launcher fan myself, but that's just me — choose whichever weapon you'd like.

5. After you've chosen the weapon, you see the Generic Entity dialog box turn into the model for that weapon, as shown in Figure 23-9.

6. Select the Count value in the Properties area. Enter a value into the Value box.

   This number determines how much starting ammo the player gets for that weapon when he picks it up. The maximum you can enter is 999.

7. Click the Set button.

Figure 23-9: The rocket launcher in your level, just waiting to be picked up

"Why Is My Weapon White?"

When you define your entity as a weapon, the entity turns into the weapon you chose, looking exactly as it would in-game but with a wireframe box around it. If all you see is an all-white version of your weapon, you're experiencing a common problem among Tempest users, which is that the path to the weapon bitmaps is wrong. There's an easy fix, though.

1. Click Customize in the upper toolbar, then click Configure Paths.

2. Select the Bitmaps tab.

3. Click the Add button.

4. Browse to the directory under your Quake III Arena folder that contains the weapon models. This should be Quake III Arena\baseq3\models\weapons2.

5. Click the Add subpaths check box.

6. Click the Use Path button.

7. Click OK in the Bitmaps dialog box.

You should now be able to see your weapon textured properly.

Items such as ammo for weapons, armor, and health are all added in the same way weapons are. You can find all these items in the Entity Editor. The key information and variables for each item are explained in the Description area. Experiment with and learn about these entities by adding some ammo, armor, and health to your map.

Tutorial: Bringing on the pain (Or adding lava and other triggers)

You've got all the basics: the walls, the textures, the lights, a weapon, and a Player Start. Now you have the urge to get a little fancy. Adding some lava to your map is just the thing—not only does it add something different to your level than just walls, but you also learn how to use *triggers*, or entities that react to actions in the game.

Triggers like lava or fog that can kill you add interesting gameplay elements by introducing danger to some areas of your map. Want to make a powerful weapon even more challenging to get to? How about placing it on a narrow ledge and making the player jump over a deadly, endless pit filled with fog to get to it? Or how about creating an area of your level where players have to fight each other without falling into the deadly lava below? Firing a rocket at your opponent's feet and catapulting him off a delicate bridge to a fiery death below can be a satisfying experience. But I digress.

Adding lava shows us how to use the trigger_hurt entity. As you can guess by the entity's name, we're going to make sure that falling into lava is not a pleasant experience. Creating this is a two-step process: First we create the lava, and then we create the trigger that makes it painful.

Follow these steps to create the lava:

1. Adjust the height grid by right-clicking in the viewport and choosing Manipulate; then mouse over the height grid's circle and bring it down to a height of about 16.

   You may need to change the grid size to a smaller number; 8 is usually convenient.

Note   Using the height grid to set a height that a brush snaps to is just one way of manipulating brushes. You'll learn more about changing the height and width of brushes in later tutorials.

2. Click the Box Brush, and drag out a box.

   You can put this brush anywhere in your level, but I used the Top viewport and dragged a rectangular brush from one side of my level to another, like a river of lava, as shown in Figure 23-10.

Figure 23-10: A river of lava in the Tempest editor. We'll make this deadly with a trigger brush.

3. In the Shader Nav dialog box, select Liquids.

4. Choose a lava texture.

Any of them will do for our purposes, so just choose the first one.

Now that you've created the lava area, we need to create the trigger that makes it painful when a player hits it. Without that, the lava is just another brush in the world, albeit a liquid one. (Try testing this by compiling and playing your level before you move on to the next steps. Then do the same after you've added the trigger_hurt entity.)

1. Click Box Brush, and drag out a second box that's just about the same size as the one you just created. Place it near the lava brush.

My preference is to make this second box a few grid units smaller so that it fits inside the lava.

2. In the Shader Nav area, choose the Common set of textures, and then choose Trigger.

Applying this texture tells the game that this is a special brush that causes some kind of event to happen (in this case, hurt the player when it's touched).

3. Bring up the Entity Editor dialog box. Scroll down the list, and choose trigger_hurt.

4. In the Description box, notice the key called dmg in the trigger_hurt entity.

The value for this key tells the trigger how much health to take off the player every second or so. If you want the lava to instantly kill the victim, enter a value of 999. If you enter a value smaller than 125, the player loses the amount of health you specify every second he spends in the lava.

5. Use the Move tool to move the trigger brush so that it's exactly where the lava brush is. If you made it a grid unit or two smaller, fit the trigger brush inside the lava brush like two Russian dolls fitting one inside the other.

6. To make the lava look a bit more realistic, add some brushes around it to "contain" it, making it look like a pool. Don't be afraid to get creative here!

Tip

Players never actually see trigger brushes. They're rendered invisible in the game. You can think of the lava-textured brush as a representative of the trigger brush. It's the brush that the player actually sees, but it's not the one that does the damage.

In order to work properly, trigger brushes like our lava damage have to be almost the same size and in the same place as the brush that the player actually sees. It's easier to create and edit the trigger brush a few grid steps away from the first brush and then move it on top of the first brush. When two brushes are sitting in the same spot, selecting and working with them can be difficult.

Compile your level and take a swim in your new lava pool, shown in Figure 23-11. Dangerous, isn't it?

Figure 23-11: Your lava is ready for a clumsy player to try to cross.

Advanced Editing: Slicing, Dicing, and the Fine Art of Texturing

At this point in your budding level design career, you probably want more power in manipulating the geometry you create. So far, we've really only created simple brushes and then moved them, but now you're about to use the other ignored tools in that toolbar as you learn to edit the geometry you create.

Tutorial: A gothic skylight

For this tutorial, you may want to create a new map, one where the initial box you make is about 512 units high (twice as high as your first room). But instead of just texturing the ceiling with either a sky texture or a regular texture, let's do a combination of both by creating and manipulating some brushes.

Commonly Used Common Textures

The set of Common textures contains unique textures used to tell the game how a brush reacts when touched by an object. Here's a quick guide to some of the most commonly used common textures.

✦ **NoDrop:** If a player dies and drops his weapon, and it falls into a NoDrop brush, the weapon disappears and can't be picked up by anyone. This is useful especially in space maps where a player may die falling off the edge and drop his weapon. If there weren't a NoDrop brush at the bottom of the level, all the dropped weapons could collect and slow down the game.

✦ **Slick:** Applied to a brush, it makes the surface slippery.

✦ **Clip:** This texture turns the brush into an invisible wall used to mark off areas where you don't want a player to go. It can also be used to pad fixtures and details in your level that jut out, causing players to get stuck on them. A clip brush can help players slide around the offending geometry without getting stuck.

✦ **Mirror:** This brush is used to create a mirror in the level. Be careful! Creating mirrors in Quake III Arena can really drag down the frame rate, and you should use this feature sparingly, if at all.

✦ **Caulk:** This texture is applied to parts of the level that are hidden behind curves. It's a special kind of texture that tells the game to "blend the curve that hides this with the face of this texture so that it looks smooth."

1. Create your initial room, 512 units high;

   Refer to the first tutorial in this chapter if you need help.

2. Texture the floor and the walls. For a change of pace, try using the Gothic textures in the Shader Nav.

3. Texture the ceiling with a non-sky texture of your choice.

   You'll find some interesting ones under the gothic_trim group.

4. Give the Top viewport some more room.

   You'll be working in this one for a few steps.

5. In the Perspective viewport, select the ceiling brush.

6. Right-click, choose Convert To, and then select Editable Brush.

Tip Whenever you need to edit a brush — resize it, scale it, and so on — remember to right-click on the brush, select Convert To, and choose Editable Brush.

7. Click the Brush Manipulate button above the number strip.

You see small green circles on the edges of the brush in the viewports, as shown in Figure 23-12. If you don't see these, try right-clicking in the viewport, choosing Manipulate, and then clicking Brush Manipulate again.

8. In the Top viewport, click and hold the bottom green circle, and move it upward. Notice in the Perspective viewport that the brush is getting narrower.

9. When you finish making it narrower, click Brush Manipulate again to deselect that tool.

10. Select the brush again if it's not already selected.

11. On the menu, choose Edit ➪ Clone. Click OK, because we want to copy this brush.

This makes an exact copy of the brush, complete with textures.

Tip   The clone tool is one of the most useful tools in level design. By selecting multiple pieces of textured geometry, you can instantly reproduce them with the clone tool and then move them wherever you want. This comes in handy when creating Capture the Flag levels, where the level is often a mirror image.

12. Click the Move button in the Transformation tools, and move the new brush down to the opposite side of the room.

13. Clone the new brush, and move it so that it's in the gap in the ceiling you created.

14. Click Brush Manipulate, and make the brush narrower so that it fits into the gap.

You can use the edges of the other two brushes in the Top viewport as your guide.

15. Texture this brush with a sky texture.

16. Compile and load your level to be sure that there are no leaks, that is, no gaps in the ceiling between the three pieces.

Take a look at your new level by loading it into Quake III Arena. In Figure 23-12, only the sky is illuminating the level through the new gap in the ceiling. Feel free to add some lights in those dark corners to brighten up the level a bit. We'll add some stairs and curves to this map in the next couple of tutorials.

Tip   You can use the Clone tool on anything in Tempest, including lights.

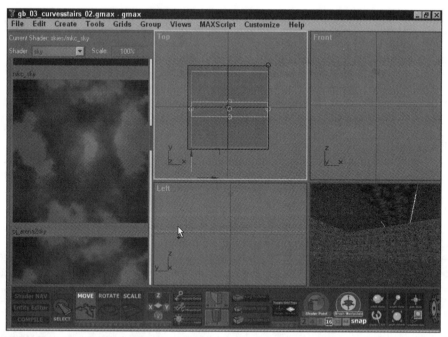

Figure 23-12: Creating an open ceiling. Note the green circles on the brush—they allow you to manipulate the brush.

Tutorial: Getting into gear

Although the tools in the lower toolbar are quick and easy to use when it comes to editing geometry, the most powerful set of editing tools is hidden behind that small gear on the right side of the toolbar. Click it, and you are presented with the Command Panel, an interface exactly like that of gmax's editing interface. (You can also open the Command Panel by pressing the 3 key.) In fact, the tools here are exactly the same as those covered in the earlier chapters, so we just cover them briefly with a simple tutorial on making a ramp up to a second floor in your level. We also learn how to use the Shader Paint tool as well.

1. Drag two brushes to make the second floor of your map; the ramp needs something to lead up to. Leave a gap between the two brushes about the width of the sky texture; this is where your ramp goes.

   Figure 23-13 shows what your ramp should look like.

Tip

Create and texture one brush, and then use the Clone tool to copy and move it.

Leakage

When a gap exists in the geometry of your level that allows the outside world in Tempest to creep into your level, you have a leak, and it stops the compile process cold. To understand what a leak really is, think of your level as a spaceship: It must be completely sealed off from the vacuum of space, or in this case, the emptiness of the void in which your level sits. The game must calculate the paths for all lighting in your level, and if a leak exists, it tries to compile a light path to get through that leak and out to infinity. (After all, there's literally nothing outside of your level, much like the infinite universe our hypothetical spaceship sits in. Pretty heavy, huh?) Because trying to calculate something to infinity tends to be impossible, when the compiler detects a leak, it stops compiling the map and warns you in the text file that pops up after a compile.

So how do you prevent a leak? By making sure that every brush that walls off your level to the empty void outside touches the brushes near it, creating a sealed-off space. Brushes inside this space make up the inner parts of your level, and it won't matter if they touch other brushes. But the outer walls of your level must not leave a gap that light can get through. It doesn't matter whether these brushes have sky textures on them. Although thinking of the sky as open when you texture a brush with it is easy, it's still considered a "solid" brush. Brushes using the Common set of textures, however, are not considered solid and can't be used to prevent leaks.

As your levels become more complex, leaks can easily develop. As you build geometry and add rooms, you should check your level often by compiling it. The compiler warns you about leaks, and you'll see the leak area in your viewports by following the white line that Tempest draws from a light source to the leak. If you check often enough, it can save you time and energy when trying to hunt them down.

2. Drag a brush between these two, then right-click it, select Convert To, and choose Editable Brush.

3. Resize it using the Brush Manipulate tool. The length doesn't matter, but you probably want it to be no longer than half the length of your map. Make it the same height as the two brushes on either side of it, and fit it exactly between these two (use the Top viewport as your guide). When you're finished resizing it, click Brush Manipulate to deselect the tool.

4. Click the gear in the lower right (or press 3 on your keyboard) to bring up the Command Panel.

5. Click the second tab, the Modify tab.

6. From the Modifier drop-down list, choose Taper from the Selection Modifiers.

7. In the Taper Axis options, choose the Effect to occur only on the X-axis.

   8. In the Taper parameter, decrease the numbers to begin tapering the brush. You'll see it taper in the viewports. Keep tapering until you get close to having a small flat area on the brush, as shown in Figure 23-13.

   Use the viewports as your guide.

   9. In the Modifier Stack, right-click Taper and choose Collapse All after you're satisfied with the effect. Choose Yes when it asks you to confirm.

   10. Notice that the modifier now shows the ramp as being an Editable Poly.

   If we were to leave it like that, it would never show up in the game. We need to convert it back to an Editable Brush.

   11. From the Modifier List, choose Turn to Brush at the bottom of the list.

   12. Right-click this new modifier again, and choose Collapse All. After you've confirmed the action, you see the Modifier Stack show that it's an editable brush again.

   13. Click the gear to close the editing panel, and bring up the Shader Nav to texture the brush.

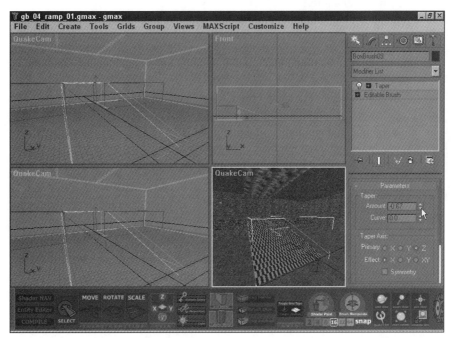

Figure 23-13: Tapering a brush using the Command Panel in Tempest. This panel is much like gmax's Command Panel, so the tools should be familiar.

Tutorial: Multi-textured brushes

When I textured my ramp, I chose one of the blocky textures from the end of the gothic_floor list. I like this texture as a floor, and because I want the second story of my level to match up, I applied it to the tops of the brushes on either side of the ramp. But I also wanted to keep the cool decorated block textures on the front of the brushes. How did I do this? With the Shader Paint tool. Let's learn how to apply multiple textures to different faces of a single brush.

1. Right-click on each of the blocks making up the second story of your level, choose Convert To, and then choose Editable Brush.

2. Open the Command Panel (click the gear at the bottom right, or press 3).

3. Click the plus (+) sign next to Editable Brush in the Modifier Stack.

   A list drops down to reveal a Face option.

4. Click Face.

5. Click the Shader Paint tool.

   A small menu appears in the Command Panel, and each face of the brush is now clickable.

6. To choose a new texture, open the Shader Nav and scroll down to a new texture.

7. Click the texture you'd like to apply; to make the floor look like a continuation of the ramp, choose the texture you applied to the ramp.

8. In the Perspective viewport, a small circle appears over the face of a selected texture. Click the circle to apply the texture to that face.

9. Repeat the process with the brush on the other side of the ramp.

The result should look like Figure 23-14.

Figure 23-14: Using Shader Paint to apply multiple textures to one brush

More on Functions

So far, you've worked with a couple of different types of entities. Lights are one kind of entity, and the trigger you created in the lava pool was another kind of entity. You may have scrolled through the entity list and wondered what the other entities were all about.

Tutorial: Adding a door

In the following tutorial, you'll learn how to create a function entity by creating a door that opens when a player gets close to it.

1. Drag a rectangular brush (something door-like).

   We will texture this and then resize the brush so that it fits the texture.

2. Open the Shader Nav.

3. Scroll down to gothic_door, and then choose one of the door textures. The third one is a good choice.

4. Apply the texture.

5. Right-click the brush, and convert it to an editable brush. Then click Brush Manipulate.

   Here's where we're going to resize and add texture to the door.

6. Use the green manipulators to change the height and width of the brush until only half of the door texture is seen on one side. In other words, you're creating one half of the door. Notice that if the brush is too big, you'll see the texture repeat or tile. Bring the sides and top out or in accordingly until you get a single half of the door on the brush.

7. Clone the brush, and then manipulate its width to get the other half of the door. Figure 23-15 shows a door brush.

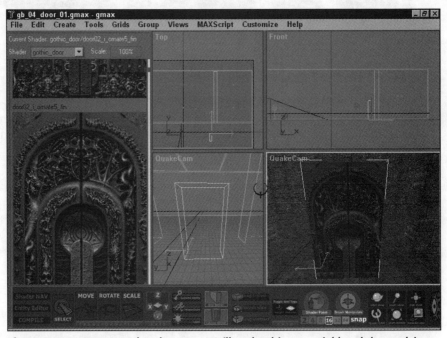

Figure 23-15: Doors are brushes, too. We'll make this a special brush by applying the func_door entity to it.

8. Manipulate the brushes so that they are 4 units thick.

9. Move the halves of the door so that they are near the opposite end of the room from the ramp, centered over the middle dividing line on the grid.

10. Drag a brush that divides a segment of the room on the opposite side of the ramp. We're making a hole for the door.

11. Using the center of the grid as a guide (if you've got height grid toggled on, you'll see it divide the map), make your brush 8 units wide, as tall as the ceiling, and make it stretch from one side of the map to one side of the door.

12. Texture the brush, then clone it, and move the cloned copy to the opposite side of the room, creating the other wall.

13. Repeat these steps to create the part of the wall that sits above the door. Select one half of the door, and then open the Entity Editor.

14. Choose func_door from the drop-down list, set it, and repeat this for the other half of the door.

15. The func_door function is set by default to open upward for a single door.

    We want our door, however, to split in half so that each half moves apart. We can easily change the function to do just that.

16. With the left half of the door selected, choose the angle key in the parameter list, and enter **-270**. For the right half, enter **-90**.

17. The doors need to move apart at the same time to look right. To do this, choose the Team key from the parameters list in the Entity Editor. Enter a name in the value box; "door1" works fine. Repeat with the other half of the door. By assigning the same name in both Team keys, you tell the editor that the doors must work in tandem.

Compile your map, and take a look.

Working with angles

Choosing the angle in which your door moves when it opens requires knowing the coordinate system that Tempest is using. The Y-axis always points north in Tempest, while the X-axis always points east. If the beginning of the X-axis is assigned an angle of 0, you can move counter-clockwise around like a compass, assigning angles of 90, 180, 270, and so on. See Figure 25-16 for a better visual reference.

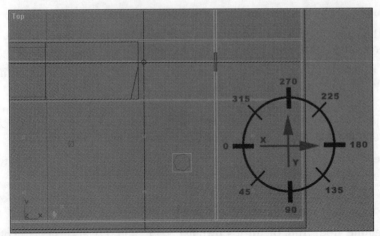

Figure 23-16: The axes of the world in Tempest are aligned like a compass. When specifying angles, use this guide to determine which value you need.

Importing Models

Walk around any of the Quake III Arena levels, and you'll notice that they aren't made up of only brushes and textures. Part of what makes a map stand out is the models used. Arena Gate, for example, has two large statues in the outer courtyard of Major and Visor that help decorate the level. These extra items are models, and you can add them to your own maps.

Fortunately for Q3A level designers, almost every model you see in the game is something you can use in your own levels — you just have to add it. A wide variety of models is available to choose from, ranging from statues like those in Arena Gate to wall-mounted images of Baphomet to small skull-shaped lamps used to decorate and light the rooms. In the tutorial that follows, you'll learn how to add one of the many skull lamps found in Q3A to your own level.

Tutorial: Adding torches

Let's brighten up our room and add a little creepiness to it by placing one of those tall skull torches in a corner. You'll also see in this tutorial how a little lighting can go a long way toward creating the right atmosphere.

1. Find a nice spot in your map to add a floor torch.

   A corner usually looks good.

2. Click the Generic Entity button in the middle of the bottom toolbar. (Move the entity a little if you need to so that it's not buried in the floor if you've got snap turned on.)

3. Open the Entity Editor.

4. Scroll down and choose misc_model.

5. Click the Model parameter to select it.

6. Click Load Model.

7. Browse to your Quake III Arena directory, and then drill down to the baseq3\models\mapobjects\storch\directory.

8. Choose tall_torch.md3, and click OK.

9. You should now see a tall skull torch on your map. If you want to change which way the torch faces, choose the Angle parameter.

   In this example, we're going to place the torch so that it's angled.

10. Enter **45** in the Value area, and click Set.

    Your model turns in the new angle.

11. Close the Entity Editor.

12. Move the torch with the Move tool (don't forget to select it first) to position it just where you want it.

The final result should look like Figure 23-17.

Figure 23-17: Torches like this one add some nice atmosphere to your level.

Compile your map, and take a look at your torch. If your level so far is anything like mine, you'll probably notice that while the torch has a moving flame on top of it, it doesn't actually give off any light and illuminate the corner. To make it look as if your torch is giving off light, as in Figure 23-18, add a light with moderate intensity (refer to the lighting tutorial if you need help) just in front of the torch and recompile.

Figure 23-18: The final placement. Martha Stewart could use some decorating like this, right?

Tutorial: Advanced texture manipulation

Let's put some finishing touches on your level by adding a few pillars to give it some style. After placing a pillar, we'll use Tempest's texture editing tools to get the texture looking right on its surface.

1. Select the Cylinder Brush tool.

2. Drag a cylinder in the Perspective window.

   Any radius will do because we're going to manipulate it to get it looking the way we want.

3. Convert the cylinder to an editable brush, and then select Brush Manipulate.

4. Using the manipulators, heighten the cylinder so that it almost reaches the ceiling, and move it a few steps off the floor.

   We're going to add a foundation to the top and bottom, just like the pillars found in Roman ruins.

5. Open the Shader Nav.

6. From the gothic_trim group, select the stucco7top texture and apply it.

7. Notice that the texture repeats because it's smaller in height than the pillar. To change that, open the Command Panel with the 3 key or by clicking the gear.

8. From the Modify panel, click the plus (+) sign to open the Editable Brush list.

9. Choose Face.

10. In the Perspective window, click the cylinder. You'll select one face that makes up the whole cylinder, which is actually made up of several polygons. Using the camera views, select all faces of the cylinder by clicking on each while holding down the Ctrl key.

11. In the mapping rollout below the Modify Stack, click the up arrow next to V Scale. Notice that the texture stretches. Keep clicking until the texture no longer repeats, and it covers the pillar appropriately, as in Figure 23-19.

    (You can simply enter numbers manually to move this along faster; I entered 1 in place of 0 before the decimal point.)

12. Deselect the pillar, and create brushes that cap it at the top and bottom, touching the ceiling and the floor.

    There's another stucco texture in the gothic_trim group that would be good for these.

Messing with Textures

The Mapping rollout from the Modify menu in the Command Panel contains a few tools used to manipulate textures:

   ✦ **U Shift:** Moves a texture horizontally

   ✦ **V Shift:** Moves a texture vertically

   ✦ **Rotation:** Rotates the texture at an angle specified

   ✦ **U Scale:** Stretches or compresses the texture horizontally

   ✦ **V Scale:** Stretches or compresses the texture vertically

These tools can be used when your textures need some fine adjustments to fit on the brushes you create.

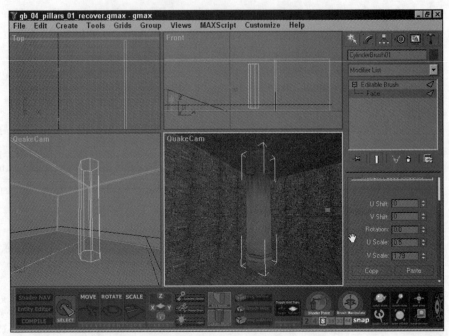

Figure 23-19: Select the faces that make up the pillar, and use the Modifier Stack to edit the texture.

Enter the Arena: Finding Help in the Map Community

Creating levels is probably the most popular way that the fan community gets involved in Quake III Arena. If you find yourself with the urge to create bigger and better maps now that you've gotten a taste of what it's like to make your own, a whole world out there is waiting to help you. The Quake III Arena community is packed with tutorials, resources, and Web sites that will help you make better levels. And who knows? Maybe you'll find that level design is your hidden talent, and the world may see one of your levels in the next best-selling game.

To help further your budding level artist career, check out these resources. Some of them deal specifically with a different level editor (Q3Radiant), but many of the resources on making levels in general can still be applied to Tempest.

Tempest discussion at gmax support forums

http://www.gmaxsupport.com

The gmax discussion forums have a separate forum just for Tempest discussion. The moderators and regular posters have developed a substantial network of people who help each other learn how to use Tempest. If you have a Tempest question, someone there can probably answer it.

Quake3World forums

http://www.quake3world.com/forums/

Quake3World has been a pillar of the Quake III community since the game came out in 1999. A very well-respected group of both amateur and professional level designers hang out there and are always willing to answer questions.

..::LvL

http://www.planetquake.com/lvl

...::LvL is a great place to check out maps by other level designers. The site features a free beta map submission system—if you're looking for feedback on your map, submit it to the site, where other level designers and players can download it, critique it, and give you an idea of what worked and what didn't.

QMap

http://www.qmap.org

This is another first-person shooter mapping site dedicated to spreading the word about level design. The site has forums where you can get help with your mapping techniques and learn from others.

Claudec's Tutorial Index

http://www.claudec.com/lair_of_shaders/tutorials.shtml

This is perhaps the single-most useful fan-created site on level design. Claudec has taken every known tutorial on the Web and compiled a massive index to each one. Lighting, triggers, basic rooms, models—you name it, there's a tutorial listed here for it. Although most of the tutorials are geared for those using Q3Radiant, Tempest users still get lots of help from them, because many cover the essentials of good level design.

Summary

If you've ever wanted to create your own arenas to play with, share with friends, and use as a canvas, Tempest definitely gets you started. Like many things in life, level design is easy to learn, yet it takes a long time to master.

In this chapter, you used Tempest to learn the following skills:

✦ Creating a simple room with CSG hollow

✦ Applying textures

✦ Manipulating brushes

✦ Importing and working with models

✦ Editing textures and geometry with gmax's Command Panel

✦ Compiling and playing your level in Quake III Arena

In the next chapter, you'll learn how to create new scenery for Flight Simulator 2002.

✦   ✦   ✦

Creating Custom Content for Flight Simulator 2002

✦ ✦ ✦ ✦

In This Chapter

Using the
MakeMDL tool

Using MakeMDL
Recognized Names

Working with textures

Creating scenery
objects

✦ ✦ ✦ ✦

Of all the various flight simulators that are available, Microsoft's Flight Simulator is the most popular and most flown flight simulator. It has also been around the longest. Included with Flight Simulator 2002 Professional Edition are the tools needed to create your own custom content.

Using the Flight Simulator Editing Tools

Flight Simulator includes several unique tools for editing almost every aspect of aircraft and their environment. If you visit the official Flight Simulator Web pages at http://zone .msn.com/flightsim/FS02DevDeskSDK00.asp, you'll find a host of different Software Development Kits (SDKs) for customizing everything from the plane's interior to the ATC voices.

The SDKs that are currently available on the Flight Simulator Insider Web site include the following:

✦ ABL SDK

✦ Aircraft Container SDK

✦ Aircraft Panels SDK

✦ ATC Voicepack SDK

✦ Autogen SDK

✦ Cab File SDK

✦ Custom Terrain Textures SDK

✦ FSEdit SDK

✦ MakeMDL SDK

✦ MDL Format SDK

✦ Panels and Gauges SDK

✦ Multiplayer/Flight Instructor SDK

✦ Netpipes SDK

✦ Special Effects SDK

✦ Traffic Database Builder Utility

Each of these SDKs includes detailed documentation

The key tool that relates to gmax is MakeMDL SDK. Using this tool, you can export gmax-created objects to a format that Flight Simulator can use.

Note   As you read this chapter, keep in mind two other Microsoft simulator products that work in similar ways. The latest Combat Flight Simulator also ships with a gmax game pack and the means to export to the M3D file format. Train Simulator is another simulator in this same vein. Its gmax game pack enables you to create custom train cars using gmax.

Using the MakeMDL Tool

If you install the complete version of Flight Simulator 2002 Professional, you'll find the MakeMDL tool in the gmax folder where Flight Simulator is installed. If you are using a newer version of gmax, such as 1.2, you'll want to copy the MakeMDL.exe file into the gmax\plugins directory where the new installation is. This makes the MakeMDL tool available within gmax.

The MakeMDL tool, shown in Figure 24-1, consists of five panels — Main, LOD, Options, Scenery, and Output.

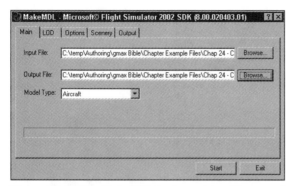

Figure 24-1: The MakeMDL tool consists of five panels.

The Main panel

The Main panel of the MakeMDL tool can export two file types:

✦ **MDL,** which is used for aircraft

✦ **BGL,** which is used for scenery

The Input File is the source file that you want to load into Flight Simulator, and the Output File is the name of the file that Flight Simulator will read.

Flight Simulator has strict naming conventions that it follows. Each file name begins with a name followed by an underscore character and a three-digit number that defines the Level of Detail (LOD) for the object, followed by an underscore and a letter (A-Z) to maintain different versions of the models. Interior models also include "_interior" and shadow models include "_shadow" at the end of their file names.

The LOD panel

In the LOD panel, shown in Figure 24-2, you can select to include several different models each at a different resolution depending on the size of the model on the screen. For example, if you have a complex model that is off in the distance, it would be a waste of the computer's calculations to compute all the complexity of the model if it is too far away to be seen. By creating a lower resolution version of the complex model and loading it into the LOD panel, you can speed the display of all models in the scene.

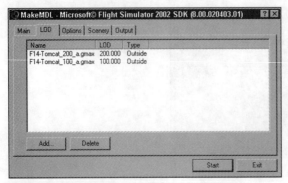

Figure 24-2: The LOD panel can load different resolution models.

The three-digit number specified in the naming convention correlates to the LOD level, where the lower numbers correspond to the lower resolution models and higher numbers are higher resolution models.

The Options panel

In the Options panel, shown in Figure 24-3, are several options that you can set to determine how the MakeMDL tool will function. These options are described in Table 24-1.

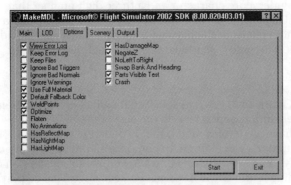

Figure 24-3: Using the Options panel, you can control the export settings.

Table 24-1
MakeMDL Options

Option	Description
View Error Log	Creates an error log and makes it visible in Windows Notepad.
Keep Error Log	Saves the error log along with the file.
Keep Files	Keeps intermediate .ASM files as the files are being created.
Ignore Bad Triggers	Ignores any unknown animations.
Ignore Bad Normals	Ignores any normals that are misplaced.
Ignore Warnings	Ignores any warnings that appear.
Use Full Material	Uses all material attributes. Uses only diffuse color if disabled.
Default Fallback Color	Uses the default fallback color instead of the material's diffuse color.
Weld Points	Welds all points within a 4-millimeter threshold.
Optimize	Optimizes the mesh during export.
Flatten	Flattens the input mesh into a single mesh object.
No Animations	Ignores all animations with the file.
HasReflectMap	Identifies that any texture ending with "_T" has a reflection map.
HasNightMap	Identifies that any texture ending with "_LM" has a night map.
HasLightMap	Identifies that any texture ending with "_L" has a light map.
HasDamageMap	Identifies that any texture ending with "_D" has a damage map.
NoLeftToRight	Ignores any left to right transformations.
NegateZ	Flips the Z-axis for the model.
Swap Bank and Heading	Swaps the bank and heading values for all animations.
Parts Visible Test	Tests the visible part (used only for aircraft).
Crash	Creates a crash tree for this object.

The Scenery panel

The Scenery panel, shown in Figure 24-4, is only used for objects that are exported as scenery. It is used to define the location of the scenery object in Longitude and Latitude values. You can also specify the Heading and View Distance.

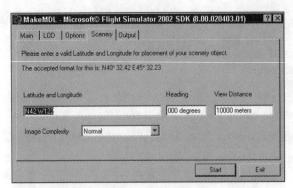

Figure 24-4: You can enter the longitude and latitude values in the Scenery panel.

The Output panel

The Output panel, shown in Figure 24-5, is where all status and errors are reported and should be checked whenever you export a model using the MakeMDL tool.

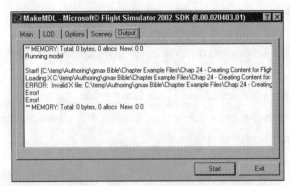

Figure 24-5: The Output panel displays any errors that occurred during the export process.

MakeMDL Recognized Names

As you build scenery and aircraft models in gmax, the MakeMDL tool recognizes several part names. If you use these names, then the Flight Simulator game engine can work with the various part names and even add some functionality and animations to them.

The following are aircraft part names that can be recognized by default:

pilot	r_wingtip	nose
l_wing	lwingtip	nose1
r_wing	rwingtip	engine0
l_wingfold	tail	engine1
r_wingfold	l_tail	engine2
l_wing_tip	r_tail	engine3
r_wing_tip	tail_l	l_engine
l_wingtip	tail_r	r_engine

Working with Textures

All aircraft and scenery objects created in gmax can include textures, but the textures can change based on the conditions created by Flight Simulator. Objects can use five different textures to display these various conditions. The available textures include the following:

- ✦ **Base Texture:** This is the default texture. It should end with "_T." This is represented in the gmax Material Editor as the Diffuse map.

- ✦ **Damage Texture:** This texture is used when the aircraft gets damaged (it is not used on scenery objects). This map should be named the same as the base texture except that it ends with "_D."

- ✦ **Night Map Texture:** This texture is used for night conditions. This is represented in the gmax Material Editor as the Ambient Color map.

- ✦ **Light Map Texture:** This texture is used for enabling lights during night conditions. This is represented in the gmax Material Editor as the Self-Illumination map. This map should be named the same as the base texture except that it ends with "_l."

- ✦ **Reflection Map Texture:** This texture provides a reflection map that shines off the surface. This is represented in the gmax Material Editor as the Reflection map.

All textures can be saved using the Bitmap (BMP) or Targa (TGA) image formats and need to be 256×256 pixels. These image formats can be applied to the model in gmax, but a convert DDS image file that has the same name also needs to be created using the Image Tool utility. You can find this utility in the gmax directory where Flight Simulator 2002 Professional was installed.

The Image Tool, shown in Figure 24-6, enables you to load BMP and TGA images and save them as DDS files. Flight Simulator uses the DirectX (DDS) files with its game engine to display textures.

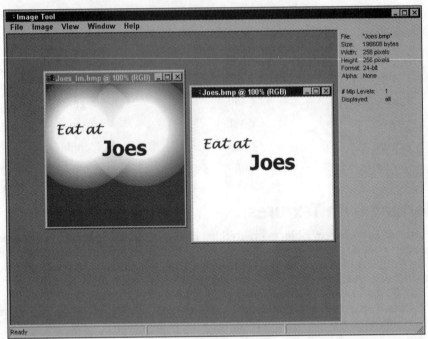

Figure 24-6: The Image Tool utility can convert BMP and TGA files to DDS files.

Creating Scenery Objects

When creating scenery objects, there are several things that you need to check before you start that can save you lots of trouble later.

Setting units

Before beginning to create objects, you first need to check the units setup used by gmax. Flight Simulator expects the units to be set to meters. You can check this in the Units Setup dialog box by selecting Customize ➪ Units Setup and selecting the Metric option and the Meters selection in the drop-down list. Select Customize ➪ Preference menu option to open the Preference Settings dialog box, and select the System Unit Scale so that 1 Unit equals 1 meter.

With these settings, your models should appear correctly in Flight Simulator. If these settings are wrong, then your objects appear mis-scaled. With the correct units set up, all parameter values are expressed in meters.

Positioning objects

The position of the object in the scene is based on the location of the object's Pivot Point. You can control the location of this point using the Hierarchy panel in gmax. Another way to set its position is with the Transform Type-In dialog box, which can be opened with the F12 key. In this dialog box, enter a value of **0** in the Absolute: World column for the X, Y, and Z-axes.

Tip   Corresponding coordinate fields for the X, Y, and Z-axes are available in the status bar at the bottom of the gmax window. You can also enter coordinate values in these fields.

Determining Longitude and Latitude coordinates

The easiest way to find the longitude and latitude coordinates for the location where you wish to place a scenery object is to use Flight Simulator itself. To do this, fly to the location where you'd like to place your custom scenery object and select Views ➪ New View ➪ Top Down to get a top-down view of the location. Then select Aircraft ➪ Slew Mode; move the aircraft to the exact location where the scenery object will go; and record the longitude, latitude, and heading values that are displayed in the upper-right corner. Figure 24-7 shows this view.

Figure 24-7: In Slew mode, you can see the longitude, latitude, and heading values for scenery locations.

Tutorial: Creating a billboard

What is the big difference between airport runways and freeways? The answer is billboards. If I were an airplane parts manufacturer, I'd buy the prime real estate surrounding runways and place my strategic billboards everywhere. (But it might work better if I were an insurance dealer, because such a billboard would be waiting for some stray airplane to crash into it.)

To add a billboard to the edge of a runway, follow these steps:

1. In gmax, open the Billboard.gmax file from the Chap 24 directory on the CD-ROM.

   This file includes the billboard object. The appropriate texture files have also been prepared and also are waiting in the Chap 24 directory.

2. Check the Units setup by selecting Customize ➪ Units Setup and then selecting the Metric option and Meters in the drop-down list. Then close the Units Setup dialog box, and open the Preference Settings dialog box with the Customize ➪ Preferences menu option. Set the Unit Scale so that 1 Unit equals 1 meter.

3. Because the object is already created, you need only to position it. Open the Hierarchy panel, and click the Pivot button. Then click the Affect Pivot Only button to see exactly where the pivot point is. Click the Affect Pivot Only button when finished to deselect it.

   For this object it is already at the bottom of the billboard post where it should be.

4. Enter values of **0** in the X, Y, and Z-axes coordinate fields at the bottom of the gmax window.

   This will correctly position the billboard above ground.

5. You must now apply the materials: Press the M key to open the gmax Material Editor. Click the New button, and select the Multi-Material material. Set up the Multi-Material with two materials. Name the first material "Sign" and click on its Material button. Then, click the Diffuse mapping button to the right of the Diffuse color swatch, and double-click the Bitmap mapping type from the gmax Material Navigator that appears. Then locate the Joes.tga file from the Chap 24 directory on the CD-ROM, and click OK. Click the Go to Parent button, name the second material "Post," and change its color to black.

6. Select next the mapping button next to the Ambient color swatch (make sure the lock button is off), and select the Joes_lm.bmp image file. Then click the Apply button to apply this material to the billboard object. This applies the first material to the sign, which has a Material ID of 1. The post is black because its Material ID is 2.

7. In Flight Simulator, use the Slew view to locate the Longitude, Latitude, and Heading values for the location where you want to place this billboard (and don't put it in the middle of the runway!).

8. Back in gmax, select File ⇨ Export to open the MakeMDL tool. In the Scenery panel, enter the recorded longitude, latitude, and heading values. In the Main panel, select Scenery as the Model Type, and click the Start button.

   The exported model is automatically saved to the Program Files\FS2002\AddonScenery directory.

9. Open the Image Tool utility and convert all the textures to DDS files with the same names. Then copy the billboard textures to the Program Files\FS2002\AddonScenery\Textures directory.

By following these steps, you can start Flight Simulator and fly to the location where the billboard was placed.

Working with Aircraft

The MakeMDL exporter works for aircraft as well as scenery. You need only to select Aircraft from the drop-down list in the Main panel. Aircraft models are exported as MDL files.

Tip If you've created an aircraft in FSDS, you can import it into gmax using the DXF format as a go-between. First export the model from FSDS using the DXF format, and then import it into gmax using the DXF format.

The aerodynamic performance of the aircraft is defined in a configuration file. The configuration files are simple text files with parameters that define how the aircraft act. You can learn more about these files in the Aircraft Container SDK.

Tutorial: Exporting an MDL Aircraft

In this example, we'll export an aircraft using the Combat Flight Simulator (CFS) game pack. This game pack works just like the Flight Simulator game pack and provides an export option.

Note The CFS game pack is part of the Aircraft and Vehicle SDK that can be found on the CFS Insider Web page at http://microsoftgamesinsider.com/CFSInsider/Tools/default.htm.

To export an aircraft to the MDL format, follow these steps:

1. Open the F14 Tomcat.gmax file from the Chap 24 directory on the CD-ROM. This file includes a model of the F14 Tomcat created by Viewpoint Datalabs.

2. In gmax, select File ⇨ Export and choose the M3D format in the File Type drop-down list. Name the aircraft F14_Tomcat. Navigate to the Program Files\Microsoft Games\Combat Flight Simulator 3\Aircraft directory and create a new directory for this aircraft. Save the aircraft in this directory.

3. Open the Image Tool utility and convert all the texture maps used on the aircraft to DDS files. Then copy all the original texture files and the DDS image files to the directory where you saved the aircraft model.

Figure 24-8 shows the F13 Tomcat aircraft in gmax, ready to be exported.

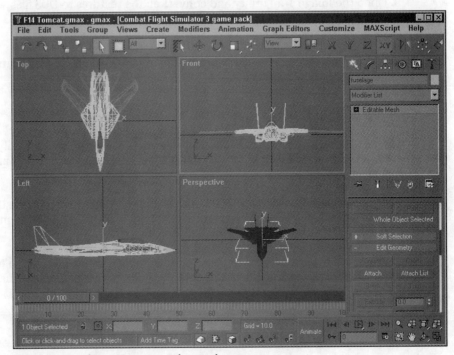

Figure 24-8: The CFS game pack can also export content.

Finding Online Resources for Flight Simulator 2002

If you look online, you'll find that gmax is just one of a vast number of content creator tools available for Flight Simulator. A wealth of information is available for creating aircraft and you'll find no shortage of people willing to help you as you get started.

Developer's Desk at Flight Simulator Insider

http://zone.msn.com/flightsim/FS02DevDeskSDK00.asp

These are the official pages for Flight Simulator. You can find the SDKs in the Developer Desk pages.

Combat Flight Simulator Insider

http://microsoftgamesinsider.com/CFSInsider/Tools/default.htm

The Tools pages of the Combat Flight Simulator Insider provide the tools required to customize content for Combat Flight Simulator.

FSPlanet

http://www.fsplanet.com/

This is a very popular site that includes a huge repository of resources from aircraft and scenery to virtual cockpits and video clips. All content is rated, making it easy to find the best add-ons.

FlightSim.com

http://www.flightsim.com/cgi/kds/main/menuch00.htm

This is a good site for general news and announcements concerning flight simulation in general.

AVSim

http://www.avsim.com/

AVSim is another good site and includes forums covering many different aspects of content creation.

Train Simulator Insider

http://microsoftgamesinsider.com/TrainSimulator/default.htm

The Train Simulator game pack is very similar to the Flight Simulator. You can download the Train Simulator game pack from this site's Tools pages.

Summary

Using the MakeMDL tool, you can export custom aircraft and scenery for Flight Simulator. In this chapter, the following topics have been covered:

✦ Using the MakeMDL interface, including the various panels

✦ Creating scenery objects in gmax for export to Flight Simulator

The next chapter begins an adventure with Dungeon Siege.

✦　　✦　　✦

Creating Adventures with Dungeon Siege®

◆ ◆ ◆ ◆

In This Chapter

Understanding the
Dungeon Siege
Tool Kit™

Using Siege Max™
to export custom
terrains and nodes

Working with objects
and animating
characters

Finding online
resources

◆ ◆ ◆ ◆

Dungeon Siege® is a game created by the fine people at Gas Powered Games and distributed by Microsoft Game Studios. The person behind all the hoopla at Gas Powered Games is Chris Taylor, who previously created a small game called Total Annihilation (TA). This game became a phenomenon, and active TA gamers still can be found today. The key to TA is its expandability. That same functionality has found its way to Dungeon Siege.

The key to creating new levels in Dungeon Siege is a freely available set of tools bundled together in what is called the Dungeon Siege Tool Kit™. Using this tool kit (which includes a robust gmax game pack) allows you to create new levels, monsters, weapons, characters, and scenery. You can even define new adventures with tasks to be accomplished and far-off places to see.

Using the Dungeon Siege Tool Kit™

The Dungeon Siege Tool Kit (DSTK) is freely available, but it requires that Dungeon Siege be installed. This tool kit actually doesn't come on the Dungeon Siege CDs, but you can download it for free from `http://www.microsoft.com/games/dungeonsiege/8.asp`.

Note

The latest release of the Dungeon Siege Tool Kit is version 1.1a. This version includes several bug fixes that make the Tool Kit more stable.

The latest version includes support for several new Art Packs. These Art Packs include default character types that you can modify and export. They provide a good starting point for creating your own content. You can find more details on the Art Packs at `http://www.dungeonsiege.com/dstk_art_packs.shtml`.

The Dungeon Siege Tool Kit includes the following tools:

- ✦ DS Anim Viewer™
- ✦ DS Mod™
- ✦ Siege Editor™
- ✦ Siege Max™

The DSTK comes with a standard installation executable. After installing the tool kit, you can access all the tools from the Windows Start menu.

Caution

The Dungeon Siege Tool Kit requires that the latest upgrade patch be applied to Dungeon Siege before it can be installed and used. You can find the latest patches on the Dungeon Siege Web site.

Siege Editor™

The first place to start in the DSTK is with the Siege Editor, shown in Figure 25-1. Using this tool, you can create new levels and scenarios, add new functionality to the characters and objects in the game, and modify many aspects of the game.

Tip

The Siege Editor requires a video card that can run 3D graphics in a window, which can be tricky for some older video cards that like to have full control over the window. If you're having trouble running the Siege Editor, try lowering the resolution and running Siege Editor again.

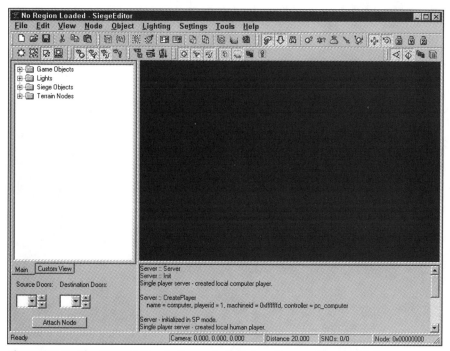

Figure 25-1: The Siege Editor is the main interface for creating worlds for Dungeon Siege.

Siege Max™

Siege Max is the gmax game pack for Dungeon Siege. It provides additional functionality for previewing models and for exporting meshes and animations. Siege Max also includes several unique tools for preparing the meshes to interface with the other aspects of the Dungeon Siege game. All this additional functionality can be accessed via a pop-up quadmenu that appears when you right-click an object in one of the viewports. Figure 25-2 shows this quadmenu.

DS Anim Viewer™ and DS Mod™

The DS Anim Viewer tool lets you view the animations applied to a mesh. The Animation Viewer is accessible from within Siege Max, which is convenient for working with objects. Pressing the H key while the Animation Viewer is active opens a help file for the Animation Viewer.

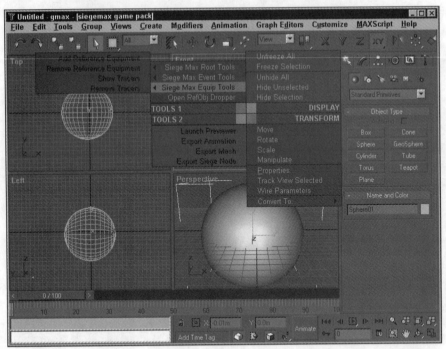

Figure 25-2: The Siege Max tool is the gmax interface with some clever additions.

The DS Mod tool is a version of Dungeon Siege that contains a console that gives you access to the playing parameters. It provides a place where you can test out your new level.

Working with the Siege Editor™

Before you can see any of your new content in Dungeon Siege, you need a way to get the content into the game. The gate to this brave new world is the Siege Editor. Using the Siege Editor, you can build level regions and populate them with custom objects and characters.

Note   The Siege Editor is a fairly complex piece of software, and an entire book could be written to describe how to use it. Its coverage in this chapter is introductory and touches only on those main issues that are required to work with your gmax created content. For more detailed coverage of the Siege Editor, refer to its user manual.

The Siege Editor also includes the ability to control the lighting and mood of the scene and to place triggers in the level, which react based parameters you set. You can also use the Siege Editor to define quests scenarios.

Finding the Correct Node

All nodes used in Dungeon Siege can be found within the file view pane, but locating the node that you want can be tricky. If you understand the naming convention that Dungeon Siege uses, it can help you in locating the correct node. All nodes end with the .SNO extension, which stands for Siege Node.

Most node names consist of five different components that are separated by the underscore character. These components relate directly to the directory structure where the file is found. The first component is represented by a single letter that identifies the type — "t" for terrains. The second component refers to the set. For example, "grdn" is the garden set, "dgn01" is the dungeon1 set, and "xxx" is the generic set. The third component is the node type. Each set has several different node types that define where it would fit. For example, the "crypt1" set has "corner," "cap," "floor," "room," "stair," and "wall" node types. The next category is a number that explains the node's size. The final category is the unique name for the node. For example, the file named "t_dgn01_str_flr-08x08.sno" is a terrain node for the Dungeon01 set of stairs that are 8 by 8 meters.

Learning the Siege Editor™ interface

The Siege Editor interface is split into several panes. You can dynamically change the space allotted to each pane by dragging its border. The various interface elements include the following, as shown in Figure 25-3:

✦ **Menus and Toolbars:** These contain standard interface elements for executing commands.

✦ **Main View Window:** Objects and map details are shown in this window. You can navigate about this window using the mouse.

✦ **File View Pane:** This pane shows a file list of the available resources; you can switch between the Main View and the Custom View using the tabs at the bottom of the pane.

✦ **Console Pane:** This pane displays as text all the commands that take place and provides some valuable feedback as you build levels.

✦ **Status Bar:** Located at the bottom of the interface, this bar holds information such as the camera's position, distance, and the number of nodes.

Navigating the view window

Because the main view window is the place where you get to see the pieces of the level come together, you'll need to know how to change the camera's view. All navigation within this window is accomplished using the mouse.

Main view window

File View Pane

Menus and toolbars

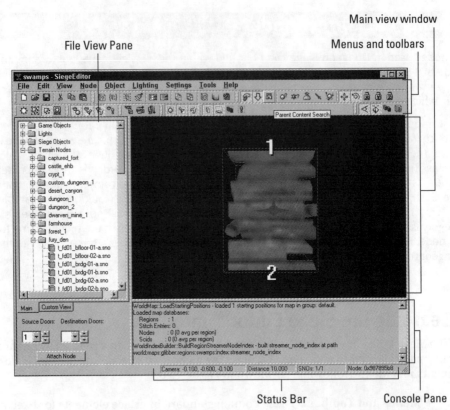

Status Bar   Console Pane

Figure 25-3: The Siege Editor interface includes several panes that provide information.

To pan the view, hold down the right mouse button while moving the mouse. To zoom in on the view, scroll the mouse scroll wheel. To pan the vertical height, hold down the Shift key and the right mouse button while moving the mouse. You can also hold down both mouse buttons while moving the mouse. To rotate the view, click and hold the middle scrollable mouse wheel while moving the mouse.

Tip   If you don't have a mouse with a middle scrolling wheel, you'll be unable to zoom or rotate the view.

Working with maps, regions, and nodes

Now that you have a familiarity with the Siege Editor interface, you can start building a map. Within each map are regions, and regions are made up of nodes. To create a new map, select File ⇨ New Map or press the New button on the main toolbar. This makes the New Map dialog box appear, as shown in Figure 25-4. For a new map, enter a Name, which will be listed as the folder, and a Screen Name, which is the name that will appear in Dungeon Siege.

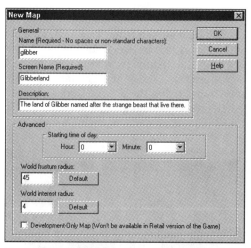

Figure 25-4: The New Map dialog box lets you name each new map.

The next step is to create a region within the map, which is accomplished with the File ➪ New Region menu command. Regions also need a name, as well as a unique Range and ID numbers. Accepting the defaults ensures that these values are unique. The New Region dialog box, shown in Figure 25-5, also includes a file view for selecting the starting node.

Figure 25-5: Maps are made of regions that are created in the New Region dialog box.

Connecting nodes

Regions are made of nodes, and nodes can be selected from the file view pane and added to the starting node by connecting the doors between the nodes. If you select the starting node that appears within the main view window, as shown in Figure 25-6, its edges are surrounded by numbers. These numbers are the Source Doors, and you can cycle through these doors using the Source Doors spinner located under the file view pane. The selected door is highlighted in red and has a red arrow pointing away from it.

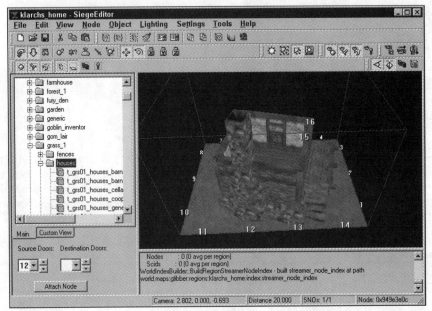

Figure 25-6: The node doors are listed by number and can be connected with other nodes.

With a node door selected, you can select a node to connect to it in the file view pane and then click on the Destination Doors spinner to rotate through the connected node's doors. After the node is correctly placed, you can select the new node and connect more nodes to it. Figure 25-7 shows a house node with three new river nodes attached to it. This process can continue until you're satisfied with the region.

Caution

As you connect nodes using doors, be careful not to overlap the nodes. If two nodes are overlapped, then the map may not function correctly in the game and you'll lose your current region. Remember to save often.

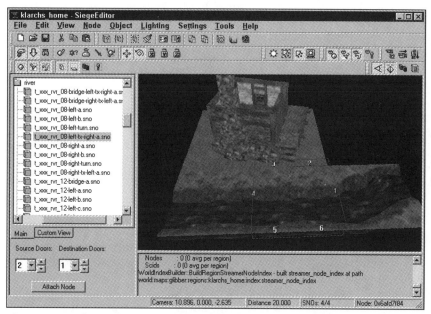

Figure 25-7: Three new river nodes have been connected to the house node.

Previewing nodes

If you want to look at a node before placing it, you can view it in the Previewer. Right-clicking on a node in the file view pane and selecting Mesh Previewer opens the Mesh Previewer window, shown in Figure 25-8. You can use the same mouse command for zooming and panning in this window as in the main view window.

Using the Node Matcher

Within the Siege Editor's Tools menu are several helpful tools that can make building a map much easier. One of these tools in the Node Matcher, shown in Figure 25-9.

If you have a funny shaped node that you're trying to work with, the Node Matcher can provide a list of nodes from a given folder that match the selected door. With a door selected, choose Tools ⇨ Node Matcher to run the Node Matcher. You can select the number of folders to check to limit the search; then when you click the Match Selected button, a list of nodes that match the given door node appears.

If you select a node from the list and press the Attach button, the node is attached to the source node.

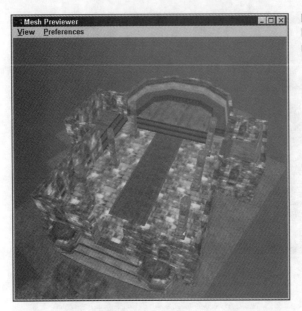

Figure 25-8: The Mesh Previewer lets you see a node before you connect it.

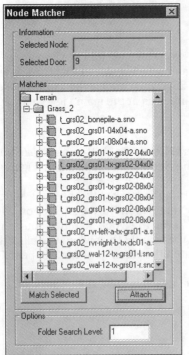

Figure 25-9: The Node Matcher tool displays a list of nodes that match the selected door.

Tutorial: Building a stone house region

For this example, we'll create a simple stone house region by connecting several nodes.

To create a simple stone house region, follow these steps:

1. Select File ➪ New Map to create a new map. In the New Map dialog box, enter a Name, Screen Name, and a Description of the map, and click OK.

2. Select File ➪ New Region to create a new region within the map you just made. In the New Region dialog box, select the map name, give the region a name, select the Terrain Nodes\grass_1\houses\t_grs01_houses_generic-a-stone.sno node as the starting node, and click OK.

3. Click the house object in the main view window to select it. Use the spinner arrows to select 15 in the Source Door field. In the file view, select the Terrain Nodes\grass_1\houses\t_grs01_houses_generic-a-roof-shingle.sno node, and click the arrows on the Destination Doors field to attach the roof node to the house.

4. Select number 7 as the Source Door, choose the Terrain Nodes\generic\floor\t_xxx_flr_04x08-v0.sno node in the file view pane, and select 1 as the Destination Door.

   This adds some grass to one side of the house.

5. With the same node selected in the file view pane, select 5 as the Source Door and 4 as the Destination Door. Repeat for Source 14 to Destination 4 and Source 12 to Destination 1.

6. In the file view pane, select Terrain Nodes\generic\river\t_xxx_rvr_08-left-b.sno, then choose the Source Door 8 and the Destination Door 2, and repeat for Source 9 and Destination 3. Then select the newest river node, Source 1 and Destination 4, to complete the river.

Figure 25-10 shows the resulting house and river. This is just a simple example, but it gives you the idea of how to connect nodes.

Working with node properties

Each node that is placed in a region has a set of properties associated with it. You can view these properties by selecting Node ➪ Properties. This opens the Node Properties dialog box. Using this dialog box, you can set some general node settings such as Occludes Light and Bounds Camera. This dialog box also includes a panel for setting the Fade options and a Node Set panel for selecting the set that is used to texture the node.

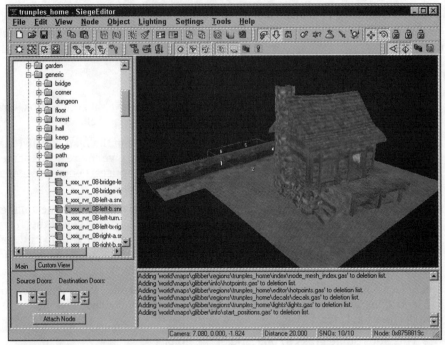

Figure 25-10: A house and a river made from connecting nodes

Selecting a node and changing its set in the Node Set panel changes the textures that are applied to the node. This makes it possible to reuse nodes and to quickly change their set textures without having to rebuild a region. For example, if you held down the Ctrl key while selecting all the nodes in a region and changed its Node Set from "grass1" to "ice_caves," then all the grassy areas of the region would be changed to snow. Note that all nodes have a changeable node set. The nodes that are guaranteed to have more than one node set are the "Generic Set" nodes which are recognizable by the "xxx" portion of their name.

Placing and positioning objects

After the terrain nodes are established, you can add objects to the scene to enhance the look of a region. Objects can be placed anywhere within the scene, but you need to carefully place them so they look realistic. For example, having a sword floating in mid-air might be fun, but it is not very realistic.

The first step to placing objects is to check the Objects ➪ Mode menu and make sure that you're in Placement mode. The other available modes are Movement and Rotate. If a check mark appears next to Placement mode, then you can simply locate the object that you wish to place in the file view pane and click in the main view window where you want it to go. Figure 25-11 shows five bushes that have been placed next to the house.

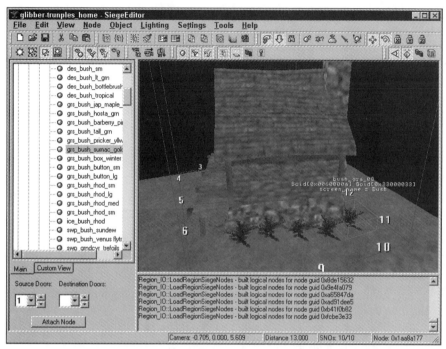

Figure 25-11: Objects can be placed anywhere within the scene.

Caution

If Placement mode is enabled and an object is selected in the file view, then an object is created every time you click in the main view window. Remember to turn off Placement mode if you're not actively using it.

When an object is selected, it is highlighted with a green box and its name appears above it. Selected objects can be moved if Movement mode (Objects ➪ Mode ➪ Movement) is enabled by simply dragging the object to their new location. Holding down the Ctrl key while clicking several objects lets you select multiple objects. These objects can then be grouped together with the Objects ➪ Grouping menu command.

By default, all objects are placed on the ground, but if you disable the Object ➪ Mode ➪ Auto Snap to Ground option, then you can move objects upward by holding down the Shift key as you drag the object.

Once objects are placed in the scene, you can easily rotate them using the arrow keys if the Rotate mode is enabled. The left and right arrows spin the object at 45-degree increments about its local Y-axis. The up and down arrows rotate the object through the ground plane about its local Z-axis.

Using Object Properties

With an object selected, you can open the Object Properties dialog box, shown in Figure 25-12, by choosing Object ⇨ Properties or by right-click on the object and selecting Properties from the pop-up menu.

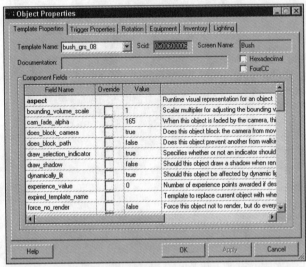

Figure 25-12: The Object Properties dialog box includes several panels for working with objects.

The first panel in the Object Properties dialog box is Template Properties. These properties are specific parameters and values that the game engine uses to determine how to interact with the object. If you look at the description column, you'll see questions like the following:

✦ Does this object block the camera from moving through it?

✦ Does this object prevent another from walking through it?

✦ Should this object draw a shadow when rendered?

✦ What is the value of this object in gold pieces?

✦ Can this item be used by a ghost?

✦ What icon should be used for megamap representation?

With these types of questions (and many more), you can see the type of control you have over objects in the scene. You can change any of these property values by clicking in the Value column and selecting a new value.

The Rotation panel is used to rotate objects in the scene. This panel consists of three dials that control the Pitch (X), Yaw (Y), and Roll (Z) of the object.

If you plan on adding lots of the same object to the scene, it will look funny if they all are positioned exactly the same and are sized the same. The Object ➪ Next Object menu command can help with this. It opens the Next Object Placement Settings dialog box, where you can select a random rotation along any axis and a random scale with minimum and maximum values. Using this to create a grove of trees results in each one being slightly different.

The Object menu also includes commands for hiding and unhiding objects, an Object List dialog box that lists all the objects in the current region, and a Content Search dialog box for searching for objects by name or description.

Tutorial: Adding objects to the scene

The little house out by the river that we pieced together in the preceding tutorial looks great, but it needs some decorating and a door. In this tutorial, you'll place some objects in the scene.

To add some objects to the current scene, follow these steps:

1. Open the glibber-trunples_home region into the Siege Editor with the File ➪ Open command.

2. In the file view pane, locate and select the Game Objects\landscape\foliage\grs_bush_sumac_gold object. With the middle scrollable wheel on the mouse, rotate the scene until you can see the back wall of the house.

3. Make sure that the Object ➪ Mode ➪ Placement Mode option is enabled, and click along the back of the house to place five sumac bushes in a row.

4. Then scroll around to the front of the house, and place the Game Objects\door\normal\glb_wooden_farmhouse object in the scene.

5. With the Object ➪ Mode ➪ Movement Mode option enabled, drag the door over in front of the house. Disable the Object ➪ Mode ➪ Auto Snap to Ground option, press the Shift key, and drag the door upward until it is positioned even with the doorframe.

6. With the door object still selected, choose Object ➪ Properties and click the Rotate panel. Drag the Yaw (Y) dial until its value reads 270, and close the Object Properties dialog box.

Figure 25-13 shows the house with a door positioned in front of it.

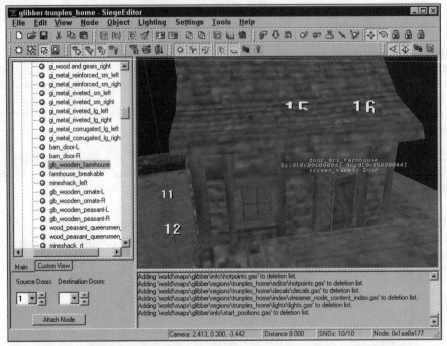

Figure 25-13: Objects added to the scene enhance the realism of the level.

Setting starting positions

The Starting Position object defines where the character appears when the map is first loaded. Because every map must have at least one of these objects, one is created automatically when a region is first created. It is a red star-like object, as shown in Figure 25-14.

Tip

You can find the Starting Position object in the Siege Objects folder of the file view pane.

There can be as many as eight of these objects within a scene, one for each character in the game.

Working with monsters and triggers

A region with no monsters or challenges makes the adventure a field trip. This scenario is quickly solved by adding monsters (or groups of monsters) and triggers to a region. Monsters are added to a region just like other objects, but the properties that can be set on monsters are unique to monsters.

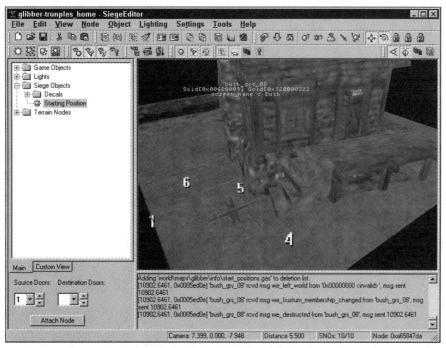

Figure 25-14: The Starting Position object defines where the character first appears in the region.

Adding monsters

Each monster placed in a scene includes several configurable ranges. These ranges define the behavior of the monster. For example, the Range Engage and the Melee Engage perimeters are the areas within which the monster detects and attacks with either ranged weapons or melee weapons. You can also set a Sight Range, a Comfort Range, and the monster's Personal Space (and you best not enter a monster's personal space).

All of these ranges, along with the monster's attacks, armor, inventory, movements, and so on can be configured in the Object Properties dialog box. Figure 25-15 shows a Big Chicken monster with several circles designating the various ranges.

Monsters can be found in the file view pane under the Game Objects\actors folder.

Setting triggers

Triggers can be found in the Game Objects\gizmos\triggers folder. They also are placed like other objects. Opening the Object Properties dialog box with a trigger object selected opens straight to the Trigger Properties panel, shown in Figure 25-16. Using the settings in this panel, you can define the Conditions for the trigger to fire and the Actions that happen when it does.

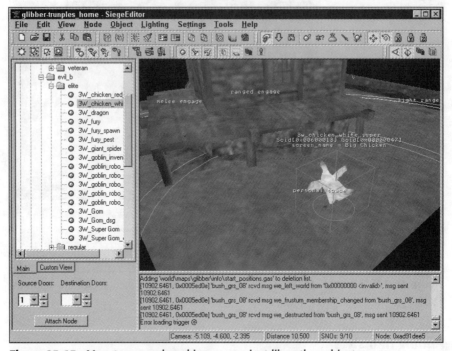

Figure 25-15: Monsters are placed in a scene just like other objects.

Setting lighting and mood

You have complete control over several types of lighting in your worlds. These light types include Ambient, Directional, and Point lights. Ambient lighting is controlled using Lighting ➪ Ambient. This command opens a dialog box where you can set the ambient intensity values for General, Object, and Actor settings. You can also select a color for each of these settings.

Directional lights are added with Lighting ➪ Edit Directional Lights. This command also opens a dialog box where you can create a new directional light with the New button. New lights get a number that appears in a list. If you select a light and click the Edit button, the Directional Light Properties dialog box opens where you can set the directional light's color, intensity, and direction. Several other options are available, including an On Timer option that causes the directional light color to change with the time of day.

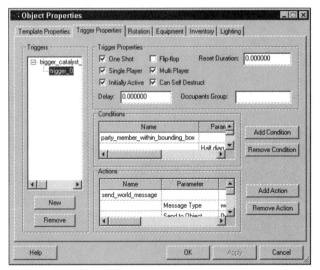

Figure 25-16: The Trigger Properties panel of the Object Properties dialog box defines what happens when the trigger is activated.

In addition to ambient and directional light, you can also add Point and Spot lights to your scene from the file view list. These two light types are located under the Lights folder. After they are placed in the scene and positioned like other objects, you can open the Properties for these objects and, in the Lighting panel, set the parameter values for these light objects.

Tip　All light sources (except for ambient) have an option to enable or disable shadows. This means that if a character walks by this type of light, the character casts a shadow. Be aware that only one light source at a time will cause a character to cast a shadow, so if you have several light sources affecting an object, include one that enables shadows.

Under the Tools menu is the Mood Editor tool. Using this tool, shown in Figure 25-17, you can set the weather, fog, and music for a particular mood. These moods can then be applied to a region.

Exporting maps to Dungeon Siege®

When you're finished tinkering with your level, you can turn it into a playable Dungeon Siege level by exporting it to the .dsmap format. To do this, select Files ⇨ Save Map as .dsmap. This opens a dialog box in which you can select the map to convert. In the next dialog box, you can enter a name, the map title, and a description. Click the Start button to begin exporting. The exporter completes the process and returns any errors that may have been encountered.

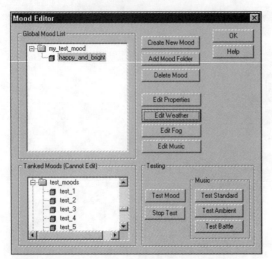

Figure 25-17: Establishing a mood controls ambiance details like weather, fog, and music.

The final exported dsmap appears along with a text file that includes a list of all the files that are included. To play the map in Dungeon Siege, you need to copy the dsmap file into the Dungeon Siege\Maps directory. It will then show up in the Load Map screen in Dungeon Siege.

Working with Siege Max™

Now that you have a rough understanding of how the Siege Editor works, we'll turn our sights toward Siege Max. Siege Max lets you create custom terrains, objects, and monsters instead of just repackaging the existing Dungeon Siege pieces.

Setting units and snap settings

The first task in creating custom content using Siege Max is to set the units to be something that Dungeon Siege can work with. If you forget to set the units correctly, your objects will appear huge in the Siege Editor (if they appear at all).

Dungeon Siege uses the metric system as its unit of measure. You can set the units in Siege Max to meters by selecting Customize ➪ Units Setup to open the Units Setup dialog box; then select the Metric option and Meters from the drop-down list.

You also need to set the units scaling. To do this, open the Preference Settings dialog box using Customize ➪ Preferences; in the General panel, set the System Unit Scale so that 1 unit equals Millimeters.

Because the nodes in the Siege Editor need to line up exactly, you'll want to enable the Snap settings, which can be done by opening the Grid and Snap Settings dialog box found also under the Customize menu. In this dialog box, select the Home Grid panel and change the Grid Spacing to 0.1 meter; in the Snaps panel, enable the Grid Points snap option.

After you close the Grid and Snap Settings dialog box, you can enable snapping by clicking the 3D Snap button at the bottom of the window (or by pressing the S key).

Creating custom terrain nodes

Terrain nodes are the building blocks used to create the various landscapes in Dungeon Siege. Each separate piece needs to have "doors" defined along its edges that can be linked to other nodes.

To make linking the various nodes easier, the Dungeon Siege makers have standardized node sizes. All node doors should be 2, 4, 8, 12, 24, or 32 meters in length, with 4 square meter blocks being the most common.

The standard also extends to texture maps with a 128×128 resolution map being applied to a 4-square-meter node and a 256×256 resolution map being applied to an 8-square-meter node. All larger nodes should be made from textures that are broken up into 256×256 multiples, so four 256×256 maps could be applied to a 16-square-meter node. Textures need to be saved using the PSD, BMP, or RAW formats, with PSD being the preferred format.

Using the SNO Tool Kit

After you've created a model that you wish to make into a node, you can make it a node by applying the Siege Max SNO modifier to the object. This modifier includes a single rollout that holds a single button labeled Open SNO Tool Kit.

The SNO Tool Kit, shown in Figure 25-18, includes several tools for defining doors and specifying the node type.

Clicking the Edit Doors button in the SNO Tool Kit places you in edge selection mode. In this mode, you can select edges in the viewports and click the insert or append buttons in the SNO Tool Kit dialog box to create a door. The doors are numbered with red numbers in the viewport. At the center of each door in the viewport is a small yellow line pointing away from the object. This defines the direction of the door, which needs to be away from the object. If you need to change this direction, you can use the Flip Door button.

Figure 25-18: The SNO Tool Kit lets you define the door locations.

The Siege Node Tools rollout includes several buttons for defining how the node is rendered. The options include

✦ **Floor (flr):** Floor sections are areas where the characters can walk.

✦ **Water (wtr):** Water sections are rendered differently in Dungeon Siege to look like water.

✦ **Ignored (ign):** Ignored faces are not moved when the Cleanup and Round Off Siege Node tool is used.

✦ **Locked (lck):** Locked sections are exported with vertex normals that are parallel to the Z-axis ensuring that the boundaries between nodes are smooth.

✦ **No Round (nrd):** These sections are not rounded off when the Cleanup and Round Off Siege Node tool is used.

The Floor, Water, and Ignored options put you in face subobject mode, where you can select the faces to receive the various attributes. Once selected, you can click the Add Selected button to apply the definition.

The Locked and No Round options enter vertex subobject mode, where you can select the vertices to which to apply either of these conditions.

The Cleanup and Round Off Siege Node button should be clicked only after the attributes have been applied. They move the faces to the nearest 0.1 meter that are not ignored and align the vertex normals that are locked so they are parallel to the Z-axis.

Exporting terrains

To export the terrain node, right-click the terrain object and select Export Siege Node from the pop-up quadmenu. This opens a dialog box in which you can save the terrain node.

Tip　Remember to name all custom terrain nodes beginning with "t_". This enables the Siege Editor to place them in the correct folders within the file view list of the Siege Editor.

Tutorial: Exporting a sample terrain node

For this sample node tutorial, we'll create a simple plane object with a texture applied.

To create and export a terrain node, follow these steps:

1. Select Customize ⇨ Units Setup, and then select the Metric option and Meters in the drop-down list. Select Customize ⇨ Preferences, and set 1 unit equal to Millimeters. Select Customize ⇨ Grid and Snap Settings, and enable the Grid Points option in the Snaps panel. Then select the Home Grid panel, and set the Grid Spacing to 0.1m. Press the S key to enable spacing.

2. In the Create panel, select the Plane button and drag in the Top view to create a plane object. Enter the value of 4m in both the Length and Width fields in the Parameters rollout. In the Command Panel, name the object, "t_clover-field."

Caution　If you forget to name the object correctly, the exporting process will fail.

3. Press the M key to open the gmax Material Editor, and click the New button. Select the Standard material, and click OK. Then click on the mapping button next to Diffuse color, and double-click the Bitmap map type in the gmax Material Navigator to open a file dialog box. Locate and select the b_t_clover-field.psd image found in the Chap 25 directory on the CD-ROM. Then click the Apply button to apply the material to the selected object.

4. Open the Modify panel, and in the Modifier List, select the Siege Max SNO modifier. In the Siege Max SNO rollout that appears, click the Open SNO Tool Kit button.

5. In the SNO Tool Kit dialog box, click the Edit Doors button. Hold down the Ctrl key, and select all the edges along the left side of the plane object. Then click the Append New Door button. Repeat this step for the top, right, and bottom edges to create four doors.

6. In the lower part of the SNO Tool Kit, click the flr button, select all the faces that make up the plane object, and then click the Add Selected button to mark all faces of the plane object as a floor. Finally, click the Cleanup and Round Off Siege Node button, and close the SNO Tool Kit dialog box.

7. Right-click on the plane object, and select Export Siege Node from the pop-up quadmenu. The node will be exported with the name that you gave the object to the My Documents\Dungeon Siege\Bits\Art\Terrain folder.

Figure 25-19 shows the plane object in gmax before it is exported. The exported file is saved to the \gmax\gamepacks\SiegeMax\Scenes\ArtAssets\Terrains directory.

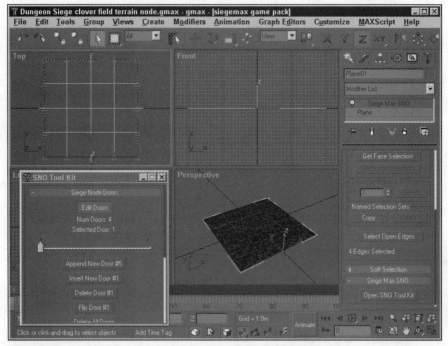

Figure 25-19: Terrain nodes can be created using Siege Max.

Creating custom objects

Custom objects can include objects such as plants and rocks, but it can also include new weapons and armor. The Dungeon Siege makers suggest that you keep the number of polygons that make up the objects under 100. All textures are limited to 256×256 or less. The best format for texture maps is the PSD format.

Before exporting the object, you need to give it a name that begins with "m_." This tells the Siege Editor that the object is a mesh object. For weapons, the name should begin with "m_w_," and bitmap textures need to begin with "b_."

Using the Reference Object Dropper

When you begin to build a new object such as a weapon, it can be difficult to know exactly how big it should be, even with the units set correctly. To fix this problem, Siege Max includes a cool tool that drops a reference object on the screen. These reference objects let you measure up your custom object to a droog, dwarf, or pack mule.

You can access this tool by right-clicking in the viewport and selecting the Open RefObj Dropper menu command. This opens the Dropper dialog box, shown in Figure 25-20. To use the dropper, simply double-click an object from the Available Objects list and then click in the viewport to place the reference object. You can delete all dropped objects with the Delete Objects button.

Figure 25-20: The Dropper dialog box can place reference objects in the scene.

Using the Item Tool Kit

You can create two different types of objects — objects that are used in the game (such as weapons) and items that aren't used (but are gathered or placed to enhance the scene). Items that are used in the game need special points identified. These points tell the game engine how to deal with the object. For example, one of the key points to a sword is the tip. By marking the tip of the sword, the game engine can correctly display any animations that involve the sword.

The key points can be added to an object using the Item Tool Kit, shown in Figure 25-21, which is opened by right-clicking an object and selecting the Open Item Tool Kit menu option. The key points that can be added using this dialog box include a Grip, a Dummy Root, and Attach points consisting of light, tip, notch, tracer01, and tracer02.

Figure 25-21: The Item Tool Kit lets you define key object points used to animate the object.

Caution The Open Item Kit menu option is available only if the object is named correctly with an "m_" at the beginning of its name.

The grip and dummy root objects are placed on the object at its pivot point. You can move these locations by moving the object's pivot point using the Hierarchy panel. The grip point defines the location where the character holds the weapon or object, and the dummy root defines the place where the object touches the ground. After all key points are created for the object, you need to link the key points to the object and link the mesh object to the dummy root.

Exporting objects

If you've named and linked the object correctly, then the exporting process is as simple as right-clicking the object and selecting Export Mesh from the pop-up quadmenu. Before exporting, you may want to select the Launch Previewer menu option, which loads the DS Anim Viewer application, as shown in Figure 25-22. This previewer displays the object on the ground as it would be found in the Dungeon Siege world.

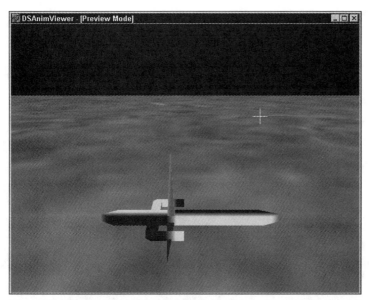

Figure 25-22: The Anim Viewer utility displays a preview of the custom object.

Tutorial: Exporting a sword object

About the last thing that Dungeon Siege needs is another sword, but the goal here is to teach you the process for exporting custom objects. To create and export a sword object, follow these steps:

1. In Siege Max, open the simple sword.gmax file from the Chap 25 directory on the CD-ROM. This file contains a simple sword.

2. Check the polygon count to make sure the sword isn't too complicated. In the Utilities panel, click on the Polygon Counter button to see a dialog box that tells how many polygons make up the sword. It weighs in at 80 polygons, which is fine.

Tip The Dungeon Siege makers suggest that objects shouldn't exceed 100 polygons.

3. Check the scale of the object. This is an important step because if the scale is off, the object may be too small to see or too large to be realistic. The size for this sword is about one meter in length; you can check this with the Tape dummy object in the Create panel. Once you think the scale is correct, right-click on the object and select the Ref Object Dropper. Then double-click the Droog character and click in the Front viewport to place the character. Figure 25-23 shows that the sword is about the right size for the Droog to hold.

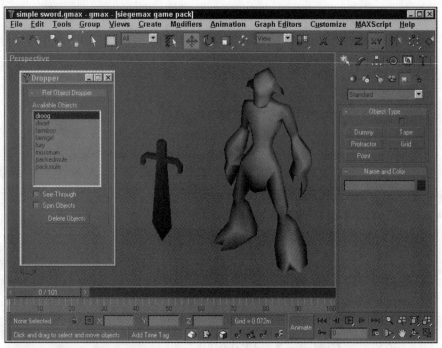

Figure 25-23: Using the Ref Object Dropper, you can check the scale of object relative to a Dungeon Siege character.

Click on the Delete Objects button in the Dropper dialog box to remove the Droog and close the Dropper dialog box.

4. In the Name and Color rollout in the Modify panel, type the object name, "m_w_swd_simplegold01." The "m" identifies this object as a mesh object, the "w" is for weapon class, and the final part is the object's unique name.

Note   For objects, the "m_" is required in order for the Item Tool Kit to appear.

5. The way the sword is oriented, it will be pointing into the ground. To orient it so it lies flat, click on the Select and Rotate button on the main toolbar and rotate the sword about its Z-Axis until it is parallel to the grid plane.

6. The Dummy Root marks the position of the object in the Dungeon Siege world. You can add a Dummy Root by selecting the object, right-clicking, and selecting the Item Object Tool Kit. This dialog box includes a button labeled Add Dummy Root to Item. Click this button and the Dummy Root is positioned below the sword. The object is named "dummyroot_m_w_swd_simplegold01," and it is positioned directly beneath the sword's pivot point.

7. With the Dummy Root in place, you can see the sword in the Animation Preview window, but you need to apply a material to the texture first. Press the M key to open the Material Editor, click the New button, and select a Standard material. Raise the Specular Level to 90. Click on the map button to the right of the Diffuse color swatch and double-click on the Bitmap mapping type in the Material Navigator. Locate the gold.psd texture in the Chap 25 directory on the CD-ROM. This is a simple 16×16 pixel image file. Click the Apply button to apply this material to the sword.

Caution   If an object doesn't include a texture, it cannot be exported.

8. Right-click on the sword and select Launch Previewer from the pop-up quad-menu. Figure 25-24 shows the sword in this window.

9. The next step is to identify the grip and tracer points on the sword. These points tell the game engine how to position the sword when a character picks it up and how to animate the weapon as a character wields it. The grip dummy object will be created at the object's pivot point, so first you need to move the pivot point to the center of the sword's handle. Open the Hierarchy panel, click the Pivot button, and click the Affect Pivot Only button. With the Select and Move button selected, move the pivot point to the center of the sword's handle and deselect the Affect Pivot Only button.

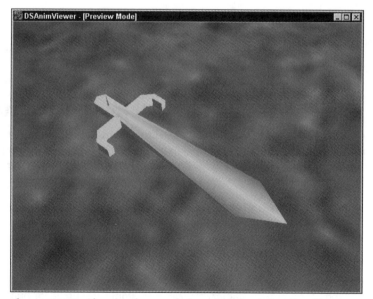

Figure 25-24: The simple sword viewed in the Animation Viewer.

10. Right-click on the sword and select Object Item Tool Kit. In the Helpers dialog box that appears, click the Add Grip to Item button. This creates a grip dummy object named "grip_m_w_swd_simplegold01."

11. With the sword selected, select trace01 from the list in the Helpers dialog box and click the Add Attach Point to Item button. A point dummy object named "AP_trace01" is added to the scene at the object's pivot point. Select and move the point to the tip of the sword.

    Repeat this step to create another trace point named "AP_trace02" and move it to the base of the sword's blade.

12. The next step is to link all the dummy objects in the correct order. With the Select and Link button enabled, link the two tracer points to the sword's mesh object. Then link the sword object to its grip and finally the grip to the Dummy Root. You can open the Select Objects dialog box (H) and click on the Display Subtree option to check your linking.

13. The final step is to export the object. Right-click on the sword and select Export Mesh from the pop-up quadmenu. This saves the file into the My Documents\Dungeon Siege\Bits\Art\Meshes\Weapons\Sword directory.

Note The exporter is smart enough to know if the correct directory hasn't been created or if the texture map is in the wrong directory. The exporter offers to fix these issues for you automatically.

Once exported, the object is ready to be used in a level, but one more step is needed before you can add it to your list of objects. That is defining the characteristics of the object that will be used in the game. You can define object characteristics through Template files.

Defining object characteristics through Template files

If you've created a beautiful sword, you'll need to assign it a value and let the game engine know how much damage is done when your character uses it to fight back a monster. All the details that affect the characteristics of the object are defined using template files.

These files are standard text files (with a .gas extension) that include a scripted syntax of variables that the game engine understands. For example, the variable of "screen_name" defines the name that appears in the game and "f damage_max" defines the value for maximum damage afflicted by the weapon.

Note Building templates is an advanced aspect of customizing Dungeon Siege that is beyond the scope of this chapter. You can find ample resources for building templates at www.DungeonSiege.com.

Locating the Template files

Before you can work with the Template files, you need to find them. They just happen to be located together in a nice neat resource package named Logic.dsres (dsres stands for Dungeon Siege Resource). You can unpackage all these files using the Siege Editor. Simply select the File ➪ Convert .dsmap to Files menu command. A dialog box appears where you can select the resource file to unpackage.

Note

The process of packaging and unpackaging files in Dungeon Siege is referred to as *tanking* and *untanking* files.

The Logic.dsres file is located in the Resources directory where Dungeon Siege is installed. Using the Siege Editor command, all the template files will be unpackaged to the My Documents\Dungeon Siege\Bits directory. The template files will have a .gas extension. They can be opened and read by a simple text editor such as Notepad.

Editing Template files

Once you've located the correct template file, the easiest way to edit is to locate an object that is similar in nature to the new object, and then copy its template definition and paste it into the same .gas file. You can edit the new entry to reflect the new object.

Tip

Be sure when you create a new template by copying and pasting that you rename the template. Each template must have a unique name.

Tutorial: Building a Template for the sword object

Before you can add the sword object you created to a level, you need to have it appear in the Siege Editor. Before it can appear in the Siege Editor, you need to define a template for it.

To create a template for the sword object, follow these steps:

1. In the Siege Editor, select the File ➪ Convert .dsmap to Files menu command. In the dialog box that appears, locate the Logic.dsmap from the default installation of Dungeon Siege in the Resources directory and click the OK button. This untanks all the template files into the My Documents\Dungeon Siege\ Bits directory.

2. In Windows Notepad, open the wpn_sword.gas file found in My Documents\ Dungeon Siege\Bits\world\contentdb\templates\regular\interactive.

3. At the bottom of the wpn_sword.gas file, copy the last template and paste at the end of the document.

4. In the pasted template, change the template name by adding an 01 on the end of the name. Edit the doc and screen_name variables to be "Simple Gold Sword" and change the model variable to match the sword's mesh name, "m_w_swd_simplegold01."

5. Save the file using the File ➪ Save menu command.

6. Close and reopen the Siege Editor. In the hierarchy panel, locate the Simple Gold Sword located in the Game Objects ➪ weapons ➪ swords folder.

Figure 25-25 shows the simple sword object positioned to the side of the house.

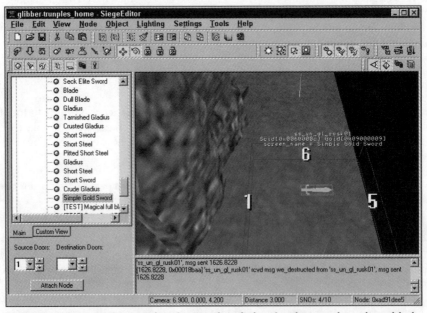

Figure 25-25: Once its template is completed, the simple sword can be added to scenes in the Siege Editor.

Working with characters

Objects are great to add to a Dungeon Siege map, but the real fun is in creating monsters and other characters. The biggest difference between characters and objects is that characters can be animated.

Just like objects, characters require exact names, but the mesh simply needs to be named "skinmesh" in gmax and all parts of the character need to belong to the same Editable Mesh object. The game engine then uses the character's file name to determine where the character appears. Character files that include animations should start with "a_" and the mesh files should begin with "m_".

Another big difference between objects and characters is that character meshes include bones. The bone names have to follow the naming convention listed in Table 25-1.

Table 25-1 Character Bones	
Bone Name	**Connects to**
Bip01_Head	None
Bip01_Neck	Bip01_Head
Bip01_R_Clavicle	Bip01_Neck
Bip01_R_Upperarm	Bip01_R_Clavicle
Bip01_R_Forearm	Bip01_R_Upperarm
Bip01_R_Hand	Bip01_R_Forearm
Bip01_R_Finger	Bip01_R_Hand
Bip01_L_Clavicle	Bip01_Neck
Bip01_L_Upperarm	Bip01_L_Clavicle
Bip01_L_Forearm	Bip01_L_Upperarm
Bip01_L_Hand	Bip01_L_Forearm
Bip01_L_Finger	Bip01_L_Hand
Bip01_Spine03	Bip01_Neck
Bip01_Spine02	Bip01_Spine03
Bip01_Spine	Bip01_Spine02
Bip01_Pelvis	Bip01_Spine
Bip01_R_Thigh	Bip01_Pelvis
Bip01_R_Calf	Bip01_R_Thigh
Bip01_R_Foot	Bip01_R_Calf
Bip01_R_Toe	Bip01_R_Foot
Bip01_L_Thigh	Bip01_Pelvis
Bip01_L_Calf	Bip01_L_Thigh
Bip01_L_Foot	Bip01_L_Calf
Bip01_L_Toe	Bip01_L_Foot

Note These bone names relate to a two-legged, two-armed character, and we all know that many monsters don't look human-like. Dungeon Siege can support other bone structures, but consistent names are still required. Check the Dungeon Siege online documentation for information on other bone structures.

To character meshes, like Terrain nodes, you can apply a mesh-specific modifier called the Siege Max ASP modifier. This modifier makes subobject selection within the mesh possible just like those for Editable Mesh objects. It also makes a button labeled Open ASP Tool Kit available. Clicking on this button opens the ASP Tool Kit dialog box, as shown in Figure 25-26. This tool kit includes buttons that let you easily select sections of the mesh and options that define how they are rendered in the game engine.

Figure 25-26: Using the ASP Tool Kit dialog box, you can identify certain subobject selections.

For characters, you need to supply a root object and grips just as you do for objects. The Root object is added or animated using the Siege Max Root Tools pop-up quadmenu option. The weapon grip is typically linked to the right hand bone and the shield is linked to the left hand bone. Care should be taken to align the grip so its Z-axis points away from the body, which is how the weapon will point.

Once set up, you can export your character using the Export Mesh popup quad-menu option.

Animating characters

Before animating your characters, you need to set the Frame Rate to match the game engine's or your characters will look like they're on fast forward. Dungeon Siege seems to work well with a Frame Rate set to 12 FPS. You can change the Frame Rate by clicking on the Time Configuration button in the Time Controls. This opens the Time Configuration dialog box, where you can set the FPS.

Files that include animated characters need to have a name that begins with "a_" and ends with a specified attack and animation type. The attack types are "fs" and a number. The animation types are two- or three-letter codes as listed in Table 25-2.

Table 25-2 Attack and Animation Types	
Type Value	*Description*
fs0	Barehanded attack with no weapon
fs1	Single-handed weapon, such as a dagger
fs2	Single-handed weapon and a shield
fs3	Long two-handed weapon, such as an axe
fs4	Short two-handed weapon, such as a sword
fs5	Two-handed staff weapon
fs6	Bow and arrow
fs7	Crossbow
fs8	Shield only
at	Attack animation
dfs	Default fighting stance animation
dff	Default fighting fidget animation
de	Die animation
ds	Default stance animation
dsf	Default stance fidget animation
mg	Magic animation
rl	Running loop animation
wl	Walking loop animation
fl	Flying loop animation
rv	Reveal animation

So, for example, if I (initials, klm) had a character named Bear in the DeadlyWorld mod that is animated making a barehanded attack, the file name would be "a_c_klm_DeadlyWorld_fs0_at."

Note   Stance animations should have only a single frame.

Tutorial: Animating a skeleton

To get some experience animating a character, we're going to look to the default source characters found in the gmax\gampacks\Siege Max\Scenes\ArtAssets\Characters directory.

To animate a skeleton model, follow these steps:

1. In Siege Max, open the m_c_ecm_sk_pos_a0.gmax file from the ArtAssets\ Characters directory where gmax is installed. This file contains a skeleton model that's been boned and skinned. You can also find several animations of this skeleton in the same directory.

2. In the Time Controls, click on the Time Configuration button and set the Frame Rate to 12 FPS. Also, set the End Time to 10 to create eleven frames for the animation.

3. Select the skeleton mesh and right click on the skeleton and select Siege Max Root Tools ⇨ Add/Reset Root Marker. This will add a large blue arrow under the mesh.

4. Click the Animate button at the bottom of the gmax interface to enable animation mode, drag the Time Slider to frame 5 and click on the Select and Move button. Then maximize the Front viewport.

5. Select the right upper arm bone and drag it upward, then repeat this for the left arm. Then select all the bones by dragging an outline over them and move them upward slightly. Then select the Select and Rotate button, select the right thigh bone and drag it outward, then repeat for the left thigh bone.

6. Drag the Time Slider to frame 10 and return all the bones to their original position. An easy way to do this is to select the key at frame 0 and drag it to frame 10 while holding down the Shift key. This will copy the key from one frame to another.

7. The final animation should have the skeleton doing jumping jacks. Click the Animate button to disable animation mode.

8. Choose the File ⇨ Save As menu option and save the file as "a_c_ecm_fs1_dsf-01.gmax". Select and right click on the skeleton mesh to access the popup quadmenu. Select Export Animation and the animation file is exported.

Caution   Check your mesh before exporting and make sure it is named "skinmesh" or the Export Animation option will not be available.

Figure 25-27 shows the skeleton figure doing jumping jacks while waiting to join the action.

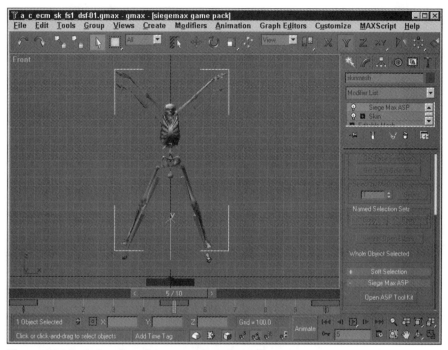

Figure 25-27: Animating characters gives them life.

Finding Dungeon Siege® Online Resources

If you've made it through this chapter, you're probably asking, "Where do I go from here?" The answer is online. If you search the Web, you'll find a huge number of sites that include all sorts of Dungeon Siege materials including endless numbers of new Siegelets, tutorials, custom objects, characters, weapons, and spells. The complete list would be long, but I'll include several of the major sites to get you started.

Dungeon Siege®

http://www.dungeonsiege.com/index.shtml

The official Dungeon Siege site is a great place to start. From here, you can download the DSTK and any new patches that appear for the game. It also offers news to keep you up to date and Siege University, a comprehensive list of tutorials that provide the details I didn't have room for.

Planet Dungeon Siege

http://www.planetdungeonsiege.com/

Planet Dungeon Siege includes an active set of forums where you can find answers to any question plus a detailed look at all aspects of the game.

SiegeNetwork

`http://www.siegenetwork.com/index.php`

The SiegeNetwork is a great place to get news on the latest Siegelets under development. It includes forums and a wealth of modding tutorials.

The Dungeon Siege 'Net Guide

`http://www.dsnetguide.com/`

The Dungeon Siege 'Net Guide includes a rated listing of the available Siegelets. It includes a helpful list of tips and tricks that will help you as a game player and as a mod creator.

Dungeon Siege Realms

`http://www.dsrealms.com/app/default.asp`

Dungeon Siege Realms is another useful site that requires registration and a login.

Summary

Using the tools that come in the Dungeon Siege Tool Kit, you can create custom content to populate your Dungeon Siege worlds. This chapter included a whirlwind tour of some very complex tools. You can find more information on using these tools and creating Dungeon Siege content online.

This chapter covered the following topics:

✦ Learning the basics of the Siege Editor for creating new maps and regions

✦ Using Siege Max to create new textured nodes and objects

✦ Animating characters

✦ Finding more information online.

In the next chapter, you'll learn how to mod in the world of Trainz.

✦   ✦   ✦

Creating New Scenery for Trainz

CHAPTER

26

◆ ◆ ◆ ◆

In This Chapter

Using content creation tools

Editing Trainz

Installing and using the Trainz Asset Creation Studio

Working with Trainz objects

Sharing content

◆ ◆ ◆ ◆

Auran's Trainz is a train simulator that lets players take control of thousands of pounds of metal. Train simulators have a unique advantage over flight simulators in that they are close to the ground, so you have lots more interesting things to see. You can really feel the speed of a train as it roars down the track.

Trainz is built on top of Auran Jet, a structured 3D gaming platform. Using the features of Auran Jet, you can easily manipulate new graphics and models on the fly making the platform highly configurable. Tying the Auran Jet platform in with gmax is a logical extension to the platform.

Many different aspects of Trainz can be edited using gmax including locomotives and rolling stock objects, scenery, and trackside accessories. This chapter focuses on creating those objects that rely on gmax, although other aspects of the game can also be edited. For these other editable aspects, I refer you to the game documentation.

Note

Two train simulation games include gmax game packs — Auran's Trainz and Microsoft's Train Simulator (MSTS). I've chosen to cover Trainz, not because I think it is better (I'll let you make that call) but because the Train Simulator game pack is similar to the Flight Simulator package and the Trainz game pack is different.

Content Creation Tools

The first place to start if you're interested in editing Trainz is to visit the Content Creation page on the Trainz Web site located at `www.auran.com/trainz/contentcreation.htm`. This page includes many of the external tools that are needed to edit Trainz content, including the latest version of gmax.

Most of these tools are covered throughout this chapter, but the following is a rundown of the tools available:

- ✦ **Content Dispatcher:** A utility used to package and upload content to the Trainz Download Station
- ✦ **Content Foundry:** A utility used to create the config.txt files and paths needed by content
- ✦ **Trainz Content Creation Procedures:** A detailed reference manual of all the settings that can be added within the config.txt files and the directories where the content should be placed
- ✦ **Highland Valley Scripts:** Sample scripts for the Highland Valley scenario
- ✦ **Trainz Asset Creation Studio:** The game pack for Trainz that endows gmax with the ability to export meshes in a format that Trainz can read
- ✦ **Trainz Custom:** Sample files of custom content
- ✦ **Source Files:** Example gmax files of several different custom assets
- ✦ **Paint Shed Content Creation Guide:** Reference documentation for the Paint Shed product

Of these various tools, we mainly focus on the Trainz Asset Creation Studio tool and its export capabilities. The remaining tools are well-documented and fairly easy to use.

Trainz Paint Shed

Trainz Paint Shed is an extension product for Trainz that includes 20 locomotives, 14 new rolling stock items, and the ability to change colors and add decals to the custom paint templates. So, if you want to name your favorite engine "The Green Monster" and give it a custom paint job, this product is for you.

A special edition of Paint Shed is available with Ultimate Trainz Collection (UTC). This edition includes additional locos and rolling stock. UTC is the current version of Trainz at the time of writing.

Trainz Paint Shed does not allow locomotives and rolling stock included with Trainz to be repainted.

Editing Trainz

Most of the editing that takes place in Trainz can be done from within the game itself. When Trainz first loads, the menu consisting of four distinct areas, as shown in Figure 26-1, appears. Each of these menu options loads a separate module.

✦ **My Collection:** Presents a list of the available engines and rollingstock. In this module, you can zoom in and out and rotate around the train cars. You can also get information on the various train cars, but editing is limited to the ability to edit the running numbers that appear on the train cars.

✦ **Driver:** This module lets you create a consist (a list of train cars), choose a terrain, and select the game settings. From here, you can actually get the train rolling down the track. Editing in this module is limited to creating consists and choosing a starting point.

✦ **Surveyor:** This module is a full-featured level editor. Using the Surveyor module, you can create a new Terrain map and edit an existing one. For most features in the Surveyor, you can load new custom pieces that can be used.

✦ **Scenarios:** This module includes a list of specific tasks that need to be accomplished.

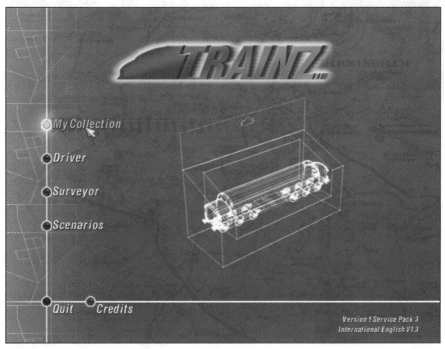

Figure 26-1: Menu options available in Trainz

Working with the Surveyor

Of these four modules, most of the editing takes place in the Surveyor. When the Surveyor first loads, all the available terrains are listed to the right and all custom maps are listed with a C to the right of the name, as shown in Figure 26-2. The overview maps for the selected terrain are displayed to the left.

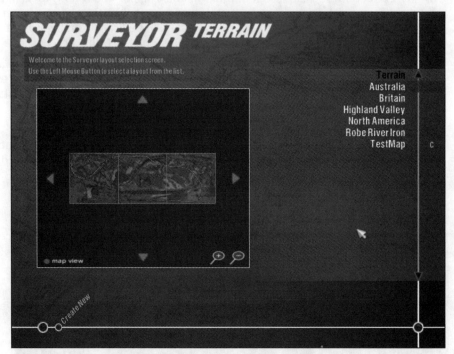

Figure 26-2: The Surveyor module lets you edit existing maps or create new ones.

Loading an existing map into the Surveyor lets you edit it, or new maps can be created by clicking the Create New button in the bottom-left corner. New maps begin with a blank grid, but by using the tabs positioned to the right in the Surveyor, you can add topology, objects, and tracks, paint different landscapes, or even change the color of the sky.

The six tabbed panels to the right in the Surveyor are

✦ **Topology:** Enables you to raise and lower sections of the grid to produce hills, mountains, and valleys.

✦ **Paint:** Offers the ability to paint different landscape textures on the grid surface.

✦ **Objects:** Includes 3D objects that can be placed and oriented within the scene.

✦ **Tracks:** Provides a way to draw railway tracks within the scene.

✦ **Tools:** Includes tools for working with rulers and cameras. It also includes a means to copy areas, textures, and objects, and paste them in a different location.

✦ **World:** Provides a way to set the world conditions such as weather, time of day, cloud looks, and water looks.

Clicking on any of these tabs causes a panel of options to rollout from the right like the Objects panel that is visible in Figure 26-3.

Figure 26-3: A new map being created in the Surveyor module

Note   Using the Surveyor is well documented in the Trainz game documentation.

Within most of these panels are collections of textures and 3D objects broken into several regions. Using gmax and the Trainz Asset Creation Studio, you can create custom 3d scenery objects and have them appear within the Surveyor module.

Adding graphics to the Surveyor

Several of the Surveyor panels hold libraries of images, and you can add to these libraries easily enough by placing the image (along with its config.txt file) in the appropriate directory. The acceptable image formats are fairly rigid in Trainz; they must conform to the number of pixels, bit-depth, and image format.

Tip   The two formats used by Trainz for bitmaps are the Targa (TGA) and Bitmap (BMP) formats. These image files should not be compressed because decompression adds work for the CPU in "real-time."

All custom image files can be placed in the Auran\Trainz\World\Custom directory in the following folders:

✦ **Ground:** These textures are used for ground surfaces. These images must be 128×128, 24-bit Bitmap (BMP) files. Custom ground textures are made available in the Paint panel of the Surveyor.

✦ **Displacements:** These images are used to displace the surface where black (or dark) sections aren't moved and white (or light) sections are displaced. These images must be 256×256, 24-bit Bitmap (BMP) files. Displacement maps are made available in the Advanced section of the Topology panel of the Surveyor.

✦ **Environment\Sky:** These textures are used to represent the sky and consist of three different images — one for the sky, one for the night sky, and one for the stormy sky. All three of these images must be 256×256, 24-bit Targa (TGA) files, except for the night sky image, which should be 32-bit. Custom sky textures are made available in the World panel of the Surveyor.

✦ **Environment\Water:** These textures are used to represent the water and consist of two different images — one for the water surface and one for the water reflection. The water surface image should be 128×128, 32-bit Targa (TGA) files, and the water reflection images should be 128×128, 8-bit Bitmap (BMP) files. Custom water textures are made available in the World panel of the Surveyor.

Creating config files

If you create an image using the correct format, place it in the right directory, and start up Trainz eager to see your custom content, it will not be visible. In fact, on the Trainz splash screen, you'll see a warning note, saying that the correct KUID was not found. The KUID number is a special identifier that references the image.

As Trainz loads, it examines every object in its path and looks for its corresponding config.txt file. This configuration file contains all the settings details about the custom content; if it is missing, the custom content is not loaded.

Note The only custom content item that doesn't need a config.txt file is a displacement map.

Creating these config files is easy, and they can be done using a standard text editor. The file always needs to be saved as config.txt in the same folder as the custom content. The config.txt file at a minimum needs to include a KUID number and a kind statement, but other settings are helpful and useful.

Note The kind statement identifies the type of object, so a compliment like "This object looks very nice today," although kind, won't work.

In addition to the required fields, each asset type has its own settings that can be included in the config.txt file. A complete list of config.txt settings for each asset type can be found in the Trainz Content Creation Procedures document. For example, the config.txt file for a ground texture must include a KUID and a kind type of groundtexture, but it can also include an RGB value for specifying the underlying ground color, a username and description, and a category class, region, and era.

Note If you're interested in configuring your train engine's performance, study the config variables for the engine kind found in the Content Creation Procedures documentation. The config variables include all the parameters used to define how the engine works, such as mass, fuel, motor resistance, brake ratio, and air-drag coefficient.

Table 26-1 shows a listing of generic settings that can be included in all config.txt files.

Table 26-1 Trainz Content ID Ranges		
Setting	**Value**	**Description**
kuid	kuid <KUID:*xxxxx:yyyyyy*>	*xxxxx* is the UserID number for the person uploading the file, and *yyyyyy* is the Content ID number that follows Auran's range guidelines.
Kind	engine, bogey, traincar, enginesound, hornsound, interior, pantograph, water, environment, map, groundtexture, scenery, track, bridge, mospeedboard, mosignal, mojunction, moturntable, mocrossing, activity	The asset type.
Username	"Big Blue Engine"	The name of the asset.

Continued

Table 26-1 *(continued)*

Setting	Value	Description
Description	"This is my favorite train car from my model set."	A description of the asset.
Region	Australia	The country region where the asset is from.
trainz-build	1.3	The Trainz version number that the asset was built for.
category-class	AD	The class code for this asset.
category-region-0	US	A list of regions ranging from 0.
category-era-0	1920s	A list of eras ranging from 0.
author	"klm"	Name of the asset creator.
contact-email	`"bigblue@trainz.com"`	Email address of the creator.
contact-website	`"www.trainz.com"`	Web address of the creator's site.

Using KUID Numbers

Auran has created a network that makes it easy to upload and share the objects you build with the Trainz community. All the uploaded content is available online at Planet Auran.

As you can imagine, thousands of objects are available online, and keeping track of all these objects poses a problem. How do I know that the bridge model that took me 40 hours to create won't be overwritten by some beginning user's lame bridge that happens to share the same name?

Auran has come up with a brilliant strategy to keep track of all these different objects. Their plan is to tag each object with a unique KUID number. These numbers are listed within the config.txt file that accompanies every object. The format for the KUID number within the config.txt file is:

```
kuid <KUID:xxxxx:yyyyyy>
```

where xxxxx is the UserID number for the person uploading the file and yyyyyy is the Content ID number that follows Auran's range guidelines. A unique User ID is given to all users who register their software with Planet Auran. This is required before you can upload content.

A complete list of the Content IDs is listed in the Content Creation Procedures documentation that is available on Auran's Web site, but a small sampling is included in Table 26-2.

Table 26-2
Trainz Content ID Ranges

ID Range	Content Type
1-9999	Locomotives (use the locomotive's road number if possible)
10000-14999	Passenger cars
15000-19999	Freight cars
20000-20999	Routes
21000-21999	Textures
22000-22999	Foliage
23000-23999	Signposts
24000-24999	Signaling
25000-25999	Residential buildings
26000-26999	Commercial buildings
27000-27999	Industrial buildings
28000-28999	Railroad buildings
29000-29999	Objects that move on land, such as cars
30000-30999	Objects that move on sea, such as boats
31000-31999	Objects that move in air, such as airplanes
32000-32999	Bridges
33000-33999	Tunnels
35000-35999	People
36000-36999	Animals
37000-37999	Splines (including roads and power lines)
38000-38999	Rails
39000-39999	Civil buildings, such as hospitals and schools
40000-40999	Military buildings
41000-49999	Reserved for future use (do not use this range)
50000-50999	Bogies/trucks
51000-52999	Engine specifications
53000-53999	Engine sounds

Continued

Table 26-2 *(continued)*	
ID Range	**Content Type**
54000-54999	Horn sounds
55000-56999	Interior
57000-57999	Pants (pantographs)
58000-58999	Public fun places, such as stadiums and amusement parks
60000-99999	Miscellaneous objects
100000-	Numbers beyond 100,000 are automatically assigned by Trainz (do not use this range)

Creating image reference files

If your asset includes a texture, then you'll also need an image reference file. This file is also a text file that includes two settings—Primary and Tile. The value of the Primary setting is simply the texture's filename, and the Tile value is set to "st." The file is then saved with a name that is the same as the image file with .texture.txt tacked on the end. Trainz uses this reference file to locate the texture image and determine how to tile it across the object.

Using the Content Foundry

If you download and install the Trainz V1.3 Content Update Pack from the Trainz Web site, you'll find a new application called Content Foundry located in the Auran\Trainz directory. The Content Foundry can help you create config.txt files automatically.

When the Content Foundry is first run, it displays a registration page like the one shown in Figure 26-4. Registration requires your User ID. This User ID can be obtained via email from the Planet Auran Web page. It is also used in the KUID numbers that identify your assets.

After you're registered, the Content Foundry loads. It is a simple interface, shown in Figure 26-5. To use it, simply select the asset class from the drop-down list, enter a name and description, and click the Create button. The config.txt file, along with copies of all the other files that are needed, are created automatically and placed in a folder that matches the name you entered under the Auran\Trainz\World\Custom directory.

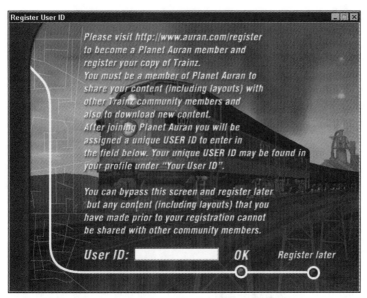

Figure 26-4: The registration screen requires your User ID to be entered.

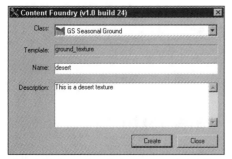

Figure 26-5: The Content Foundry utility automatically creates config.txt files for you.

The other files are not meant to be included with the asset, but should be replaced with the actual files after they are ready. For example, if the GA Arid Ground option is selected in the Content Foundry and the name of "desert" is given to the asset, then clicking the Create button opens Windows Explorer with the following three files created: config.txt, replace.bmp, and replace.texture.txt, as shown in Figure 26-6. After replace.bmp is replaced with the correct texture image and the replace.texture.txt file is renamed, the asset is ready for loading into Trainz.

Tip

Be sure to check your config.txt file before uploading content. Although the Content Foundry makes building the necessary files easy, overlooking something is also easy.

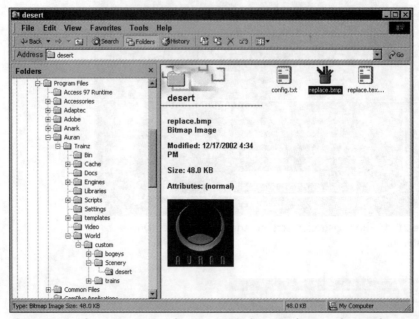

Figure 26-6: The Content Foundry opens Windows Explorer to the newly created folder.

Tutorial: Creating a green water texture

Although most water is blue, sea green water is also common, especially in algae-filled ponds. For this example, you'll create a green water texture and load it into Trainz where you can access it from the Surveyor module.

Note

This example creates all the necessary text files manually, but you can try the Content Foundry also.

To create a green water texture, follow these steps:

1. Open Adobe PhotoShop, and create a sea green texture image. Resize the image so that it is exactly 128×128 pixels. Then save the file as a 32-bit Targa (TGA) file. Name the file Sea_Green_Water.tga.

2. In PhotoShop, create a second image to be used for the water reflection that is also 128×128 pixels. Save this file as an 8-bit grayscale Bitmap (BMP) file. Name the file Sea_Green_Water_Reflection.bmp.

3. Create an image reference text file for the texture image by opening a text editor and typing the following:

```
Primary=Sea_Green_Water.tga
Tile=st
```

Save the text file as Sea_Green_Water.texture.txt. Then create a similar text file for the reflection image.

4. Create a config.txt file by typing the following in a text file:

```
kuid <KUID:xxxxx:21001>
kind water
normal Sea_Green_Water
reflection Sea_Green_Water_Reflection
```

where xxxxx is your User ID. Save the file as config.txt.

5. Place all the files together in a folder named Sea_Green_Water, and move the folder to the Auran\Trainz\World\custom\Environment directory.

6. Restart Trainz, open the Surveyor module, and look in the World panel.

Figure 26-7 shows the Surveyor module with our custom sea green water texture selected.

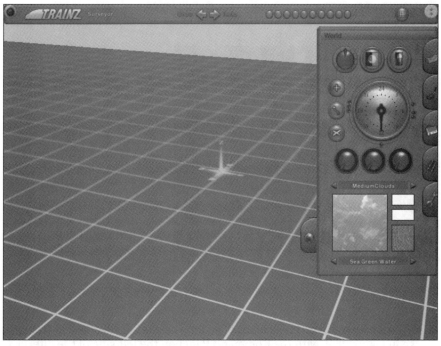

Figure 26-7: With the sea green water texture, we can make fluorescent ponds look real.

Installing the Trainz Asset Creation Studio

The Trainz Asset Creation Studio (ACS) is a gmax game pack for Trainz. It can be used to create scenery objects that you can use to populate and customize your Trainz terrains.

Look in the gmax directory on the Trainz CD-ROM to find an installation of gmax, along with a zip file for the Trainz Asset Creation Studio (ACS) that includes the game pack installation for Trainz. After the installation completes, an icon for the Trainz Asset Creation Studio is placed on your desktop.

Note During the ACS installation, you can specify the gmax directory that you want to use. This is important because the default installation on the Trainz CD is gmax 1.1, and you'll want to use the latest version of gmax.

When you run the Trainz Asset Creation Studio, a splash screen, shown in Figure 26-8, appears. The gmax Driver Setup dialog box appears where you can select the display driver to use. The options include the default Heidi driver (that works in software), the OpenGL driver, or Direct3D. Auran recommends the Direct3D driver and provides a utility to change the default display driver under the Start menu.

Cross-Reference The various display drivers are covered in Chapter 3, "Making a Custom Face, er, Interface."

Figure 26-8: The splash screen for the Trainz game pack

After you select a driver, gmax loads. The interface is a little different from gmax, as shown in Figure 26-9, with the Command Panel on the left side of the interface and the Tab Panel active. Another change is that ten common modifiers are available as buttons at the top of the Modify panel.

Caution For the Trainz game pack, the Command Panel tab icons are reversed with the Utilities icon on the left (that actually opens the Create panel) and the Create icon on the right (that actually opens the Utilities panel).

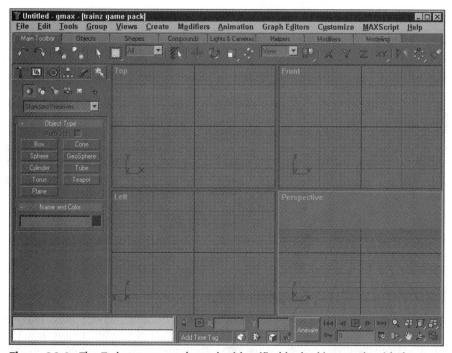

Figure 26-9: The Trainz game pack can be identified by looking on the title bar.

Note Before installing the ACS, you should check Auran's Web site at www.auran.com/ trainz/contentcreation.htm for the latest updates.

Except for the subtle repositioning of the different interface elements, the only other real change is that the Export dialog box has been modified to export models to several unique Trainz formats. These formats include the following:

✦ **.IM:** Indexed Mesh file

✦ **.PM:** Progressive Mesh file

✦ **.KIN:** Animation file

Working with Trainz Objects

If you have a favorite engine that you like to take out of the roadhouse, then you're probably interested in adding new scenery to your favorite route. You really have no limitations on the types of objects that you can add as scenery, but keep in mind that scenery is added at the size represented in gmax, so you need to check the units before exporting the scenery.

Setting and measuring units

gmax can work with either Metric or English units. You can change them using the Customize ➪ Units Setup menu command, which opens the Units Setup dialog box.

Cross-Reference   The Units Setup dialog box is covered in Chapter 3, "Making a Custom Face, er, Interface."

If you've created an object and you're not sure of its height, you can measure it using the Tape object found in the Helpers subcategory of the Create panel. After selecting the Tape button, click one end of the object and drag to the other end. The Length value is displayed in the Parameters rollout.

Objects are represented in the Trainz world at a 1:1 ratio with their sizes in gmax, so you probably won't want a building that is only 2 meters high or a billboard that is 70 meters high.

Editing existing source files

On the Auran Web site is a zip file of source objects called source_files. This file includes the gmax files for several example objects that can be customized. Using these source files, you can edit existing custom objects and practice getting used to the constraints of the Trainz objects. They also provide a good reference point if you get stuck.

Tutorial: Adding a windmill object

One of the items found among the source files is a windmill object. You can find this object in the Scenery\Animation_sample directory. In this directory is the gmax file that you can open within the Trainz Asset Creation Studio. From there, you can modify and export it.

To add a modified windmill to the Surveyor, follow these steps:

1. Locate and open the oz_windmill_tower.gmax file from the Source_files directory. If you extract the entire Source_files.zip file, it will be located in the Source_files\Scenery\Animation_sample\windmill_oz directory.

2. Select Customize ➪ Units Setup, and select the Metric option and Meters.

3. Select Edit ➪ Select All and click the Zoom Extents All button in the lower-right corner of the gmax window to zoom in on the windmill object.

4. In the Create panel, select the Helpers category and click the Tape button. Click in the Front viewport at the base of the windmill, and drag to the top of the windmill.

The Length value shown in the Parameters rollout indicates that this windmill is only about 0.5 meter tall.

5. Select the entire windmill again, and click the Select and Scale button. Then drag in the Front viewport until the coordinate text fields in the status bar show a value of 2000.

6. Use the Tape helper object to measure the windmill again. After scaling, it should be about 12.5 meters tall.

7. Select the entire windmill again, and with the Select and Move button selected, enter a value of 0 in the X, Y, and Z coordinate text fields in the status bar.

This centers the position of the windmill again. Figure 26-10 shows the resulting windmill after you've clicked the Zoom Extents All button again.

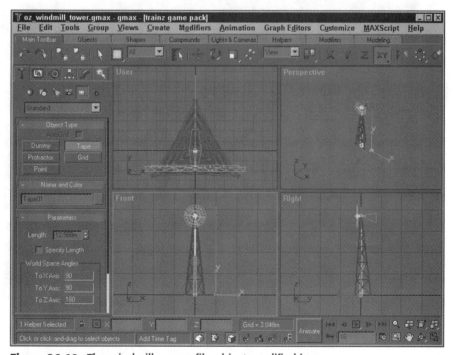

Figure 26-10: The windmill source file object modified in gmax

8. Delete the tape objects, and select File ➪ Export. Save the file as windmill in a windmill folder.

9. Open the Utility panel, and click the Resource Collector button. Click the Browse button, locate the windmill directory, and click the Use Path button. Enable the Collect Bitmaps option, and click the Begin button.

   This gathers and copies all the bitmap files to the windmill directory.

10. Create the necessary config.txt and image reference text files, and copy them all into the windmill directory.

11. Copy the entire windmill directory to the Auran\Trainz\World\Custom\ Scenery directory, and restart Trainz.

    The windmill appears in the Objects panel of the Surveyor module under the Custom category.

Figure 26-11 shows the windmill objects added to the scene.

Figure 26-11: The windmill object added to the current scene in the Surveyor module

Creating Trainz objects

All geometric objects can be used to create scenery including primitives, meshes, patches, and even compound objects, but it doesn't make much sense to add a camera to an object.

You'll want to combine all separate objects into a single object prior to exporting. If you convert one of the objects to an Editable Mesh object, then you can use the Attach or Attach List buttons found in the Modify panel to make all objects subobject elements of the same object.

If you apply any modifiers to the object, you want to collapse the modifiers to a single Editable Mesh before exporting the object. This can be done by right-clicking any of the modifiers or object types listed in the Modifier Stack and selecting Collapse To Editable Mesh.

Mapping Trainz objects

Before an object can be exported, all its faces must include mapping coordinates. If an object includes faces without mapping coordinates, the exporter throws an error, as shown in Figure 26-12, and the export is not completed.

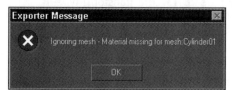

Figure 26-12: Exporting an object without mapping coordinates is bad news.

Trainz allows only Bitmap maps and not the Checker map. If you apply a Checker map to an object, the exporter throws an error.

To enable mapping coordinates for all primitive and patch objects, you need to enable the Generate Mapping Coordinates option at the bottom of the Parameters rollout. For other object types like Editable Meshes, you can add mapping coordinates to any faces or objects without them with the UVW Map modifier.

Another export limitation is that each object can have only one Multi-Material applied to it, but if you use the Multi-Material correctly, you only need one.

All bitmaps that are applied to objects as maps need to be multiples of 64 pixels in each direction. The Trainz game engine optimizes the use of maps and can efficiently work with maps that conform to this standard. So maps that are 64×64 are fine, as are 128×128, 256×256, 64×256, and so on.

Positioning Trainz objects

Before exporting Trainz objects, you need to position them correctly or they won't appear within the Surveyor module. The home grids in gmax make this positioning easy to do. The X- and Y-axes need to have coordinate values of 0, and the object needs to be positioned along the Z-axis so that all portions of the object are above the XY plane.

Open the Move Transform Type-In dialog box, shown in Figure 26-13, by selecting the Select and Move button on the main toolbar and right-clicking the same button (or by pressing the F12 key). Then you can quickly zero out the X- and Y-axes by right-clicking their respective spinners.

Tip   An even quicker way to set these values to 0 is to enter the value in the Transform Type-In field found on the status bar at the bottom of the gmax window.

Figure 26-13: The Transform Type-In dialog box can quickly set the X- and Y-axes values to 0.

The Pivot Point for the object should also be located at the center of the object. This can be done easily by opening the Hierarchy panel, clicking the Pivot button, clicking the Affect Pivot Only button, and then clicking the Center to Object button. This moves the pivot point for the object to the center of the object.

Exporting Trainz objects

After your objects are ready to be included in the world, you need to export them using File ➪ Export. The Trainz format is selected by default in the File Type drop-down list.

Tip   Before you export your object, you should save a version of the object as a gmax file so you can return to work on it later.

The exported object appears as several files when exported. All these files need to be saved to a single folder that is named the same as the exported object. For example, an object exported as "Farm House" needs to be saved into a folder named also "Farm House."

When naming objects, remember to include an underscore in the file name wherever you want a space to appear. A file saved as "Farm_House" will be displayed in the Surveyor as "Farm House."

The content folder needs to contain all the files used to create the object including all bitmaps. gmax includes a utility useful for gathering together all the needed files. The Resource Collector can be found as a button in the Utility panel, shown in Figure 26-14. To use this utility, click the Browse button, locate the folder where you want to compile all the files for this object, enable the Collect Bitmaps and Copy options, and then click the Begin button. This copies all the reference files to the specified folder.

Figure 26-14: The Resource Collector utility is useful for gathering all the various files.

Loading Trainz objects

The final step is to place the folder with all the object files in a place where the Trainz application can find them. If you create a directory under the Trainz installation directory called World\Custom\Scenery and place the object folder in it, Trainz will find it when it is restarted. For example, if the object you created is a farm house that has been exported to the name "Farm_House" and saved in a folder named "Farm_House," then the folder should be placed in the Trainz\Custom\Scenery\Farm_House directory.

Custom subdirectories found under Auran\Trainz\World\Custom can include the following:

✦ **Trains:** Locomotive or car body meshes, shadow meshes, train icons, and "alpha number" files

✦ **Bogeys:** The wheel mechanisms for locos or cars

✦ **Engines:** Engine config.txt files that give locos and cars their physics and performance boundaries

✦ **Maps:** Custom maps generated from the Surveyor module

✦ **Ground:** Ground textures.

✦ **Environment:** Sky and water textures

✦ **Pants:** The mechanisms on top of trains that conduct electricity via overhead wires (short for *pantographs*)

✦ **Scenery:** Objects used to populate the terrain

✦ **Splines:** Used to create repeating objects such as fences and roads

✦ **Track:** Railway tracks including rails, tunnels, and bridges

✦ **Trackside:** Objects that are placed on or near the tracks, such as signs

✦ **Scenarios:** Written in a special script to define a task to be accomplished

✦ **Interiors:** Inside sections of the train engine

Tutorial: Adding a cow scenery object

I remember taking a train ride on the remote northern island of Hokkaido in Japan crowded with tourists, and I was disturbed by some commotion that caused all the tourists to crowd to the left side of the train and stare out the window. My curiosity drove me to the window, where I looked in vain for the cause of all the excitement. I was puzzled because all I could see were some simple cows grazing in a meadow. As I puzzled, I overheard some tourists remark that they'd never actually seen cows "in the wild." So it turned out that the cows were what all the excitement was about.

Now that I have a chance, I'd hate to deny any city-dwelling tourist the chance to see cows in their rustic habitat. This example creates a cow object that can be populated as scenery.

To add a cow model to the Trainz scenery, follow these steps.

1. Open the file named cow.gmax from the Chap 26 directory on the CD-ROM.

This file includes an excellent cow model created by Viewpoint Datalabs. Although the cow model includes different parts, all these parts have been attached together into an Editable Mesh object.

2. Since this is a high-res model, you check to see how heavy the file is. In the Utilities panel, click on the Polygon Counter button. This opens the Polygon Counter dialog box, where you can see the number of polygons that make up the model. The selected cow model weighs in at 3,973 polygons, definitely in the heavyweight class.

3. Putting the cow on a diet can be done easily with the Optimize modifier. With the cow selected, choose the Modifiers ⇨ Mesh Editing ⇨ Optimize menu command. In the Parameters rollout, enable the options to preserve Material and Smooth Boundaries and also enable the Auto Edge option. Then set the Face Threshold to 20. The cow will be more blocky, but the game engine will thank you.

4. Press the M key to open the gmax Material Editor, click the New button, and select Multi-Material from the New Material dialog box. In the Multi/Sub-Object Basic Parameters rollout, click the Set Number button and set the number of materials to 3.

5. Click the color swatch for the first material, and set it to brown. Set the second and third material colors to white and black, respectively. Then select the cow model, and click the Apply button.

6. Open the Modify panel, and select Element subobject mode. Select the udder element. In the Surface Properties rollout, set the Material ID to 2. Repeat this step for the four hoof elements, and set their Material ID to 3. Click the map button next to the Diffuse color for the brown material, and select the cow_hide.tga bitmap.

7. In the Modify panel, click the UVW Map button to apply the UVW Map modifier to the cow model. In the Parameters rollout, select the Spherical option.

8. With the Select and Move button selected, drag the cow upward in the Front view until its hoofs are just above the grid center point. Then enter values of 0 in both the X and Y text fields in the status bar. Figure 26-15 shows the cow model when completed in gmax.

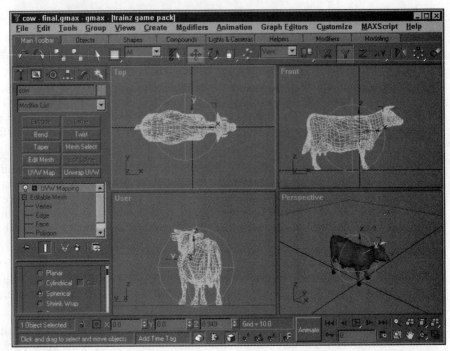

Figure 26-15: After material, modifiers, and positioning, the cow model is ready to be exported.

9. Select the File ⇨ Export command to open the Export dialog box. Use the Create a New Folder button to create a new folder named Cow, and save the object as Cow.im.

10. In a text editor, create a file named config.txt that includes a KUID and a single line a text that says, "kind scenery" and save the file in the Cow folder. Then create a texture reference file.

11. Move the Cow folder to the Trainz\Custom\Scenery directory where Trainz is installed, and restart Trainz. Select the Surveyor module, select a terrain, open the Objects panel, and select the Custom region to see the cow object.

Figure 26-16 shows a terrain with several cows added to the landscape.

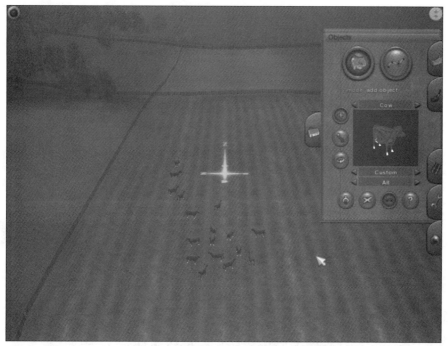

Figure 26-16: This terrain now has cows, compliments of gmax.

Creating Trains

Train objects interact with the game engine exclusively. When creating a train object, you need to define several points that identify various locations on the train to the game engine. These points help maintain correct alignment as the train moves along the track (it wouldn't be a very good simulation if the train were misaligned with the tracks).

Create the alignment points in gmax using the Point helper object located in the Create panel, under the Helpers category. These points must be named as shown in Table 26-3.

Table 26-3
Train Alignment Points

Point Name	Description
a.limfront	Marks the front coupling of the train car.
a.limback	Marks the rear coupling of the train car. The origin should be an equal distance from the limfront and limback points.
a.bog0	Marks the front bogey attachment location.
a.bog1	Marks the rear bogey attachment location.
a.exhaust*	Marks the exhaust ports; * is a number starting with 0.
a.light*	Marks the lights; * is a number starting with 0.
a.ditch*	Marks the ditch lights; * is a number starting with 0.
a.cabfront	Marks the location of the front of the cab.
a.pant*	Marks the pantograph attachment location; * is a number starting with 0.
a.driver*	Marks the driver location; * is a number starting with 0.

Note   Carriage cars need only limfront, limback, bog0 and bog1 points.

One of the easiest ways to begin modeling trains is to load one of the trains from the Source_files directory and to modify the original train, keeping all its attachment points. Custom trains must be placed in the Auran\Trainz\World\ custom\trains directory.

Adding Sound and Smoke Effects

Sound files can be associated with train and scenery objects. Trainz accepts .WAV sound files. By specifying the kind in the config.txt file, you can add a sound effect to the scene. Within the config.txt file you can specify the sound's volume, attachment, range, distance, and repeat-delay parameters. For example, we could easily create the sound of a cow mooing and attach it to the previous cow model.

Another way to add realism to your scene is with smoke effects. These effects can be added to scenery objects such as a factory or a house chimney as well as a train. The smoke's origin is marked by an attachment point named a.smoke. Smoke emanates from the attachment point's location along the positive Y-axis. For example, if you want steam to come from a steam locomotive that you created, position an attachment point (Create panel, Helper category in gmax) inside the smokestack so its Y-axis points upward and out of the smokestack.

You can define how the smoke looks by editing the object's config.txt file. Smoke parameters include color, acceleration, looping, start, rate, and lifetime. Using these variables, you can create any effect from white, fluffy steam to thick, black smoke (without damaging the fragile environment).

Sharing Content

If you've completed a new level and you want to share it with other Trainz users, you can run the Content Dispatcher.exe file in the Trainz directory. This file begins with a registration process where you can receive a User ID that lets you access the community section of the Planet Auran Web site.

Working with the Content Dispatcher

From the Planet Auran Web site, you can download custom content created by other users and share your new content with them. The Content Dispatcher, shown in Figure 26-17, will verify that the content is free of errors. The assets can then be packaged together for uploading to the Planet Auran Web site.

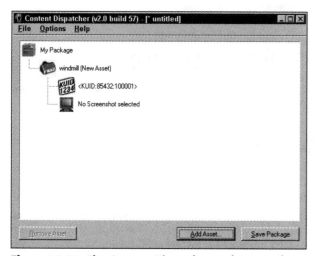

Figure 26-17: The Content Dispatcher packages and uploads your custom assets.

Debugging with the Content Dispatcher

The Content Dispatcher performs another helpful key role. Any errors that are associated with a given asset can be detected and reported. Using this report, you can fix any errors that your assets have. To get a report of the errors for your current custom content, click Add Assets; the errors are shown next to all assets that have errors, like those shown in Figure 26-18. Clicking the error icon opens a dialog box that revels the error.

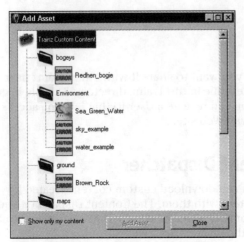

Figure 26-18: The Add Assets dialog box shows any errors with your content.

Locating Online Trainz Resources

This chapter is just a small sampling of the customization possible with Trainz. You can find additional resources online.

Auran's Trainz Web site

http://www.auran.com/trainz/

This is the first stop for information and resources on Trainz. Auran's Web site is the official Trainz headquarters. It includes a Download Station where you can access the huge repository of uploaded content. The Download Station requires you to register and obtain an ID number to upload and download.

Trainz Luvr

http://trainz.luvr.net/

This Web site is a fan site covering all aspects of Trainz. You can find content and an extensive Knowledge Base with answers to just about any question you might want to ask.

Train Simulator Insider

`http://microsoftgamesinsider.com/TrainSimulator/default.htm`

The Train Simulator Insider Web pages are dedicated to Microsoft's Train Simulator, another excellent simulator for people who love trains.

Summary

Trainz is a simulator for trains. Using the Trainz Asset Creation Studio, you can customize scenery that can be used to edit and populate the new levels you can make.

This chapter covered these topics:

✦ Creating custom texture images

✦ Learning to install and use the Trainz Asset Creation Studio

✦ Discovering how to use gmax to create new scenery objects for Trainz's Surveyor module

✦ Exporting gmax objects to Trainz

The next chapter explores the various — wait, there isn't a next chapter! You might want to read the appendixes, which cover installing and configuring gmax, the keyboard shortcuts, and the contents of the CD-ROM. Hope you enjoyed this book. Thanks for reading.

✦   ✦   ✦

Appendixes

P A R T

VI

◆ ◆ ◆ ◆

In This Part

Appendix A
Installing and
Configuring gmax

Appendix B
gmax Keyboard
Shortcuts

Appendix C
What's on the
CD-ROM

◆ ◆ ◆ ◆

Installing and Configuring gmax

◆ ◆ ◆ ◆

In This Appendix

Understanding
hardware
requirements

Installing gmax

Registering the
software

Setting the
display driver

◆ ◆ ◆ ◆

Although this material may seem like it should have been covered in Chapter 1, you're an experienced game player and I'm sure you've installed (and uninstalled) your share of games and applications. I didn't want to weigh down the first chapter with information that you might not need.

Then again, gmax is unsupported and has several gotchas that I can warn you of. I've included this appendix to guide you through the installation and configuration process and to answer some questions that might arise along the way.

Hardware Requirements

To get the best performance from gmax, you need a fairly meaty machine. If you're running any of the games that include a gmax game pack, then you more than likely have a computer that is more powerful than most, so you're probably alright when it comes to hardware.

A good default system to use would be a Pentium IV or an AMD Athlon-based computer with 1GB or more of RAM (and 2GB of swap space) and a decent-sized hard drive and monitor. If need be, you can get by with a 300 MHz Pentium (or AMD) packing as little as 128MB of RAM (with 300MB of swap space), but you may spend lots of time watching your computer churn furiously to keep up.

Concerning operating systems, gmax can run on Windows 98, Windows 2000, or any version of Windows newer than Windows 98.

Note   One big drawback to running gmax on Windows 98 or ME is that it can run only a single instance at a time. Windows 2000 and XP users can run multiple instances of gmax at the same time.

One element of your system that will probably have the greatest impact on the performance of gmax is the graphics card. Any good graphics card has specialized hardware that will take lots of the workload off your computer's CPU, freeing it up to do other tasks. And it makes your games run better, too. gmax is fairly graphics-intensive, and a little extra money in the graphics card department will go a long way toward boosting your performance.

The good news is that hardware accelerated graphics cards are becoming cheaper — you can get great cards for $200–$300. When searching for a graphics card, make sure it can support a resolution of at least 1024×768 at 16-bit color and that it comes with drivers for OpenGL 1.1 or later and Direct3D/Direct X. You'll also want a minimum of 32MB on the graphics card or 64MB for 3D graphics acceleration.

For the complete install, you will need just under 100MB of hard drive space (not counting any game packs that you may wish to install). You can get by with less if you choose not to install the help and tutorial files. The help files are especially useful if you plan on working with MAXScript.

Another handy piece of hardware to have is a scrollable mouse. A scrollable mouse makes moving through menus and the Command Panel easier, plus it gives you a third button, which can be used to navigate the viewports.

Portions of gmax (specifically the help files) will require Internet Explorer 5 or newer and Macromedia's Flash Player. Flash Player is included as part of the installation process.

Downloading gmax

gmax is a freely available program that can be downloaded off the Web from Discreet's Web site at www.discreet.com/products/gmax or from File Planet at www.FilePlanet.com.

On the CD-ROM   For convenience, gmax is included on the book's CD-ROM. The version included is gmax 1.2. Be sure to check the Discreet Web site to see whether a newer version has been released before installing.

The gmax installation has been split into several small files to make the download easier. These files include:

✦ gmax 1.2 Installer (19MB)

✦ gmax Help files (15MB)

✦ gmax Tutorials (14MB)

✦ gmax Sample Textures (3MB)

Of these files, you really need only the gmax 1.2 Installer, but the Help files and Tutorials do come in handy.

Installing gmax

After you've downloaded the necessary files (or decided to run them from the CD-ROM), installing gmax is straightforward.

Caution gmax 1.2 will install over the top of gmax 1.1, but it will not install over the top of any versions prior to 1.0. If you have an installed version of 1.0 on your computer, you need to uninstall that version before installing version 1.2.

Here's what you need to do:

1. Locate the gmax12.exe file from your downloaded directory (or from the CD-ROM), and double click it to execute the self-extractor.

2. In the WinZip Self-Extractor dialog box that appears, click the Setup button to begin the installation.

3. A Welcome screen appears, advising you to shut down other applications before proceeding. Click the Next button to move on. This screen also includes a button to view the Readme file. Reading this is a good idea, because it has last-minute information.

4. The next screen is the Software License Agreement. Choose your country, and read the corresponding License Agreement. After you've read the agreement, click the now-enabled "I accept" button. Then click the now-enabled Next button to move on.

5. Next is the Destination Folder screen. By default, gmax will be installed in c:\gmax, but you can choose a different destination by clicking the Browse button and navigating to a different directory. When you're happy with the installation location, click the Next button to continue.

6. The next screen is the point-of-no-return, Start Copying Files screen. Click the Next button to begin copying files to your hard drive. It takes a few minutes for gmax to install completely.

7. After this is completed, you can click the Finish button to exit the gmax setup. Installing gmax will not require that you reboot your computer.

Note The first step of the installation process checks for existing gmax components. If you run the gmax installation program after gmax has already been installed, it offers the options to Repair or Remove gmax.

Registering the Software

After gmax is installed, you need to register the software through Discreet before you can use it. When you first run gmax, a dialog box appears asking for a Registered User Identification Code. You can obtain a code by registering the software online at `www.discreet.com/products/gmax/register`. Registering online requires that you have an e-mail address where they can send you the ID code.

Once you've gotten your ID code, you can enter it into the text box that appears in the dialog box. The Continue button becomes active when a valid ID is entered. Clicking the Exit button closes the dialog box, and gmax will not run.

Installing Game Packs

Most games that include a gmax game pack also include a version of gmax, but these versions are typically out of date. When installing a game pack, you should first download the latest gmax version from the Discreet site. A game pack typically recognizes the existing version of gmax and uses it instead of the gmax version that comes with the game.

Several of the game packs have their own setup wizard, but others are included within a zip file. Check the game-specific chapters in Part V for detailed information on the various game packs.

You can check to see which game packs are installed by looking in the \gamepacks directory. Dungeon Siege, Tempest (for Quake), Trainz,, and Command & Conquer: Renegade all place their game packs in this directory.

 Caution   Flight Simulator works a little differently from the other games and places its components in the \plugins directory.

Setting the Display Driver

When gmax is first run, you'll see the gmax Driver Setup dialog box, which lets you select the display driver to use. Choosing the correct display driver is important for getting the best performance out of your computer. If you are unsure of which display driver to use (it really depends on your graphics card), choose the HEIDI option, which is a software driver. You can change the display driver in gmax later by choosing Customize ➪ Preferences, selecting the Viewports panel, and clicking the Choose Driver button. The Graphics Driver Setup dialog box opens. If you change the graphics driver, you need to restart gmax before the new driver is used.

You can choose one of three drivers to use in gmax: Software, Direct3D, or OpenGL. There is also an option to select a custom driver.

Tip You can also start gmax with a specific display driver from the command line using the –h option. For example, 3dsgmax.exe –h causes the gmax Driver Setup dialog box to appear when you run gmax.

Software

The software display driver option is gmax's own built-in software graphics driver called HEIDI. Because it is a software driver, it does not take advantage of any special graphics hardware that your graphics card supports, so your computer's CPU does all the work. The nice thing about this option is that it works on any computer, even if you don't have a very good graphics card.

After you've installed gmax, start it up using software drivers to make sure that everything installed correctly. From there, try out the different graphics drivers to see whether you can move up to something faster.

Note Viewport antialiasing works in gmax only when using the software display drivers.

OpenGL

If your graphics card supports OpenGL in hardware, then this is definitely the driver to use. OpenGL works under all Windows operating systems and is typically present on high-end graphics cards. In order for gmax to use OpenGL, the drivers must support OpenGL 1.1 or later.

Direct3D

Direct3D uses the hardware capabilities of the graphics cards that are present and simulates anything else it needs in software. You must have at least the 8.0 version of DirectX installed for these drivers to work with gmax, but most of the gmax games use DirectX 8 or later. Simulating different features makes Direct3D run on a wide range of computers, but it can also be much slower. If your graphics card's drivers support all of Direct3D in hardware, then using this driver might give you good performance. If it switches to software mode, however, it will be much slower than HEIDI. The Direct3D display driver does not work on video cards that have less than 32MB of memory.

✦ ✦ ✦

gmax Keyboard Shortcuts

T he key to working efficiently with gmax is learning the keyboard shortcuts. If you know the keyboard shortcuts, you can maximize the viewports using Expert Mode (Ctrl+X) and use the keyboard and mouse to access all commands.

Almost every separate window has its own set of keyboard shortcuts. You can use the Keyboard Shortcut Override Toggle button at the bottom of the gmax window (it looks like a keyboard key) to make the keyboard shortcuts for the other windows take precedence over the main window's shortcuts.

For example, in the main gmax window, the A key toggles the Angle Snap feature on and off, but in the Track View window, the A key adds keys. If Track View is open and the Keyboard Shortcut Override Toggle is enabled, then the Add Keys function will be performed. If the Keyboard Shortcut Override Toggle is off, then Angle Snap will be activated.

If you want to change any of the keyboard shortcuts, the Customize User Interface dialog box includes a Keyboard panel for making changes. You can open this dialog box using the Customize ⇨ Customize User Interface command.

Cross-Reference

Chapter 3, "Making a Custom Face, er Interface," offers more details on creating custom keyboard shortcuts.

Main Interface Shortcuts

The following tables present the various shortcut keys for the main interface.

In This Appendix

Overriding the keyboard shortcuts

Main interface shortcuts

Dialog box shortcuts

Miscellaneous shortcuts

◆ ◆ ◆ ◆

Menus	
Command	*Shortcut*
New Scene	Ctrl+N
Open File	Ctrl+O
Save File	Ctrl+S
Undo Scene Operation	Ctrl+Z
Redo Scene Operation	Ctrl+A
Hold	Alt+Ctrl+H
Fetch	Alt+Ctrl+F
Delete Objects	Delete
Select by Name	H
Transform Type-In	F12
Align	Alt+A
Normal Align	Alt+N
Place Highlight	Ctrl+H
Spacing Tool	Shift+I
Undo Viewport Operation	Shift+Z
Redo Viewport Operation	Shift+A
Viewport Background	Alt+B
Update Background Image	Alt+Shift+Ctrl+B
Match Camera to View	Ctrl+C
Redraw All Views	1
Expert Mode Toggle	Ctrl+X
Show/Hide Command Panel	3
Show/Hide Floating Toolbars	4
Show/Hide Main Toolbar	Alt+6
Show/Hide Tab Panel	2, Y
Lock User Interface	Alt+0 (zero)
MAXScript Listener	F11
File Menu	Alt+F
Edit Menu	Alt+E

Command	Shortcut
Tools Menu	Alt+T
Group Menu	Alt+G
Views Menu	Alt+V
Create Menu	Alt+C
Modifiers Menu	Alt+O
Animation Menu	Alt+A
Graph Editors Menu	Alt+D
Customize Menu	Alt+U
MAXScript Menu	Alt+M
Help Menu	Alt+H

Main Toolbar

Command	Shortcut
Rectangle, Circle, Polygon Selection Cycle	Ctrl+F
Restrict to X	F5
Restrict to Y	F6
Restrict to Z	F7
Restrict Plane Cycle	F8
gmax Material Editor	M

Viewports

Command	Shortcut
Front View	F
Back View	K
Top View	T
Bottom View	B
Left View	L

Continued

Viewports *(continued)*

Command	Shortcut
Right View	R
Perspective View	P
User View	U
Camera View	C
Selection Brackets Toggle	J
Light View	Shift+4
Disable Viewport	D
Dynamic Resizing	Drag viewport borders
Transform Gizmo Toggle	X
Transform Gizmo Size Down	-
Transform Gizmo Size Up	=
Wireframe/Smooth+Highlights	F3
View Edged Faces	F4
Bounding Box	Shift+B
Texture Correction	Ctrl+T
Default Lighting	Ctrl+L
See-Through Display	Alt+X
Unhide by Name	5
Freeze Selection	6
Unfreeze All	7
Show/Hide Cameras	Shift+C
Show/Hide Geometry	Shift+O
Show/Hide Grids	G
Show/Hide All Grids	Shift+G
Show/Hide Helpers	Shift+H
Show/Hide Lights	Shift+L
Show/Hide Particle Systems	Shift+P
Show/Hide Space Warps	Shift+W
Access Quadmenu	Q
Select Objects	Right mouse click

Status Bar

Command	Shortcut
Selection Lock Toggle	Spacebar
Degradation Override	O
Adaptive Perspective Grid	Shift+Ctrl+A
Snap	S
Angle Snap	A
Snap Percent	Shift+Ctrl+P

Time Controls

Command	Shortcut
Animate Mode	N
Play/Pause Animation	/
Backup Time One Unit	,
Forward Time One Unit	.
Go to Start Frame	Home
Go to End Frame	End

Viewport Navigation

Command	Shortcut
Zoom Extents	Alt+Ctrl+Z
Zoom Extents All	Shift+Ctrl+Z
Zoom Mode	Z
Zoom Region Mode	Ctrl+W
Zoom Viewport In	[
Zoom Viewport Out	]
Zoom In 2X	Shift+Numlock +
Zoom Out 2X	Shift+Numlock -
Pan View	Ctrl+P

Continued

Viewport Navigation *(continued)*

Command	Shortcut
Interactive Pan	I
Rotate View Mode	Ctrl+R, V
Min/Max Toggle	W

Quadmenus

Command	Shortcut
Animation Quadmenu	Alt+right mouse click
Modeling Quadmenu	Ctrl+right mouse click
Snap Quadmenu	Shift+right mouse click

Subobjects

Command	Shortcut
Subobject Level Cycle	Insert
Shade Selected Faces	F2
Delete Subobject	Delete
Select Subobject Toggle	Ctrl+B

Hierarchies

Command	Shortcut
Select Ancestor	Page Up
Select Child	Page Down
Select Entire Hierarchy	Double-click parent

Editable Mesh	
Command	*Shortcut*
Detach	Ctrl+D
Cut Mode	Alt+C
Chamfer Mode	Ctrl+C
Extrude Mode	Ctrl+E
Edge Turn	Ctrl+T
Weld Selected	Ctrl+W
Weld Target Mode	Alt+W

Editable Poly	
Command	*Shortcut*
Cut	Alt+C
Bevel Mode	Ctrl+V
Extrude Poly Face	Alt+E
Meshsmooth	Ctrl+M
Collapse Poly Object	Alt+Ctrl+C
Cap Object	Alt+P

Dialog Box Shortcuts

Use the following shortcut keys to work with the various dialog boxes. The dialog box must be selected for these shortcuts to work. It is possible for modeless dialog boxes to have the dialog box visible but not selected.

Track View	
Command	*Shortcut*
Edit Keys Mode	E
Function Curves Mode	F5, F
Add Keys	A

Continued

Track View (continued)

Command	Shortcut
Move Keys	M
Expand Track	Enter, T
Expand Objects Track	O
Filters	Q
Scroll Down	Ctrl+Down arrow
Scroll Up	Ctrl+Up arrow
Lock Selection	Spacebar
Nudge Keys Left	Left arrow
Nudge Keys Right	Right arrow
Move Highlight Down	Down arrow
Move Highlight Up	Up arrow
Backup Time One Unit	,
Forward Time One Unit	.
Undo Scene Operation	Ctrl+Z
Redo Scene Operation	Ctrl+A
Apply Ease Curve	Ctrl+E
Apply Multiplier Curve	Ctrl+M
Lock Tangents Toggle	L
Apply Controller	C
Copy Controller	Ctrl+C
Paste Controller	Ctrl+V
Make Controller Unique	U

Free-Form Deformations

Command	Shortcut
Switch to Control Point Level	Alt+Shift+C
Switch to Lattice Level	Alt+Shift+L
Switch to Set Volume Level	Alt+Shift+S
Switch to Top Level	Alt+Shift+T

Edit UVWs

Command	Shortcut
Load UVW	Alt+Shift+Ctrl+L
Edit UVWs	Ctrl+E
Unwrap Options	Ctrl+O
Update Map	Ctrl+U
Break Selected Vertices	Ctrl+B
Lock Selected Vertices	Spacebar
Filter Selected Faces	Alt+F
Get Face Selection From Stack	Alt+Shift+Ctrl+F
Detach Edge Vertices	D, Ctrl+D
Planar Map Faces/Patches	Enter
Hide Selected	Ctrl+H
Freeze Selected	Ctrl+F
Pixel Snap	Ctrl+S
Mirror Horizontal	Alt+Shift+Ctrl+N
Mirror Vertical	Alt+Shift+Ctrl+M
Move Horizontal	Alt+Shift+Ctrl+J
Move Vertical	Alt+Shift+Ctrl+K
Texture Vertex Contract Selection	-
Texture Vertex Expand Selection	+
Texture Vertex Move Mode	Q
Texture Vertex Rotate Mode	Ctrl+R
Texture Vertex Weld Selected	Ctrl+W
Texture Vertex Target Weld	Ctrl+T
Pan	Ctrl+P
Zoom	Z
Zoom Extents	X
Zoom Region	Ctrl+X
Zoom Selected Elements	Alt+Shift+Ctrl+Z
Zoom to Gizmo	Shift+Spacebar

Miscellaneous Shortcuts

In addition to specific shortcuts for the main interface and the dialog boxes, gmax provides several general shortcuts that can be used in many places.

General Shortcuts	
Command	*Shortcut*
Cut Value	Ctrl+X
Copy Value	Ctrl+C
Paste Value	Ctrl+V
Apply Settings	Enter
Highlight Next Text Field	Tab
Highlight Previous Text Field	Shift+Tab
Highlight Any Text Field	Double-click current value
Nudge Selection	Arrow keys
Display Quadmenus	Right-click
Display First Tab	Alt+1

✦   ✦   ✦

What's on the CD-ROM

✦   ✦   ✦   ✦

In This Appendix

System requirements

Using the CD with Windows

What's on the CD

Troubleshooting

✦   ✦   ✦   ✦

Throughout the book, you'll find many tutorials that help you to understand the principles being discussed. All the example files used to create these tutorials are included on the CD-ROM that came with this book. In addition to these files, you'll find a copy of gmax and many of the tools needed to create the custom content.

This appendix provides you with information on the contents of the CD that accompanies this book. For the latest and greatest information, please refer to the ReadMe file located at the root of the CD.

System Requirements

Make sure that your computer meets the minimum system requirements listed in this section. If your computer doesn't match up to these requirements, you may have a problem using the contents of the CD.

For Windows® 2000 or Windows® 98:

- ✦ Intel® or AMD processor at 300 MHz or better
- ✦ 128MB RAM or greater
- ✦ At least 300MB of swap space
- ✦ Graphics card supporting $1024 \times 768 \times 16$-bit color (Open GL and Direct3D hardware acceleration supported)
- ✦ Windows-compliant pointing device
- ✦ A CD-ROM drive
- ✦ Internet Explorer 5.0 (IE 5.5 recommended and available for download)
- ✦ Macromedia Flash Player (included with the gmax installer)

Using the CD with Windows

To install the items from the CD to your hard drive, follow these steps:

1. Insert the CD into your computer's CD-ROM drive.
2. A window appears with the following options: Install, Browse, eBook, Links, and Exit.

   Install: Gives you the option to install the supplied software and/or the author-created samples on the CD-ROM.

   Browse: Enables you to view the contents of the CD-ROM in its directory structure.

   eBook: Enables you to view an electronic version of the book.

   Links: A Web page of links to all the game tools.

   Exit: Closes the autorun window.

If you do not have autorun enabled or if the autorun window does not appear, follow these steps to access the CD:

1. Click Start ➪ Run.
2. In the dialog box that appears, type *d*:**setup.exe**, where *d* is the letter of your CD-ROM drive.

   This brings up the autorun window described earlier.
3. Choose the Install, Browse, eBook, Links, or Exit option from the menu.

   See Step 2 in the preceding list for a description of these options.

What's on the CD

The following sections provide a summary of the software and other materials you'll find on the CD.

Author-created materials

The example files used in the tutorials throughout the book are included in the "Chapter Example Files" directory. Within this directory are separate subdirectories for each chapter. Supplemental files such as models and images are also included in these directories.

gmax Game Packs

Each game pack on the CD extends the features of gmax and enables you to create custom content in the formats that the various games need. Game packs are included for the following games:

✦ Trainz

✦ Dungeon Siege

✦ Train Simulator

Note   Check each game's Web site for the latest updates to these game packs.

gmax is also available on the CD-ROM. This version of gmax is the latest version available at the time of printing. This version needs to be registered in order to work. The registration process is covered in Appendix A and can easily be done at Discreet's Web site.

Trial, demo, or evaluation versions are usually limited either by time or functionality (such as being unable to save projects). Some trial versions are very sensitive to system date changes. If you alter your computer's date, the programs "time out" and are no longer functional.

eBook version of *gmax Bible*

All the text for the book is included on the CD-ROM in PDF format (Adobe's Portable Document Format), along with Adobe Acrobat Reader (also included on the CD). Using the electronic version of the book, you can search the text. You can also see the book's figures in color.

Troubleshooting

If you have difficulty installing or using any of the materials on the companion CD, try the following solutions:

✦ **Turn off any anti-virus software that you may have running.** Installers sometimes mimic virus activity and can make your computer incorrectly believe that it is being infected by a virus. (Be sure to turn the anti-virus software back on later.)

✦ **Close all running programs.** The more programs you're running, the less memory is available to other programs. Installers also typically update files and programs; if you keep other programs running, installation may not work properly.

✦ **Check the ReadMe:** Please refer to the ReadMe file located at the root of the CD-ROM for the latest product information at the time of publication.

If you still have trouble with the CD, please call the Customer Care phone number: (800) 762-2974. Outside the United States, call (317) 572-3994. You can also contact Customer Service by e-mail at techsupdum@wiley.com. Wiley Publishing, Inc., will provide technical support only for installation and other general quality control items; for technical support on the applications themselves, consult the program's vendor or author.

✦   ✦   ✦

Glossary

3DS file A 3D file format used by the DOS version of 3D Studio.

Adaptive Degradation A gmax feature that maintains an animation's frame rate by selectively reducing a scene's complexity.

align To move two objects so that their edges, centers, or pivots are equally positioned.

ambient light Created by light that is deflected off walls and objects; provides overall lighting to the entire scene and keeps shadows from becoming completely black.

ancestors All the *parent objects* above a *child object*.

animation The process of simulating motion by displaying many separate images in succession.

arc A primitive shape that is a portion of a circle.

array An ordered group of objects or data that can be referred to by number.

artificial light Usually reserved for indoor scenes where light bulbs provide the light.

Asset Browser An interface where you can preview materials, objects, and scenes. The Asset Browser can also be used to surf the Internet for scene components.

attenuation A property that determines how light fades over distance.

auto backup A configurable feature that automatically saves the current scene periodically.

backface cull For wireframe displays, this option hides the edges of the faces pointing away from the current view.

Base object A mesh or patch object whose vertices are interpolated with the vertex positions of a second mesh or patch object (called the *Target object*) to create a Morph animation.

bevel Occurs when an object edge is replaced by a face.

Bézier curve A type of curved line where the curvature of the line is controlled by control vertices and handles.

BMP file An image format used commonly on Windows systems.

bone system A hierarchy of bone objects.

Boolean object A new object created by combing two or more objects using a union, subtraction, or intersection operation.

Boolean value A value that has only two states: on and off.

bounding box A non-rendered box that completely surrounds a selected object and defines its extents.

bump map A type of material map that defines areas to be modified by comparing the intensity of the pixels in the map.

camera An object that can be positioned within a scene to provide a unique viewpoint.

caps Fill in the surface at each end of an extruded shape.

chamfered object An object whose edges have been smoothed out.

child object An object that is linked to and controlled by a *parent object*.

circumscribed polygon A polygon positioned outside of a circle that touches the midpoint of each polygon edge.

clipping planes Each side of the edge is connected to a face.

clone A duplicate copy of an object.

collapse The process of reducing all the modification steps involved in creating an object to a single base object.

Command Panel The main interface dialog, usually positioned to the right, that holds the settings for the selected object.

compound objects Unique objects that are created with special functionality including Morph, Connect, Loft, ShapeMerge and Boolean types.

constraints Specialized controllers that limit the extraneous motion of objects during animation.

container A special track that can hold multiple tracks.

control lattice A lattice of points that has direct control over the surface to which it is connected.

Control Vertex (CV) A vertex that controls the shape of a CV Curve or CV Surface.

controllers Affect the position, rotation, and scaling of objects in preset ways. Also, *plug-ins* that set the keys for animation sequences.

cropping The process of cutting out a portion of an image.

data types Different classes of values that you can store in *variables*.

descendants All the *child objects* below a *parent object*.

Direct3D A 3D rendering display technology language created by Microsoft and frequently used in games to render 3D objects.

diffuse color The main color radiated by an object under normal white light.

display driver The 3D rendering language that "drives" the display of 3D objects on the screen. Common display drivers for gmax include Heidi, Direct3D, and OpenGL.

dolly A motion applied to cameras and/or lights that moves the object closer to or further from the intended target.

dummy object A non-rendering object that can be linked to structures to make the structure easier to animate.

DXF file A 3D file format used commonly on older AutoCAD systems.

ease curve A curve that is applied to a function curve that softens the curves shape causing animations to ease into and out of a position.

edge Line that run between two vertices.

editable mesh, poly, patch, and spline objects Objects that are comprised of sub-objects that can be edited and that are not parametric.

end effector The object included at the end of an IK chain that controls the movements of the chain.

execute The process of performing instructions in a script; also referring to as *running* a script.

expert mode An interface mode in which the Command Panel, menus, toolbars, and lower interface controls are removed. This mode is initiated with the Views ⇨ Expert Mode menu command (Ctrl+X).

expression Defines how an object is transformed. The results of an expression are computed for every frame and used to affect various *parameters* in a scene.

extents The maximum dimension along each axis.

extruding The process of adding height to a *spline* or adding depth to a polygon face.

Face subobject A mesh subobject that has only three edges.

Field of View A measurement of how much of the scene is visible; directly related to the *focal length*.

Fillet The parameter that determines the amount of roundness applied to an edge of a chamfered object.

fins An extruded section that extends from the face of a bone object to show direction.

flyout A button that holds additional buttons.

focal light The distance between the film and the camera lens.

Follow object An object that defines the motion of an applied IK solution.

Forward Kinematics system A default *hierarchy* established using the Link tool, where control moves down the hierarchy from *parent object* to *child object*. Causes objects at the bottom of a linked structure to move along with their parents.

frame rate The rate at which images are displayed to produce an animation. Common rates are 30 fps (NTSC), 25 fps (PAL), and 24 fps (Film).

Free Form Deformations (FFD) A deformation method that is accomplished by surrounding an object with a matrix of movable control points.

function curve Displayed in the Track View, these editable curves display the animation values as a function of time.

functions *Expressions* that are given a *parameter* and return a value.

fusing The process of collapsing two separate vertices into one.

gamma settings A means by which colors can be consistently represented, regardless of the monitor that is being used.

gamma value A numerical offset required by an individual monitor in order to be consistent with a standard.

GeoSphere An optimized sphere primitive with regular-shaped faces.

ghosting A feature that displays "ghost" objects before and/or after an object along its animation path.

Gizmo objects Wireframe control objects that are displayed in the viewport and provide an actual structure for working with a modifier.

grid A non-rendered object that relates the viewport space to actual physical dimensions and helps align and position objects.

group A collection of objects that acts as one single object.

Heidi display driver A 3D rendering display technology language that runs as software to render 3D objects. This technology is proprietary to gmax.

helix Like a spring coil shape; the one shape of all the Shape primitives that exists in 3D.

helpers A unique class of objects that aren't visible, but are useful as you create other objects such as Dummy and Point objects.

hierarchy The complete set of related *parent* and *child* objects.

hold and fetch A temporary snapshot of the current scene (hold) that can be recalled at any moment (fetch) without dealing with files.

Hot and Cool materials A material that has been assigned within a scene and is automatically updated in the scene when the material parameters change (hot) or that isn't updated immediately, but held in the Material Editor until it is applied (cool).

hotspot The portion of a spotlight where the light intensity is at a maximum.

IK Solver An inverse kinematics solution that can be applied to a linked hierarchy of objects that define how the objects move relative to one another.

inscribed polygon A polygon positioned within a circle that touches all the polygon's vertices.

instanced modifier A single modifier that is applied to several objects at the same time.

interface The controls, menus, and buttons that are used to access the program's features.

Inverse Kinematics system A method of defining the connections between parts for easier animation. Enables *child objects* to control their *parent objects*.

JPEG file An image format used commonly on the Web. This format supports variable compression ratios.

key A definition of a specific object state that exists during an animation.

keyboard shortcuts Keys that are pressed to execute a standard feature without relying on a menu.

Kinematics A branch of mechanics that deals with the motions of a system of objects. In Max, these systems are defined by links between objects.

linking The process of attaching one object to another so that they move together.

Listener window An interface where MAXScript commands can be executed.

loft object An object created by sweeping a defined cross-section along the length of a spline path.

map A bitmap image that is pasted on or wrapped around an object.

mapping coordinates A definition on how a map should be positioned and oriented on the surface of an object.

Material Editor The interface where materials are defined, created, and applied.

MAXScript A type of a computer language specifically created for dealing with graphics.

Mesh object An object type that consists of interconnected polygons.

modeless dialog box A dialog box that doesn't need to be closed before you can work with objects in the background.

modifier Special functions used to change various aspects of an object.

Modifier Stack A list, displayed as a drop-down list, of all the modifiers that have been applied to an object. Lets you revisit any modifier and change its parameters.

Morph objects Used to create a Morph animation by interpolating the vertices in one object to the vertex positions of a second object. The original object is called the *Base object,* and the second object is called the *Target object.*

multiplier A value that increases the intensity of the parameter such as lights.

named selection A selection of objects that are identified with a name that has been created by entering it in the Named Selection field on the main toolbar. Named selections can be recalled quickly at any time.

natural light Used for outside scenes; uses the sun and moon for its light source.

nested groups Groups that contain other groups.

Ngon shape Very similar to the circle shape except that you can specify the number of sides and the corner radius, as well as whether it is an *inscribed* or *circumscribed polygon.*

normal A vector that is perpendicular to the polygon face.

Note Tracks Simple notes on when a track was altered or what it does.

omni light A type of light that sends light equally in all directions from a central point.

opacity The amount by which an object refuses to allow light to pass through it, typically measured as a percentage. The opposite of *transparency.*

opaque objects Objects that you cannot see through, like rocks and trees.

open edge Only one face connects to the edge.

OpenGL A common 3D rendering display technology language used to render and display 3D objects.

operator The part of an expression that tells how to deal with the *variables.*

orthographic view Displayed from looking straight down an axis at an object, which reveals only one plane and shows the actual height and width of the object. Available orthographic viewports in gmax include Front, Back, Top, Bottom, Left, and Right.

Out-of-range type Defines how an animation continues beyond the specified range.

parameters The *variables* that control an object.

parameter wiring A configurable method where the reactions of one object can control the reaction of another object.

Parametric objects Objects that are mathematically defined and can be changed by modifying their parameters.

parent object An object that controls any secondary objects, or *child objects,* linked to it.

Patch object An object type that consists of surfaces that are controlled by their adjoining vertices and edges.

path A spline that is used to define how an object is animated or how a loft proceeds.

persistence A feature of many, but not all, dialog boxes, where the values added to the dialog box remain set whenever the dialog box is reopened during the same gmax session. The settings remain after being applied until they are changed. You can reset all the values at once by clicking the Reset All Parameters button.

perspective Distortion of images taken with a wide *Field of View.* Causes linear dimensions to appear larger if they are closer than similar dimensions lying at a farther distance.

pivot point The point about which transforms are applied.

pixels Small square dots that collectively make up an entire screen.

Plasma A version of 3ds max that is uniquely designed to produce 3D graphics for the Web. gmax can export files to the Plasma (P3D) format.

plug-in An external program that integrates seamlessly with the gmax interface to provide additional functionality.

PNG file The Portable Network Graphic image format used commonly on the Web. This format supports 32-bit graphics.

polygon subobject A mesh subobject that has more than three vertices and two or more faces.

precedence The order of importance among several nodes, joints, or operations. Data with a higher precedence is executed first.

primitive objects The simplest building blocks used to create a model. Created by selecting the primitive object type (such as a box, sphere, cylinder, or cone) and then dragging in one of the viewports to define the primitive object's dimensions.

projection map A type of material map that is used with lights.

properties Pieces of data inside a larger object. Also referred to as *members*.

PSD file An image format used by Photoshop. This format supports Photoshop layers.

quadmenu A pop-up menu of options that is accessed by right-clicking, consisting of four different sets of menus surrounding the current cursor location.

ray trace shadow A type of *shadow* that is calculated by following the path of every light ray striking a scene.

reference Similar to an instance in that changes to the original affect all the instances, except that changes made to the instances don't affect the original object.

reflection What you see when you look in a mirror. Reflection values control how much a material reflects its surroundings.

refraction A property that defines how light bends as it moves through a transparent material. The amount of refraction that a material produces depends on the *Index of Refraction*.

rollout A panel that holds parameters and settings. Can be collapsed and expanded by clicking on the rollout title.

Root object The top *parent object* that has no parent and controls the entire *hierarchy*.

run The process of performing instructions in a script; also referred to as *executing* a script.

script A list of commands or actions that you want gmax to perform.

segments The lines or edges that run between two vertices.

shadow The area behind an object where the light is obscured.

shadow map A type of *shadow* that is an actual bitmap that the renderer produces and combines with the finished scene to produce an image.

smoothing groups A specified region listed by a number that defines how the edges of the region should be smoothed.

SMPTE A standard time measurement used in video and television. The acronym stands for Society of Motion Picture and Television Engineers.

snap To automatically move a vertex to a predefined location, such as a grid point or the corner of an object, when close.

specular highlights Highlights on a shiny object where light reflects off its surface.

spinners Interface controls that allow you to enter values or interactively increase or decrease the value by clicking the up and down arrows to the right.

spline A special type of line that curves according to mathematical principles.

strings Groups of characters within *variables*.

subobjects The geometric parts that make up the objects, such as vertices, edges, faces, polygons, elements, or combinations of object parts.

Target object A mesh or patch object whose vertex positions are interpolated with the vertices of the original mesh or patch object (called the *Base object*) to create a Morph animation.

Terminator The last object in an *Inverse Kinematics system* that is affected by the child's movement.

TGA file A 32-bit image format that supports alpha channel transparency. This format also uses the .vda, .icd, and .vst extensions.

tick $\frac{1}{4800}$ of a second.

TIF file Tagged Image Format, an image format commonly found on Macintosh systems.

tiling The process of laying texture images end to end to cover the entire surface of an object.

tooltips Text labels that identify buttons.

torus A ring with a circular cross section. Also referred to as a "doughnut."

Track View A window that includes a hierarchical list of all tracks included in a scene. These tracks can be edited and manipulated.

trajectory The actual *spline* path that an object follows when it is animated.

Transform gizmo An apparatus that enables you to visually constrain the transform motion of an object.

transforming objects The fundamental process of "repositioning" or changing an object's position, rotation, and scale.

transparency The amount of light that is allowed to pass through an object. The opposite of *opacity*.

transparent objects Objects that you can see through, like glass and clear plastic.

UVW coordinates Coordinates that are used to control the placement of a material map on the surface of an object. UVW coordinates are similar to the XYZ coordinate system, except that they apply to maps.

variables Placeholders for different values.

viewport A small window that displays a scene from one perspective.

wireframe A render type that displays only the lines that make up an object.

World object An imaginary object that holds all objects.

XRef An external object that is referenced in the current scene.

Index

Symbols and Numerics

% Along Path value, Path Parameters rollout, 610
& (ampersand), Logical And operator, 649
* (asterisk)
    Dot Product vector operator, 649
    multiple-character wildcard, 140
    Multiplication operator, 649
    Scalar Multiplication vector operator, 649
^ (caret), Raise to the Power operator, 649
. (Component vector operator), 649
$ (dollar sign), Light view, 528
— (double hyphen), MAXScript comment indicator, 237
... (ellipsis), menu items, 20
= (equal sign)
    Equal to logical operator, 649
    increase gizmo size, 192
' (feet), 78
/ (forward slant), Division operator, 649
> (greater than logical operator), 649
>= (greater than or equal to logical operator), 649
" (inches), 78
<= (Less than or equal to logical operator), 649
< (Less than logical operator), 649
| (Logical Or operator), 649
- (minus sign)
    decrease gizmo size, 192
    Negation operator, 648
    Subtraction operator, 648
    Vector Subtraction vector operator, 649
+ (plus sign)
    Addition operator, 648
    MAXScript variables, joining, 234
    Pick Target rollout, 366
    Save File As dialog box, 105
    Vector Addition vector operator, 649
? (question mark)
    MAXScript previous command indicator, 227
    single-character wildcard, 140
** (Raise to the Power operator), 649
_ (underscore), MAXScript variable name, 234
2d Icons icon set, 74

2D map, 494
2D shape, 285
2D Snap Toggle button, Prompt Line, 45, 213
2.5D Snap Toggle button, Prompt Line, 45, 213
2-Sided option, Shader Basic Parameters rollout, 482
3D Snap Toggle button, Prompt Line, 45, 213
3D space
    Orthographic views, 50–51
    overview, 49
    Perspective view, 51
    representing on 2D computer screen, 50
3D Studio Mesh file format (3DS), 108
3D Studio Projects file format (PRJ), 108
3D Studio Shape file format (SHP), 108, 286
3ds max software
    compared to gmax, 12–14
    versions, 4
15mm lens, 551
20mm lens, 551
24mm lens, 551
28mm lens, 551
35mm lens, 542, 551
50mm lens, 551
57 Chevy bending over a hill.gmax, 420
80mm lens, 542
85mm lens, 551
135mm lens, 551
200mm lens, 542, 551

A

ABL SDK (Flight Simulator software development kit), 705
About gmax command, Help menu, 31
Absolute coordinates, Transform Type-In dialog box, 194
Absolute toggle, Envelope Properties, 448
Absolute transform assignments option, MacroRecorder menu, 229
Absolute Value function, 651
Access Quadmenu command, 798
Acquire button, UVW Map modifier, 506
ACS. See Asset Creation Studio

Activate Grid Object command, Views menu, 25
Activate Home Grid command, Views menu, 25
activating grid, 212
Active option, Keyboard panel, 60
Active Viewport Only option, Time Configuration dialog box, 557
ActiveShade view option, Viewport Configuration dialog box, 86
ActiveX Control form element, Visual MAXScript, 253
Adaptive (Cubic) button, Bevel Deformation, 388
Adaptive (Linear) button, Bevel Deformation, 388
Adaptive option, Interpolation rollout, 288
Adaptive Path Steps option, Skin Parameters rollout, 382
Adaptive Perspective Grid command, 799
Add Attribute to Type drop-down list, 573
Add Color button, Object Color dialog box, 270
Add Custom Attribute command, Animation menu, 29
Add Custom Colors button, Object Color dialog box, 270
Add Default Lights to Scene command, Views menu, 26
Add Default Lights to Scene dialog box, 524
Add Keys button
    Edit Keys Mode, 585
    Function Curves Mode, 589
    Motion panel, 565
    Track View window, 590, 593
Add Keys command, 801
Add Link button, Link Parameters rollout, 612
Add LookAt Target button, LookAt Constraint rollout, 615
Add Note Track button, Global Track View Toolbar, 581
Add Parameter dialog box, 573
Add Point button
    Keyboard Entry rollout, 291
    Output rollout, 500
Add Time Tag, Time Configuration dialog box, 558

Add Visibility Track button
   Edit Keys Mode, 585
   Track View window, 590
Addition operator (+), 648
Additional Help command, Help
   menu, 31
Adjust Pivot rollout, 205–206
Adjust Transformation rollout, 207
Adobe Illustrator, 286
Adobe Photoshop image file (PSD),
   126, 132, 497
Advanced Quad Menu Options dialog
   box, 67–68
Affect Backfacing option, Soft Select
   rollout, 264
Affect Hierarchy Only mode, Adjust
   Pivot rollout, 206
Affect Object Only mode, Adjust Pivot
   rollout, 206
Affect Pivot Only mode, Adjust Pivot
   rollout, 205–206
Affect Region modifier, 435
aiming, camera, 547
Aircraft Container SDK (Flight
   Simulator software
   development kit), 705
Aircraft Panels SDK (Flight Simulator
   software development
   kit), 705
airplane, animating, 566
Alias/Wavefront software company, 5
Alien landscape.gmax, 436
Align button, main toolbar, 34
Align Camera command, Tools menu,
   24, 549
Align command, Tools menu, 24, 208,
   796
Align Curves button, Function Curves
   Mode, 589
Align Keys button
   Edit Keys Mode, 585
   Track View window, 590
Align Normal command, Tools
   menu, 24
Align Selection dialog box, 208
Align to Camera button, main
   toolbar, 34
Align to Object/Pivot button, Adjust
   Pivot rollout, 206
Align to View command
   main toolbar, 34
   Tools menu, 24, 210
   Views menu, 25
Align to World button, Adjust Pivot
   rollout, 206
aligning, camera, 549
alignment points, Trainz, 782
Alignment section, UVW Map
   modifier, 506
Alike option, Selection rollout, 298

All IDs button, Edit UVW dialog box,
   511
All Selection Filter, 137
Allow Upside Down option, Path
   Parameters rollout, 610
alpha channel, Virtual Frame Buffer,
   134
Alpha From RGB Intensity option,
   Output rollout, 500
Alt key, navigating menu with, 20–21
Always Deform option, Advanced
   Parameters rollout, 449
Always Transform Children of the
   World option, Inverse
   Kinematics panel, 458
Ambient color, gmax Material Editor,
   468
ambient light, 522, 524–525
Ambient mapping, 503
ampersand (&), Logical And operator,
   649
Amplitude value, Ring Array, 174–175
and operator, 239
Angle Snap command, main toolbar,
   211, 799
Angle Snap Toggle button, Prompt
   Line, 45, 214
Animate button
   enabling, 558
   keys, automatic creation of, 559
   parameter animation keys,
     copying, 561
   Time Slider button, 560
Animate Mode command, 799
animate on construct, MAXScript,
   246
Animation file (.KIN), 115, 771
Animation menu
   Add Custom Attribute
     command, 29
   Bones Option command, 28
   Constraints submenu, 28
   Create Bones menu command, 28
   Dummy command, 28–29
   IK Solvers submenu, 28
   objects, animating, 569
   Point command, 28–29
   Wire Parameters command, 29
Animation Menu command, 797
Animation Modifiers, Modifiers menu,
   28, 417
Animation panel, Preference Settings
   dialog box
   Local Center During Animate
     option, 90
   MIDI Time Slider controls, 90
   Set Defaults button, 91
   Sound Plug-In, assigning, 91
Animation Quadmenu command, 800
animation sequence, controlling, 43

animation types, Dungeon Siege Tool
   Kit, 753
Animations section, Advanced Quad
   Menu Options dialog
   box, 68
animator, 5
anti-alias, 498
Applied IK method, 13, 459–460
Apply Colors Now button, Colors
   panel, 71
Apply Controller command, 802
Apply Ease Curve button, Function
   Curves Mode, 589, 802
Apply Multiplier Curve button,
   Function Curves Mode,
   589, 802
Apply Only to Keys option, Inverse
   Kinematics rollout, 457
Apply Settings command, 804
Apply Source and Display to option,
   Viewport Background
   dialog box, 56
Apply to All Duplicates option,
   Duplicate Name dialog
   box, 106
Arc Cosine function, 650
Arc primitive object, 289, 291
Arc Rotate command, Viewport
   Navigation button, 52
Arc Rotate Selected command,
   Viewport Navigation
   button, 52
Arc Rotate SubObject command,
   Viewport Navigation
   button, 52
Arc Sine function, 650
Arc Subdivision section, Import DXF
   File dialog box, 110
Arc Tangent function, 650
Archive command, File menu, 21
Archive System, 94
archiving files, 107
Area Selection option, Selection
   rollout, 298
array
   definition, 155
   MAXScript, 241
Array button, main toolbar, 34
Array command, Tools menu, 23
Array dialog box
   circular array, 170–171
   linear array, 168–170
   opening, 168
   spiral array, 172–173
Array Dimensions section, Array
   dialog box, 169
array parameter format, 573
artificial light, 522
as keyword, MAXScript, 241

Aspect Ratio section, Viewport Background dialog box, 56
Asset Browser command, Help menu, 31
Asset Browser tool, Utilities panel, 41–42
Asset Browser utility, Utilities panel
    Explorer pane, 127
    file types supported, 125
    Internet, connecting to, 127
    Thumbnail pane, 127
    Virtual Frame Buffer window, 126
    Web pane, 127
Asset Creation Studio (ACS), 770–771
Asset Manager Utility, 472
Assign Controller button
    Global Track View Toolbar, 580
    Motion panel, 40, 605
    Track View window, 598
Assign Controller rollout, 565, 620
Assign Position Controller dialog box, 621–622
Assign Random Colors option, Object Color dialog box, 270
Assign to Children option, IK Solver, 440
Assign to Root option, IK Solver, 440
Assign Vertex Color tool, Utilities panel, 41–42
Assigned To field, Keyboard panel, 60
asterisk (*)
    Dot Product vector operator, 649
    multiple-character wildcard, 140
    Multiplication operator, 649
    Scalar Multiplication vector operator, 649
at. See attack animation
ATC Voicepack SDK (Flight Simulator software development kit), 705
Atmospheric effects, absence of, 14
Attach button
    Edit Geometry rollout, 324
    Geometry rollout, 300, 352
Attach command, Group menu, 178
Attach Controls dialog box, 638–639
Attach List dialog box, 324
Attach Mult. button, Geometry rollout, 301
Attachment constraint, 606
Attachment Parameters rollout, 606
attack animation (at), Dungeon Siege, 753
attack types, Dungeon Siege Tool Kit, 753
Attenuate Lights option, Preference Settings dialog box, 96
Attenuation Parameters rollout, 532–533
Auran software, 8

Auran's Trainz Web site, 784
Auto Backup feature, Files panel, 93
Auto Smooth option, Import DXF File dialog box, 110
Auto Termination option, Auto Termination rollout, 453
Auto Window/Crossing by Direction option, Preference Settings dialog box, 88
AutoBackup directory path, 76–77
AutoCAD ACI palette, 270
AutoCAD file, 108–110
Autogen SDK (Flight Simulator software development kit), 706
AutoGrid feature, 212
Automatic Sub-Material Assignment option, Preference Settings dialog box, 88
Automatic Unit Conversion option, Preference Settings dialog box, 78, 87
AutoPlay Preview Files setting, Preference Settings dialog box, 88
AvSim (Web site), 717
Axis Constraint settings, Transform Managers, 196
Axis constraints toolbar, 191
Axis tool, Tempest Toolbar, 669
Aztec pyramid.gmax, 336

B
Back orthographic viewport, 50
Back View option, Viewport Configuration dialog box, 86, 797
Backface Cull on Object Creation option, Preference Settings dialog box, 96
Backface Cull option, Object Properties dialog box, 148
Background button, gmax Material Editor, 470
background image
    creating with digital camera, 56
    loading into viewport, 55
Backgrounds library, gmax Material Navigator, 479
Backup on Save option, Files panel, 92
Backup Time One Unit command, 799, 802
.bak file extension, 92
Balloon and pump.gmax, 655
Bank Amount value, Path Parameters rollout, 610
Banking option, Skin Parameters rollout, 382

barehanded attack with no weapon (fs0), Dungeon Siege, 753
Barycentric coordinates, 606
Barycentric Morph controller, 621, 636–637
Base Texture, MakeMDL SDK, 711
Benard, Jean-Luc (Trainz software designer), 8
Bend modifier, 426–427
Bevel button
    Face subobject, 334–335
    Geometry rollout, 358
Bevel Deformation window, 388
Bevel Mode command, 801
Bézier controller, 627–628
Bézier option, Creation Method rollout, 290
Bézier Position, default Position controller, 621
Bézier Scale, default Scale controller, 621
Bias option, Optimize modifier, 416
Bind button, Geometry rollout, 304, 352
Bind First option, Geometry rollout, 301
Bind Last option, Geometry rollout, 301
Biting crocodile.gmax, 576
Bitmap Fit button, UVW Map modifier, 506
Bitmap form element, Visual MAXScript, 252
bitmap image file (BMP), 65, 126, 132, 497
Bitmap map type
    coordinates, 494–495
    definition, 13, 494
    noise, 496–497
    rotation, 496
Bitmap Parameters rollout, 497–499
Bitmap Path Editor utility, Utilities panel, 129
Bitmaps panel, Configure Paths dialog box, 76–77
black handles, 254
Blend transparency option, 81
Blinn Shader, 482–485
.blk file extension, 638
Block controller, 637–639
Block Parameters dialog box, 638
blue channel, Virtual Frame Buffer, 134
blurriness, 496
BMP. See bitmap image file
Boat on rough seas.gmax, 607
Bogeys custom subdirectory, Trainz, 778
Bone Class ID, 138
Bone Parameters rollout, 441

bones, Dungeon Siege Tool Kit, 751
Bones Option command, Animation
          menu, 28
bones system
     child bone, 440
     creating, 440
     object, converting into bone, 444
     root bone, 440
     weights, specifying, 448
Bookshelf.gmax, 315
Boolean button, Geometry rollout,
          301
Boolean object Class ID, 138
Boolean object type
     Cut operation, 376
     definition, 13, 365
     Intersection operation, 376
     Subtraction operation, 376
     tips for working with, 377
     Union operation, 376
Boolean operations, editing Spline
          subobject, 309–310
Boolean parameter format, 573
Both button, Light Navigation
          Control, 529
Bottom orthographic viewport, 50
Bottom View command, 797
Bottom view option, Viewport
          Configuration dialog box,
          86
Bounding Box command, 798
Bounding Box snap point, 214
Bounding Box Viewport Rendering
          Level, 80
bow and arrow (fs6), Dungeon Siege,
          753
Box Brush tool, Tempest Toolbar, 670
Box primitive Class ID, 138
Box primitive object, creation
          method, 272
Box, Standard Primitives, 274
Brass swan-front view.jpg, 57
Break button, Geometry rollout, 300,
          326–327
Break Selected Vertices button, Edit
          UVW dialog box, 510, 803
Bricks library, gmax Material
          Navigator, 479
broadsword.gmax, 162
Brush Manipulate tool, Tempest
          Toolbar, 670
Brush Slice tool, Tempest Toolbar,
          670
brush, Tempest game pack, 667
Bubble button, Soft Select rollout, 264
Bubble parameter, Affect Region
          modifier, 435
Budget value, Polygon Counter utility,
          342
Bugs Head Software logo.gmax, 373

BuildCube.gmax, 255
building blocks, Tempest game pack,
          673–674
built-in collection, 241
Bulge Angle Deformer, Gizmos rollout,
          450
bump map, 492, 504
button
     appearance, changing, 64
     color, creation mode, 268
     dragging between toolbars, 62
Button form element, Visual
          MAXScript, 252
By Vertex option, Selection rollout,
          322, 350

C

Cab File SDK (Flight Simulator
          software development
          kit), 706
CAD drawing, using as background
          image, 56
camera
     aiming, 547
     aligning, 549
     animating, 569
     clipping, 552
     cone, 552
     controlling, 545–547
     field of view, 542, 550
     focal length, 542
     lens setting, 542, 550
     perspective, 542
     selecting for viewport, 543
     telephoto lens, 542
     type, 551
     viewpoint, 541
     wide-angle lens, 542
Camera controls, Tempest game
          pack, 671
Camera Controls tool, Tempest
          Toolbar, 671
Camera Match utility, absence of, 14
Camera Navigation controls, 546–547
Camera Tracker utility, absence of, 14
Camera View command, 798
Cameras category button, Create
          panel, 542
Cameras category panel, Create
          panel, 267
cameras collection, 241
Cameras object category, Create
          panel, 38
Cameras Selection Filter, 137
Cameras_16a.bmp, 65
Cameras_16i.bmp, 65
Cameras_24a.bmp, 65
Cameras_24i.bmp, 65
Cancel Expert Mode command, Views
          menu, 27

Cap Holes modifier, 415–416
Cap Object command, 801
capsule-shaped envelope, bone
          object, 446
career, in gaming industry, 5
caret (^), Raise to the Power
          operator, 649
Carousel.gmax, 176
Case Sensitive option, Select Objects
          dialog box, 140
Category drop-down list
     Keyboard panel, 60
     Quads panel, 66
     Toolbar panel, 62
Caulk texture, Tempest game pack,
          689
CCW. See counterclockwise
Ceiling function, 651
Center button, UVW Map modifier,
          506
Center Face snap point, 214
center point, 197
Center to Object/Pivot button, Adjust
          Pivot rollout, 206
Centered parameter, Text primitive,
          292
Center-End-End method, Arc
          primitive, 291
Centers option, Spacing Tool dialog
          box, 166
centimeters (cm), 78
CFS. See Combat Flight Simulator 3
Chamfer button
     editing vertices, 304
     Vertex subobject mode, 327
Chamfer Mode command, 801
Channel Display drop-down list,
          Virtual Frame Buffer, 134
Character Bones, Dungeon Siege, 751
character, Dungeon Siege Tool Kit,
          750–753
Character Studio, 4
Characteristic graph, Noise
          Controller dialog box, 629
Check Box form element, Visual
          MAXScript, 253
Check Button form element, Visual
          MAXScript, 253
Checker map type
     Bitmap map type, compared to,
          494
     definition, 13
     gmax Material Navigator, 493
Checker Parameters rollout, 501–502
checkerboard, creating, 346
Chess game.gmax, 201
Chess game–Opponents View.gmax,
          544
child, definition, 180

Chop option, creating hemisphere with, 275
Circle command, 797
Circle primitive object, 289, 291
Circular selection method, 140
Circular Selection Region button, main toolbar, 33
circumscribed polygon, 291
Clamp option, Output rollout, 500
Class IDs, Filter Combinations dialog box, 137
classof command, 235
Claudec's Tutorial Index, 703
Clear Keys option, Inverse Kinematics rollout, 457
Clip manually option, Parameters rollout, 552
Clip texture, Tempest game pack, 689
clipping, camera, 552
clipping pane, 83
clockwise (CW), 295
Clone command, Tools menu, 23
Clone Options dialog box
    copy, 158
    creating, 156–157
    instance, 158
    opening, 156
    reference, 158
Clone Part of the Mesh dialog box, 322
cloning
    definition, 155
    subobject mode, 322
Close button, editing Splines, 312
Closed option, Geometry rollout, 301
closed spline, 319
.clr file extension, 71, 74
cm. See centimeters
Collapse button
    Motion panel, 565
    Vertex subobject mode, 329
Collapse Poly Object command, 801
Collapse To option, Modifier Stack, 320
Collapsing the Stack, Modifier Stack, 402
Collect Bitmaps option, Resource Collector utility, 129
collect keyword, MAXScript, 242
collection, MAXScript, 240–241
college degree, game development, 6
color
    object property, 146
    vertices, 330
color cues feature, 48
Color option, Import DXF File dialog box, 109
color parameter format, 573
Color Picker form element, Visual MAXScript, 253

color representation, 94
Color Selection drop-down list, Preference Settings dialog box, 89
Color Selector: Add Color dialog box, 270
Color Selector dialog box, 214
Color Vertices Weights option, Display rollout, 449
Colors panel, Customize User Interface dialog box, 29, 71–72
Combat Flight Simulator 3 (CFS), 10–11, 706
Combat Flight Simulator Insider (Web site), 717
Combine button, Edit Named Selections dialog box, 144
Combo Box form element, Visual MAXScript, 253
Command & Conquer: Renegade, 10
Command Panel
    Create panel, 38
    Display panel, 41
    example, 37
    Hierarchy panel, 39–40
    Modify panel, 39
    Motion panel, 40–41
    removing from interface, 27
    rollout, 36–37
    Utilities panel, 41–42
Command panel, Tempest game pack, 691–693
Command Panel toggle, Show UI menu, 29
comment, MAXScript, 237
Common Logarithm function, 651
company logo, creating, 295
Compare button, Shape Commands rollout, 390
Compare dialog box, 390
Compile tool, Tempest Toolbar, 668
Component vector operator (.), 649
Compound Objects modeling type, 262, 365
compound shape, 287
Compounds default toolbar, Tab Panel, 72
Compounds toolbar, Tab Panel, 35
Compress on Save option, Files panel, 92
compressed file, 107
computer graphics conference, 6
Computer-Aided Design, 109
Concrete library, gmax Material Navigator, 479
Conditional If function, 651
conditional statement, MAXScript, 240
Cone Angle helper, 575–576

cone, camera, 552
Cone object type, Surface constraint, 608
Cone primitive object, creation method, 272
Cone, Standard Primitives, 277
conferences, gaming industry, 6
config file, Trainz, 762–763
Configure Button Sets button
    Modify Panel, 73
    Utility Panel, 73
Configure Driver button, Preference Settings dialog box, 100–101
Configure Modifier Sets dialog box, 73
Configure Paths command, Customize menu, 29
Configure Paths dialog box
    Files panel, 93
    fonts, 292
    opening, 75–77
    XRef Scenes and Objects tab, 124–125
Conform object, absence of, 13
Connect button, editing vertices, 303
Connect object type
    creating, 368
    definition, 13, 365
    examples, 369
Connect option, Geometry rollout, 301
Console Pane, Siege Editor interface, 724
Constant Cross-Section option, Skin Parameters rollout, 382
Constant option, Param Curve Out-of-Range Types dialog box, 599
Constant Velocity option, Path Parameters rollout, 610
Constraints, 40
Constraints menu
    Attachment constraint, 606
    Link constraint, 613
    LookAt constraint, 614–615
    Path constraint, 609–610
    Position constraint, 611–612
    purpose, 605
    Surface constraint, 608
Constraints submenu, Animation menu, 28
Container Track Icon, 582
Content Dispatcher, Trainz, 758, 783–784
Content Foundry, Trainz, 758, 766–768
Content ID ranges, Trainz, 763–766
Contents panel, File Properties dialog box, 131
continuous tangent, 593

Contour option, Skin Parameters rollout, 382

Contract Selection button, Edit UVW dialog box, 510

controllers
automatically assigned, 620–621
default, 623–624
Float controllers, 620
manually assigned, 621–623
Point3 controllers, 620
purpose, 40, 619
Scale controllers, 620
Transform controllers, 620, 625–626
types, 620

Controllers Track Icon, 582

controlling camera, 545–547

Convert Degrees radians function, 651

Convert From button, Motion panel, 565

Convert Radians degrees function, 651

Convert to Editable Mesh command, 321

Convert to Editable Patch command, 348

Convert to Editable Poly command, 321

Convert To submenu, 262

Cookie Cutter option, ShapeMerge object type, 372

Coordinate fields, 44

coordinate system, 196

coordinates
Bitmap map type, 494–495
entering, 194
Status Bar, 44

Coordinates button, Edit UVW dialog box, 510

Coordinates rollout, UVW coordinate system, 494

coplanar patch vertices, 351

Copy command, MAXScript Editor window, 228

Copy Controller button, Track View window, 580, 598, 802

Copy CurvePoints option, Output rollout, 500

Copy Maps button, Bitmap Path Editor dialog box, 129

Copy option, Pick Targets rollout, 366

Copy Time button
Edit Time Mode, 586
Track View window, 591

Copy Value command, 804

CorelDRAW, 286

Corner option, Creation Method rollout, 290

corner patch vertices, 351

Cosine function, 650

Count value, Spacing Tool dialog box, 165

counterclockwise (CCW), 295

cow.gmax, 157

Crash option, MakeMDL, 709

Create Bones command, Animation menu, 28

Create button, Face subobject, 334
Face subobject, 334
Geometry rollout, 352

Create Key dialog box, 560

Create Line button, Geometry rollout, 300

Create menu, 28, 269, 797

Create Morph Key button, Morph rollout, 367

Create panel
Command Panel, 38
Standard Primitives, 274

Create Shape button, Geometry rollout, 357

Create Shape dialog box, 333

Create Shape from Edges button, Edge subobject mode, 333

creating files, 103–104

creating grid, 212

creating light, 525–526

creation method, primitive objects, 271–272

Creation Method rollout, 274, 288–289

crocodile model, 152, 576

Cropping/Placement dialog box, 498–499

Cross Product vector operator (x), 649

Cross Sections on Top option, Display rollout, 449

crossbow (fs7), Dungeon Siege, 753

Crossing Selection method, 140

Crossing/Window Selection button, Prompt Line, 45

CrossInsert button, editing vertices, 304

CrossSection modifier, Modifier Stack drop-down list, 317, 409

Crucible.gmax, 317

CSG Hollow tool, Tempest Toolbar, 670

CSG Subtrack tool, Tempest Toolbar, 670

Cubic Morph controller, 636

.cui file extension, 62, 74

Curious Labs (Poser modeling tool), 110

Current Frame field button, Time Control, 43, 556

Current Time, Time Configuration dialog box, 558

Custom form element, Visual MAXScript, 253

custom icon, adding, 64–65

custom interface
locking, 75
saving, 74–75

Custom, Key Tangent, 563

custom object, Dungeon Siege Tool Kit, 742–743

Custom panel, File Properties dialog box, 131

custom parameters, creating, 572–573

Custom tangent type, Key Info dialog box, 593

Custom Terrain Textures SDK (Flight Simulator software development kit), 706

custom toolbar, creating, 63–64

Custom units system, 77

Customize menu
Configure Paths command, 29
Customize User Interface dialog box, 29
Grid and Snap Settings command, 30
keyboard shortcut, 797
Load Custom UI command, 29, 74
Lock UI Layout command, 29
Preferences command, 29
Revert to Startup UI Layout command, 29
Save Custom UI command, 29, 74
Show UI menu, 29
Units Setup command, 30
Viewport Configuration command, 30

Customize Modifier Sets button, Modifier Stack, 399

Customize User Interface dialog box
Colors panel, 71–72
Customize menu, 29
Keyboard panel, 60–61
Menus panel, 68–70
opening, 29, 59
Quads panel, 66–68
Toolbar panel, 62–65

Cut button, Edge subobject mode, 332–333

Cut command, MAXScript Editor window, 228, 801

Cut Mode command, 801

Cut Time button
Edit Time Mode, 586
Track View window, 591

Cut Value command, 804

CW. See clockwise

Cycle button, editing vertices, 304

Cycle option, Param Curve Out-of-Range Types dialog box, 599

Cycles parameter, Ring Array, 174
Cycles value, Ring Array, 175
Cylinder Brush tool, Tempest Toolbar, 670
Cylinder object type, Surface constraint, 608
Cylinder primitive object, creation method, 272
Cylinder, Standard Primitives, 276
Cylinders showing modifier stack order.gmax, 401
Cylindrical Environment mapping type, 495

D

Damage Texture, MakeMDL SDK, 711
Dart and Dartboard.gmax, 570
data type, MAXScript, 234–235
DDS. See DirectX file
de. See die animation
Deactivate All Maps command, Views menu, 27
deer.gmax, 178
Default Fallback Color option, MakeMDL, 709
default fighting fidget animation (dff), Dungeon Siege, 753
default fighting stance animation (dfs), Dungeon Siege, 753
default light, 524
Default Lighting command, 798
Default Lighting toggle, Viewport Rendering Options, 82
default stance animation (ds), Dungeon Siege, 753
default stance fidget animation (dsf), Dungeon Siege, 753
default UI color interface scheme, 71
DefaultFillLight, 524
DefaultUI keyboard shortcut set, 61
DefaultUI standard interface, 74
Define Stroke dialog box, 98–99
Deformation window interface, 383–386
Degradation Override button, Prompt Line, 45, 799
Delete button
    Geometry rollout, 301
    MAXScript Editor window, 228
    Toolbar panel, 62
Delete Control Point button
    Deformation dialog box, 385
    Fit Deformation dialog box, 389
Delete Controller button, Global Track View Toolbar, 580
Delete Curve button, Fit Deformation dialog box, 389
Delete Ease/Multiplier Curve button
    Function Curves Mode, 589
    Track View window, 594

Delete Keys button
    Edit Keys Mode, 585
    Function Curves Mode, 589
    Motion panel, 565
    Track View window, 590
Delete Link button, Link Parameters rollout, 612
Delete LookAt Target button, LookAt Constraint rollout, 615
Delete Mesh modifier, 413
Delete Morph Target button, Pick Targets rollout, 366
Delete Objects command, 796
Delete Patch modifier, 412
Delete Point button, Output rollout, 500
Delete Spline modifier, 314, 412
Delete Subobject command, 800
Delete Time button
    Edit Time Mode, 586
    Track View window, 591
deleting command from quadmenu, 67
Destination Doors spinner, Dungeon Siege Tool Kit, 726
Detach as Clone, Detach dialog box, 326
Detach button, Geometry rollout, 301, 357
Detach command, Group menu, 178, 801
Detach dialog box, 326
Detach Edge Vertices command, 803
Detach to Element, Detach dialog box, 326
Developer's Desk at Flight Simulator Insider (Web site), 717
df. See default fighting fidget animation
dfs. See default fighting stance animation
dialog box, modeless compared to persistent, 49
die animation (de), Dungeon Siege, 753
Diffuse color, gmax Material Editor, 468
Diffuse control, Blinn Shader, 483
Diffuse mapping, 503
digital camera, creating background image with, 56
Dining Room.gmax, 202
Direct Light, 522
Direct3D, 793
Directional Light Parameters rollout, 533
DirectX file (DDS), 711
Disable Textures option, Viewport Rendering Options, 82

Disable View option, Viewport Rendering Options, 82
Disable Viewpoint command, 798
disc
    eBook, 807
    gmax game packs, 807
    gmax version 1.2, 4
    installing, 806
    system requirements, 805
    troubleshooting, 807–808
    tutorial files, 806
discontinuous tangent, 593
Discreet (software company), 4, 6, 12
Displace modifier, 435
Displacement Mapping, absence of, 14
displacement mapping, 505
Displacements folder, Trainz, 762
Display, default quadmenu, 46
Display Alpha Channel button, Virtual Frame Buffer, 134
Display as Box option, Object Properties dialog box, 147
Display as Box property, 147
Display Cross Hair Cursor option, Preference Settings dialog box, 88
Display First Tab command, 804
Display Floater command, Tools menu, 23
Display Floater dialog box, 149–150
Display Gamma value, 95
Display Mesh option, Mesh Settings rollout, 288
Display Obsolete File Message option, Files panel, 93
Display options, Skin Parameters rollout, 382
Display panel, Command Panel categories, adding, 151
    Display Color rollout, 150
    Display Properties rollout, 152
    Freeze rollout, 152
    Hide by Category rollout, 150
    Hide rollout, 152
    Link Display rollout, 152
    Link Replaces Object option, 152
    links, 182
    opening, 41
Display Properties, Object Properties dialog box, 22
Display Quadmenus command, 804
Display Selected with Edged Faces option, Viewport Rendering Options, 82
Display World Axis option, Preference Settings dialog box, 97
Display X-Axis button, Deformation dialog box, 385

Display XY Axes button, Deformation dialog box, 385
Display Y-Axis button, Deformation dialog box, 385
displaying text backwards, 292
Divide button, Edge subobject mode, 332
Division operator (/), 649
Dizzy dragonfly and following camera.gmax, 616
Dizzy dragonfly.gmax, 610
docking feature, 48
docking panels, 47
docking toolbars, 47
dodecahedron, 335
dog.gmax, 53–55
$ (dollar sign), Light view, 528
Dolly button, Light Navigation Control, 529
Dolly Camera button, Camera Navigation Control, 546
Dolly Camera + Target button, Camera Navigation Control, 546
Dolly Target button, Camera Navigation Control, 546
Dolphin.gmax, 486
Donut primitive object, 289, 294
Dot Product vector operator (*), 649
— (double hyphen), MAXScript comment indicator, 237
downloading, Dungeon Siege Tool Kit, 720
downloading gmax, 790–791
Drag Type option, Creation Method rollout, 290
drag-and-drop feature, 48
dragon object, 142
dragonfly, animating, 610, 616
Drag/Rotate pop-up menu command, Material Editor, 472
Draw All Envelopes option, Display rollout, 449
Draw Links as Lines option, Preference Settings dialog box, 96
Drawing Exchange Format (DXF), 108–110
Driver option, Trainz, 759
Driver Setup dialog box, 100
Drop-Down List form element, Visual MAXScript, 253
ds. See default stance animation
DS Anim Viewer, Dungeon Siege Tool Kit, 721–722
DS Mod, Dungeon Siege Tool Kit, 721–722
dsf. See default stance fidget animation
.dsmap format, 737, 749

Dummy command, Animation menu, 28–29
Dummy object, 185, 281
Dungeon Siege, 9–10
Dungeon Siege 'Net Guide (Web site), 756
Dungeon Siege Realms (Web site), 756
Dungeon Siege Tool Kit
    animation types, 753
    attack types, 753
    bones, 751
    character, creating, 750–753
    custom object, creating, 742–743
    Destination Doors spinner, 726
    downloading, 720
    DS Anim Viewer, 721–722
    DS Mod, 721–722
    interface, Siege Editor, 723
    Item Tool Kit, 743–744
    lighting, 736–737
    map, 724, 737–738
    monster, adding, 735–736
    Node Matcher, 727–728
    Node Properties dialog box, 729
    Node Set panel, 730
    nodes, 723, 726
    object, 730–731, 744
    Object Properties dialog box, 732–733
    online resources, 755–756
    Previewer, 727
    Reference Object Dropper, 743
    region, creating, 725
    Siege Editor, 720–722
    Siege Max, 721, 738–739
    SNO Tool Kit, 739–741
    Source Doors spinner, 726
    Starting Position object, 734
    template file, 748–749
    terrain, exporting, 741
    trigger, adding, 735
    view window, 723–724
Duplicate Name dialog box, 106
DXF. See Drawing Exchange Format
Dynamic module, absence of, 13
Dynamic Resizing command, 798

E

E. See Natural Logarithm Predefined Variable
Ease Curve Out-of-Range Types dialog box, 589, 594
Ease option, Rotational Joints rollout, 454
Easter eggs.gmax, 475
Edge Distance option, Soft Select rollout, 264
Edge snap point, 214
Edge subobject mode, 321
Edge Turn command, 801

Edged Faces option, Rendering Method panel, 80
edges, editing, 331–333, 355
Edges Only option, Object Properties dialog box, 148
Edges option, Spacing Tool dialog box, 166
Edit Box form element, Visual MAXScript, 253
Edit Button Appearance command, button pop-up menu, 64
Edit Envelopes button, Skin modifier, 446–448
Edit Geometry rollout
    Attach button, 324
    Explode button, 324
    Grid Align button, 325
    Remove Isolated Vertices button, 324–325
    View button, 325
Edit Keys button, Global Track View Toolbar, 581
Edit Keys Mode command, 801
Edit keys mode, Track View window, 584–585, 590–591
Edit Macro dialog box, 64–65
Edit menu
    Edit Named Selection command, 21
    Fetch command, 22
    Hold command, 22
    Object Properties command, 22
    Preference Settings dialog box, 22
    Redo command, 22
    Select All command, 21
    Select By Color and/or Name command, 21
    Select Invert command, 21
    Select None command, 21
    Undo command, 22
Edit Menu command, 796
Edit Mesh modifier, 320, 413–414
Edit Named Selection command, Edit menu, 21
Edit Named Selections dialog box, 143–144
Edit Patch modifier, 348, 408–409
Edit Ranges button, Global Track View Toolbar, 581
Edit ranges mode, Track View window, 587
Edit Spline modifier, 297, 314, 409
Edit Time button, Global Track View Toolbar, 581
Edit time mode, Track View window, 586–587, 591–592
Edit Triangulation button, Editable Poly object, 340
Edit UVWs dialog box, 509–511, 803

Editable Mesh object
    Editable Poly object, compared
        to, 320
    subobject modes, 321–322
editable object, 263
Editable Patch object, converting
        object into, 348
Editable Poly object, 320, 333
Editable Poly subobject modes, 322
Editable Spline
    converting shape into, 296
    Geometry rollout, 299
    Modifier Stack, 297
effects specialist, 5
85mm lens, 551
80mm lens, 542
Element subobject mode, 321, 333
elements, spacing, 254
Ellipse primitive object, 289, 293
ellipsis (...), menu items, 20
Enable Color Map option, Output
        rollout, 500
Enable Ease/Multiplier Curve Toggle
        button, Function Curves
        Mode, 589
Enable Gamma Correction option,
        Gamma panel, 94
Enable option, MacroRecorder menu,
        229
Enable Viewport Tooltips toggle,
        Preference Settings dialog
        box, 88
End Offset value, Spacing Tool dialog
        box, 165
End Time, Time Configuration dialog
        box, 558
End-End-Middle method, Arc
        primitive, 291
Endpoint snap point, 214
engine0, MakeMDL SDK recognized
        name, 711
engine1, MakeMDL SDK recognized
        name, 711
engine2, MakeMDL SDK recognized
        name, 711
engine3, MakeMDL SDK recognized
        name, 711
Engines custom subdirectory, Trainz,
        778
Entity Editor tool, Tempest Toolbar,
        668
Entity option, Import DXF File dialog
        box, 109
entity, Tempest game pack, 668
Envelope Properties section,
        Parameters rollout,
        447–448
Envelope subobject, Skin modifier,
        446

Envelopes on Top option, Display
        rollout, 449
Environment custom subdirectory,
        Trainz, 778
environment map, 494
Environment maps, Resource
        Collector utility, 128
EnvironmentWater folder, Trainz, 762
EnvironmentSky folder, Trainz, 762
= (equal sign)
    Equal to logical operator, 649
    increase gizmo size, 192
E3 Expo, 6
Euler XYZ Rotation controller,
        633–634
Evaluate All command, MAXScript
        Editor window, 228
Evaluate button, Expression
        Controller dialog box, 644
Event Handler panel, Visual
        MAXScript window,
        251–252
examples
    aligning camera, 549–550
    animation, 559, 570
    Applied IK method, 459
    applying materials, 486
    Attachment constraint, 607
    Auto Backup feature, 93
    basic bones system, 442–444
    Boolean objects, 377–379
    circular array, 171
    clones, 157–160
    Connect object, 370–371
    creating camera, 544–545
    custom interface, saving, 75
    custom material library, 479
    custom toolbar, creating, 63
    Displace modifier, 436
    dummy objects, 185–187
    Dungeon Siege nodes, connecting,
        729
    Dungeon Siege object, 733,
        745–748
    Dungeon Siege skeleton,
        animating, 754–755
    Dungeon Siege template, 749–750
    Dungeon Siege terrain, exporting,
        741–742
    editable mesh, 330–331
    Editable Poly object, 336
    Editable Splines, 312–313
    editing splines, 306–307
    Expression controller, 656–658
    Fast View setting, Viewport
        Configuration dialog box,
        83–85
    Float Expression controller,
        645–647, 655

Free Form Deformation modifier,
        425–426
function curves, 595–597
GeoSpheres, 278
gmax Material Editor, 475–476
groups, 178–179
human figure, importing, 111–112
IK Limb Solver, 462–463
imported meshes, correcting
        problems with, 340–341
inverse kinematics system,
        building, 455–456
keyboard shortcuts, customizing,
        61
Lathe modifier, 317
Light Navigation controls, 530
linear array, 168–170
Link constraint, 613–614
linking objects, 181–182
Loft object, 391–392
Loft object with different cross
        sections, 382–383
LookAt constraint, 615–616
looping path, 566–567
Macro Recorder, 230–231
MakeMDL SDK aircraft, 715–716
MakeMDL SDK billboard, 714–715
manipulator helper, 576–577
MAXScript animation program,
        245–250
MAXScript interpreter, 225–226
MAXScript Utility rollout, 222
MeshSmooth modifier, 422–423
mirroring, 162
Morph modifier, 418–419
Morph object, 367–368
Multi-Material material, 489
multiple materials, assigning to
        one object, 491
new menu, adding, 69–70
Noise modifier, 430
Normal Align feature, 209–210
object, converting into bones
        system, 444–445
object parameters, modifying,
        279–280
objects, hiding, 152
Omni lights, 535–536
Orientation constraint, 617
patch grid, 346–347
Patch object, 360–362
PatchDeform modifier, 420
Path constraint, 610
Placing Highlights feature,
        527–528
Projector Map, 538
Pythagorean Theorem, 282
raytraced shadows, 538–539
                                    Continued

examples *(continued)*
reference images, loading for modeling, 56–57
Ring Array system, 175–177
rotating objects, 202–203
scaling objects, 204
selecting objects, 142
ShapeMerge object, 373–374
Skin modifier, 449–450
Snap feature, 215–216
Snapshot tool, 164
Soft Selection, 266
sound, adding, 601–602
Spacing tool, 166–167
spiral array, 172–173
spline Boolean operations, 315–316
Stack order, 400
strokes, defining, 99–100
Surface constraint, 609
surface tools, 410–412
Target Spot light, 536–537
Tempest advanced textures, 700–701
Tempest building blocks, creating, 673–674
Tempest Command panel, 691–693
Tempest functions, 695–698
Tempest gothic skylight, adding, 688–691
Tempest level, compiling and loading, 679–680
Tempest models, 698–700
Tempest multiple textures, applying, 694–695
Tempest Player Start, adding, 678–679
Tempest textures, applying, 674–677
Tempest trigger, adding, 685–688
Trainz scenery, 778–780
Trainz source file, 772–774
Trainz texture, 768–769
transforming camera, 547–548
transforming objects, 200–202
Twist modifier, 428–429
2D splines and shapes, 295
Unwrap UVW modifier, 512–514
UVW Map modifier, 505–506
variables, 235–236
Vertex Paint modifier, 516
Viewport Navigation buttons, 53–55
Visual MAXScript editor, 254–258
Volume Select modifier, 407–408
XRef proxy, 122–123
XRef Scene, adding, 119
Exclude Left End Point button, Edit Time Mode, 587

Exclude Right End Point button, Edit Time Mode, 587
Exit command, File menu, 21
Exit Isolation button, 23
Expand Objects Track command, 802
Expand Selection button, Edit UVW dialog box, 510
Expand Track command, 802
Expert Mode command, Views menu, 27, 796
Explicit Map Channel mapping type, 494
Explicit scene object names option, MacroRecorder menu, 229
Explicit subobject sets option, MacroRecorder menu, 229
Explode button, Edit Geometry rollout, 324
Explode command, 178, 312
Explorer pane, Asset Browser utility, 127
Exponential function, 651
Export dialog box, 115
Export directory path, 76–77
exporting files, 108
exporting objects, Trainz, 776–777
expression
building, 643
entering for spinner, 641
functions, 650–651
mathematical, 575
MAXScript, 237–239
operators, 648–650
predefined variables, 647–648
return types, 652
sample, 653–654
variables, 642–643
Expression controller, 630
Expression Controller dialog box, 642, 644, 654–655
Expression Debug Window, 644
Expressions directory path, 76
Extend button, editing Splines, 311
Extended primitives, absence of, 12
Extended view option, Viewport Configuration dialog box, 86
external reference (XRefs), 21, 116
Extract Operand button, Parameters rollout, 371
Extrude button
Edge subobject mode, 332
Geometry rollout, 357
Extrude Mode command, 801
Extrude modifier, 315, 415
Extrude Poly Face command, 801
extruding splines, 315
Extrusion spinner, 332, 357

F
F. *See* Frame Number Predefined Variable
Fabric library, gmax Material Navigator, 479
Face Extrude modifier, 414
Face snap point, 214
Face subobject, 321, 333
faces, reducing number of, 342
faceted sphere, 275
Facets+Highlights Viewport Rendering Level, 80
Fade style, Animations section, 68
Falloff cone, 535
Falloff curve, Envelope Properties, 448
Falloff Distance button, Edit UVW dialog box, 510
Falloff parameter, Affect Region modifier, 435
Falloff Type button, Edit UVW dialog box, 510
Falloff value, Soft Select rollout, 264
Far Range value, Parameters rollout, 552
Fast, Key Tangent, 563
Fast View setting, Viewport Rendering Options, 83–85
feet ('), 78
Fence selection method, 140
Fence Selection Region button, main toolbar, 33
Ferris wheel.gmax, 171
Fetch command, Edit menu, 22, 403, 796
FFD. *See* Free Form Deformation modifier
FFD (Box) modifier, 424–425
FFD (Cyl) modifier, 424–425
field of view (FOV), 85, 542, 546, 550
15mm lens, 551
50mm lens, 551
57 Chevy bending over a hill.gmax, 420
Figure skater skating a figure eight.gmax, 613
file
archiving, 107
consolidating into one location, 128–129
creating, 103–104
exporting, 108
finding, 127–128
formats, 108
importing, 108
objects, merging, 106
opening, 105
saving, 104–105

scene file, 103
viewing information about, 130–131
File Archive dialog box, 107
File Finder utility, Utilities panel, 127–128
File menu
keyboard shortcut, 796
MAXScript Editor window, 228
opening, 21
Visual MAXScript window, 252
File Properties dialog box, 21, 131
File View Pane, Siege Editor interface, 724
Files button, Viewport Background dialog box, 56
Files panel, Preference Settings dialog box
Auto Backup feature, 93
Backup on Save option, 92
Compress on Save option, 92
Configure Paths dialog box, 93
Display Obsolete File Message option, 93
Increment on Save option, 92
log files, 94
Recent Files in File Menu option, 93
Save Viewport Thumbnail Image option, 92–93
Zoom Extents on Import option, 94
Fillet button, editing vertices, 304
Fillet Radius 1 value, Star primitive object, 294
Fillet Radius 2 value, Star primitive object, 294
Film frame rate standard, 557
filter color mapping, 504
Filter Combinations dialog box, 137
Filter Environment Backgrounds option, Preference Settings dialog box, 97
Filter Selected Faces button, Edit UVW dialog box, 511, 803
Filters button, Global Track View Toolbar, 580, 802
Filters dialog box, 597–598
Find Maps button, Bitmap Path Editor dialog box, 129
finding files, 127–128
firecracker.gmax, 230
first-person shooter genre, 6
fish, animating, 247–250
Fish scene.gmax, 245
Fit button, UVW Map modifier, 506
Fit Deformation window, 388–389
fl. See flying loop animation
Flamingo leg.gmax, 463

Flamingo skin.gmax, 449
Flash icon set, 74
flash shade renderer, 14
Flatten option, MakeMDL, 709
Flight Simulator 2002 Professional, 7–8
Flight Simulator Insider Web site, 706
FlightSim.com (Web site), 717
Flip button, Surface Properties rollout, 340
Flip Horizontal button, Edit UVW dialog box, 510
Flip Normal Mode button, Surface Properties rollout, 340
Flip Normals option, Skin Parameters rollout, 382
Flip Vertical button, Edit UVW dialog box, 510
Float controllers, 620
Float Expression controller, 642, 655
float parameter format, 573
floating feature, 48
floating panel, 32, 47
floating toolbar, 47
Floating Toolbars toggle, Show UI menu, 29
Floor function, 651
flying loop animation (fl), Dungeon Siege, 753
flyout, 32
Flyout Time spinner, Preference Settings dialog box, 89
focal length, camera, 542
Follow option, Spacing Tool dialog box, 166
Following a rocket.gmax, 548
Following eyes.gmax, 645
Font drop-down list, 292
Fonts directory path, 76
for loop, MAXScript, 242–243
Force 2-Sided option, Viewport Rendering Options, 82, 325
form elements, Visual MAXScript, 252–253
Forward Direction, Time Configuration dialog box, 558
forward kinematics, 452
Forward Time One Unit command, 799, 802
FOV. See field of view
FOV parameter, Parameters rollout, 550
Fractal Design Painter 3D, 495
Fractal Noise option, Noise Controller dialog box, 629
fractional units, entering, 78

Frame Number Predefined Variable (F), 648
Frame Rate, Time Configuration dialog box, 557
Frames option, Time Display, 557
Frame:Ticks option, Time Display, 557
Free camera object, 542–543, 551
Free Direct light, 525
free download, gmax, 4
Free Form Deformation (FFD) modifier, 423–424
Free Form Deformers, Modifiers menu, 28
Free Spot light, 525
Freeze button, Edit UVW dialog box, 511
Freeze Nonselected Curves button, Function Curves Mode, 589
Freeze option, Object Properties dialog box, 149
Freeze rollout, Display panel, 152
Freeze Selection command, 798, 803
Frequency value, Noise Controller dialog box, 629
friction, 13
Front orthographic viewport, 50
Front view option, Viewport Configuration dialog box, 86, 199, 797
fs0. See barehanded attack with no weapon
fs1. See single-handed weapon
fs2. See single-handed weapon and a shield
fs3. See long two-handed weapon
fs4. See short two-handed weapon
fs5. See two-handed staff weapon
fs6. See bow and arrow
fs7. See crossbow
fs8. See shield only
FSEdit SDK (Flight Simulator software development kit), 706
FSPlanet (Web site), 717
Full Compile, Tempest game pack, 681
Function curves mode, Track View window, 581, 588–589, 592–595, 801
function, MAXScript, 243–245
list, 644, 650–651
MAXScript, 243–245
Tempest game pack, 668, 695–698
Fuse button, editing vertices, 302–303

G

Game Developer's Conference (GDC), 4, 6
game packs, installing, 792

Gamma panel, Preference Settings dialog box
    Enable Gamma Correction option, 94
    Input Gamma setting for Bitmap files option, 95
.gas file extension, 748
Gas Powered Games, 9, 719
GDC. *See* Game Developer's Conference
Gear and prop.gmax, 459
Gears tool, Tempest Toolbar, 671
General Panel, Object Properties dialog box, 146–147
General panel, Preference Settings dialog box
    Auto Window/Crossing by Direction option, 88
    Automatic Sub-Material Assignment option, 88
    AutoPlay Preview Files setting, 88
    Color Selection drop-down list, 89
    Display Cross Hair Cursor option, 88
    Enable Viewport Tooltips toggle, 88
    Flyout Time spinner, 89
    Horizontal Text in Vertical Toolbars option, 89
    Load Plug-Ins When Used option, 88
    opening, 86–87
    Origin control, 87
    Reference Coordinate System setting, 88
    Resulting Accuracy, 87
    Rollup Threshold value, 89
    Save UI Configuration on Exit switch, 89
    Scene Undo spinner, 87
    System Unit Scale option, 87
    Use Large Toolbar Buttons option, 89
    Use Spinner Snap option, 89
    warnings, disabling, 88
    Wrap Cursor Near Spinner option, 89
General Path panel, Configure Paths dialog box, 75–77
Generate Mapping Coordinates option
    Mesh Settings rollout, 288
    Parameters rollout, 494
Generate Path button, Fit Deformation dialog box, 389
Generic Entity tool, Tempest Toolbar, 669
Generic units, 77
Genie lamp.gmax, 159

Geodesic Base Type option, Parameters rollout, 278
Geometry category panel, Create panel, 267
Geometry drop-down list, Standard Primitives, 267
Geometry object category, Create panel, 38
Geometry rollout
    Attach button, 300, 352
    Attach Mult. button, 301
    Bind button, 352
    Bind First option, 301
    Bind Last option, 301
    Boolean button, 301
    Break button, 300
    Closed option, 301
    Connect option, 301
    Create button, 352
    Create Line button, 300
    Delete button, 301
    Detach button, 301
    Editable Splines, 299
    Hide button, 301
    Insert button, 301
    Linear option, 301
    Refine button, 301
    Reorient option, 300, 302
    Show Selected Segs option, 302
    Unbind button, 352
    Unhide button, 301
    View Steps value, 354
    Weld button, 353
    Weld Target button, 354
Geometry Selection Filter, 137
GeoSphere primitive object, creation method, 272
GeoSphere, Standard Primitives, 277–278
Get Face Selection From Stack command, 803
Get Shape button, Fit Deformation dialog box, 389
ghosting, 97, 567–658
gizmo, 192–193
Gizmos rollout, 450–451
Global Settings rollout, Light Lister dialog box, 527
Global Track View Toolbar buttons, Track View window, 580–581
Global Tracks track, 637
Glossiness control, Blinn Shader, 483–485
glossiness mapping, 504
Glossiness value, gmax Material Editor, 469
gmax Driver Setup dialog box, 792–793
.gmax file extension, 103

gmax File Finder tool, Utilities panel, 41–42
gmax Material Editor
    Ambient color, 468
    Background button, 470
    compared to 3ds max, 13
    creating material, 471
    Diffuse color, 468
    dragging and dropping, 471–472
    Glossiness value, 469
    gmax Material Navigator button, 470
    Go Forward to Sibling button, 470, 481
    Go to Parent button, 470, 481
    main toolbar, 34, 797
    map, rendering, 472
    opacity, 468–469
    opening, 469
    picking material from scene, 474
    reflection, 469
    refraction, 469
    removing material, 475
    resetting material, 474
    Roughness property, 469
    sample slot, 471, 473
    Self-Illumination color, 468
    Show Map in Viewport button, 470
    Soften value, 469
    Specular color, 468
    Specular Level value, 469
    transparency, 469
gmax Material Navigator
    Find material text field, 476
    gmax Material Editor, 470
    library, 476, 479
    Library Name field, 477
    List option, 478
    loading material into gmax Material editor, 478
    main toolbar, 34
    map types, 493
    Material Name field, 477
    opening, 476
    purpose, 474
    submaterial, 480–482
gmax prototype, 6
gmaxFinder dialog box, 127–128
gmax.log, 94
gmaxStart directory path, 76
gmax12.exe, 791
Go Forward to Sibling button, gmax Material Editor, 470, 481
Go to End button, Time Controls, 43, 556, 799
Go to Parent button, gmax Material Editor, 470, 481
Go to Start button, Time Controls, 43, 556, 799

gothic skylight, Tempest game pack, 688–691
Graph Editors menu, 29, 797
graphics card requirements, 790
Graphics Driver Setup dialog box, 792
gravity, 13
Greater than logical operator (>), 649
Greater than or equal to logical operator (>=), 649
green channel, Virtual Frame Buffer, 134
Grid Align button, Edit Geometry rollout, 325
Grid and Snap Settings command, Customize menu, 30
Grid and Snap Settings dialog box, 211–214
Grid button, Create panel, 212
Grid Coordinate System, Transform Managers, 197
Grid Divisions tool, Tempest Toolbar, 670
Grid Lines snap point, 214
Grid Nudge Distance, Preference Settings dialog box, 97
Grid Points snap point, 214
grid size, Status Bar, 44
Grid view option, Viewport Configuration dialog box, 86
Grids command, Views menu, 25
Ground custom subdirectory, Trainz, 778
Ground folder, Trainz, 762
Ground library, gmax Material Navigator, 479
group
    closing, 178
    creating, 177
    opening, 178
    removing, 178
Group Box form element, Visual MAXScript, 253
Group command, 177
Group drop-down list
    Keyboard panel, 60
    Toolbar panel, 62
Group menu, 25, 797
group name, object property, 146

H
Hailing taxi man with incorrect normals.gmax, 341
hard drive space requirements, 790
hardware requirements, gmax, 789–790
HasDamageMap option, MakeMDL, 709
HasLightMap option, MakeMDL, 709

HasNightMap option, MakeMDL, 709
HasReflectMap option, MakeMDL, 709
HD IK Solver, absence of, 13
Headlights on 57 Chevy.gmax, 536
Heart Shaped NURMS.gmax, 423
heart.gmax, 266
Hedras, absence of, 12
Heidi Drivers directory path, 76
HEIDI software driver, 793
Height parameter, Helix primitive shape, 294
Helix primitive object, 289, 294–295
Help directory path, 76
Help menu
    About gmax command, 31
    Additional Help command, 31
    Asset Browser command, 31
    MAXScript Editor window, 228
    MAXScript Reference, 30
    screen appearance, 31
    User Reference, 30
Help Menu command, 797
Helpers category panel, Create panel, 267, 281–282
Helpers default toolbar, Tab Panel, 72
Helpers object category, Create panel, 38
Helpers Selection Filter, 137
Helpers toolbar, Tab Panel, 35
hemisphere, 275
HI. See Hierarchy Independent
HI IK Solver, absence of, 13
hide and seek with crocodile teeth.gmax, 152
Hide button
    Edit UVW dialog box, 511
    Geometry rollout, 301
    Selection rollout, 322–323
Hide by Category rollout, Display panel, 150
Hide option, Object Properties dialog box, 149
Hide rollout, Display panel, 152
Hide Selected command, 803
Hide/Freeze tab, Display Floater dialog box, 149–150
hierarchy, object
    definition, 180
    displaying, 183–184
    selecting, 185
Hierarchy Independent (HI), 13
Hierarchy panel, Command Panel, 39–40, 180, 184–185
Highland Valley Scripts, Trainz, 758
Highlight Any Text Field command, 804
Highlight Next Text Field command, 804

Highlight Previous Text Field command, 804
highlights, placing, 527
high-polygon count model, 342
history of gmax, 4
Hold command, Edit menu, 22, 403, 796
Home Grid, 211
Horizontal Text in Vertical Toolbars option, Preference Settings dialog box, 89
Hot material, 474
Hotkey field, Keyboard panel, 60
Hotspot cone, 535
house, creating, 512
hue, saturation, and value (HSV) color system, 270
human figure
    figure skater, 613–614
    hailing taxi, 341
    importing from Poser, 111–113
    kissing couple, 209
    morphing facial expressions, 418
Hyper Pogo Stick with Sound.gmax, 601
Hyper Pogo Stick.gmax, 595
Hyperbolic Cosine function, 651
Hyperbolic Sine function, 650
Hyperbolic Tangent function, 651

I
ui directory, 71
icon, adding custom, 64–65
Icon Directory dialog box, 74
Icons icon set, 74
Icosa option, Parameters rollout, 278
Id Software, 6
Ignore Backfacing option, Selection rollout, 322, 350
Ignore Bad Normals option, MakeMDL, 709
Ignore Bad Triggers option, MakeMDL, 709
Ignore Extents option, Object Properties dialog box, 148
Ignore Visible Edges option, Selection rollout, 322
Ignore Warnings option, MakeMDL, 709
IK. See inverse kinematics
IK Chain Assignment rollout, 440–441
IK Chain Object Class ID, 138
IK display Options rollouts, 463
IK Limb, 440
IK Limb Solver, 13, 460–463
IK Solver, 440
IK Solvers submenu, Animation menu, 28
.IM. See Indexed Mesh file

image reference file, Trainz, 766
Import dialog box
    Convert Units option, 108
    file formats, 108
Import directory path, 76–77
Import DXF File dialog box, 109
Import Settings dialog box, 108
importing files, 108
Impossible Creatures, 11
in coordsys construct, MAXScript, 249
inches ("), 78
Increment on Save option, Files panel, 92
Index of Refraction, Extended Parameters rollout, 505
Indexed Mesh file (.IM), 115, 771
Infinite Bounds option, editing Splines, 311
Inherits rollout, Hierarchy panel, 185, 200
Input Gamma setting for Bitmap files option, Gamma panel, 95
inscribed polygon, 291
Insert Bézier Point button, Deformation dialog box, 385
Insert button, Geometry rollout, 301
Insert Corner Point button, Deformation dialog box, 385
Insert Time button
    Edit Time Mode, 587
    Track View window, 591
installing gmax, 791
Instance, definition, 155
Instance option, Pick Targets rollout, 366
instanced modifier, 400
integer parameter format, 573
Interactive IK method, 13, 457–458
Interactive Pan command
    keyboard shortcut, 800
    Viewport Navigation button, 51
interface design, importance of, 17–18
interface elements, types of
    Command Panel, 19
    Dialog Boxes and Editors, 20
    Floating Toolbars, 20
    Main Toolbar, 18
    Menus, 18
    Quadmenus, 20
    Status Bar, 19
    Tab Panel, 20
    Time Controls, 19
    Track Bar, 19
    using as part of game pack, 18
    Viewport Navigation Controls, 19
    Viewports, 19

Interiors custom subdirectory, Trainz, 778
Internet, connecting to, 127
Interpolation rollout, 288
Intersection option, Preference Settings dialog box, 97, 144, 309
inverse kinematics (IK), 13, 39–40, 439, 452
Inverse Kinematics panel, Preference Settings dialog box, 89–90, 457–458
Inverse Kinematics rollout, Hierarchy panel, 457
inverse kinematics system, building
    binding objects, 454
    joint constraints, 453–454
    joints, copying, 454
    linking objects, 452
    pivot points, 452
    terminator, 452–453
Invert option, Output rollout, 500
Isolate command, Tools menu, 23, 144
Italics parameter, Text primitive, 292
Item Tool Kit, Dungeon Siege Tool Kit, 743–744

J

Joint Angle Deformer, Gizmos rollout, 450
.JPEG file extension, 126, 132, 497
Justified parameter, Text primitive, 292

K

.kbd file extension, 61, 74
Keep Error Log option, MakeMDL, 709
Keep Files option, MakeMDL, 709
Keep Initial Offset option, LookAt Constraint rollout, 615
Kerning parameter, Text primitive, 292
Key dialog boxes, 563
Key Entire Hierarchy section, Link Parameters rollout, 613
Key Info dialog box, 593
Key Info rollout
    Link constraints, 613
    TCB controller, 632
Key Info section, Attachment Parameters rollout, 606
Key Mode section, Link Parameters rollout, 613
Key Mode Toggle button, Time Controls, 43, 556
Key Properties menu, 562
Key Steps group, Time Configuration dialog box, 558
Key Tangents, Key dialog boxes, 563

Key Time field, Track View window, 583
keyboard command, appearance on menu, 20
Keyboard Entry rollout, Create panel, 273, 289
Keyboard panel, Customize User Interface dialog box, 29, 49, 60–61
keyboard shortcuts
    customizing, 60–61
    defaults, 61
    list of, 795–804
    printing out, 61
keys, 558, 590
kilometers (km), 78
.KIN. See Animation file
Kissing couple.gmax, 209
KUID number, Trainz, 762–764

L

Label form element, Visual MAXScript, 253
Lamp.gmax, 530
Large Toolbar Buttons option, Preference Settings dialog box, 32
Lathe modifier, 316–317, 412–413
Layer option, Import DXF File dialog box, 109
Layout menu, Visual MAXScript window, 252
Layout panel, Viewport Configuration dialog box, 86
LC. See Lights and Cameras
leaf, creating, 361
leakage, 692
Left orthographic viewport, 50
Left parameter, Text primitive, 292
Left view option, Viewport Configuration dialog box, 86, 199, 797
legs, 5
l_engine, MakeMDL SDK recognized name, 711
Length, Time Configuration dialog box, 558
lens, camera, 542, 550
Less than logical operator (<), 649
Less than or equal to logical operator (<=), 649
Level of Detail, setting for viewports, 342
level, Tempest game pack, 679–680
library, material, 476
licensing, 6
Light Falloff button, Light Navigation Control, 529
Light Hotspot button, Light Navigation Control, 529

Light Lister dialog box, 24, 524, 526–527
Light Map Texture, MakeMDL SDK, 711
Light Navigation controls, 528–5529
light, Tempest game pack, 681–683
Light tool, Tempest Toolbar, 669
Light View command, 798
lighting
  ambient, 522, 524–525
  artificial, 522
  Attenuation Parameters rollout, 532–533
  creating, 525–526
  default, 524
  Directional Light Parameters rollout, 533
  Dungeon Siege Tool Kit, 736–737
  Falloff cone, 535
  Free Direct light, 525
  Free Spot light, 525
  General Parameters rollout, 531–532
  Hotspot cone, 535
  importance of, 521
  listing, 526–527
  natural, 522
  Omni light, 525
  Projector Map, 538
  Projector Parameters rollout, 533
  raytraced shadows, 522–523, 538
  shadow maps, 522–523
  Shadow Parameters rollout, 534–535
  Spotlight Parameters rollout, 533
  Target Direct light, 525
  Target Spot light, 525
  transforming, 526
lights, animating, 569
Lights and Cameras (LC), Filter Combinations dialog box, 137
Lights & Cameras toolbar, Tab Panel, 35, 72
Lights category panel, Create panel, 267
lights collection, 241
Lights object category, Create panel, 38
Lights rollout, Light Lister dialog box, 527
Lights Selection Filter, 137
limitations of gmax, compared to 3ds max
  Atmospheric effects, 14
  Camera Match utility, 14
  Camera Tracker utility, 14
  Conform object, 13
  Displacement Mapping, 14
  Dynamic module, 13

Extended primitives, 13
HD IK Solver, 13
Hedras, 13
HI IK Solver, 13
Material editor, 13
Mesher object, 13
Motion Capture controller, 14
Non-Uniform Rational B-Splines modeling, 13
Pyramid primitive object, 13
Raytrace Materials, 14
reasons for, 12
Reflection Mapping, 14
rendering, 14
Scatter object, 13
Schematic View, 14
Section spline tool, 13
Shaders, 14
Sunlight system, 14
Terrain object, 13
Torus Knots, 13
Video Post interface, 14
Limited option, Rotational Joints rollout, 454
Lincoln Logs booleans.gmax, 377
Line primitive object, 289–291
linear array, 168–170
Linear controller, 628
Linear Interpolation option, Skin Parameters rollout, 382
Linear, Key Tangent, 563
Linear option
  Geometry rollout, 301
  Param Curve Out-of-Range Types dialog box, 599
link
  creating, 180–181
  displaying, 182
Link button, main toolbar, 141, 180–181
Link constraint, 613
Link Display rollout, Display panel, 152, 182–183
Link Information button, Hierarchy panel, 39–40, 185
Link Inheritance utility, 200
Link Parameters rollout, 612–613
Link Replaces Object option
  Display panel, 152
  Link Display rollout, 183
Link to World button, Link Parameters rollout, 612
linked hierarchy, 155, 439. *See also* bones system
Linked Solar System.gmax, 181
Linked XForm modifier, 419
List Box form element, Visual MAXScript, 253
List controller, 630

Lit Wireframes Viewport Rendering Level, 80
Load button, Toolbar panel, 62
Load Custom UI command, Customize menu, 29
Load Plug-Ins When Used option, Preference Settings dialog box, 88
Load UVW command, 803
loading objects, Trainz, 777
Local Center During Animate option, Preference Settings dialog box, 90
Local Coordinate System, Transform Managers, 197–198
local keyword, MAXScript, 244
Lock Aspect button, Fit Deformation dialog box, 389
Lock Handles option, Selection rollout, 298, 350
Lock Selected Vertices button, Edit UVW dialog box, 511, 803
Lock Selection button, Global Track View Toolbar, 581, 802
Lock Selection Set button, Status Bar, 44
Lock Tangents button
  Function Curves Mode, 589
  Key Info dialog box, 593, 802
Lock UI Layout command, Customize menu, 29
Lock User Interface command, 796
Lock Zoom/Pan option, Viewport Background dialog box, 56
locking axes, 199
locking current interface, 75
Locks rollout, 185, 200
Loft object type
  Bevel Deformation window, 388
  definition, 13, 365
  Deformation window interface, 383–386
  Fit Deformation window, 388–389
  Get Path button, 379
  Get Shape button, 379
  modifying, 390
  path parameters, 381
  paths, editing, 391
  Scale Deformation window, 387
  shapes, comparing, 390
  skin parameters, 381–382
  Surface constraint, 608
  surface parameters, 380–381
  surface tool, compared to, 392–393
  Teeter Deformation window, 387
  Twist Deformation window, 387
  vertex order, 380
Lofted drapes.gmax, 391
Lofted slip-proof hanger.gmax, 382

log file, 94
Logical And operator (&), 649
Logical Or operator (|), 649
Logic.dsres, 749
long two-handed weapon (fs3),
        Dungeon Siege, 753
LookAt axis, LookAt Constraint
        rollout, 615
LookAt constraint, 614–615
loop, MAXScript, 242–243
Loop option
    Param Curve Out-of-Range Types
        dialog box, 599
    Path Parameters rollout, 610
    Time Configuration dialog box,
        557–558
Looping airplane.gmax, 566
low-polygon count model, 342
Low-Res Environment Background
        option, Preference
        Settings dialog box, 97
l_tail, MakeMDL SDK recognized
        name, 711
..::LvL (map community), 703
l_wing, MakeMDL SDK recognized
        name, 711
l_wingfold, MakeMDL SDK recognized
        name, 711
lwingtip, MakeMDL SDK recognized
        name, 711
l_wingtip, MakeMDL SDK recognized
        name, 711
l_wing_tip, MakeMDL SDK recognized
        name, 711

M

m. *See* meters
Macro Recorder, MAXScript menu, 30,
        229
Macro script, 232–233
macros command, 232
magic animation (mg), Dungeon
        Siege, 753
main toolbar
    Align button, 34
    Align to Camera button, 34
    Align to View button, 34
    Array button, 34
    Circular Selection Region
        button, 33
    Fence Selection Region button, 33
    floating panel, changing to, 32
    gmax Material Editor button, 34
    gmax Material Navigator
        button, 34
    Mirror Selected Objects
        button, 34
    Named Selection Set drop-down
        list, 34
    Normal Align button, 34

Open Track View button, 34
Place Highlight button, 34
Rectangular Selection Region
        button, 33
Redo button, 33
Reference Coordinate System
        drop-down list, 33
Restrict to X button, 34
Restrict to XY Plane button, 34
Restrict to XZ Plane button, 34
Restrict to Y button, 34
Restrict to YZ Plane button, 34
Restrict to Z button, 34
Select and Link button, 33
Select and Manipulate button, 33
Select and Move button, 33
Select and Non-Uniform Scale
        button, 33
Select and Rotate button, 33
Select and Squash button, 33
Select and Uniform Scale
        button, 33
Select by Name button, 33
Select Object button, 33
selecting objects, 138
Selection Filter drop-down list, 33
Snapshot button, 34
Spacing Tool button, 34
tooltips, 32
Undo button, 33
Unlink Selection button, 33
Use Pivot Point Center button, 33
Use Selection Center button, 33
Use Transformer Coordinate
        Center button, 33
viewing entire, 32
main toolbar toggle, Show UI
        menu, 29
Main view window, Siege Editor
        interface, 724
Make Controller Unique command
    Global Track View Toolbar, 581
    keyboard shortcut, 802
    Track View window, 598
Make First button, editing vertices,
        303
Make Planar button, Vertex subobject
        mode, 329
Make Symmetrical button,
        Deformation dialog box,
        385
Make Unique button, Modifier Stack,
        399–400
MakeMDL SDK (Flight Simulator
        software development kit)
    aircraft, 715
    Flight Simulator Insider Web site,
        706
    latitude and longitude, 713
    LOD panel, 707–708

Main panel, 707
    object, positioning, 713
    online resources, 717
    Options panel, 708–709
    Output panel, 710
    recognized names, 710–711
    Scenery panel, 709–710
    textures, 711–712
    units, 712
manipulator helper, 575–576
Manual Update toggle, Text primitive,
        293
map
    bump, 492
    compared to material, 470
    definition, 486
    Dungeon Siege Tool Kit, 724,
        737–738
    material, 492
    projection, 493
Map Button form element, Visual
        MAXScript, 252
map gizmo, 506
Maple leaf.gmax, 361
mapping coordinates, Trainz, 775–776
Maps custom subdirectory, Trainz,
        778
Maps rollout
    Ambient mapping, 503
    bump mapping, 504
    Diffuse mapping, 503
    displacement mapping, 505
    filter color mapping, 504
    glossiness mapping, 504
    opacity mapping, 504
    opening, 486, 493
    reflection mapping, 505
    refraction mapping, 505
    self-illumination mapping, 504
    Specular Level mapping, 504
    Specular mapping, 503
Maps Track Icon, 582
Mask Viewport to Safe Region option,
        Preference Settings dialog
        box, 96
Master Block Parameters dialog box,
        637–638
Master Block section, Assign
        Constant Controller dialog
        box, 637
Master Point controller, 639–640
Master Track Key Info dialog box, 639
Match Bitmap button, Viewport
        Background dialog box, 56
Match Camera to View command,
        Views menu, 26, 549, 796
Match Viewport button, Viewport
        Background dialog box, 56
Material Button form element, Visual
        MAXScript, 252

Material Editor. *See* gmax Material
	Editor
material ID
	automatic assignment of, 490
	Editable Mesh object, 490
	Multi-Material material, 487–488
Material IDs option, Surface
	Properties rollout, 340,
	359
material map, 492
Material Name, object property, 146
materials, animating, 569
Materials directory path, 76–77
Materials Track Icon, 582
matlibs directory, 479
MaxColors color interface scheme, 71
MaxColorsGrey color interface
	scheme, 71–72
Maximize View Camera Control, 671
Maximum Edge Length option,
	Optimize modifier, 416
Maximum Value function, 651
MaxKeys keyboard shortcut set, 61
MaxKeysClassic keyboard shortcut
	set, 61
MAXScript, computer language,
	219–220
MAXScript Editor window, 228
MAXScript interpreter, 224
MAXScript Listener command, 30, 796
MAXScript Listener window
	appearance of, 223
	Edit menu, 224
	File menu, 224
	Help menu, 224
	interpreter, 224
	Macro Recorder menu, 224
	Search menu, 224
MAXScript menu
	Macro Recorder command, 221,
		228–230
	MAXScript Listener command,
		221, 797
	New Script command, 220
	Open Script command, 220
	Run Script command, 221
	viewing, 30
MAXScript Mini Listener, 44–46, 227
MAXScript panel, Preference Settings
	dialog box, 101–102
MAXScript Reference, Help menu, 30
MAXScript tool, Utilities panel, 41–42
MAXScript Utility rollout, 221–222
MaxStart standard interface, 74
MaxStart.ui, 75
Maxzip archive program, 94
Maya Personal Learning Edition, 5
maze environment, creating, 119–120
maze.gmax, 119–120, 164
.mcr file extension, 221

MDL Format SDK (Flight Simulator
	software development
	kit), 706
measurement system, 77
measuring units, Trainz, 772
Melting ice cream cone.gmax, 407
members, large objects, 235
Menu command
	executing, 20
	Quads panel, 66
menus
	Alt key, navigating menu with,
		20–21
	Animation menu, 28–29
	Create menu, 28
	Customize menu, 29–30
	Edit menu, 21–22
	ellipsis, 20
	File menu, 21
	Graph Editors menu, 29
	Group menu, 25
	Help menu, 30–31
	importance of, 20–21
	keyboard command, 20
	MAXScript menu, 30
	menu command, 20
	Modifiers menu, 28
	small black arrow, 20
	submenus, 20
	toggle menu option, 20
	Tools menu, 23–24
	Track View menu, 29
	Views menu, 25–27
Menus and toolbars, Siege Editor
	interface, 724
Menus panel, Customize User
	Interface dialog box
	Action drop-down list, 68
	adding new menu, 69–70
	Group drop-down list, 68
	Menus pane, 68
	opening, 29
	Separator pane, 68
Mercury space capsule.gmax, 410
Merge Animation dialog box, 571–572
Merge dialog box, 106
Merge option, Operations group, 372
Mesh clown head.gmax, 330
Mesh Editing modifiers, 28, 413
mesh object
	converting objects into, 319–320
	editing, 324–325
Mesh Select modifier, 402, 404, 488
Mesh Settings rollout, 287–288
Mesher object, absence of, 13
Meshes modeling type, 262
MeshSmooth button, Subdivide
	rollout, 338, 801
MeshSmooth modifier, 421–422

Metal library, gmax Material
	Navigator, 479
Metal Shader, 485
meters (m), 78
Methane Molecule.gmax, 215
Metric units system, 77
mg. *See* magic animation
Microid, 11
Microsoft, 10–11. *See also* Combat
	Flight Simulator 3; Flight
	Simulator 2002
	Professional; Train
	Simulator
middle mouse button, defining, 98–99
MIDI Time Slider controls, Preference
	Settings dialog box, 90
Midpoint snap point, 214
millimeters (mm), 78
Minimum Value function, 651
Min/Max Toggle command
	Camera Navigation Control, 547
	keyboard shortcut, 800
	Light Navigation Control, 529
	Viewport Navigation button, 52
minus sign (-)
	decrease gizmo size, 192
	Negation operator, 648
	Subtraction operator, 648
	Vector Subtraction vector
		operator, 649
Mirror Both button, editing Splines,
	310
Mirror command, Tools menu, 23
Mirror dialog box, 161–162
Mirror Horizontally button
	Edit UVW dialog box, 510, 803
	editing Splines, 310
	Fit Deformation dialog box, 389
Mirror modifier, 435
Mirror Selected Objects button, main
	toolbar, 34
Mirror texture, Tempest game pack,
	689
Mirror Vertically button
	Edit UVW dialog box, 510, 803
	editing Splines, 310
	Fit Deformation dialog box, 389
mm. *See* millimeters
MM:SS:Ticks option, Time Display,
	557
.mnu file extension, 68, 74
mod creator, 5
model
	Tempest game pack, 698–700
	Trainz, 771
modeler, 5
modeless dialog box, 49
Modeling default toolbar, Tab Panel,
	72
Modeling Quadmenu command, 800

Modeling toolbar, Tab Panel, 35
modeling types, 262
modifier gizmo, 402
Modifier List drop-down list, Modifier
        Stack, 397–398
Modifier Stack, Modify panel
    Collapsing the Stack, 402
    copying and pasting, 399
    Customize Modifier Sets button,
        399
    dragging and dropping, 400
    Editable Spline, 297
    Make Unique button, 399–400
    Modifier List drop-down list,
        397–398
    Modifiers menu, 397–398
    Pin Stack button, 399
    purpose, 397
    Remove Modifier from the Stack
        button, 399
    Show End Result on/off toggle
        button, 399
    Stack order, 400
    subobjects, 402
    Topology Dependency warning
        dialog box, 403
    viewing, 39
Modifiers default toolbar, Tab Panel,
        72
Modifiers menu, 28, 397–398, 797
Modifiers toolbar, Tab Panel, 35
Modifiers Track Icon, 582
Modify panel, Command Panel, 39
Modify Subtree button
    Edit Keys Mode, 585
    Edit Time Mode, 587
Modulus Value function, 651
mono channel output, 498
Monochrome button, Virtual Frame
        Buffer, 134
monster, Dungeon Siege Tool Kit,
        735–736
Morph Angle Deformer, Gizmos
        rollout, 450
Morph button, Create panel, 366
Morph modifier, 417
Morph object type
    Base object, 366
    definition, 13, 365
    Morph key, 367
    Target object, 366
Morpher modifier, 367
Morphing alien head.gmax, 367
Morphing facial expressions.gmax,
        418
Motion Blur, Object Properties dialog
        box, 22
Motion Capture controller, absence
        of, 14
Motion panel, Command Panel

Assign Controllers rollout, 565
    opening, 40–41
    Parameters button, 564
    PRS Parameters rollout, 565
    Trajectories button, 565
Move button
    Edit UVW dialog box, 510
    Output rollout, 500
Move Control Point button,
        Deformation dialog box,
        385
Move Gizmo, 193
Move Highlight Down command, 802
Move Highlight Up command, 802
Move Horizontal button
    Edit UVW dialog box, 510
    Function Curves Mode, 589.803
Move Keys button
    Edit Keys Mode, 585
    Function Curves Mode, 589
    Track View window, 590, 593, 802
Move option, Pick Targets rollout, 366
Move Vertical button
    Edit UVW dialog box, 510, 803
    Function Curves Mode, 589
.ms file extension, 221
M3D file format, 10
Multi-Material material
    definition, 13, 487
    editing, 487–488
    material ID, 487–488
Multiplayer/Flight Instructor SDK
        (Flight Simulator software
        development kit), 706
multiple materials, assigning to one
        object, 490–492
multiple textures, Tempest game
        pack, 694–695
Multiplication operator (*), 649
Multiplier Curve Out-of-Range Types
        button, Function Curves
        Mode, 589
Multi/Sub-Object Basic Parameters
        rollout, 487–488
Multi/Sub-Object material type, 340,
        359
Musical notes.gmax, 538
My Collection option, Trainz, 759

N
name
    material, 473
    object property, 146
    selecting object by, 139–140
    variable, 234
Name and Color rollout, Create panel,
        38, 269
Name Group dialog box, 177
Named Selection Sets drop-down list,
        34, 143, 298, 323

Nasa decal on rocket.gmax, 507
National Television Standards
        Committee (NTSC), 557
natural light, 522
Natural Logarithm function, 651
Natural Logarithm Predefined
        Variable (E), 648
Near Range value, Parameters rollout,
        552
NegateZ option, MakeMDL, 709
Negation operator (-), 648
Netpipes Instructor SDK (Flight
        Simulator software
        development kit), 706
New button
    Quads panel, 67
    Toolbar panel, 62
New Map dialog box, Siege Editor
        interface, 724
New Material dialog box, 471
New Region dialog box, Siege Editor
        interface, 725
New Scene command, 796
Next Frame button, Time Controls, 43
Next Frame/Key button, Time
        Control, 556
Next Wired Parameter wiring
        parameter, 575
NGon primitive object, 289, 291
Night Map Texture, MakeMDL SDK,
        711
Ninja star.gmax, 306
No Animations option, MakeMDL, 709
Node Matcher, Dungeon Siege Tool
        Kit, 727–728
node parameter format, 573
Node Properties dialog box, Dungeon
        Siege Tool Kit, 729
Node Set panel, Dungeon Siege Tool
        Kit, 730
nodes, Dungeon Siege Tool Kit, 723,
        726
NoDrop texture, Tempest game pack,
        689
noise, Bitmap map type, 496–497
Noise controller, 622, 629
Noise modifier, 429
Noise Position track, 622
Noise rollout, 496–497
Noise Strength, 622
NoLeftToRight option, MakeMDL, 709
non-parametric object, 263
Non-Scaling Object Size value,
        Preference Settings dialog
        box, 97
Non-Uniform Rational B-Splines
        (NURBS) modeling, 12
Non-Uniform Rational MeshSmooth
        (NURMS), 339, 421
non-uniform scaling, 191

normal, 24
Normal Align button
    main toolbar, 34
    UVW Map modifier, 506
Normal Align command, 208, 796
Normal Align dialog box, 208–209
Normal Bevel button, Bevel
        Deformation, 388
Normal Compile, Tempest game pack,
        681
Normal modifier, 415
Normalize Spline modifier, 314, 413
Normalized Time Predefined Variable
        (NT), 648
nose, MakeMDL SDK recognized
        name, 711
nose1, MakeMDL SDK recognized
        name, 711
not operator, 239
Note Tracks Track Icon, 582
Notes dialog box, 599–600
NT. See Normalized Time Predefined
        Variable
NTSC. See National Television
        Standards Committee
Nudge Keys Left command, 802
Nudge Keys Right command, 802
Nudge Selection command, 804
number of children, object property,
        146
Number of elements parameter, Ring
        Array, 174
number of faces, object property, 146
number of objects selected, 44
number of vertices, object property,
        146
Numerical Expression Evaluator
        dialog box, 6441
NURBS. See Non-Uniform Rational B-
        Splines modeling
NURMS. See Non-Uniform Rational
        MeshSmooth

O

object. See also selecting objects
    cloning, 23, 156
    color, 270
    converting, 262–263
    dummy, 185
    Dungeon Siege Tool Kit, 730–731,
        744
    exporting, 115
    grouping, 177
    hierarchy, 141, 177
    importing, 110–114
    linking, 141, 180–181
    material, assigning to, 473
    moving, 190
    naming, 269

naming group of, 143
    parameters, 279
    properties, 135, 146
    rotating, 190
    scaling, 190
    Trainz, 775
Object Color dialog box, 270
Object Level tab, Display Floater
        dialog box, 149–150
Object Properties command, Edit
        menu, 22
Object Properties dialog box
    Backface Cull option, 148
    Display as Box option, 147
    Dungeon Siege Tool Kit, 732–733
    Edges Only option, 148
    Freeze option, 149
    General Panel, 146–147
    Hide option, 149
    Ignore Extents option, 148
    opening, 22
    See-Through option, 148
    Show Frozen in Gray option, 148
    Trajectory option, 148
    User-Defined Panel, 149
    Vertex Color option, 148
    Vertex Ticks option, 148
Object Type rollout
    AutoGrid check box, 286
    opening, 212
    Shapes category, 286
    Start New Shape option, 286–287
Objects default toolbar, Tab Panel, 72
Objects panel, Trainz, 761
Objects toolbar, Tab Panel, 35
Objects Track Icon, 582
Octa option, Parameters rollout, 278
Odd Only check box, Edit Macro
        dialog box, 64
Offset values, Transform Type-In
        dialog box, 194
Omni light, 525
135mm lens, 551
onion-skins, traditional animation, 97
online resources
    Dungeon Siege Tool Kit, 755–756
    Quake III Arena, 703
    software conferences, 6
    Tempest game pack, 702–703
    Trainz, 784–785
On/Off controller, 635
Opacity control, Blinn Shader,
        483–484
opacity, gmax Material Editor,
        468–469, 504
Open File command, 796
open spline, 319
Open Track View button, main
        toolbar, 34

Open Track View command, Graph
        Editors menu, 184
OpenGL, 793
opening files, 105
operating system requirements, 789
operators, 648–650
Optimize modifier, 342, 416

Optimize option
    Interpolation rollout, 288
    MakeMDL, 709
Optimize Shapes and Paths option,
        Skin Parameters rollout,
        381
or operator, 239
Orbit button
    Camera Navigation Control, 547
    Light Navigation Control, 529
Orbit View Camera Control, 671
Origin control, Preference Settings
        dialog box, 87
origin dimensions, object property,
        146
Orthographic Projection option,
        Parameters rollout, 551
Outline button, editing Spline
        subobject, 308–309
Output rollout, 500
Output Sub-Mesh Selection option,
        Operations group, 372

P

Paint panel, Trainz, 760
Paint Shed Content Creation Guide,
        Trainz, 758
Paint Weights button, 449
Pair of dice.gmax, 491
PAL. See Phase Alternate Line
Pan button
    Deformation dialog box, 385
    Status Bar, 584
Pan Camera button, Camera
        Navigation Control, 547,
        803
Pan command, Viewport Navigation
        button, 51
Pan Light button, Light Navigation
        Control, 529
Pan View Camera Control, 671, 799
panel, floating and docking, 47
Panels and Gauges SDK (Flight
        Simulator software
        development kit), 706
Pants custom subdirectory, Trainz,
        778
Pan/Zoom option, Preference Settings
        dialog box, 98
Param Curve Out-of-Range Types
        dialog box, 599

Parameter controllers
  Barycentric Morph controller,
    636–637
  Block controller, 637–639
  Cubic Morph controller, 636
  Master Point controller, 639–640
  On/Off controller, 635
  RGB controller, 635–636
  Track View window, 634
Parameter Out-of-Range Types
    button, Global Track View
    Toolbar, 581
Parameter Wiring dialog box, 574–575
Parameters button, Motion panel,
    40–41
Parameters rollout
  Connect object, 370
  Create panel, 273
  Ring Array, 174
Parametric Deformer modifiers, 28,
    426
parametric object, 263
parent
  definition, 180
  object property, 146
Parent Coordinate System, Transform
    Managers, 197
Parent Space group, IK Solver
    Properties rollout, 462
Park bench.gmax, 370
Particle Systems, 14
Particles default toolbar, Tab
    Panel, 72
Parts Visible Test option, MakeMDL,
    709
Paste command, MAXScript Editor
    window, 228
Paste Controller button
  Global Track View Toolbar, 580
  keyboard shortcut, 802
  Track View window, 598
Paste Time button, Edit Time Mode,
    586
Paste Value command, 804
Patch grid
  creating, 346
  definition, 345
Patch Grid Parameters rollout, 346
Patch modeling type, 262, 345
Patch object, 345
Patch quilt.gmax, 489
Patch seashell.gmax, 360
Patch Select modifier, 402, 404
Patch subobject, 348–350, 357
patch vertices
  connecting objects, 352–353
  connecting to edges, 352
  connecting to vertices, 352
  coplanar, 351
  corner, 351

creating, 352
deleting, 353
detaching, 352
Geometry rollout, 350
hiding, 353
unhiding, 353
welding multiple to one vertex,
    353–354
PatchDeform modifier, 420
Patch/Spline Editing, Modifiers menu,
    28, 408
Path Commands rollout, 390
Path constraint, 609–610
Path Parameters rollout, 381, 609–610
PathDeform modifier, 420–421
% Along Path value, Path Parameters
    rollout, 610
Percent Snap button, Prompt Line, 45,
    211, 214
Perpendicular snap point, 214
persistent dialog box, 49
Perspective button, Camera
    Navigation Control, 546
perspective, camera, 542
Perspective Sensitivity value,
    Preference Settings dialog
    box, 97
Perspective view option, Viewport
    Configuration dialog box,
    86, 798
Phase Alternate Line (PAL), 557
Phase parameter, Ring Array, 174
Phase value, Ring Array, 175
Phong Shader, 485
physical properties, 13
PI Predefined Variable (Pi), 648
Pick Button form element, Visual
    MAXScript, 253
Pick Coordinate System, Transform
    Managers, 197
Pick Path button, Spacing Tool dialog
    box, 165–166
Pick Points button, Spacing Tool
    dialog box, 165–166
Pick Shape button, Pick Operand
    rollout, 371
Pick Target button
  IK Solver Properties rollout, 462
  Pick Targets rollout, 366
Pick Texture button, Edit UVW dialog
    box, 510
picking material from scene, gmax
    Material Editor, 474
Pie Slice option, Arc primitive, 291
pilot, MakeMDL SDK recognized
    name, 711
Pin Stack button, Modifier Stack, 399
Pinch button, Soft Select rollout, 264

Pinch parameter, Affect Region
    modifier, 435
Ping Pong option, Param Curve Out-
    of-Range Types dialog
    box, 599
Ping-Pong Direction, Time
    Configuration dialog box,
    558
Pivot button, Hierarchy panel, 39–40,
    184, 205
Pivot Point Center button, Transform
    Center flyout, 196–198
Pivot snap point, 214
pixel averaging, 498
Pixel Snap command, 803
Place Highlight command, Tools
    menu, 24, 34, 527, 796
Planar from Object XYZ mapping
    type, 494
Planar from World XYZ mapping type,
    494
Planar Map button, Parameters
    rollout, 512
Planar Map Faces/Patches command,
    803
Planar Threshold value, 322
Plane Angle helper, 575–576
Plane primitive object, creation
    method, 272
Plane, Standard Primitives, 277
Planet Dungeon Siege, 755–756
Plasma file format (P3D), 108, 115
Play Animation button, Time Control,
    556
Play Selected button, Time Control,
    556
Playback section, Time Configuration
    dialog box, 557
Player Start, Tempest game pack,
    678–679
Player Start tool, Tempest Toolbar,
    669
Play/Pause Animation button, Time
    Controls, 43, 799
Play/Pause Selected button, Time
    Controls, 43
PlugCFG directory path, 76
Plug-In Info button, Summary Info
    dialog box, 130
Plug-In Keyboard Shortcut Toggle
    button, Prompt Line, 45
Plug-Ins panel, Configure Paths dialog
    box, 76–77
+ (plus sign)
  Addition operator, 648
  MAXScript variables, joining, 234
  Pick Target rollout, 366
  Save File As dialog box, 105
  Vector Addition vector operator,
    649

PM. *See* Progressive Mesh file
.PNG file extension, 126, 132, 497
pogo stick, animating, 595
Point command, Animation menu, 28–29
Point filters Class ID, 138
Point object, 281
Point3 controllers, 620
Point3 data type, 235
Point3 Expression controller, 642
Point3 return type, 652
Poly Select modifier, 404
Polygon Counter utility, 342
Polygon Selection Circle command, 797
Polygon subobject mode, 321, 333
Polys modeling type, 262
portfolio, creating, 6
Poser modeling tool
    3DS file, 111–112
    DXF file, 113–114
    importing human figures, 110–111
Position constraint, 611–612
Position Expression controller, 642
Position ranges mode, Track View window, 581, 587–588
Position, Rotation, and Scale (PRS), 566
Position track controllers
    Bézier controller, 627–628
    Expression controller, 630
    Linear controller, 628
    List controller, 630
    Noise controller, 629
    Position XYZ controller, 630–631
    purpose, 620
    TCB controller, 632–633
Position XYZ controller, 630–631
positioning objects, Trainz, 776
Position/Rotation.Scale Transform controller, 625
Power function, 651
Precedence value, Object Parameters rollout, 455
predefined variables, 647–648
Preference Settings dialog box
    controllers, 620
    opening, 22, 29, 86–87
Preferences command, Customize menu, 29
Preserve modifier, 437
Previewer, Dungeon Siege Tool Kit, 727
Previous Frame button, Time Controls, 43
Previous Frame/Key button, Time Control, 556
primitive, definition, 262, 267
Primitives modeling type, 262

PRJ. *See* 3D Studio Projects file format
processor requirements, 789
Progress Bar form element, Visual MAXScript, 253
Progressive Mesh file (PM), 115, 771
projection map, 493
Projection option, Preference Settings dialog box, 97
Projector maps, Resource Collector utility, 128, 538
Projector Parameters rollout, 533
Prompt Line
    buttons, 44–45
    removing from interface, 27
Prompt Line, Track View window, 583
Properties button, Edit Keys Mode, 585, 589
Protractor object, 281–282
proxy, XRef, 121–123
PRS. *See* Position, Rotation, and Scale
PRS Parameters, Link constraints, 613
PRS Parameters rollout, Motion panel, 565
PSD. *See* Adobe Photoshop image file
pull-down menu. *See* menus
puppet, creating with bones, 443
Push modifier, 430–431
Pyramid primitive object, absence of, 12
Pyramidal Filtering option, Bitmap Parameters rollout, 498

Q
Qmap (map community), 703
.qmo file extension, 67, 74
Quad Patch, 345–346, 356, 608
Quad Sides option, Skin Parameters rollout, 382
quadmenus
    customizing, 66–68
    displaying, 46–47
Quads panel, Customize User Interface dialog box
    Advanced Options button, 67
    Category drop-down list, 66
    command, adding to quadmenu, 67
    Group drop-down list, 66
    Menu command, 66
    New button, 67
    opening, 29
    Rename button, 67
    Separator command, 66
    Show All Quads option, 67
Quake Cam Camera Control, 671
Quake III Arena. *See* Tempest game pack
Quake3World (map community), 703

? (question mark)
    MAXScript previous command indicator, 227
    single-character wildcard, 140
Quick Compile, Tempest game pack, 681

R
Radio Buttons form element, Visual MAXScript, 253
Radius parameter, Ring Array, 174
Raise to the Power operator (^ or **), 649
Ramp in value, Noise Controller dialog box, 629
Ramp out value, Noise Controller dialog box, 629
Random Noise Position noise function, 651
RayTraced library, gmax Material Navigator, 479
raytraced shadows, 522–523, 538
real-time scene update, 342
Recent Files in File Menu option, Files panel, 93
Rectangle command, 797
Rectangle primitive object, 289, 293
Rectangular selection method, 140
Rectangular Selection Region button, main toolbar, 33
red channel, Virtual Frame Buffer, 134
red, green, and blue (RGB) color system, 270
Redo command, 22, 33, 273–274
Redo Scene Operation command, 796, 802
Redo View Change command, Views menu, 25, 52
Redo Viewpoint Operation command, 796
Redraw All Views command, Views menu, 26, 796
Reduce Keys button
    Edit Time Mode, 587
    Track View window, 591
Reference Coordinate System, Transform Managers, 33, 88, 196
Reference, definition 155
reference images, loading for modeling, 56–57
Reference Object Dropper, Dungeon Siege Tool Kit, 743
Reference option, Pick Targets rollout, 366
Refine button
    Bone Parameters rollout, 441
    Cut operation, 376
    Geometry rollout, 301
reflection, gmax Material Editor, 469

Reflection Map Texture, MakeMDL SDK, 711
reflection mapping, 505
ReflectionMaps library, gmax Material Navigator, 479
refraction, gmax Material Editor, 469
refraction mapping, 505
region
    Dungeon Siege Tool Kit, 725
    selecting object by, 140
Region command, Edit menu, 140
Region Fit button, UVW Map modifier, 506
Region Zoom command, Viewport Navigation button, 51
Registered User Identification Code, 792
Relative option, Path Parameters rollout, 610
Relative Repeat option, Param Curve Out-of-Range Types dialog box, 599
Relative toggle, Envelope Properties, 448
Relative transform operations option, MacroRecorder menu, 229
Relax modifier, 432
Relax option, Surface Properties rollout, 359–360
Remove Inside option, Cut operation, 376
Remove Isolated Vertices button, Edit Geometry rollout, 324–325
Remove Modifier from the Stack button, Modifier Stack, 399
Remove Outside option, Cut operation, 376
Remove UVW utility, 517
removing material, gmax Material Editor, 475
Rename button
    Quads panel, 67
    Toolbar panel, 62
Render Map dialog box, 472
rendering, absence of, 14
Rendering Control, Object Properties dialog box, 22
Rendering default toolbar, Tab Panel, 72
r_engine, MakeMDL SDK recognized name, 711
RenX game pack, 10
Re-Orient check box, Array dialog box, 169
Reorient option, Geometry rollout, 300, 302
Re-scale Time button, Time Configuration dialog box, 558

Reset Background Transform command
    Viewport Background dialog box, 56
    Views menu, 26, 55
Reset button
    Shape Commands rollout, 390
    UVW Map modifier, 506
Reset Curve button
    Deformation dialog box, 385
    Fit Deformation dialog box, 389
    Output rollout, 500
Reset Rotation pop-up menu command, Material Editor, 472
Reset Scale button, Adjust Transformation rollout, 207
Reset Transform button, Adjust Transformation rollout, 207
Reset XForm utility, 207
resetting material, gmax Material Editor, 474
Resource Collector utility, Utilities panel, 41–42, 128–129
Restore Active View command, Views menu, 25
Restore Active Viewport command, Views menu, 52
Restrict Axis button, Axis constraints toolbar, 191, 199
Restrict Plane Cycle command, 797
Restrict to X button, main toolbar, 34, 199, 797
Restrict to XY Plane button, main toolbar, 34, 199
Restrict to Y button, main toolbar, 34, 199, 797
Restrict to YZ Plane button, main toolbar, 34, 199
Restrict to Z button, main toolbar, 34, 199, 797
Restrict to ZX Plane button, main toolbar, 34, 199
Resulting Accuracy, Preference Settings dialog box, 87
Retriangulate button, Editable Poly object, 340
return types, 652
reveal animation (rv), Dungeon Siege, 753
Reverse button, editing Spline subobject, 308
Reverse Direction, Time Configuration dialog box, 558
Reverse Time button
    Edit Time Mode, 586
    Track View window, 591

Revert to Startup UI Layout command, Customize menu, 29, 75
Review Strokes dialog box, 98–99
RGB. See red, green, and blue color system
RGB channel output, 498
RGB controller, 635–636
Right orthographic viewport, 50
Right parameter, Text primitive, 292
Right view option, Viewport Configuration dialog box, 86, 199, 798
right-click quadmenus, displaying, 46–47
Rigid Patch Handles option, Advanced Parameters rollout, 449
Rigid Vertices option, Advanced Parameters rollout, 449
Ring Array system, 174–177
Ripple modifier, 432–433
rl. See running loop animation
rocket, following with camera, 548
Roll Camera button, Camera Navigation Control, 546
Roll Light button, Light Navigation Control, 529
roller coaster.gmax, 167
rollout, Command Panel, 36–37
rollout space, Visual MAXScript window, 254
Rollup Threshold value, Preference Settings dialog box, 89
root, definition, 180
Rotate 90 Degrees CCW button, Fit Deformation dialog box, 389
Rotate 90 Degrees CW button, Fit Deformation dialog box, 389
Rotate button, Edit UVW dialog box, 510
Rotate Mapping Coordinates dialog box, 496
Rotate View Mode command, 800
rotation, 190
Rotation and Scale track controllers
    Euler XYZ Rotation controller, 633–634
    Scale XYZ controller, 634
    Smooth Rotation controller, 634
Rotation controllers, 620
Rotation Expression controller, 642
Rotation Increment value, Preference Settings dialog box, 97
Rotational Joints rollout, 453–454
Roughness property, gmax Material Editor, 469

r_tail, MakeMDL SDK recognized name, 711
running loop animation (rl), Dungeon Siege, 753
rv. *See* reveal animation
r_wing, MakeMDL SDK recognized name, 711
r_wingfold, MakeMDL SDK recognized name, 711
rwingtip, MakeMDL SDK recognized name, 711
r_wingtip, MakeMDL SDK recognized name, 711
r_wing_tip, MakeMDL SDK recognized name, 711

S

S. *See* Seconds Predefined Variable
Save Active View command, Views menu, 25
Save Active Viewport command, Views menu, 52
Save button, Toolbar panel, 62
Save Custom UI command, Customize menu, 29
Save File As dialog box, 104–105
Save File command, 796
Save UI Configuration on Exit switch, Preference Settings dialog box, 89
Save Viewport Thumbnail Image option, Files panel, 92–93
saving files, 104–105
Scalar Multiplication vector operator (*), 649
scalar return type, 652
Scale button, Edit UVW dialog box, 510
Scale Control Point button, Deformation dialog box, 385
Scale controllers, 620
Scale Deformation window, 387
Scale Expression controller, 642
Scale Horizontal button, Edit UVW dialog box, 510
Scale Keys button
    Edit Keys Mode, 585
    Function Curves Mode, 589
    Track View window, 590, 593
Scale Point button, Output rollout, 500
Scale Time button
    Edit Time Mode, 587
    Track View window, 591
Scale Transform Type-In dialog box, 207
Scale Values button, Function Curves Mode, 589

Scale Vertical button, Edit UVW dialog box, 510
Scale XYZ controller, 634
scaling
    definition, 190
    measurement units, 78
    non-uniform, 191
Scatter object, absence of, 13
Scenarios custom subdirectory, Trainz, 778
Scenarios option, Trainz, 759
scene file, 103
Scene Undo spinner, Preference Settings dialog box, 87
Scenery custom subdirectory, Trainz, 778
Scenes directory path, 76–77
Schematic view option, Viewport Configuration dialog box, 86
Scheme drop-down list, Colors panel, 71
Screen Coordinate System, Transform Managers, 196
Screen Environment mapping type, 495
Script controller, 625–626
script execution, 237
scripted mouse tool, 233
scripted right-click menu, 233
scripted utility, 233
Scripts directory path, 76–77
Scroll Down command, 802
Scroll Up command, 802
scrollable mouse, 790
SDK. *See* software development kit
Search menu, MAXScript Editor window, 228
Seconds Predefined Variable (S), 648
Section spline tool, absence of, 12
Seed value, Noise Controller dialog box, 629
See-Through Display command, 798
See-Through option, Object Properties dialog box, 148
segment, editing, 307–308
Segment End option, Selection rollout, 298
Select All command, Edit menu, 21, 138
Select Ancestor command, 800
Select and Link button, main toolbar, 33
Select and Manipulate button, main toolbar, 33
Select and Move button, main toolbar, 33, 138, 190, 192
Select and Non-Uniform Scale button, main toolbar, 33, 191

Select and Rotate button, main toolbar, 33, 138, 190, 192
Select and Scale button, main toolbar, 138
Select and Squash button, main toolbar, 33, 191
Select and Uniform Scale button, main toolbar, 33, 190, 192
Select Background Image dialog box, 56
Select Bitmap Image File dialog box, 497
Select By Color and/or Name command, Edit menu, 21
Select by Color button, Object Color dialog box, 270
Select By ID dialog box, 340
Select by Material button, Material Editor, 145
Select By menu command, Edit menu, 138
Select by Name button, main toolbar, 33, 796
Select by Name field, Track View window, 583
Select Camera dialog box, 543
Select Child command, 800
Select Entire Hierarchy command, 800
Select Invert command, Edit menu, 21, 138
Select Missing Maps button, Bitmap Path Editor dialog box, 129
Select None command, Edit menu, 21, 138
Select Objects button, main toolbar, 33, 798
Select Objects dialog box
    Case Sensitive option, 140
    links, 182–183
    opening, 139
    Select by Name text field, 139–140
    Select Dependents option, 140
Select Open Edges button, Edge subobject mode, 333, 350
Select Spline modifier, 314
Select Subobject Toggle command, 800
Select Time button
    Edit Time Mode, 586
    Track View window, 591
Select Tool tool, Tempest Toolbar, 668
selected object, Status Bar, 44
selecting objects, 145
    by name, 139–140
    by region, 140
    Class IDs, 138
    multiple, 141

Continued

selecting objects (continued)
  selection brackets, 136
  selection filter, 137–138
  Viewport Configuration dialog
    box, 136
Selecting Single option, Snapshot
  dialog box, 163–164
Selection Brackets Toggle command,
  798
Selection Center, Transform
  Managers, 196
Selection Center button, Transform
  Center flyout, 197–198
Selection Filter drop-down list, main
  toolbar, 33, 137
Selection Floater command, Tools
  menu, 23, 271
Selection Lock Toggle button, Status
  Bar, 143, 799
Selection Modifiers, Modifiers menu
  applying, 404–407
  viewing, 28
Selection Region button, main
  toolbar, 140
Selection rollout, subobjects,
  322–323, 349–350
selection set, 143–144
Selection-relative scene object names
  option, MacroRecorder
  menu, 229
Selection-relative subobject sets
  option, MacroRecorder
  menu, 230
Self-Illumination color, gmax Material
  Editor, 468
Self-Illumination control, Blinn
  Shader, 483
self-illumination mapping, 504
Separator command, Quads panel, 66
Set Controller Defaults dialog box, 91,
  624
Set Defaults button, Preference
  Settings dialog box, 91
Set Number button, Multi/Sub-Object
  Basic Parameters rollout,
  487–488
Set Orientation button, LookAt
  Constraint rollout, 615
Set Path button, Bitmap Path Editor
  dialog box, 129
SG. See Smoothing Group
Shade Selected command, Views
  menu, 26
Shade Selected Faces option,
  Viewport Rendering
  Options, 82, 136, 800
Shader Basic Parameters rollout, 482
Shader Nav tool, Tempest Toolbar,
  668, 677

Shader Paint tool, Tempest Toolbar,
  670
Shaders, 14, 482, 667, 677
shadow maps, 522–523
Shadow Parameters rollout, 534–535
Shape and Path Steps option, Skin
  Parameters rollout, 381
Shape Commands rollout, 390
shape primitives, 286–287
Shape view option, Viewport
  Configuration dialog box,
  86
ShapeMerge object type
  Cookie Cutter option, 372
  definition, 13, 365
  Merge option, 372
  spline shape, 371
Shapes and Splines modeling type,
  262
Shapes category panel, Create panel,
  267
Shapes default toolbar, Tab Panel, 72
Shapes object category, Create panel,
  38
Shapes Selection Filter, 137
Shapes toolbar, Tab Panel, 35
shield only (fs8), Dungeon Siege, 753
short two-handed weapon (fs4),
  Dungeon Siege, 753
shortcuts, keyboard, 49, 795–804
Show All Gizmos option, Display
  rollout, 449
Show All Quads option, Quads panel,
  67
Show All Tracks wiring parameter,
  575
Show All Vertices option, Display
  rollout, 449
Show command panel switchings
  option, MacroRecorder
  menu, 230
Show Cone option, Parameters
  rollout, 552
Show Dependencies command, Views
  menu, 26
Show End Result on/off toggle button,
  Modifier Stack, 399
Show Frozen in Gray option, Object
  Properties dialog box, 148
Show Ghosting command, Views
  menu, 26, 567
Show Home Grid command, Views
  menu, 25
Show Horizon option, Parameters
  rollout, 552
Show Key Times, Views menu, 26, 566
Show Map button, Edit UVW dialog
  box, 510
Show Map in Viewport button, gmax
  Material Editor, 470

Show menu item selections option,
  MacroRecorder menu, 230
Show Normals option, Selection
  rollout, 322–323
Show Selected Key Statistics button,
  Status Bar, 584
Show Selected Key Statistics field,
  Track View window, 583
Show Selected Segs option, Geometry
  rollout, 302
Show Tangents button, Function
  Curves Mode, 589
Show tool selections option,
  MacroRecorder menu, 230
Show Transform Gizmo command,
  Views menu, 26, 192
Show UI menu, Customize menu, 29
Show Vertex Numbers option,
  Selection rollout, 299, 312
Show Vertices as Dots option,
  Preference Settings dialog
  box, 96
Show/Hide All Grids command, 798
Show/Hide Cameras command, 798
Show/Hide Command Panel
  command, 796
Show/Hide Floating Toolbars
  command, 796
Show/Hide Geometry command, 798
Show/Hide Grids command, 798
Show/Hide Helpers command, 798
Show/Hide Lights command, 798
Show/Hide Main Toolbar command,
  796
Show/Hide Particle Systems
  command, 798
Show/Hide Space Warps command,
  798
Show/Hide Tab panel command, 796
SHP. See 3D Studio Shape file format
Shrink-Wrap Environment mapping
  type, 495
Siege Editor, Dungeon Siege Tool Kit,
  720–722
Siege Max, Dungeon Siege Tool Kit, 9,
  721, 738–739
SiegeNetwork, 756
Siggraph, 6
Simple house.gmax, 512
Sine function, 650
single-handed weapon and a shield
  (fs2), Dungeon Siege, 753
single-handed weapon (fs1), Dungeon
  Siege, 753
Skew modifier, 433
Skin modifier
  Envelope subobject, 446
  using with bone system, 446
Skin Paint Strength value, 449
Skin Parameters rollout, 381

Skys library, gmax Material Navigator, 479

Slice modifier, 434

Slice option, creating hemisphere with, 276

Slice Plane mode, 328

Slick texture, Tempest game pack, 689

Slide Keys button
Edit Keys Mode, 585
Track View window, 590

Slider form element, Visual MAXScript, 253

Slider helper, 575–576

Sliding Joints rollout, 453–454

Slow, Key Tangent, 563

small black arrow, menu items, 20

smoke effects, Trainz, 783

Smooth Angle value, 110

Smooth, Key Tangent, 563

Smooth modifier, 415

Smooth option, Creation Method rollout, 290

Smooth Rotation controller, 634

Smooth Viewport Rendering Level, 80

Smooth+Highlights Viewport Rendering Level, 80

Smoothing Group (SG), 340

Smoothness value, Path Parameters rollout, 610

SMPTE. See Society of Motion Picture Technical Engineers

SMPTE option, Time Display, 557

Snap button, main toolbar, 211, 799

Snap Frames button, Global Track View Toolbar, 581

Snap Percent command, 799

Snap Quadmenu command, 800

Snap Strength setting, Color Selector dialog box, 214

Snap tool, Tempest Toolbar, 670

Snapshot button, main toolbar, 34

Snapshot command, Tools menu, 23

Snapshot dialog box, 163–164

SNO Tool Kit, Dungeon Siege Tool Kit, 739–741

snowman, creating, 204

Snowman camera.gmax, 549

Snowman highlight.gmax, 527

Society of Motion Picture Technical Engineers (SMPTE), 557

Soft Selection Curve, Soft Select rollout, 264–265

Soft Selection rollout, 264, 299, 323, 350

Soften value, gmax Material Editor, 469

software development kit (SDK), 7

software registration, 792

solar system, creating, 181

Sort by Color setting, Selection Floater command, 271

sound effects, Trainz, 782

Sound Options dialog box, 600–601

Sound Track Icon, 582

Sounds directory path, 76

Source Doors spinner, Dungeon Siege Tool Kit, 726

source file, Trainz, 758, 772

Space library, gmax Material Navigator, 479

Space Warps default toolbar, Tab Panel, 14, 72

Spacebar, Lock Selection Set button, 44

Spacing Tool button, main toolbar, 34, 796

Spacing Tool command, Tools menu, 24

Spacing Tool dialog box, 165–166

Spacing value, Spacing Tool dialog box, 165

Special Effects SDK (Flight Simulator software development kit), 706

Specify Length option, Tape object, 281

Specular color, gmax Material Editor, 468

Specular control, Blinn Shader, 483

Specular Level control, Blinn Shader, 483–484

Specular Level mapping, 504

Specular Level value, gmax Material Editor, 469

Specular mapping, 503

Speed setting, Time Configuration dialog box, 558

sphere, converting to Editable Patch, 358

Sphere button, Standard Primitives, 268

Sphere data type, 235

Sphere object type, Surface constraint, 608

Sphere primitive object, creation method, 272

Sphere, Standard Primitives, 275–276

SphereArray.gmax, 222

sphere.max, 84

Spherical Environment mapping type, 495

Spider web.gmax, 312

spider.gmax, 455

spinner
controlling, 48–49
entering expression for, 641
importance of, 27

Spinner form element, Visual MAXScript, 253

Spinner Snap Toggle button, Prompt Line, 45, 213

Spinning prop.gmax, 559

Spiral Staircase.gmax, 172

spline
definition, 285
extruding, 315

Spline Select modifier, 402, 404

spline subobject
editing, 308
naming, 298
selecting, 297

Splines custom subdirectory, Trainz, 778

Split option
Cut operation, 376
Slice Plane mode, 328

Spotlight Parameters rollout, 533

Spring Back option, Rotational Joints rollout, 454

Square Root function, 651

Squash option, creating hemisphere with, 275

Stack order, Modifier Stack, 400

Stained glass window.gmax, 539

standard gmax palette, 270

standard interface, reverting to, 75

Standard materials, 13, 482

Standard Primitives
Box, 274
Cone, 277
Create panel, 274
Cylinder, 276
Geometry drop-down list, 267
GeoSphere, 277–278
Plane, 277
Sphere, 275–276
Teapot, 279
Torus, 276–277
Tube, 278

Star primitive object, 289, 294

stars, creating, 535

Start Offset value, Spacing Tool dialog box, 165

Start Time field, Link Parameters rollout, 558, 612

Starting Position object, Dungeon Siege Tool Kit, 734

Starting Quadrant option, Advanced Quad Menu Options dialog box, 67

startup interface, reverting to, 75

StartupScripts directory path, 76

Statistics tab, Properties dialog box, 131

Status Bar, 27, 44, 583–584, 724

Steel-eyed dragon.gmax, 142

Step, Key Tangent, 563

Stipple transparency option, 81

stock lenses, 551

Stones library, gmax Material Navigator, 479
Stoplight.gmax, 657
Stretch style, Animations section, 68
String data type, 235
Stripping paths option, Bitmap Path Editor dialog box, 129
Stroke option, Preference Settings dialog box, 98
Stroke Point Size, 98
Stroke Preferences command, 98
Strokes Utility, 98
Subdivide button, Patch object, 355
Subdivide rollout, Editable Poly object, 338–339
Subdivision Surfaces, Modifiers menu, 28
submaterial, 480–482
submenu, 20, 67
subobject
    Mesh Select modifier, 404
    Patch Select modifier, 404–405
    Poly Select modifier, 405
    revealing, 264
    selecting, 263
    Spline Select modifier, 405
    Volume Select modifier, 405–407
Sub-Object button, Motion panel, 565
Subobject Level Cycle command, 800
subobject mode, 321–322
Subtract button, Edit Named Selections dialog box, 144
Subtraction operator (-), 648
Subtraction option, Shape Boolean operation, 309
Summary Info command, File menu, 21
Summary Info dialog box, 130
Summary panel, File Properties dialog box, 131
Summary tab, Properties dialog box, 131
Summed Area Filtering option, Bitmap Parameters rollout, 498
Sunlight system, absence of, 14
Superman logo.gmax, 405
Surface constraint, 608
Surface Controller Parameter rollout, 608
Surface modifier, 317, 409–410
Surface, Modifiers menu, 28
Surface Parameters rollout, Loft object, 380–381
Surface Properties rollout
    Editable Mesh object, 333
    Face subobject, 340
    Patch subobject mode, 358–359

Relax option, 359–360
Vertex subobject mode, 329, 355
surface tools, 317, 392–393
Swap Bank and Heading option, MakeMDL, 709
Swap Deform Curves button, Deformation dialog box, 385
Switch to Control Point Level command, 802
Switch to Lattice Level command, 802
Switch to Set Volume Level command, 802
Switch to Top Level command, 802
Swivel Angle value, IK Solver Properties rollout, 462
system requirements, disc, 805
System Unit Scale option, Preference Settings dialog box, 87
system units, 77–78
Systems category panel, Create panel, 267
Systems object category, Create panel, 38

T
T. See Ticks Predefined Variable
Tab Panel
    modifying, 72
    opening, 35
Tab Panel toggle, Show UI menu, 29
tagged image format file (TIF), 126, 132, 497
tail, MakeMDL SDK recognized name, 711
tail_l, MakeMDL SDK recognized name, 711
tail_r, MakeMDL SDK recognized name, 711
Tangent function, 650
Tangent snap point, 214
tanking, 749
Tape object, 281
Taper modifier, 427
Targa image file (TGA), 132, 497
Target button, Light Navigation Control, 529
Target camera object, 542–543, 551
Target Direct light, 525
Target Spot light, 525
Target Weld button, Edit UVW dialog box, 510
TCB. See Tension, Continuity, and Bias
TCB controller, 632–633
TCB Rotation, default Rotation controller, 621
Team Elemental, 9

Teapot primitive object, creation method, 272
Teapot, Standard Primitives, 279
Teapot.gmax, 235
Teddy bear.gmax, 445
Teeter Deformation window, 387
telephoto lens, camera, 542
Tempest game pack
    brush, 667
    building blocks, creating, 673–674
    Camera controls, 671
    Caulk texture, 689
    Clip texture, 689
    Command panel, 691–693
    configuring, 665
    downloading, 663
    entity, 668
    Full Compile, 681
    function, 668
    functions, 695–698
    gothic skylight, adding, 688–691
    installing, 664
    level, compiling and loading, 679–680
    light, adding, 681–683
    Mirror texture, 689
    models, 698–700
    multiple textures, applying, 694–695
    NoDrop texture, 689
    Normal Compile, 681
    online communities, 702–703
    Player Start, adding, 678–679
    Quake III Arena, loading, 666–667
    Quick Compile, 681
    shader, 667, 677
    Slick texture, 689
    Tempest toolbar, 668–671
    testing, 666
    texture, definition, 667
    textures, applying, 674–677, 700–701
    trigger, 668, 685–688
    viewports, 672
    weapon, adding, 683–685
template file, Dungeon Siege Tool Kit, 748–749
Tennis Master Series, 11
Tension, Continuity, and Bias (TCB), 606
Terminator option, Object Parameters rollout, 453
terrain, Dungeon Siege Tool Kit, 741
Terrain object, absence of, 13
Tessellate button, Editable Poly object, 337–338
Tessellate modifier, 415

Tessellation button, Subdivide rollout, 339

Testing Pythagoras.gmax, 282

Tetra option, Parameters rollout, 278

Text primitive object, 289, 292–293

Texture Correction option, Viewport Rendering Options, 82, 798

Texture Falloff Space button, Edit UVW dialog box, 510

texture map, 494

texture map parameter format, 573

texture, Tempest game pack, 667, 674–677, 700–701

Texture Vertex Contract Selection command, 803

Texture Vertex Expand Selection command, 803

Texture Vertex Move Mode command, 803

Texture Vertex Rotate Mode command, 803

Texture Vertex Target Weld command, 803

Texture Vertex Weld Selected command, 803

TGA. See Targa image file

35mm lens, 542, 551

3D Snap Toggle button, Prompt Line, 45, 213

3D space
    Orthographic views, 50–51
    overview, 49
    Perspective view, 51
    representing on 2D computer screen, 50

3D Studio Mesh file format (3DS), 108

3D Studio Projects file format (PRJ), 108

3D Studio Shape file format (SHP), 108, 286

three-dimensional space, 199

3ds max software
    compared to gmax, 12–14
    versions, 4

3DS. See 3D Studio Mesh file format

three-sided spline, 288

Threshold values, IK Solver Properties rollout, 462

thumbnail image, 93

Thumbnail pane, Asset Browser utility, 127

tick, 557

Ticks per Second Predefined Variable (TPS), 648

Ticks Predefined Variable (T), 648

TIF. See tagged image format file

tiling, 495

Time Configuration button, Time Controls, 43, 556

Time Configuration dialog box, 557

Time Controls
    list, 556
    Time Slider, 555
    viewing, 43–44, 555

Time Display section, Time Configuration dialog box, 557

Time rollout, 500

Time Ruler, Track View window, 582

Time Slider, Time Controls
    definition, 44
    Morph key, 367

Time Tag field, time Configuration dialog box, 558

Timer form element, Visual MAXScript, 253

Tire rolling down a hill.gmax, 608

Toggle Animation Mode button, Time Controls, 43

Toggle Grid Type tool, Tempest Toolbar, 670

toggle menu option, 20

toolbar, floating and docking, 47

Toolbar panel, Customize User Interface dialog box
    button appearance, changing, 64
    custom icon, adding, 64–65
    custom toolbar, creating, 63–64
    importance of, 62–63
    opening, 29, 62

Tools1, default quadmenu, 46

Tools2, default quadmenu, 46

Tools menu
    Align Camera command, 24
    Align command, 24
    Align Normal command, 24
    Align to View command, 24
    Array command, 23
    Clone command, 23
    Display Floater command, 23
    Isolate command, 23
    Light Lister command, 24
    Mirror command, 23
    Place Highlight command, 24
    Selection Floater command, 23
    Snapshot command, 23
    Spacing Tool command, 24
    Transform Type-In command, 23

Tools Menu command, 797

Tools panel, Trainz, 761

tooltips, main toolbar, 32

Top orthographic viewport, 50

Top view option, Viewport Configuration dialog box, 86, 199, 797

Topology Dependency warning dialog box, Modifier Stack, 403

Topology panel, Trainz, 760

Torus Knots, absence of, 12

Torus object type, Surface constraint, 608

Torus primitive object, creation method, 272

Torus, Standard Primitives, 276–277

TPS. See Ticks per Second Predefined Variable

Track Bar menu command, 44

Track Bar, Show UI menu, 29

Track custom subdirectory, Trainz, 778

Track Icons, Track View window, 582

Track View menu, Graph Editors menu, 29

Track view option, Viewport Configuration dialog box, 86

Track View Pick dialog box, 637–638

Track View Utilities button, Global Track View Toolbar, 581

Track View window
    controllers, 598, 620, 623
    Edit keys mode, 584–585, 590–591
    Edit ranges mode, 587
    Edit time mode, 586–587, 591–592
    expressions, 654
    filters, 597
    Function curves mode, 588–589, 592–595
    Global Track View Toolbar buttons, 580–581
    note tracks, 599–600
    opening, 145, 579
    out-of-range values, 599
    Position ranges mode, 587–588
    selecting objects, 145
    status bar buttons, 583–584
    Time Ruler, 582
    Track Icons, 582
    tracks, list of, 581

TrackBar, Time Configuration dialog box, 558, 561–562

tracks, list of, 581

Tracks panel, Trainz, 761

Trackside custom subdirectory, Trainz, 778

Traffic Database Builder Utility (Flight Simulator software development kit), 706

train object, Trainz, 781–782

Train Simulator, 11, 706

Train Simulator Insider (Web site), 717, 785

Trains custom subdirectory, Trainz, 778

Trainz
    alignment points, 782
    Asset Creation Studio, installing, 770–771
    config file, 762–763
    Content Dispatcher, 758, 783–784
    Content Foundry, 758, 766–768
    Content ID ranges, 763–766
    Displacements folder, 762
    Driver option, 759
    EnvironmentWater folder, 762
    EnvironmentSky folder, 762
    exporting objects, 776–777
    file formats, 115
    Ground folder, 762
    Highland Valley Scripts, 758
    image reference file, 766
    KUID number, 762–764
    loading objects, 777
    mapping coordinates, 775–776
    measuring units, 772
    models, exporting, 771
    My Collection option, 759
    object, creating, 775
    Objects panel, 761
    online resources, 784–785
    overview, 8–9
    Paint panel, 760
    Paint Shed Content Creation Guide, 758
    positioning objects, 776
    Scenarios option, 759
    smoke effects, 783
    sound effects, 782
    source file, editing, 772
    Source files, 758
    Tools panel, 761
    Topology panel, 760
    Tracks panel, 761
    train objects, creating, 781–782
    Trainz Asset Creation Studio, 758
    Trainz Content Creation Procedures, 758
    Trainz Custom, 758
    World panel, 761
Trainz Luvr (Web site), 784
Trajectories button, Motion panel, 40–41, 565
Trajectory option, Object Properties dialog box, 148
transform buttons, 192
Transform, default quadmenu, 46
Transform Center flyout, Transform Managers, 197–198
Transform Center point, 190

Transform Center settings, Transform Managers, 196
Transform controllers, 620, 625–626
Transform Coordinate button, Transform Center flyout, 197–198
Transform Coordinate Center, Transform Managers, 196
Transform Degrade option, Skin Parameters rollout, 382
Transform Gizmo, 97, 192–194, 798
Transform Managers, main toolbar
    Axis Constraint settings, 196
    axis constraints, 199
    Grid Coordinate System, 197
    Local Coordinate System, 197–198
    Parent Coordinate System, 197
    Pick Coordinate System, 197
    Pivot Point Center, 196
    Reference Coordinate System, 196
    Screen Coordinate System, 196
    Selection Center, 196
    Transform Center flyout, 197–198
    Transform Center settings, 196
    Transform Coordinate Center, 196
    View Coordinate System, 196
    World Coordinate System, 196
Transform Type-In command, Tools menu, 23, 194–195, 796
transformation
    coordinate fields, 44
    types, 190–191
Transformation Rule setting, Orientation constraint, 617
Transformation Tools tool, Tempest Toolbar, 669
translation, 190
transparency, gmax Material Editor, 469
Treasure chest of gems.gmax, 279
Tree.gmax, 122
Tri Patch, 345–346, 356
trigger
    Dungeon Siege Tool Kit, 735
    Tempest game pack, 668, 685–688
Trim button, editing Splines, 311
Truck Camera button, Camera Navigation Control, 547
Truck Light button, Light Navigation Control, 529
Tube primitive object, creation method, 272
Tube, Standard Primitives, 278
Turn button, Edge subobject mode, 332
Turns parameter, Helix primitive shape, 294

tutorials
    aligning camera, 549–550
    animation, 559, 570
    Applied IK method, 459
    applying materials, 486
    Attachment constraint, 607
    Auto Backup feature, 93
    basic bones system, 442–444
    Boolean objects, 377–379
    circular array, 171
    clones, 157–160
    Connect object, 370–371
    creating camera, 544–545
    custom interface, saving, 75
    custom material library, 479
    custom toolbar, creating, 63
    Displace modifier, 436
    dummy objects, 185–187
    Dungeon Siege nodes, connecting, 729
    Dungeon Siege object, exporting, 745–748
    Dungeon Siege objects, adding to scene, 733
    Dungeon Siege skeleton, animating, 754–755
    Dungeon Siege template, 749–750
    Dungeon Siege terrain, exporting, 741–742
    editable mesh, 330–331
    Editable Poly object, 336
    Editable Splines, 312–313
    editing splines, 306–307
    Expression controller, 656–658
    Fast View setting, Viewport Configuration dialog box, 83–85
    Float Expression controller, 645–647, 655
    Free Form Deformation modifier, 425–426
    function curves, 595–597
    GeoSpheres, 278
    gmax Material Editor, 475–476
    groups, 178–179
    human figure, importing, 111–112
    IK Limb Solver, 462–463
    imported meshes, correcting problems with, 340–341
    inverse kinematics system, building, 455–456
    keyboard shortcuts, customizing, 61
    Lathe modifier, 317
    Light Navigation controls, 530
    linear array, 168–170
    Link constraint, 613–614
    linking objects, 181–182

Loft object, 391–392

Loft object with different cross sections, 382–383

LookAt constraint, 615–616

looping path, 566–567

Macro Recorder, 230–231

MakeMDL SDK aircraft, 715–716

MakeMDL SDK billboard, 714–715

manipulator helper, 576–577

MAXScript animation program, 245–250

MAXScript interpreter, 225–226

MAXScript Utility rollout, 222

MeshSmooth modifier, 422–423

mirroring, 162

Morph modifier, 418–419

Morph object, 367–368

Multi-Material material, 489

multiple materials, assigning to one object, 491

new menu, adding, 69–70

Noise modifier, 430

Normal Align feature, 209–210

object, converting into bones system, 444–445

object parameters, modifying, 279–280

objects, hiding, 152

Omni lights, 535–536

Orientation constraint, 617

patch grid, 346–347

Patch object, 360–362

PatchDeform modifier, 420

Path constraint, 610

Placing Highlights feature, 527–528

Projector Map, 538

Pythagorean Theorem, 282

raytraced shadows, 538–539

reference images, loading for modeling, 56–57

Ring Array system, 175–177

rotating objects, 202–203

scaling objects, 204

selecting objects, 142

ShapeMerge object, 373–374

Skin modifier, 449–450

Snap feature, 215–216

Snapshot tool, 164

Soft Selection, 266

sound, adding, 601–602

Spacing tool, 166–167

spiral array, 172–173

spline Boolean operations, 315–316

Stack order, 400

strokes, defining, 99–100

Surface constraint, 609

surface tools, 410–412

Target Spot light, 536–537

Tempest advanced textures, 700–701

Tempest building blocks, creating, 673–674

Tempest Command panel, 691–693

Tempest functions, 695–698

Tempest gothic skylight, adding, 688–691

Tempest level, compiling and loading, 679–680

Tempest models, 698–700

Tempest multiple textures, applying, 694–695

Tempest Player Start, adding, 678–679

Tempest textures, applying, 674–677

Tempest trigger, adding, 685–688

Trainz scenery, 778–780

Trainz source file, 772–774

Trainz texture, 768–769

transforming camera, 547–548

transforming objects, 200–202

Twist modifier, 428–429

2D splines and shapes, 295

Unwrap UVW modifier, 512–514

UVW Map modifier, 505–506

variables, 235–236

Vertex Paint modifier, 516

Viewport Navigation buttons, 53–55

Visual MAXScript editor, 254–258

Volume Select modifier, 407–408

XRef proxy, 122–123

XRef Scene, adding, 119

TV-hyperspace deformation.gmax, 425

28mm lens, 551

24mm lens, 551

20mm lens, 551

twinkling stars, creating, 535

Twist Deformation window, 387

Twist modifier, 428

Twisting bridge.gmax, 428

Two cars in a sphere stunt.gmax, 186

2d Icons icon set, 74

2D map, 494

2D shape, 285

2D Snap Toggle button, Prompt Line, 45, 213

2.5D Snap Toggle button, Prompt Line, 45, 213

two-handed staff weapon (fs5), Dungeon Siege, 753

200mm lens, 542, 551

2-Sided option, Shader Basic Parameters rollout, 482

Type 1 PostScript fonts, 292

Type of Object section, Array dialog box, 169

type of objects selected, 44

U

U values button, Edit UVW dialog box, 511

UI. See user interface

.ui file extension, 74

UI Type drop-down list, 573

Unbind button
  editing vertices, 304
  Geometry rollout, 352

Underline parameter, Text primitive, 292

Underscore (_), MAXScript variable name, 234

Undo command, 22, 33, 228, 273–274

Undo Scene Operation command, 796, 802

Undo View Change command, Views menu, 25, 52

Undo Viewpoint Operation command, 796

Unfreeze All command, 798

Unfreeze button, Edit UVW dialog box, 511

Ungroup command, Group menu, 25, 178

Unhide button
  Edit UVW dialog box, 511
  Geometry rollout, 301

Unhide by Name command, 798

Uniform check box, Array dialog box, 169

Unify button, Surface Properties rollout, 340

Unify Normals option, Import DXF File dialog box, 114–115

Union option, Shape Boolean operation, 309

Unit Vector function, 651

Units Setup command, Customize menu, 30

Units Setup dialog box, 77–78

Unlink Selection button, main toolbar, 33

Unreal Tournament 2003, 11

untanking, 749

Unwrap Options dialog box, 511, 803

Unwrap UVW modifier, 509–511

Update Background Image command, Views menu, 26, 55, 796

Update Background While Playing option, Preference Settings dialog box, 97

Update During Spinner Drag command, Views menu, 27

Update Map button, Edit UVW dialog box, 510, 803

Update Materials option, Resource Collector utility, 129

Update Viewports option, Inverse Kinematics rollout, 457

Upnode axis, LookAt Constraint rollout, 615

U.S. Standard units, 77

Use Dual Plane option, Preference Settings dialog box, 95

Use Full Material option, MakeMDL, 709

Use Large Toolbar Buttons option, Preference Settings dialog box, 89

Use Pivot Point Center button, main toolbar, 33

Use Secondary Threshold option, Inverse Kinematics panel, 458

Use Selection Brackets option, Viewport Rendering Options, 82

Use Selection Center button
    Array dialog box, 170
    main toolbar, 33

Use Soft Selection parameter, Soft Select rollout, 264

Use Spinner Snap option, Preference Settings dialog box, 89

Use TrackBar option, Time Configuration dialog box, 558

Use Transformer Coordinate Center button, main toolbar, 33

User Grids panel, 211

user interface (UI), 29

User Reference, Help menu, 30

User view option, Viewport Configuration dialog box, 86, 798

User-Defined Panel, Object Properties dialog box, 149

Utilities panel, Command Panel
    Asset Browser window, 125–127
    opening, 41–42

UV Coordinates, Modifiers menu, 28

.UVW file extension, 509

UVW Map modifier, 14, 505–506

UVW Unwrap, 14

UVW XForm modifier, 14, 508

V

V values button, Edit UVW dialog box, 511

Value Display field, Track View window, 583

Value panel, Visual MAXScript window, 251

variable
    defining, 642–643
    MAXScript, 233–235
    name, 234

Vector Addition vector operator (+), 649

Vector Component function, 651

Vector If function, 651

Vector Length function, 651

vector return type, 652

Vector Subtraction vector operator (-), 649

vertex
    chamfering, 327–328
    create, 325
    delete, 325

Vertex Color Channel mapping type, 494

Vertex Color option, Object Properties dialog box, 148

vertex number, 303

vertex order, Loft object type, 380

Vertex Paint modifier, 416, 515

Vertex Paint on Heart.gmax, 516

Vertex snap point, 214

Vertex subobject mode, 321, 350

Vertex subobject, Modifier Stack, editing, 302

Vertex Ticks option, Object Properties dialog box, 148

vertices, editing, 302–305

Video Post interface, absence of, 14

View Align button, UVW Map modifier, 506

View button, Edit Geometry rollout, 325

View Coordinate System, Transform Managers, 196

View Edged Faces command, 798

View Error Log option, MakeMDL, 709

View File dialog box, 132

View Image File command, File menu, 21

View Steps value, Geometry rollout, 354

view window, Dungeon Siege Tool Kit, 723–724

viewing entire, main toolbar, 32

Viewline Length value, LookAt Constraint rollout, 615

Viewpoint Background command, 796

viewpoint, camera, 541

Viewpoint Datalabs, 342–343

Viewport Arc Rotate Snap Angle, Preference Settings dialog box, 97

Viewport Background command, Views menu, 25–26, 55–56

Viewport Background dialog box, 524

Viewport Clipping option, Viewport Rendering Options, 83

Viewport Configuration command, Customize menu, 30

Viewport Configuration dialog box
    Default Lighting option, 524
    Field of View, 85
    Layout panel, 86
    opening, 30, 78
    Preference Settings dialog box, 96
    Rendering Method panel, 79
    Transparency options, 81
    2 Lights option, 524
    Viewport Rendering Level options, 80–81
    Viewport Rendering Options, 81

Viewport Navigation buttons
    Arc Rotate, 52
    Arc Rotate Selected, 52
    Arc Rotate SubObject, 52
    flyout buttons, color coding, 52
    Interactive Pan, 51
    Min/Max Toggle, 52
    Pan, 51
    Region Zoom, 51
    removing from interface, 27
    selecting, 52
    tutorial, 53–55
    Zoom, 51
    Zoom All, 51
    Zoom Extents, 51
    Zoom Extents All, 51
    Zoom Extents All Selected, 51
    Zoom Extents Selected, 51

Viewport Navigation Controls, Views menu, 25

viewport refresh rate, 120

Viewport Rendering Level options, Viewport Configuration dialog box, 80–81

Viewport Rendering Options, Viewport Configuration dialog box
    Default Lighting toggle, 82
    Disable Textures option, 82
    Disable View option, 82
    Display Selected with Edged Faces option, 82
    Fast View setting, 84–85
    Force 2-Sided option, 82

importance of, 81
Shade Selected Faces option, 82
Texture Correction option, 82
Use Selection Brackets option, 82
Viewport Clipping option, 83
Z-Buffer Wireframe Objects
    option, 82
viewport, Tempest game pack, 672
Viewports panel, Preference Settings
    dialog box
Attenuate Lights option, 96
Backface Cull on Object Creation
    option, 96
Configure Driver button, 100–101
Display World Axis option, 97
Draw Links as Lines option, 96
Filter Environment Backgrounds
    option, 97
ghosting, 97
Grid Nudge Distance, 97
Intersection option, 97
Low-Res Environment
    Background option, 97
Mask Viewport to Safe Region
    option, 96
Non-Scaling Object Size value, 97
Pan/Zoom option, 98
Perspective Sensitivity value, 97
Projection option, 97
Rotation Increment value, 97
Show Vertices as Dots option, 96
Stroke option, 98
Transform Gizmo, 97
Update Background While Playing
    option, 97
Use Dual Plane option, 95
Viewport Arc Rotate Snap
    Angle, 97
Viewport Configuration dialog
    box, 96
Views menu
Activate Grid Object
    command, 25
Activate Home Grid command, 25
Add Default Lights to Scene
    command, 26
Align to View command, 25
Cancel Expert Mode command, 27
Deactivate All Maps command, 27
Expert Mode command, 27
Grids command, 25
Match Camera to View
    command, 26
Redo View Change command, 25
Redraw All Views command, 26
Reset Background Transform
    command, 26
Restore Active View command, 25

Save Active View command, 25
Shade Selected command, 26
Show Dependencies command, 26
Show Ghosting command, 26
Show Home Grid command, 25
Show Key Times command, 26
Show Transform Gizmo
    command, 26
Undo View Change command, 25
Update Background Image
    command, 26
Update During Spinner Drag
    command, 27
Viewport Background command,
    25–26
Viewport Navigation Controls, 25
Views Menu command, 797
Virtual Frame Buffer, 126, 133–134
visibility, Envelope Properties, 448
Visual MAXScript window
    editor window, 251–252
    opening, 228, 250–251
.vms file extension, 251
Volume Select modifier, 402, 404

W

W values button, Edit UVW dialog
    box, 511
walking loop animation (wl), Dungeon
    Siege, 753
warnings, disabling, 88
Wave modifier, 433
weapon, Tempest game pack, 683–685
Web pane, Asset Browser utility, 127
Weld button, editing vertices,
    302–303, 353
Weld Points option, MakeMDL, 709
Weld Selected button
    Edit UVW dialog box, 510, 801
    vertices, 329
Weld Target button, Geometry
    rollout, 354
Weld Target mode, 329, 801
Weld Vertices section, Import DXF
    File dialog box, 110,
    113–114
Westwood Studios, 10
wide-angle lens, camera, 542
wildcards, Select by Name text field,
    140
Window Selection method, 140
Windows Default Colors, Colors
    panel, 71
Windows Explorer, viewing Properties
    dialog box information,
    131
Windows TrueType fonts, 292

Wire Parameters command,
    Animation menu, 29, 574
Wireframe Viewport Rendering
    Level, 80
Wireframe/Smooth+Highlights
    command, 798
wl. See walking loop animation
Wood library, gmax Material
    Navigator, 479
World Coordinate System, Transform
    Managers, 196
World Falloff Space button, Edit UVW
    dialog box, 510
World panel, Trainz, 761
World Track Icon, 582
Wrap Cursor Near Spinner option,
    Preference Settings dialog
    box, 89
Write Keyboard Chart button,
    Keyboard panel, 60

X

x (Cross Product vector operator),
    649
X field, status bar, 195
XForm modifier, 436
XRef Objects dialog box
Convert Selected button, 120
Ignore Animation option, 121
Modifier Stack, 124
Select From Scene button, 121
Select In Scene button, 121
Update Materials option, 121
Update Now button, 121
Use Proxy option, 121–123
XRef Scenes and Objects tab,
    Configure Paths dialog
    box, 124–125
XRef Scenes dialog box
Automatic option, 117–118
Convert Selected button, 117
Enabled option, 117
Ignore section, 118
Merge button, 117
purpose, 116
Unbind button, 118
Update Now button, 117
XRefs. See external reference
XRefs panel, Configure Paths dialog
    box, 76–77
XY plane, 199

Y

Y field, status bar, 195
YZ plane, 199

Z

Z field, status bar, 195

Z-Buffer Wireframe Objects option,
    Viewport Rendering
    Options, 82

.zip file extension, 107

Zoom All command, Viewport
    Navigation button, 51

Zoom command
    Deformation dialog box, 386
    keyboard shortcut, 803
    Status Bar, 584
    Viewport Navigation button, 51

Zoom Extents All command
    Camera Navigation Control, 546
    keyboard shortcut, 799
    Light Navigation Control, 529
    Viewport Navigation button, 51

Zoom Extents All Selected command
    Camera Navigation Control, 546
    Light Navigation Control, 529
    Viewport Navigation button, 51

Zoom Extents Camera Control, 671

Zoom Extents command
    Deformation dialog box, 385
    keyboard shortcut, 799, 803
    Viewport Navigation button, 51

Zoom Extents Horizontal button,
    Deformation dialog box,
    386

Zoom Extents on Import option, Files
    panel, 94

Zoom Extents Selected command,
    Viewport Navigation
    button, 51

Zoom Extents Vertical button,
    Deformation dialog box,
    386

Zoom Horizontal button, Deformation
    dialog box, 386

Zoom Horizontal Extents button,
    Status Bar, 584

Zoom In 2X command, 799

Zoom Mode command, 799

Zoom Out 2X command, 799

Zoom Region command
    Deformation dialog box, 386

    keyboard shortcut, 803
    Status Bar, 584

Zoom Region Mode command, 799

Zoom Selected Elements command,
    803

Zoom Selected Object
    Status Bar, 584
    Track View window, 583

Zoom Time button, Status Bar, 584

Zoom Value Extents button, Status
    Bar, 584

Zoom Vertical button, Deformation
    dialog box, 386

Zoom View Camera Control, 671

Zoom Viewpoint In command, 799

Zoom Viewpoint Out command, 799

ZX plane, 199

Wiley Publishing, Inc.
End-User License Agreement

READ THIS. You should carefully read these terms and conditions before opening the software packet(s) included with this book "Book". This is a license agreement "Agreement" between you and Wiley Publishing, Inc. "WPI". By opening the accompanying software packet(s), you acknowledge that you have read and accept the following terms and conditions. If you do not agree and do not want to be bound by such terms and conditions, promptly return the Book and the unopened software packet(s) to the place you obtained them for a full refund.

1. **License Grant.** WPI grants to you (either an individual or entity) a nonexclusive license to use one copy of the enclosed software program(s) (collectively, the "Software" solely for your own personal or business purposes on a single computer (whether a standard computer or a workstation component of a multi-user network). The Software is in use on a computer when it is loaded into temporary memory (RAM) or installed into permanent memory (hard disk, CD-ROM, or other storage device). WPI reserves all rights not expressly granted herein.

2. **Ownership.** WPI is the owner of all right, title, and interest, including copyright, in and to the compilation of the Software recorded on the disk(s) or CD-ROM "Software Media". Copyright to the individual programs recorded on the Software Media is owned by the author or other authorized copyright owner of each program. Ownership of the Software and all proprietary rights relating thereto remain with WPI and its licensers.

3. **Restrictions On Use and Transfer.**

    (a) You may only (i) make one copy of the Software for backup or archival purposes, or (ii) transfer the Software to a single hard disk, provided that you keep the original for backup or archival purposes. You may not (i) rent or lease the Software, (ii) copy or reproduce the Software through a LAN or other network system or through any computer subscriber system or bulletin- board system, or (iii) modify, adapt, or create derivative works based on the Software.

    (b) You may not reverse engineer, decompile, or disassemble the Software. You may transfer the Software and user documentation on a permanent basis, provided that the transferee agrees to accept the terms and conditions of this Agreement and you retain no copies. If the Software is an update or has been updated, any transfer must include the most recent update and all prior versions.

4. **Restrictions on Use of Individual Programs.** You must follow the individual requirements and restrictions detailed for each individual program in the About the CD-ROM appendix of this Book. These limitations are also contained in the individual license agreements recorded on the Software Media. These limitations may include a requirement that after using the program for a specified period of time, the user must pay a registration fee or discontinue use. By opening the Software packet(s), you will be agreeing to abide by the licenses and restrictions for these individual programs that are detailed in the About the CD-ROM appendix and on the Software Media. None of the material on this Software Media or listed in this Book may ever be redistributed, in original or modified form, for commercial purposes.